Phil Edmonston

LEMON-AID 2010

NEW CARS and TRUCKS

Phil Edmonston

LEMON-AID 2010

NEW CARS and TRUCKS

DUNDURN PRESS
TORONTO

Editing: Andrea Battiston, Andrea Douglas, Jenny Govier
Design: Jack Steiner
Printer: Webcom

1 2 3 4 5 13 12 11 10 09

Canada Council for the Arts

Canada

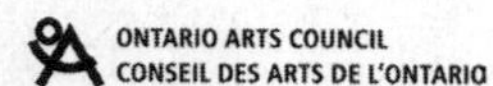

We acknowledge the support of the Canada Council for the Arts and the Ontario Arts Council for our publishing program. We also acknowledge the financial support of the Government of Canada through the Book Publishing Industry Development Program and The Association for the Export of Canadian Books, and the Government of Ontario through the Ontario Book Publishers Tax Credit program, and the Ontario Media Development Corporation.

Care has been taken to trace the ownership of copyright material used in this book. The author and the publisher welcome any information enabling them to rectify any references or credits in subsequent editions.
J. Kirk Howard, President

Printed and bound in Canada.
www.dundurn.com

Dundurn Press
3 Church Street, Suite 500
Toronto, Ontario, Canada
M5E 1M2

Gazelle Book Services Limited
White Cross Mills
High Town, Lancaster, England
LA1 4XS

Dundurn Press
2250 Military Road
Tonawanda, NY
U.S.A. 14150

CONTENTS

Squeezing the Most Out of *Lemon-Aid*

Read Part One before visiting the dealer. You will learn about the elements that make a vehicle a good buy, from the standpoint of price, safety, reliability, performance, and fuel-economy. Tips for negotiating the contract are also a must-read. Part Two outlines the best way to get a refund when things go wrong. Your rights and the dealer's obligations are spelled out in detail, and we provide a sample claim letter that you can copy to get action fast. A summary of little-known secret warranties and winning court cases completes your legal arsenal. Part Three and Appendix I describe the best and worst buys for the past two model years and predict how the 2010 models will perform. Appendix II lists 20 easy ways to save fuel, and Appendix III serves up a specially culled list of informative and amusing websites. Appendix IV gives you some tips on buying a vehicle in the States, and Appendix V includes some of the latest secret warranties and confidential service bulletins. Finally, the model index at the back of the book groups models by rating and allows you to go straight to our discussion of a particular model.

Part Two

Part Three

Appendix II

Appendix III

Appendix IV

Appendix V

KEY DOCUMENTS

Lemon-Aid is a feisty owner's manual that has no equal anywhere. We don't want you stuck with a lemon, or to wind up paying for repairs that are the automaker's fault and are covered by secret "goodwill" warranties. That's why we are the only book that includes many hard-to-find, confidential, and little-known documents that automakers don't want you to see.

In short, we know you can't win what you can't prove.

The following charts, documents, and service bulletins are included so that you can stand your ground and be treated fairly. Photocopy and circulate whichever document will prove helpful in your dealings with automakers, dealers, service managers, insurance companies, or government agencies. Remember, most of the summarized service bulletins outline repairs or replacements that should be done for free.

Part One

RAW DEALS AND GOOD BUYS

Part Two

WARRANTIES AND WEASELS

Part Three

RATINGS: THE GOOD, THE BAD, AND THE RISKY

AMERICAN VEHICLES

Appendix I

MINI-REVIEWS AND PREVIEWS

Appendix V

SECRET WARRANTIES AND CONFIDENTIAL SERVICE BULLETINS

Phil Edmonston

LEMON-AID

2010

NEW CARS and TRUCKS

Introduction

"SEE THE U.S.A. IN YOUR CHEVROLET"?

GM: Government Motors

General Motors, like the other two geezers of the Old Three, is a vast retirement home, with a small loss-making auto subsidiary. The UAW is the AARP in an Edsel: It has three times as many retirees and widows as "workers".... GM has 96,000 employees [as of December 2008] but provides health benefits to a million people.

MARK STEYN
NATIONAL REVIEW
DECEMBER 20, 2008

Chrysler Fire Sale

Bill Colter, owner of Performance Chrysler-Jeep-Dodge in Phoenix, says he had 300 new vehicles in stock at the beginning of May—before learning that his store will be dropped as a Chrysler LLC dealership as of June 9. He sold 70 to 80 vehicles in the past week, discounting them up to 40 percent from sticker with factory and his own incentives. "We have been losing money on virtually every car; but if we have to give them away, we will," Colter says.

ARLENA SAWYERS
AUTOMOTIVE NEWS
JUNE 1, 2009

Dinah Shore's 1952 hit Chevy jingle should be replaced by Canadian singer-poet Leonard Cohen's song "It's Closing Time."

Detroit's automakers are dead men walking, so anyone planning to tour the country in a Chevrolet—or any American vehicle—had better hurry. General Motors has ditched Pontiac, after sounding the death knell for Opel, Hummer, Saab, Saturn, and Vauxhall. Even GMC, the automaker's upscale Chevrolet truck division, is on GM's endangered species list.

Lemon-Aid predicted the bankruptcy of Chrysler and GM several years ago, after almost 40 years of rating auto companies. So it was no surprise to us when, in June 2009, GM threw in the towel and followed Chrysler into bankruptcy.

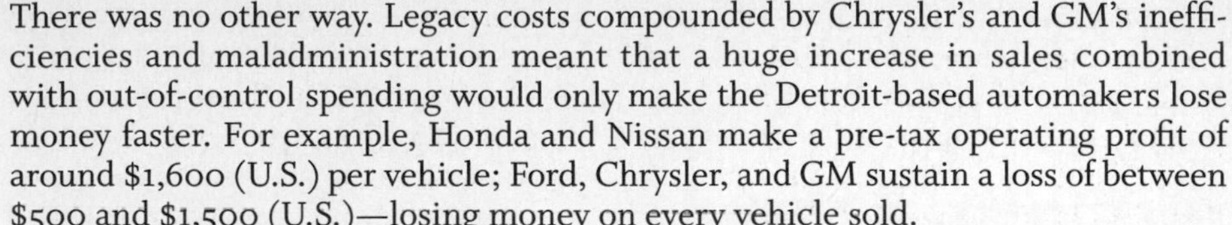

There was no other way. Legacy costs compounded by Chrysler's and GM's inefficiencies and maladministration meant that a huge increase in sales combined with out-of-control spending would only make the Detroit-based automakers lose money faster. For example, Honda and Nissan make a pre-tax operating profit of around $1,600 (U.S.) per vehicle; Ford, Chrysler, and GM sustain a loss of between $500 and $1,500 (U.S.)—losing money on every vehicle sold.

How GM's Wheels Fell Off

"GM" now stands for "Government Motors" following its Chapter 11 bankruptcy filing and partial ownership by the U.S. and Canadian governments and the United Auto Workers (UAW). The company has sold barely half as many cars as it did last year; it dumped Hummer, Pontiac, Saab, Saturn, and Opel; its GMAC financing is on life support; and it has capriciously fired 1,200 dealers. In effect, General Motors has poured sugar into its own gas tank.

General Motors' 96,000 U.S. employees will be pared down to 38,000, and its 12,000 Canadian workers will lose 7,000 jobs by 2014. The dealer network will be cut by half, and only four divisions will remain: Buick, Cadillac, Chevrolet, and GMC. By cutting workers and models, GM hopes to make money in a North American auto market that will retail only 9.5 million vehicles annually instead of 17 million. And the company expects that rationalizing its production using more co-ventures with other automakers will quickly bring in new GM models at little financial risk.

On the other hand, GM insiders say the automaker is hoarding billions of its federal government bailout dollars to build more factories in China to export small cars to North America. Expect fireworks at GM's future board meetings when the governments and the UAW discover that bailout funds went to create jobs in China.

Quo Vadis, Chrysler?

GM's extensive restructuring goals make Chrysler's roll of the dice with a Fiat partnership look extremely risky and short-sighted. With Chrysler hitching its wagon (and minivan) to Fiat, it will be like two drunks propping each other up.

CHRISIS-LER

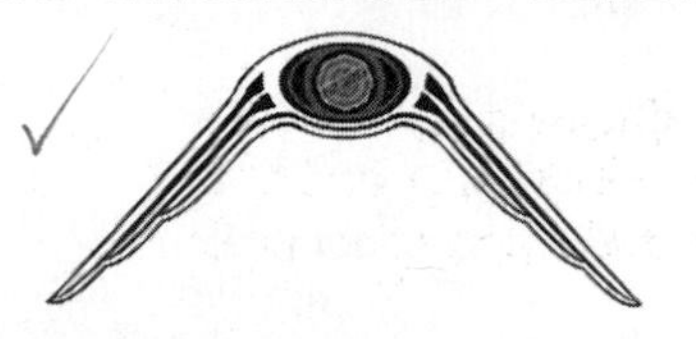

What we have with Chrysler and Fiat is two automakers known for making crappy cars combining into one huge company to make more crappy cars and SUVs. Fiat's econoboxes are frugal—and feeble. They won't come on the market for several years. North American mechanics have no idea how to repair Fiats, and their parts supply has always been problematic. Few shoppers will risk their money on a Chrysler-Fiat combo, and it's even less likely that Chrysler's large-platform factories in Canada will build the cars—no matter what the two companies promise.

Chrysler is no longer a viable entity, no matter to whom it is partnered. (Remember, not even Mercedes could afford to support Chrysler's cash burn, and it recently dumped its 19 percent stake in the company.) The Obama administration shouldn't scapegoat Chrysler or GM bondholders for forcing either company into Chapter 11. Whether you get 10 or 15 cents back from each dollar invested, a bad deal is still a bad deal. Investors, workers, and the Canadian and U.S. governments should not have put a penny into the automakers. Crafty Fiat won't risk one lira on Chrysler, and will probably still get 35 percent of the restructured company. Fiat knows.

It's as if Leonard Cohen means to succinctly sum up Chrysler's and GM's plight, once again, when he sings "Everybody Knows."

Ford's Future

At least Ford has a future, for the time being. It is burning through less cash than GM or Chrysler and has enough reserves to buy time as it awaits an infusion of new small cars imported from its European and Japanese partners. Ford has cut its $25.8 billion (U.S.) debt by $9.9 billion (which will cut interest payments by $500 million a year) and has modified its contract with the unions to produce even more savings.

Ford's 2010 Fusion is a European Fiesta on stilts. Its North American future is cloudy. A new Focus is more reliable and better performing.

The only downside to this marketing plan is that Ford has never had a successful European transplant in North America. (Remember the Cortina, Merkur, Land Rover, and Jaguar models?)

Nevertheless, its reducing of liabilities and the corresponding interest burden is a strong positive for the company. In fact, Ford is the only one of the Detroit Three automakers that has not taken government bailout money to stave off bankruptcy.

Good Buys in a Bad Economy

Bad news for Detroit is good news for car buyers. New- and used-car prices have plummeted. Recently built large trucks and SUVs now cost less than half their original list prices because of soaring fuel costs that have abated but are headed up again.

Smart car buyers should be patient as vehicle prices fall during the coming months and millions of unsold vehicles pile up on dealers' lots. As in the lyrics from a well-known Rolling Stones' cover, time is on my side (yes, it is). Now through the summer of 2010 is the best time to buy a new car or truck, if you are careful and

follow *Lemon-Aid*'s tips in Part One for buying a cheap, reliable, and recession-proof car.

As the Canadian dollar flies higher toward parity with the American greenback and new-car prices sink lower, Canadian shoppers are in the driver's seat to get new vehicles discounted by 30–40 percent. Cash and access to credit makes price haggling a breeze, particularly with almost half of GM Canada's dealers terminated—with back lots full of unsold iron. Hundreds of Chrysler's dumped dealers are in even worse shape. They are caught in a perfect storm of uncertainty, with millions of unsold new vehicles, omnipresent bankruptcies, and a worldwide economic depression.

GM's Tahoe and Yukon (above) have been dropped this year, and Hummer may hum only for the Chinese in China.

Used prices are even more of a bargain. For example, an all-equipped 2006 Yukon Denali (rated Average) that sold for $63,645 can now be bought for less than $20,000. At the other end of the choices available, a fuel-frugal 2006 Ford Focus ZX5 SES four-door hatchback (also Average) that listed new for $21,800 can now be picked up for $7,500. Incidentally, I have used the 2006 model year as an example of a good year to buy most cars, vans, SUVs, and trucks because it was a watershed year for across-the-board safety and quality improvements.

Interestingly, cars and trucks that are currently coming off three- and five-year leases have added to the savings possible when buying used. Dealers gave these vehicles inordinately high buy-back residual values, resulting in owners dumping the cars at the end of their lease and buying something else more affordable. This has created a glut of reliable, overpriced, low-mileage vehicles that will be massively discounted. And these price cuts will be sweetened through the summer of 2010.

Lemon-Aid Guide Improvements

Because the auto industry is in such a transformative, chaotic state, we have made a number of changes to *Lemon-Aid New Cars and Trucks 2010* to make it easier to read and more content-rich as Detroit's fortunes go into free fall. For the first time, the guide rates new cars, SUVs, trucks, and vans, taking into account the possibilities that warranties and resale values may be worthless on some models and that servicing and the parts supply may be problematic on others. There's also a user-friendly layout that includes reviews and previews of additional models.

In this 2010 edition, you'll find descriptions of the best and worst vehicles for new drivers or seniors, tips on getting dealers to bid for your business, and reasons why hybrids and diesel-equipped cars get much less fuel economy than promised. Additionally, we will suggest which vehicles are the safest, most reliable, and cheapest to fuel, service, and insure—without breaking your budget or getting snagged when dealers or automakers close their doors. And, for when things go terribly wrong, we include sample complaint letters, negotiation tips, and the jurisprudence needed to help you get your money back—from the seller or from Ottawa.

Not all small cars are good buys. Daimler's Smart econocar was never a "smart" car for crashworthiness or performance. Honda's Fit is a better buy.

This year's guide also combines test results with owner feedback to provide a critical comparison of 2009–10 vehicles. In Appendix I, "Mini-Reviews and Previews," we rate vehicles that have been on the market for only a short time or are sold in small numbers, like the 2010 Chevrolet Camaro, for example.

If improvements and additional safety features don't justify the higher costs of newer models (and most don't), we say so, as we promote safer, more reliable, and cheaper alternatives. Front, offset, side, and rollover crash test results are also included, along with an exhaustive list of useful and useless accessories and optional safety features. We show how much profit dealers make on each vehicle, and what is a fair price as dealer inventories bulge with unsold new cars and trucks.

We are also watching cross-border prices carefully, as we have done in the past. We know new-car prices in the States will tumble more quickly as inventory piles up there, and we expect to see new cars and trucks discounted by at least 50 percent.

Lemon-Aid is a practical owner's manual that has no equal anywhere. We don't want you to get stuck with a lemon, or to wind up with a car that can't be serviced. Plus, you shouldn't pay for repairs that are the automaker's fault and that are covered by secret "goodwill" warranties. We show you how to get an automaker or government refund for your repairs by exposing many hard-to-find, confidential, and little-known documents that automakers don't want you to see.

In short, *Lemon-Aid* is your anchor for honest and practical information in a stormy sea where it seems all boats are sinking.

Phil Edmonston
October 2009

RAW DEALS AND GOOD BUYS

I'm Going Bankrupt!

I work every day the store is open, nine to ten hours a day. I know most of our customers and all our employees. Sunshine Dodge is my life. On Thursday, May 14, 2009 I was notified that my Dodge franchise will be taken away from my family and given to another dealer at no cost to them. My new vehicle inventory consists of 125 vehicles with a financed balance of 3 million dollars. This inventory becomes impossible to sell with no factory incentives. Without the Dodge franchise we can no longer sell a new Dodge as "new," nor will we be able to do any warranty service work. Additionally, my Dodge parts inventory (approximately $300,000) is virtually worthless without the ability to perform warranty service. There is no offer from Chrysler to buy back the vehicles or parts inventory. Our facility was recently totally renovated at Chrysler's insistence, incurring a multi-million dollar [invoice]. We did NOTHING wrong. This atrocity will most likely force my family into bankruptcy.

GEORGE JOSEPH
SUNSHINE DODGE
MAY 2009

The Death of Detroit

Ailing Detroit automakers need Dr. Kevorkian more than additional Washington and Ottawa handouts. Unfortunately, the American and Canadian governments (federal and provincial) have thrown good money after bad by purchasing up to 72 percent of GM in June 2009 as they get more deeply mired in Motor City quicksand. As a member of the federal parliament in the 1990s, I railed against throwing money into this swamp, yet Ottawa and Quebec gave GM's now-defunct factory in Boisbriand, Quebec, $220 million to stay open. History is repeating itself.

Don't believe the auto analysts that this downturn is only temporary. Auto sales are toxic and will worsen as already bankrupt Chrysler gets nibbled to death by its creditors and fired car dealers use a phalanx of lawyers to litigate the automakers to a standstill.

Talk to your neighbours. Whom do you know who plans to buy a new Detroit-made car or truck?

A recent study from automotive market research firm CNW surveyed 6,000 American shoppers who were intending to buy a new car within six months, and discovered that about 90 percent of them would switch brands rather than buy from a bankrupt automaker.

Let's see, that means Chrysler and GM could lose more than four out of five potential U.S. clients while their sales are barely half of last year's total.

The poll also showed that customers were more likely to abandon Detroit automakers than foreign ones, with Chrysler faring the worst—a full 91 percent of buyers said they wouldn't buy a Chrysler product if the company went bankrupt. Ford and GM did only slightly better, with 80 percent of buyers saying they would go elsewhere if either company closed its doors.

Recession-Proof Buys

Don't get turned off by all of the bad news. Now is the time to buy a new or used vehicle, if you are careful and follow *Lemon-Aid*'s advice on how to grab a recession-proof car or truck.

Bad news for Detroit is good news for car buyers. Three-year-old large trucks and SUVs now cost less than half their original list prices because of higher fuel costs, hard-to-find credit, and poor sales. Now that fuel prices have dropped from last year's highs, most vehicle prices have remained in the basement and many new cars are selling at a 30–40 percent discount. Prices are expected to remain low through the first quarter of 2010.

Says one terminated car dealer, "If new is sold at auction for cheap, that inventory can be remarketed for far less than whatever the factory sends along. Prices will be depressed for some time—at least until the distressed inventory can be cleared."

10 tips for big savings

There are 10 ways you can save money by purchasing a recession-proof vehicle from a dependable dealer as you ride out this economic downturn amid mass bankruptcies and changing alliances:

1. Buy a new or used vehicle that is relatively uncomplicated, is easy to service, and has been sold in large numbers over a decade or so. This will ensure that independent garages can provide service and parts, because many parts suppliers and dealers will have shut their doors.
2. Look for a vehicle that's finishing its model run. But steer clear of models that were axed because of poor reliability or mediocre performance, like GM's front-drive minivans.
3. Stay away from European cars, vans, and SUVs. Dealership networks are weak, parts are inordinately expensive and hard to find, and few garages will invest in expensive diagnostic equipment needed to service complicated emissions

and fuel-delivery systems. The old axiom that there is a right way, a wrong way, and a European way to troubleshoot a car still holds true.

4. Don't buy a hybrid or a diesel. They are failure-prone, complicated to service, and dealer-dependent, and they don't provide the fuel economy or savings they hype. Furthermore, with gas still comparatively cheap, there really is no imperative to complicate your life with a complex piece of machinery. Diesel complexity comes from emissions regulations passed several years ago, requiring the use of cleaner-burning engines and hard-to-service fuel systems.
5. Don't buy most Chrysler or Dodge models, with the exception of a well-inspected Jeep Wrangler or Liberty or a minivan, which are the best of the bad. Chrysler is the weakest of the Detroit Three, and its prices will fall dramatically in the late fall. Be careful, though. Most of the Chrysler lineup is afflicted with serious safety- and performance-related defects, and its automatic transmissions, brakes, and air conditioners are practically biodegradable.
6. Don't buy GM's front-drive models or vehicles imported from China. As a rule, they are less reliable than the rear-drives and have poorly performing powertrains and brakes. Furthermore, crash test ratings for many China-made vehicles are listed as "Poor," and their assembly quality is neanderthal, at best. Start shopping for a GM car or truck in the first quarter of 2010, when prices are lowest and an additional 1,000 dealers will be fired, leaving hundreds of thousands of unsold cars and trucks.
7. Consider Ford—the automaker has offered more reliable and better-performing buys since it started cost cutting and selling off large chunks of the company several years ago. The added cash was invested in new models and better quality control that has made some Not Recommended models (such as the 2000–04 Focus) into Average (2004–10 Focus) or better buys. Today, Ford is the only Detroit builder with a model that *Lemon-Aid* rates as Recommended.
8. Don't buy from dual dealerships. The vehicle and parts inventory is split between two companies, and the represented auto companies see the dealerships as less than loyal and will cut them little slack in vehicle deliveries and warranty assistance.
9. Don't buy any vehicle that has been stored longer than three months; the Transport Canada–required date-of-manufacture plate will give you the month and year the car left the factory. Don't buy any vehicle that requires an extended warranty due to a reputation for past failures. It is likely warranties will be worthless when companies merge or shut down. And, as cash gets scarce, automakers and dealers will find more reasons to deny warranty coverage as they try to cover their payrolls, instead.

10. Use your credit card for the down payment, and put down as little money as possible. Use credit instead of cash to pay for repairs and maintenance charges.

Detroit's Misery and the Agony of Others

2010 is shaping up to be a terrible year for new-car sales, from Saskatoon to Seoul. All car companies are losing money at a record-breaking pace in every vehicle-marketing niche. The Japanese Big Three—Toyota, Honda, and Nissan—are posting record-breaking losses, and Hyundai, Kia, and BMW (MINI Cooper) are barely keeping their heads above water. Finally, Mitsubishi, one Japanese auto dealer with a good array of popular vehicles, is starved for new products.

European automakers have not done all that well, either. Mercedes-Benz sales have done poorly due to the general perception that the company makes overly engineered, poor-quality vehicles. Volkswagen, Audi, and Porsche sales have declined because of the entry of better-quality Japanese products, and Volvo/Saab sales have tanked as more buyers learn that Ford/GM do not speak "European car," except for Canada-based Magna buying into Opel (with Russia's help).

2009 was a nightmare year for Detroit-built cars and trucks, as the number of units sold in North America headed to less than 10 million vehicles annually (from 17 million). By mid-year, Chrysler, Ford, and General Motors sales were tracking far behind the Asian and European automakers, despite never-before-seen 20 percent discounts on Detroit models.

March of the Penguins

What hypocrisy! Auto companies are no different from apple vendors: Some stock is fresh, and some is rotten. All automakers and dealers have one goal in common, and that is to convince buyers that they are getting the safest, most reliable, and best vehicle money can buy—even if it's not true. GM doesn't want to hear about its 1995–2004 history of engine intake manifold gasket failures; Ford won't admit that it has been bedevilled by premature engine and automatic transmission burnouts from the early '90s through 2005; and Chrysler hypes its Hemi engines while denying that its automatic transmissions, which equip most of its lineup, are biodegradable crap.

After 40 years writing *Lemon-Aid*, I know car manufacturers run from the truth and look upon independent critics with hostile suspicion. In fact, there's an interesting and entertaining phenomenon that occurs every time I attend the annual auto shows in Montreal, Toronto, and Vancouver. As I walk by automakers' kiosks, each fronting dozens of beautifully spiffed new cars and trucks, and give comments to the press, manufacturers' reps follow me cautiously,

Auto shows promote a herd mentality where truth is the first casualty.

almost in lock-step fashion. Decked out in similarly styled suits and walking in unison, they play out a scene reminiscent of the movie *March of the Penguins*, except no one lays an egg (at least, not literally).

But this year is different. There are few auto shows. And, before I entered into a radio studio during my annual *Lemon-Aid* book promotion tour, a Detroit Three confidential letter was handed to me, asking for my assistance in "letting bygones be bygones and help[ing] us turn this thing around."

My answer is simple: NO! Detroit automakers have cheated and abused Canadians for almost half a century. I am a witness to that past, and will not forget its lessons. Auto executives will sell their souls for a few dollars and then pretend that all of their failings were caused by external forces. You want absolution? Go to Deepak Chopra, or some fawning car columnist.

All car journalists (an oxymoron?) know it's tough rating new and used vehicles without selling out to the car industry. That's why most do. This fact has been repeatedly confirmed by some of the best writers and broadcasters who are critical of automobile manufacturers.

Yet the road to auto harlotry is so subtle that few writers or broadcasters can resist compromising their integrity: The kids need private schooling; the mortgage must be paid. The smooth-talking executive car pimps are always there to say how much the company admires your work, but then they tell your editor or program director how much better your stories would be with more "balance."

And then these hustlers invite you on their trips to Asia and Europe, where they give you geishas, hats, jackets, laptop computers, specially prepared vehicles, and interviews with the top brass. They even sponsor annual journalism awards to make sure their coterie of friendly scribes spouts the party line.

You feel like nobility, but you're really a whore.

These smug automakers are in serious need of a reality check.

Here are the dismal facts published in 2006 by the authors of *Branding Iron: Branding Lessons from the Meltdown of the U.S. Auto Industry*:

The headlines offer a simplistic interpretation. They say that legacy costs, poor cost control, ill-advised investments in other automakers and in undistinguished products, all of which are serious issues, caused the trouble.

That's wrong. Or, worse, incomplete and myopic. It's the same kind of myopia that created the problem in the first place. Like many a crisis, this one has been brewing for decades. And the cost-cutting quick fixes proposed by many industry experts won't solve it. Why not? Because it's not the root cause. What is killing US automakers is their inability to attract growing numbers of customers to its numerous brands, many of which seem almost irrelevant today.

I have seen so much as I approach my fifth decade of automobile consumer advocacy. Back in the '70s, American Motors gave away free TVs with its new car, just before shutting its doors; five years ago, GM gave away free Dell computers; and recently, VW hawked free guitars. Detroit Three automakers continue to build poor-quality cars and trucks, although there appears to be some improvement over the past three years. The gap between Asian and American automobile quality has narrowed; however, this may reflect only a lowered benchmark following recent Honda, Nissan, and Toyota powertrain, electrical system, and body fit glitches. Nevertheless, Toyota and Lexus continue to dominate J.D. Power and Associates' dependability surveys, while American and European makes are mostly ranked below the industry average.

Buying a New Car, Truck, SUV, or Van

First, keep in mind that you are going to spend much more money than you may have anticipated—almost $31,000 for the average vehicle transaction, according to Dennis DesRosiers, a Toronto-based auto consultant. This is because of the many hidden fees, like freight charges and so-called administrative costs, that are added to the bottom line. But with cut-throat discounts, and armed with tips from this guide, you can bring this amount down to less than $25,000.

According to the Canadian Automobile Association (CAA), the average household owns two vehicles, which are each driven about 20,000 km annually and cost an average of $800 a year for maintenance.

Also, the CAA says in its *2009 Driving Costs* brochure that the annual cost of driving a 2009 Chevrolet Cobalt LT works out to $6,516 per year, or $17.85 a day, when factoring in insurance costs, licensing fees, depreciation, and financing. The cost rises to $23.63 per day when a 2009 Dodge Grand Caravan SE is used as a comparison vehicle.

Keep in mind that it's practically impossible to buy a bare-bones car or minivan because automakers cram them with costly, non-essential performance and convenience features in order to maximize their profits. Nevertheless, money-wasting gadgets like electronic navigation and sophisticated entertainment systems can easily be passed up with little impact on safety or convenience.

Full-torso side curtain airbags and electronic stability control, however, are important safety options that are well worth the extra expense.

Before paying big bucks, though, you should know what your real needs are and how much you can afford to spend. Don't confuse needs with styling (do you have a bucket bottom to conform to those bucket seats?) or trendy with essential (will a cheaper Mazda5 mini-minivan or Chrysler's Caliber hatchback suit you as well as or better than a Caravan or mid-sized car?). Visiting the showroom with your spouse or a level-headed relative or friend will help you steer a truer course through all the non-essential options you'll be offered.

Women don't receive the same welcome at auto showrooms as men do because they make the salesmen (yes, usually less than 10 percent of the sales staff are women) work too hard to make a sale. Most sales agents admit that female shoppers are far more knowledgeable about what they want and more patient in negotiating the contract's details than men, who tend to be mesmerized by many of the techno-toys available and often skip over the fine print and bluff their way through the negotiations.

Knowing that women often approach their purchases differently than men, you would think that smart dealerships would cater to this difference. But this is not the case. Marion W., a volunteer *Lemon-Aid* regional reporter from British Columbia, writes of her showroom experience:

> As a new young widow, shopping alone for the first time, I am totally shocked at the treatment I am receiving at the hands of car salespeople. Whatever happened to sexual equality?
>
> One salesperson had the gall to ask me if I had my husband's permission to buy a car! Another salesperson cornered my 12-year-old son and asked him on the sly if I had the money to buy that particular vehicle. Many dealerships don't even bother to approach me to ask if I would like help, and several have refused to let me drive their vehicles, giving me some pretty flaky reasons why I can't. I have a perfect driving record, so there should be no excuse....

In increasing numbers, women have discovered that minivans and SUVs are more versatile than passenger cars and station wagons. And, having spotted a profitable trend, automakers are offering increased versatility combined with unconventional styling in so-called "crossover" vehicles. These blended cars are part sedan and part station wagon, with a touch of sport-utility added for function and fun. For example, the Chrysler Pacifica is a smaller, sporty crossover vehicle that looks like a miniature SUV. It is a competent performer, but factory-related deficiencies and poor sales forced the Pacifica off the market in 2009.

What Can I Afford?

Determine how much money you can spend, and then decide which vehicles in that price range interest you. Have several models in mind so that the overpriced one won't tempt you too much. As your benchmarks, use the ratings, alternative models, estimated purchase costs, and residual value figures shown in Part Three of this guide. Remember, logic and prudence are the first casualties of showroom hype, so carefully consider your actual requirements and how much you can budget to meet them before comparing models and prices at a dealership. Write down your first, second, and third choices relative to each model and the equipment offered. Browse the automaker websites both in Canada and in the States, and consult *canadiandriver.com* for the Canadian manufacturer's suggested retail price (MSRP), promotions, and package discounts. Look for special low prices that may apply only to Internet-generated referrals. Once you get a good idea of the price variations, get out the fax machine or PC at home or work (a company letterhead is always impressive), and then make the dealers bid against each other (see page 71). Call the lowest-bidding dealership, ask for an appointment to be assured of getting a sales agent's complete attention, and take along the downloaded info from the automaker's website to avoid arguments.

Can I Get More for Less?

Easy as pie. Sometimes a cheaper twin will fill the bill. "Twins" are nameplates made by different auto manufacturers, or by different divisions of the same company, that are virtually identical in body design and mechanical components—such as the Chevrolet Cobalt and Pontiac Pursuit.

Let's look at the savings possible with "twinned" Chrysler minivans. A 2003 Grand Caravan that originally listed for $29,300 is now worth about $5,000. An upscale 2003 Town & Country that performs similarly to the Grand Caravan, with just a few additional gizmos, first sold for $42,700 and is now worth about $6,500. Where once $13,400 separated the two minivans, the price difference is now only $1,500—and you can expect the gap to close to almost nil over the next few years. Did the little extras really justify the Town & Country's higher price, or make it a better buy than the Grand Caravan? Obviously, the marketplace thinks not.

And don't get taken in by the "Buy Canadian!" chanting from Chrysler, Ford, and General Motors, as well as by Canadian Auto Workers (CAW) President Ken Lewenza. It's pure hypocrisy. While Detroit-based automakers are beating their chests over the need to buy American, they buy Japanese and South Korean companies and then market the foreign imports from Asian factories as their own. This practice has resulted in bastardized nameplates whose parentage isn't always easy to nail down. For example, is the Aveo a Chevy or a Daewoo? (It's a Daewoo, and not that reliable, to boot.)

Vehicles that are produced through co-ventures between Detroit automakers and Asian manufacturers have better quality control than vehicles manufactured by companies that were bought outright, and this looks like one of the factors that may save the American auto industry. For example, Toyota and Pontiac churn out identical Matrix and Vibe compacts in Ontario and the United States; however, the cheaper, Ontario-built Matrix has the better reputation for quality. On the other hand, Jaguar and Volvo quality have stagnated or declined since Ford bought the companies, and GM-owned Saab hasn't done much better. As for Daimler's takeover of Chrysler, what innovative, high-quality products did we see? Very little.

Sometimes choosing a higher trim line that packages many options as standard features will cost you less when you take all the features into account. It's hard to compare these bundled prices with the manufacturer's base price and added options, though. All of the separate prices are inflated and must be negotiated downward individually, while fully equipped vehicles don't allow for options to be deleted or priced separately. Furthermore, many of the bundled options are superfluous, and you probably wouldn't have chosen them to begin with.

Buying a GM front-drive minivan is like diving into a shark tank with 10 pounds of raw hamburger strapped to your butt.

Minivans, for example, often come in two versions: a base commercial, or cargo, version and a more luxurious model for private use. The commercial version doesn't have as many bells and whistles, but it's more likely to be in stock and will probably cost much less. And if you're planning to convert it, there's a wide choice of independent customizers that will likely do a better—and less expensive—job than the dealer. Of course, you will want a written guarantee from the dealer or customizer, or sometimes both, that no changes will invalidate the manufacturer's warranty. Also, look on the lot for a low-mileage (less than 10,000 km) current-year demonstrator that is carried over unchanged as a 2010 version. You will get an end-of-model-year rebate, a lower price for the extra mileage, and sundry other sales incentives that apply. Remember, if the vehicle has been registered to another company or individual, it is not a demo and should be considered used and be discounted accordingly (by at least 25 percent). You will also want to carry out a CarProof search and to have a complete printout of the vehicle's service history.

Leasing without Losing

Why Leasing May Cost More

There are many reasons why leasing is a bad idea. It's often touted as an alternative used to make high-cost vehicles more affordable, but for most people, it's really more expensive than buying outright. Lessees usually pay the full MSRP on a vehicle loaded with costly options, plus hidden fees and interest charges that wouldn't be included if the vehicle was purchased instead of leased. Researchers have found that some fully loaded entry-level cars leased with high interest rates and deceptive "special fees" could cost more than what some luxury models would cost to buy. A useful website that takes the mystery out of leasing is *www.federalreserve.gov/pubs/leasing* (Keys to Vehicle Leasing), run by the U.S. Federal Reserve Board. It goes into incredible detail, comparing leasing versus buying, and has a handy dictionary of the terms you're most likely to encounter.

Decoding "Lease-Talk"

Take a close look at the small print found in most leasing ads. Pay particular attention to words relating to the model year, condition of the vehicle ("demonstration" or "used"), equipment, warranty, interest rate, buy-back amount, down payment, security payment, monthly payment, transportation and preparation charges, administration fees ("acquisition" and "disposal" fees), insurance premiums, number of free kilometres, and excess kilometre charges.

Leasing Advantages

Leasing in Canada once made up almost 35 percent of all motor vehicle sales transactions because of rising interest rates and prices. Now, with lower new-car prices and generally low interest rates, the major Detroit automakers have backed away from leases, leaving the market to the Asians and Europeans. But leasing is still a fairly popular option, leading to 48-month leases and a proliferation of entry-level models that are now being leased in addition to the traditional "luxe" toys. Insiders say that almost all vehicles costing $60,000 or more are leased vehicles.

Experts agree: If you must lease, keep your costs to a minimum by leasing for the shortest time possible, by assuming the unexpired portion of an existing lease (see "Using Leasebusters," later in this section), and by making sure that the lease is close-ended (meaning that you walk away from the vehicle when the lease period ends)—an option used by 75 percent of lessees, according to the CAA.

Leasing does have a few advantages, though. First, it saves some of your capital, which you can invest to get a return greater than the leasing interest charges. Second, if you are taking a chance on a new model that hasn't been proven, you know that yours can be dumped at the dealer when the lease expires. But using that tactic raises more questions: What are you doing choosing such a risky venture in the first place? Will you have the patience to wait in the service bay while your luxury lemon is being repaired for the umpteenth time? Finally, do you want to be saddled with a four-year contract where the dealer is the judge and jury as to whether you go carless or not?

Some Precautions and an Alternative

On both new and used purchases, be wary of unjustified hidden costs, like a $495 "administrative" or "disposal" fee, an "acquisition" charge, or boosted transport and freight costs that can collectively add several thousand dollars to a vehicle's retail price. Also, look at the lease transfer fee charged by the leasing company or dealer or both. This fee can vary considerably. For example, Ford Credit, GMAC Financial Services, and BMW Financial Services charge $175, $450, and $1,500, respectively. Ford and BMW dealers can also impose a transfer fee.

Instead of leasing, consider purchasing used. Look for a three- to five-year-old off-lease vehicle with 60,000–100,000 km on the clock and some of the original warranty left. Such a vehicle will be just as reliable for less than half the cost of one bought new or leased. Parts will be easier to find, independent servicing should be a breeze, insurance premiums will come down from the stratosphere, and your financial risk will be lessened considerably if you end up with a lemon.

Breaking a Lease

Not an easy thing to do, and you may wind up paying $3,000–$8,000 in cancellation fees.

The last thing you want to do is stop your payments, especially if you've leased a lemon: The dealer can easily sue you for the remaining money owed, and you will have to pay the legal fees for both sides. You won't be able to prove the vehicle was defective or unreliable, because it will have been seized after the lease payments stopped. So there you are, without the vehicle to make your proof and on the receiving end of a costly lawsuit.

Lawyers advise three ways of breaking a lease. First, you can ask for free Canadian Motor Vehicle Arbitration Plan (CAMVAP) arbitration (see page 110). A second recourse, if there's a huge debt remaining, is to send a lawyer's letter cancelling the contract by putting the leasing agency and automaker on notice that the vehicle is unacceptable. This should lead to some negotiation. If this fails, inspect the vehicle, have it legally tendered back to the dealer, and then sue for what you owe plus your inconvenience and assorted sundry expenses. You can use the small claims court on your own if the amount in litigation is less than the court's claim limit.

The third way to get out of a lease is to legally transfer the lease using a firm like Leasebusters.

Using Leasebusters

Leasebusters (*www.leasebusters.com*) is a Canadian company that puts you in touch with people who are willing to take over your lease. Before listing your vehicle, the company will evaluate your present lease obligations, online and free of charge, to determine if a lease transfer is a wise idea.

Leasebusters has been in business for over a decade and says about 80 percent of the leased vehicles they offer are disposed of within 60 days. For $295 plus GST (or GST and QST in Quebec), Leasebusters provides a how-to-exit-a-car-lease guide, a large display ad, and an aggressive advertising campaign to shop your lease around.

Here is how the process works through Leasebusters: All lease transfers are credit-approved legal transfers sanctioned by the lessor. Typically, the original selling dealership must participate in the transfer because they are the selling agent for the lessor and, in many cases, own the leasing agency. The order of operations for the person accepting the lease is as follows:

- Go see the vehicle (inspect, test drive, and discuss the vehicle with the original lessee).
- Make a deal, in principal, with the original lessee (including who pays for transfer fees, inspections, security deposits, cash incentives, and/or down payments). The deal is subject to credit approval.
- Complete a credit application and submit it to the original selling dealership.
- Wait for a credit decision after the dealership submits the deal to the lessor.
- Coordinate a delivery and signing date with the dealership and the original lessee upon receipt of credit approval.
- Pay the fee that will be charged for the transfer by either or both the dealer and the lessor.

Assuming an existing lease from another driver has many advantages and a few pitfalls. First, you get a vehicle that may be depreciated by almost 40 percent of its original value, and you don't have to pay for freight, pre-delivery inspection (PDI), air tax, gas tax, or other charges—increasing your savings even more. And of course, you reduce retail sales tax (RST) and goods and services tax (GST) and get the balance of all factory warranties. Second, you can have a short-term fling with an exotic vehicle without risking a long-term commitment. This is especially advantageous when leasing imports and "luxe" toys where servicing and performance aren't up to the advertised hype.

On the downside, you may be asked to assume the obligation to pay for a lease that was a bad deal in the first place. However, if you can get the previous lessee to put additional money up front as compensation, the deal may be acceptable. Furthermore, servicing by the dealer will likely be obligatory in order to maintain the warranty, which will add to overall maintenance costs.

The leasing agency or dealer may claim extra money when the lease expires, because the vehicle may miss some original equipment or show "unreasonable" wear and tear (dings, paint problems, and excessive tire wear are the most common reasons for extra charges). Prevent this from happening by having the vehicle inspected prior to the lease takeover. Remember, some leasing companies will hold the original lessee liable for the lease until the end of the term; once a buyer is approved to take over the lease, the next lessee will be added on to the original contract, making the current lessee like a co-signer on the lease.

Buying the Right Car or Truck

Keep It Simple

Our driving needs are influenced by where we live, our lifestyles, and our ages (see pages 28–30 for a discussion of vehicles best suited to mature drivers). The ideal car should be crashworthy and easy to drive, have minimal high-tech features to distract and annoy, and not cost much to maintain.

In the city, a small wagon or hatchback is more practical and less expensive than a mid-sized car like the Honda Accord or Toyota Camry. Furthermore, have you seen the newer Civic and Elantra? What once were small cars are now quite large, relatively fuel-efficient, and equipped with more horsepower than you'll ever likely need. Nevertheless, if you're going to be doing a lot of highway driving, transporting small groups of people, or loading up on accessories, a medium-sized sedan, wagon, or small sport-utility could be the best choice for price, comfort, and reliability.

Don't let spikes in fuel prices stampede you into buying a vehicle unsuitable to your driving needs. If you travel less than 20,000 km per year, mostly in the city, choose a small car equipped with a 4-cylinder engine that produces between 120 and 140 hp to get the best fuel economy (5.9 L/100 km, or almost 40 mpg) without sacrificing performance. Anything more powerful is just a waste. Extensive highway driving, however, demands the cruising performance, extra power for additional accessories, and durability of a larger, 6-cylinder engine. Believe me, fuel savings will be the last thing on your mind if you buy an underpowered vehicle.

Be especially wary of the towing capabilities bandied about by automakers. They routinely exaggerate towing capability and seldom mention the need for expensive optional equipment, or that the top safe towing speed may be only 72 km/h (45 mph), as is the case with some minivans. Generally, 3.0L to 3.8L V6 engines will safely accommodate most towing needs. The 4-cylinder engines may handle light loads, but it will likely be a white-knuckle experience when merging with highway traffic or travelling over hilly terrain.

Remember, you may have to change your driving habits to accommodate the type of vehicle you purchase. Front-drive braking is quite different from braking with a rear-drive, and braking efficiency on ABS-equipped vehicles is compromised if you pump the brakes. Also, rear-drive vans handle like trucks, and you may scrub the right rear tire during sharp right-hand turns until you get the hang of making wider turns. Limited rear visibility is another problem with larger vans, forcing drivers to carefully survey side and rear traffic before changing lanes or merging with traffic.

Front-Drives

Front-drives direct engine power to the front wheels, which pull the vehicle forward while the rear wheels simply support the rear. The biggest benefit of front-drives is foul-weather traction. With the engine and transmission up front, there's lots of extra weight pressing down on the front-drive wheels, increasing tire grip in snow and on wet pavement. But when you drive up a steep hill, or tow a boat or trailer, the weight shifts and you lose the traction advantage.

Although I recommend a number of front-drive vehicles in this guide, I don't like them as much as rear-drives. Granted, front-drives provide a bit more interior room (no transmission hump), more carlike handling, and better fuel economy than do rear-drives, but damage from potholes and fender-benders is usually more extensive, and maintenance costs (especially premature front tire and brake wear) are much higher than with rear-drives.

Rear-Drives

Rear-drives direct engine power to the rear wheels, which push the vehicle forward. The front wheels steer and also support the front of the vehicle. With the engine up front, the transmission in the middle, and the drive axle in the rear, there's plenty of room for larger and more durable drivetrain components. This makes for less crash damage, lower maintenance costs, and higher towing capacities than with front-drives.

On the downside, rear-drives don't have as much weight over the front wheels as do the front-drives, and therefore, they can't provide as much traction on wet or icy roads and tend to fishtail unless they're equipped with an expensive traction-control system.

Chevrolet's 2010 resurrected Camaro should be a big rear-drive winner for GM.

Four-Wheel Drive (4×4)

Four-wheel drive (4×4) directs engine power through a transfer case to all four wheels, which pull and push the vehicle forward, giving you twice as much traction. On most models, when four-wheel drive isn't engaged, the vehicle reverts to rear-drive. The large transfer-case housing makes the vehicle sit higher, giving you additional ground clearance.

Keep in mind that extended driving over dry pavement with 4×4 engaged will cause the driveline to bind and result in serious damage. Some buyers are turning instead to rear-drive pickups equipped with winches and large, deep-lugged rear tires.

Many 4×4 customers driving SUVs set on truck platforms have been turned off by the typically rough and noisy driveline, a tendency for the vehicle to tip over when cornering at moderate speeds, vague or trucklike handling, high repair costs, and poor fuel economy.

All-Wheel Drive (AWD)

Essentially, this is four-wheel drive that's on all the time. Used mostly in sedans and minivans, AWD never needs to be deactivated when running over dry pavement and doesn't require the heavy transfer case that raises ground clearance and cuts fuel economy. AWD-equipped vehicles aren't recommended for off-roading because of their lower ground clearance and fragile driveline parts, which aren't as rugged as 4×4 components. But anyhow, you shouldn't be off-roading in a car or minivan in the first place.

Safety and Comfort

Do You Feel Comfortable in the Vehicle?

The advantages of many sports cars and minivans quickly pale in direct proportion to your tolerance for a harsh ride, noise, a claustrophobic interior, and limited visibility. Minivan owners often have to deal with a high step-up, a cold interior, lots of buffeting from wind and passing trucks, and poor rear visibility. With these drawbacks, many buyers find that after falling in love with the showroom image, they end up hating their purchase—all the more reason to test drive your choice over a period of several days to get a real feel for its positive and negative characteristics.

Check to see if the vehicle's interior is user-friendly. For example, can you reach the sound system and AC controls without straining or taking your eyes off the road? Are the controls just as easy to operate by feel as by sight? What about dash glare onto the front windshield, and headlight aim and brightness? Can you drive with the window or sunroof open and not be subjected to an ear-splitting roar? Do rear-seat passengers have to be contortionists to enter or exit, as is the case with many two-door vehicles?

To answer these questions, you need to drive the vehicle over a period of time to test how well it responds to the diversity of your driving needs, without having some impatient sales agent yapping in your ear. If this isn't possible, you may find out too late that the handling is less responsive than you'd wanted.

You can conduct the following showroom tests: Adjust the seat to a comfortable setting, buckle up, and settle in. Can you sit 25 cm away from the steering wheel and still reach the accelerator and brake pedals? When you look out the windshield and use the rear- and side-view mirrors, do you detect any serious blind spots? Will optional mirrors give you an unobstructed view? Does the seat feel comfortable enough for long trips? Can you reach important controls without moving your back from the seatback? If not, shop for something that better suits your needs.

Which Safety Features Are Best?

Automakers have loaded 2009–10 models with features that wouldn't have been imagined several decades ago, because safety devices appeal to families and some, like airbags, can be marked up by 500 percent. Yet some safety innovations, such as anti-lock brake systems (ABS) and adaptive cruise control (ACC), don't deliver the safety payoffs promised by automakers and may create additional dangers. For example, anti-lock breaks often fail and are expensive to maintain, while adaptive cruise control may slow the vehicle down when passing another car on the highway. Some of the more-effective safety features are head-protecting side airbags, electronic stability control (ESC), adjustable brake and accelerator pedals, standard integrated child safety seats, seat belt pretensioners, adjustable head restraints, and sophisticated navigation and communication systems.

Seat belts provide the best means of reducing the severity of injury arising from both low- and high-speed frontal collisions. In order to be effective, though, seat belts must be adjusted properly and feel comfortably tight without undue slack. Owners often complain that seat belts don't retract enough for a snug fit, are too tight, chafe the neck, or don't properly fit children. Some automakers have corrected these problems with adjustable shoulder-belt anchors that allow both tall and short drivers to raise or lower the belt for a snug, more comfortable fit. Another important seat belt innovation is the pretensioner (not found on all seat belts), a device that automatically tightens the safety belt in the event of a crash.

Crashworthiness

A vehicle with a high crash protection rating is a lifesaver. In fact, crashworthiness is the one safety improvement over the past 40 years that everyone agrees has paid off handsomely without presenting any additional risks to drivers or passengers. By surrounding occupants with a protective cocoon and deflecting crash forces away from the interior, auto engineers have successfully created safer vehicles without increasing vehicle size or cost. And purchasing a vehicle with the idea that you'll be involved in an accident someday is not unreasonable. According to IIHS, the average car will likely have two accidents before ending up as scrap, and it's twice as likely to be in a severe front-impact crash as a side-impact crash.

Since some vehicles are more crashworthy than others, and since size doesn't always guarantee crash safety, it's important to buy a vehicle that gives you the best protection from frontal, frontal offset, and side collisions while keeping its rollover potential to a minimum.

For example, the Chrysler Caravan and Ford Freestar minivans are similarly designed, but your chances of surviving a high-speed frontal offset collision are greater with the Freestar than with a Caravan or any other Chrysler minivan. (But the chances that your wallet will survive a trip to the service bay are less certain.)

Two Washington-based agencies monitor how vehicle design affects crash safety: the National Highway Traffic Safety Administration (NHTSA) and the Insurance Institute for Highway Safety (IIHS). Crash information from these two groups doesn't always correspond because, while IIHS's results incorporate all kinds of accidents, including offset crashes and bumper damage sustained from low-speed collisions, NHTSA's figures relate only to 56 km/h (35 mph) frontal collisions and some side collisions. The frontal tests are equivalent to two vehicles of equal weight hitting each other head-on while travelling at 56 km/h, or to a car slamming into a parked car at 114 km/h (71 mph). Bear in mind that a vehicle providing good injury protection may also cost more to repair, because its structure, not the occupants, absorbs most of the collision forces. That's why safer vehicles don't always have lower insurance rates.

Don't get taken in by the five-star crash rating hoopla touted by automakers. There isn't any one vehicle that can claim a prize for being the safest. Vehicles that do well in NHTSA side and front crash tests may not do very well in IIHS offset crash tests, or may have poorly designed head restraints that can increase the severity of neck injuries. Or a vehicle may have a high number of airbag failures, such as the bags deploying when they shouldn't or not deploying when they should.

Before making a final decision on the vehicle you want, look up its crashworthiness and overall safety profile in Part Three.

Cars versus trucks

Occupants of large vehicles have fewer severe injury claims than do occupants of small vehicles. This was proven conclusively in a 1996 NHTSA study, which showed that collisions between light trucks or vans and small cars resulted in car occupants having an 81 percent higher fatality rate than the occupants of the light trucks or vans did.

Vehicle weight offers the most protection in two-vehicle crashes. In a head-on crash, for example, the heavier vehicle drives the lighter one backward, which decreases forces inside the heavy vehicle and increases forces in the lighter one. All heavy vehicles, even poorly designed ones, offer this advantage in two-vehicle collisions. However, they may not offer good protection in single-vehicle crashes.

Crash test figures show that SUVs, vans, and trucks also offer more protection to adult occupants than do passenger cars in most crashes because their higher set-up allows them to ride over other vehicles (Ford's 2002 4×4 Explorer lowered its bumper height to prevent this hazard). Conversely, because of their high centre of gravity, easily overloaded tires, and unforgiving suspensions, these vehicles have a disproportionate number of single-vehicle rollovers, which are far deadlier than frontal or side collisions. In the case of the early Ford Explorer, Bridgestone/Firestone CEO John Lampe testified in August 2001 that 42 of the 43 rollovers involving Ford Explorers in Venezuela were on competitors' tires—shifting the rollover blame to the Explorer's design and crashworthiness.

Interestingly, a vehicle's past crashworthiness rating doesn't always guarantee that subsequent model years will be just as safe or safer. Take Ford's Escort as an example. It earned five stars for front-passenger collision protection in 1991, and then earned fewer stars every year thereafter, until the model was discontinued in 2002. The Dodge Caravan is another example. It was given five stars for driver-side protection in 2000 but has earned four stars ever since.

Rollovers

Although rollovers represent only 3 percent of crashes (out of 10,000 annual U.S. road accidents), they cause one-third of all traffic deaths from what are usually single-vehicle accidents.

Rollovers occur less frequently with passenger cars and minivans than with SUVs, trucks, and full-sized vans (especially the 15-passenger variety). That's why electronic vehicle stability systems aren't as important a safety feature on passenger cars as on minivans, vans, pickups, and SUVs. All of the rollover ratings for prior years and models can be found at *www.nhtsa.dot.gov/ncap*.

More Safety Considerations

There are no more easy safety solutions that protect us from ourselves. According to NHTSA's figures, 50 percent of car-crash and 70 percent of pickup-crash fatalities weren't wearing seat belts. This statistic is all the more troubling because everyone knows that safety belt use saves lives. Clearly, half of us don't give a damn.

Although there has been a dramatic reduction in fatalities and injuries over the past three decades, safety experts feel that additional automobile safety features will henceforth pay small dividends, and they expect the highway death and injury rate to start trending upward. They say it's time to target the driver, after reviewing NHTSA's studies that show 76 percent of almost 7 million annual crashes on North American highways are caused by driver error, 14 percent can be attributed to driver impairment (drugs, alcohol, or illness), and 8 percent are caused by the environment (poorly maintained roads and bad weather conditions). Just 2 percent are caused by vehicle problems such as inferior tires or poor design.

This means that safety programs that concentrate primarily on motor vehicle standards won't be as effective as measures that target both the driver and the vehicle—such as more-sophisticated "black box" data recorders; more-stringent licensing requirements, including graduated licensing and de-licensing programs directed at teens and seniors; and stricter law enforcement.

Incidentally, police studies have shown that there's an important side benefit to arresting traffic-safety scofflaws: They often net dangerous career criminals or seriously impaired drivers before they have the chance to harm others. Apparently, sociopaths and substance abusers don't care which laws they break.

Beware of unsafe designs

Although it sounds hard to believe, automakers will deliberately manufacture a vehicle that will kill or maim simply because, in the long run, it costs less to stonewall complaints and pay off victims than to make a safer vehicle. I learned this lesson after listening to the court testimony of GM engineers—who deliberately placed fire-prone "sidesaddle" gas tanks in millions of pickups to save $3 per vehicle—and after reading the court transcripts of *Grimshaw v. Ford* (fire-prone Pintos) from 1981. Reporter Anthony Prince wrote the following assessment of Ford's indifference in an article titled "Lessons of the Ford/Firestone scandal: Profit motive turns consumers into road kill," *People's Tribune* (Online Edition); Vol. 26, No. 11, November 2000:

> Rejecting safety designs costing between only $1.80 and $15.30 per Pinto, Ford had calculated the damages it would likely pay in wrongful death and injury cases and pocketed the difference. In a cold and calculating "costs/benefits" analysis, Ford projected that the Pinto would probably cause 180 burn deaths, 180 serious burn injuries, [and] 2,100 burned vehicles each year. Also, Ford estimated civil suits of $200,000 per death, $67,000 per injury, [and] $700 per vehicle for a grand total of $49.5 million. The costs for installing safety features would cost approximately $137 million per year. As a result, the Pinto became a moving target, its unguarded fuel tank subject to rupture by exposed differential bolts shoved into it by rear-end collisions at speeds of as little as 21 miles per hour [34 km/h]. Spewing gasoline into the passenger compartment, the car and its passengers became engulfed in a raging inferno.

And here are more recent examples of corporate greed triumphing over public safety: Pre-1997 airbag designs that maim or kill women, children, and seniors; anti-lock brake systems that don't brake; flimsy front seats and seatbacks; the absence of rear head restraints; and fire-prone GM pickup fuel tanks and Ford cruise-control deactivation switches. Two other examples of hazardous engineering designs that put profit ahead of safety are failure-prone Chrysler, Ford, and GM minivan sliding doors and automatic transmissions that suddenly shift into Neutral, allowing the vehicle to roll away when parked on an incline or causing it to break down in traffic.

Active safety

Advocates of active safety stress that accidents are caused by the proverbial "nut behind the wheel" and believe that safe driving can be best taught through schools or private driving courses. Active safety components are generally those mechanical systems—such as anti-lock brake systems (ABS), high-performance tires, and traction control—that may help a driver to avoid accidents if they're skillful and mature.

I am not a fan of ABS. The systems are often ineffective, failure-prone, and expensive to service. Yet they are an essential part of most systems' electronic stability control (ESC), which is a proven lifesaver. Essentially, ABS prevents a vehicle's wheels from locking when the brakes are applied in an emergency situation, thus reducing skidding and the loss of directional control. When braking on wet or dry roads, your stopping distance will be about the same as with conventional braking systems. But in gravel, slush, or snow, your stopping distance will be greater.

The theory of active safety has several drawbacks. First, drivers who are under the influence of alcohol or drugs cause about 40 percent of all fatal accidents. All the high-performance options and specialized driving courses in the world will not provide much protection from impaired drivers who draw a bead on your vehicle. And because active safety components get a lot of use—you're likely to need anti-lock brakes 99 times more often than you'll need an airbag—they have to be well designed and well maintained to remain effective. Finally, consider that independent studies show that safe driving taught to young drivers doesn't necessarily reduce the number of driving-related deaths and injuries (*Lancet*, July 2001; 1978 DeKalb County, Georgia, Study):

> In 1980, the U.S. Department of Transportation conducted a study designed to prove the value of driver education in the nation's high schools. It's commonly referred to as the DeKalb Study, from the county in Georgia where the research took place. The DeKalb Study compared the accident records of 9,000 teens that had taken driver education in the county's high schools with 9,000 teens that had no formal driver training. The final results showed no significant difference between the two groups. In other words, DeKalb County, Georgia, paid a large amount of money for absolutely no value.

Passive safety

Passive safety assumes that you will be involved in life-threatening situations and should be either warned in time to avoid a collision or automatically protected from rolling over, losing traction, or bearing the brunt of collision forces. Head-protecting side airbags, electronic stability control, daytime running lights, and a centre-mounted third brake light are four passive safety features that have paid off handsomely in reduced injuries and lives saved.

Passive safety features also assume some accidents aren't avoidable and that, when those accidents occur, vehicles should provide as much protection as possible to drivers, passengers, and other vehicles that may be struck—without depending on the driver's reactions. Passive safety components that have consistently been proven to reduce vehicular deaths and injuries are seat belts, laminated windshields, and vehicle structures that enhance crashworthiness by absorbing or deflecting crash forces away from the vehicle's occupants.

Safety Features That Kill

In the late '60s, Washington forced automakers to include essential safety features like collapsing steering columns and safety windshields in their cars. As the years have passed, the number of mandatory safety features increased to include seat belts, airbags, and crashworthy construction. These improvements met with public approval until quite recently, when reports of deaths and injuries caused by ABS and airbag failures showed that defective components and poor engineering negated the potential life-saving benefits associated with having these devices.

For example, one out of every five ongoing NHTSA defect investigations concerns inadvertent airbag deployment, deactivation of the front passenger airbag, failure of the airbag to deploy, or injuries suffered when the bag did go off. In fact, airbags are the agency's single-largest cause of current investigations, exceeding even the full range of brake problems, which runs second.

Side Airbags—Good and Bad

Side and side curtain airbags are designed to protect drivers and passengers in rollovers and side-impact crashes, which are estimated to account for almost one-third of vehicular deaths. They also have been shown to help keep unbelted occupants from being ejected in rollovers. Head-protecting side airbags can reduce serious crash injuries by 45 percent. Side airbags without head protection reduce injuries by only 10 percent. Ideally, you want a side airbag system that protects both the torso and head.

Because side airbags aren't required by federal regulation in Canada or the States, neither government has developed any tests to measure their safety for children or small adults. IIHS hopes its test results will goad government regulators and automakers into standardizing the design of side airbags and increasing their effectiveness and safety.

There is a downside to increased side airbag protection: Sit properly in your seat, or face serious injury from the deploying side airbag. Preliminary safety studies show side airbags may be deadly to children or to any occupant sitting too close to the airbag, resting his or her head on the side pillar, or holding onto the roof-mounted assist handle. Research carried out in 1998 by safety researchers (Anil Khadikar, Biodynamics Engineering Inc., and Lonney Pauls, Springwater Micro Data Systems, *Assessment of Injury Protection Performance of Side Impact Airbags*) shows there are four hazards that pertain to most airbag systems:

1. Inadvertent airbag firing (short circuits, faulty hardware or software)
2. Unnecessary airbag firing (sometimes the opposite-side airbag will fire; the airbag may deploy when a low-speed side-swipe wouldn't have endangered occupant safety)
3. A small child, say, a three-year-old, restrained in a booster seat could be seriously injured
4. Out-of-position restrained occupants could be seriously injured

The researchers conclude with the following observation: "Even properly restrained vehicle occupants can have their upper or lower extremities in harm's way in the path of an exploding [side] airbag."

The 1998 study and dozens of other scientific papers confirm that small or tall restrained drivers face death or severe injury from frontal and side airbag deployments for the simple reason that they are outside of the norm of the 5'8", 180-pound, male test dummy. These studies also debunk the safety merits of anti-lock brakes, so it's no surprise they go unheralded by Transport Canada and other government and private safety groups.

And don't forget NHTSA's side airbag warning issued on October 14, 1999:

> Side impact airbags can provide significant supplemental safety benefits to adults in side impact crashes. However, children who are seated in close proximity to a side airbag may be at risk of serious or fatal injury, especially if the child's head, neck, or chest is in close proximity to the airbag at the time of deployment.

Protecting yourself

Because not all airbags function, or malfunction, the same way, *Lemon-Aid* has done an exhaustive analysis of U.S. and Canadian recalls, crash data, and owner complaints to determine which vehicles and which model years use airbags that may seriously injure occupants or deploy inadvertently. That data can be found in Part Three's model ratings.

Additionally, you should take the following steps to reduce the danger from airbag deployment:

- Buy a vehicle with head-protecting side curtain airbags for front and rear passengers.
- Make sure that seat belts are buckled and all head restraints are properly adjusted (to about ear level).
- Choose vehicles with head restraints that are rated "Good" by IIHS (see Part Three).
- Insist that passengers who are frail or short, or who have recently had surgery, sit in the back and properly position themselves away from side airbags.
- Ensure that the driver's seat can be adjusted for height and has tracks with sufficient rearward travel to allow short drivers to remain at a safe distance (over 25 cm) away from the bag's deployment and still be able to reach the accelerator and brake.
- Consider buying pedal extensions to keep you at a safe distance away from a deploying airbag if you are short-statured.

Top 20 Safety Defects

The U.S. federal government's online safety complaints database contains well over 100,000 entries, going back to vehicles made in the late '70s. Although the database was originally intended to record only incidents of component failures that relate to safety, you will find every problem imaginable dutifully recorded by clerks working for NHTSA.

A perusal of the listed complaints shows that some safety-related failures occur more frequently than others and often affect one manufacturer more than another. Here is a summary of the most commonly reported failures, in order of frequency:

1. Airbags not deploying when they should, or deploying when they shouldn't
2. ABS total brake failure; wheel lock-up
3. Tire-tread separation
4. Electrical or fuel-system fires
5. Sudden acceleration
6. Sudden stalling
7. Sudden electrical failures
8. Transmission failing to engage, or suddenly disengaging
9. Transmission jumping from Park to Reverse or Neutral; vehicle rolling away when parked
10. Steering or suspension failures
11. Seat belt failures
12. Collapsing seatbacks
13. Defective sliding door, door locks, and latches
14. Poor headlight illumination; glare
15. Dash reflecting onto windshield
16. Hood flying up
17. Wheel falling away
18. Steering wheel lifting off
19. Transmission lever pulling out
20. Exploding windshields

Vehicles for Older Drivers

Canada's Safety Council says that more than 30 percent of Canada's population was over age 50 in 2002, and half of Canadians aged 65 or older living in private households drive motor vehicles—though most drive only a few times a week. Furthermore, drivers over 80 are the fastest-growing segment of the driving population. Husbands do the bulk of family driving, which usually involves short trips (11–17 km per day, on average) for medical appointments and visits to family, friends, and shopping malls. This puts older women, who tend to outlive their husbands, in a serious bind because of their lack of driving experience—particularly in rural areas, where driving is a necessity rather than a choice. Says Statistics Canada (*www12.statcan.ca/census-recensement/2006/as-sa/97-551/p10-eng.cfm*):

> The fertility decline that began in the 1960s and the steady increase in life expectancy, which affected every part of Canada, contributed to the almost uninterrupted aging of all provincial and territorial populations over the last 40 years. The aging trend can be expected to accelerate throughout the country when the first baby-boomers turn 65 years in 2011.

I am 65, so I know that older drivers, like most other drivers, want cars that are reliable, relatively inexpensive, and fuel efficient. Additionally, we require vehicles that compensate for some of the physical challenges associated with aging (I'm getting fatter, slower, and much more taciturn, I'm told) and provide protection for accidents more common with mature drivers (side impacts, for example). Furthermore, as drivers get older, they find that the very act of getting into a car (sitting down while moving sideways, without bumping their heads or twisting their necks) demands considerable acrobatic skill.

Access and Comfort for Older Drivers

I've been told that some drivers with arthritic hands have to insert a pencil into their key ring to twist the key in the ignition. Make sure your ignition lock doesn't require that much effort. Power locks and windows are a must, especially if the vehicle will be operated with hand controls. A remote keyless entry will allow entry without having to twist a key in the door lock. A vehicle equipped with a buttonless shifter will be less difficult to activate for arthritis sufferers and drivers with limited upper-body mobility. Cruise control can be helpful for those with lower-body mobility challenges.

Get a vehicle that's easy to enter and exit. Check for door openings that are wide enough to get into and out of easily, both for you and for any wheelchairs or scooters that may need to be loaded. Make sure the door catches when opened on a slight incline so that it doesn't close as you are exiting. If necessary, your trunk or rear cargo area should have a low liftover and room to stow your wheelchair or scooter. Bench seats are preferable because they're roomier and easier to access; getting a power-adjustable driver's seat with memory is also a good idea. Make sure the seat is comfortable and has plenty of side bolstering.

Forget minivans, unless you invest in a step-up, choose one with an easily reached inside-grip handle, and don't mind bumping the left-side steering-column stalk with your knee each time you slide into the driver's seat. Incidentally, General Motors' 2009 minivans offer a Sit-N-Lift option, which is a motorized, rotating lift-and-lower passenger seat that's accessed through the middle door and can be taken out when not needed.

Drivers with limited mobility, or those who are recovering from hip surgery, give kudos to the Cadillac Escalade SUV and GM Venture/Montana minivans; Toyota's Echo, Yaris, Matrix, and Avalon; and small SUVs such as the Honda CR-V, Hyundai Tucson, and Toyota RAV4. Of this group, only the recently discontinued GM minivans give me cause for concern, because of their poor reliability. Incidentally,

NHTSA warns drivers with physical disabilities against the use of special steering-control devices on airbag-equipped vehicles.

Safety Features for Older Drivers

The driver's seat should be mounted high enough to give a commanding view of the road (with slower reaction times, seniors need earlier warnings). Driver's seats must offer enough rearward travel to attenuate the force of an exploding airbag, which can be particularly hazardous to older or small-statured occupants, children, or anyone recovering from surgery. Adjustable gas and brake pedals are a must for short-legged drivers.

And while we're discussing airbags, remember that they are calibrated to explode during low-speed collisions (at less than 10 km/h) and that reports of injuries caused by their deployment are commonplace. Therefore, always put at least 25 cm between your upper torso and the steering wheel.

Look for handles near the door frame that can be gripped for support when entering or leaving the vehicle, bright dashboard gauges that can be seen in sunlight, and instruments with large-sized controls.

Remote-controlled mirrors are a must, along with adjustable, unobtrusive head restraints and a non-reflective front windshield (many drivers put a cloth on the dash-top to cut the distraction). Make sure that the brake and accelerator pedals aren't mounted too close together.

As far as safety features are concerned, a superior crashworthiness rating is essential, as well as torso- and head-protecting side airbags, since most intersection collisions involving mature drivers occur when drivers are making a turn into oncoming traffic. The extra head protection can make a critical difference in side impacts. For example, Toyota's 2004 RAV4 with $680 head-protecting side airbags earned a "Best Pick" designation from the Insurance Institute for Highway Safety (IIHS). When tested without the head protection, it received a "Poor" rating in the side test.

Don't be overly impressed by anti-lock brakes, since their proper operation (no tapping on the brakes) runs counter to everything you have been taught, plus they aren't that reliable. Look for headlights that give you a comfortable view at night, as well as easily seen and heard dash-mounted turn signal indicators. Ensure that the vehicle's knobs and switches are large and easy to identify. Having an easily accessed, full-sized spare tire and a user-friendly lug wrench and jack stand is also important.

Other Buying Considerations

When "New" Isn't New

Nothing will cause you to lose money more quickly than buying a new car that's older than advertised, has previously been sold and then taken back, has accident damage, or has had the odometer disconnected or turned back.

Even if the vehicle hasn't been used, it may have been left outdoors for a considerable length of time, causing the deterioration of rubber components, premature body and chassis rusting, or severe rusting of internal mechanical parts, which leads to brake malfunction, fuel line contamination, hard starting, and stalling.

You can check a vehicle's age by looking at the date-of-manufacture plate usually found on the driver-side door pillar. If the date of manufacture is 7/09, your vehicle was probably one of the last 2009 models made before the September changeover to the 2010s. Redesigned vehicles or those new to the market are exceptions to this rule. They may arrive at dealerships in early spring or midsummer and are considered to be next year's models. They also depreciate more quickly, owing to their earlier launching, but this difference narrows over time.

Sometimes a vehicle can be too new and cost you more in maintenance because its redesign glitches haven't yet been worked out. As Honda's North American manufacturing chief, Koki Hirashima, so ably put it, carryover models generally have fewer problems than vehicles that have been significantly reworked or just introduced to the market. Newly redesigned vehicles get quality scores that are, on average, 2 percent worse than vehicles that have been around for a while, says J.D. Power. Some surprising poor performers: the 2002 Jaguar X-Type, 2002 Nissan Altima, 2002 Toyota Avalon and Camry, and 2001 Honda Civic. More recently, the 2004 Nissan Quest and Toyota Sienna failed to live up to expectations.

Because they were the first off the assembly line for that model year, most vehicles assembled between September and February are called "first-series" cars. "Second-series" vehicles, made between March and August, incorporate more assembly-line fixes and are better built than the earlier models, which may depend on ineffective "field fixes" to mask problems until the warranty expires. Second-series vehicles will sell for the same price or less, but they will be a far better buy because of their assembly-line upgrades and more generous rebates. Service bulletins for Chrysler's new Caliber and Charger; GM's Solstice, Torrent, and Sky roadsters; and the Ford Fusion, Zephyr, and Milan show these vehicles all had serious quality shortcomings during their first year on the market. It usually takes a couple of years for the factory to get most of the quality glitches corrected.

There's also the very real possibility that the new vehicle you've just purchased was damaged while being shipped to the dealer and was later fixed in the service bay during the pre-delivery inspection. It's estimated that this happens to about

10 percent of all new vehicles. Although there's no specific Canadian legislation allowing buyers of vehicles damaged in transit to cancel their contracts, B.C. legislation says that dealers must disclose damages of $2,000 or more. In a more general sense, Canadian common-law jurisprudence does allow for cancellation or compensation whenever the delivered product differs markedly from what the buyer expected to receive. Ontario's revised *Consumer Protection Act* is particularly hard-nosed in prohibiting this kind of misrepresentation.

Fuel Economy Follies

Poor gas mileage is one of the top complaints among owners of new cars and minivans. Drivers say gas mileage is seldom as high as it's hyped to be; in fact, it's likely to be 10–20 percent less than advertised with most vehicles. (Gas mileage, measured in mpg, is the opposite of metric fuel consumption, measured in L/100 km. In other words, you want gas mileage to be high and consumption to be low.) *Consumer Reports* magazine estimates that 90 percent of vehicles sold don't get the gas mileage advertised, and their reporters target hybrids built by Honda and Toyota as the worst offenders. (Incidentally, Honda dropped its Insight hybrid for three years and is just returning to the market with its 2010 version.)

Why such a contradiction between promise and performance?

It's simple: Automakers cheat on their tests. They submit their own test results to the government after testing under optimum conditions. Transport Canada then publishes these self-serving "cooked" figures as its own research. One Ford service bulletin is remarkably frank in discounting the validity of these tests:

> Very few people will drive in a way that is identical to the EPA [sanctioned] tests.... These [fuel economy] numbers are the result of test procedures that were originally developed to test emissions, not fuel economy.

Stephen Akehurst, a senior manager at Natural Resources Canada, which tests vehicles and publishes the annual *Fuel Consumption Guide*, admits that his lab tests vehicles under ideal conditions. He says that actual driving may burn about 25 percent more fuel than what the government tests show. Too bad we never see this fact hyped in the automakers' fuel economy ads.

Some examples: One of the biggest gas-guzzlers tested, the Lincoln Aviator, burned 44 percent more than the *Fuel Consumption Guide*'s estimate. A Nissan Quest burned twice as much fuel as was advertised in the *Guide*. Only the Hyundai Elantra did well. It burned a full litre less than predicted by the guys in the white lab coats.

Although good fuel economy is important, it's hardly worth a harsh ride, excessive highway noise, side-wind buffeting, anemic acceleration, and a cramped interior. You may end up with much worse gas mileage than advertised and a vehicle that's underpowered for your needs.

If you never quite got the hang of metric fuel economy measurements, use the approximate fuel conversion table at right to establish how many miles to a U.S. gallon of gas your vehicle provides.

FUEL ECONOMY CONVERSION TABLE

L/100 KM	MPG (U.S.)	L/100 KM	MPG (U.S.)	L/100 KM	MPG (U.S.)
5.2	45	7.1	33	11.2	21
5.3	44	7.4	32	11.8	20
5.5	43	7.6	31	12.4	19
5.6	42	7.8	30	13.1	18
5.7	41	8.1	29	13.8	17
5.9	40	8.4	28	14.7	16
6.0	39	8.7	27	15.7	15
6.2	38	9.0	26	16.8	14
6.4	37	9.4	25	18.1	13
6.5	36	9.8	24	19.6	12
6.7	35	10.2	23	21.4	11
6.9	34	10.7	22	23.5	10

"Miracle" Fuels

The lure of cheap, "clean" fuel has never been stronger, and the misrepresentations as to the advantages of different fuels have never been greater. Take a look at the following list of flavour-of-the-month alternate fuels that have been proposed by politicians and businesses, and consider that, except for diesel, not a single other alternate fuel is economically viable.

Ethanol and flex-fuel vehicles (FFVs)

Ethanol is the trendy "fuel of the year" for automakers, oil companies, and politicians who have their heads stuck up their tailpipes. All three groups recite the mantra that increased ethanol use will cut fuel costs, make us less dependent on foreign oil sources (goodbye, Big Oil; hello, Big Corn), and create a cleaner environment. Unfortunately, this is simply not true—it's reminiscent of the misguided embrace of the 1997 Kyoto Accord by governments who promised they would be effective in cutting emissions that lead to global warming. Ironically, research now shows signatories to the Accord produce more emissions than non-signatories.

FFVs are all the rage with the Detroit Three, and they're being promoted over hybrids and diesel engines because the switchover is less costly for automakers. They only have to modify the fuel-delivery system on their vehicles and then lobby the federal government to pay billions of dollars for new pipelines, tankers, and gas stations. Millions of their vehicles already on the market can run on a mixture of 85 percent ethanol and 15 percent gasoline (called E85), but oil companies won't supply the fuel because charging high gasoline prices is more profitable. Furthermore, governments won't pony up the billions of dollars needed to construct new ethanol pipelines (at an estimated cost of $1.6 million per kilometre for 322,000 km) and to convert filling stations that would provide real competition for gas-selling stations ($240,000 for a new tank and pump). At the moment, most E85 FFVs are gasoline-powered because ethanol retailers can't be found (only 608 out of 168,987 filling stations sell ethanol in the States; there are only a couple in Canada that do). Yet the automakers get important tax credits because they have converted much of their production to run on ethanol fuel (in theory), though most of the vehicles will burn gasoline.

Brazil, a huge ethanol producer since the late '70s, doesn't need a pipeline because most of its sugar cane fields are located where they can be distilled and the resulting ethanol marketed—thereby forgoing expensive transportation costs. In North America, most of the corn and other ethanol-producing crops are found in the U.S. Midwest and Central and Western Canada, far away from major population areas.

Indeed, ethanol is smokeless, burns cleaner, and (theoretically) leads to less engine maintenance. Plus, you can drink it (diluted, or with a chaser).

But will the increased use of ethanol make North America much less dependent on gasoline? No way—not if you do the math: About 4 billion gallons of ethanol is produced annually in the States, but they burn an average of 140 billion gallons of gasoline each year.

Accepting that ethanol filling stations are practically nonexistent and are expected to stay that way, here are some other jaw-dropping facts that ensure ethanol won't be the fuel of the future: The fuel costs almost as much as gasoline in some places (unless you distill it yourself); gas mileage *drops* by up to 30 percent when ethanol is used; cold-weather performance is mediocre; and the product is highly corrosive, with a particular fondness for snacking on plastic and rubber components.

Hybrids

You have to be quite stupid to plunk down about $30,000 for a hybrid vehicle in the hope of saving gas—or the environment. Already the waiting lines have thinned out as fuel prices drop in North America.

As practical as the promise of ethanol fuel for everybody, hybrids use a pie-in-the-sky alternative fuel system that requires expensive and complex electronic and mechanical components to achieve the same fuel economy that a bare-bones Honda Civic or Toyota Yaris can achieve at half the initial purchase price—and without polluting the environment with exotic toxic metals leached from used battery packs.

Want the real-world hybrid fuel economy and cost-of-ownership numbers?

Consumer Reports tested six pairs of vehicles, with each pair including a conventional vehicle and the equivalent hybrid model, and published the astounding results in its April 2006 edition. *CR* found that in each category of car, truck, and SUV, the extra cost for the hybrid version was unacceptably *higher* than the cost of the same vehicle equipped with a conventional propulsion system.

Other disadvantages of hybrids are their mechanical and electronic complexities, dependence on specialized dealers for basic servicing, high depreciation rates and insurance costs, overblown fuel-efficiency numbers (owners report getting 40 percent less mileage than promised), and $3,000 cost to replace their battery packs.

ESTIMATED COSTS FOR 2006 GASOLINE-FUELED VEHICLES VS. HYBRIDS

Over a 5-year period, the smallest estimated U.S.–dollar operating cost difference was between the two Honda Civics ($3,700), followed by Toyota's Corolla and Prius ($5,250). The biggest gap between two similar models was registered by the gasoline-powered Toyota Highlander SUV and its hybrid version ($13,300 U.S.), with the Lexus RX330 and RX400h posting a $13,100-higher cost for the hybrid version. The first two figures are the manufacturers' suggested retail prices.

	GASOLINE	HYBRID	HIGHER OPERATING COST
Ford Escape SUV	$22,818	$29,140	$ 8,350
Honda Accord EX	$25,862	$31,540	$10,250
Honda Civic	$18,444	$22,400	$ 3,750
Lexus RX330/RX400h	$37,960	$46,755	$13,100
Toyota Highlander	$32,650	$39,835	$13,300
Toyota Corolla/Prius	$16,607	$22,305	$ 5,250

Source: *Consumer Reports*, April 2006

Finally, consider this: Hybrid vehicles like the Toyota Prius use rare-earth minerals such as neodymium in the lightweight permanent magnets that power their motors. Neodymium is a radioactive substance found almost exclusively in China, which has begun restricting its sale for domestic use. It's ironic that "green-minded" motorists may trade a dependence on Middle Eastern oil for a troubling dependence on Chinese-sourced neodymium.

Diesels

Diesel fuel is cleaner these days and far more fuel-efficient than ever before. Among the alternate fuels tested by independent researchers, diesel comes closest to the estimated fuel economy figures. It's also widely available and requires neither a steep learning curve in the service bay nor exotic replacement parts. Additionally, unlike hybrids, diesel-equipped vehicles are reasonably priced and hold their value quite well.

As with the changeover to unleaded gasoline two decades ago, owners of diesel-equipped Detroit-made vehicles can expect horrendously expensive maintenance costs, considerable repair downtime, and the worsening of the diesel's poor reliability trend, which was seen over the past decade with Ford's Powerstroke and General Motors' Duramax.

Fuel economy misrepresentation

So if you can't make a gas-saving product that pours into your fuel tank or attaches to the fuel or air lines, you have to use that old standby and, well, lie. Hell, if automakers and government fuel-efficiency advocates can do it, why not dealers?

Fuel economy misrepresentation is actionable, and there is Canadian jurisprudence that allows for a contract's cancellation if the gas-mileage figures are false (see Part Two). Most people, however, simply keep the car they bought and live with the fact that they were fooled.

There are a few choices you can make that will lower fuel consumption. First off, choose a smaller version of the vehicle style you are interested in buying. Secondly, choose a manual transmission or an automatic with a fuel-saving Fifth gear. Thirdly, an engine with a cylinder-deactivation feature or variable valve timing will increase fuel economy by 8 and 3 percent, respectively.

Excessive Maintenance Fees

Maintenance inspections and replacement parts represent hidden costs that are usually exaggerated by dealers and automakers to increase their profits on vehicles that either rarely require fixing or are sold in insufficient numbers to support a service bay.

Alan Gelman, a well-known Toronto garage owner and host of CFRB radio's *Car Talk*, warns drivers:

> There are actually two maintenance schedules handed out by car companies and dealers. The dealer inspection sheets often call for far more extensive and expensive routine maintenance checks than what's listed in the owner's manual. Most of those checks are padding; smart owners will stick with the essential checks listed in the manual and have them done by cheaper, independent garages.

Getting routine work done at independent facilities will cost about one-third to one-half the price usually charged by dealers. Just be sure to follow the automaker's suggested schedule so no warranty claim can be tied to botched servicing. Additionally, an inexpensive ALLDATA service bulletin subscription (see Appendix III) will keep you current as to your vehicle's factory defects, required check-ups, and recalls; will tell you what's covered by little-known "goodwill" warranties; and will save you valuable time and money when troubleshooting common problems.

Whom Can You Trust?

Very few people or newspapers, it appears.

The government lies to us about fuel economy and airbag dangers. Automakers lie to us about the reliability and "real" prices of their products. Car dealers routinely charge us for services covered by "goodwill" extended warranties and put pricing information in such small print in newspapers that no one can read it. And many car journalists lie to us when they say that they're unbiased, aren't intimidated by their editors and automaker reps, and can't be, ahem…bribed.

Most investigative stories done on the auto industry in Canada (such as exposés on secret car warranties, dangerous airbags, and car company shenanigans) have been written by business columnists, freelancers, or "action line" troubleshooters rather than by reporters on the auto beat. This is because most auto beat reporters are regularly beaten into submission by myopic editors and greedy publishers who don't give them the time or the encouragement to do hard-hitting investigative exposés. In fact, it's quite impressive that we do have a small cadre of reporters who won't be cowed. Links to some of the best Canadian and American sites can be found in Appendix III.

Here are some examples:

- The non-profit Automobile Protection Association (*www.apa.ca*) is a consumer protection website. The group specializes in exposing unsafe and unreliable cars and trucks.
- Toronto-based Kurt Binnie's *OnTheHoist.com* is a well-written site replete with auto information from consumer advocacy and car enthusiast perspectives (not an easy balance). Binnie buttresses information files and frequent blog entries with URLs from around the world that run the gamut from the well-known to the obscure. He is particularly effective as a price analyst who tracks down auto companies' suggested retail prices, customer and dealer rebates, and sales incentives and discount programs and then compares them on both sides of the border. His website is an essential free tool for effective price haggling.
- The CanadianDriver website (*www.canadiandriver.com*) offers a cornucopia of Canadian car critics who are relatively independent of industry influence.

Canada also has a number of auto experts and consumer advocates who are not afraid to take on the auto industry and follow good stories, no matter where they lead. Here are some of my favourites:

- Jeremy Cato and Michael Vaughan are two of Canada's best-known automotive and business journalists. This duo epitomizes the best combination of auto journalism and business reporting by asking the tough questions automakers hate to answer.
- Mohamed Bouchama, president of Car Help Canada, shakes up the auto industry by rating new and used cars, providing legal advice, and teaching consumers the art of complaining on *AutoShop* every Sunday evening on Toronto's CP24.
- I have known and respected the *Toronto Star*'s Ellen Roseman for more than 30 years. She is one of Canada's foremost consumer advocates and business columnists, and never pulls back from an important story—no matter how loudly advertisers squeal. She teaches, does TV and radio, and maintains a blog to give her readers current information on all types of consumer issues.
- Phil Bailey is a Lachine, Quebec, garage owner with almost five decades of experience with European, Japanese, and American cars. In his insightful comments on the car industry, he's as skillful with his pen as he is with a wrench, and he's got the everyday garage experience that make him and Toronto CFRB broadcaster Alan Gelman such unimpeachable auto industry critics.

These reporters and consumer advocates represent the exception, not the rule. Even the most ardent reporters frequently have to jump through hoops to get their stories out, simply because their editors or station managers have bought into many of the fraudulent practices so common to the auto industry. Haranguing staff for more "balance" is the pretext du jour for squelching hard-hitting stories that implicate dealers and automakers. News editors don't want truth; they want copy and comfort. They'll spend weeks sifting through Prime Minister Stephen Harper's trash bins looking for conflicts of interest while ignoring the auto industry scams threaded throughout their own advertisers' ads and commercials.

Want proof? Try to decipher the fine print in *The Globe and Mail*'s or the *Toronto Star*'s new car ads, or better yet, tell me what the fine print scrolled at breakneck speeds on television car commercials really says. Where is the investigative reporter who will submit these ads to an optometrists' group to confirm that the message is unreadable?

Think about this: Dealers posing as private parties and selling used cars from residences ("curbsiders") are periodically exposed by dealer associations and "crusading" auto journalists. Yet these scam artists place dozens or more ads weekly in the classified sections of local newspapers that employ these same muckraking reporters. The same phone numbers and billing addresses reappear in the ads, sometimes days after the scam has been featured in local news reports. The ad order-takers know who these crooks are. News editors know that their own papers are promoting these scammers. Why isn't there an ad exposé by reporters working for these papers? Why don't they publish the fact that it's mostly new-vehicle dealers who supply curbsiders with their cars? That's what I'd call balanced reporting. Although car columnists claim that their integrity is not for sale, there's no doubt that it can be rented. Travel junkets and public relations and advertising contracts all sweeten the pot for these pseudo-journalists.

Two of my favourite auto journalists, Dan Neil, automotive writer for the liberal *Los Angeles Times*, and Robert Farago, a long-time columnist, auto critic, and creator of *The Truth About Cars*, a British-based website, were both punished for writing the truth.

Neil's paper was hit with a $10 million (U.S.) loss after General Motors and its dealers pulled their ads in response to his sharp criticism of GM for a series of poor management decisions that lead to the flop of its 2005 G6 model:

> GM is a morass of a business case, but one thing seems clear enough, and Lutz's mistake was to state the obvious and then recant: The company's multiplicity of divisions and models is turning into a circular firing squad...someone's head ought to roll, and the most likely candidate would be the luminous white noggin of Lutz...[the G6] is not an awful car. It's entirely adequate. But plainly, adequate is not nearly enough....
>
> *LOS ANGELES TIMES*
> APRIL 6, 2005

The *Times* stood by Neil, a Pulitzer Prize–winning automobile columnist. GM's ads eventually returned after a hiatus of several months.

Farago didn't fare as well. In late August 2005, he was canned and stayed canned. His column was permanently axed, without explanation, by the uber-liberal *San Francisco Chronicle* after his criticism of Subaru's Tribeca, an SUV wannabe that never will be:

> I'm not sure if the *Chronicle* removed my description of the SUV's front end as a "flying vagina" (the editors ignored my request for a copy of the published review), but even without it my analysis of the B9 was not bound to please its manufacturer....
>
> In fact, the Subaru B9 Tribeca is both subjectively (to the best of my knowledge and experience) and empirically a dreadful machine that besmirches the reputation of its manufacturer. Sure, the B9 handles well. The review pointed this out. But to suggest that it's an SUV worthy of its manufacturer's hype ("The end of the SUV as we know it" and "The ideal balance of power and refinement") is to become a co-conspirator in Subaru's attempts to mislead the public....
>
> And here's the thing: I believe the media in general, and newspapers in particular, have an obligation to tell the truth about cars. You know all those puff pieces that fill up the odd blank spot in every single automotive section in this great country of ours? ... And that's why so many car enthusiasts have turned to the web. Other than Dan Neil at the *Los Angeles Times*, there are no print journalists ready, willing and able to directly challenge the auto manufacturers' influence with the plain, unvarnished truth (including the writers found in the happy clappy buff books). Car lovers yearn for the truth about cars. Sites like *www.jalopnik.com* are dedicated to providing it. And that's why the mainstream press' cozy little Boys' Club is doomed....

The "Car of the Year" Scam

Once you've established a budget and selected some vehicles that interest you, the next step is to ascertain which ones have high safety and reliability ratings. Be wary of the "Car of the Year" ratings found in enthusiast magazines and on most websites; their supposedly independent tests are a lot of baloney. Mark Toljagic and Frank Williams, two freelance Canadian auto journalists published in the *Toronto Star*'s "Wheels" section, agree. Williams says:

> You'd be forgiven for thinking COTY awards are little more than a gift to car advertisers, who provide a self-appointed number of "elite" journalists with priority access to press cars, and then co-promote a new product with an old publication. It's certainly an excellent excuse for carmakers like Renault (Alliance), Chevrolet (Citation), Plymouth (RIP, Volare) and Ford (Probe) to sell cars by touting their COTY award like they'd won the Nobel Prize.
>
> If not pissing off your paymasters is the priority, it is perhaps significant that *Car and Driver*'s 2006 "10 Best" awards considered 52 cars in new categories, including

> "Best Luxury Sports Car," "Best Sports Coupe," "Best Roadster," "Best Sports Car" and "Best Muscle Car." Perhaps *C&D* hopes persnickety pistonheads will spend so much time debating which car belongs in what category they'll be too tired to dispute the winners.

Doggedly independent, Toljagic penned the following observations about press junkets from a lakeside château in Salzburg, Austria, where all expenses were paid by Lexus:

> Waves of automotive writers from the U.S., Canada, Europe and Asia were treated to business-class flights, their own luxury suites, gourmet meals, a cigar lounge and an evening at the Fortress Restaurant overlooking Mozart's hometown of Salzburg.... While there are economies of scale to be realized in conducting one global event, it still doesn't come cheap. Toyota estimates the cost to fête each journalist to be about $10,000.... Airline points are major currency for freelancers. Auto companies assign the points to the writer, so it's easy to rack up impressive totals that can be used at vacation time.

Imagine: *Car and Driver* rated the Ford Focus as a "Best Buy" during its first three model years, while government and consumer groups decried the car's dozen or so recall campaigns and the huge number of owners' safety and reliability complaints.

There are dozens of organizations and magazines that rate cars for everything from their overall reliability and frequency of repairs (J.D. Power and *Consumer Reports*) to their crashworthiness and appeal to owners (NHTSA, IIHS, and Strategic Vision's Total Quality Survey (TQS)). These ratings don't always match.

Getting Reliable Info

Funny, as soon as they hear that you're shopping for a new car, all your relatives, co-workers, and friends want to tell you what to buy.

After a while, you'll get so many conflicting opinions that it'll seem as if any choice you make will be wrong. Before making your decision, remember that you should invest a month of research into your $30,000-plus new-car-buying project. This includes two weeks for basic research and another two weeks to actually bargain with dealers to get the right price and equipment. The following sources provide a variety of useful information that will help you ferret out what vehicle best suits your needs and budget.

Auto shows

Auto shows are held from January through March throughout Canada, starting in Montreal and ending in Vancouver. Although you can't buy or drive a car at the show, you can easily compare prices and the interior and exterior styling of different vehicles. In fact, show officials estimate that about 20 percent of auto show visitors are actively seeking info for an upcoming new-car purchase. Interestingly, while the shows are open, dealer traffic nosedives, making for much more generous deals in showrooms. Business usually picks up following the show.

Online services

Anyone with access to the Internet can now obtain useful information relating to the auto industry in a matter of minutes at little or no cost. This can be accomplished in two ways: by subscribing to an online service, like America Online (AOL), that offers consumer forums and easy Internet access; or by going directly to the Internet through a low-cost Internet service provider (ISP) and using a search engine like Google that helps you find thousands of helpful sites. Also, an extensive listing of informative and helpful sites can be found in Appendix III.

Shopping on the Internet

The key word here is "shopping," because *Consumer Reports* magazine has found that barely 2 percent of Internet surfers actually buy a new or used car online. Yet over 80 percent of buyers admit to using the Internet to get prices and specifications before visiting the dealership. Apparently, few buyers want to purchase a new or used vehicle without first seeing what's offered and knowing all money paid will be accounted for.

New-vehicle shopping through automaker and independent websites is a quick and easy way to compare prices and model specifications, but you will have to be careful. Many so-called independent sites are merely fronts for dealers and automakers, tailoring their information to steer you into their showroom or convince you to buy a certain brand of car. One independent Canadian site for finding real discounted prices is *OnTheHoist.com*.

Shoppers now have access to information they once were routinely denied or had trouble finding, such as dealers' price markups and incentive programs, the book value for trade-ins, and considerable safety data. Canadian shoppers can get Canadian invoice prices and specs by contacting APA by phone or fax, or online by visiting *www.canadiandriver.com*.

Other advantages to online shopping are as follows: Some dealers offer a lower price to online shoppers; the entire transaction, including financing, can be done on the Internet; and buyers don't have to haggle—they merely post their best offers electronically to a number of dealers in their area code (for more convenient servicing of the vehicle) and then await counteroffers. But here are three caveats: (1) You will have to go to a dealer to finalize the contract, and be preyed upon by the financing and insurance (F&I) sales agents; (2) as far as bargains are concerned, *Consumer Reports* says its test shoppers obtained lower prices more frequently by visiting the dealer's showroom and concluding the sale there; and (3) only one-third of online dealers respond to customer queries.

Auto Quality Rankings

Consumer groups and non-profit auto associations like APA and Car Help Canada (see Appendix III) are your best bets for the most unbiased auto ratings for Canadians. They're not perfect, though, so it's a good idea to consult both groups and look for ratings that match.

Consumer Reports (*CR*) is an American publication that once had a tenuous affiliation with the Consumers' Association of Canada. Its ratings, extrapolated from Consumers Union's annual U.S. member survey, don't quite mirror the Canadian experience. Components that are particularly vulnerable to our harsh climate usually don't perform as well as the *CR* reliability ratings indicate, and poor servicing caused by a weak dealer body in Canada can make some service-dependent vehicles a nightmare to own here, whereas the American experience may be less problematic.

Based on more than one million responses from subscribers to *Consumer Reports* and *ConsumerReports.org*, *CR*'s annual auto reliability findings are impressively comprehensive, though they may not always be correct. Statisticians agree that *CR*'s sampling method leaves some room for error, but, with a few notable exceptions, the ratings are fair, conservative, and consistent guidelines for buying a reliable vehicle. Not so for child safety seats. A January 2007 *CR* report said that 10 out of 12 seats it tested failed disastrously at impact speeds of 56–61 km/h. NHTSA checked *CR*'s findings and discovered that the side-impact speeds actually exceeded 112 km/h. *CR* admitted it made a mistake.

My only criticisms of the auto ratings are that many Asian models, like Toyota and Honda, are not as harshly scrutinized as their American counterparts, yet service bulletins and extended "goodwill" warranties have shown for years that they also have serious engine, transmission, brake, and electrical problems. *Consumer Reports* confirms this anomaly in its April 2006 edition, where it admits that Asian vehicle quality improvement has "slowed" since 2002.

When and Where to Buy

When to Buy

This year, with Chrysler and GM sorting out their respective bankruptcies, new-car sales and prices will continue to trend downward well into 2010 as the Detroit automakers flood the market with millions of heavily discounted unsold cars and trucks. The longer you wait, the more money you will save, regardless of whether you buy from an American, Japanese, South Korean, or European automaker.

Shoppers who can wait until the summer or early fall of 2010 can double-dip from additional automakers' dealer incentive and buyer rebate programs—which can mean thousands of dollars in additional savings. Remember, too, that vehicles made between March and August offer the most factory upgrades.

Allow yourself at least two weeks to finalize a deal if you aren't trading in your vehicle, or longer if you sell your vehicle privately. Visit the showroom at the end of the month, just before closing, when the salesperson will want to make that one last sale to meet the month's quota. If sales have been terrible, the sales manager may be willing to do some extra negotiating in order to boost sales staff morale.

Where to Buy

If all you care about is getting a low price, shopping in auto-factory towns will get you the cheapest vehicles because assembly-line workers buy heavily discounted cars in order to "flip" them. Large towns have more of a selection, and dealers offer a variety of payment plans that will likely suit your budget.

Good dealers aren't always the ones with the lowest prices, though. Buying from someone who you know gives honest and reliable service is just as important as getting a good price. Check a dealer's honesty and reliability by talking with motorists who drive vehicles purchased from that dealer (identified by the nameplate on the vehicle's trunk). If these customers have been treated fairly, they'll be glad to recommend their dealer. You can also ascertain the quality of new-vehicle preparation and servicing by renting one of the dealer's vehicles for a weekend, or by getting your trade-in serviced.

How can you tell which dealers are the most honest and competent? Well, judging from the thousands of reports I receive each year, dealerships in small suburban and rural communities are fairer than big-city dealers because they're more vulnerable to negative word-of-mouth testimonials and to poor sales—when their vehicles aren't selling, good service takes up the slack. Their prices may also be more competitive, but don't count on it.

Unfortunately, as part of their bankruptcy restructuring, Chrysler and General Motors are now closing down dealerships principally in suburban and rural areas because the dealers cannot generate sufficient sales volume to meet the automakers' profit targets.

Dealers selling more than one manufacturer's product line present special problems. Their overhead can be quite high, and the cancellation of a dual dealership by an automaker in favour of setting up an exclusive franchise elsewhere is an ever-present threat. Parts availability may also be a problem because dealers with two separate vehicle lines must split their inventory and may, therefore, have an inadequate supply on hand.

The quality of new-vehicle service is directly linked to the number and competence of dealerships within the network. If the network is weak, parts are likely to be unavailable, repair costs can go through the roof, and the skill level of the mechanics may be subpar, since better mechanics command higher salaries. Among foreign manufacturers, Asian automakers have the best overall dealer representation across Canada, except for Mitsubishi and Kia.

Kia's dealer network is weak but growing nevertheless through strong sales after having been left by its former owner, Hyundai, to fend on its own for many years. Mitsubishi, on the other hand, is floundering, despite having a good array of quality products. Its major problem is that Canadian dealers piggybacked their sales outlets on bankrupt Chrysler franchises.

All of the European automakers are losing money, including BMW, MINI, Mercedes, Porsche, and VW (to a much lesser extent). However, their profits are expected to grow in 2010 as higher fuel prices and the quest for better highway performance drives shoppers to the European vehicles. But servicing, already woefully inadequate, for the many European makes in Canada is expected to worsen as the economic downturn continues.

Despite the above drawbacks, you can always get better treatment by patronizing dealerships that are accredited by auto clubs such as the Canadian Automobile Association (CAA) or consumer groups like the Automobile Protection Association (APA) or Car Help Canada. Auto club accreditation is no ironclad guarantee that a dealership will exhibit courteous, honest, or competent business practices; however, if you're insulted, cheated, or given bad service by one of their recommended garages (look for the accreditation symbol in a dealer's phone book ads, on the Internet, or on their shop windows), the accrediting club is one more place to take your complaint to apply additional mediation pressure. And as you'll see in Part Two, plaintiffs have won substantial refunds by pleading that an auto club is legally responsible for the actions of a garage it recommends.

Automobile Brokers and Vehicle-Buying Services

Brokers are independent agents who act as intermediaries to find the new or used vehicle you want at a price below what you'd normally pay. They have their Rolodex of contacts, speak the sales lingo, know all of the angles and scams, and can generally cut through the bull to find a fair price—usually within days. Their services may cost a few hundred dollars, but you may save a few thousand. Additionally, you save the stress and hassle associated with the dealership experience, which for many people is like a trip to the dentist.

Brokers get new vehicles through dealers, while used vehicles may come from dealers, auctions, private sellers, and leasing companies. The broker's job is to find a vehicle that meets a client's expressed needs and then to negotiate its purchase (or lease) on behalf of that client. The majority of brokers tend to deal exclusively in new vehicles, with a small percentage dealing in both new and used vehicles. Ancillary services vary among brokers and may include such things as comparative vehicle analysis and price research.

The cost of hiring a broker can be charged either as a flat fee of a few hundred dollars or as a percentage of the value of the vehicle (usually 1–2 percent). The flat fee is usually best because it encourages the broker to keep the selling price low. Reputable brokers are not beholden to any particular dealership or make, and they'll disclose their flat fee up front or tell you the percentage amount they'll charge on a specific vehicle.

Finding the right broker

Good brokers are hard to find, particularly in western Canada. Buyers who are looking for a broker should first ask friends and acquaintances if they can recommend one. Word-of-mouth referrals are often the best because people won't refer others to a service with which they were dissatisfied. Your local credit union or the regional CAA office is a good place to get a broker referral. For instance, Alterna Savings recommends a car-buying service called Dealfinder.

Dealfinder

For most buyers, going into a dealer showroom to negotiate a fair price is intimidating and confusing. Numbers are thrown at you, promises made and broken, and after getting the "lowest price possible," you realize your neighbour paid a couple thousand dollars less for the same vehicle.

No wonder smart consumers are turning away from the "showroom shakedown" and letting professional buyers, like Ottawa-based Dealfinder Inc. (*www.dealfinder.ca*), separate the steak from the sizzle and real prices from "come-ons." In fact, simply by dealing with the dealership directly, Dealfinder can automatically save you the $200+ sales agent's commission, before negotiations even begin.

For a $159 (plus GST) flat fee, Dealfinder acts as a price consultant after you have chosen the vehicle you want. The agency then shops dealers for the new car or truck of your choice in any geographic area you indicate. It gets no kickbacks from retailers or manufacturers, and if you can negotiate and document a lower price than Dealfinder, the fee will be refunded. What's more, you're under no obligation to buy the vehicle they recommend, since there is absolutely no collusion between Dealfinder and any manufacturer or dealership.

Dealfinder is a small operation that has been run by Bob Prest for over 17 years. He knows the ins and outs of automobile price negotiation and has an impressive list of clients, including some of Canada's better-known credit unions. His reputation is spread by word-of-mouth recommendations and the occasional media report. He can be reached by phone at 1-800-331-2044, or by email at *dealfinder@magma.ca*.

Choosing a Reliable, Cheap Vehicle

Quality: Down with the Economy

North America's year-old recession has not only produced millions of unsold new vehicles but also caused a serious decline in the quality of the vehicles that have been sold. Industry insiders tell *Lemon-Aid* that the 2009–10 new cars and trucks have serious factory-related glitches and fit and finish deficiencies partly because disheartened autoworkers, facing unemployment and pension losses, simply don't care about quality anymore.

Another big factor is related to the transportation and storage of unsold vehicles. Some vehicles have been stored in ports, parking lots, and fields where fuel tanks rust prematurely, electrical components and connections corrode, braking systems leak or seize, and rubber strips and gaskets rot—all problems that can affect the safety, reliability, and performance of any vehicle that's kept outdoors and unattended for long periods of time.

Your best protection against buying a new car that has sustained environmental damage, or one that has been "redated" (last year's model sold as this year's version), is to make sure the car is "fresh." This is done by checking the federally required date-of-manufacture plate or sticker that's usually found on the door jamb on the driver's side (where oil stickers are often stuck). Transport Canada says automakers must indicate the month and year of manufacture as each vehicle leaves the assembly line. So, it isn't rocket science to find a vehicle that was recently built.

Worker gloom and environmental damage aside, overall vehicle safety and body fit and finish on both domestic and imported vehicles are better today than they were three decades ago. Premature rusting is less of a problem, and reliability is improving. Repairs to electronic systems and powertrains, however, are outrageously expensive and complicated. Owners of cars and trucks made by GM, Ford, and Chrysler still report serious engine and automatic transmission deficiencies, often during the vehicle's first year in service. Other common defects include electrical system failures caused by faulty computer modules; malfunctioning ABS systems, brake rotor warpage, and early pad wearout; failure-prone air conditioning and automatic transmissions; and faulty engine head gaskets, intake manifolds, fuel systems, suspensions, and steering assemblies.

Nothing shows the poor quality control of the Detroit Three automakers as much as the poor fit and finish of body panels. Next time you are stuck in traffic, look at the trunk lid or rear hatch alignment of the vehicle in front of you. Chances are, if it's a Chrysler, Ford, or GM model, the trunk or hatch will be so misaligned that there will be a large gap on one side. Then look at most Asian products: Usually you will see perfectly aligned trunks and hatches, without any large gaps on either side.

That, in a nutshell, is Detroit's problem.

Detroit's "Good" Products

Don't get the impression that Detroit automakers can't make reasonably good vehicles. Chrysler's PT Cruiser and the Jeep Wrangler are good values; Ford's Mustang, Crown Victoria, Grand Marquis, and its much-improved 2004–10 Focus carry little risk; and GM's full-sized rear-drive vans are fairly reliable. Nevertheless, the Asian competition still makes better products.

General Motors' products are quite a mixed bag: Its full-sized vans and SUVs, small cars, and joint ventures with Toyota and Suzuki have all performed well, but its trucks and recently released mid-sized family cars are mediocre, at best—and its just discontinued, bargain basement minivans are poison.

Most studies done by consumer groups and private firms show that, in spite of improvements attempted over the past two decades, vehicles made by Chrysler, Ford, and (to a lesser extent) GM still don't measure up to Japanese and some South Korean products, such as Hyundai's, in terms of quality and technology. This is particularly evident in SUVs and minivans, where Honda and Toyota have long retained the highest reliability and dependability ratings, despite a handful of missteps with powertrain quality.

Chrysler

Chrysler's bailout, bankruptcy, and betrothal to Fiat is like giving a transfusion to an Italian corpse. In effect, Washington has forced the merger of the world's two worst automakers into one giant piece of excrement.

Don't buy a Chrysler unless it's a Jeep Wrangler or Liberty or a well-inspected Ram pickup with a manual transmission and a diesel engine. That's it. All the other products are failure-prone and costly to maintain, though the minivans are the best of a bad lot.

Ford

Ford sold off most its assets and borrowed billions of dollars just before the recession hit. The fact that it hasn't yet gone bankrupt means that Ford not only has kept its own loyal customers but also is well poised to poach Chrysler's and GM's sales.

Ford's management is less dysfunctional than what we see at Chrysler and GM. Moreover, the company has improved its quality control during the past several years and brought out popular new products like the Edge and Fusion. Lincoln's reliable and profitable Town Car will likely remain for a few more years as Ford's only rear-drive Lincoln, such is its popularity with seniors and fleet managers.

What not to buy from Ford? Anything imported from Europe or China. Remember that piece of trash called the Ford Cortina, or the mishmash of letters and numbers called the Merkur XR4Ti?

General Motors

First the flowers, then the flower pot. GM's eight divisions have been whittled down to four, its money-losing Opel unit has been sold to Magna, and the company says it will get out of bankruptcy shortly.

Don't believe that last part. GM has lost its customer base. Major quality deficiencies still affect most of its lineup, notably American-built front-drives and imported pickups. Owners cite unreliable powertains, poor braking performance, electrical problems, and subpar fit and finish as the main offenders.

Unlike Ford, GM has thousands of angry workers and terminated dealers who just don't believe in the company anymore. Henceforth, GM will stand for "Government Motors," with governments owning 72.5 percent of the new company, the UAW owning 17.5 percent, and the remaining 10 percent going to GM bondholders to wipe out $27 billion in unsecured debt. When GM does finally get back on its feet, I expect only Chevrolet to survive—with an expanded lineup that includes China-built small cars and trucks.

The company's increased reliance on factories in China to build economy cars for North America is a scary thought. Imagine, not only are North Americans' bailout funds being used to create jobs in China, but we also will have the dubious pleasure of driving some of the worst-made automobiles in the world, imported from the country that sold us lead-laced-paint-coated kids' toys and poisoned pet food ingredients. Move over Fiat, here come Chery's economy and Brilliance's "brilliant" crashworthiness. (Don't just take my word that these are bad cars—watch the crash videos.)

An interesting conclusion relative to Chinese manufacturing, according to several independent studies—like those done by Christensen Associates, Inc. (*www.camcinc.com/library/SoYou'reBuyingFromChina.pdf*) and by Paul Midler in *Poorly Made in China: An Insider's Account of the Tactics Behind China's Production Game* (John Wiley & Sons, 2009)—is that safety and quality are trumped by price. Your car has no brakes? No problem. We will give you a 10 percent discount and shoot the company president.

Asian Automakers

Don't buy into the myth that parts for imports are overpriced or hard to find. It's actually easier to find parts for Japanese vehicles than for domestic ones because of the large number of units produced, the presence of hundreds of independent suppliers, the ease with which relatively simple parts can be interchanged among different models, and the large reservoir of used parts stocked by junkyards. When a part is hard to find, the annual *Mitchell* manuals are useful guides to substitute parts that can be used for many different models. They're available in some libraries, most auto parts stores, and practically all junkyards.

Sadly, customer relations have been the Japanese automakers' Achilles' heels. Dealers are spoiled rotten by decades of easy sales, and have developed a "take it or leave it" showroom attitude, which is often accompanied by a woeful ignorance of their own model lineups. This was once a frequent complaint of Honda and Toyota shoppers, though recent APA undercover surveys show a big improvement among Toyota dealers.

Where attitudes have gotten worse is in the service bay, where periodic maintenance visits and warranty claims end up costing more than expected. Well-known factory-related defects (Honda engine oil leaks and Toyota engine and tranny problems) are corrected under extended warranties, but you always have the feeling you owe the "family."

There's no problem with discourteous or ill-informed South Korean automakers. Instead, poor quality has been their bugaboo. Yet, like Honda's and Toyota's recoveries following start-up quality glitches, Hyundai, South Korea's biggest automaker, has made considerable progress in bringing quality up almost to Toyota's and Honda's level.

Up to the mid-'90s, South Korean vehicles were merely cheap, poor-quality knock-offs of their Japanese counterparts. They would start to fall apart after their third year because of subpar body construction, unreliable automatic transmission and electrical components, and parts suppliers who put low prices ahead of reliability and durability. This was particularly evident with Hyundai's Pony, Stellar, Excel, and early Sonata models. During the past several years, though, Hyundai's product lineup has been extended and refined, and quality is no longer a worry. Also, Hyundai's comprehensive base warranty protects owners from most of the more-expensive breakdowns that may occur.

Hyundais are easily repaired by independent garages, and their rapid depreciation doesn't mean much because they cost so little initially and entry-level buyers are known to keep their cars longer than most, thereby easily amortizing the higher depreciation rate.

Kia, a struggling, low-quality, small South Korean compact automaker bought by Hyundai in October 1998, has come a long way. At first it languished under Hyundai's "benign neglect," as Hyundai spent most of its resources on its own cars and SUVs. But, during the past few years, Hyundai has worked hard to improve Kia reliability and fit and finish by using more Hyundai parts in each Kia redesign and by improving quality control on the assembly line. Nevertheless, Kia's SUV and minivan quality is spotty, at best.

Not all that's Asian is good. Kia's Sedona is an icon of poor quality.

European Models

Lemon-Aid doesn't recommend many European cars; there are way too many with serious and expensive quality and servicing problems. Heck, even the Germans have abandoned their own products. For example, a 2002 J.D. Power survey of 15,000 German car owners found that German drivers are happiest at the wheel of a Lexus, a Japanese car. This survey included compact and luxury cars as well as off-roaders. Toyota won first place on quality, reliability, and owner satisfaction, while Nissan's Maxima headed the luxury class standings. BMW was the first choice among European offerings.

For those who feel the German survey was a fluke, there's also a 2003 study of 34,000 car owners with vehicles up to eight years old, published by Britain's Consumers' Association. It found that less than half of British owners would recommend a British-made Rover or Vauxhall to a friend. The most highly rated cars in the study were the Japanese Subaru, Isuzu, and Lexus: Over 85 percent of drivers would recommend them.

Here's another surprise: Although it builds some of the most expensive cars and SUVs in the world, Mercedes' quality isn't always first-class. After stumbling badly when it first launched its rushed-to-production American-made SUV for the 1998 model year, the automaker has sent out many urgent service bulletins that seek to correct a surprisingly large number of production deficiencies affecting its entire lineup, including C-Class and E-Class models. Dealers' lots continue to be overloaded with unsold inventory, so vehicles are being sold with steep discounts and bargain-basement leasing terms.

Mercedes executives admit that the company's cars and SUVs have serious quality shortcomings, and have vowed to correct them. But such a turnaround is complicated by M-B's huge financial losses from Chrysler and Smart. The "oh, so cute" Smart division has lost billions and doesn't compare with the more refined and safer Asian competition.

While Mercedes sorts through its woes, shoppers who can't resist having a German nameplate should buy a VW Jetta, or a BMW 3 Series or 5 Series and take special courses to learn how to manage the cars' iDrive multifunctional cockpit controller.

Volkswagen's quality isn't quite as bad as Mercedes', and its sales have been on the upswing. True, VW has always been early on the scene with great concepts, but their ideas have often been accompanied by poor execution and a weak servicing network. With its failure-prone and under-serviced Eurovan and Camper, the company hasn't been a serious minivan player since the late '60s, and VW's Rabbit and Golf small cars were resounding duds. Even the company's forays into luxury cruisers have been met with underwhelming enthusiasm and general derision.

But not all the news is bad. For 2009–10, VW's small cars and diesel-equipped models will continue to be strong sellers. Resale values are strong, and prices will be even more competitive.

Nevertheless, with European models, your service options are limited and customer-relations staffers can be particularly insensitive and arrogant. You can count on lots of aggravation and expense because of the unacceptably slow distribution of parts and their high markups. Because these companies have a quasi-monopoly on replacement parts, there are few independent suppliers you can turn to for help. And auto wreckers, the last-chance repository for inexpensive car parts, are unlikely to carry European parts for vehicles that are either more than three years old or manufactured in small numbers.

These vehicles also age badly. The weakest areas remain the drivetrains, electronic control modules, electrical and fuel systems, brakes, accessories (including the sound system and AC), and body components.

Cutting Costs

Watch the Warranty

There's a big difference between warranty promise and warranty performance. Most automakers offer bumper-to-bumper warranties that are good for at least the first 3 years/60,000 km, and most models get powertrain coverage up to 5 years/100,000 km. It's also becoming an industry standard for car companies to pay for roadside assistance, a loaner car, or hotel accommodations if your vehicle breaks down while you're away from home and it's still under warranty. *Lemon-Aid* readers report few problems with these ancillary warranty benefits.

Don't buy more warranty than you need

As part of its bailout program for the auto industry, Ottawa has given Detroit automakers millions of dollars to pay for warranty claims on most 2009–10 models, but some vehicles purchased before March 2008 may not be included in the government payout. This means that there will be no government warranty backup for those vehicles if the well goes dry.

If you pick a vehicle rated Recommended by *Lemon-Aid*, the manufacturer's warranty won't be that important and you won't need to spend money on additional warranty protection. On those vehicles that have a history of engine and transmission breakdowns, budget about $1,500 for an extended powertrain warranty backed by an insurance policy. If the vehicle has a sorry repair history, you will likely need a $2,000 comprehensive warranty. But first ask yourself this question: "Why am I buying a vehicle that's so poorly made that I need to spend several thousand dollars to protect myself until the warranty company grows tired of seeing my face?"

Just like the weight-loss product ads you see on TV, what you see isn't always what you get. For example, bumper-to-bumper coverage usually excludes stereo components, brake pads, clutch plates, and many other expensive parts. And automakers will pull every trick in the book to make you pay for their factory screw-ups. These tricks include blaming your driving or your vehicle's poor maintenance, penalizing you for using an independent garage or the wrong fuel, or simply stating that the problem is "normal" and it's really you who is out of whack.

Part Two has all the answers to the above lame excuses. There, you will find plenty of court decisions and sample claim letters that will make automakers and their dealers think twice about rejecting your claim.

Don't pay for repairs covered by "secret" warranties

Automobile manufacturers are reluctant to publicize their secret warranty programs because they feel that such publicity would weaken consumer confidence in their products and increase their legal liability. The closest they come to an admission is to send out a "goodwill policy," "special policy," or "product update" service bulletin intended for dealers' eyes only. These bulletins admit liability and propose free repairs for defects that include faulty paint, air conditioning malfunctions, and engine and transmission failures.

If you're refused compensation, keep in mind that secret warranty extensions are, first and foremost, an admission of manufacturing negligence. You can usually find them in technical service bulletins (TSBs) that are sent daily to dealers by automakers. Your bottom-line position should be to accept a pro rata adjustment from the manufacturer, whereby you, the dealer, and the automaker each accept a third of the repair costs. If polite negotiations fail, challenge the refusal in court on the grounds that you should not be penalized for failing to make a reimbursement claim under a secret warranty that you never knew existed!

Service bulletins are written by automakers in "mechanic speak" because service managers relate better to them that way. They're great guides for warranty inspections (especially the final one), and they're useful in helping you decide when it's best to trade in your car. Manufacturers can't weasel out of their obligations by claiming that they never wrote such a bulletin.

If your vehicle is out of warranty, show these bulletins to less-expensive, independent garage mechanics so they can quickly find the trouble and order the most recent upgraded part, ensuring that you don't replace one defective component with another.

Canadian service managers and automakers may deny at first that the bulletins even exist, or they may shrug their shoulders and say that they apply only in the States. However, when they're shown a copy, they usually find the appropriate Canadian part number or bulletin in their files. The problems and solutions don't change from one side of the border to another. Imagine American and Canadian tourists' cars being towed across the border because each country's technical service bulletins were different. Mechanical fixes do differ in cases where, for example, a bulletin is for California only, or it relates to a safety or emissions component used only in the States. But these instances are rare, indeed. What is quite gratifying is to see some automakers, like Honda, candidly admit in their bulletins that "goodwill" repair refunds are available. What a shame other automakers aren't as forthcoming!

The best way to get bulletin-related repairs carried out is to visit the dealer's service bay and to attach the specific ALLDATA-supplied service bulletin covering your vehicle's problems to a work order.

Getting your vehicle's service bulletins

Free summaries of automotive recalls and technical service bulletins listed by year, make, model, and engine can be found at the ALLDATA (*www.alldata.com/TSB*) and NHTSA (*www.safercar.gov*) websites. But, like the NHTSA summaries, ALLDATA's summaries are so short and cryptic that they're of limited use. You can download the complete contents of all the bulletins applicable to your vehicle from ALLDATA at *www.alldatadiy.com* if you pay the $26.95 (U.S.) annual subscription fee. Bulletins for Acura and BMW are not available, because these automakers have requested that ALLDATA keep their service bulletin information confidential.

Trim Insurance Costs

Insurance premiums can average between $900 and $2,000 per year, depending on the type of vehicle you own, your personal statistics and driving habits, and whether you can obtain coverage under your family policy.

There are some general rules to follow when looking for insurance savings. For example, vehicles older than five years do not necessarily need collision coverage, and you may not need loss-of-use coverage or a rental car. Other factors that should be considered are as follows:

- A low damageability rating and an average theft history also can reduce rates by 10–15 percent. These rankings can be checked at *www.ibc.ca/en/Car_Insurance/Buying_a_New_Car/HCMU.asp*. Don't be surprised, though, if there appears to be no rhyme or reason for the disparity in the ratings of similar vehicles. Insurance statistics aren't as scientific as insurers pretend—they often charge whatever the market will bear.
- When you phone for quotes, make sure you have your serial number in hand. Many factors—such as the make of the car, the number of doors, if there's a sports package, and the insurer's experience with the car—can affect the quote. And be honest, or you'll find your claim denied, the policy cancelled, or your premium cost boosted.

- Where you live and work also determine how much you pay. Auto insurance rates are 25–40 percent lower in London, Ontario, than in downtown Toronto because there are fewer cars in London and fewer kilometres to drive to work. Similar disparities are found in B.C. and Alberta.
- Taking a driver-training course can save you thousands of premium dollars.
- You may be able to include your home or apartment insurance as part of a premium package that's eligible for additional discounts.

InsuranceHotline.com, based in Ontario but with quotes for other provinces, says that it pays to shop around for cheap auto insurance rates. In February 2003, the group discovered that the same insurance policy could vary in cost by a whopping 400 percent. For example, a 41-year-old married female driving a 2002 Honda Accord and a 41-year-old married male driving a 1998 Dodge Caravan, both with unblemished driving records, should pay no more than $1,880, but some companies surveyed asked as much as $7,515.

"Hidden" Costs

Depreciation

This is going to be the sales killer in 2009–10: low resale values on models sold by bankrupt car companies, or vehicles that have been dropped, like Pontiac, Saab, Saturn, and Hummer. No one wants to be stuck with a relatively new vehicle that can't be sold for a fair price. And, with job uncertainty and pensions threatened, one's vehicle may be the only place where you have some equity to tide you over the rough spots.

Depreciation is the biggest—and most often ignored—expense that you encounter when you trade in your vehicle or when an accident forces you to buy another vehicle before the depreciated loss can be amortized. Most new cars depreciate a whopping 30–45 percent during the first two years of ownership. For 2009 models, expect prices to tumble by another 15 percent.

The best way to use depreciation rates to your advantage is to choose a vehicle listed as being both reliable and economical to own and then keep it for eight to 10 years. Generally, by choosing a lower-depreciating vehicle—such as one that keeps at least half its value over three years—you are storing up equity that will give you a bigger down payment and fewer loan costs with your next purchase.

Gas Pains

With gas prices once again headed toward the $1.00 a litre mark, motorists are scratching their heads trying to find easy ways to cut gas consumption. Here are three simple suggestions (and 20 more tips are found in Appendix II):

1. Buy a used compact car for half its original price. Savings on taxes, freight fees, and depreciation: about $15,000.
2. Buy low-octane fuel from Internet-referred gas stations. You can save about 15 cents a litre.
3. Keep your vehicle properly tuned for a 10 percent savings from improved fuel economy.

Gas-saving gadgets and government mileage figures? Don't trust 'em. Ottawa hoodwinks us with gas mileage figures that are impossible to achieve.

The government's *Fuel Consumption Guide* is a work of fiction intended to make automakers, bureaucrats, and motorists feel "green" and empowered.

More dirt on diesels

The only reasons to buy a diesel-equipped vehicle are for their potential to deliver outstanding fuel economy and for their much lower maintenance and repair costs when compared with similar-sized vehicles powered by gasoline engines. Unfortunately, independent data suggests that both claims by automakers may be false.

Let's examine the fuel-savings issue first. In theory, when compared with gasoline powerplants, diesel engines are up to 30 percent more efficient in a light vehicle and up to 70 percent cheaper to run in a heavy-duty towing and hauling truck or SUV. They become more efficient as the engine load increases, whereas gasoline engines become less so. This is the main reason diesels are best used where the driving cycle includes a lot of city driving—slow speeds, heavy loads, frequent stops, and long idling times. At full throttle, both engines are essentially equal from a fuel-efficiency standpoint. The gasoline engine, however, leaves the diesel in the dust when it comes to high-speed performance.

On the downside, fleet administrators and owners report that diesel fuel economy in real driving situations is much less than what's advertised—a complaint also voiced by owners of hybrids. Many owners say that their diesel-run rigs get about 30 percent less mileage than what the manufacturer promised.

Also undercutting fuel-savings claims is the fact that, in some regions, the increased cost of diesel fuel—because of high taxes and oil company greed, some say—makes it more expensive than regular fuel.

The diesel engine's reputation for superior reliability may have been true in the past, but no longer. This fact is easily confirmed if you cross-reference owner complaints with confidential automaker service bulletins and independent industry polling results put out by J.D. Power and others, a task done for you in Part Three's ratings section.

Many owners of diesel-equipped vehicles are frustrated by chronic breakdowns, excessive repair costs, and poor road performance. It's practically axiomatic that bad injectors have plagued Dodge Cummins, Ford Power Stroke, and GM Duramax engines.

Defective injectors were often replaced in the past at the owner's expense and at a cost of thousands of dollars. Now, GM and Ford are using special programs to cover replacement costs long after the base warranty has expired. Chrysler has been more recalcitrant in making payouts, apparently because fewer vehicles may be involved and costs can be quite high (their lift pumps and injectors may be faulty).

Hybrid cars

Automakers are offering hybrid vehicles like the Toyota Prius and Honda Civic and Accord Hybrids that use an engine/electric motor for maximum fuel economy and low emissions while providing the driving range of a comparable small car. Yet this latest iteration of the electric car still has serious drawbacks, which may drive away even the most green-minded buyers:

- Real-world fuel consumption may be 40 percent higher than advertised.
- Cold weather can cut fuel economy by almost 10 percent.
- AC and other options can increase fuel consumption by 20 percent.
- Electrical systems can deliver a life-threatening 275–500 volts if tampered with through incompetent servicing or during an emergency rescue.
- Battery packs can cost up to $3,000 (U.S.), and fuel savings equal the hybrid's extra costs only after about 20,000 km of use.
- Hybrids cost more to insure, and they depreciate as much as non-hybrid vehicles.
- Hybrids make you a captive customer where travel is dependent on available service facilities.

If you find the limitations of an electric hybrid too daunting, why not simply buy a more fuel-efficient small car? Here are some environmentally friendly cars recommended by Toronto-based Environmental Defence Canada (*www.environmentaldefence.ca*) and by *Lemon-Aid*:

- Ford Focus
- Honda Civic and Fit
- Hyundai Accent and Tucson
- Mazda3 and Mazda5
- Nissan Sentra and Versa

- Toyota Corolla and Yaris
- VW Golf/Jetta TDI

Test for "Real" Performance

Take the phrase "carlike handling" with a large grain of salt. A van isn't supposed to handle like a car. Since many rear-drive models are built on a modified truck chassis and use steering and suspension components from their truck divisions, they tend to handle more like trucks than cars, in spite of automakers' claims to the contrary. Also, what you see isn't necessarily what you get when you buy or lease a new sport-utility, van, or pickup, because these vehicles seldom come with enough standard features to fully exploit their versatility. Additional options are usually a prerequisite to make them safe and comfortable to drive or capable of towing heavy loads. Consequently, the term "multipurpose" is a misnomer unless you are prepared to spend extra dollars to outfit your car or minivan. Even fully equipped, these vehicles don't always provide the performance touted by automakers.

Rust Protection

Except for unsold Detroit cars and trucks parked at ports around the country for almost a year, most vehicles built today are much less rust-prone than they were several decades ago, thanks to more-durable body panels and better designs. When rusting occurs now, it's usually caused by excessive environmental stress (road salt, etc.), a poor paint job, or the use of new metal panels that create galvanic corrosion or promote early paint peeling—two causes that are excluded from most rustproofing warranties.

Invest in undercoating, and remember that the best rustproofing protection is to park the vehicle in a dry, unheated garage or under an outside carport and then wash it every few weeks. Never bring it in and out of a heated garage during the winter months, since it is most prone to rust when temperatures are just a bit above freezing; keep it especially clean and dry during that time. If you live in an area where roads are heavily salted in winter, or in a coastal region, have your vehicle's undercoating sprayed annually.

Annual undercoating, which costs less than $100, will usually do as good a job as rustproofing. It will protect vital suspension and chassis components, make the vehicle ride more quietly, and allow you to ask a higher price at trade-in time. The only downside, which can be checked by asking for references, is that the undercoating may give off an unpleasant odour for months, and it may drip, soiling your driveway.

Whether you are rustproofing the entire vehicle or just undercoating key areas, make sure to include the rocker panels (make a small mark inside the door panels on the plastic hole plugs to make sure that they were removed and that the inside was actually sprayed), the rear hatch's bottom edge, the tailgate, and the wheelwells. It's also a smart idea to stay at the garage while the work is being done to see that the overspray is cleaned up and all areas have been sufficiently covered.

Surviving the Options Jungle

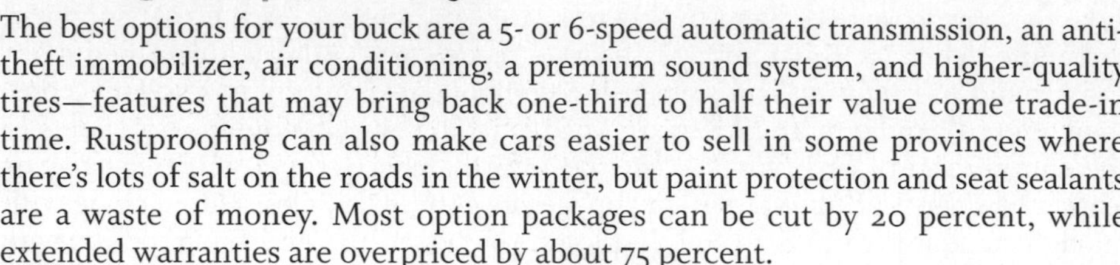

The best options for your buck are a 5- or 6-speed automatic transmission, an anti-theft immobilizer, air conditioning, a premium sound system, and higher-quality tires—features that may bring back one-third to half their value come trade-in time. Rustproofing can also make cars easier to sell in some provinces where there's lots of salt on the roads in the winter, but paint protection and seat sealants are a waste of money. Most option packages can be cut by 20 percent, while extended warranties are overpriced by about 75 percent.

Dealers make more than three times as much profit selling options as they do selling most cars (50 percent profit versus 15 percent profit). No wonder their eyes light up when you start perusing their options list. If you must have some options, compare prices with independent retailers and buy where the price is lowest and the warranty is the most comprehensive. Buy as few options as possible from the dealer, since you'll get faster service, more comprehensive guarantees, and lower prices from independent suppliers. Remember, extravagantly equipped vehicles hurt your pocketbook in three ways: They cost more to begin with and return only a fraction of what they cost when the car is resold; they drive up maintenance costs; and they often consume extra fuel.

A heavy-duty battery and suspension, and perhaps an upgraded sound system, will generally suffice for American-made vehicles; most imports already come well equipped. An engine block heater with a timer isn't a bad idea, either. It's an inexpensive investment that ensures winter starting and reduces fuel consumption by allowing you to start out with a semi-warm engine.

When ordering parts, remember that purchases from American outlets can be slapped with a small customs duty if the part isn't made in the United States. And then you'll pay the inevitable GST levied on the part's cost and customs duty. Finally, your freight carrier may charge a $15–$20 brokerage fee for representing you at the border.

Smart Options

The problem with options is that you often can't refuse them. Dealers sell very few bare-bones cars and minivans, and they option-pack each vehicle with features that can't be removed. You'll be forced to dicker over the total cost of what you are offered, whether you need the extras or not. So it isn't a case of "yes" or "no," but more a decision of "at what cost?"

Adjustable Pedals and Extensions

This device moves the brake and accelerator pedals forward or backward about 10 cm (4 in.) to accommodate short-statured drivers and protect them from airbag-induced injuries.

If the manufacturer of your vehicle doesn't offer optional power-adjustable pedals, there are several companies selling inexpensive pedal extensions by mail order through the Internet; for example, go to HDS Specialty Vehicles' website at *hdsmn.stores.yahoo.net*. If you live in Toronto or London, Ontario, check out Kino Mobility (*www.kinomobility.com*).

Adjustable Steering Wheel

This option allows easier access to the driver's seat and permits a more-comfortable driving position. It's particularly useful if more than one person will drive the vehicle.

Air Conditioning

AC systems are far more reliable than they were a decade ago, and they have a lifespan of five to seven years. Sure, replacement and repair costs can hit $1,000, but that's very little when amortized over an eight- to 10-year period. AC also makes your car easier to resell.

Does AC waste or conserve fuel when a vehicle is driven at highway speeds? Edmunds, a popular automotive information website, conducted fuel-efficiency tests and concluded that there wasn't that much difference between open or closed windows, a finding confirmed by *Consumer Reports*. See *www.edmunds.com/advice/fueleconomy/articles/106842/article.html*:

> While the A/C compressor does pull power from the engine wasting some gas, the effect appears to be fairly minimal in modern cars. And putting the windows down tends to increase drag on most cars, canceling out any measurable gain from turning the A/C off. But this one depends on the model you're driving. When we opened the sunroof in our SUV, the mileage did decrease even with the A/C off. Still, in our experience, it's not worth the argument because you won't save a lot of gas either way. So just do what's comfortable.

AC provides extra comfort, reduces wind noise (from not having to roll down the windows), and improves window defogging. Factory-installed units are best, however, because you'll get a longer warranty and improve your chances that everything was installed properly.

Anti-Theft Systems

You'd be a fool not to buy an anti-theft system, including a lockable fuel cap, for your much-coveted-by-thieves Japanese compact or sports car. Auto break-ins and thefts cost Canadians more than $400 million annually, meaning that there's a one in 130 chance that your vehicle will be stolen but only a 60 percent chance that you'll ever get it back.

Since amateurs are responsible for stealing most vehicles, the best theft deterrent is a visible device that complicates the job while immobilizing the vehicle and sounding an alarm. For less than $150, you can install both a steering-wheel lock and a hidden remote-controlled ignition disabler. Satellite tracking systems like GM's OnStar feature are also very effective.

Battery (Heavy-Duty)

The best battery for northern climates is the optional heavy-duty type offered by many manufacturers for about $100. It's a worthwhile purchase, especially for vehicles equipped with lots of electric options. Most standard batteries last only two winters; heavy-duty batteries give you an extra year or two for about 20 percent more than the price of a standard battery.

Make sure your new vehicle comes with a fresh battery—one manufactured less than six months earlier. Batteries are stamped with a date code, either on the battery's case or on an attached label. The vital information is usually in the first two characters—a letter and a numeral. Most codes start with a letter indicating the month: A for January, B for February, and so forth. The numeral denotes the year: Say, 0 for 2000. For example, "B3" stands for February 2003.

Don't order an optional battery with cold cranking amps (CCA) below the one specified for your vehicle, or one rated 200 amps or more above the specified rating. It's a waste of money to go too high. Also, buy a battery with the longest reserve capacity you can find; a longer capacity can make the difference between driving to safety and paying for an expensive tow.

Replacement batteries are very competitively priced and easy to find. Sears' DieHard batteries usually get *Consumer Reports*' top ratings. A useful link for finding the right battery with the most CCA for your car and year is *www.autobatteries.com/basics/selecting.asp*.

Central Locking Control

Costing around $200, this option is most useful for families with small children, car-poolers, or drivers of minivans who can't easily slide across the seat to lock the other doors.

Child Safety Seat (Integrated)

Integrated safety seats are designed to accommodate any child more than one year old or weighing over 9 kg (20 lb.). Since the safety seat is permanently integrated into the seatback, the fuss of installing and removing the safety seat and finding someplace to store it vanishes. When not in use, it quickly folds out of sight, becoming part of the seatback. Two other safety benefits: You know that the seat has been properly installed, and your child gets used to having his or her "special" seat in back, where it's usually safest to sit.

Electronic Stability Control (ESC)

The latest IIHS studies conclude that as many as 10,000 fatal crashes could be prevented if all vehicles were equipped with ESC. Its June 2006 report concluded that stability control is second only to seat belts in saving lives because it reduces the risk of fatal single-vehicle rollovers by 80 percent and the chance of having other kinds of fatal collisions by 43 percent.

Electronic stability control was first used by Mercedes-Benz and BMW on the S-Class and 7 Series models in 1995 and then was featured on GM's 1997 Cadillacs and Corvettes. It helps prevent the loss of control in turns, on slippery roads, or when you must make a sudden steering correction. The system applies the brakes to individual wheels or cuts back the engine power when sensors find the vehicle is beginning to spin or skid. It's particularly useful in maintaining stability with SUVs, but it's less useful with passenger coupes and sedans.

It's worrisome that there won't be any federal standard governing the performance of these systems before 2012, considering that not all electronic stability control systems work as they should. In tests carried out by *Consumer Reports* on 2003 models, the stability control system used in the Mitsubishi Montero was rated "unacceptable," BMW's X5 3.0i system provided poor emergency handling, and Acura's MDX and Subaru's Outback VDC stability systems left much to be desired.

Engines (Cylinder Deactivation)

Choose the most powerful 6- or 8-cylinder engine available if you're going to be doing a lot of highway driving, if you plan to carry a full passenger load and luggage on a regular basis, or if you intend to load up the vehicle with convenience features like air conditioning. Keep in mind that minivans, SUVs, and trucks with 6-cylinder or larger engines are easier to resell and retain their value the longest. For example, Honda's '96 Odyssey minivan was a sales dud in spite of its bulletproof reliability, mainly because buyers didn't want a minivan with an underpowered 4-cylinder powerplant. Some people buy underpowered vehicles in the mistaken belief that increased fuel economy is a good trade-off for decreased engine performance. It isn't. That's why there's so much interest in peppy 4-cylinders hooked to 5-speed transmissions and in larger engines with a "cylinder deactivation" feature.

In fact, cylinder deactivation is one feature that appears more promising than most other fuel-saving add-ons. For example, *AutoWeek* magazine found the overweight Jeep Commander equipped with a "Multiple Displacement System" still managed a respectable 13.8 L/100 km (17 mpg) on the highway in tests published in its March 2006 edition.

Honda employs a similar method, which cuts fuel consumption by 20 percent on the Odyssey. It runs on all six cylinders when accelerating, and on three cylinders when cruising. So far, there have been neither reliability nor performance complaints.

Engine and Transmission Cooling System (Heavy-Duty)

This relatively inexpensive option provides extra cooling for the transmission and engine. It can extend the life of these components by preventing overheating when heavy towing is required. It is a must-have feature for large cars made by Chrysler, Ford, or General Motors.

Extended Warranties

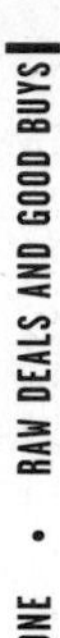

A smart buy if the dealer will discount the price by 50 percent and you are able to purchase the extra powertrain coverage only. However, you are throwing away \$1,500–\$2,000 if you buy an extended warranty for cars, vans, or trucks rated Recommended in *Lemon-Aid* or for vehicles sold by automakers that have written "goodwill" warranties covering engine and transmission failures. If you can get a great price for a vehicle rated just Average or Above Average but want protection from costly repair bills, patronize garages that offer lifetime warranties on parts listed in this guide as being failure-prone, such as powertrains, exhaust systems, and brakes.

Buy an extended warranty only as a last resort, and make sure you know what it covers and for how long. Budget \$1,000 after dealer discounting for the powertrain warranty. Incidentally, auto industry insiders say the average markup on these warranties varies from 50 to 65 percent, which seems almost reasonable when you consider that appliance warranties are marked up from 40 to 80 percent.

Flat-Folding Rear Seats

Fold-down rear seats give sedans and coupes additional room to carry long or bulky items. Split-folding rear seats are the most useful because they allow you to carry another passenger in the rear with one of the seats folded.

Keyless Entry (Remote)

This safety and convenience option saves you from fiddling with your key in a dark parking lot, or taking off a glove in cold weather to unlock or lock the vehicle. Try to get a keyless entry system combined with anti-theft measures such as an ignition kill switch or some other disabler. Incidentally, many automakers no longer make vehicles with an outside key lock on the passenger's side.

Paint Colour

Choosing a popular colour can make your vehicle easier to sell at a good price. DesRosiers Automotive Consultants say that blue is the preferred colour overall, but green and silver are also popular with Canadians. Manheim auctioneers say that green-coloured vehicles brought in 97.9 of the average auction price, while silver ones sold at a premium 105.5 percent. Remember that certain colours require particular care.

Black (and other dark colours): These paints are most susceptible to sun damage because of their heavy absorption of ultraviolet rays.

Pearl-toned colours: These paints are the most difficult to work with. If the paint needs to be retouched, it must be matched to look right from both the front- and side-angle views.

Red: This colour also shows sun damage, so keep your car in a garage or shady spot whenever possible.

White: Although grime looks terrible on a white car, white is the easiest colour to care for. But the colour is also very popular with car thieves, because white vehicles can be easily repainted another colour.

Power-Assisted Sliding Doors, Mirrors, Windows, and Seats

Merely a convenience feature with cars, power-assisted windows and doors are a necessity with minivans—crawling across the front seat a few times to roll up the passenger-side window or to lock the doors will quickly convince you of their value. Power mirrors are convenient on vehicles that have a number of drivers, or on minivans. Power seats with memory are particularly useful, too, if more than one person drives a vehicle. Automatic window and seat controls currently have few reliability problems, and they're fairly inexpensive to install, troubleshoot, and repair. As a safety precaution, make sure the window control has to be lifted. This will ensure no child is strangled from pressing against the switch. Power-sliding doors on minivans are even more of a danger. They are failure-prone on all makes and shouldn't be purchased by families with children.

Side Airbags

A worthwhile feature if you are the right size and properly seated, side airbags are presently overpriced and aren't very effective unless both the head and upper torso are protected. Side airbags are often featured as a $700 add-on to the sticker price, but you would be wise to bargain aggressively.

Stow 'n Go Seating

Pioneered by Chrysler in its minivans, Stow 'n Go seating allows the second- and third-row seats to be folded into, not onto, the floor. Folding the seats is a one-hand operation, and the head restraints don't need to be removed. Pop the spring-loaded seats back up, and there's an in-floor storage bin under each seat. One caveat: These seats sacrifice comfort for versatility. But check them out.

Suspension (Heavy-Duty)

Always a good idea, this inexpensive option pays for itself by providing better handling, allowing additional ride comfort (though a bit on the firm side), and extending shock life by an extra year or two.

Tires

There are three rules to remember when purchasing tires. First, neither brand nor price is a reliable gauge of performance, quality, or durability. Second, choosing a tire recommended by the automaker may not be in your best interest, since traction and long tread life are often sacrificed for a softer ride and maximum EPA mileage ratings. And third, don't buy any new tire that's older than two years, since the rubber compound may have deteriorated because of poor handling and improper storage (if they've been stored near electrical motors). You can check the date of manufacture on the side wall of the tire.

Two types of tires are generally available: all-season and performance. "Touring" is just a fancier name for all-season tires. All-season radial tires cost from $90 to $150 per tire. They're a compromise, since according to Transport Canada, they won't get you through winter with the same margin of safety as snow tires will and don't provide the same durability on dry surfaces as do regular summer tires. In areas with low to moderate snowfall, however, these tires are adequate as long as they're not pushed beyond their limits.

Mud or snow tires provide the best traction on snowy surfaces, but traction on wet roads is actually decreased. Treadwear is also accelerated by the use of softer rubber compounds. Beware of using wide tires for winter driving; 70-series or wider give poor traction and tend to float over snow.

Spare tires

Be wary of space-saver spare tires. They often can't match the promised mileage, and they seriously degrade steering control. Furthermore, they are usually stored in spaces inside the trunk that won't hold a normal-sized tire. The location of the stored spare can also have safety implications. Watch out for spares stowed under the chassis or mounted on the rear hatch. Frequently, the attaching cables and bolts rust out or freeze, so the spare falls off or becomes next to impossible to use when you need it.

Self-sealing and run-flat tires

Today there are two technologies available to help maintain vehicle mobility when a tire is punctured: self-sealing and self-supporting/run-flat tires.

Self-sealing: Ideal if you drive long distances. Punctures from nails, bolts, or screws up to 3/16 of an inch in diameter are fixed instantly and permanently with a sealant. A low air-pressure warning system isn't required. Expert testers say a punctured self-sealing tire can maintain air pressure for up to 200 km—even in freezing conditions. The Uniroyal Tiger Paw NailGard ($85–$140, depending on the size) is the overall winner in a side-by-side test conducted by The Tire Rack (*www.tirerack.com*).

Self-supporting/run-flat: Priced from $175 to $350 per tire, 25 to 50 percent more than the price of comparable premium tires, Goodyear's Extended Mobility Tire (EMT) run-flat tires were first offered as an option on the 1994 Chevrolet Corvette and then became standard on the 1997 model. These tires reinforce the side wall so it can carry the weight of the car for 90 km, or about an hour's driving time, even after all air pressure has been lost. You won't feel the tire go flat; you must depend on a $250–$300 optional tire-pressure monitor to warn you before the side wall collapses and you begin riding on your rim. Also, not all vehicles can adapt to run-flat tires; you may need to upgrade your rims. Experts say run-flats will give your car a harder ride, and you'll likely notice more interior tire and road noise. The car might also track differently. The Sienna's standard Dunlop run-flat tires have a terrible reputation for premature wear. At 25,000 km, one owner complained that her Sienna needed a new set at $200 each. You can expect a backlog of over a month to get a replacement. Goodyear and Pirelli run-flat tires have been on the market for some time now, and they seem to perform adequately.

Which tires are best?

There is no independent Canadian agency that evaluates tire performance and durability. However, the U.S.-based NHTSA rates treadwear, traction, and resistance to sustained high temperatures, etches the ratings onto the side walls of all tires sold in the States and Canada, and regularly posts its findings on the Internet (*www.nhtsa.dot.gov*). NHTSA also logs owner complaints relative to different brands. *Lemon-Aid* summarizes these complaints in the ratings of specific models in Part Three. However, you may get more-recent complaint postings, service bulletins, and tire recall notices at *www-odi.nhtsa.dot.gov/complaints*. On the Internet, you may also check out independent owner performance ratings as compiled by Tire Rack, a large tire retailer, at *www.tirerack.com/tires/surveyresults/index.jsp*.

Traction Control

This option limits wheelspin when accelerating. It is most useful with rear-drive vehicles and provides surer traction in wet or icy conditions.

Trailer-Towing Equipment

Just because you need a vehicle with towing capability doesn't mean that you have to spend big bucks. But you should first determine what kind of vehicle you want to do the job and whether your tires will handle the extra burden. For most towing needs (up to 900 kg/2,000 lb.), a passenger car, small pickup, or minivan equipped with a 6-cylinder engine will work just as well as a full-sized pickup or van (and will cost much less). If you're pulling a trailer that weighs more than 900 kg, most passenger cars won't handle the load unless they've been specially outfitted according to the automaker's specifications. Pulling a heavier trailer (up to 1,800 kg/4,000 lb.) will likely require a large vehicle equipped with a V8 powerplant.

Automakers reserve the right to change limits whenever they feel like it, so make any sales promise about towing an integral part of your contract. A good rule of thumb is to reduce the promised tow rating by 20 percent. In assessing towing weight, factor in the cargo, passengers, and equipment of both the trailer and the towing vehicle. Keep in mind that five people and luggage add 450 kg (almost 1,000 lb.) to the load, and that a full 227 L (60 gal.) water tank adds another 225 kg (almost 500 lb.). The manufacturer's gross vehicle weight rating (GVWR) takes into account the anticipated average cargo and supplies that your vehicle is likely to carry.

Automatic transmissions are fine for trailering, although there's a slight fuel penalty. Manual transmissions tend to have greater clutch wear caused by towing than do automatic transmissions. Both transmission choices are equally acceptable. Remember, the best compromise is to shift the automatic manually for maximum performance going uphill and to maintain control while not overheating the brakes when descending mountains.

Unibody vehicles (those without a separate frame) can handle most towing chores as long as their limits aren't exceeded. Front-drives aren't the best choice for pulling heavy loads in excess of 900 kg, since they lose some steering control and traction with all the weight concentrated in the rear.

Whatever vehicle you choose, keep in mind that the trailer hitch is crucial. It must have a tongue capacity of at least 10 percent of the trailer's weight; otherwise, it may be unsafe to use. Hitches are chosen according to the type of tow vehicle and, to a lesser extent, the weight of the load.

Most hitches are factory-installed, even though independents can install them more cheaply. Expect to pay about $200 for a simple boat hitch and a minimum of $600 for a fifth-wheel version.

Equalizer bars and extra cooling systems for the radiator, transmission, engine oil, and steering are prerequisites for towing anything heavier than 900 kg. Heavy-duty springs and brakes are a big help, too. Separate brakes for the trailer may be necessary to increase your vehicle's maximum towing capacity.

Transmissions

Despite its many advantages, the manual transmission is an endangered species in North America, where manuals equip only 8–10 percent of all new vehicles (mostly econocars, sports cars, and budget trucks), and that figure is slated to fall to 6 percent by 2012 as more vehicles adopt fuel-saving CVT transmissions, among other powertrain innovations. One theory on why the manual numbers keep falling: North American drivers are too busy with cell phones, text messaging, and cappuccinos to shift gears. Interestingly, European buyers opt for a manual transmission almost 90 percent of the time. (And they also drink cappuccinos, but usually not in 20 oz. paper takeout cups.)

Automakers are currently offering hybrid, manumatic transmissions that provide the benefits of an automatic transmission while also giving the driver the NASCAR-styled fun of clutchless manual shifting. Or, if all you want is fuel savings, there are now 5- and 6-speed automatic models—and even 7- and 8-speed versions—that are fuel-sippers.

Some considerations: The brake pads on stick-shift vehicles tend to wear out less rapidly than those on automatics do; a transmission with five or more forward speeds is usually more fuel-efficient than one with three forward speeds (hardly seen anymore); and manual transmissions add a mile or two per gallon over automatics, although this isn't always the case, as *Consumer Reports* recently discovered. Their road tests found that the 2008 Toyota Yaris equipped with an automatic transmission got slightly better gas mileage than a Yaris powered by a manual tranny.

Unnecessary Options

All-Wheel Drive (AWD)

Mark Bilek, editorial director of *Consumer Guide*'s automotive website (*consumerguideauto.howstuffworks.com*), is a critic of AWD. He says AWD systems generally encourage drivers to go faster than they should in adverse conditions, which creates trouble stopping in emergencies. Automakers like AWD as "a marketing ploy to make more money," Bilek contends. My personal mechanic adds, "Four-wheel drive will only get you stuck deeper, farther from home."

Anti-Lock Brakes (ABS)

Like adaptive cruise control and backup warning devices, ABS is another safety feature that's fine in theory but mostly impractical under actual driving conditions. (If you want the highly recommended electronic stability control (ESC), you must use anti-lock brakes.) The system maintains directional stability by preventing the wheels from locking up. This will not reduce the stopping distance, however. In practice, ABS is said to make drivers overconfident. Many still pump the brakes and render them ineffective; total brake failure is common; and repairs are frequent, complicated, and expensive to perform.

Cruise Control

Automakers provide this \$250–\$300 option, which is mainly a convenience feature, to motorists who use their vehicles for long periods of high-speed driving. The constant rate of speed saves some fuel and lessens driver fatigue during long trips. Still, the system is particularly failure-prone and expensive to repair, can lead to driver inattention, and can make the vehicle hard to control on icy roadways. Malfunctioning cruise-control units are also one of the major causes of sudden acceleration incidents. At other times, cruise control can be very distracting, especially to inexperienced drivers who are unaccustomed to sudden speed fluctuations.

Adaptive cruise control is the latest evolution of this feature. It senses a vehicle ahead of you and then automatically downshifts, brakes, or cuts your vehicle's speed. This commonly occurs when passing another car or when a car passes you, and it can make for a harrowing experience. Mercedes was the first out with the feature in 2000, followed by BMW in 2002. The BMW 5 Series sells it for \$2,500, Cadillac's DTS costs \$1,200 more with the device, and the Toyota Avalon XLS tacks on \$700 for the option.

Lots of fun when you are in the passing lane.

Electronic Instrument Readout

If you've ever had trouble reading a digital watch face or resetting your VCR, you'll feel right at home with this electronic gizmo. Gauges are presented in a series of moving digital patterns that are confusing, distracting, and unreadable in direct sunlight. This system is often accompanied by a trip computer and vehicle monitor that determine fuel use and how many kilometres you can drive until the tank is empty, indicate average speed, and signal component failures. Figures are frequently in error or slow to catch up.

Fog Lights

A pain in the eyes for other drivers, fog lights aren't necessary for most drivers who have well-aimed original-equipment headlights on their vehicles.

Gas-Saving Gadgets and Fuel Additives

The accessory market has been flooded with hundreds of atomizers, magnets, and additives that purport to make vehicles less fuel-thirsty. However, tests on over 100 gadgets and fuel or crankcase additives carried out by the U.S. Environmental Protection Agency have found that only a handful produce an increase in fuel economy, and the increase is tiny. These gadgets include warning devices that tell the driver to ease up on the throttle or shift to a more fuel-frugal gear, hardware that reduces the engine power needed for belt-driven accessories, cylinder deactivation systems, and spoilers that channel airflow under the car. The use of any of these products is a quick way to lose warranty coverage and fail provincial emissions tests.

GPS Navigation Systems

This navigation aid links a Global Positioning System (GPS) satellite unit to the vehicle's cellular phone and electronics. Good GPS devices cost $125–$1,500 (U.S.) when bought from an independent retailer. As a dealer option, you will pay $1,000–$2,000 (U.S.). For a monthly fee, the unit connects drivers to live operators who will help them with driving directions, give repair or emergency assistance, or relay messages. If the airbag deploys or the car is stolen, satellite-transmitted signals are automatically sent from the vehicle to operators who will notify the proper authorities of the vehicle's location.

Many of the systems' functions can be performed by a cellular telephone, and the navigation screens may be obtrusive, distracting, washed out in sunlight, and hard to calibrate. A portable Garmin GPS unit is more user-friendly and much cheaper.

High-Intensity Headlights

These headlights are much brighter than standard headlights, and they cast a blue hue. Granted, they provide additional illumination of the roadway, but they are also annoying to other drivers, who will flash their lights—or give you the middle finger—thinking that your high beams are on. These lights are easily stolen and expensive to replace. Interestingly, European versions have a device to maintain the light's spread closer to the road so that other drivers aren't blinded.

ID Etching

This $150–$200 option is a scam. The government doesn't require it, and thieves and joyriders aren't deterred by the etchings. If you want to etch your windows for your own peace of mind, several private companies will sell you a $15–$30 kit that does an excellent job (try *www.autoetch.net*), or you can wait for your municipality or local police agency to conduct one of their periodic free VIN ID etching sessions in your area.

Paint and Fabric Protectors

Selling for $200–$300, these "sealants" add nothing to a vehicle's resale value. Although paint lustre may be temporarily heightened, this treatment is less effective and more costly than regular waxing, and it may also invalidate the manufacturer's guarantee at a time when the automaker will look for any pretext to deny your paint claim.

Auto fabric protection products are nothing more than variations of Scotchgard, which can be bought in aerosol cans for a few dollars—a much better deal than the $50–$75 charged by dealers.

Power-Assisted Minivan Sliding Doors

Not a good idea if you have children. These doors have a high failure rate, opening or closing for no apparent reason and injuring children caught between the door and post.

Reverse-Warning System

Selling for about $500 as part of an option package, this safety feature warns the driver of any objects in the rear when backing up. Although a sound idea in theory, in practice the device often fails to go off or sounds an alarm for no reason. Drivers eventually either disconnect or ignore it.

Rollover-Detection System

This feature makes use of sensors to determine if the vehicle has leaned beyond a safe angle. If so, the side airbags are automatically deployed and remain inflated to make sure occupants aren't injured or ejected in a rollover accident. This is a totally new system that has not yet been proven. It could have disastrous consequences if the sensor malfunctions, as has been the case with front and side airbag sensors over the past decade.

Rooftop Carrier

Although this inexpensive option provides additional baggage space and may allow you to meet all your driving needs with a smaller vehicle, a loaded roof rack can increase fuel consumption by as much as 18 percent. An empty rack can cut fuel economy by about 10 percent.

Rustproofing

Rustproofing is no longer necessary, since automakers have extended their own rust warranties. In fact, you have a greater chance of seeing your rustproofer go belly up than having your untreated vehicle ravaged by premature rusting. Even if the rustproofer stays in business, you're likely to get a song and dance about why the warranty won't cover so-called internal rusting, or why repairs will be delayed until the sheet metal is actually rusted through.

Be wary of electronic rustproofing. Selling for $425 to $700, these electrical devices claim to inhibit vehicle corrosion by sending out a pulse current to the grounded body panels, protecting areas that conventional rust-inhibiting products can't reach. There is much debate as to whether these devices are worth the cost, or if they work at all.

Sunroof

Unless you live in a temperate region, the advantages of having a sunroof are far outweighed by the disadvantages. You aren't going to get better ventilation than a good AC system would provide, and a sunroof may grace your environment with painful booming wind noises, rattles, water leaks, and road dust accumulation. A sunroof increases gas consumption, reduces night vision because overhead highway lights shine through the roof opening, and can lose you several centimetres of headroom.

Tinted Glass

On the one hand, tinting jeopardizes safety by reducing your night vision. On the other hand, it does keep the interior cool in hot weather, reduces glare, and hides the car's contents from prying eyes. Factory applications are worth the extra cost, since cheaper aftermarket products (costing about $150) distort visibility and peel away after a few years. Some tinting done in the United States can run afoul of provincial highway codes that require more transparency.

Cutting the Price

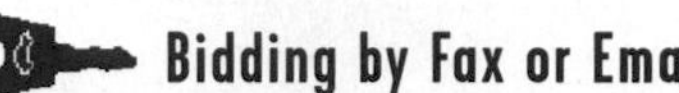

Bidding by Fax or Email

Dealers are more receptive to fax and email bidding this year because showroom traffic has dwindled because of the economic recession. The process is quite easy: Simply fax or email an invitation for bids to area dealerships, asking them to give their bottom-line price for a specific make and model. Be clear that all final bids must be sent within a week. When all the bids are received, the lowest bid is sent to the other dealers to give them a chance to beat that price. After a week of bidding, the lowest price gets your business. Incidentally, with the Canadian loonie headed to parity with the American dollar, try doing an Internet search for American prices and then using that lower figure to haggle with Canadian dealers.

Dozens of *Lemon-Aid* readers have told me how this bidding approach has cut thousands of dollars from the advertised price and saved them from the degrading song-and-dance routine between the buyer, sales agent, and sales manager ("he said, she said, the sales manager said").

A *Lemon-Aid* reader sent in the following suggestions for buying by fax or email:

> First, I'd like to thank you for writing the *Lemon-Aid* series of books, which I have used extensively in the fax-tendering purchase of my '99 Accord and '02 Elantra. I have written evidence from dealers that I saved a bare minimum of $700 on the Accord (but probably more) and a whopping $900 on the Elantra through the use of fax-tendering, over and above any deals possible through Internet-tendering and/or showroom bargaining.
>
> Based on my experience, I would suggest that in reference to the fax-tendering [or email-tendering] process, future *Lemon-Aid* editions emphasize:
>
> - Casting a wide geographical net, as long as you're willing to pick the car up there. I faxed up to 50 dealerships, which helped tremendously in increasing the

number of serious bidders. One car was bought locally in Ottawa, the other in Mississauga.

- Unless you don't care much about what car you end up with...be very specific about what you want. If you are looking at just one or two cars, which I recommend, specify trim level and all extended warranties and dealer-installed options in the fax letter. Otherwise, you'll end up with quotes comparing apples and oranges, and you won't get the best deal on options negotiated later. Also, specify that quotes should be signed—this helps out with errors in quoting.
- Dealerships are sloppy—there is a 25–30 percent error rate in quotes. Search for errors and get corrections, and confirm any of the quotes in serious contention over the phone.
- Phone to personally thank anyone who submits a quote for their time. Salespeople can't help themselves, they'll ask how they ranked, and often want to then beat the best quote you've got. This is much more productive than faxing back the most competitive quote (I know, I've tried that too).

SAMPLE FAX BID REQUEST

WITHOUT PREJUDICE

Date: ______________________________

Dear Sir or Madam,

I will be purchasing a new 2005 Toyota Sienna or a new 2005 Honda Odyssey and am issuing a request for quotation to several dealerships. I am willing to travel to complete a deal.

The quoted price is to *include* my requested options as well as any applicable pre-delivery inspection, administration, documentation, freight, and delivery fees. I understand that tire tax, air conditioning tax, battery tax, and provincial and federal sales tax are extra and are not required on your quotation. The dealer may sell off the lot or order the vehicle.

Please complete the attached form and either fax or email it back to me before the deadline of *5:00pm, April 14, 2005*. All respondents will be contacted after the deadline to confirm their bid. The winning bidder will then be contacted soon after to complete the transaction.

I will accept an alternate price quotation for a demonstration model with similar options, but this is not a mandatory requirement.

Please direct any questions via email to me at ___________ and I will respond promptly. Alternately you may call me at my office at _________.

Sincerely,
Joe Buyer

Another reader, in British Columbia, was successful with this approach (the fax bid request they used appears on the previous page):

> I purchased your 2005 edition *SUVs, Vans, and Trucks* earlier this year from Chapters. Thanks for all the information that helped me decide to purchase a new Honda Odyssey EX-L for a super price from a good dealer. After completing my research (and vacillating for a few weeks) I ended up issuing a faxed "request for quotation" (RFQ) from several dealerships. I can tell you that some of them were not happy and tried to tell me that Honda Canada was clamping down on this activity. In the end, one dealership did not respond and one "closer" salesperson called to attempt to get me in their dealership so he could "assess my needs." I told him that my needs were spelled out very specifically in my request but he refused to give me a price. In the end, I received five quotations by phone, fax, and email. I purchased my van in Chilliwack for about $2,200 off list. It turned out that the salesperson just started selling cars two months ago and was very appreciative of my business. The whole deal was completed in half an hour. I was in full control but treated every respondent fairly. I did not play dealers off one another and went with the lowest first offer.

Getting a Fair Price

"We Sell Below Cost"

This is no longer a bait-and-switch scam. Many dealers who are going out of business are desperate to sell their inventory, sometimes for 40 percent below the MSRP. Assuming the vehicle's cost price was 20 percent under the MSRP, astute buyers are getting up to a 20 percent discount. I've listed the profit margins below for various vehicle categories, excluding freight, PDI, and administrative fees, which you should bargain down or not pay at all.

South Korean, Chrysler, and General Motors prices are the most negotiable, while Japanese and European vehicle prices are much firmer. In addition to the dealer's

DEALER MARKUP

DEALER MARKUP (AMERICAN VEHICLES)	
Small cars:	10%–12%
Mid-sized cars:	13%–15%
Large cars:	16%–18%
Sports cars:	15%–20%
High-end sports cars:	20+%
Luxury cars:	20+%
High-end luxury cars:	20+%
Minivans:	15%
High-end minivans:	16%–20%

DEALER MARKUP (JAPANESE VEHICLES)	
Small cars:	10%%
Mid-sized cars:	11%–13%
Large cars:	15%
Sports cars:	15%–20%
High-end sports cars:	20+%
Luxury cars:	20+%
High-end luxury cars:	20+%
Minivans:	12%–15%
High-end minivans:	15%–17%

markup, some vehicles may also have a 3 percent carryover allowance paid out in a dealer incentive program. Finance contracts may also tack on a 3 percent dealer commission.

Holdback

Ever wonder how dealers who advertise vehicles for "a hundred dollars over invoice" can make a profit? They are counting mostly on the manufacturer's holdback.

In addition to the MSRP, the invoice price, dealer incentives, and customer rebates (available to Canadians at *www.apa.ca*), another key element in every dealer's profit margin is the manufacturer's holdback—the quarterly payouts dealers depend on when calculating gross profit.

The holdback was set up over 45 years ago by General Motors as a guaranteed profit for dealers tempted to bargain away their entire profit to make a sale. It usually represents 1–3 percent of the sticker price (MSRP) and is seldom given out by Asian or European automakers, which use dealer incentive programs instead. There are several free Internet sources for holdback information: The most recent and comprehensive are *www.edmunds.com* and *www.kbb.com*, two websites geared toward American buyers. Although there may be a difference in the holdback percentage between American automakers and their Canadian subsidiaries, it's usually not significant.

Some GM dealers maintain that they no longer get a holdback allowance. They are being disingenuous—the holdback may have been added to special sales "incentive" programs, which won't show up on the dealer's invoice. Options are the icing on the cake, with their average 35–65 percent markup.

Can You Get a Fair Price?

Yes, but you'll have to keep your wits about you and time your purchase well into the model year—usually in late winter or spring.

New-car negotiations aren't wrestling matches where you have to pin the sales agent's shoulders to the mat to win. If you feel that the overall price is fair, don't jeopardize the deal by refusing to budge. For example, if you've brought the contract price 10 percent or more below the MSRP and the dealer sticks you with a $200 "administrative fee" at the last moment, let it pass. You've saved money and the sales agent has saved face.

Of course, someone will always be around to tell you how he or she could have bought the vehicle for much less. Let that pass, too.

To come up with a fair price, subtract two-thirds of the dealer's markup from the MSRP and then trade the carryover and holdback allowance for a reduced delivery and transportation fee. Compute the options separately, and sell your trade-in privately. Buyers can more easily knock $4,000–$7,000 off a $20,000 base price if they wait until Chrysler and GM hold their new year "fire" sales in early 2010 and ratchet up the competition. Remember, choose a vehicle in stock, and resist getting unnecessary options.

Beware of Financing and Insurance Traps

Once you and the dealer have settled on the vehicle's price, you aren't out of the woods yet. You'll be handed over to an F&I (financing and insurance) specialist, whose main goal is to convince you to buy additional financing, loan insurance, paint and seat cover protectors, rustproofing, and extended warranties. These items will be presented on a computer screen as costing only "a little bit more each month."

Compare the dealer's insurance and financing charges with those from an independent agency that may offer better rates and better service. Often, the dealer gets a kickback for selling insurance and financing. And guess who pays for it? Additionally, remember that if the financing rate looks too good to be true, you're probably paying too much for the vehicle. The F&I closer's hard-sell approach will take all your willpower and patience to resist, but when he or she gives up, your trials are over.

Add-on charges are the dealer's last chance to stick it to you before the contract is signed. Dealer pre-delivery inspection (PDI) and transportation charges, "documentation" fees, and extra handling costs are ways that the dealer gets extra profits for nothing. Dealer preparation is often a once-over-lightly affair, with a car seldom getting more than a wash job and a couple of dollars' worth of gas in the tank. It's paid for by the factory in most cases, but, when it's not, it should cost no more than 2 percent of the car's selling price. Reasonable transportation charges are acceptable, although dealers who claim that the manufacturer requires the payment often inflate them.

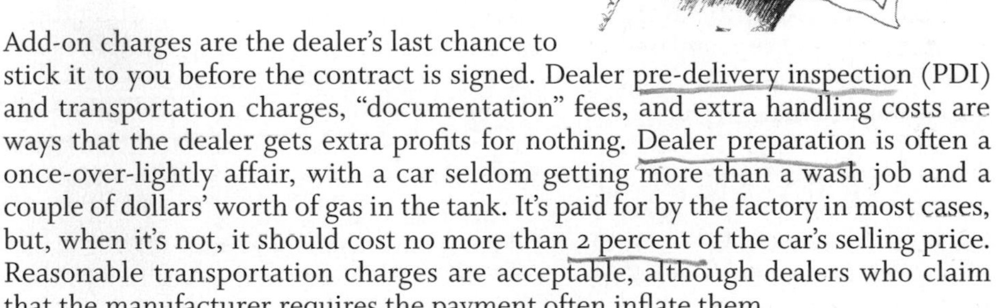

"No Haggle" Pricing Is "Price Fixing"

All dealers bargain. They hang out the "No dickering; one price only" sign simply as a means to discourage customers from asking for a better deal. Like parking lots and restaurants that claim they won't be responsible for lost or stolen property, they're bluffing. Still, you'd be surprised by how many people believe that if it's posted, it's non-negotiable.

No-haggle pricing is not only a deceptive practice, but it's also illegal under federal price-fixing statutes. Several *Lemon-Aid* readers say some Honda dealers refuse to negotiate prices via email or fax (see page 71) or through third-party auto brokers because Honda Canada has threatened to yank their franchise if they do so. Following *Lemon-Aid*'s formal complaint last year, the feds opened a formal investigation of Honda's practice. They closed the probe six months later because the new *Competition Act* says that a price-fixing practice actually has to be proven as having affected the prices customers would have paid.

Lemon-Aid was luckier with its Toyota complaint. In June 2004, Toyota Canada abandoned its Access no-haggle price strategy sales system after settling out of court a price-fixing probe undertaken by the federal Competition Bureau.

Price Guidelines

When negotiating the price of a new vehicle, remember that there are several price guidelines and dealers use the one that will make them the most profit on each transaction. Two of the more-common prices quoted are the MSRP (what the automaker advertises as a fair price) and the dealer's invoice cost (which is supposed to indicate how much the dealer paid for the vehicle). Both price indicators leave considerable room for the dealer's profit margin, along with some extra padding in the form of inflated transportation and preparation charges. If you are presented with both figures, go with the MSRP, since it can be verified by calling the manufacturer. Any dealer can print up an invoice and swear to its veracity. If you want an invoice price from an independent source, contact *apa.ca* or *carhelpcanada.com*.

Buyers who live in rural areas or in western Canada are often faced with grossly inflated auto prices compared to those charged in major metropolitan areas. A good way to get a more-competitive price without buying out of province is to check online what prices are being charged in different urban areas. Show the dealer printouts that list selling prices, preparation charges, and transportation fees, and then ask for his or her price to come closer to the advertised prices.

Another tactic is to take a copy of a local competitor's car ad to a competing dealer selling the same brand and ask for a better price. Chances are they've already lost a few sales due to the ad and will work a little harder to match the deal; if not, they're almost certain to reveal the tricks in the competitor's promotion to make the sale.

Dealer Incentives and Customer Rebates

Sales incentives haven't changed much in the past 30 years. When vehicles are first introduced in the fall, they're generally overpriced; early in the new year, they'll sell for about 20–30 percent less. After a year, they may sell for 40 percent less through a combination of dealer sales incentives (manufacturer-to-dealer), cash rebates (manufacturer-to-customer), zero percent interest financing (manufacturer's-finance-company-to-customer), and discounted prices (dealer-to-customer).

In most cases, the manufacturer's rebate is straightforward and mailed directly to the buyer from the automaker. There are other rebate programs that require a financial investment on the dealer's part, however, and these shared programs tempt dealers to offset losses by inflating the selling price or pocketing the manufacturer's rebate. Therefore, when the dealer participates in the rebate program, demand that the rebate be deducted from the MSRP, not from some inflated invoice price concocted by the dealer.

Some rebate ads will include the phrase "from dealer inventory only." So if your dealer doesn't have the vehicle in stock, you won't get the rebate.

Sometimes automakers will suddenly decide that a rebate no longer applies to a specific model, even though their ads continue to include it. When this happens, take all brochures and advertisements showing your eligibility for the rebate plan to provincial consumer protection officials. They can use false advertising statutes to force automakers to give rebates to every purchaser who was unjustly denied one.

If you are buying a heavily discounted vehicle, be wary of "option packaging" by dealers who push unwanted protection packages (rustproofing, paint sealants, and upholstery finishes), or who levy excessive charges for preparation, filing fees, loan guarantee insurance, and credit life insurance.

Rebates and Quality

Forget the old adage "You get what you pay for." Many reliable, top-performing vehicles come with rebates—especially now that auto sales are down more than 40 percent for 2009. Rarely will Toyota and Honda offer more than $1,500 rebates, but Chrysler, Ford, and GM routinely hand out $5,000–$7,000 discounts and other sales incentives. The rest of the auto manufacturers fall somewhere in between. To come out ahead, you have to know how to play this rebate game by choosing quality first.

Customer and dealer incentives are frequently given out to stimulate sales of year-old models that are unpopular, scheduled to be redesigned, or headed for the axe. By choosing carefully which rebated models you buy, it's easy to realize important savings with little risk. For example, GM's $2,000 incentives are good deals when applied to its reasonably reliable compact cars (Aveo excepted) but not worth it when applied to the company's glitch-prone Saturn models and small trucks. Ford's Explorer and Expedition and Freestar minivan rebates ($4,000 plus) also aren't sufficient to offset the greater risk of factory-related defects afflicting these poor-quality models. Post-bankrupt Chrysler's sizeable rebates can be a good deal only when applied to minivans and Jeeps like the Wrangler and Liberty, but they're not advisable as a reason to buy the company's less-reliable cars and SUVs.

Chrysler's little Caliber econobox has been slammed by *Consumer Reports* for being underpowered, with a hard ride, poor handling, and a tacky interior. Not a good buy, no matter what rebates are given.

Prices Go Up; Prices Go Down

Generally, vehicles are priced according to what the market will bear and then are discounted as the competition heats up (Chrysler's larger rear-drive cars and its PT Cruiser and GM's SUVs are prime examples). This year, though, all vehicles are cheaper than ever due to historically bad sales seen in 2008–09. A vehicle's stylishness, scarcity, or general popularity doesn't count for much when unemployment is pandemic, credit is scarce, and many dealers are going bust with hundreds of unsold new vehicles in their inventories.

Cash is once again king, and the once overpriced and hard-to-find popular models are now heavily discounted, or have been dropped entirely, sending their resale values plummeting. For example, Chrysler's rear-drive Hemi-engine-equipped Magnum and 300 had prevailing market values about $1,000 higher than their suggested selling prices when launched in 2004. They were a unique entry in a hot market niche, and were in short supply. But all that doesn't matter any more. Sales of these models have dropped by more than 40 percent during the last four years, and new models are sold with 30–40 percent discounts.

This year, the best prices will come early in the first quarter of 2010 and will continue through the summer. This includes Chevrolet's brand new 2010 Camaro. On the other hand, if your choice has an unusually low sticker price, find out why it's so unpopular and then decide if the savings are worth it. Vehicles that don't sell because of the recession or their weird styling are no problem, but poor quality control (think Chrysler's cars and some Kias) can cost you big bucks.

Leftovers

Again this year, almost all the cars and trucks are leftovers. Dealers are drowning in a sea of unsold vehicles. Most are new and eligible for substantial factory rebates. But are these leftovers really bargains?

They might be, if you can amortize the first year's depreciation by keeping the vehicle for eight years or more. But if you're the kind of driver who trades every two or three years, you're likely to come out a loser by buying an end-of-the-season vehicle. The simple reason is that, as far as trade-ins are concerned, a leftover is a "used" vehicle that has depreciated at least 30 percent in its first year. The savings the dealer gives you may not equal that first year's depreciation (a cost you'll incur without getting any of the first year's driving benefits). If the dealer's discounted price matches or exceeds the 30 percent depreciation, you're getting a pretty good deal.

Ask the dealer for all work orders relating to the vehicle, including the PDI checklist, and make sure that the odometer readings follow in sequential order. Remember as well that most demonstrators should have less than 5,000 km on the ticker and that the original warranty has been reduced from the day the vehicle was first put on the road. Also, make sure the vehicle is relatively "fresh" (about three months old) and check for warranty damage. With demos, have the dealer extend the warranty or lower the price about $100 for each month of warranty that has expired. If the vehicle's file shows that it was registered to a leasing agency or any other third party, you're definitely buying a used vehicle disguised as a demo. You should walk away from the sale—you're dealing with a crook.

Cash versus Financing

Up until this year, car dealers preferred financing car sales, instead of getting cash, because of the kickbacks lenders gave them. This is no longer the case, because fewer companies are lending money, and those that do are giving back very little to dealers and don't want to give loans for more than two-thirds of the purchase price. Dealers are scrambling for equity and will sell their vehicles for less than what they cost if the buyer pays cash.

If you aren't offered much of a discount for cash, financial planners say it can be smarter to finance the purchase of a new vehicle if a portion of the interest is tax-deductible. The cash that you free up can then be used to repay debts that aren't tax-deductible (mortgages or credit card debts, for example).

Rebates versus Low or Zero Percent Financing

Low-financing programs have the following disadvantages:

- Buyers must have exceptionally good credit.
- Shorter financing periods mean higher payments.
- Cash rebates are excluded.
- Only fully equipped or slow-selling models are eligible.
- Buyers pay full retail price.

Remember, to get the best price, first negotiate the price of the vehicle without disclosing whether you are paying cash or financing the purchase (say you haven't yet decided). Once you have a fair price, you can then take advantage of the financing.

Getting a Loan

Borrowers must be at least 18 years old (the age of majority), have a steady income, prove that they have discretionary income sufficient to make the loan payments, and be willing to guarantee the loan with additional collateral or with a parent or spouse as a co-signer.

Before applying for a loan, you should have established a good credit rating via a paid-off credit card and have a small savings account with your local bank, credit union, or trust company. Prepare a budget listing your assets and obligations. This will quickly show whether or not you can afford a car. Next, prearrange your loan with a phone call. This will protect you from much of the smoke-and-mirrors showroom shenanigans.

Incidentally, if you do get in over your head and require credit counselling, contact Credit Counselling Service (CCS), a not-for-profit organization located in many of Canada's major cities (*www.creditcanada.com*).

Hidden Loan Costs

Don't trust anyone. The APA's undercover shoppers have found that most deceptive deals involve major banking institutions rather than automaker-owned companies.

In your quest for an auto loan, remember that the Internet offers help for people who need an auto loan and want quick approval but don't want to face a banker. The Bank of Montreal (*www.bmo.com*), RBC (*www.rbc.com*), and other banks allow vehicle buyers to post loan applications on their websites. Loans are available to any web surfer, including those who aren't current BMO or RBC customers.

Be sure to call various financial institutions to find out the following:

- The annual percentage rate on the amount you want to borrow, and for the duration of your repayment period
- The minimum down payment that the institution requires
- Whether taxes and licence fees are considered part of the overall cost and, thus, are covered by part of the loan
- Whether lower rates are available for different loan periods, or for a larger down payment
- Whether discounts are available to depositors, and if so, how long you must be a depositor before qualifying

When comparing loans, consider the annual rate and then calculate the total cost of the loan offer; that is, how much you'll pay above and beyond the total price of the vehicle.

Dealers may be able to finance your purchase at interest rates that are competitive with the banks' because of the rebates they get from the manufacturers and some lending institutions. Don't believe dealers that say they can borrow money at as much as five percentage points below the prime rate. Actually, they're jacking up the retail price to more than make up for the lower interest charges. Sometimes, instead of boosting the price, dealers reduce the amount they pay for the trade-in. In either case, the savings are illusory.

When dealing with banks, keep in mind that the traditional 36-month loan has now been stretched to 48 or 60 months. Longer payment terms make each month's payment more affordable, but over the long run, they increase the cost of the loan considerably. Therefore, take as short a term as possible.

Be wary of lending institutions that charge a "processing" or "document" fee ranging from $25 to $100. Sometimes consumers will be charged an extra 1–2 percent of the loan up front in order to cover servicing. This is similar to lending institutions adding "points" to mortgages, except that with auto loans, it's totally unjustified. In fact, dealers in the States are the object of several state lawsuits and class actions for inflating loan charges.

Some banks will cut the interest rate if you're a member of an automobile owners' association or if loan payments are automatically deducted from your chequing account. This latter proposal may be costly, however, if the chequing account charges exceed the interest-rate savings.

Loan Protection

Credit insurance guarantees that the vehicle loan will be paid if the borrower becomes disabled or dies. There are three basic types of insurance that can be written into an installment contract: credit life, accident and health, and comprehensive. Some car companies, like Hyundai, will make some of your loan payments if you become unemployed. Most bank and credit union loans are already covered by some kind of loan insurance, but dealers sell the protection separately at an extra cost to the borrower. For this service, the dealer gets a hefty 20 percent commission. The additional cost to the purchaser can be significant. The federal GST is applied to loan insurance, but RST may be exempted in some provinces.

Collecting on these types of policies isn't easy. There's no payment if your unemployment was due to your own conduct or an illness is caused by some condition that existed prior to your taking out the insurance. Generally, credit insurance is unnecessary if you're in good health, you have no dependants, and your job is secure. Nevertheless, if you need to cancel your financial obligations, the same company that started up Leasebusters (refer to page 16) now offers FinanceBusters (*www.financebusters.com*). They offer a similar service to a lease takeover, but for customers who have vehicle loans.

Personal loans from financial institutions (particularly credit unions) now offer lots of flexibility, like fixed or variable interest rates, a choice of loan terms, and no penalties for prepayment. Precise conditions depend on your personal credit rating.

Leasing contracts are less flexible. There's a penalty for any prepayment, and rates aren't necessarily competitive.

Financing Scam: "Your Financing Was Turned Down"

This may be true, now that credit has become more difficult to get. But watch out for the scam that begins after you have purchased a vehicle and left your trade-in with the dealer. A few days later, you are told that your loan was rejected and that you now must put down a larger down payment and accept a higher monthly payment. Of course, your trade-in has already been sold.

Protect yourself from this rip-off by getting a signed agreement that stipulates that financing has been approved and that monthly payments can't be readjusted. Tell the dealer that your trade-in cannot be sold until the deal has closed.

The Contract

How likely are you to be cheated when buying a new car or truck? APA staffers posing as buyers visited 42 dealerships in four Canadian cities in early 2002. Almost half the dealers they visited (45 percent) flunked their test, and (hold onto your cowboy hats) auto buyers in western Canada were especially vulnerable to dishonest dealers. Either dealer ads left out important information or vehicles in the ads weren't available or were selling at higher prices. Fees for paperwork and vehicle preparation were frequently excessive.

Now, eight years later, we know dealers are much more honest. Ahem...maybe.

The Devil's in the Details

Watch what you sign, since any document that requires your signature is a contract. Don't sign anything unless all the details are clear to you and all the blanks have been filled in. Don't accept any verbal promises that you're merely putting the vehicle on hold. And when you are presented with a contract, remember it doesn't have to include all the clauses found in the dealer's pre-printed form. You and the sales representative can agree to strike some clauses and add others.

When the sales agent asks for a deposit, make sure that it's listed on the contract as a deposit, try to keep it as small as possible (a couple hundred dollars at the most), and pay for it by credit card—in case the dealer goes belly up. If you decide to back out of the deal on a vehicle taken from stock, let the seller have the deposit as an incentive to cancel the contract (believe me, it's cheaper than hiring a lawyer and probably equal to the dealer's commission).

Scrutinize all references to the exact model (there's a heck of an upgrade from base to LX or Limited), prices, and delivery dates. Make sure you specify a delivery date in the contract that protects the price.

Contract Clauses You Need

You can put things on a more-equal footing by negotiating the inclusion of as many clauses as possible from the sample additional contract clauses found on the following page. To do this, write in a "Remarks" section on your contract and then add, "See attached clauses, which form part of this agreement." Then attach a photocopy of the "Additional Contract Clauses" and persuade the sales agent to initial as many of the clauses as possible. Although some clauses may be rejected, the inclusion of just a couple of them can have important legal ramifications later on if you want a full or partial refund.

ADDITIONAL CONTRACT CLAUSES

1. **Original contract:** This is the ONLY contract; i.e., it cannot be changed, retyped, or rewritten, without the specific agreement of both parties.
2. **Financing:** This agreement is subject to the purchaser obtaining financing at _____% or less within _______ days of the date below.
3. **"In-service" date and mileage:** To be based on the closing day, not the day the contract was executed, and will be submitted to the automaker for warranty and all other purposes. The dealership will have this date corrected by the automaker if it should become necessary.
4. **Delivery:** The vehicle is to be delivered by ______, failing which the contract is cancelled and the deposit will be refunded.
5. **Cancellation:**
   (a) The purchaser retains the right to cancel this agreement without penalty at any time before delivery of the vehicle by sending a notice in writing to the vendor.
   (b) Following delivery of the vehicle, the purchaser shall have two days to return the vehicle and cancel the agreement in writing, without penalty. After two days and before thirty-one days, the purchaser shall pay the dealer $25 a day as compensation for depreciation on the returned vehicle.
   (c) Cancellation of contract can be refused where the vehicle has been subjected to abuse, negligence or unauthorized modifications after delivery.
   (d) The purchaser is responsible for accident damage and traffic violations while in possession of the said vehicle.
6. **Protected price:** The vendor agrees not to alter the price of the new vehicle, the cost of preparation, or the cost of shipping.
7. **Trade-in:** The vendor agrees that the value attributed to the vehicle offered in trade shall not be reduced, unless it has been significantly modified or has suffered from unreasonable and accelerated deterioration since the signing of the agreement.
8. **Courtesy car:**
   (a) In the event the new vehicle is not delivered on the agreed-upon date, the vendor agrees to supply the purchaser with a courtesy car at no cost. If no courtesy vehicle is available, the vendor agrees to reimburse the purchaser the cost of renting a vehicle.
   (b) If the vehicle is off the road for more than five days for warranty repairs, the purchaser is entitled to a free courtesy vehicle for the duration of the repair period. If no courtesy vehicle is available, the vendor agrees to reimburse the purchaser the cost of renting a vehicle of equivalent or lesser value.
9. **Work orders:** The purchaser will receive duly completed copies of all work orders pertaining to the vehicle, including warranty repairs and the pre-delivery inspection (PDI).
10. **Dealer stickers:** The vendor will not affix any dealer advertising, in any form, on the vehicle.
11. **Fuel:** Vehicle will be delivered with a free full tank of gas.
12. **Excess mileage:** New vehicle will not be acceptable and the contract will be void if the odometer has more than 50 km at delivery/closing.
13. **Tires:** Original equipment Firestone, Bridgestone, or Goodyear tires are not acceptable.

____________	____________________	____________________
Date	Vendor's Signature	Buyer's Signature

"We Can't Do That"

Dealers and automakers facing bankruptcy can do almost anything to get your business. Don't take the dealer's word that "We're not allowed to do that"—heard most often in reference to your reducing the PDI or transportation fee. Some dealers have been telling *Lemon-Aid* readers that they are "obligated" by the automaker to charge a set fee and could lose their franchise if they charge less. This is pure hogwash. No dealer has ever had their franchise licence revoked for cutting prices. Furthermore, the automakers clearly state that they don't set a bottom price, since doing so would violate Canada's *Competition Act*—that's why you always see them putting disclaimers in their ads saying the dealer can charge less.

The Pre-delivery Inspection

The best way to ensure that the PDI (written as "PDE" in some regions) will be done is to write in the sales contract that you'll be given a copy of the completed PDI sheet when the vehicle is delivered to you. Then, with the PDI sheet in hand, verify some of the items that were to be checked. If any items appear to have been missed, refuse delivery of the vehicle. Once you get home, check out the vehicle more thoroughly, and send a registered letter to the dealer if you discover any incomplete items from the PDI.

Selling Your Trade-In

When to Sell

Used cars are worth more than ever because new cars are suspect (in terms of price and insecurities about warranties being honoured and dealer/automaker backup). New prices are lower than ever before, and used prices are rising. This makes it hard for most owners to figure out when is the best time to sell or buy another vehicle. It doesn't take a genius to figure out that the longer one keeps a vehicle, the less it costs to own.

If you're happy with your vehicle's styling and convenience features and it's safe and dependable, there's no reason to get rid of it. But when the cost of repairs becomes equal to or greater than the cost of payment for a new car (about $2,000 a year), you need to consider trading it in. Shortly after your vehicle's fifth birthday (or whenever you start to think about trading it in), ask a mechanic to look at it to give you some idea of what repairs, replacement parts, or maintenance work it will need in the coming year. Find out if dealer service bulletins show that it will need extensive repairs in the near future (see Appendix III for how to order bulletins from ALLDATA). If it's going to require expensive repairs, you should trade the vehicle right away; if expensive work isn't predicted, you may want to keep it. Auto owners' associations provide a good yardstick. They figure that the annual cost of repairs and preventive maintenance for the average vehicle is about $800. If your vehicle is five years old and you haven't spent anywhere near $4,000 in maintenance, it would pay to invest in your old vehicle and continue using it for another few years.

Consider whether your vehicle can still be serviced easily. If it's no longer on the market, the parts supply is likely to dry up and independent mechanics will be reluctant to repair it.

Don't trade for fuel economy alone. Most fuel-efficient vehicles, such as front-drives, offset the savings through higher repair costs. Also, the more fuel-efficient vehicles may not be as comfortable to drive because of their excessive engine noise, lightweight construction, stiff suspension, and torque steer.

Reassess your needs. Has your family grown to the point that you need a new vehicle? Are you driving less? Are you taking fewer long trips? Let your car or minivan show its age, and pocket the savings if its deteriorating condition doesn't pose a safety hazard and isn't too embarrassing. If you're in sales and are constantly on the road, it makes sense to trade every few years—in that case, the vehicle's appearance and reliability become a prime consideration, particularly since the increased depreciation costs are mostly tax-deductible.

Getting the Most for Your Trade-In

Customers who are on guard against paying too much for a new vehicle often sell their trade-ins for too little. Before agreeing to any trade-in amount, read Part Three of *Lemon-Aid Used Cars and Trucks*. The guide will give your vehicle's dealer price and private selling price, and it offers a formula to figure out regional price fluctuations.

Now that you've nailed down your trade-in's approximate value, here are some tips on selling it with a minimum of stress:

- Never sign a new-vehicle sales contract unless your trade-in has been sold—you could end up with two vehicles.
- Negotiate the price from retail (dealer price) down to wholesale (private sales).
- If you haven't sold your trade-in after two weekends, you might be trying to sell it at the wrong time of year or have it priced too high.

Make Money—Sell Privately

If you must sell your vehicle and want to make the most out of the deal, consider selling it yourself and putting the profits toward your next purchase. You'll likely come out hundreds of dollars ahead—buyers will pay more for your vehicle because they don't pay the 5 percent GST on a private sale. The most important thing to remember is that there's a large market for used vehicles in good condition in the $5,000–$7,000 range. Although most people prefer buying from individuals rather than from used-car lots, they may still be afraid that the vehicle is a lemon. By using the following suggestions, you should be able to sell your vehicle quite easily:

1. Know its value. Study dealers' newspaper ads and compare them with the prices listed in *Lemon-Aid*. Undercut the dealer's price by $300–$800, and be ready to bargain down another 10 percent for a serious buyer. Remember, prices can fluctuate wildly depending on which models are trendy, so watch the want ads carefully.
2. Enlist the aid of the salesperson who's selling you your new car. Offer him or her a few hundred dollars to find you a buyer. The fact that one sale hinges on the other, along with the prospect of making two commissions, may work wonders.
3. Post notices on bulletin boards at your office or local supermarkets, and place a "For Sale" sign in the window of the vehicle itself. Place a newspaper ad only as a last resort.
4. Don't give your address right away to a potential buyer responding to your ad. Instead, ask for the telephone number where you may call that person back.
5. Be wary of selling to friends or family members. Anything short of perfection, and you'll be eating Christmas dinner alone.
6. Don't touch the odometer. If you do, you may get a few hundred dollars more—and a criminal record.
7. Paint the vehicle. Some specialty shops charge only $300 and give a guarantee that's transferable to subsequent owners.
8. Make minor repairs. This includes a minor tune-up and patching up the exhaust. Again, if any repair warranty is transferable, use it as a selling point.
9. Clean the vehicle. Go to a reconditioning firm, or spend the weekend scrubbing the interior and exterior. First impressions are important. Clean the chrome, polish the body, and peel off old bumper stickers. Remove butts from the ashtrays and clean out the glove compartment. Make sure all tools and spare parts have been taken out of the trunk. Don't remove the radio or speakers—the gaping holes will lower the vehicle's worth much more than the cost of the sound equipment. Replace missing or broken dash knobs and window cranks.
10. Change the tires. Recaps are good buys.
11. Let the buyer examine the vehicle. Insist that it be inspected at an independent garage, and then accompany the prospective buyer to the garage. This gives you protection if the buyer claims you misrepresented the vehicle.
12. Don't mislead the buyer. If the vehicle was in an accident or some financing is still to be paid, admit it. Any misleading statements may be used later against you in court. It's also advisable to have someone witness the actual transaction in case of a future dispute.
13. Keep important documents handy. Show prospective buyers the sales contract, repair orders, owner's manual, and all other documents that show how the vehicle has been maintained. Authenticate your claims about fuel consumption.
14. Write an effective ad, if you need to use one.

Selling to Dealers

Selling to a dealer means that you're likely to get 20 percent less than if you sold your vehicle privately, unless the dealer agrees to participate in an accommodation sale based upon you buying a new vehicle from them. Most owners will gladly pay some penalty to the dealer, however, for the peace of mind that comes with knowing that their eventual buyer won't lay a claim against them. This assumes that the dealer hasn't been cheated by the owner—if the vehicle is stolen, isn't paid for, has had its odometer spun back (or forward to a lower setting), or is seriously defective, the buyer or dealer can sue the original owner for fraud. Sell to a dealer who sells the same make. He or she will give you more because it's easier to sell your trade-in to customers who are interested in only that make of vehicle.

Drawing Up the Contract

The province of Alberta has prepared a useful bill of sale applicable throughout Canada that can be accessed at *www.servicealberta.gov.ab.ca/pdf/mv/BillOfSaleReg3126.pdf*. Your bill of sale should identify the vehicle (including the serial number) and include its price, whether a warranty applies, and the nature of the examination made by the buyer.

The buyer may ask you to put in a lower price than what was actually paid in order to reduce the sales tax. If you agree to this, don't be surprised when a Revenue Canada agent comes to your door. Although the purchaser is ultimately the responsible party, you're an accomplice in defrauding the government. Furthermore, if you turn to the courts for redress, your own conduct may be put on trial.

Summary

Purchasing a used vehicle and keeping it at least five years saves you the most money. It takes about eight years to realize similar depreciation savings when buying new. Giving the biggest down payment you can afford, using zero percent financing programs, and piling up as many kilometres and years as possible on your trade-in are the best ways to save money with new vehicles. Remember that safety is another consideration that depends largely on the type of vehicle you choose.

Buy Safe

Here are some safety features to look for:

1. A high NHTSA and IIHS crashworthiness rating for front, offset, and side collisions (pay particular attention to the side rating if you are a senior driver), plus a low rollover potential due to electronic stability control
2. Good-quality tires; be wary of "all-season" tires and Bridgestone/Firestone makes. Follow *tirerack.com* consumer recommendations.

3. Three-point seat belts with belt pretensioners and adjustable shoulder belt anchorages
4. Integrated child safety seats and seat anchors, safety door locks, and override window controls
5. Depowered dual airbags with a cut-off switch; side airbags with head protection; unobtrusive, effective head restraints that don't push your chin into your chest; and pedal extenders
6. Front driver's seat with plenty of rearward travel and a height adjuster
7. Good all-around visibility; a dash that doesn't reflect onto the windshield
8. An ergonomic interior with an efficient heating and ventilation system
9. Headlights that are adequate for night driving and don't blind oncoming traffic
10. Dash gauges that don't wash out in sunlight or produce windshield glare
11. Adjustable head restraints for all seating positions
12. Delaminated side-window glass
13. Easily accessed sound system and climate controls
14. Navigation systems that don't require a degree from MIT to calibrate
15. Manual sliding doors in vans (if children are being transported)

Buy Smart

1. Buy the vehicle you need and can afford, not the one someone else wants you to buy, or one loaded with options that you'll probably never use. Take your time. Price comparisons and test drives may take a month, but you'll get a better vehicle and price in the long run.
2. Buy in winter or later in the new year to double-dip from dealer incentives and customer rebate or low-cost financing programs.
3. Sell your trade-in privately.
4. Arrange financing before buying your vehicle.
5. Test drive your choice by renting it overnight or for several days.
6. Buy through the Internet or by fax, or use an auto broker if you're not confident in your own bargaining skills, you lack the time to haggle, or you want to avoid the "showroom shakedown."
7. Ask for at least a 25 percent discount off the MSRP, and cut PDI and freight charges by at least 50 percent. Insist on a specific delivery date written in the contract, as well as a protected price in case there's a price increase between the time the contract is signed and when the vehicle is delivered. Also ask for a free tank of gas.
8. Order a minimum of options, and seek a 30–40 percent discount on the entire option list.
9. Put the vehicle's down payment on your credit card.
10. Avoid leasing. If you must lease, choose the shortest time possible, drive down the MSRP, and refuse to pay an "acquisition" or "disposal" fee.
11. Look at Japanese vehicles made in North America, co-ventures with American automakers, and rebadged imports. They often cost less than imports and are just as reliable. However, some European imports may not be as reliable as you might imagine—Mercedes' M-Class sport-utilities, for example. Get extra

warranty protection from the automaker if you're buying a model that has a poorer-than-average repair history. Use auto club references to get honest, competent repairs at a reasonable price.

Now that you know how to get a recession-proof vehicle for the least amount of money, Part Two will show you how to get your money back if that "dream car" turns into a nightmare, or if the dealer goes bankrupt.

Part Two

WARRANTIES AND WEASELS

Ottawa (Auto-wa?)

The Canadian government is putting up $185.3 million to back warranties of new Chrysler and General Motors vehicles in case the companies go bankrupt. Industry Minister Tony Clement announced in Ottawa the [Canadian Warranty Commitment Program] fund would back vehicles sold after Tuesday [April 7, 2009,] and last throughout the troubled companies' restructuring period....

UPI.COM
APRIL 8, 2009

Canadian Auto Warranty Services (CAWS)

[W]atch out, police say. The people calling you don't actually have any idea about the warranty on your car. They don't even know if you have a car.

They're cold calling you from call centres in the U.S. and trying to sell you on a warranty that many mechanics may not honour....

The provinces of Saskatchewan and British Columbia have both issued CAWS orders to cease and desist selling "warranties" in both provinces because the company is not licensed to do so under the provincial statutes that govern the sale of insurance in those provinces.

[Michael] Carter [general counsel for CAWS] cites a great misunderstanding, caused by a third-party call centre in Florida that accidentally started calling Saskatchewan residents on behalf of CAWS.

"We originally didn't care about Saskatchewan," Carter said. "It was too small. Our attorneys had looked at B.C., Alberta and Ontario." "We mistakenly took [Saskatchewan's cease and desist order] lightly because we said: 'Look, there are either a million or less than a million people there.' Had we known that it would have metastasized into B.C. we probably would have done it properly."

BRETT POPPLEWELL
TORONTO STAR, "WHEELS"
FEBRUARY 14, 2009

Worthless Warranties

Get ready for a tsunami of auto warranty rejections, a serious decline in Detroit Three quality, and independent warranty sellers misrepresenting their products—or going belly up. Think British Leyland in the '60s, American Motors a decade later, and Renault a few years after that. It doesn't matter that the Canadian government is backing Chrysler's and GM's warranties with almost $200 million. GM's warranty payouts alone topped $4.5 billion (U.S.) in 2007, according to its Securities and Exchange Commission filings. And how are we going to make quality "Job 1" when many autoworkers have lost that one job?

Paint delamination is a common defect that automakers often blame on everything from bird droppings to ultraviolet light—or they simply say the warranty has expired. The courts haven't been very receptive to these kinds of excuses.

In a June 4, 2009, interview with *Globe and Mail* auto journalist Jeremy Cato, GM Canada's public affairs director, Stew Low, said that GM operations, warranty approvals, and quality control will continue unchanged, despite the company's Chapter 11 bankruptcy filing. Keep in mind, this is the same motor mouthpiece who two years ago swore to *The Globe* and to the *Toronto Star* that GM didn't have an intake manifold gasket design defect in a decade's worth of V6-engine-equipped cars, trucks, and minivans (1995–2004). Six months later, GM settled a Canadian class action lawsuit over the engines for tens of millions of dollars. Low never recanted.

I gave pro bono testimony for that case, and found some of the plaintiffs. I will always remember how GM's lawyers, engineers, PR flacks, and consultants (among them, auto consultant Dennis DesRosiers) tried to make a silk purse out of a sow's ear. Hard feelings, Mr. Low? Yes, indeed. You lied. Why should anyone believe what you say today?

Bankruptcy Means Never Having to Say You're Sorry

Chrysler's and GM's bankruptcies mean that their warranties technically no longer exist, consumer product liability lawsuits don't have deep-pocket defendants, dealers have lost franchise contracts, suppliers have lost purchasers, and many autoworkers have lost jobs and some of their pensions.

Runzheimer International consultants say that one out of every 10 American vehicles produced by the Detroit Three is a lemon. I would guess that owners of Ford and GM vehicles with faulty plastic engine intake manifold gaskets and slipping automatic transmissions, or of Toyotas with unreliable powertrains that hesitate when accelerating in traffic, would put the lemon estimate much higher.

And, what about 2006–07 Corvette owners whose cars' roofs have broken off and flown away?

GM PAINTED ROOF ADHESIVE SEPARATION

BULLETIN NO.. 05112C DATE: JUNE 7, 2006

This program is in effect until March 31, 2007.

CONDITION: On certain 2005–06 Chevrolet Corvette vehicles, the painted roof panel may separate from its frame in some areas if it is exposed to stresses along with high temperature and humidity. The occupants of the vehicle may notice one or more of these symptoms: a snapping noise when driving over bumps, wind noise, poor roof panel fit, roof panel movement/bounce when a door or hatch is closed, or a water leak in the headliner.

CORRECTION: Dealers are to apply adhesive foam to ensure proper adhesion, or in a small number of vehicles, replace the roof panel.

In this post-bankruptcy period, there's even less motivation to make a good car; the government will now pay for factory goofs. Nothing has changed. Automakers will continue to vote themselves fat paycheques, and consumer complaints will still be treated like excrement stuck to the corporate shoe.

A/T—SHIFT FLARE/HARSH 2–3 SHIFTS

BULLETIN NO.: 09-07-30-004 DATE: JANUARY 27, 2009

FLARE AND/OR HARSH 2–3 SHIFTS (INSTALL THREE FLUID SEAL RINGS)

2007–09 Cadillac Escalade, Escalade ESV, Escalade EXT; 2007–09 Chevrolet Silverado; 2007–09 GMC Sierra, Yukon Denali, Yukon XL Denali; 2008–09 Chevrolet Suburban; 2008–09 GMC Yukon XL; 2009 Chevrolet Avalanche, Tahoe; 2009 GMC Yukon.

CONDITION: Some customers may comment on a flare or harsh 2–3 shift or a bump/delay in 2–3 shift.

CAUSE: This condition may be caused by leaking 1–2–3–4 and 3–5–R clutch fluid seal rings.

The federal government shouldn't pay for this three-million-vehicle factory screw-up.

Four Ways to Get Your Money Back

If you've bought an unsafe vehicle or one that was misrepresented, or you've had to pay for repairs to correct factory-related defects, this section's for you. Its intention is to help you get your money back—without going to court or getting frazzled by a dealer's broken promises or "benign neglect." But if going to court is your only recourse, you'll find the jurisprudence you need to cite in your complaint to get an out-of-court settlement or to win your case without spending a fortune on lawyers and research.

Remember the "money-back guarantee"? Well, that's long gone. Automakers are reluctant to offer any warranty that requires them to take back a defective car or minivan, because they know that there are a lot of lemons out there. Fortunately, our provincial consumer protection laws have filled the gap when the base warranty expires, so now any sales contract for a new or used vehicle can be cancelled—or free repairs can be ordered—in the following situations:

- Vehicle is unfit for the purpose for which it was purchased
- Vehicle was misrepresented
- Repairs are covered by a secret warranty or a "goodwill" warranty extension
- Vehicle hasn't been reasonably durable, considering how well it was maintained, the mileage driven, and the type of driving that was done (this is particularly applicable to engine, transmission, and paint defects)

The four legal concepts enumerated above can lead to the sales contract being cancelled, the purchase price being partially refunded, and damages being awarded. For example, if the seller says that a minivan can pull a 900 kg (2,000 lb.) trailer and you discover that it can barely tow half that weight or won't reach a reasonable speed while towing, you can cancel the contract for misrepresentation. The same principle applies to a seller's exaggerated claims concerning a vehicle's fuel economy or reliability, as well as to "demonstrators" that are in fact used cars with false (rolled-back) odometer readings. GM's and Chrysler's secret paint warranties and Ford's Windstar engine and transmission "goodwill" programs have all been successfully challenged in small claims court. And reasonable durability is an especially powerful legal argument that allows a judge to determine what the dealer and auto manufacturer will pay to correct a premature failure long after the original warranty has expired.

Unfair Contracts

Sales contracts aren't fair, nor are they meant to be. Dealers' and automakers' lawyers spend countless hours making sure their clients are well protected with ironclad contracts.

Called "standard form contracts," or "contracts of adhesion," these agreements are looked upon by judges with a great deal of skepticism. They know these are contracts in which you have little or no bargaining power, such as loan documents, insurance contracts, and automobile leases. So when a dispute arises over terms or language, provincial consumer protection statutes require that judges interpret these contracts in the way most favourable to the consumer.

"Hearsay" Not Allowed

It's essential that printed evidence and/or witnesses (relatives are not excluded) are available to confirm that a false representation actually occurred, that a part is failure-prone, or that its replacement is covered by a secret warranty. Stung by an increasing number of small claims court defeats, automakers are now asking small claims court judges to disallow evidence from *Lemon-Aid*, service bulletins, or memos on the pretext that such evidence is hearsay (not proven) unless confirmed by an independent mechanic or unless the document is recognized by the automaker's or dealer's representative at trial ("Is this a common problem? Do you recognize this service bulletin? Is there a case-by-case 'goodwill' plan covering this repair?"). This is why you should bring in an independent garage mechanic or body expert to buttress your allegations. Sometimes, though, the service manager or company representative will make key admissions if questioned closely by you, a court mediator, or the trial judge. That questioning can be particularly effective if you call for the exclusion of witnesses until they're called (let them mill around outside the courtroom wondering what their colleagues have said).

Automakers often blame owners for having pushed their vehicle beyond its limits. Therefore, when you seek to set aside the contract or get a repair reimbursed, it's essential that you get the testimony of an independent mechanic and co-workers in order to prove that the vehicle's poor performance isn't caused by negligent maintenance or abusive driving.

It Should Have Lasted Longer!

The reasonable durability claim is your ace in the hole. It's probably the easiest allegation to prove, since all automakers have benchmarks as to how long body components, trim and finish, and mechanical and electronic parts should last (see the "Reasonable Part Durability" chart on page 104). Vehicles are expected to be reasonably durable and merchantable. What "reasonably durable" means depends on the price paid, the kilometres driven, the purchaser's driving habits, and how well the vehicle was maintained by the owner. Judges carefully weigh all these factors in awarding compensation or cancelling a sale.

Whatever the reason you use to get your money back, don't forget to conform to the "reasonable diligence" rule that requires you to file suit within a reasonable time after the vehicle's purchase or after you've discovered the defect. If there have been no negotiations with the dealer or automaker, this period cannot exceed a few months. If either the dealer or the automaker has been promising to correct the defects for some time, or has carried out repeated unsuccessful repairs, the delay for filing the lawsuit can be extended.

Refunds for Other Expenses

It's a lot easier to get the automaker to pay to replace a defective part than it is to obtain compensation for a missed day of work. Manufacturers seldom pay for consequential expenses like a ruined vacation, a vehicle not living up to its advertised hype, or an owner's mental distress, because they can't control the amount of the refund. Courts, however, are more generous, having ruled that all expenses (damages) flowing from a problem covered by a warranty or service bulletin are the manufacturer's or dealer's responsibility under both common law (which covers all provinces except Quebec) and Quebec civil law. Fortunately, when legal action is threatened—usually through small claims court—automakers quickly up their ante to include most of the owner's expenses because they know the courts will be more generous.

One precedent-setting judgment (cited in *Sharman v. Ford*, found on page 125) giving generous damages to a motorist fed up with his "lemon" Cadillac was rendered in 1999 by the British Columbia Supreme Court in *Wharton v. Tom Harris Chevrolet Oldsmobile Cadillac Ltd.* ([2002] B.C.J. No. 233, 2002 BCCA 78d). In that case, Justice Leggatt threw the book at GM and the dealer in awarding the following amounts:

> (a) Hotel accommodations: $ 217.17
>
> (b) Travel to effect repairs at 30 cents per kilometre: The plaintiff claims some 26 visits from his home in Ucluelet to Nanaimo. Some credit should be granted to the defendants since routine trips would have been required in any event. Therefore, the plaintiff is entitled to be compensated for mileage for 17 trips (approximately 400 km from Ucluelet to Nanaimo return) at 30 cents per kilometre.
>
> $2,040.00
>
> TOTAL: $2,257.17
>
> [20] The plaintiffs are entitled to non-pecuniary damages for loss of enjoyment of their luxury vehicle and for inconvenience in the sum of $5,000.

Warranties

It's really not that hard to get a refund if you take it one step at a time. Vehicle defects are covered by two warranties: the *expressed* warranty, which has a fixed time limit, and the *implied*, or *legal*, warranty, which is entirely up to a judge's discretion.

Expressed Warranties

The manufacturer's or dealer's warranty is an "expressed" promise that a vehicle will perform as represented and be reasonably reliable, subject to certain conditions. Regardless of the number of subsequent owners, this promise remains in force as long as the warranty's original time/kilometre limits haven't expired. The expressed warranty given by most sellers is often full of empty promises, and it allows the dealer and manufacturer to act as judge and jury when deciding whether a vehicle was misrepresented or is afflicted with defects they'll pay to correct. Rarely does it provide a money-back guarantee.

Some of the more familiar lame excuses used in denying expressed warranty claims are "You abused the car," "It was poorly maintained," "It's normal wear and tear," "It's rusting from the outside, not the inside," and "It passed the safety inspection." Ironically, the expressed warranty sometimes says that there is no warranty at all, or that the vehicle is sold "as is." And, when the warranty's clauses (or lack of) don't deter claimants, some dealers simply say that a verbal warranty or representation as to the vehicle's attributes is unenforceable.

Fortunately, these attempts to weasel out of the warranty and limit the seller's liability seldom make it through judicial review. Justice Searle put it this way in the *Chams* decision (see pages 127–133):

Ford's warranty attempts to limit its liability to what it grants in the warranty. It is ancient law that one who attempts to limit his liability by, for example, excluding common law remedies, must clearly bring that limitation to the attention of the person who might lose those remedies. The evidence in this case is clear the buyer of even a new car does not get a warranty booklet until after purchasing the car although he "would be" told the highlights sooner.

Implied Warranties

Thankfully, car owners get another kick at the can with the implied warranty ("of fitness"). As clearly stated in the unreported Saskatchewan decision *Maureen Frank v. General Motors of Canada Limited* (found exclusively in *Lemon-Aid* on page 117)—in which the judge declared that paint discoloration and peeling shouldn't occur within 11 years of the purchase of a vehicle—the implied warranty is an important legal principle. It's solidly supported by a large body of federal and provincial laws, regulations, and jurisprudence, and it protects you primarily from hidden dealer- or factory-related defects. But the concept also includes misrepresentation and a host of other scams.

This warranty also holds dealers to a higher standard of conduct than private sellers because, unlike private sellers, dealers are presumed to be aware of the defects present in the vehicles they sell. That way, they can't just pass the ball to the automaker or to the previous owner and then walk away from the dispute. For instance, in British Columbia, a new-car dealer is required to disclose damage requiring repairs costing more than 20 percent of the price (under *the Motor Dealer Act Regulations*).

Why the implied warranty is so effective

- It establishes the concept of "reasonable durability" (see "How Long Should a Part or Repair Last?" page 103), meaning that parts are expected to last for a reasonable period of time, as stated in jurisprudence, judged by independent mechanics, or expressed in extended warranties given by the automaker in the past (7–10 years/160,000 km for engines and transmissions).
- It covers the entire vehicle and can be applied for whatever period of time the judge decides.
- It can order that the vehicle be taken back, or that a major repair cost be refunded.
- It can help plaintiffs claim compensation for supplementary transportation, inconvenience, mental distress, missed work, screwed-up vacations, insurance paid while the vehicle was in the repair shop, repairs done by other mechanics, and exemplary, or punitive, damages in cases where the seller was a real weasel.
- It is frequently used by small claims court judges to give refunds to plaintiffs " in equity" (out of fairness) rather than through a strict interpretation of contract law.

Expressed and Implied Warranties: Fuel Economy Claims

Canadian courts are cracking down on lying dealers and deceptive sales practices, and the misrepresenting of fuel economy figures is squarely in the judiciary's sights. Ontario's *Consumer Protection Act, 2002* (*www.e-laws.gov.on.ca/html/statutes/english/elaws_statutes_02c30_e.htm*), for example, lets a vehicle buyer cancel a contract within one year of entering into an agreement if their dealer made a false, misleading, deceptive, or unconscionable representation. This includes using exaggeration, innuendo, or ambiguity as to a material fact, or failing to state a material fact if such use or failure deceives or tends to deceive consumers.

This law means that new- or used-car dealers cannot make the excuse that they were fooled about the condition or performance of a vehicle, or that they were simply providing data supplied by the manufacturer. The law clearly states that both parties are jointly liable and that dealers are *presumed* to know the history, quality, and true performance of what they are selling.

Details like fuel economy *can* lead to a contract's cancellation if the dealer gives a higher-than-actual figure. In *Sidney v. 1011067 Ontario Inc. (c.o.b. Southside Motors)*, a precedent-setting case that was filed before Ontario's *Consumer Protection Act* was toughened in 2002, the buyer was awarded $11,424.51 plus prejudgment interest because of a false representation made by the defendant regarding fuel efficiency. The plaintiff claimed that the defendant advised him that the vehicle had a fuel efficiency of 800–900 km per tank of fuel when, in fact, the maximum efficiency was only 500 km per tank.

This consumer victory is particularly important as fuel prices soar and everyone from automakers to sellers of ineffective gas-saving gadgets make outlandishly false fuel economy claims. Not surprisingly, sellers try to use the expressed warranty to reject claims, while smart plaintiffs ignore the expressed warranty and argue for a refund under the implied warranty, instead.

Expressed and Implied Warranties: Tire Failures

Consumers have gained additional rights following Bridgestone/Firestone's massive tire recall in 2001. Because of the confusion and chaos surrounding Firestone's handling of the recall, Ford's 575 Canadian dealers stepped into the breach and replaced the tires with any equivalent tires dealers had in stock, no questions asked.

This is an important precedent that tears down the traditional liability wall separating tire manufacturers from automakers in product liability claims. In essence, whoever sells the product can now be held liable for damages. In the future, Canadian consumers will have an easier time holding the dealer, automaker, and tiremaker liable, not just for recalled products but also for any defect that affects the safety or reasonable durability of that product.

This is particularly true now that the Supreme Court of Canada (*Winnipeg Condominium v. Bird Construction* [1995] 1S.C.R.85) has ruled that defendants are liable in negligence for any designs that resulted in a risk to the public for safety or health. The Supreme Court reversed a long-standing policy and provided the public with a new cause of action that had not existed before in Canada. Prior to this Supreme Court ruling, companies dodged liability for falling bridges and crashing planes by warranty exclusion and "entire-agreement" contract clauses. In the *Winnipeg Condominium* case, the Supreme Court held that repairs made to prevent serious damage or accidents could be claimed from the designer or builder for the cost of repair in tort from any subsequent purchaser. Consumers with tire or other claims relating to the safety of their vehicles would be wise to insert the above court decision (with explanation) in their claim letter and then mail or fax it to the automaker's legal affairs or product liability department. A copy should also be deposited with the clerk of the small claims court, if you have to use that recourse.

Other Warrantable Items

Safety restraints, such as airbags and seat belts, have warranty coverage extended for the lifetime of the vehicle, following an agreement made between U.S. automakers and importers. In Canada, though, some automakers try to dodge this responsibility because they are incorporated as separate Canadian companies. That distinction didn't fly with B.C.'s Court of Appeal in the 2002 *Robson* decision (*www.courts.gov.bc.ca/jdb-txt/ca/02/03/2002bcca0354.htm*). In that class action petition, the court declared that both Canadian companies *and* their American counterparts can be held liable in Canada for deceptive acts that violate the provincial *Trade Practices Act* (in this case, Chrysler and GM paint delamination):

> At this stage, the plaintiffs are only required to demonstrate that they have a "good arguable case" against the American defendants. The threshold is low. A good arguable case requires only a serious question to be tried, one with some prospect of success: see *AG Armeno Mines, supra*, at para. 25 [*AG Armeno Mines and Minerals Inc. v. PT Pukuafu Indah* (2000), 77 B.C.L.R.(3d) 1 (C.A.)].

Aftermarket products and services—such as gas-saving gadgets, rustproofing, and paint protectors—can render the manufacturer's warranty invalid, so make sure you're in the clear before purchasing any optional equipment or services from an independent supplier.

How fairly a warranty is applied is more important than how long it remains in effect. Once you know the normal wear rate for a mechanical component or body part, you can demand proportional compensation when you get less than normal durability—no matter what the original warranty said.

Some dealers tell customers that they need to have original-equipment parts installed in order to maintain their warranty. A variation on this theme requires that routine servicing—including tune-ups and oil changes (with a certain brand of oil)—be done by the selling dealer, or the warranty is invalidated.

Nothing could be further from the truth. Canadian law stipulates that whoever issues a warranty cannot make that warranty conditional on the use of any specific brand of motor oil, oil filter, or any other component, unless it's provided to the customer free of charge.

Beware the Warranty Runaround

Sometimes dealers will do all sorts of minor repairs that don't correct the problem, and then, after the warranty runs out, they'll tell you that major repairs are needed. You can prevent this nasty surprise by repeatedly bringing your vehicle into the dealership before the warranty ends. During each visit, insist that a written work order include the specific nature of the problem as *you* see it and that the work order carry the notation that this is the second, third, or fourth time the same problem has been brought to the dealer's attention. Write it down yourself, if need be. This allows you to show a pattern of nonperformance by the dealer during the warranty period and establishes that it's a serious and chronic problem. When the warranty expires, you have the legal right to demand that it be extended on those items consistently reappearing on your handful of work orders. *Lowe v. Fairview Chrysler* (see page 133) is an excellent judgment that reinforces this important principle. In another lawsuit, *François Chong v. Marine Drive Imported Cars Ltd. and Honda Canada Inc.* (see page 140), a Honda owner forced Honda to fix his engine six times—until they got it right.

A retired GM service manager gave me another effective tactic to use when you're not sure that a dealer's warranty "repairs" will actually correct the problem for a reasonable period of time after the warranty expires. Here's what he says you should do:

> When you pick up the vehicle after the warranty repair has been done, hand the service manager a note to be put in your file that says you appreciate the warranty repair; however, you intend to return and ask for further warranty coverage if the problem reappears before a reasonable amount of time has elapsed—even if the original warranty has expired. A copy of the same note should be sent to the automaker.... Keep your copy of the note in the glove compartment as cheap insurance against paying for a repair that wasn't fixed correctly the first time.

Extended (Supplementary) Warranties

You have to tread very carefully here. During Chrysler's and GM's bankruptcies, hundreds of small, independent supplementary warranty sellers invaded the marketplace. Their specialty: making automated "robo-calls" to pitch dubious auto warranties to scared owners. Asking to be put on a "do not call" list is not always effective, but threatening legal action helps. One fed-up owner of a 10-year-old vehicle writes (*www.complaintsboard.com/complaints/national-auto-warranty-service-c73231.htm*):

> I have no relationship with this company, but I'm about to send them a registered letter telling them that if they call me again I will bill them for my time and the use of my phone equipment for their marketing calls, and that their agreement to my terms will be signaled by their next call to my phone number. Failure to pay will result in a suit for collection in Maryland.

The manufacturer, the dealer, or an independent third party may sell supplementary warranties that provide extended coverage, and this coverage is automatically transferred when a vehicle is sold. They cost between $1,500 and $2,000 and should be purchased only if the vehicle you're buying has a reputation for being unreliable or expensive to service (see Part Three) or if you're reluctant to use the small claims courts when factory-related trouble arises. Don't let the dealer pressure you into deciding right away.

Dealers love to sell you extended warranties, whether you need them or not, because up to 60 percent of the warranty's cost represents dealer markup. Out of the remaining 40 percent comes the sponsor's administration costs and profit margin, calculated at another 15 percent. What's left to pay for repairs is a minuscule 25 percent of the original amount. The only reason that automakers and independent warranty companies haven't been busted for operating this Ponzi scheme is that only half of the vehicle buyers who purchase extended service contracts actually use them.

Those who *do* need help often find it difficult to collect a refund, because independent companies frequently go out of business or limit the warranty's coverage through subsequent mailings. Provincial laws cover both situations. If the bankrupt warranty company's insurance policy won't cover your claim, take the dealer to small claims court and ask for the repair costs and a refund of the original warranty payment. Your argument for holding the dealer responsible is a simple one: By accepting a commission to act as an agent of the defunct company, the dealer also took on the obligations of that company. As for limiting the coverage after you have already bought the warranty policy, this practice is illegal and allows you to sue both the dealer and the warranty company for a refund of both the warranty and the repair costs.

Emissions-Control Warranties

These little-publicized warranties can save you big bucks if major engine or exhaust components fail prematurely. They come with all new vehicles and cover major components of the emissions-control system for up to 8 years/130,000 km, no matter how many times the vehicle is sold. Unfortunately, although owner's manuals vaguely mention the emissions warranty, most don't specify which parts are covered. The U.S. Environmental Protection Agency has intervened on several occasions, with hefty fines against Chrysler and Ford, and ruled that all major motor and fuel-system components are covered. These components include fuel metering, ignition spark advance, restart, evaporative emissions, positive crankcase ventilation (PVC), engine electronics (computer modules), and catalytic converter systems as well as parts like hoses, clamps, brackets, pipes, gaskets, belts, seals, and connectors. Canada, however, has no governmentally defined list, so it's up to each manufacturer and the small claims courts to decide which emissions-control components are covered.

Some of the confidential technical service bulletins listed in Part Three show parts failures that are covered under the emissions warranty (stinky exhausts caused by defective catalytic converters, for example), even though motorists are routinely charged for their replacement. Ford of Canada has issued one bulletin where owners of 2002–05 Ford Taurus and Sable models will get refunds for fuel gauge repairs under the emissions warranty. Faulty fuel gauges are a common problem with all automakers, with repairs costing $300–$500.

Make sure to get your emissions system checked out thoroughly by a dealer or an independent garage before the emissions warranty expires or before having the vehicle inspected by provincial emissions inspectors. In addition to ensuring that you'll pass provincial tests, this precaution could save you up to $1,000 if your catalytic converter and other emissions components are faulty.

Exposing "Secret" Warranties

Few vehicle owners know that secret warranties exist. The closest automakers come to an admission is sending out a "goodwill policy," "product improvement program," or "special policy" technical service bulletin (TSB) to dealers or first owners of record. Consequently, the only motorists who find out about these policies are the original owners who haven't moved or haven't leased their vehicles. The other motorists who get compensated for repairs are the ones who read *Lemon-Aid* each year, wave TSBs, and yell the loudest.

Remember, second owners and repairs done by independent garages are included in these secret warranty programs. Large, costly repairs, such as blown engines, burned transmissions, and peeling paint, are often covered.

Here are a few examples of the most comprehensive secret warranties that have come across my desk during the last several years.

All Years, All Models

Automatic transmissions

Problem: Faulty automatic transmissions that self-destruct, shift erratically, gear down to "limp home mode," are slow to shift in or out of Reverse, or are noisy. **Warranty coverage:** If you have the assistance of your dealer's service manager, expect an offer of 50–75 percent (about $2,500). File the case in small claims court, and a full refund will be offered up to 7 years/160,000 km. Acura, Honda, Hyundai, Lexus, and Toyota coverage varies between seven and eight years.

Brakes

Problem: Premature wearout of brake pads, calipers, and rotors. Produces excessive vibration, noise, and pulling to one side when braking. **Warranty coverage:** *Calipers and pads:* "Goodwill" settlements confirm that brake calipers and pads that fail to last 2 years/40,000 km will be replaced for 50 percent of the repair cost; components not lasting 1 year/20,000 km will be replaced for free. *Rotors:* If they last less than 3 years/60,000 km, they'll be replaced at half the price; replacement is free up to 2 years/40,000 km.

Interestingly, early brake wearout, once mainly a Detroit failing, is now quite common with Asian makes, as well. Apparently, brake suppliers to all automakers are using cheaper calipers, pads, and rotors that can't handle the heat generated by normal braking on heavier passenger cars, trucks, and vans. Consequently, drivers find routine braking causes rotor warpage that produces excessive vibrations, shuddering, noise, and pulling to one side when braking.

Engines

Problem: At around 60,000–100,000 km, the engine may overheat, lose power, and burn extra fuel or, possibly, self-destruct. Under the best of circumstances, the repair will take a day and cost about $800–$1,000. **Warranty coverage:** If you have the assistance of your dealer's service manager, expect a full refund up to 7 years/160,000 km, although initial offers will hover at about 50 percent of the costs. Ford Windstars and GM minivans are particularly afflicted with this defect. If you threaten small claims court action, cite the *Chams* decision (see pages 127–133).

No matter which automaker you're dealing with, filing your claim in small claims court always sweetens the company's settlement offer. Furthermore, you likely won't have to step inside a courtroom to get your refund, since most small claims court filings are settled at the pretrial mediation stage.

Exhaust systems

Problem: A nauseating "rotten-egg" exhaust smell permeates the interior. **Warranty coverage:** At first, owners are told they need a tune-up. And then they are told to change fuels and to wait a few months for the problem to correct itself. When this fails, the catalytic converter will likely be replaced and the power control module recalibrated.

Chrysler, Ford, General Motors, Honda, Hyundai, and Mazda

Paint

Problem: Faulty paint jobs that cause paint to turn white, peel off of horizontal panels, or produce thin white scratches. Recent Mazda CX-9, Mazda3, Mazda5, and Mazda6 models are most affected (particularly the blue and black-cherry colours). **Warranty coverage:** Automakers will offer a free paint job or partial compensation up to six years with no mileage limitation. Thereafter, all these manufacturers offer 50–75 percent refunds on the small claims courthouse steps.

In *Frank v. GM*, the Saskatchewan small claims court set an 11-year benchmark for paint finishes, and three other Canadian small claims judgments have extended the benchmark to seven years, second owners, and pickups.

> I wanted to let you and your readers know that the information you publish about Ford's paint failure problem is invaluable. Having read through your "how-to guide" on addressing this issue, I filed suit against Ford for the "latent" paint defect. The day prior to our court date, I received a settlement offer by phone for 75 percent of what I was initially asking for.
>
> This settlement was for a 9-year-old car. I truly believe that Ford hedges a bet that most people won't go to the extent of filing a lawsuit because they are intimidated or simply stop progress after they receive a firm no from Ford.
>
> M.P.

How Long Should a Part or Repair Last?

How do you know when a part or service doesn't last as long as it should, and whether you should seek a full or partial refund? Sure, you have a gut feeling based on your use of the vehicle, how you maintained it, and the extent of work that was carried out on it. But you'll need more than emotion to win compensation from garages and automakers.

You can definitely get a refund if a repair or part lasts longer than its guarantee but not as long as is generally expected. But you'll have to show what the auto industry considers to be "reasonable durability." Automakers, mechanics, and the courts all have their own benchmarks as to what's a reasonable period of time or amount of mileage one should expect a part or adjustment to last. Consequently, I've prepared this table to show what most automakers consider to be reasonable durability, as expressed by their original and "goodwill" warranties.

Many of the guidelines on the following page were extrapolated from Chrysler and Ford payouts to thousands of dissatisfied customers over the past decade, in addition to Chrysler's original seven-year powertrain warranty (applicable from 1991 to 1995 and reapplied from 2001 to 2004). Other sources for this chart were

REASONABLE PART DURABILITY

ACCESSORIES

Part	Durability
Air conditioner	7 years
Cruise control	5 years/100,000 km
Power doors, windows	5 years
Radio	5 years

BODY

Part	Durability
Paint (peeling)	7–11 years
Rust (perforations)	7–11 years
Rust (surface)	5 years
Water/wind/air leaks	5 years

BRAKE SYSTEM

Part	Durability
Brake drum	120,000 km
Brake drum linings	35,000 km
Brake rotor	60,000 km
Brake calipers/pads	30,000 km
Master cylinder	100,000 km
Wheel cylinder	80,000 km

ENGINE AND DRIVETRAIN

Part	Durability
CV joint	6 years/160,000 km
Differential	7 years/160,000 km
Engine (diesel)	15 years/350,000 km
Engine (gas)	7 years/160,000 km
Radiator	4 years/80,000 km
Transfer case	7 years/160,000 km
Transmission (auto.)	7 years/160,000 km
Transmission (man.)	10 years/250,000 km
Transmission oil cooler	5 years/100,000 km

EXHAUST SYSTEM

Part	Durability
Catalytic converter	8–10 years/100,000 km or more
Muffler	2 years/40,000 km
Tailpipe	3 years/60,000 km

IGNITION SYSTEM

Part	Durability
Cable set	60,000 km
Electronic module	5 years/80,000 km
Retiming	20,000 km
Spark plugs	20,000 km
Tune-up	20,000 km

the Ford and GM transmission warranties outlined in their secret warranties; Ford, GM, and Toyota engine "goodwill" programs laid out in their internal service bulletins; and court judgments where judges have given their own guidelines as to what is reasonable durability.

Safety features—with the exception of anti-lock brake systems (ABS)—generally have a lifetime warranty. Chrysler's 10-year "free-service" program, part of its 1993–99 ABS recall, can serve as a handy benchmark as to how long one can expect these components to last on more-recent models.

Airbags are a different matter. Those that are deployed in an accident—and the personal injury and interior damage their deployment will likely have caused—are covered by your accident insurance policy. However, if there is a sudden deployment for no apparent reason, the automaker and dealer should be held jointly responsible for all injuries and damages caused by the airbag. You can prove their liability by downloading data from your vehicle's data recorder. This will likely lead to a more-generous settlement from the two parties and prevent your insurance premiums from being jacked up.

Use the manufacturer's emissions warranty as your primary guideline for the expected durability of high-tech electronic and mechanical pollution-control components, such as powertrain control modules (PCM) and catalytic converters. Look first at your owner's manual for an indication of which parts on your vehicle are covered. If you come up with few specifics, ask the auto manufacturer for a list of specific components covered by the emissions warranty.

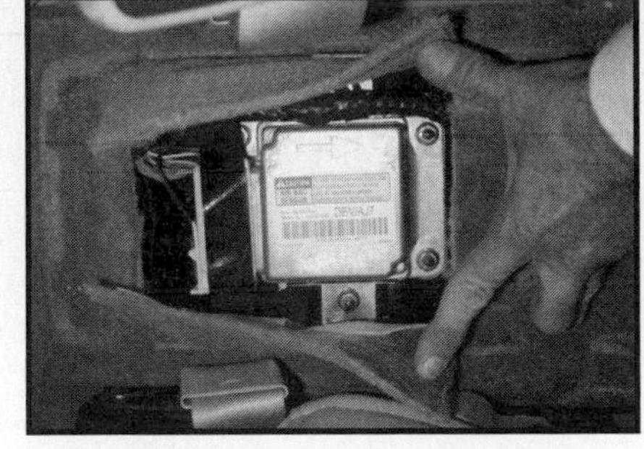

"Black box" data can prove that the brakes, airbag, or other component failed.

Recall Repairs

Vehicles are recalled for one of two reasons: Either they are unsafe or they don't conform to federal pollution-control regulations. Whatever the reason, recalls are a great way to get free repairs and to keep your car safe—if you know which ones apply to you and you have the patience of Job.

A recall doesn't mean your vehicle will become a long-term problem. Most vehicles will undergo two or three recalls during their life cycle. Indeed, recalls happen in even the best automotive neighbourhoods, with manufacturers from Acura to Rolls-Royce subject to government-mandated recalls. Even quality-snob Toyota has sustained two large recalls on 16 models in the last couple of years (affecting some 1.27 million vehicles, including the Prius hybrid).

More than 390 million unsafe vehicles have been recalled by automakers for the free correction of safety-related defects since American recall legislation was passed in 1966 (a weaker Canadian law was enacted in 1971). During that time, NHTSA estimates that about 28 percent of the recalled vehicles never made it back to the dealership for repairs because owners were never informed, they just didn't consider the defect to be that hazardous, or they gave up waiting for corrective parts. Yet one study that estimated the effect of recalls on safety found that a 10 percent increase in the recall rate of a particular model will reduce the number of accidents involving that model by around 2 percent (*ms.cc.sunysb.edu/~hbenitezsilv/recall.pdf*).

The automaker has three options for correcting the defect: repair, replace, or refund. This probably means a trip to the dealer. However, in the case of a tire or child seat recall, you may mail in the defective item or go to the retailer that sold the product.

If you've moved, it's smart to pay a visit to your local dealer. Give the dealer your address to get a "report card" on which recalls, free service campaigns, and warranties apply to your vehicle. Simply give the service advisor the vehicle identification number (VIN)—found on your insurance card or on the dash, just below the windshield on the driver's side—and have the number run through the automaker's computer system. Ask for a computer printout of the vehicle's history (or have it faxed to you, if you're so equipped), and make sure you're listed in the automaker's computer as the new owner. This process ensures that you'll receive notices of warranty extensions and emissions and safety recalls.

There are limitations on automotive recalls. Vehicle manufacturers are not required to perform free recalls on vehicles that are more than 10 years old. Getting repairs when the automaker says you are too late often takes a small claims court filing. But these cases are easy to win and are usually settled out of court. U.S. recalls may be voluntary or ordered by the U.S. Department of Transportation, and they can be nationwide or regional. In Canada, all recalls are considered voluntary. Transport Canada can only order automakers to notify owners that their vehicles may be unsafe; it can't force them to correct the problem. Fortunately, most U.S.-ordered recalls are carried out in Canada, and when Transport Canada makes a defect determination on its own, automakers generally comply with an owner notification letter and a recall campaign.

Voluntary recall campaigns—frequently called "Special Service" or "Safety Improvement" campaigns—are a real problem. The government does not monitor the notification of owners; dealers and automakers routinely deny there's a recall, thereby dissuading most claimants; and the company's so-called fix, not authorized by any governing body, may not correct the hazard at all. Also, the voluntary recall may leave out many of the affected models or unreasonably exclude certain owners.

Wherever you live or drive, don't expect to be welcomed with open arms when your vehicle develops a safety- or emissions-related problem that's not yet part of a recall campaign. Automakers and dealers generally take a restrictive view of what constitutes a safety or emissions defect, and they frequently charge for repairs that should be free under federal safety or emissions legislation. To counter this tendency, look at the following list of typical defects that are clearly safety-related. If you experience similar problems to these, insist that the automaker fix the problem at no expense to yourself, including paying for a car rental:

- Airbag malfunctions
- Corrosion affecting the safe operation of the vehicle
- Disconnected or stuck accelerators
- Electrical shorts
- Faulty windshield wipers
- Fuel leaks
- Problems with original axles, driveshafts, seats, seat recliners, or defrosters
- Seat belt problems
- Stalling, or sudden acceleration
- Sudden steering or brake loss
- Suspension failures
- Trailer coupling failures

Regional recalls

Don't let any dealer refuse you recall repairs because of where you live. In order to cut recall costs, many automakers try to limit a recall to vehicles in a certain designated region. This practice doesn't make sense, since cars are mobile and an unsafe, rust-cankered steering unit can be found anywhere—not just in certain rust-belt provinces or American states.

In 2001, Ford attempted to limit to five American states its recall of faulty Firestone tires. Public ridicule of the company's proposal led to an extension of the recall throughout North America.

In July 2004, Ford announced a regional recall to install protective spring shields on almost one million 1999, 2000, and 2001 model year Taurus and Sable sedans to correct defective front springs that can break and puncture a tire. As it did for Windstars and Aerostars recalled earlier for the same problem, Ford says it will send recall letters only to owners whose vehicles are registered in high-corrosion areas or where salt is used on roads.

Safety Defect Information

If you wish to report a safety defect or want recall info, you may access Transport Canada's website at *www.tc.gc.ca/roadsafety/safevehicles/defectinvestigations/index.htm*. You can get recall information in French or English, as well as general information relating to road safety and importing a vehicle into Canada. Web surfers can now access the recall database for 1970 to current model year vehicles, but unlike NHTSA's website, owner complaints aren't listed, defect investigations aren't disclosed, voluntary warranty extensions (secret warranties) aren't shown, and service bulletin summaries aren't provided. You can also call Transport Canada at 1-800-333-0510 to get additional information.

If you're not happy with Ottawa's treatment of your recall inquiry, try NHTSA's website at *www.nhtsa.dot.gov/cars/problems*. It's more complete than Transport Canada's—NHTSA's database is updated daily and covers vehicles built since the '50s. You'll get immediate access to four essential database categories applicable to your vehicle and model year: the latest recalls, current and closed safety investigations, defects reported by other owners, and a brief summary of TSBs.

Four Steps to a Refund

Step 1: Informal Negotiations

Most vehicle owners won't take the steps outlined in the previous sections; instead, they'll try to settle things informally with a phone call. This tactic rarely works. Customer service agents (who recite policies but don't make them) will tell you the vehicle's warranty doesn't apply. This brush-off usually convinces 90 percent of complainers to drop their claims after some angry venting.

Nevertheless, don't take no for an answer. Contact someone higher up who has the authority to bend policies to satisfy your request. Speak in a calm, polite manner, and try not to polarize the issue. Talk about cooperating to solve the problem. Let a compromise emerge—don't come in with a hardline set of demands.

An independent estimate of the vehicle's defects and the cost of repairing them is essential if you want to convince the dealer that you're serious in your claim and that you stand a good chance of winning your case in court. Come prepared to use your estimate to challenge the dealer who agrees to pay half the repair costs and then tries to jack up the price 100 percent so that you wind up paying the whole shot.

Don't insist on getting the settlement offer in writing, but make sure that you're accompanied by a friend or relative who can confirm the offer in court if it isn't honoured. Be prepared to act upon the offer without delay so that if the dealer or automaker withdraws it, they won't be able to blame your hesitancy.

Dealer and service manager help

Service managers have more power than you may realize. They make the first determination of what work is covered under warranty or through post-warranty "goodwill" programs, and they're directly responsible to the dealer and manufacturer for their decisions. (Dealers hate manufacturer audits that force them to pay back questionable warranty decisions.) Service managers are paid to save the dealer and automaker money while mollifying irate clients—an almost impossible balancing act. Nevertheless, when a service manager agrees to extend warranty coverage, it's because you've raised solid issues that neither the dealer nor the automaker can ignore. All the more reason to present your argument in a confident, forthright manner with your vehicle's service history and *Lemon-Aid*'s "Reasonable Part Durability" chart (see page 104) on hand.

Also bring as many technical service bulletins and owner complaint printouts as you can find from websites like NHTSA's. It's not important that they apply directly to your problem; they establish parameters for giving out after-warranty assistance, or "goodwill." Don't use your salesperson as a runner, because the sales staff are generally quite distant from the service staff and usually have less pull than you do.

If the service manager can't or won't set things right, your next step is to convene a mini-summit with the service manager, the dealer principal, and the automaker's rep. By getting the automaker involved, you run less risk of having the dealer fob you off on the manufacturer, and you can often get an agreement where the dealer and automaker pay two-thirds of the repair costs.

Step 2: Send a Registered Letter, Fax, or Email

Don't worry, no one feels comfortable writing a complaint. But if you haven't sent a written claim letter, fax, or email, you haven't really complained—or at least

NEW-VEHICLE COMPLAINT LETTER/FAX/EMAIL

WITHOUT PREJUDICE

Date: ______________________________

Name and address of dealer: ______________________________

Name and address of manufacturer: ______________________________

Please be advised that I am not satisfied with my ____________ (indicate year, make, model, and serial number of vehicle). The vehicle was purchased on (indicate date) and currently indicates __________ km on the odometer. The vehicle presently exhibits the following defects:

1. Premature rusting
2. Paint peeling/discoloration
3. Water leaks
4. Other defects (explain)

(List previous attempts to repair the vehicle. Attach a copy of a report from an independent garage, showing cost of estimated repairs and confirming the manufacturer's responsibility.)

I hereby request that you correct these defects free of charge under the terms of the implied warranty provisions of provincial consumer protection statutes as applied in *Kravitz v. General Motors* (1979), I.S.C.R., and *Chabot v. Ford* (1983), 39 O.R. (2d).

If you do not correct the defects noted above to my satisfaction and within a reasonable length of time, I will be obliged to ask an independent garage to __________________ (choose [a] estimate or [b] carry out) the repairs and claim the amount of $___________ (state the cost, if possible) by way of the courts without further notice or delay.

I have dealt with your company because of its competence and honesty. I close in the hope of hearing from you within five (5) days of receiving this letter, failing which I will exercise the alternatives available to me. Please govern yourself accordingly.

Sincerely,

(signed with telephone or fax number)

that's the auto industry's mindset. Send the dealer and manufacturer a polite registered letter or fax that asks for compensation for repairs that have been done or need to be done, insurance costs during the vehicle's repair, towing charges, supplementary transportation costs like taxis and rented cars, and damages for your inconvenience (see the sample complaint letter).

Specify five days (but allow 10 days) for either party to respond. If no satisfactory offer is made or your claim is ignored, file suit in small claims court. Make the manufacturer a party to the lawsuit, especially if an emissions warranty, a secret warranty extension, a safety recall campaign, or extensive chassis rusting is involved.

Step 3: Get the Government Involved

In this post-bankruptcy era, the federal government partially owns General Motors and Chrysler. That's why it's a good idea to send your local MP and the federal

Minister of Industry a copy of your complaint. After all, the feds have given $185.3 million to automakers for warranty claims. It's in the government's interest to know if those claims are being paid. Plus, it won't hurt to have a discreet inquiry sent to the manufacturer by your MP or by someone in the Minister's office.

Step 4: Mediation and Arbitration

If the formality of a courtroom puts you off, or you're not sure that your claim is all that solid and don't want to pay the legal costs to find out, consider using mediation or arbitration offered by these groups: the Better Business Bureau (BBB), the Automobile Protection Association (APA), the Canadian Automobile Association (CAA), small claims court (mediation is often a prerequisite to going to trial), provincial and territorial government-run consumer mediation services, and the Canadian Motor Vehicle Arbitration Plan (CAMVAP):

> I just won my case with Chrysler Canada over my 2003 Ram SLT 4×4 quad cab truck. I've been having PCV valves freezing up (5 PCVs in 9,000 km). After one month in the shop, I went to CAMVAP to put in my claim, went to arbitration, and won. They have agreed to buy back my truck.

CAMVAP (1-800-207-0685; *www.camvap.ca*) is the best known and most efficient organization offering free arbitration. Decisions are usually reached within a few months. Awards are no longer confidential (thanks to pressure exerted by the Quebec government), and the stipulation that no appeals are allowed doesn't seem enforceable, as CAMVAP says on its own website:

> If you believe that the award or result of your hearing was improper because the arbitrator erred in law or erred in his or her assessment of the facts, then you may want to consider an appeal to the courts.

Getting Outside Help

Don't let poor preparation scuttle your case. Ask government or independent consumer protection agencies to evaluate how well prepared you are before going to your first hearing. Also, use the Internet and media sources to ferret out additional facts and to gather support (*www.lemonaidcars.com* is a good place to start).

Auto Industry Groups

Ontario consumers may file an online complaint with the Ontario Motor Vehicle Industry Council (OMVIC) at *www.omvic.on.ca/services/consumers/file_complaint_info.htm*. Sure, OMVIC is the dealer's self-defence lobby—made up of around 9,000 registered dealers and 20,000 registered salespeople—but it has the following mandate:

> [T]o maintain a fair, safe and informed marketplace in Ontario by protecting the rights of consumers, enhancing industry professionalism and ensuring fair, honest and open competition for registered motor vehicle dealers.

The way your complaint is handled will test the veracity of the above-stated goals.

Alberta has a similar self-regulating auto industry group, the Alberta Motor Vehicle Industry Council (AMVIC) (*www.amvic.org*). During 2004, 873 consumer files were opened with AMVIC and 844 were closed. Their investigators laid 403 charges under the *Fair Trading Act* and the Canadian *Criminal Code*. Court fines of $13,400 were levied under the *Fair Trading Act*, and the courts ordered $289,281 in restitution payments. Also, AMVIC obtained $1,687,180 by mediation in restitution for victims of unfair trade practices.

Classified Ads and Television Exposés

Put an ad in the local paper describing your plight, and ask for information from people who may have experienced a problem similar to your own. This approach alerts others to the potential problem, helps build a base for a class action or a group meeting with the automaker, and puts pressure on the local dealer and manufacturer to settle with you. Sometimes the paper's news desk will assign someone to cover your story after your ad is published, or you may gain attention by setting up a website.

Television producers and their researchers need articulate consumers with issues that are easily filmed and understood. If you want media coverage, you must summarize your complaint and have visual aids that will hold the viewer's interest (viewers should be able to understand the issues with the sound turned off). Paint delamination? Show your peeling car. Bought a lemon vehicle? Show your repair bills. Holding a demonstration? Make it a "lemon" parade: Target one of the largest dealers, give your group a nifty name, and then drive past the dealership in vehicles decorated with "lemon" signs.

Federal and Provincial Consumer Affairs

The wind left the sails of the consumer movement over two decades ago, leaving consumer agencies understaffed and unsupported by the government. Federal consumer protection is a government-created PR myth. Although the beefed-up *Competition Act* has some bite in regard to misleading advertising and a number of other illegal business practices, the government has been more reactive than proactive in applying the law. The *Act* also had some teeth pulled by an amendment that forces the government to prove in civil court that not only did price fixing occur, but that it also was successful in influencing prices. There is now a passive mindset among many pro-consumer government staffers throughout Canada, who are tired of getting their heads kicked in by businesses, deadwood bosses, and budget cutters.

Nevertheless, you can lodge a formal complaint with the Competition Bureau if you encounter misleading advertising, odometer tampering, or price fixing. Use the online Enquiry/Complaint Form found at *www.competitionbureau.gc.ca*. Five years ago, an online complaint sent by *Lemon-Aid* made Toyota cease its Access price-fixing practices and pay out almost $2 million as a settlement fee. On the other hand, Ottawa just rejected *Lemon-Aid*'s petition that Honda was fixing prices by warning dealers not to transact business with auto brokers. The threat to dealers was proven, but the proof that prices went up could not be made (who could prove that?). Interestingly, the recession has cured the problem. Hungry dealers will take business from any third party.

Consumer affairs offices can still help with investigation, mediation, and some litigation. Strong and effective consumer protection legislation has been left standing in most of the provinces, and resourceful consumers can use these laws in conjunction with media coverage to prod provincial consumer affairs offices into action. Furthermore, provincial bureaucrats aren't as well shielded from criticism as their federal counterparts. A call to your MPP or MLA, or to their executive assistants, can often get things rolling.

Invest in Protest

You can have fun and put additional pressure on a seller or garage by putting a "lemon" sign on your car and parking it in front of the dealer or garage, by creating a lemon website, or by forming a self-help group like the Chrysler Lemon Owners Group (CLOG) or the Ford Lemon Owners Group (FLOG). After forming your group, you can have the occasional parade of creatively decorated cars visit area dealerships as the local media are convened. Just remember to keep your remarks pithy and factual, don't interfere with traffic or customers, and remain peaceful.

One other piece of advice from this consumer advocate with more than 40 years of experience and hundreds of pickets and mass demonstrations under his belt: Keep a sense of humour, and never break off negotiations.

Finally, don't be scared off by threats that it's illegal to criticize a product or company. Unions, environmentalists, and consumer groups do it regularly (it's called "informational picketing"), and the Supreme Court of Canada in *R. v. Guinard* reaffirmed this right in February 2002. In that judgment, an insurance policyholder posted a sign on his barn claiming the Commerce Insurance Company was unfairly refusing his claim. The municipality of St-Hyacinthe, Quebec, told him to take the sign down. He refused, maintaining that he had the right to state his opinion. The Supreme Court agreed. This judgment means that consumer protests, signs, and websites that criticize the actions of corporations cannot be banned simply because they say unpleasant things.

Typical Refund Scenarios

Sudden Acceleration, Chronic Stalling, and ABS and Airbag Failures

Incidents of sudden acceleration or chronic stalling are quite common. However, they are very difficult to diagnose, and individual cases can be treated very differently by federal safety agencies. Sudden acceleration is considered to be a safety-related problem—stalling isn't. Never mind that a vehicle's sudden loss of power on a busy highway puts everyone's lives at risk (as is the case with 2001–03 VW and Audi ignition coil failures). The same problem exists with engine and transmission powertrain failures, which are only occasionally considered to be safety-related. ABS and airbag failures, however, are universally considered to be life-threatening defects. If your vehicle manifests any of these conditions, here's what you need to do:

1. Get independent witnesses to confirm that the problem exists. Your primary tools include an independent mechanic's verification, passenger accounts, downloaded data from your vehicle's data recorder, and lots of Internet browsing using *www.lemonaidcars.com* and Google's search engine. Notify the dealer or manufacturer by fax, email, or registered letter that you consider the problem to be a factory-induced, safety-related defect. Make sure you address your correspondence to the manufacturer's product liability or legal affairs department. At the dealership's service bay, make sure that every work order clearly states the problem as well as the number of previous attempts to fix it. (You should end up with a few complaint letters and a handful of work orders confirming that this is an ongoing deficiency.) If the dealer won't give you a copy of the work order because the work is a warranty claim, ask for a copy of the order number "in case your estate wishes to file a claim, pursuant to an accident." (This wording will get the service manager's attention.) Leaving a paper trail is crucial for any claim you may have later on, because it shows your concern and persistence, and it clearly indicates that the dealer and manufacturer have had ample time to correct the defect.
2. Note on the work order that you expect the problem to be diagnosed and corrected under the emissions warranty or a "goodwill" program. It also wouldn't hurt to add the phrase on the work order or in your claim letters that "any deaths, injuries, or damage caused by the defect will be the dealer's and manufacturer's responsibility" because the work order (or letter, fax, or email) constitutes you putting them on "formal notice."
3. If the dealer does the necessary repairs at little or no cost to you, send a follow-up confirmation that you appreciate the "goodwill." Also, emphasize that you'll be back if the problem reappears—even if the warranty has expired—because the repair renews your warranty rights applicable to that defect. In other words, the warranty clock is set back to its original position. Understand that you won't likely get a copy of the repair bill, either, because dealers don't like to admit that there was a serious defect present and don't feel that they owe you a copy of the work order if the repair was done *gratis*. You can, however,

subpoena the complete vehicle file from the dealer and manufacturer (this costs about $50) if the case goes to small claims or a higher court. This request has produced many out-of-court settlements when the internal documents show extensive work was carried out to correct the problem.

4. If the problem persists, send a letter, fax, or email to the dealer and manufacturer saying so, look for ALLDATA service bulletins to confirm that your vehicle's defects are factory-related, and report the failure by calling Transport Canada or NHTSA or by logging on to NHTSA's website. Also, call the Nader-founded Center for Auto Safety in Washington, D.C. (Tel: 202-328-7700) to get a lawyer referral and an information sheet covering the problem.
5. Now come two crucial questions: Repair the defect now or later? Use the dealer or an independent? Generally, it's smart to use an independent garage if you know the dealer isn't pushing for free corrective repairs from the manufacturer, if weeks or months have passed without any resolution of your claim, if the dealer keeps repeating that it's a maintenance item, and if you know an independent mechanic who will give you a detailed work order showing the defect is factory-related and not caused by poor maintenance. Don't mention that a court case may ensue, since this will scare the dickens out of your only independent witness. An added bonus is that the repair charges will be about half of what a dealer would demand. Incidentally, if the automaker later denies warranty "goodwill" because you used an independent repairer, use the argument that the defect's safety implications required emergency repairs, carried out by whoever could see you first.
6. Dashboard-mounted warning lights usually come on prior to airbags suddenly deploying, ABS brakes failing, or engine glitches causing the vehicle to stall out. (Sudden acceleration usually occurs without warning.) Automakers consider these lights to be critical safety warnings and generally advise drivers to *immediately* have their vehicle serviced to correct the problem when any of the warning lights come on (advice that can be found in the owner's manual). This fact bolsters the argument that your life was threatened, emergency repairs were required, and your request for another vehicle or a complete refund isn't out of line.
7. Sudden acceleration can have multiple causes, isn't easy to duplicate, and is often blamed on the driver mistaking the accelerator for the brakes or failing to perform proper maintenance. Yet NHTSA data shows that with the 1992–2000 Explorer, for example, a faulty cruise-control or PCV valve and poorly mounted pedals are the most likely causes of the Explorer's sudden acceleration. So how do you satisfy the burden of proof showing that the problem exists and it's the automaker's responsibility? Use the legal doctrine called "the balance of probabilities" by eliminating all of the possible dodges the dealer or manufacturer may employ. Show that proper maintenance has been carried out, you're a safe driver, and the incident occurs frequently and without warning.
8. If any of the above defects causes an accident, or if the airbag fails to deploy or you're injured by its deployment, ask your insurance company to have the vehicle towed to a neutral location and clearly state that neither the dealer nor the automaker should touch the vehicle until your insurance company

and Transport Canada have completed their investigation. Also, get as many witnesses as possible and immediately go to the hospital for a check-up, even if you're feeling okay. You may be injured and not know it because the adrenalin coursing through your veins is masking your injuries. A hospital exam will easily confirm that your injuries are accident-related, which is essential evidence for court or for future settlement negotiations.

9. Peruse NHTSA's online accident and service bulletin database to find reports of other accidents caused by the same failure, bulletins that indicate part upgrades, current defect investigations, and reported failures that have resulted in recalls or closed investigations.
10. Don't let your insurance company bully you. Refuse to let them settle the case if you're sure the accident was caused by a mechanical failure. Even if an engineering analysis fails to directly implicate the manufacturer or dealer, you can always plead the aforementioned balance of probabilities. If the insurance company settles, your insurance premiums will soar and the manufacturer will get away with the perfect crime.

Defective Tires

Tire companies are far easier to deal with than automobile manufacturers because, under the legal doctrine of *res ipsa loquitur* ("the thing speaks for itself," meaning, in negligence cases, that liability is shown by the failure), tires aren't supposed to fail. When they do, smart claimants can use the *Robson v. General Motors B.C.* class action judgment to bring in the American corporation, and you can also refer to the Supreme Court of Canada judgment *Winnipeg Condominium No. 36 v. Bird Construction Co. Ltd.* (1995; 1 S.C.R.85), which ruled that defendants are liable in negligence for any designs that result in a public safety or health risk. This decision reversed a long-standing policy and provided the public with a new cause of action that had not existed before in Canada.

No wonder tire and auto companies routinely avoid liability by imputing blame to someone or something else, like punctures, impact damage, overloading, overinflating, or under-inflating.

If you have a tire failure that conceivably puts your life in peril, consider the 10 steps outlined previously in "Sudden Acceleration, Chronic Stalling, and ABS and Airbag Failures," and add the following:

1. Access NHTSA on the Internet (see Appendix III) for current data about which tires are failure-prone and which companies are under investigation, conducting recalls, or carrying out "silent" recalls.
2. Keep the tire. If the tiremaker says an analysis must be done, permit only a portion of the tire to be taken away.
3. Plead the balance of probabilities, using friends and family to refute the tire company's contention that you caused the failure.
4. Ask for damages that are adequate to replace all the tires on your vehicle, including mounting costs.

5. Include in your damage claim any repairs needed to fix the body damage caused by the tire's failure.

Paint and Body Defects

The following settlement advice applies mainly to paint defects, but you can use these tips for any other vehicle defect that you believe is the automaker's or dealer's responsibility. If you aren't sure whether the problem is a factory-related deficiency or a maintenance fault, have it checked out by an independent garage or get a technical service bulletin summary for your vehicle. The summary may include specific bulletins relating to diagnosis and correction as well as information about ordering the upgraded parts needed to fix your problem.

Four good examples of favourable paint judgments are *Shields v. General Motors of Canada*, *Bentley v. Dave Wheaton Pontiac Buick GMC Ltd. and General Motors of Canada*, *Maureen Frank v. General Motors of Canada Limited*, and the most recent, *Dunlop v. Ford of Canada*.

In *Dunlop v. Ford of Canada* (No. 58475/04; Ontario Superior Court of Justice, Richmond Hill Small Claims Court; January 5, 2005; Deputy Judge M.J. Winer), the owner of a 1996 Lincoln Town Car that was purchased used in 1999 for $27,000 was awarded $4,091.64. Judge Winer cited the *Shields* decision (following) and gave these reasons for finding Ford of Canada liable:

> Evidence was given by the Plaintiff's witness, Terry Bonar, an experienced paint auto technician. He gave evidence that the [paint] delamination may be both a manufacturing defect and can be caused or [sped] up by atmospheric conditions. He also says that [the paint on] a car like this should last ten to 15 years, [or even for] the life of the vehicle....
>
> It is my view that the presence of ultraviolet light is an environmental condition to which the vehicle is subject. If it cannot withstand this environmental condition, it is defective....

In *Shields v. General Motors of Canada* (No. 1398/96; Ontario Court, General Division, Oshawa Small Claims Court; July 24, 1997; Robert Zochodne, Deputy Judge), the owner of a 1991 Pontiac Grand Prix had purchased the vehicle used with over 100,000 km on its odometer. Beginning in 1995 the paint began to bubble and flake, and it eventually peeled off. Deputy Judge Zochodne awarded the plaintiff $1,205.72 and struck down every one of GM's arguments that the peeling paint was caused by acid rain, UV rays, or some other environmental factor. Here are some other important aspects of this 12-page judgment that GM didn't appeal:

1. The judge admitted many of the technical service bulletins referred to in *Lemon-Aid* as proof of GM's negligence.
2. Although the vehicle had 156,000 km on its odometer when the case went to

court, GM still offered to pay 50 percent of the paint repairs if the plaintiff dropped his suit.

3. The judge ruled that the failure to protect the paint from the damaging effects of UV rays is akin to engineering a car that won't start in cold weather. In essence, vehicles must be built to withstand the rigours of the environment.
4. Here's an interesting twist: The original warranty covered defects that were present at the time it was in effect. The judge, taking statements found in the GM technical service bulletins, ruled that the UV problem was factory-related, existed during the warranty period, and, therefore, represented a latent defect that appeared once the warranty expired.
5. The subsequent purchaser was not prevented from making the warranty claim, even though the warranty had long since expired, from both time and mileage standpoints, and he was the second owner.

The small claims judgment in *Bentley v. Dave Wheaton Pontiac Buick GMC Ltd. and General Motors of Canada* (Victoria Registry No. 24779; British Columbia Small Claims Court; December 1, 1998; Judge Higinbotham) builds upon Ontario's *Shields v. General Motors of Canada* decision and cites other jurisprudence as to how long paint should last on a car. If you're wondering why Ford and Chrysler haven't been hit by similar judgments, remember that they usually settle out of court.

From *Maureen Frank v. General Motors of Canada Limited* (No. SC#12 (2001); Saskatchewan Provincial Court, Saskatoon, Saskatchewan; October 17, 2001; Provincial Court Judge H.G. Dirauf):

> On June 23, 1997, the Plaintiff bought a 1996 Chevrolet Corsica from a General Motors dealership. At the time, the odometer showed 33,172 km. The vehicle still had some factory warranty. The car had been a lease car and had no previous accidents.
>
> During June of 2000, the Plaintiff noticed that some of the paint was peeling off from the car and she took it to a General Motors dealership in Saskatoon and to the General Motors dealership in North Battleford where she purchased the car. While there were some discussions with the GM dealership about the peeling paint, nothing came of it and the Plaintiff now brings this action claiming the cost of a new paint job.
>
> During 1999, the Plaintiff was involved in a minor collision causing damage to the left rear door. This damage was repaired. During this repair some scratches to the left front door previously done by vandals were also repaired.
>
> The Plaintiff's witness, Frank Nemeth, is a qualified auto body repairman with some 26 years of experience. He testified that the peeling paint was a factory defect and that it was necessary to completely strip the car and repaint it. He diagnosed the cause of the peeling paint as a separation of the primer surface or colour coat from the electrocoat primer. In his opinion no primer surfacer was applied at all. He testified that once the peeling starts, it will continue. He has seen this problem on General Motors vehicles. The defect is called delamination.

> Mr. Nemeth stated that a paint job should last at least 10 years. In my opinion, most people in Saskatchewan grow up with cars and are familiar with cars. I think it is common knowledge that the original paint on cars normally lasts in excess of 15 years and that rust becomes a problem before the paint fails. In any event, paint peeling off, as it did on the Plaintiff's vehicle, is not common. I find that the paint on a new car put on by the factory should last at least 15 years.
>
> It is clear from the evidence of Frank Nemeth (independent body shop manager) that the delamination is a factory defect. His evidence was not seriously challenged. I find that the factory paint should not suffer a delamination defect for at least 15 years and that this factory defect breached the warranty that the paint was of acceptable quality and was durable for a reasonable period of time.
>
> There will be judgment for the Plaintiff in the amount of $3,412.38 plus costs of $81.29.

Some of the important aspects of the *Frank* judgment are as follows:

1. The judge accepted that the automaker was responsible, even though the car had been bought used. The subsequent purchaser wasn't prevented from making the warranty claim, even though the warranty had long since expired, from both time and mileage standpoints, and she was the second owner.
2. The judge stressed that the provincial warranty can kick in when the automaker's warranty has expired or isn't applied.
3. By awarding full compensation to the plaintiff, the judge didn't feel that there was a significant "betterment" or improvement added to the car that would warrant reducing the amount of the award.
4. The judge decided that the paint delamination was a factory defect.
5. The judge also concluded that without this factory defect, a paint job should last up to 15 years.
6. GM offered to pay $700 of the paint repairs if the plaintiff dropped the suit; the judge awarded five times that amount.
7. Maureen Frank won this case despite having to confront GM lawyer Ken Ready, who had considerable experience arguing other paint cases for GM and Chrysler.

Other paint and rust cases

Martin v. Honda Canada Inc. (March 17, 1986; Ontario Small Claims Court, Scarborough; Judge Sigurdson): The original owner of a 1981 Honda Civic sought compensation for the premature "bubbling, pitting, [and] cracking of the paint and rusting of the Civic after five years of ownership." Judge Sigurdson agreed with the owner and ordered Honda to pay the owner $1,163.95.

Thauberger v. Simon Fraser Sales and Mazda Motors (3 B.C.L.R., 193): This Mazda owner sued for damages caused by the premature rusting of his 1977 Mazda GLC. The court awarded him $1,000. Thauberger had also previously sued General

Motors for a prematurely rusted Blazer truck and was awarded $1,000 in the same court. Both judges ruled that the defects couldn't be excluded from the automaker's expressed warranty or from the implied warranty granted by British Columbia's *Sale of Goods Act*.

Whittaker v. Ford Motor Company (1979) (24 O.R. (2d), 344): A new Ford developed serious corrosion problems despite having been rustproofed by the dealer. The court ruled that the dealer, not Ford, was liable for the damage for having sold the rustproofing product at the time of purchase. This is an important judgment to use when a rustproofer or paint protector goes out of business or refuses to pay a claim, because the decision holds the dealer jointly responsible.

See also:

- *Danson v. Chateau Ford (1976) C.P.* (Quebec Small Claims Court; No. 32-00001898-757; Judge Lande)
- *Doyle v. Vital Automotive Systems* (May 16, 1977; Ontario Small Claims Court, Toronto; Judge Turner)
- *Lacroix v. Ford* (April 1980; Ontario Small Claims Court, Toronto; Judge Tierney)
- *Marinovich v. Riverside Chrysler* (April 1, 1987; District Court of Ontario; No. 1030/85; Judge Stortini)

Using the Courts

When to Sue?

If the dealer you've been negotiating with agrees to make things right, give him or her a deadline to complete the repairs and then have an independent garage check them over. If no offer is made within 10 working days, file suit in court. Make the manufacturer a party to the lawsuit only if the original, unexpired warranty is still in place; if your claim falls under the emissions warranty, a TSB, a secret warranty extension, or a safety recall campaign; or if there is extensive chassis rusting caused by poor engineering.

Which Court?

Most claims can be handled without a lawyer in small claims court, especially now that courts' jurisdictions vary from $5,000 to $25,000. Still, it's up to you to decide what remedy to pursue—that is, whether you want a partial refund or a cancellation of the sale. To determine the refund amount, add the estimated cost of repairing the existing mechanical defects to the cost of prior repairs. Don't exaggerate your losses or claim for repairs that are considered to be routine maintenance. A suit for the cancellation of a sale involves practical problems. The court requires that the vehicle be "tendered," or taken back, to the seller at the time the lawsuit is filed. This leaves you without transportation for as long as the case continues, unless you purchase another vehicle in the interim. If you lose the case, you must then take back the old vehicle and pay the accumulated storage fees. You could go from having no vehicle to having two—one of which is a clunker!

Generally, if the cost of repairs or the sales contract amount falls within the small claims court limit (discussed later), file the case there to keep your costs to a minimum and to get a speedy hearing. Small claims court judgments aren't easily appealed, lawyers aren't necessary, filing fees are minimal (about $125), and cases are usually heard within a few months. In fact, your suit is almost always best argued in the provincial small claims court to keep costs and frustrations down and to get a quick resolution within a few months.

> Mr. Edmonston, I emailed you earlier in the year seeking help on my small claims case against Ford. I'm happy to report that I won my case and received a $1,900 settlement cheque from Ford in the mail yesterday! As you may recall I have a 1991 Explorer that has a significant paint peel problem.
>
> MARK G.

Here's another reason not to be greedy: If you claim more than the small claims court limit, you'll have to go to a higher court—where costs quickly add up, lawyers routinely demand 30 percent of your winnings or settlement, and delays of a few years or more are commonplace.

Small Claims Courts

Crooked automakers scurry away from small claims courts like cockroaches from bug spray, not because the courts can issue million-dollar judgments or force litigants to spend millions in legal fees (they can't), but because dealers and manufacturers don't want the bad publicity arising from the filings and eventual judgments. Other disincentives are that small claims courts can award sizeable sums to plaintiffs not represented by lawyers, and they make jurisprudence that other judges on the same bench are likely to follow.

For example, in *Dawe v. Courtesy Chrysler* (Dartmouth Nova Scotia Small Claims Court; SCCH #206825; July 30, 2004), Judge Patrick L Casey, Q.C., rendered an impressive 21-page decision citing key automobile product liability cases from the past 80 years, including *Donoghue*, *Kravitz*, and *Davis*. The court awarded $5,037 to the owner of a new 2001 Cummins engine–equipped Ram pickup with the following problems: It wandered all over the road; lost power, or jerked and bucked; shifted erratically; lost braking ability; bottomed out when passing over bumps; allowed water to leak into the cab; produced a burnt-wire and oil smell in the interior as the lights would dim; and produced a rear-end whine and wind noise around the doors and under the dash. Dawe had sold the vehicle and reduced his claim to meet the small claims threshold. Anyone with engine, transmission, or suspension problems or water leaking into the interior will find this judgment particularly useful.

Interestingly, "small claims" court is quickly becoming a misnomer, now that Alberta, Nova Scotia, British Columbia, Yukon, and (as of January 1, 2010) Ontario allow claims of up to $25,000 and other provinces permit $5,000–$20,000 filings. See the following table, and check your provincial or territorial court's website for specific rules and restrictions.

SMALL CLAIMS COURT LIMITS

PROVINCE/TERRITORY	CLAIM LIMIT	COURT WEBSITE
Alberta	$25,000	*www.albertacourts.ab.ca*
British Columbia	$25,000	*www.courts.gov.bc.ca*
Manitoba	$10,000	*www.manitobacourts.mb.ca*
New Brunswick	$ 6,000	*www.gnb.ca/cour*
Newfoundland and Labrador	$ 5,000	*www.court.nl.ca*
Northwest Territories	$10,000	*www.nwtcourts.ca*
Nova Scotia	$25,000	*www.courts.ns.ca*
Nunavut	$20,000	*www.nucj.ca*
Ontario	$25,000	*www.ontariocourts.on.ca*
Prince Edward Island	$ 8,000	*www.gov.pe.ca/courts*
Quebec	$ 7,000	*www.justice.gouv.qc.ca*
Saskatchewan	$20,000	*www.sasklawcourts.ca*
Yukon	$25,000	*www.yukoncourts.ca*

There are small claims courts in most counties of every province, and you can make a claim in the county where the problem happened or where the defendant lives and conducts business. Simply go to the small claims court office and ask for a claim form. Remember, you must identify the defendant correctly, which may require some help from the court clerk (look for other recent lawsuits naming the same party). Crooks often change their company's name to escape liability; for example, it would be impossible to sue Joe's Garage (1999) if your contract is with Joe's Garage, Inc. (1984).

At this point, it wouldn't hurt to hire a lawyer or a paralegal for a brief walk-through of small claims procedures to ensure that you've prepared your case properly and that you know what objections will likely be raised by the other side. If, instead, you'd like a lawyer to do all the work for you, there are a number of law firms around the country that specialize in small claims litigation. "Small claims" doesn't mean "small legal fees," however. In Toronto, some law offices charge a flat fee of $1,000 for a basic small claims lawsuit and trial.

Remember that you're entitled to bring to court any evidence relevant to your case, including written documents such as a bill of sale or receipt, contract, or letter. If your car has developed severe rust problems, bring a photograph (signed and dated by the photographer) to court. You may also have witnesses testify in court. It's important to discuss a witness's testimony prior to the court date. If a witness can't attend the court date, he or she can write a report and sign it for representation in court. This situation usually applies to an expert witness, such as an independent mechanic who has evaluated your car's problems.

If you lose your case in spite of all your preparation and research, some small claims court statutes allow cases to be retried, at a nominal cost, in exceptional circumstances. If a new witness has come forward, additional evidence has been discovered, or key documents (that were previously not available) have become accessible, apply for a retrial.

Alan MacDonald, a *Lemon-Aid* reader who won his case in small claims court, gives the following tips on beating Ford over a faulty automatic transmission:

> I want to thank you for the advice you provided in my dealings with the Ford Motor Company of Canada Limited and Highbury Ford Sales Limited regarding my 1994 Ford Taurus wagon and the problems with the automatic transmission (Taurus and Windstar transmissions are identical). I also wish to apologize for not sending you a copy of this judgment earlier...(*MacDonald v. Highbury Ford Sales Limited,* Ontario Superior Court of Justice in the Small Claims Court London, June 6, 2000, Court File #0001/00, Judge J.D. Searle).
>
> In 1999, after only 105,000 km, the automatic transmission went. I took the car to Highbury Ford to have it repaired. We paid $2,070 to have the transmission fixed, but protested and felt the transmission failed prematurely. We contacted Ford, but to no avail: Their reply was we were out of warranty, period. The transmission was so poorly repaired (and we went back to Highbury Ford several times) that we had to go to Mr. Transmission to have the transmission fixed again nine months later at a further $1,906.02.
>
> It is at that point that I contacted you, and I was surprised, and somewhat speechless (which you noticed) when you personally called me to provide advice and encouragement. I am very grateful for your call. My observations with going through small claims court involved the following: I filed in January of 2000, the trial took place on June 1 and the judgment was issued June 6.
>
> At pretrial, a representative of Ford (Ann Sroda) and a representative from Highbury Ford were present. I came with one binder for each of the defendants, the court and one for myself (each binder was about 3 inches thick—containing your reports on Ford Taurus automatic transmissions, ALLDATA Service Bulletins, Taurus Transmissions Victims (Bradley website), Center for Auto Safety (website), Read This Before Buying a Taurus (website), and the Ford Vent Page (website)).
>
> The representative from Ford asked a lot of questions (I think she was trying to find out if I had read the contents of the information I was relying on). The Ford representative then offered a 50 percent settlement based on the initial transmission work done at Highbury Ford. The release allowed me to still sue Highbury Ford with regards to the

necessity of going to Mr. Transmission because of the faulty repair done by the dealer. Highbury Ford displayed no interest in settling the case, and so I had to go to court.

For court, I prepared by issuing a summons to the manager at Mr. Transmission, who did the second transmission repair, as an expert witness. I was advised that unless you produce an expert witness you won't win in a car repair case in small claims court. Next, I went to the law school library in London and received a great deal of assistance in researching cases pertinent to car repairs. I was told that judgments in your home province (in my case Ontario) were binding on the court; that cases outside of the home province could be considered, but not binding, on the judge.

The cases I used for trial involved *Pelleray v. Heritage Ford Sales Ltd.*, Ontario Small Claims Court (Scarborough) SC7688/91 March 22, 1993; *Phillips et al. v. Ford Motor Co. of Canada Ltd. et al*, Ontario Reports 1970, 15th January 1970; *Gregorio v. Intrans-Corp.*, Ontario Court of Appeal, May 19, 1994; *Collier v. MacMaster's Auto Sales*, New Brunswick Court of Queen's Bench, April 26, 1991; *Sigurdson v. Hillcrest Service & Acklands (1977)*, Saskatchewan Queen's Bench; *White v. Sweetland*, Newfoundland District Court, Judicial Centre of Gander, November 8, 1978; *Raiches Steel Works v. J. Clark & Son*, New Brunswick Supreme Court, March 7, 1977; *Mudge v. Corner Brook Garage Ltd.*, Newfoundland Supreme Court, July 17, 1975; *Sylvain v. Carroseries d'Automobiles Guy Inc. (1981)*, C.P. 333, Judge Page; [and] *Gagnon v. Ford Motor Company of Canada, Limited et Marineau Automobile Co. Ltée. (1974)*, C.S. 422–423.

In court, I had prepared the case, as indicated above, [and] had my expert witness and two other witnesses who had driven the vehicle (my wife and my 18-year-old son). As you can see by the judgment, we won our case and I was awarded $1,756.52, including pre-judgment interest and costs.

Key Court Decisions

The following Canadian and U.S. lawsuits and judgments cover typical problems that are likely to arise. Use them as leverage when negotiating a settlement or as a reference should your claim go to trial. Legal principles applying to Canadian and American law are similar; however, Quebec court decisions may be based on legal principles that don't apply outside that province. You can find a comprehensive listing of Canadian decisions from small claims courts all the way to the Supreme Court of Canada at *www.canlii.org* (Canadian Legal Information Institute).

Additional court judgments can be found in the legal reference section of your city's main public library or at a nearby university law library. Ask the librarian for help in choosing the legal phrases that best describe your claim.

LexisNexis (*global.lexisnexis.com/ca*) and FindLaw (*www.findlaw.com*) are two useful Internet sites for legal research. Their main drawback, though, is that you may need to subscribe or use a lawyer's subscription to access jurisprudence and other areas of the sites. However, there *is* a free online summary of class actions filed in Canada at *classactionsincanada.blogspot.com*. It's run by Ward Branch, one of the legal counsels in the $1.2 billion class action filed against General Motors for defective engine intake manifold gaskets.

An excellent reference book that will give you plenty of tips on filing, pleading, and collecting your judgment is Justice Marvin A. Zuker's *Ontario Small Claims Court Practice 2010* (Carswell, 2009). Judge Zuker's annual publication is easily understood by non-lawyers and uses court decisions from across Canada to help you plead your case successfully in almost any Canadian court.

Product Liability

Almost three decades ago, before *Robson*, the Supreme Court of Canada in *Kravitz v. GM* clearly affirmed that automakers and their dealers are jointly liable for the replacement or repair of a vehicle if independent testimony shows that it is afflicted with factory-related defects that compromise its safety or performance. The existence of secret warranty extensions or technical service bulletins also help prove that the vehicle's problems are the automaker's responsibility. For example, in *Lowe v. Fairview Chrysler* (see page 133), technical service bulletins were instrumental in showing in 1989 that Chrysler had a history of automatic transmission failures similar to what we see in Ford and GM today.

In addition to replacing or repairing the vehicle, an automaker can also be held responsible for any damages arising from the defect (see *Wharton*, page 95). This means that loss of wages, supplementary transportation costs, and damages for personal inconvenience can be awarded. However, in the States, product liability damage awards often exceed millions of dollars, while Canadian courts are far less generous.

When a warranty claim is rejected on the pretext that you "altered" the vehicle, failed to carry out preventive maintenance, or drove abusively, manufacturers *must* prove to the court that there's a link between their allegation and the failure (see *Julien v. General Motors of Canada Ltd.* (1991), 116 N.B.R. (2d) 80).

Before settling any claim with GM or any other automaker, read the latest information from dissatisfied customers who've banded together and set up their own self-help websites (see Appendix III).

Implied Warranty (Reasonable Durability)

This is that powerful "other" warranty that they never tell you about. It applies during and after the expiration of the manufacturer's or dealer's expressed or written warranty and requires that a part or repair will last a "reasonable" period of time. Look at the "Reasonable Part Durability" chart on page 104 for some guidelines on what you should expect.

Judges usually apply the implied or legal warranty when the manufacturer's expressed warranty has expired and the vehicle's manufacturing defects remain uncorrected. The landmark Canadian decisions upholding implied warranties in auto claims have been *General Motors Products of Canada Ltd. v. Kravitz*, [1979] 1 S.C.R. 790, and *Donoghue v. Stevenson*, [1932] A.C. 562 (H.L.).

In *Donoghue*, the court had to determine if the manufacturer of a bottle of ginger beer owed a duty to a consumer who suffered injury as a result of finding a decomposed snail in the bottle after consuming part of the bottle's contents. Lord Atkin, in finding liability against the manufacturer, established the principle of negligence. His reasons have been followed and adopted in all the common-law countries:

> The rule that you are to love your neighbour becomes in law, you must not injure your neighbour; and the lawyer's question, who is my neighbour? receives a restricted reply. You must take reasonable care to avoid acts or omissions which you can reasonably foresee would be likely to injure your neighbour. Who, then, is my neighbour?
>
> The answer seems to be—persons who are so closely and directly affected by my act that I ought reasonably to have them in contemplation as being so affected when I am directing my mind to the acts or omissions which are called in question....

Over 45 years later in Quebec, *Kravitz* said essentially the same thing. In that case, the court said the seller's warranty of quality was an accessory to the property and was transferred with it on successive sales. Accordingly, subsequent buyers could invoke the contractual warranty of quality against the manufacturer, even though they did not contract directly with it. This precedent is now codified in articles 1434, 1442, and 1730 of Quebec's *Civil Code* (see *Tardif v. Hyundai Motor America* at *www.canlii.org/fr/qc/qccs/doc/2004/2004canlii7992/2004canlii7992.html* for a full analysis of warranties, hidden defects, and misrepresentation relating to Hyundai's inability to be truthful about its horsepower ratings).

Minivan Doors (Windstar "Mental Distress")

In *Sharman v. Formula Ford Sales Limited, Ford Credit Limited, and Ford Motor Company of Canada Limited* (Ontario Superior Court of Justice; Oakville, Ontario; No. 17419/02SR; 2003/10/07), Justice Shepard awarded the owner of a 2000 Windstar $7,500 for mental distress resulting from the breach of the implied warranty of fitness plus $7,207 for breach of contract and breach of warranty. The problem with the Windstar was that its sliding door wasn't secure and leaked air and water after many attempts to repair it. The judge cited the *Wharton* decision as support for his award for mental distress:

> The plaintiff and his family have had three years of aggravation, inconvenience, worry, and concern about their safety and that of their children. Generally speaking, our contract law did not allow for compensation for what may be mental distress, but

> that may be changing. I am indebted to counsel for providing me with the decision of the British Columbia Court of Appeal in *Wharton v. Tom Harris Chevrolet Oldsmobile Cadillac Ltd.*, [2002] B.C.J. No. 233, 2002 BCCA 78. This decision was recently followed in *T'avra v. Victoria Ford Alliance Ltd.*, [2003] B.C.J. No. 1957.
>
> In *Wharton*, the purchaser of a Cadillac Eldorado claimed damages against the dealer because the car's sound system emitted an annoying buzzing noise and the purchaser had to return the car to the dealer for repair numerous times over two-and-a-half years. The trial court awarded damages of $2,257.17 for breach of warranty with respect to the sound system, and $5,000 in non-pecuniary damages for loss of enjoyment of their luxury vehicle and for inconvenience, for a total award of $7,257.17....
>
> In the *Wharton* case, the respondent contracted for a "luxury" vehicle for pleasure use. It included a sound system that the appellant's service manager described as "high end." The respondent's husband described the purchase of the car in this way: "[W]e bought a luxury car that was supposed to give us a luxury ride and be a quiet vehicle, and we had nothing but difficulty with it from the very day it was delivered with this problem that nobody seemed to be able to fix.... So basically we had a luxury product that gave us no luxury for the whole time that we had it."
>
> It is clear that an important object of the contract was to obtain a vehicle that was luxurious and a pleasure to operate. Furthermore, the buzzing noise was the cause of physical, in the sense of sensory, discomfort to the respondent and her husband. The trial judge found it inhibited listening to the sound system and was irritating in normal conversation. The respondent and her husband also bore the physical inconvenience of taking the vehicle to the appellant on numerous occasions for repairs....
>
> In my view, a defect in manufacture that goes to the safety of the vehicle deserves a modest increase. I would assess the plaintiff's damage for mental distress resulting from the breach of the implied warranty of fitness at $7,500.

Free Engine Repairs

In the following judgments, Ford was forced to reimburse the cost of engine head gasket repairs carried out under the implied warranty—long after the expressed warranty had expired.

Dufour v. Ford Canada Ltd. (April 10, 2001; Quebec Small Claims Court, Hull; No. 550-32-008335-009; Justice P. Chevalier): Ford was forced to reimburse the cost of engine head gasket repairs carried out on a 1996 Windstar 3.8L engine.

Schaffler v. Ford Motor Company Limited and Embrun Ford Sales Ltd. (Ontario Superior Court of Justice, L'Orignal Small Claims Court; Court File No. 59-2003; July 22, 2003; Justice Gerald Langlois): The plaintiff bought a used 1995 Windstar in 1998. The engine head gasket was repaired for free three years later under Ford's seven-year extended warranty. In 2002, at 109,600 km, the head gasket failed again, seriously damaging the engine. Ford refused a second repair.

Justice Langlois ruled that Ford's warranty extension bulletin listed signs and symptoms of the covered defect that were identical to the problems written on the second work order ("persistent and/or chronic engine overheating; heavy white smoke evident from the exhaust tailpipe; flashing 'low coolant' instrument-panel light even after coolant refill; and constant loss of engine coolant"). The judge concluded that the dealer knew of the problem well within the warranty period and was therefore negligent. The plaintiff was awarded $4,941 plus 5 percent interest. This award included $1,070 for two months' car rental.

John R. Reid and Laurie M. McCall v. Ford Motor Company of Canada (Superior Court of Justice, Ottawa Small Claims Court; Claim No. 02-SC-077344; July 11, 2003; Justice Tiernay): A 1996 Windstar bought used in 1997 experienced engine head gasket failure in October 2001 at 159,000 km. Judge Tiernay awarded the plaintiffs $4,145 for the following reasons:

> A Technical Service Bulletin dated June 28, 1999, was circulated to Ford dealers. It dealt specifically with "undetermined loss of coolant" and "engine oil contaminated with coolant" in the 1996–98 Windstar and five other models of Ford vehicles. I conclude that Ford owed a duty of care to the Plaintiff to equip this vehicle with a cylinder head gasket of sufficient sturdiness and durability that would function trouble-free for at least seven years, given normal driving and proper maintenance conditions. I find that Ford is answerable in damages for the consequences of its negligence.

Chams v. Ford Motor Company of Canada, Limited, and Courtesy Ford Lincoln Sales, Limited (Ontario Superior Court of Justice, Small Claims Court; London, Ontario; Claim No. 5868, Court File No. 103/04; November 22, 2004; Deputy Justice J.D. Searle):

Reasons for Judgment

1. J.D. SEARLE DEPUTY J.:—The defendant Ford Motor Company of Canada, Limited, hereinafter referred to as "Ford" is a corporation based in Oakville, Ontario and is a manufacturer of motor vehicles. The defendant Courtesy Ford Lincoln Sales Limited, hereinafter referred to as "Courtesy" is a corporation which carries on the business of a Ford dealer in the city of London in the county of Middlesex.
2. Samir Chams resides in the city of London. In 1997 he purchased from Courtesy a low kilometerage 1995 Ford Windstar van with a 3.8 liter engine. By 1998 at the latest Ford was aware the head gaskets of such engines had a defect which could destroy the engine. In 2000 it offered to the plaintiff and other owners an "additional warranty" for this defect but limited the warranty to seven years from the date the vehicle first went into service or 160,000 kilometers, whichever came first. Upon receiving notice of the additional warranty in 2000 the plaintiff took his van to Courtesy but no problems were manifest. For the plaintiff the original warranty had expired by passage of time. The additional warranty expired on March 08, 2002 by passage of time.

3. On January 11, 2004, some 22 months after the additional warranty expired, the plaintiff's engine overheated and was destroyed within a matter of minutes. The van had only 80,000 kilometers on the odometer. In due course the engine was replaced at a cost of over $4,000.00 paid by the plaintiff. As the court understands the plaintiff's case he is suing outside the expired warranty. Against Ford he alleges manufacturing defect. Against Courtesy he alleges negligence in 2000 in not replacing the defective head gasket to avoid possible engine destruction or at least telling him that was an option at his own expense. He also invokes manufacturer's warranty.
4. Ford contends it has no responsibility beyond its warranty and the destruction of the engine was from a cause or causes other than the head gasket. The court finds the highly probable cause of destruction of the engine was failure of the head gasket. The allegation of alternate causes is speculation not supported by the evidence. Pure economic loss does not apply because there was damage to property. See also *Winnipeg Condominium Corporation No. 36 v. Bird Construction Co. Ltd.* [1995] 1 S.C.R. 85.
5. Courtesy contends it was not negligent: the additional warranty issued by Ford only applied to cases with manifest problems and to merely replace a head gasket at a cost to the customer of $1,200.00 to $1,400.00 in the absence of manifest problems did not make economic sense.
6. In the Nova Scotia case of *Ford v. Kenney* (2003, unreported) Boudreau J. of the Nova Scotia Supreme Court was hearing an appeal from a decision of the Small Claims Court Adjudicator. At page 5 of the oral reasons His Lordship said:

   > Ford Motor Company has the right to decide which vehicles they are going to provide repairs to and which vehicles they are not. That doesn't mean that they couldn't be successfully challenged by that on negligent—proper negligent manufacturing evidence, but there was not that evidence in this case.

7. *Campbell v. Ford* is a judgment of the Nova Scotia Small Claims Court rendered on January 31, 2002 and not reported. The plaintiff's 1995 Ford Windstar van was showing signs of head gasket problems and the head gasket was replaced at 168,000 [km] at the $1,600.00 expense of the plaintiff. At 207,000 kilometers the engine was destroyed. The engine was rebuilt or replaced at a much greater cost. In both instances the vehicle was beyond the kilometerage caps of both the original and additional warranties.
8. The Adjudicator dismissed the replacement of the head gasket as pure economic loss but said of the engine rebuilding or replacement:

   > It is certainly arguable that if the head gasket failed and it was due to negligence of the designer/manufacturer and that failure in turn caused physical damage to the property of the Claimant, consequential damage to the engine itself, that may well be a recoverable head of damage and the basis for an action in negligence.

   > The Adjudicator found there was insufficient admissible and reliable evidence to establish a causal connection between the gasket failure sought

to be corrected at 168,000 kilometers and the destruction of the engine at 207,000 kilometers. The important point is that the Adjudicator was discussing the potential liability of Ford quite apart from its original or additional warranties.

9. *Beshara v. Barry* is an Ontario Small Claims Court judgment of Tierney J. with reasons released a few days before trial in the case at bar and not yet reported. The unrepresented plaintiff sued the president of Ford for the estimated cost of replacing an engine similar to the one in the case at bar. The action was dismissed because the failure occurred after the expiry of Ford's original and additional warranties and the negligence alleged was that of the repairer and not Ford. The repairer was not a party.
10. The foregoing cases were furnished to the court by the agent for Ford. In each case involving Ford that company was successful. The court did additional research.
11. In *Kozoriz v. Chrysler Canada Ltd.* [1992] O.J. No. 3937 the problem was a transaxle seal which failed at 16,000 kilometers. Thereafter there was frequent leaking and repair work. As the van neared the 80,000 kilometer warranty expiry the 80,000 kilometer inspection was done at a Chrysler dealership and no problem was found with the trans-axle seal or the transmission. A few days later in Iowa there was an expensive failure of these apparently related parts. Tierney J. of the Ontario Small Claims Court found both parts failed due to a nearly continuous leak of the seal since 16,000 kilometers.
12. Chrysler pleaded the failure occurred after the expiry of the 80,000 kilometer warranty. In part the warranty described itself as "[a] guarantee of the quality and engineering excellence...". Judge Tierney found that to be equivalent to a warranty that the product was free of defect. He found the axle seal was defective almost immediately and failed after only 16,000 kilometers and the defect led to the transmission damage after the expiry of the warranty. At page 3:

    > Those damages occurred as a direct result of the manufacturer's breach of warranty. For that reason, it is my view that the amounts are recoverable as damages for breach of contract, even though the actual breakdown occurred after the warranty period had expired.

13. A similar case is *Shields v. General Motors of Canada Ltd.* [1997] O.J. No. 5434 (Ont. Sm. C.C.). A 1991 Pontiac with a three year warranty began losing an extensive amount of its paint in 1995. Zochodne, D.J. found the problem was a failure to ensure proper bonding when the vehicle was being painted originally. At page 6:

    > The defect, which I have found, that is the lack of primer surfacer, occurred at the time the vehicle was manufactured. At that point, however, the defect was latent. The defect became patent when the paint began to bubble, flake and then peel off the vehicle.

    That being the case His Honour found the warranty must respond to the loss. Judgment was in favour of the plaintiff.

14. *Schaffler v. Ford Motor Co. of Canada and Embrum Ford Sales Ltd.* [2003] O.J. No. 3165 (Ont. Sm. C.C.) is yet another Ford Windstar case involving an engine identical to the one involved in the case at bar. On March 02 of 2000, August 06 of 2001 and October 16 of 2001 the plaintiff took the van to Embrum with problems involving coolant levels, one of the indicia of head gasket failure. On those dates the respective kilometerages were 59,850, 84,000 and 89,000. The additional warranty expired by passage of time on August 07, 2002. Two months later there was serious damage to the engine as a result of head gasket failure.
15. Deputy Judge Langlois found the dealer liable for failure to diagnose the head gasket problem and Ford liable on its additional warranty which had been invoked by the plaintiff within the additional warranty period although the major damage occurred after expiry of the warranty.
16. It is distressing to note that although Barry Holmes was able in the case at bar to produce cases from both Ontario and Nova Scotia when Ford was successful he produced none where Ford was not successful. That includes the *Schaffler* case of one year ago and in which he was Ford's representative. In the case at bar he was Ford's agent and only witness.
17. In the case at bar the plaintiff received notice in 2000 from Ford of a potential problem with the head gasket in his van. His response was to take the van to Courtesy and enquire what should he done about it. Although they are only estimates the van was 5.5 years from the original warranty start date and had traveled 49,000 kilometers. Courtesy took in the van and gave the plaintiff and his family a ride home. About one half hour later Courtesy called and said the van was ready to be picked up. There was no paperwork introduced at trial evidencing this occurrence and it is probable none exists. William Taylor was the service manager and a helpful and credible witness at trial. He was not surprised at the absence of paperwork and said by way of summary that "[w]e do not charge for conversation."
18. It is probable that what happened is this: the plaintiff took his van to Courtesy, did not have the Ford notice with him, told Courtesy he had received a notice about head gaskets, asked what should [be] done and got a ride home. Courtesy was readily able to identify the van by its vehicle identification number and pull up its file on the vehicle, including at least references to technical service bulletins and notices affecting the plaintiff's vehicle and others in its class.
19. Having received no report from the plaintiff nor made any observations themselves the Courtesy service people would not be aware of any of the mostly gross symptoms Ford said could trigger warranty work on the head gasket. According to Mr. Taylor Courtesy had done "a lot" of gasket-related work under the warranty program in 1999 and 2000. In the absence of reports or observations of at least one of the gross symptoms Courtesy would inspect the head gasket only if the customer paid. The court finds the absence of paperwork on this visit by the plaintiff makes it a near certainty there was no gasket inspection.
20. One of the four symptoms listed in the Ford notice received by the plaintiff in 2000 was "constant loss of coolant" and another was flashing of the "low coolant" sensor light. Neither the plaintiff nor his wife testified to the existence of either of these symptoms and Courtesy does not note, except perhaps

informally on the back of a work order, whether coolant has been "topped up." The plaintiff's vehicle was well maintained and in otherwise good condition throughout with much of the servicing done at Courtesy and some oil changes at a large department store if Mrs. Chams was shopping there.

21. Based on what Courtesy knew at the time of this visit Mr. Taylor would not recommend changing the head gasket for two reasons: the cost would be $1,200.00 to $1,400.00 to head off a problem which was only potential and there is a risk of non-payment and alienation if the work is done and the customer starts contending it is warranty work. The mechanic who owns and operates the independent vehicle repair shop which eventually replaced the plaintiff's engine said that due to the problems which can arise from it he will not permit his shop to change a head gasket for the sole purpose of changing the head gasket.
22. Nothing more relevant to an engine problem happened until Sunday, January 11, 2004. The Chams family fueled the van and moved it a short distance to a car wash. While entering the wash the plaintiff noticed the engine temperature digital readout was climbing. It maximized after the wash when they were back on the street. Mr. Chams pulled into the next "Petro" or "petrol" station and looked under the hood but saw nothing awry. He drove about two blocks to his house where the engine would not restart.
23. He asked a friend knowledgeable about motor vehicles to come over. That person observed coolant coming from the exhaust and coolant mixed with oil under the hood. The van was towed to Courtesy that day or early the next.
24. The diagnosis was "coolant in cylinders, no start, no heat, intermittent hydraulic lock. No start due to coolant leak inside engine. Suspect head cracked." The recommendation was replacement of the engine with a rebuilt engine. The kilometerage was noted to be 80,671. The charge for the inspection was $79.00 plus tax, later voluntarily waived by Mr. Taylor in recognition of several members of the Chams family being good customers and, no doubt, because of the arising of a warranty issue. Further, according to Mr. Chams he had urged a friend with a similar vehicle to his to go to the dealer in 2000 and the result was the replacement of the head gasket.
25. Courtesy advised Mr. and Mrs. Chams the problem was not covered by warranty. The occurrence was 22 months after the expiry of the additional warranty. Mr. and Mrs. Chams spent time unsuccessfully trying to get Ford and Courtesy to take responsibility for the problem. Either directly or indirectly the Chams had the van towed to Automotive Solutions. That is a London vehicle repair shop owned and operated by Mohamed Omar who employs two class "A" automotive mechanics in the shop and who himself is in the final stage of his apprenticeship. Mr. Omar testified.
26. The van was stored at Automotive Solutions for about three months until a rebuilt engine and ancillary equipment was purchased by Mr. Chams and installed by Automotive Solutions on and about May 01.
27. When he studied the engine of the Chams van, seemingly in the company of one of his licensed mechanics, Mr. Omar observed the engine appeared not to have been apart before. The head gasket was found to [be] "blown." Coolant was mixed with oil. The coolant had leaked into the inner part of the engine through

the No. 1 cylinder where it could mix with the oil. Oil mixing with coolant can cause the head gasket to "blow." One purpose of the head gasket is to prevent coolant getting into the interior of the engine.

28. In the opinion of Mr. Omar if the head gasket failed in 2000 the vehicle could not be driven until 2004. Head gaskets in most cars do not fail by 80,000 kilometers. He was aware the 3.8 liter Ford engine had a head gasket problem and he has worked on "a few" with such a problem. He is not "100% sure" of the reason for the failure of the Chams engine.
29. William Taylor is the Courtesy service manager. Courtesy did "a lot" of head gasket related repairs to 3.8 liter engines in 1999 and 2000. He understands the problem is a head gasket wrongly configured or "too weak." He has not seen the Chams engine but testified that theoretically the damage could be caused by a defective head gasket, a cracked head or the timing cover.
30. Barry Holmes was Ford's agent and only witness. He is a licensed mechanic and is employed by Ford in its product liability department. His direct evidence was largely on the Ford warranty and there was little or no evidence by him on defect or otherwise the cause of the major engine damage. On cross examination he said he did not know the failure rate of the head gaskets in the affected 3.8 liter engines. On further examination he acknowledged it was possibly 85% but he was not sure and had not brought that information to court with him. The court does not accept that denial of knowledge. The court notes its comments above with respect to cherry picking of cases. Mr. Holmes is a Ford product liability employee. The figure of 85% figured in another case involving a Ford 3.8 liter engine. The case at bar is at least the third nearly identical case in which Mr. Holmes has been noted in the reasons for judgment as Ford's agent or witness or both. The court finds that Ford knows it has had a failure rate of at least 85% in this head gasket which is a component which can quickly destroy an engine if it fails. That makes it nearly a certainty that unless the offending gasket is replaced in time the engine will be destroyed by its failure.
31. As to warranty this court finds, as was found in the *Shields* case, (*supra*), the defect was in existence and known to the giver of the warranty not only during the period of the additional warranty but also during the period of the original warranty. Ford is therefore liable on its warranty.
32. As to negligence there can be no doubt the gasket has had a design or manufacturing defect which has existed since the time of design or manufacture. It is that defect which caused the destruction of the plaintiff's engine and made its replacement necessary.
33. Ford's warranty attempts to limit its liability to what it grants in the warranty. It is ancient law that one who attempts to limit his liability by, for example, excluding common law remedies, must clearly bring that limitation to the attention of the person who might lose those remedies. The evidence in this case is clear the buyer of even a new car does not get a warranty booklet until after purchasing the car although he "would be" told the highlights sooner.
34. Courtesy was not negligent nor in breach of any other obligation to the plaintiff. Ford would not entertain repairs under either of its warranties unless certain "symptoms" had become manifest before the work was done. The court has no doubt Mr. Chams would have declined if Courtesy had asked if he would pay

$1,200.00 to $1,400.00 to replace the head gasket in 2000 when his vehicle was manifesting no problem. The action is therefore dismissed against Courtesy with costs of $375.00 payable by Ford. This court will leave the fancy dancing of Bullock orders and the like to the higher courts.

35. At trial the focus was understandably on liability with damages consigned to the periphery. The rebuilt engine and ancillary parts were obtained from a NAPA dealer. The net NAPA bill is $2,375.67 but to that must be added a down payment of $250.00 and from it must be deducted a core deposit of $300.00. The old core is still available for credit. The radiator and water pump are valid expenses in that they are essential to obtaining a NAPA warranty on the rebuilt engine.
36. One legitimate Automotive Solutions bill is for $776.25 for towing and storage. The other is for $1,383.45 for labour, fluids, minor parts and an alternator. Storage is acceptable, particularly when one notes the absence of a substitute vehicle claim or loss of use. The alternator could not be proved as related to the engine failure and so $126.50 will be deducted.
37. Damages are assessed at $4,358.87 and there will be judgment in that amount against Ford. That sum will attract interest pursuant to the provisions of the *Courts of Justice Act* from January 12, 2004. The Clerk is requested to make that calculation.
38. As to costs a sealed document has now been opened and found to be an October 18, 2004 offer by Ford to settle by waiving allowable costs which stood at $25.00 or $75.00 at the time of the offer.
39. The trial was scheduled for two days but was completed in one. Mr. Ferguson was helpful to the court, particularly by creating document briefs for all parties, thus collecting dozens of potential exhibits into a handful. The court agrees with Mr. Ferguson's contention that many of the [I]nternet printouts collected by or on behalf of the plaintiff and included in one of the briefs were nevertheless inadmissible. Mr. Dupuis as agent for the plaintiff put in his client's case in a way that was economical in terms of trial time but nevertheless thorough and it underscores the need for reform of the law which does not currently permit the court to award a counsel fee with respect to agents even in substantial cases. The plaintiff shall have costs fixed at $200.00 against Ford.

General Motors Intake Manifold Gasket Class Action

A Canadian class action lawsuit was launched on April 24, 2006—with *Lemon-Aid*'s help—and sought $1.2 billion in damages to compensate owners of 1995–2004 GM vehicles with defective engine intake manifold gaskets. A year later, GM Canada settled out of court for an estimated $40 million.

Automatic Transmission Failures

Lowe v. Fairview Chrysler-Dodge Limited and Chrysler Canada Limited (May 14, 1996; Ontario Court (General Division), Burlington Small Claims Court; No. 1224/95): This judgment, in the plaintiff's favour, raises important legal principles relative to Chrysler.

- Internal dealer service bulletins are admissible in court to prove that a problem exists and certain parts should be checked out.
- If a problem is reported prior to a warranty's expiration, warranty coverage for the problematic component(s) is automatically carried over after the warranty ends.
- It's not up to the car owner to tell the dealer or automaker what the specific problem is.
- Repairs carried out by an independent garage can be refunded if the dealer or automaker unfairly refuses to apply the warranty.
- The dealer or automaker cannot dispute the cost of the independent repair if it fails to cross-examine the independent repairer.
- Auto owners can ask for and win compensation for their inconvenience, which in this judgment amounted to $150.
- Court awards quickly add up: Although the plaintiff was given $1,985.94, with the addition of court costs and prejudgment interest, plus costs of inconvenience fixed at $150, the final award amounted to $2,266.04.

New-Vehicle Defects

Bagnell's Cleaners v. Eastern Automobile Ltd. (1991) (111 N.S.R. (2nd), No. 51, 303 A.P.R., No. 51 (T.D.)): This Nova Scotia company found that the new van it purchased had serious engine, transmission, and radiator defects. The dealer pleaded unsuccessfully that the sales contract excluded all other warranties except for those contained in the contract. The court held that there was a fundamental breach of the implied warranty and that the van's performance differed substantially from what the purchaser had been led to expect. An exclusionary clause could not protect the seller, who failed to live up to a fundamental term of the contract.

Burridge v. City Motor (10 Nfld. & P.E.I.R.; No. 451): This Newfoundland resident complained repeatedly of his new car's defects during the warranty period, and he stated that he hadn't used his car for 204 days after spending almost $1,500 for repairs. The judge awarded all repair costs and cancelled the sale.

Davis v. Chrysler Canada Ltd. (1977) (26 N.S.R. (2nd), No. 410 (T.D.)): The owner of a new $28,000 diesel truck found that a faulty steering assembly prevented him from carrying on his business. The court ordered that the sale be cancelled and that $10,000 in monthly payments be reimbursed. There was insufficient evidence to award compensation for business losses.

Fox v. Wilson Motors and GM (February 9, 1989; Court of Queen's Bench, New Brunswick; No. F/C/308/87): A trucker's new tractor-trailer had repeated engine malfunctions. He was awarded damages for loss of income, excessive fuel consumption, and telephone charges under the provincial *Sale of Goods Act*.

Gibbons v. Trapp Motors Ltd. (1970) (9 D.L.R. (3rd), No. 742 (B.C.S.C.)): The court ordered the dealer to take back a new car that had numerous defects and required 32 hours of repairs. The refund was reduced by mileage driven.

Johnson v. Northway Chevrolet Oldsmobile (1993) (108 Sask. R., No. 138 (Q.B.)): The court ordered the dealer to take back a new car that had been brought in for repairs on 14 different occasions. Two years after the car's purchase, the buyer initiated a lawsuit for the purchase price and general damages. General damages were awarded.

Julien v. GM of Canada (1991) (116 N.B.R. (2nd), No. 80): The plaintiff's new diesel truck produced excessive engine noise. The dealer claimed that the problem was caused by the owner's engine alterations. The plaintiff was awarded the $5,000 cost of repairing the engine through an independent dealer.

Magna Management Ltd. v. Volkswagen Canada Inc. (May 27, 1988; Vancouver (B.C.C.A.); No. CA006037): This precedent-setting case allowed the plaintiff to keep his new $48,325 VW while awarding him $37,101—three years after the car was purchased. The problems were centred on poor engine performance. The jury accepted the plaintiff's view that the car was practically worthless with its inherent defects.

Maughan v. Silver's Garage Ltd. (Nova Scotia Supreme Court; 6 B.L.R., No. 303, N.S.C. (2nd), No. 278): The plaintiff leased a defective backhoe. The manufacturer had to reimburse the plaintiff's losses because the warranty wasn't honoured. The court rejected the manufacturer's contention that the contract's exclusion clause protected the company from lawsuits for damages resulting from a latent defect.

Murphy v. Penney Motors Ltd. (1979) (23 Nfld. & P.E.I.R.; No. 152, 61 A.P.R., No. 152 (Nfld. T.D.)): This Newfoundland trucker found that his vehicle's engine problems took his new trailer off the road for 129 days during a seven-month period. The judge awarded all repair costs, as well as compensation for business losses, and cancelled the sale.

Murray v. Sperry Rand Corp. (Ontario Supreme Court; 5 B.L.R., No. 284): The seller, dealer, and manufacturer were all held liable for breach of warranty when a forage harvester did not perform as advertised in the sales brochure or as promised by the sales agent. The plaintiff was given his money back and reimbursed for his economic loss, based on the amount his harvesting usually earned. The court held that the advertising was a warranty.

Oliver v. Courtesy Chrysler (1983) Ltd. (1992) (11 B.C.A.C., No. 169): This new car had numerous defects over a three-year period, which the dealer attempted to fix to no avail. The plaintiff put the car in storage and sued the dealer for the purchase price. The court ruled that the car wasn't roadworthy and that the plaintiff couldn't be blamed for putting it in storage rather than selling it and purchasing another vehicle. The purchase price was refunded, minus $1,500 for each year the plaintiff used the car.

Olshaski Farms Ltd. v. Skene Farm Equipment Ltd. (January 9, 1987; Alberta Court of Queen's Bench; 49 Alta. L.R. (2nd), No. 249): The plaintiff's Massey-Ferguson combine caught fire after the manufacturer had sent two notices to dealers informing them of a defect that could cause a fire. The judge ruled under the *Sale of Goods Act* that the balance of probabilities indicated that the manufacturing defect caused the fire, even though there wasn't any direct evidence proving that the defect existed.

Western Pacific Tank Lines Ltd. v. Brentwood Dodge (June 2, 1975; B.C.S.C., No. 30945-74; Judge Meredith): The court awarded the plaintiff $8,600 and cancelled the sale of a new Chrysler New Yorker with badly adjusted doors, water leaks into the interior, and electrical short circuits.

Leasing

Ford Motor Credit v. Bothwell (December 3, 1979; Ontario County Court (Middlesex); No. 9226-T; Judge Macnab): The defendant leased a 1977 Ford truck that had frequent engine problems, characterized by stalling and hard starting. After complaining for one year and driving 35,000 km (21,750 mi.), the defendant cancelled the lease. Ford Credit sued for the money owing on the lease. Judge Macnab cancelled the lease and ordered Ford Credit to repay 70 percent of the amount paid during the leasing period. Ford Credit was also ordered to refund repair costs, even though the corporation claimed that it should not be held responsible for Ford's failure to honour its warranty.

Schryvers v. Richport Ford Sales (May 18, 1993; B.C.S.C., No. C917060; Justice Tysoe): The court awarded $17,578.47, plus damages, to a couple who paid thousands of dollars more in unfair and hidden leasing charges than if they had simply purchased their Ford Explorer and Escort. The court found that this price difference constituted a deceptive, unconscionable act or practice, in contravention of the *Trade Practices Act*, R.S.B.C. 1979, c. 406.

Judge Tysoe concluded that the total of the general damages awarded to the Schryvers for both vehicles would be $11,578.47. He then proceeded to give the following reasons for awarding an additional $6,000 in punitive damages:

> Little wonder Richport Ford had a contest for the salesperson who could persuade the most customers to acquire their vehicles by way of a lease transaction. I consider the actions of Richport Ford to be sufficiently flagrant and high-handed to warrant an award of punitive damages.
>
> There must be a disincentive to suppliers in respect of intentionally deceptive trade practices. If no punitive damages are awarded for intentional violations of the legislation, suppliers will continue to conduct their businesses in a manner that involves deceptive trade practices because they will have nothing to lose. In this case I believe that the appropriate amount of punitive damages is the extra profit Richport Ford endeavoured to make as a result of its deceptive acts. I therefore award punitive damages against Richport Ford in the amount of $6,000.

Salvador v. Setay Motors/Queenstown Chev-Olds (Hamilton Small Claims Court; Case No. 1621/95): Robert Salvador was awarded $2,000 plus costs from Queenstown Leasing. The court found that the company should have tried harder to sell the leased vehicle, and at a higher price, when the "open lease" expired.

Incidentally, about 3,700 dealers in 39 American states paid between $3,500 and $8,000 each in 2004 to settle an investigation of allegations that they and Ford Motor Credit Co. overcharged customers who terminated their leases early.

See also:

- *Barber v. Inland Truck Sales* (11 D.L.R. (3rd), No. 469)
- *Canadian-Dominion Leasing v. Suburban Super Drug Ltd. (1966)* (56 D.L.R. (2nd), No. 43)
- *Neilson v. Atlantic Rentals Ltd. (1974)* (8 N.B.R. (2nd), No. 594)
- *Volvo Canada v. Fox* (December 13, 1979; New Brunswick Court of Queen's Bench; No. 1698/77/C; Judge Stevenson)
- *Western Tractor v. Dyck* (7 D.L.R. (3rd), No. 535)

Return of security deposit

Dealers routinely keep much of their lease customers' security deposits when their leases expire. However, that action can always be challenged in court. In the following claim, settled out of court, Ontario lawyer Harvey Goldstein forced GMAC and a GM dealer to refund his $525 security deposit:

1. The Plaintiff Claims:
   (A) Return of his security deposit of $525.00; and a finding that no amount is owing to the Defendants;
   (B) Alternatively, damages in the above amount;
   (C) Prejudgment interest on $525.00 at the rate of 2% per month (24% per annum) from June 22, 2005, to the date of this Claim, and thereafter on the date of payment or Judgment at the rate of 4% per annum, pursuant to Section 128 of the *Courts of Justice Act*, R.S.O. (1990) as amended;
   (D) Post-judgment interest at the post-judgment rate of interest, pursuant to Section 129 of the *Courts of Justice Act*, R. S. O. (1990) as amended;
   (E) His costs of this action;
   (F) Punitive damages in an amount to be determined; and
   (G) Such further and other relief as this Honorable Court deems just and proper.
4. On or about June 10, 2005, the Plaintiff advised the Defendant North York Chevrolet Oldsmobile Ltd that he wanted it to inspect the said vehicle for chargeable damage prior to its return or that he be present when it was inspected after its return to the said Defendant.
5. The said Defendant advised that it had no control over the inspection process and that the Defendant GMAC Leaseco Limited would inspect the vehicle only after the lease expired, the vehicle was returned to the dealer and the Plaintiff was not present.

6. The Plaintiff sent an email on June 10, 2005 to the Defendant GMAC Leaseco Limited asking it for an inspection prior to the vehicle being returned.
7. The said Defendant did not respond to the request.
8. The Plaintiff called and spoke with a representative of the said Defendant on June 17, and wrote her a letter sent by fax the same day, again asking that an inspection be scheduled in his presence. The said Defendant did not respond to the letter.
9. On June 23, 2005, the Plaintiff again called the said Defendant. He was told that it had no record of the vehicle being returned to the dealership.
10. Shortly thereafter, the Plaintiff called the Defendant North York Chevrolet Oldsmobile Ltd to enquire as to the status of his security deposit. The said Defendant advised that it had no record of the vehicle being returned to it.
11. Not having heard from either Defendant, the Plaintiff called the Defendant GMAC Leaseco Limited on July 15, 2005. He was advised that he owed the said Defendant $550.00, less the amount of the security deposit held by it. He was further advised that details of its claim to that amount could be found on the said Defendant's website. He was told that it did not inspect the said vehicle until July 7, 2005, 15 days after it was left in the dealership's service bay. He was told that the vehicle was at an auction and that he could not inspect the alleged damages for which the Defendants claimed compensation. He was advised that no adjustment would be made to their claim even though the vehicle was returned with 20,000.00 kilometers less than allowed by the lease agreement. Further, he was told that the alleged damages to the vehicle were not repaired prior to sending it to auction.
12. The Plaintiff denies that the vehicle required repairs claimed by the Defendants and puts them to the strict proof thereof.
13. The Plaintiff further claims that the process by which the Defendants seek to claim compensation from him is unfair, open to abuse and contrary to the principles of natural justice. The Defendants pay the fee of the alleged independent inspectors and deny the Plaintiff the opportunity to dispute the charges in any meaningful fashion. Further, its delay in inspecting the vehicle for 15 days, leaves open the question of when, if ever, the damages occurred.

Repairs: Faulty Diagnosis

Davies v. Alberta Motor Association (August 13, 1991; Alberta Provincial Court, Civil Division; No. P9090106097; Judge Moore): The plaintiff had a used 1985 Nissan Pulsar NX checked out by the AMA's Vehicle Inspection Service prior to buying it. The car passed with flying colours. A month later, the clutch was replaced, and then numerous electrical problems ensued. At that time, another garage discovered that the car had been involved in a major accident, had a bent

frame and a leaking radiator, and was unsafe to drive. The court awarded the plaintiff $1,578.40 plus three years of interest. The judge held that the AMA set itself out as an expert and should have spotted the car's defects. The AMA's defence—that it was not responsible for errors—was thrown out. The court held that a disclaimer clause could not protect the association from a fundamental breach of contract.

False Advertising: Vehicle Not as Ordered

When you're buying a new vehicle, the seller can't misrepresent the vehicle through a lie or a failure to disclose important information. Anything that varies from what one would commonly expect, or from the seller's representation, must be disclosed prior to signing the contract. Typical scenarios are odometer turnbacks, accident damage, used or leased cars sold as new, new vehicles that are the wrong colour or the wrong model year, or vehicles that lack promised options or standard features.

Goldie v. Golden Ears Motors (1980) Ltd. (Port Coquitlam; June 27, 2000; British Columbia Small Claims Court; Case No. CO8287; Justice Warren): In a well-written eight-page judgment, the court awarded plaintiff Goldie $5,000 for engine repairs on a 1990 Ford F-150 pickup in addition to $236 court costs. The dealer was found to have misrepresented the mileage and sold a used vehicle that didn't meet Section 8.01 of the provincial motor vehicle regulations (unsafe tires, defective exhaust, and headlights).

In rejecting the seller's defence that he disclosed all information "to the best of his knowledge and belief," as stipulated in the sales contract, Justice Warren stated the following:

> The words "to the best of your knowledge and belief" do not allow someone to be willfully blind to defects or to provide incorrect information. I find as a fact that the business made no effort to fulfill its duty to comply with the requirements of this form.... The defendant has been reckless in its actions. More likely, it has actively deceived the claimant into entering into this contract. I find the conduct of the defendant has been reprehensible throughout the dealings with the claimant.

This judgment closes a loophole that sellers have used to justify their misrepresentation, and it allows for the cancellation of the sale and damages if the vehicle doesn't meet highway safety regulations.

Lister v. Scheilding (c.o.b. Kar-Lon Motors) [1983] (O.J. No. 907 (Co. Ct.)): Here, the plaintiff was entitled to rescind the contract because of the defendant's false representation. The defendant failed to state that the motor had been changed and was not the original motor.

MacDonald v. Equilease Co. Ltd. (January 18, 1979; Ontario Supreme Court; Judge O'Driscoll): The plaintiff leased a truck that was misrepresented as having an axle stronger than it really was. The court awarded the plaintiff damages for repairs and set aside the lease.

Seich v. Festival Ford Sales Ltd. (1978) (6 Alta. L.R. (2nd), No. 262): The plaintiff bought a used truck from the defendant after being assured that it had a new motor and transmission. It didn't, and the court awarded the plaintiff $6,400.

Bilodeau v. Sud Auto (Quebec Court of Appeal; No. 09-000751-73; Judge Tremblay): This appeals court cancelled the contract and held that a car can't be sold as new or as a demonstrator if it has ever been rented, leased, sold, or titled to anyone other than the dealer.

Chenel v. Bel Automobile (1981) Inc. (August 27, 1976; Quebec Superior Court (Quebec); Judge Desmeules): The plaintiff didn't receive Jacob brakes, essential to transporting sand in hilly regions, with his new Ford truck. The court awarded the plaintiff $27,000, representing the purchase price of the vehicle less the money he earned while using the truck.

Lasky v. Royal City Chrysler Plymouth (February 18, 1987; Ontario High Court of Justice; 59 O.R. (2nd), No. 323): The plaintiff bought a 4-cylinder 1983 Dodge 600, which had been represented by the salesman as being a 6-cylinder model. After putting 40,000 km on the vehicle over a 22-month period, the buyer was given her money back, without interest, under the provincial *Business Practices Act*.

Rourke v. Gilmore (January 16, 1928; *Ontario Weekly Notes*, Vol. XXXIII, p. 292): Before discovering that his new car was really used, the plaintiff drove it for over a year. For this reason, the contract couldn't be cancelled. However, the appeals court instead awarded damages for $500, which was quite a sum in 1928!

Secret Warranty Claims

It's common practice for manufacturers to secretly extend their warranties to cover components with a high failure rate. Customers who complain vigorously get extended warranty compensation in the form of "goodwill" adjustments.

François Chong v. Marine Drive Imported Cars Ltd. and Honda Canada Inc. (May 17, 1994; British Columbia Provincial Small Claims Court; No. 92-06760; Judge C.L. Bagnall): Mr. Chong was the first owner of a 1983 Honda Accord with 134,000 km on the odometer. He had six engine camshafts replaced—four under Honda "goodwill" programs, one where he paid part of the repairs, and one via a small claims court judgment. (Please note that Honda's earlier engine problems and its arrogant attitude have since moderated a bit.)

In his ruling, Judge Bagnall agreed with Chong and ordered Honda and the dealer to each pay half of the $835.81 repair bill for the following reasons:

The defendants assert that the warranty which was part of the contract for purchase of the car encompassed the entirety of their obligation to the claimant, and that it expired in February 1985. The replacements of the camshaft after that date were paid for wholly or in part by Honda as a "goodwill gesture." The time has come for these gestures to cease, according to the witness for Honda. As well, he pointed out to me that the most recent replacement of the camshaft was paid for by Honda and that, therefore, the work would not be covered by Honda's usual warranty of 12 months from date of repair. Mr. Wall, who testified for Honda, told me there was no question that this situation with Mr. Chong's engine was an unusual state of affairs. He said that a camshaft properly maintained can last anywhere from 24,000 to 500,000 km. He could not offer any suggestion as to why the car keeps having this problem.

The claimant has convinced me that the problems he is having with rapid breakdown of camshafts in his car is due to a defect, which was present in the engine at the time that he purchased the car. The problem first arose during the warranty period and in my view has never been properly identified nor repaired.

Punitive Damages

Punitive damages (also known as "exemplary damages") allow the plaintiff to get compensation that exceeds his or her losses as a deterrent to those who carry out dishonest or negligent practices. These kinds of judgments, common in the U.S., sometimes reach hundreds of millions of dollars. Canadian courts, however, seldom award substantial punitive damages.

Nevertheless, there have been a few relatively recent cases where the Supreme Court of Canada has shocked the business establishment by levying huge exemplary damage awards. One such case was the *Whiten v. Pilot Insurance Co.* decision rendered in 2002. In this case, the plaintiff's home caught fire and burned to the ground, destroying all of the home's contents and killing three pet cats. Pilot Insurance made a single $5,000 payment for living expenses and covered the family's rent for a couple of months, and then they cut off the rent payments without forewarning the family. The insurance claim went to trial, based on the respondent's allegation that the family had torched their own home, even though the local fire chief, the respondent's own expert investigator, and its initial expert all said there was no evidence whatsoever of arson. The original trial jury awarded the plaintiff compensatory damages and $1 million in punitive damages. Pilot Insurance fought this decision at the Court of Appeal, where the punitive damages award was reduced to $100,000. The case was then taken all the way to the Supreme Court, where the trial jury's unprecedented award of $1 million was restored:

The jury's award of punitive damages, though high, was within rational limits. The respondent insurer's conduct towards the appellant was exceptionally reprehensible. It forced her to put at risk her only remaining asset (the $345,000 insurance claim) plus $320,000 in costs that she did not have. The denial of the claim was designed to force her to make an unfair settlement for less than she was entitled to. The conduct

> was planned and deliberate and continued for over two years, while the financial situation of the appellant grew increasingly desperate. The jury evidently believed that the respondent knew from the outset that its arson defence was contrived and unsustainable. Insurance contracts are sold by the insurance industry and purchased by members of the public for peace of mind. The more devastating the loss, the more the insured may be at the financial mercy of the insurer, and the more difficult it may be to challenge a wrongful refusal to pay the claim.

Punitive damages are rarely awarded in Canadian courts against automakers. When they are given out, it's usually for sums less than $100,000. In *Prebushewski v. Dodge City Auto (1985) Ltd. and Chrysler Canada Ltd.*, the plaintiff got $25,000 in a judgment handed down in 2001 and confirmed by the Supreme Court in 2005. The plaintiff's 1996 Ram's running lights had shorted and caused her truck to burn to the ground, and Chrysler had refused her claim. The court basically said aggrieved car owners may sue for much more than the depreciated value of what they bought under provincial consumer protection statutes. The Supreme Court reaffirmed the power of the lower courts to assess an additional financial penalty to punish automakers that treat their customers unfairly and to ensure they don't repeat the offence.

Vlchek v. Koshel (1988; 44 C.C.L.T. 314, B.C.S.C., No. B842974): The plaintiff was seriously injured when she was thrown from a Honda all-terrain cycle on which she had been riding as a passenger. The court allowed for punitive damages because the manufacturer was well aware of the injuries likely to be caused by the cycle. Specifically, the court ruled that there is no firm and inflexible principle of law stipulating that punitive or exemplary damages must be denied unless the defendant's acts are specifically directed against the plaintiff. The court may apply punitive damages "where the defendant's conduct has been indiscriminate of focus, but reckless or malicious in its character. Intent to injure the plaintiff need not be present, so long as intent to do the injurious act can be shown."

See also:

- *Granek v. Reiter* (Ontario Court, General Division; No. 35/741)
- *Morrison v. Sharp* (Ontario Court, General Division; No. 43/548)
- *Schryvers v. Richport Ford Sales* (May 18, 1993; B.C.S.C., No. C917060; Judge Tysoe)
- *Varleg v. Angeloni* (B.C.S.C., No. 41/301)

Provincial business practices acts cover false, misleading, or deceptive representations and allow for punitive damages should the unfair practice toward the consumer amount to an unconscionable representation (see *Canadian Encyclopedic Digest (C.E.D.)*, Third Edition, s. 76, pages 140–145). And here are some specific cases to keep in mind:

- Exemplary damages are justified where compensatory damages are insufficient to deter and punish. See *Walker et al. v. CFTO Ltd. et al.* (1978; 59 O.R. (2nd), No. 104; Ontario C.A.).

- Exemplary damages can be awarded in cases where the defendant's conduct was "cavalier." See *Ronald Elwyn Lister Ltd. et al. v. Dayton Tire Canada Ltd.* (1985; 52 O.R. (2nd), No. 89; Ontario C.A.).
- The primary purpose of exemplary damages is to prevent the defendant and all others from doing similar wrongs. See *Fleming v. Spracklin* (1921).
- Disregard of the public's interest, lack of preventive measures, and a callous attitude all merit exemplary damages. See *Coughlin v. Kuntz* (1989; 2 C.C.L.T. (2nd); B.C.C.A.).
- Punitive damages can be awarded for mental distress. See *Ribeiro v. Canadian Imperial Bank of Commerce* (1992; Ontario Reports 13 (3rd)) and *Brown v. Waterloo Regional Board of Commissioners of Police* (1992; 37 O.R. (2nd)).

In the States, punitive damage awards have been particularly generous. Do you remember the Alabama fellow who won a multi-million-dollar award because his new BMW had been repainted before he bought it but the seller didn't tell him so? The case was *BMW of North America, Inc. v. Gore* (517 U.S. 559, 116 S. Ct. 1589; 1996). In this case, the U.S. Supreme Court cut the damages award and established standards for jury awards of punitive damages. Nevertheless, million-dollar awards are still quite common.

For example, an Oregon dealer learned that a $1 million punitive damages award wasn't excessive under *Gore* and under Oregon law. The Oregon Supreme Court determined that the standard it set forth in *Oberg v. Honda Motor Company* (888 P.2d 8; 1996), on remand from the Supreme Court, survived the Supreme Court's subsequent ruling in *Gore*. The court held that the jury's $1 million punitive damages award, 87 times larger than the plaintiff's compensatory damages in *Parrott v. Carr Chevrolet, Inc.* (2001 Ore. LEXIS 1; January 11, 2001), wasn't excessive. In that case, Mark Parrott sued Carr Chevrolet, Inc., over a used 1983 Chevrolet Suburban under Oregon's *Unlawful Trade Practices Act*. The jury awarded Parrott $11,496 in compensatory damages and $1 million in punitive damages because the dealer failed to disclose collision damage to a new buyer.

Now that you know how to get the best deal for less money while protecting your rights, take a look at Part Three to see which cars and trucks to pick and which ones to avoid.

Part Three

RATINGS: THE GOOD, THE BAD, AND THE RISKY

Mediocre Minivans

It's been [27] years since Chrysler's first minivan and GM and Ford haven't been able to figure out how to build a good one yet. And do they care? Has anyone been fired? Has anyone resigned in shame? Do the CEOs of GM or Ford bang their heads against their walls because they can't build a minivan? No. They never say or do anything. They don't care, either.

JERRY FLYNT
www.thecarconnection.com
JUNE 19, 2006

The Death of Detroit

This week, in its yearly roundup, *Consumer Reports* reconfirmed the obvious: "The best vehicles are built by Honda, Subaru and Toyota. They make well-rounded cars that excel across the board, getting very good scores in our road tests and high marks in reliability from subscribers in our Annual Auto Survey." It went on: "Chrysler, which tied with Suzuki for last place in our 2008 ranking, fared even worse this year."

STEVE CHAPMAN
CHICAGO TRIBUNE
MARCH 4, 2009

Honda and Toyota stole the American minivan market.

It's tough rating new vehicles without pimping for the auto industry. First, smooth-talking automaker reps invite you to lunch and tell you how much they admire your work, but then they tell you how much better it would be if your approach was more "balanced." Throw in a few free trips to Japan and Europe, where you're coddled in five-star hotels and loaned specially prepared vehicles to "test drive." Predictably, the top guys—and I do mean *guys*—have very little to say. So the PR flacks concoct writing prizes for the "best" reports—the ones that repeat the industry's mantras.

Not wanting to offend their hosts, none of these captured scribes report on the companies' "secret" car warranties, fuel economy misrepresentation, or poor crashworthiness scores. Or, those with a *National Enquirer*–like bent could mention Hyundai's theft of Toyota's quality-control reports; GM's cover-up of a decade of engine intake manifold failures; Daewoo's, Mitsubishi's, and Hyundai's CEOs being charged with criminal activity; or VW's staffers' whore-mongering for its top executives to help lubricate the flow of ideas at off-site "business conferences." But they don't.

When I go to the various auto shows, I *do* mention these things to the press. And each time I do, I risk being thrown out. Fortunately, this happens rarely. The most vivid memory I have of this is when Ford's goons threw me out of the Toronto Auto Show in the mid-'70s. Ford's president later apologized for the "overzealous" action and then settled the Rusty Ford Owners' Association's $2.8 million in rust claims. This is a useful reminder that truth and balance are not what auto shows are about, and that car executives hear better through their rears than their ears.

Lemon-Aid follows these five simple rules:

- The best rating approach is to combine a driving test with an owners' survey of past models (only *Consumer Reports* and *Lemon-Aid* do this).
- Owner responses must come from a large owner pool (over a million responses from *CR* subscribers, for example). Anecdotal responses should then be cross-referenced, updated, and given depth and specificity through NHTSA's safety complaint prism. Responses must again be cross-referenced through automaker internal service bulletins to determine the extent of a defect over a specific model and model year range and to alert owners to problems likely to occur.
- Rankings should be predicated upon important characteristics measured over a significant period of time, unlike "Car of the Year" contests, owner-perceived value, or J.D. Power–surveyed problems (which are recorded after only three months of ownership).
- Ratings must come from unimpeachable sources. There should be no conflicts of interest, such as advertising, consultant ties, or self-serving tests done under ideal conditions.
- Tested cars must be bought or rented, not borrowed from the car company, and serviced, not pampered as part of a journalists' fleet lent out for ranking purposes.

Responsible auto raters shouldn't hit up dealers or manufacturers for free "test" vehicles under any circumstances, but most auto columnists and some consumer groups compromise their integrity by doing so. Test vehicles should be rented or borrowed from an owner. I've adopted this practice from my early experience as a consumer reporter. Nissan asked me to test drive its new 1974 240Z—no strings attached. I took the car for a week, had it examined by an independent garage, spoke with satisfied and dissatisfied owners, and accessed internal service bulletins and government-logged owner safety complaints. The car's poor brake design apparently made it unsafe to drive, and I said so in my report. Nissan sued me for $4 million, fixed the brakes through a "product improvement campaign," and then dropped the lawsuit two years later. I was never offered another car.

What Makes a Good Car or Truck?

The vehicle should first live up to the promises made by the manufacturer and dealer. It must be reasonably priced, provide safe highway performance, protect occupants in a crash, be fuel-efficient, and be capable of lasting 10–15 years; it should cost no more than about $800 a year to maintain; and it should provide you with a fair resale value a few years down the road. Parts should be affordable and easily available, and servicing shouldn't be hard to find or performed incompetently.

And don't believe for one moment that the more you spend, the better the vehicle. For example, most Hondas are as good as more-expensive Acuras. The same is true of Toyota and Lexus. Even more surprising, some luxury makes, like Jaguar, give you a dressed-up Ford at a "luxury-car" price. The extra money buys you only more features of dubious value and newer, unproven technology like rear-mounted video cameras and failure-prone electronic gadgetry.

In terms of road performance, at the very minimum every vehicle must be able to merge safely onto a highway and have adequate passing power for two-lane roads. Steering feel and handling should inspire confidence. The suspension ought to provide a reasonably well-controlled ride on most road surfaces. Ideally, the passenger compartment will be roomy enough to accommodate passengers comfortably on extended trips. The noise level should not become tiresome and annoying. As a rule, handling and ride comfort are inversely proportional—good handling requires a stiff suspension, which pounds the kidneys.

Definitions of Terms

Key Facts

This year, we have added "Ground clearance" to our summary of key facts to show how well different vehicles may handle off-road areas. Also, we have included the "Origin" of each vehicle, for readers who prefer to buy vehicles made locally, and "Sales" data, for those who wish to know the sales trend for a particular model. Vehicles that aren't selling well usually carry the heftiest discounts and/or rebates; check the "Cost Analysis" section for a vehicle's predicted price negotiability.

Prices: We list the manufacturer's suggested retail price (MSRP) range, in effect at press time and applicable to standard models. You can confirm the MSRP figure by accessing each manufacturer's website. Destination charges and the predelivery inspection (PDI) fee are quasi-fraudulent "back doors" into your wallet. Offer half of the requested amount. Also, don't fall for the $99–$475 "administration fee" scam, unless the bottom-line price is so tempting that it won't make much difference. Sticking to your principles is one thing; not losing an attractive deal is another.

Tow limit: Note that towing capacities differ depending on the kind of powertrain/suspension package or towing package you buy. And remember that there's a difference between how a vehicle is rated for cargo capacity or payload and how heavy a boat or trailer it can pull. Do not purchase any new vehicle without receiving from the dealer very clear information, in writing, about a vehicle's towing capacity and the kind of special equipment you'll need to meet your requirements. Have the towing capacity and necessary equipment written into the contract.

Load capacity: This is defined as the safe combined weight of occupants and cargo (such as luggage). It is taken from the manufacturers' rating or from *Consumer Reports*' calculated safe load. Exceeding this maximum weight can adversely affect a vehicle's handling, or make it unstable.

Ratings

We rate vehicles on a scale of one to five stars, with five stars as our top ranking. We use owner complaints, confidential technical service bulletins (TSBs), and test drives to ferret out serious factory-related defects, design deficiencies, or servicing glitches.

This guide emphasizes important new features that add to a vehicle's safety, reliability, road performance, and comfort, and we point out those changes that are merely gadgets and styling revisions. Also noted are important improvements to be made in the future, or the dropping of a model line. In addition to its overall rating, each vehicle's strong and weak points are summarized.

Interestingly, some vehicles that are identical but marketed and serviced by different automakers may have different ratings. This variation occurs because servicing and after-warranty assistance may be better within one dealer network than another.

It takes about six months to acquire enough information for a fair-minded evaluation of a car's or truck's first year on the market, unless the vehicle has been available elsewhere under another name. Most new cars and trucks hit the market before all of the bugs have been worked out, so it would be irresponsible to recommend them before owner reports and internal service bulletins give them an "okay." Sadly, as we have seen with Toyota's delayed acceleration and GM's poorly shifting transmission, it may take several years to correct some factory powertrain glitches.

Recommended: This rating indicates a "Best Buy," and it's almost exclusively the domain of Asian automakers. "Recommended" vehicles usually combine a high level of crashworthiness with good road performance, few safety-related complaints, decent reliability, and a better-than-average resale value. Servicing is readily available, and parts are inexpensive and easy to find.

Above Average: Vehicles in this class are pretty good choices. They aren't perfect, but they're often more reasonably priced than their competition. Most vehicles in this category have quality construction, good durability, and plenty of safety features as standard equipment. On the downside, they may have expensive parts and servicing, too many safety-related complaints, or only satisfactory warranty performance—one or all of which may have disqualified them from the Recommended category.

Average: Some deficiencies or flaws make these good second choices. In many cases, certain components are prone to premature wear or breakdown, or don't perform as well as the competition. An "Average" rating can also be attributed to such factors as substandard assembly quality, lack of a solid long-term reliability record, a substantial number of safety-related complaints, or a deficient parts and service network.

Below Average: This rating category denotes an unreliable or poorly performing vehicle that may also have a poor safety record. Getting an extended warranty is advised.

Not Recommended: Chances of having major breakdowns or safety-related failures are omnipresent. Inadequate road performance and poor dealer service, among other factors, can make owning one of these vehicles a traumatic and expensive experience, no matter how cheaply it's sold.

Vehicles that have not been on the road long enough to assess, or that are sold in such small numbers that owner feedback is insufficient, are either "Not Recommended" or left unrated.

Quality and reliability

Lemon-Aid bases its quality and reliability evaluations in the "Rating" and "Overview" sections on owner comments, confidential manufacturer service bulletins, and government reports from NHTSA safety complaint files. We also draw on the knowledge and expertise of professionals working in the automotive marketplace, including mechanics and fleet owners. The aim is to have a wide range of unbiased (and irrefutable) data on quality, reliability, durability, and ownership costs. Allowances are made for the number of vehicles sold versus the number of complaints, as well as for the seriousness of problems reported and the average number of problems reported by each owner.

Technical Service Bulletins (TSBs) give the most probable cause of factory-related defects on previous model years that will likely be carried over to the 2010 versions. TSBs are reliable sources of information because manufacturers depend on the dealer corrections outlined in their bulletins until a permanent, cost-effective engineering solution is found at the factory, which often takes several model years with lots of experimentation.

As you read through the ratings, you'll quickly discover that most Japanese and South Korean manufacturers are far ahead of Chrysler, Ford, and GM in maintaining a high level of quality control in their vehicles (European makes are even worse performers).

Safety features and crashworthiness

Some of the main features weighed are a model's crashworthiness scores and the availability of front and side airbags, effective head restraints, assisted stability and traction control, and front and rearward visibility.

Frontal and side crash protection figures are taken from the National Highway Traffic Safety Administration's (NHTSA) New Car Assessment Program. For the front crash test, vehicles are crashed into a fixed barrier, head-on, at 57 km/h

NHTSA DRIVER SIDE-IMPACT PROTECTION (2006–07 DODGE GRAND CARAVAN WITHOUT SIDE AIRBAGS)

Save vehicles	Vehicle	Frontal Star Rating » based on risk of head & chest injury		Side Star Rating » based on risk of chest injury		Rollover Rating	
		Driver	Passenger	Front Seat	Rear Seat	2 wheel drive	4 wheel drive
☐	2006 Dodge Grand Caravan (Van)	★★★★★	★★★★★	★★★★★	★★★★★	★★★★	
☐	2007 Dodge Grand Caravan (Van)	★★★★★	★★★★★	★★★★★	★★★★★	★★★★	

IIHS DRIVER SIDE-IMPACT PROTECTION (2006–07 DODGE GRAND CARAVAN WITHOUT SIDE AIRBAGS)

OVERALL EVALUATION: P

	Injury measures			Head protection	Structure/safety cage
	Head/neck	Torso	Pelvis/leg		
Driver	A	P	G	P	A
Rear passenger	G	G	G	M	

Note: **P** = Poor; **M** = Marginal; **A** = Acceptable; **G** = Good

NHTSA gives Grand Caravans far more generous occupant protection ratings than IIHS due to different crash speeds and the use of a different barrier. It's not surprising car manufacturers prefer to cite the NHTSA scores.

(35 mph). NHTSA uses star rankings to show the likelihood, expressed as a percentage, of belted occupants being seriously injured. The higher the number of stars, the greater the protection.

NHTSA's side crash test represents an intersection-type collision with a 1,368 kg (3,015 lb.) barrier moving at 62 km/h (38.5 mph) into a standing vehicle. The moving barrier is covered with material that has "give" to replicate the front of a car.

The Insurance Institute for Highway Safety (IIHS) rates head-restraint and frontal, offset, and side crash protection as "Good," "Acceptable," "Marginal," or "Poor." In the Institute's 64 km/h (40 mph) offset test, 40 percent of the total width of each vehicle strikes a barrier on the driver's side. The barrier's deformable face is made of an aluminum honeycomb, which makes the forces in the test similar to those involved in a frontal offset crash between two vehicles of the same weight, each going just less than 64 km/h.

Though IIHS's 50 km/h (31 mph) side-impact test is carried out at a slower speed than NHTSA's side test, the barrier uses a front end shaped to simulate the typical front end of a pickup or SUV. The Institute also includes the degree of head injury in its ratings.

A vehicle's rollover resistance rating is an estimate of its risk of rolling over in a single-vehicle crash, not a prediction of the likelihood of a crash. The lowest-rated vehicles (one star) are at least four times more likely to roll over than the highest-rated vehicles (five stars) when involved in a single-vehicle crash.

Cost Analysis and Best Alternatives

Fall prices for the 2010 models aren't much higher than last year's prices, because Detroit automakers have ramped up generous discounts and rebates to move the millions of cars and trucks left over in dealer inventories. But forget about leasing. Only the Asian and European automakers are offering leasing deals.

Warranty: A manufacturer's warranty is a legal commitment. It promises that the vehicle will perform in the normal and customary manner for which it is designed. If a part malfunctions or fails (unless it's because of owner negligence or poor maintenance), the dealer must fix or replace the defective part or parts and then bill the automaker or warranty company for all of the part and labour costs. Warranties are an important factor in *Lemon-Aid*'s ratings. Unfortunately, it has been our experience that most automakers cheat on their warranty obligations and inflate the costs of scheduled maintenance work.

Most new-vehicle warranties fall into two categories: bumper-to-bumper, for a period of three to five years, and powertrain, for up to 5 years/100,000 km. Automakers sometimes charge an additional $50–$100 fee for repairs requested by purchasers of used vehicles with unexpired base warranties. For snowbirds, the federal and provincial governments can charge GST and sales tax on warranty and non-warranty repairs done south of the border—so beware. Also, keep in mind that some automakers, like Honda, may not honour your warranty if a vehicle is purchased in the States and registered in Canada.

A third kind of warranty, the 60-day "money-back" guarantee, is now offered with most GM vehicles. Although General Motors says few buyers have returned their purchase, owners report it is not for lack of trying. Taxes, extra wear and tear charges, mileage limitations and other hurdles, usually prompts dissatisfied customers to choose another vehicle in the dealer's stock.

GM gave money-back guarantees to boost Saturn sales over a decade ago. Unfortunately, new Saturn sales remained in the basement as owners cited the cars' poor reliability and mediocre highway performance. Only the recently added Saturn Outlook SUV has changed that perception.

AMERICAN VEHICLES

GM's Failure

GM's fall from grace is not about its products, per se. It's about the company's ongoing and abject failure to create compelling brands that sell products (and services) that embody the brands' promise. Never mind the LaCrosse vs. the ES350. Who would buy a Buick instead of a Lexus? Or a Chevrolet instead of a Honda? The people who would are, and the ones that don't, won't. No head-to-head model throwdown is going to change the overall dynamic, and/or the minds of people who vote with their wallet.

www.thetruthaboutcars.com/general-motors-zombie-watch
JULY 6, 2009

Government Motors

General Motors is now co-owned by the American taxpayer and labor unions. As a Briton, I find this development astonishing. It repeats the mistakes of the 1970s Labor government, which essentially killed off the British auto industry. America should avoid the same mistake.

WASHINGTON EXAMINER
MAY 4, 2009

They were once called the American Big Three. Then, defining an American car became an impossible task, with so many vehicles built overseas or assembled in Mexico or Brazil, so they were called the Big Three. Then several years ago, sales plummeted as Toyota and Volkswagen gained market share and took the top spots, and Chrysler, General Motors, and Ford became the Detroit Three. Now, with Chrysler and General Motors emerging from bankruptcy and Ford just getting its second wind, we have come into the era of Government Motors.

Over the past year, the Canadian and American governments have squandered tens of billions of dollars on the top three automakers, and have received little for their investment. *Lemon-Aid* predicted two bankruptcies and $50 billion in handouts, and a year later, that's what we got: two bankrupt automakers, thousands of closed dealerships, hundreds of suppliers closing their doors, and tens of thousands of employees without jobs.

Both car companies emerged from bankruptcy in record time, after giving the shaft to their dealers, the unions, and customers by walking away from their obligations. Now, whether Chrysler, Ford, and General Motors can compete in a new global economy will depend upon one thing: the quality of the vehicles they will build. Lemon-aid is not optimistic.

This is the scary part. Sure, the former Detroit Three can build high-performance cars, and they can even build little econoboxes. But can they build either kind of vehicle so that it is reliable? Most of the buying public thinks not. And my 40 years of writing *Lemon-Aid* says the public is right.

So what does the future hold for Chrysler, Ford, and General Motors?

Not much. We will have more bankruptcies, more begging for handouts from Ottawa and Washington, and the busting up of the different auto divisions to be sold to China, India, and various equity investors for pennies on the dollar. An industry that was riding high with 16 million cars sold annually will learn to make do with 11 million sold.

We will see many more fuel efficient vehicles in the $10,000–$14,000 range. Most of the fuel-efficient 2010 cars are co-productions with Asian and European automakers. The Asian link is a plus for reliability because many of the Asian platforms and components, like the Mazda6 parts found in Ford's Fusion, have been used and improved over many years and are much more dependable than their Detroit counterparts. In fact, *Consumer Reports* has given the Fusion high marks for safety and overall performance. But be careful: like Chrysler's Caliber and a number of other co-ventures, such as the upcoming European-derived Ford Fiesta, reliability and real-world fuel economy vary considerably.

Another trend that will be obvious this year is the ever-increasing number of models that will employ hybrid powertrains. It's an innovation that has been used for years, most successfully in the Ford Escape and Toyota Prius, though their hybrid fuel-saving claims have more in common with Harry Potter than the Society of Automotive Engineers.

Ford's Fusion looks good and performs well, but the Honda Accord gives better fuel economy and has a proven reliability record.

So, with the auto industry on its back and so many products to choose from, what should the prospective buyer of a Chrysler, Ford, or GM model do this year?

Be patient. Prices will nosedive this winter as our struggling economy tries to get back on its feet and a huge inventory of 2009 and 2010 models piles up in dealers' back lots. Car shoppers can then get some good buys at ridiculously low prices while the industry is in turmoil. On the other hand, some automakers and many dealers won't be around in the coming years to service or buy back the vehicle that today cost you so little. So, buy a vehicle that's been around for awhile, buy one that has sold in large volume, and finally, buy a vehicle that *Lemon-Aid* recommends as a "keeper" for a decade or two.

Chrysler

The Cheque Is in the Mail

The U.S. Treasury has sent the bankrupt remains of Chrysler LLC a default notice, saying the company failed to pay back a loan due June 30. Treasury sent the notice of default on Aug. 13, said old Chrysler, now known as Old Carco LLC, in a bankruptcy court filing today. The U.S. government lent Old Carco $3.34 billion to complete its bankruptcy, according to the filing.

Old Carco said it was negotiating with Treasury to "address" the default. The best assets of the old company were sold to a group led by SpA. Old Carco has now reported an $11.8 billion loss on the Fiat sale, leading to a net loss of $10.2 billion in June, court records show.

www.bloomberg.com
SEPTEMBER 4, 2009

Chrysler, as we know it, will likely be gone next year.

This company has no new products, and what it does have, nobody wants. Of the three automakers we call "American," Chrysler has the farthest to go in improving performance, quality, and reliability. Granted, the company has had beautifully styled cars like the 300 and high-performance models like the Viper; plus, its latest full-sized Ram 1500 pickup is noted for its impressive power and ride comfort. But reliability? Quality? Forget it.

2008 DODGE GRAND CARAVAN 3.8L V6

All Technical Service Bulletins

NUMBER	DATE	TITLE
23-014-09	05/07/2009	Interior—Integrated Child Seat Won't Stow Properly
23-13-09	05/06/2009	Body—Sliding Door Handle Inoperative In Freezing Temps
07-001-09	05/05/2009	Cooling System—Coolant Leak Around Radiator Cap
18-003-09A	04/04/2009	Engine Controls—MIL ON/DTC P0452/Driveability issues
08-006-09	03/19/2009	Audio System—RES Radio Clock Lockup
08-003-09	02/13/2009	Audio System—Radio Inop. After Battery Disconnect
08-002-09	02/04/2009	Instruments—Vehicle Information Center Setup
H16	01/28/2009	Campaign—Power Steering Return Hose Replacement
H30	01/20/2009	Campaign—Replacement Of Keyless Entry Transmitters
08-001-09	01/06/2009	Interior—3rd Row Power Seat Latching Problems
08-037-08	12/19/2008	Interior—3rd Row Power Folding Seat Malfunctions
18-025-08A	12/17/2008	Engine Controls—MIL ON/DTC P1607 Set
18-026-08A	12/17/2008	Engine Controls—Engine Compartment Whistling Noise

21-017-08A	12/16/2008	A/T Controls—Harsh Kickdown/Upshifts/Shift Bump
05-006-08	12/09/2008	Brakes—Abnormal Front Pad Wear/Squeal/Shudder
08-032-08	10/22/2008	Lighting—LED Turn Signal Indicator Serviceability
21-021-08	09/17/2008	A/T—Repair/Replacement Guidelines
24-008-08	09/04/2008	A/C—Airflow From Vents With A/C OFF
08-027-08	08/29/2008	Cell Phone—UConnect and Voice Recognition Inoperative
23-026-08	08/28/2008	Body—Rear Bumper Fascia Bulge/Bow or Bend
23-023-08	08/01/2008	Body—Howl/Honk Noise From A-Pillar/Windshield Area
23-022-08	07/02/2008	Body—Front Door Rattle/Door Glass Won't Roll Down
23-021-08	06/21/2008	Body—Roof Rack Howling Sound
H11	06/01/2008	Campaign—Radio Software Update
08-006-08A	05/29/2008	Electrical—Intermittent Driver Power Seat Functions
08-019-08	05/06/2008	Audio System—CD Loses Last Track After Ignition Cycle
08-018-08	05/03/2008	Computers/Controls—Cannot Data Record
H06	04/01/2008	Recall—Spark Plug Inspection/Replacement
24-004-08A	02/29/2008	A/C—Intermittent Mode Door Function
08-003-08	02/01/2008	Electrical—Hard Start/No Start/Dead Battery
14-001-08	01/16/2008	Fuel System—Slow Fuel Tank Fill/Early Nozzle Shut Off
08-032-07	12/21/2007	Instruments—Temperature Display Reverts to US Units
08-029-07	12/05/2007	Lighting—Color/Brightness Difference Between Headlamps
08-026-07A	12/05/2007	Interior—3rd Row Power Seat is Inoperative
08-024-07A	11/30/2007	Audio System—Distorted Sound From Speakers
23-046-07	10/30/2007	Body—Horizontal Paint Surface Etching
08-027-07	10/27/2007	Entertainment System—Video Screen Won't Power On
11-004-07	10/13/2007	Exhaust System—Rattle or Clunk Sound While Driving
23-044-07	10/10/2007	Body—Howling Noise From The Roof Rack
08-022-07	09/15/2007	Electrical—Courtesy Lamps ON/Liftgate Ajar Message
23-036-07	08/22/2007	Interior—Low Gloss Interior Trim Care Information
02-035-07	08/08/2007	Lighting—Information On Exterior Lamp Lens Fogging

Chrysler minivans, the automaker's most popular vehicles, have been around for decades and still suffer from inexcusable poor quality control, as do all of the company's products.

Type in "automatic transmission failures" and Google throws up a picture of a Chrysler minivan (well, not really). All kidding aside, Chrysler has gone from a company noted for engineering innovation and strong, high-performance muscle cars to stall-prone Valiants and Darts, rust-prone K-cars, and stow-in-the-floor minivan seats and cooled/heated cup holders.

About that quality thing. *Consumer Reports*' October 2009 edition says that two-thirds of Chrysler's models were below average and that the Chrysler Sebring convertible was the worst-rated car, with 2.8 times more problems than average. Other bottom-feeders: the Sebring/Avenger and Charger sedans, the Caliber hatchback, and the Liberty, Nitro, and Wrangler SUVs. *Consumer Reports* says it can't recommend any 2010 Chrysler model. Neither can *Lemon-Aid*.

The most apparent problem with Chrysler is its almost total dependence on trucks, SUVs, and minivans, aside from the few passenger cars it offers. And even those cars it does sell are huge, like the large, fuel-wasting Magnum, 300, and Charger. When gasoline was relatively cheap, "big" was profitable, but now, cheaply made small cars are more in demand—and Chrysler is coming to the party late and with little to offer.

CALIBER ★

bad buy

TECHNICAL DATA

PRICES: $15,995, *SXT:* $18.295 **FREIGHT:** $1,350 **ORIGIN:** U.S. **SALES:** Down 60%
POWERTRAIN (FRONT-DRIVE/AWD)
Engines: 2.0L 4-cyl. Turbo (158 hp) • 2.4L 4-cyl. Turbo (172 hp); Transmissions: 5-speed man. • 6-speed man. • CVT
DIMENSIONS/CAPACITY
Passengers: 2/3; Wheelbase: 104 in.; H: 60/L: 174/W: 69 in.; Headroom F/R: 5.5/4.0 in.; Legroom F/R: 41.5/26.0 in.; Cargo volume: 20 cu. ft.; Fuel tank: 51.5L/regular; Tow limit: 2,000 lb.; Load capacity: 865 lb.; Turning circle: 38 ft.; Ground clearance: 6.5 in.; Weight: 3,185 lb.

RATING: Not Recommended. **Strong points:** Expect a comfortable but firm ride; the CVT transmission usually "slips" into gear imperceptibly and can cut fuel consumption by about 5 percent; all-wheel drive works well; easy access into the interior; raised seating position is similar to a small SUV's; and rear seating space is adequate, though the Toyota Matrix is roomier. NHTSA gave the Caliber a five-star occupant protection rating in front and side collisions and four-star rollover resistance; rated "Good" in IIHS offset crash tests, but weak in others. **Weak points:** Engines lack reserve power for passing and merging and are quite noisy; CVT sometimes jerks if, when slowing down, you hit the gas and then back off; handling is mediocre, at best; interior space is disappointing due to the excess door trim and wide centre console; not much room for cargo; the sloping rear windshield and large roof pillars limit rear visibility; lots of wind noise; the cheap-looking, plastic-dependent interior is fairly spartan; subpar fit and finish; misaligned dashboard and centre panel; so-so fuel economy—the car's heft cuts into "real-world" gas mileage pretensions; and electronic stability control and traction control aren't available on all models. Rated "Marginal" in IIHS side-impact crash tests, despite the use of front and rear head curtain airbags. Head-restraint protection got a similarly low rating from the same insurance group. The AWD model is much more troublesome than the front-drive. **New for 2010:** This compact hatch gets an updated interior with a new instrument panel, door panels with softer armrests, and a center console that provides more storage space. The 1.8L engine has been dropped, leaving just the 2.0L and the 2.4L; the 2.0L is now available with a 5-speed manual transmission. All models get active front head restraints. The Caliber SRT4 is gone.

OVERVIEW: This is a bare-bones small car that doesn't cost much and gives you even less in return. From both a performance and quality perspective, the Caliber is one of the least-reliable cars Chrysler makes. Interestingly, at a time when shoppers snap up small fuel-savers, the Caliber has continued to sell poorly.

COST ANALYSIS: Look for discounts and rebates to drop prices by about 15 percent by early spring. **Best alternatives:** The Honda Civic and Fit, Mazda3 hatchback, and Nissan Versa. **Options:** Consider the Security Group option package, which includes an anti-theft alarm (you may add an engine immobilizer), brake assist, and stability control for about $500. **Rebates:** $1,000–$3,000 rebates and discounts plus zero percent financing on all models. **Depreciation:** Faster than average. **Insurance cost:** Less than average. **Parts supply/cost:** Parts are reasonably priced and easily found. **Annual maintenance cost:** Average. **Warranty:** Bumper-to-bumper 3 years/60,000 km; powertrain 5 years/100,000 km; rust perforation 5 years/160,000 km. **Supplementary warranty:** Getting an extended powertrain warranty is a smart idea. **Highway/city fuel economy:** *2.0L auto.:* 7.3/9.0 L/100 km; *2.4L man.:* 7.4/10.9 L/100 km.

OWNER-REPORTED PROBLEMS: Airbags fail to deploy; poor positioning of the AC controls and four-way flasher; car vibrates excessively when underway with the rear windows down; owners report a plethora of electrical short-circuits affecting all major components:

> While driving, the electric door locks will unlock and then lock themselves. This happens at any speed, in town or on freeways. Dealer has had car seven different times, and is unable to repair or even see the fault, although he has on different occasions found fault codes for stuck door lock switch. Dealer currently has car to try to determine the faults. Main door lock switch (drivers' side) replaced by dealer. Wiring harness repaired by dealer due to dealer-installed after market alarm system incorrectly installed. Dealer has replaced the instrument cluster. Problem is still there—I am concerned for my wife's safety, as she drives home from work after dark, and on occasion, she is unable to electrically re-lock the doors—even to the extent of having to pull over, manually push all door locks down, only to have them pop up again before she gets home.

CHALLENGER, CHARGER

bad buy ★

The Dodge Charger.

TECHNICAL DATA

PRICES: *Challenger SE:* $24,995, *Challenger SRT8:* $45,995, *Charger SE:* $29,095, *Charger SRT8:* $46,595 **FREIGHT:** $1,350 **ORIGIN:** Canada **SALES:** *Charger:* Down 50%

POWERTRAIN (REAR-DRIVE/AWD)

Engines: 2.7L V6 (178 hp) • 3.5L V6 (250 hp) • 5.7L V8 (372–376 hp) • 6.1L V8 (425 hp); Transmissions: 4-speed auto. • 5-speed auto.; *Challenger:* 6-speed man.

DIMENSIONS/CAPACITY

Passengers: 2/3; Wheelbase: 116 in.; 120 in.; *Challenger:* H: 57/L: 198/W: 76 in., *Charger:* H: 58/L: 200/W: 75 in.; Headroom F/R: *Charger:* 2.5/2.0 in.; Legroom F/R: *Charger:* 41.5/28.0 in.; Cargo volume: 16 cu. ft.; Fuel tank: 68–72L/regular; Tow limit: *Challenger:* Not recommended, *Charger:* 1,000–2,000 lb.; Load capacity: 865 lb. est.; Turning circle: 41 ft.; Ground clearance: 4.5 in.; Weight: *Challenger:* 3,720–4,140 lb., *Charger:* 3,728–4,268 lb.

RATING: Not Recommended. This duo's fastest time will be the speed it takes you to go from the dealer showroom to the service bay. **Strong points:** Styling, horsepower, and cachet. The 3.5L V6 has proven to be much more reliable than either of the two V8s, and it burns a lot less fuel. The Challenger was given five stars by NHTSA for front and side crashworthiness, and four stars for rollover resistance. The Charger earned five stars for frontal protection and four stars for rollover resistance. No testing was done for side-impact protection. IIHS rated the Charger "Good" for frontal offset protection. **Weak points:** Stay away from the Charger's 2.7L V6; it's a dog that won't hunt. You will still get horrendous gas mileage due to the car's heft, even with the cylinder deactivation feature. Expect a stiff, jarring ride; overly assisted steering that requires constant correction; and marginal rear headroom. Stability control isn't available on all models. Charger was rated "Poor" by IIHS for side-impact crashworthiness; head-restraint protection was rated "Marginal." **New for 2010:** Side curtain airbags are now standard. All Chargers get a body-colour sill plate, and SE models get a chrome grille with black inserts.

OVERVIEW: Using the same platform and engines as the Chrysler 300, the Charger and Challenger combine a potent mixture of Hemi V8 power, rear drive, and an independent suspension supplied by Mercedes. Last year, Dodge dropped in a new 5.7L Hemi Eagle engine, offering the same displacement as the previous year's 5.7L Hemi, but with variable valve timing. Combined with the company's Multi-Displacement System (MDS), which shuts down half the cylinders under light load, the new engine produces more horsepower and better fuel economy.

Although these cars are fun to drive and buy you entry into the high-performance "winner's circle," in the end, you will be the loser. High fuel, insurance, and depreciation costs will quickly thin out your wallet, and the absence of a comprehensive powertrain warranty is like performing a high-wire act without a net. The Charger, like Ford's resurrected Thunderbird, will likely have a short shelf life, judging by the number of 300s and Magnums piling up on dealers' lots. Chrysler revived the Hemi name in 2002 with a 5.7L Hemi V8 engine used in its pickups and then extended it to the 300 Ram Wagon sedan—a winning combination that revived lagging pickup, sedan, and wagon sales. But that was when fuel was relatively cheap. For 2010, bigger is definitely not better.

COST ANALYSIS: Look for discounts and rebates to drop prices by about 15–20 percent, thus putting pressure on 2010 model year prices. The 2010's standard side airbags are worth the extra cost. **Best alternatives:** The Ford Five Hundred or Mustang, or Chevy's resurrected Camaro after it has been a year on the market and de-bugged. **Options:** You'll want the 3.5L V6 engine for better all-around performance without much of a fuel penalty. **Rebates:** $3,500–$7,000 rebates and discounts, plus zero percent financing by the spring of next year. **Depreciation:** Much faster than average. A 2007 Charger that sold for $28,370 is now worth about $11,000. **Insurance cost:** Higher than average. **Parts supply/cost:** Parts are not a problem due to the many different models using the same Chrysler 300 parts. Engine and body components are expensive and complex to troubleshoot. **Annual maintenance cost:** Average; higher than average once the warranty expires. **Warranty:** Bumper-to-bumper 3 years/60,000 km; powertrain 5 years/100,000 km; rust perforation 5 years/160,000 km. **Supplementary warranty:** An extended powertrain warranty is a wise choice. **Highway/city fuel economy:** *2.7L:* 7.7/11.3 L/100 km; *3.5L:* 8.1/12.2 L/100 km; *5.7L:* 8.7/13.4 L/100 km; *6.1L:* 10.6/16.0 L/100 km.

OWNER-REPORTED PROBLEMS: *Challenger:* One vehicle shut off when the owner honked the horn and applied the brakes at the same time. The throttle sticks; vehicle loses power while under load, as in passing or going up hills as rpms race; and the rough-shifting automatic transmission causes the car to lose traction on wet roadways. *Charger:* Power distribution box under the hood caught fire and melted in one vehicle. Hard-shifting, shuddering automatic transmission; vehicle could be in Drive even though the shift lever indicates it is in Park; plastic radiator cooling fan breaks apart, shattering the fan blades and fan shroud and destroying the radiator; when accelerating, a loud whistling sound can be heard; cruise control shuts off randomly; and the solid metal door handles can burn your hand in hot weather.

AVENGER, SEBRING ★

bad buy

The Chrysler Sebring.

TECHNICAL DATA

PRICES: *LX:* $22,995, *Convertible Limited:* $40,995 **FREIGHT:** $1,350 **ORIGIN:** U.S. **SALES:** *Sebring:* Down 75%, *Avenger:* Down 60%

POWERTRAIN (FRONT-DRIVE)

Engines: 2.4L 4-cyl. (173 hp) • 2.7L V6 (186 hp) • 3.5L V6 (235 hp); Transmissions: 4-speed auto. • 6-speed manumatic

DIMENSIONS/CAPACITY

Passengers: 2/3; Wheelbase: 108.9 in.; H: 59.0/L: 190.6/W: 71.2 in.; Headroom F/R: 5.5/3.5 in.; Legroom F/R: 41/28 in.; Cargo volume: 13.6 cu. ft.; Fuel tank: 64L/regular; Tow limit: *Sebring:* 1,000 lb., *Avenger:* 2,000 lb.; Load capacity: *Sebring:* 825 lb., *Avenger:* 865 lb.; Turning circle: *Sebring:* 40.5 ft., *Avenger:* 41.0 ft.; Ground clearance: *Sebring:* 5.0 in., *Avenger:* 5.5 in.; Weight: *Sebring:* 3,335 lb., *Avenger:* 3,550 lb.

RATING: Not Recommended. **Strong points:** Adequate V6 performance; comfortable ride; crisper handling, thanks to firmer springs and shocks and lower-profile 18-inch tires; plenty of interior room; a spacious trunk with wide-opening lid for easy loading and unloading; and few owner complaints on past models. The convertible is especially attractive because of its reasonable price and slow depreciation. *Avenger:* NHTSA awarded it five stars for frontal crashworthiness and four stars for rollover resistance. IIHS gave Avenger and Sebring top marks ("Good") for frontal offset, side, and rear crash protection. *Sebring:* NHTSA gave it five stars for frontal and side crashworthiness; rollover resistance earned four stars. *Sebring convertible:* NHTSA gave four stars for frontal and rear crashworthiness; side-impact occupant protection earned five stars. Front offset and side crashworthiness were deemed "Good" by the IIHS. **Weak points:** Mediocre, lethargic, and buzzy 4-cylinder engine; and just competent, not thrilling, V6 acceleration. The 4-speed automatic can't match the 5-speeds found in competing makes. Overly soft suspension and less-responsive handling on the 4-cylinder and 2.7L V6-equipped models. Optional stability control. Five adults will feel cramped in seats that aren't sufficiently bolstered; and trunk space is limited. *Sebring convertible:* Head restraint protection rated "Marginal" by IIHS. **New for 2010:** *Avenger:* Returns unchanged. *Sebring:* The hood grooves are gone, wheels have been redesigned, the instrument panel is changed, and active head restraints have been added.

COST ANALYSIS: Look for discounts and rebates to drop prices by about 20 percent, thus putting pressure on 2010 model year prices. **Best alternatives:** The Honda Accord, Hyundai Elantra or Sonata, and Toyota Camry. For convertible aficionados, consider the Mazda Miata. **Options:** You'll want the 3.5L V6 engine for better all-around performance without much of a fuel penalty The 2.4L 4-banger also underwhelms the Caliber and Jeep Compass. **Rebates:** $3,000–$5,000 rebates and discounts plus zero percent financing. **Depreciation:** Faster than average. **Insurance cost:** Should be average. **Parts supply/cost:** Parts are expected to be reasonably priced and easily found. **Annual maintenance cost:** Predicted to be average through the third year of ownership, and then a bit higher than average once the warranty expires. **Warranty:** Bumper-to-bumper 3 years/60,000 km; powertrain 5 years/100,000 km; rust perforation 5 years/160,000 km. **Supplementary warranty:** Getting an extended powertrain warranty is a smart idea. **Highway/city fuel economy:** *2.4L:* 6.6/9.7 L/100 km; *2.7L:* 7.2/10.8 L/100 km; *3.5L:* 7.4/12.9 L/100 km.

OWNER-REPORTED PROBLEMS: Side airbags fail to deploy; inaccurate fuel gauge readings make it easy to run out of gas; brakes fail when backing up; engine surges when brakes are applied; and tapping the brakes fails to disengage the cruise control.

300, 300C ★★

The Chrysler 300C.

RATING: Below Average. These cars are scheduled to be dropped next year, if Chrysler doesn't drop first. **Strong points:** Plenty of power with the 3.5L V6; acceptable handling; and a remarkably quiet and spacious interior, along with a large trunk. The touring model gives a smoother, more comfortable ride than does

TECHNICAL DATA

PRICES: *Touring:* $27,595, *AWD:* $31,895, *C:* $41,095, *SRT8:* $49,195
FREIGHT: $1,350 **ORIGIN:** Canada
SALES: Down 50%
POWERTRAIN (REAR-DRIVE/AWD)
Engines: 2.7L V6 (178 hp) • 3.5L V6 (250 hp) • 5.7L V8 (359 hp) • 6.1L V8 (425 hp); Transmissions: 4-speed auto. • 5-speed auto.
DIMENSIONS/CAPACITY (BASE)
Passengers: 2/3; Wheelbase: 120 in.; H: 58.4/L: 196.8/W: 74.1 in.; Headroom F/R: 4.5/2.5 in.; Legroom F/R: 43.0/30.5 in.; Cargo volume: 15.6 cu. ft.; Fuel tank: 68L/regular; Tow limit: 2,000 lb.; Load capacity: 865 lb.; Turning circle: 41 ft.; Ground clearance: 5.6 in.; Weight: *300:* 3,766 lb., *AWD:* 4,041 lb.

the 300C, which is the performance-oriented variant. **Weak points:** The base 2.7L V6 is no match for the car's weight. These cars are gas-guzzlers in spite of their engine cylinder deactivation feature. Hemi-equipped models are way overpriced; resale values have fallen considerably since 2005. Standard towing capability is less than one would expect from a rear-drive. Some of the electronics derived from Mercedes' luxury models have had serious reliability problems. The car's high waistline and tall doors make for a claustrophobia-inducing interior and limit outward visibility. Stability control isn't a standard feature on all models. **New for 2010:** Side curtain airbags; the 300 Limited gets more chrome trim and heated mirrors; the 300C gains keyless ignition and a rear parking assist system.

OVERVIEW: Front-drives are out, and rear-drives are in—again—along with all-wheel drive and complicated Hemi V8 engines—all the ingredients for Chrysler's second bankruptcy. The V8 is rather exceptional, in that it features Chrysler's Multi-Displacement System, which uses eight cylinders under load and then switches to 4-cylinder mode when cruising. This is unsettling, because the last time this was offered by an American automaker (Cadillac, in the '80s), owners found their cars running on four cylinders along freeways and then switching to eight cylinders in traffic. After a torrent of lawsuits, GM went back to a conventional powertrain set-up.

COST ANALYSIS: Excess weight and large engines drive up fuel costs; consequently, resale values are dropping because buyers are shifting to smaller, more economical sedans. **Best alternatives:** Ford's Crown Victoria or a used Grand Marquis are credible rear-drive alternatives. **Options:** Consider the SXT model with the 3.5L V6 and traction/stability control. **Rebates:** Expect $5,000–$7,000 discounts or rebates and low-interest financing programs by late winter. **Depreciation:** Higher than average. For example, a 2005 Chrysler 300C SRT8 equipped with a Hemi V8 sold new for almost $50,000; today its resale value is barely $15,000. **Parts supply/cost:** Expect long delays and high costs. **Annual maintenance cost:** Higher than average. **Warranty:** Bumper-to-bumper 3 years/60,000 km; powertrain 5 years/100,000 km; rust perforation 5 years/160,000 km. **Supplementary warranty:** Get a powertrain warranty thrown into the deal. **Highway/city fuel economy:** *3.5L:* 8.1/12.2 L/100 km; *AWD:* 8.6/12.6 L/100 km; *300C (cylinder deactivation):* 8.0/13.5 L/100 km; *SRT8:* 10.6/16.0 L/100 km. Owners report that real-world fuel consumption with both engines, however, is far more than the above estimates.

OWNER-REPORTED PROBLEMS: One car caught on fire while parked and then exploded:

> My 2008 300 Touring was parked in a parking lot. The alarm started going off by itself. A fire started out of nowhere from under the hood. Then my car exploded from the front to the back through the exhaust pipe. I only had 6100 or so miles [9,800 km] on my car.

Chronic electrical shorts and stalling; automatic transmission clicking and banging into gear; transmission will suddenly slip into a lower gear; electronic stability control is ineffective on ice:

> I rented a Chrysler 300 over this past weekend. I want you to know that it was the scariest ride I've had in a while. Have you ever tested the electronic stability program on ice? It not only does not work, it is extremely dangerous. I had to drive about 600 miles [965 km] on icy and windy Wyoming roads which proved to be quite scary in the 300 with ESP.

CD player won't play a complete disc, and parts aren't available; steering knocks when turning; brakes drag and pulsate when stopping; horn won't sound if the car is not running or if not hit in the right spot:

> Excessive effort is required to operate the horn. The driver must strike the horn pad cover with much stronger than typical force, and only in certain, very specific locations before the horn will sound. In a panic, a driver will likely not meet these location/force requirements and the horn will not sound, resulting in other drivers and pedestrians not receiving a warning.

Poorly performing Goodyear Integrity tires:

> Goodyear Integrity tires hydroplane every time it rains. I have already had one accident because I couldn't stop. I've run a red traffic light and I have experimented in a parking lot and hydroplaned at 15 mph [24 km/h].

Defective rack and pinion steering:

> The driver heard a grinding noise coming from the steering wheel when turning in either direction. The dealer stated that the noise was normal and would disappear once the tires were "broken in." The noise continued well over three months. The vehicle was taken to a different dealer and they stated that the rack and pinion steering was defective. They also stated that the part to repair the steering was unavailable.

PT CRUISER ★★

Chrysler's PT Cruiser: From hero to zero in nine years.

RATING: Below Average. Chrysler said it would dump the Cruiser last year. Now it has given the car a one-year reprieve. When it finally exits, its resale value will plummet just like Oldsmobile, Saturn, and Pontiac models. **Strong points:** Excellent fuel economy (regular fuel); nimble handling around town; acceptable steering response, with good road feedback. Good braking; a versatile and spacious interior; many thoughtful interior amenities; and easy access. NHTSA awarded the PT Cruiser four stars for frontal, side, and rear crashworthiness; IIHS followed with its top "Good" rating for occupant protection in a frontal impact, but the car failed other tests. **Weak points:** The 150 hp 2.4L 4-cylinder engine is not very smooth-running when matched to the automatic transmission; it struggles when going uphill or merging with highway traffic. Going uphill or merging requires frequent downshifting and lots of patience—accelerating to 100 km/h takes about 9 seconds. The automatic transmission doesn't have much low-end torque, forcing early kickdown shifting and deft manipulation of the accelerator pedal. Rough downshifts; mediocre highway performance and handling; a firm ride; lots of engine, wind, and road noise; and limited rear visibility. Emergency handling is slow and sloppy. The turning diameter seems excessive for such a short vehicle. Hard cornering produces an unsteady, wobbly ride because of the car's height.

TECHNICAL DATA

PRICE: *Classic:* $20,500 **FREIGHT:** $1,350
ORIGIN: Mexico **SALES:** Down 65%
POWERTRAIN (FRONT-DRIVE)
Engine: 2.4L 4-cyl. (150 hp);
Transmissions: 5-speed man. • 4-speed auto.
DIMENSIONS/CAPACITY (BASE)
Passengers: 2/3; Wheelbase: 103 in.; H: 63.0/L: 168.9/W: 67.1 in.; Headroom F/R: 2.0/4.0 in.; Legroom F/R: 45.0/28.0 in.; Cargo volume: 32 cu. ft.; Fuel tank: 57L/regular; Tow limit: 1,000 lb.; Load capacity: 865 lb.; Turning circle: 41 ft.; Ground clearance: 5.0 in.; Weight: 3,147 lb.

According to IIHS, the PT Cruiser isn't very crashworthy; it got a "Poor" rating in both the side and rear tests, and the organization blasted the vehicle's inability to protect occupants:

In the side test, measures recorded on the driver dummy indicate that in a real-world crash of similar severity, rib fractures and internal organ injuries would be likely, along with a possible pelvic fracture. The rear passenger dummy's head contacted the C-pillar during the test because this car doesn't have rear-seat side airbags. Measures recorded on the dummy indicate that serious neck injuries and a fractured pelvis would be possible in a crash of this severity.

New for 2010: The lineup has been trimmed down to a single model, the Cruiser Classic. The turbocharged engine and manual transmission have both been dropped, leaving the 150 hp 2.4L 4-cylinder and 4-speed automatic as the sole powertrains.

COST ANALYSIS: Since its debut as a year 2000 model, the Cruiser has been one of the best small cars Chrysler sells, which isn't saying a lot. Minus the turbocharged engine this year, the car loses much of its performance edge, but saves fuel and maintenance costs in the process. **Best alternatives:** Chevrolet HHR, Honda Civic, Hyundai Tucson, Kia Rondo, Mazda5, and the Mini Cooper. **Options:** An anti-theft engine immobilizer would be a good idea. **Rebates:** Expect $2,000–$3,000 discounts or rebates by late winter. **Depreciation:** Faster than average. For example, the 2005 Classic sold for $22,215; now it's worth about $6,500 and will probably sell for much less than that when the model is dropped in 2010. **Parts supply/cost:** No problem. **Annual maintenance cost:** Average. **Warranty:** Bumper-to-bumper 3 years/60,000 km; powertrain 5 years/100,000 km; rust perforation 5 years/160,000 km. **Supplementary warranty:** Get an extended powertrain warranty. **Highway/city fuel economy:** 7.5/9.8 L/100 km.

OWNER-REPORTED PROBLEMS: Main complaint areas continue to be the automatic transmission, AC, and brakes. Airbags deploy for no reason or fail to deploy; gas pedal goes to the floor with no effect; vehicle suddenly shifts into First gear while cruising; headrests are too high, blocking vision; the instrument panel is hard to read; and water leaks into the interior. Other problems include sudden, unintended acceleration; sudden brake or steering lock-ups; extremely rough idling; high-speed engine surging; drivetrain whine; an annoying wind noise when driving with the rear window or sunroof open; moisture between the clearcoat and paint that turns the hood a chalky white colour; moisture accumulation in headlights; and sudden electrical shutdowns. The power windows may be hazardous to children:

> My 6-year-old stuck her head out the window... When she did, she accidentally kicked the power window button with her foot. The button was located near the floor in the backseat on the middle console. She rolled the window up on her own head and was stuck in the window. She only lived through the event because (1) her head was tilted at the time so the window rolled up on the side of her neck and not on her trachea; and (2) her 8-year-old sister in the back seat with her heard her screams and got her foot off the button and rolled the window back down. It was terrifying and painful and totally preventable. The button should be in a different place where it cannot be kicked or bumped so easily, and there should be a mechanism that allows the window to roll back down if it meets resistance.

GRAND CARAVAN, TOWN & COUNTRY ★★

The Dodge Grand Caravan.

RATING: Below Average. These minivans, along with Chrysler's Jeep division, will likely be sold separately when Chrysler faces its next bankruptcy, thereby ensuring a bit of clemency for the owners of these models. **Strong points:** Very reasonably priced and subject to deep discounting. Chrysler's top-of-the-line 4.0L engine is a better choice if you intend to do a lot of highway cruising—it's smooth and quiet with lots of much-needed low-end torque. The regular-sized minivans are the closest thing to a passenger car when it comes to ride and handling. The tight chassis and responsive steering provide a comfortable, no-surprise ride. Stiffer springs have greatly improved handling and comfort. Manoeuvrability around town is easy. Excellent braking, lots of innovative convenience features, user-friendly instruments and controls, two side sliding doors, easy entry and exit, and plenty of interior room. Dual airbags include knee bolsters to prevent front occupants from sliding under the seat belts. Remote-controlled power door locks can be programmed to lock when the vehicle is put in gear. Chrysler has developed a mechanism that releases the power door locks and turns on the interior lights when the airbag is deployed. Both vehicles were given NHTSA's top five-star rating for frontal and side crashworthiness; rollover resistance earned four stars. **Weak points:** The 41TE 4-speed automatic transmission with Overdrive shifts slowly and imprecisely. The transmission whines excessively. Power steering is vague and over-assisted as speed increases. Downshifting from the electronic gearbox provides practically no braking effect. Brake pedal feels mushy, and the brakes tend to heat up after repeated applications, causing a considerable loss of effectiveness (fade) and the warping of the front discs. The ABS system has proved to be unreliable on older vans, and repair costs are astronomical. Mediocre handling with the extended versions, though the ride is smoother over bumps. A sad history of chronic powertrain, AC, ABS, and body defects that are exacerbated by the automaker's hard-nosed attitude in interpreting its after-warranty assistance obligations. Get used to a cacophony of rattles, squeals, moans, and groans caused by the vehicle's poor construction and subpar components. Fuel consumption is worse than advertised. **New for 2010:** Active front head restraints; three-zone climate control (SE); and a slightly higher final-drive ratio for the 4.0L engine.

OVERVIEW: These versatile minivans return with a wide array of standard and optional features that include anti-lock brakes, child safety seats integrated into the seatbacks, flush-design door handles, and front windshield wiper and washer controls located on the steering-column lever for easier use. Childproof locks are standard. The Town & Country, a luxury version of the Caravan, comes equipped with a 3.8L V6 and standard luxury features that make the vehicle more fashionable for upscale buyers.

COST ANALYSIS: If you can get a discounted (20 percent) 2009 Grand Caravan, do so; they aren't that different from the 2010 models. The same advice applies to the 2009 and 2010 Town & Country. Chrysler's bankruptcy has delayed the introduction of most 2010 models until the second quarter of 2010. The company will fill the gap by adding extra shifts to pump out more 2009s and sell them with hefty discounts well into the winter. **Best alternatives:** Honda's Odyssey should be your first choice. The mini-minivan Mazda5 is also a good alternative because of its frugal 4-cylinder engine and wagonlike configuration. Full-sized GM rear-drive vans are also worth consideration. They are more affordable and practical buys if you intend to haul a full passenger load, do regular heavy hauling, are physically challenged, use lots of accessories, or take frequent motoring excursions. Don't splurge on a new luxury Chrysler minivan: Chrysler's upscale Town & Country may cost up to $10,000 more than a Grand Caravan, yet be worth only a few thousand dollars more after five years on the market. **Options:** As you increase body length, you lose manoeuvrability but gain ride comfort. The 3.8L V6 is a good choice for most city-driving situations, but don't hesitate to get the 4.0L if you're planning on lots of highway travel or carrying four or more passengers. Since its introduction, it's been relatively trouble-free. The sliding side doors make it easy to load and unload children, install a child safety seat in the middle, or remove the rear seat. On the downside, the doors can expose kids to traffic and are a dangerous, failure-prone option. Child safety seats integrated into the rear seatbacks are convenient and reasonably priced, but Chrysler's versions have had a history of tightening up excessively, or not tightening enough and allowing the

TECHNICAL DATA

PRICES: *Grand Caravan:* $26,595–$31,395, *Town & Country:* $36,995–$42,995 **FREIGHT:** $1,350 **ORIGIN:** Canada and U.S. **SALES:** *Grand Caravan:* Down 38%, *Town & Country:* Down 35%

POWERTRAIN (FRONT-DRIVE)

Engines: 3.3L V6 (180 hp) • 3.8L V6 (197 hp) • 4.0L V6 (251 hp); Transmissions: 4-speed auto. • 6-speed auto.

DIMENSIONS/CAPACITY

Passengers: 2/2/3; Wheelbase: 121 in.; H: 69/W: 77/L: 203 in.; Headroom F/R1/R2: 6/5/0 in., *Town & Country:* 3.5/4.5/0.0 in.; Legroom F/R1/R2: 41.0/30.5/27.0 in., *Town & Country:* 41/31/25 in.; Cargo volume: 61.5 cu. ft.; Fuel tank: 76L/regular; Tow limit: 3,800 lb.; Load capacity: 1,150 lb.; Turning circle: 41 ft.; Ground clearance: 5.0 in.; Weight: *Grand Caravan:* 4,600 lb., *Town & Country:* 4,755 lb.

child to slip out. Try the seat with your child before buying it. Other important features to consider are the optional defroster, power mirrors, power door locks, and power driver's seat (if you're shorter than 5'9" or expect to have different drivers using the minivan). You may wish to pass on the tinted windshields; they seriously reduce visibility. Ditch the failure-prone Goodyear original-equipment tires, and remember that a night drive is a prerequisite to check out headlight illumination, called inadequate by many. **Rebates:** The 2009 models will likely get $3,500–$4,500 rebates or discounting plus zero percent financing throughout the year. **Depreciation:** Average, but faster than average with the Town & Country. **Insurance cost:** About average for a minivan. **Parts supply/cost:** Higher than average, especially for AC, transmission, and ABS components, which are covered under a number of "goodwill" warranty programs and several recall campaigns. **Annual maintenance cost:** Repair costs are average during the warranty period. **Warranty:** The base warranty is inadequate if you plan to keep your minivan for more than five years. Bumper-to-bumper 3 years/60,000 km; powertrain 5 years/100,000 km; rust perforation 5 years/160,000 km. **Supplementary warranty:** An extended powertrain warranty is a must-have. If buying the warranty separately, bargain it down to about one-third of the $2,000 asking price. Chrysler minivans can be expected to have some powertrain, electrical system, brake, suspension, AC, and body deficiencies similar to previous versions. Quality control has been below average since these vehicles were first launched 20 years ago and, surprisingly, got much worse after the '90 model year introduced limp-prone transmissions. **Highway/city fuel economy:** *Grand Caravan 3.3L:* 8.3/12.3 L/100 km; *4.0L:* 7.9/12.2 L/100 km; *Town & Country 4.0L:* 7.9/12.2 L/100 km.

OWNER-REPORTED PROBLEMS: Owners say powertrain and sliding-door failures make them afraid to drive these minivans. Their complaints also focus on electrical glitches, erratic AC performance, and early brake wear (see *forum.chryslerminivan.net*). In one NHTSA-logged complaint, the minivan, used as a hearse, was deemed unsafe to transport...dead bodies?

> All electrical equipment stopped working on the way home from the dealership. No gauges, no power windows or doors, no turn signals, no brake lights, no A/C, no radio. The only thing[s] working were the windshield wipers which came on by themselves and I could not shut them off. All the warning lights on the dash lit up. Made it home and called the dealership. Van has less than 100 miles [160 km] on it and already in for service. Called dealership Monday afternoon, they can't find any problems, must be the TIPM (Totally Integrated Power Module). They have ordered the part, but it is on backorder until who knows when. Van has been deemed unsafe to drive until repaired. Dealership provided me with a small sedan to drive until fixed, but this van was purchased by my funeral home to use for body transportation, stretchers, caskets, etc. Sedan is totally useless for my business.

Other owners note the premature wearout of the cooling system, clutch, front suspension components, wheel bearings, air conditioning, and body parts (trim; weather stripping becomes loose and falls off; plastic pieces rattle and break easily). The front brakes need constant attention, if not to replace the pads or warped rotors after two years or 30,000 km, then to silence the excessive squeaks when braking. And don't expect engine compression to help with braking:

> As we have experienced to our horror on numerous occasions driving on the west coast (Vancouver Island), while trying to maintain vehicle control on a downhill stretch of paved road, this 4-speed electronic transmission system is incapable of providing any engine braking assistance whatsoever. The only alternative is to ride the brakes to maintain vehicle control.

SOME SERVICE TIPS: AC condenser road debris damage can be avoided by installing a condenser guard supplied by Chrysler (under warranty, of course). TSB #23-047-06 is very useful for determining when a cracked windshield should be replaced under warranty. Power liftgate failures can be easily corrected by re-calibrating the power control module, says TSB #08-045-06. NHTSA has recorded numerous complaints of airbags deploying unexpectedly—when passing over a bump in the road, or simply when turning the vehicle on—or failing to deploy in an accident:

> While driving approximately 35 mph [56 km/h], another vehicle ran a red light and crashed into the front and rear passenger doors of the contact's vehicle. The windows shattered and the side airbags failed to deploy. The driver and four other passengers received minor injuries.

Chrysler continues to downplay the safety implications of its minivan defects, whether in the case of ABS failures, inadvertent airbag deployments, or sudden transmission breakdowns. Seat belts are another recurring problem: Belts may become unhooked from the floor anchor; buckles jam or suddenly release; and the child safety seat harness easily pulls out or over-retracts, trapping children. Owners report that the minivans won't carry seven passengers safely:

> I recently purchased a 2008 Dodge Caravan and discovered that I couldn't get all the car seats in. We called several friends to see what they do, and they say that they gave up after getting bloody knuckles trying to put the seats in and now don't use one. The car manufacturers claim that because there are 7 seat belts that it is a seven passenger vehicle. This leads to parents getting frustrated because they can't fit the car seats, so they let their child go without. The back seat has 3 seat belts but it is impractical to get 3 car seats, or booster seats in. There is a gap in what the safety guidelines require and what the manufacturers are selling.

RAM 1500, 2500 PICKUP ★★★★

The Dodge Ram 2500.

TECHNICAL DATA

PRICES: *1500 ST:* $23,795, *Crew 4x4:* $36,140, *2500 Reg.:* $34,690, *Laramie 4x4:* $50,285 **FREIGHT:** $1,350 **ORIGIN:** Mexico and U.S. **SALES:** Down 23%
POWERTRAIN (REAR-DRIVE/PART-TIME/FULL-TIME AWD)
Engines: 3.7L V6 (215 hp) • 4.7L V8 (310 hp) • 5.7L V8 (390 hp); Transmissions: 4-speed auto. • 5-speed auto. • 6-speed man.
DIMENSIONS/CAPACITY (BASE)
Passengers: 3/2; Wheelbase: 141 in.; H: *1500:* 77, *2500:* 79/W: 80/L: 228 in.; Headroom F/R: 6/4 in.; Legroom F/R: 40.5/25.0 in., *2500:* 40/26 in.; Cargo volume: N/A; Fuel tank: 132L/regular; Tow limit: 5,655 lb.; Load capacity: *1500:* 1,120 lb., *2500:* 1,945 lb.; Turning circle: *1500:* 50 ft., *2500:* 51 ft.; Ground clearance: *1500:* 10.5 in., *2500:* 8.0 in.; Weight: *1500:* 5,655 lb., *2500:* 7,130 lb.

RATING: Above Average. **Strong points:** Improved ride and handling, thanks in large part to the addition of coil springs. The crew cab model comes with a cargo bed that's longer than that of most of the competition, but not as huge as the Mega Cab; a new Mega Cab/long bed configuration is also available on the Ram Heavy Duty models. More goodies: lockable storage bins in the rear fenders; in-floor cabin storage compartments; and a minor Hemi engine power boost. *2010 1500 four-door Regular Cab, 1500 four-door Crew Cab and 1500 four-door Quad Cab:* NHTSA awarded five stars for frontal crashworthiness and four stars for rollover resistance. 4×4 variants received only three stars for rollover resistance. No recent 2500 models have been tested. *All 2009 1500 models:* IIHS gave frontal offset crash protection and head restraint effectiveness a "Good" rating. **Weak points:** Hemi V8 is fuel-thirsty and complicated to service; parts are often back-ordered. Full-time AWD and electronic stability control (ESC) are optional. Mediocre braking highlighted by extended stopping distances. If you are a short driver, you may not be able to see over the raised hood. *All 2009 1500 models:* IIHS gave side crash protection a "Marginal" rating. **New for 2010:** *Ram 1500:* Although the RAM 1500 was all-new for 2009, it sees several changes for the 2010 model year. The gross combined weight rating (GCWR: maximum permissible weight of the truck, fuel, occupants, cargo and trailer) for long-wheelbase 5.7L models is up three-quarters of a ton to 15,500 lbs. V6 models get a fuel-saver "ECO" dash light to indicate fuel-efficient driving, while a deceleration fuel shut-off system is intended to improve real-world fuel economy (EPA estimates are unchanged, however). New features include an iPod connector, active head restraints, and an improved tire pressure monitoring system; options include a trailer brake controller, 22-inch wheels on R/T models, and auto-dimming mirrors. *Ram 2500/3500:* The heavy-duty Ram gets a thorough going-over, including the addition of a crew cab. The styling follows that of the Ram 1500, but with a bigger, more masculine look, while the interior is upgraded with new materials and amenities. A re-tuned suspension provides a more comfortable ride. Engines are carryovers: the 5.7L Hemi V8 (all new last year) and the 6.7L Cummins turbodiesel. Fleet customers will be able to purchase a biodiesel-capable version of the Cummins engine that runs on B20 (20 percent biodiesel/80 percent petroleum diesel). Maximum GCWR is up to 25,400 lbs., while maximum towing capacity is 18,500 lbs. *Ram 3500/4500/5500 Chassis cab:* No changes for 2010, except for diesel engine emissions components.

OVERVIEW: These trucks were considerably improved last year, and so many have been sold over the years that their maintenance and support is practically bankruptcy-proof—with the exception of the Hemi engine and the automatic transmissions, which are the most problematic components.

COST ANALYSIS: If you find a discounted (20 percent) 2009 Ram, buy it. The ideal combination is a 2009 Ram with a diesel engine and a manual transmission to dodge (pun intended) Chrysler's automatic transmission breakdowns. **Best alternatives:** Honda Ridgeline, Mazda B Series, Nissan Frontier, and the Toyota Tacoma and Tundra. **Rebates:** The 2009 and delayed 2010 models will likely get $3,500–$5,000 rebates or discounting plus zero percent financing throughout the year. **Depreciation:** Average; much faster than average for the V8-equipped models. Diesels with manual transmissions hold their value best. **Insurance cost:** Average. **Parts supply/cost:** Higher than average, especially for Hemi engine, AC, transmission, and ABS components:

> I purchased the vehicle new and the first time I used the 4×4 auto the vehicle began to fail. It would stay in 4×4 for awhile then it would engage the 4×4 lock. I have had trouble getting it fixed because of a lack of supply of the required part. Also the windshield wipers went out and it was 2 weeks before they could get that part in. I have not had any luck with the customer support at Dodge at all.

Annual maintenance cost: Repair costs are average during the warranty period; however, this doesn't include lost wages or use of the truck due to back-ordered parts. **Warranty:** The base warranty is inadequate if you plan to keep your pickup for more than five years. Bumper-to-bumper 3 years/60,000 km; powertrain 5 years/100,000 km; rust perforation 5 years/160,000 km.

Supplementary warranty: Consider buying an extended powertrain warranty. If buying the warranty separately, bargain it down to about one-third of the $2,000 asking price. **Highway/city fuel economy:** *1500 3.7L V6:* 10.0/14.8 L/100 km; *1500 4.7L V8:* 10.8/15.6 L/100 km; *1500 4.7L V8 4×4:* 16.5/22.7 L/100 km; *1500 5.7L V8 MDS:* 10.2/15.4 L/100 km; *1500 5.7L V8 4×4 MDS:* 10.8/16.2 L/100 km.

OWNER-REPORTED PROBLEMS: The chrome trim ring around the console-mounted shifter reflects the sun into the driver's eyes; at 70 km/h, the truck shakes violently and veers to the side of the road; the airbag warning light comes on for no reason; two dealers could not get the airbag sensor replacement parts; gas spews out of filler tube when filling up; wheel lug nuts sheared and wheel flew off truck; defective suspension front struts:

> Two front struts on our 2008 Dodge are leaking. This is a part covered under the extended warranty. The issue is that this part is on a national back order with Chrysler. This is an issue that for whatever reason is not considered a recall item. This item also causes the front tires to deteriorate and go flat regularly. Tires are not covered under warranty so this becomes an expense and/or burden on the owners. This is also a safety issues because the vehicle is not able to properly maintain a lane in traffic when there are changes in road texture, pot holes, or if there are road deterioration issues. These changes cause the vehicle to bounce out of control and it makes it difficult to safely maneuver the vehicle in traffic.

Sudden steering lockup; windshield wipers fall off because they no longer have a retention bolt; frequent front shock failures:

> Front shocks both blew out leaking all of their fluid out. Ride became very poor. Manufacturer should recall and redesign the front shocks.

•

> Absolutely horrible shocks/suspension road handling ability of 2008 Dodge Ram 1500. Truck would "jump" or "skip" over pot holes, seams in asphalt/cement transitions and other areas. When wet pavement was present, it would skip sideways a bit, and one time spun out. Front shocks were blown at 12,000 miles [19,300 km], but handled very poorly when bought brand new last September. Dodge denied any problems; "That is just how they ride" is what I was told. Other individuals with same model vehicle I personally know have the same problems. No aftermarket support available either.

WRANGLER ★★

RATING: Below Average. The Wrangler is one of the most off-road-capable Jeeps ever made, but it falls short when driven on-road. What this fun-to-drive, competent off-roader gives in impressive performance is taken away through its overall lack of quality and poor reliability. Still, when the new Chrysler is broken up and sold piece-meal by Fiat, the popular minivans, Jeeps, and Rams will likely be spun off into new divisions with a host of new investors. **Strong points:** An impressive off-roader that now comes with a roomier, plusher cabin and a more-rigid frame that enhances handling but makes for a stiff ride. **Weak points:** These little SUVs are selling at their full list price and are not likely to be discounted by much as the year progresses. The V6 engine is coarse and underpowered, and the 6-speed manual transmission is anything but smooth. Handling is compromised by vague steering, a stiff ride, and low cornering limits (standard stability control is a plus), and violent shaking makes the vehicle practically uncontrollable ("Death Wobble") when passing over small bumps at cruising speeds:

> While driving my Jeep Wrangler at about 35–40 mph [56–64 km/h] over a rough spot on the road, I experienced horrible front end shake that I could not control until I pulled the car over. I'm very lucky there was nobody else

TECHNICAL DATA

PRICES: *2-door:* $19,995, *2-door Rubicon:* $30,195, *4-door Unlimited:* $25,695, *4-door Rubicon:* $32,195

FREIGHT: $1,350 **ORIGIN:** U.S. **SALES:** Up 2%

POWERTRAIN (REAR-DRIVE/PART-TIME/FULL-TIME AWD)

Engine: 3.8L V6 (205 hp); Transmissions: 6-speed man. • 4-speed auto.

DIMENSIONS/CAPACITY (BASE)

Passengers: 2/3; Wheelbase: 116 in.; H: 71/W: 74/L: 173 in.; Headroom F/R: 5.5/5.0 in.; Legroom F/R: 41/28 in.; Cargo volume: 34.5 cu. ft.; Fuel tank: 70L/regular; Tow limit: 3,500 lb.; Load capacity: 850 lb.; Turning circle: 43 ft.; Ground clearance: 8 in.; Weight: *Sport:* 3,849 lb., *Rubicon:* 4,165, lb.

> in front or in back of me because I had no control of my vehicle. I looked into this online and have learned it's called the "Death Wobble" and it's happened to many other Jeep owners.

Owners report that the Wrangler's off-road prowess is compromised by poor original-equipment tires and thin body panels. Although there's not much you can do about the body panels, *www.tirerack.com* can give you invaluable, unbiased tips on the best and cheapest tires for the kind of driving you intend to do. Fuel economy? It isn't as good as advertised. **New for 2010:** The Sport trim replaces the X trim for 2010.

OVERVIEW: The Wrangler is the smallest and least expensive (we're talking bare-bones here) Jeep you can find. It's an iconic SUV that can easily handle open-air off-road driving anywhere you choose and still be presentable for Saturday night cruising downtown. How's this for versatility: The standard soft top can be folded down or the available hard top can be taken off. Then, if you want more adventure, the doors can be removed and the windshield folded down—in effect, creating many different vehicles out of one.

The two-door Wrangler is offered in Sport, Sahara, and Rubicon trim with standard four-wheel drive powered by a 202 hp 3.8L V-6 engine, hooked to a standard 6-speed manual with Overdrive or an optional 4-speed automatic, also with Overdrive. Also standard is electronic stability control with roll control, traction control, brake assist, and hill hold control. The Sahara gives you body colour flares, Infinity speakers, remote keyless entry, power windows, a security alarm, and 18-inch wheels. The Rubicon offers equipment that off-road enthusiasts usually pick up from independent suppliers, like heavy-duty axles, front and rear electronic locking differentials, 32-inch BF Goodrich mud tires, a sway bar disconnect system, rock rails, and a heavy-duty transfer case with 4:1 low-gear ratio. The available Freedom Top three-piece modular hardtop allows panels to be removed above the driver or passenger. Other options include Dual Top Group, half doors, remote start system, front seat-mounted side air bags, and a multimedia infotainment system with 30-gigabyte hard drive and navigation system. The Unlimited is the first four-door Wrangler that carries five people and their luggage. It's the only four-door convertible available that offers rear-drive or four-wheel drive, making it equally at home on the trail or in the wilds of your local shopping mall.

COST ANALYSIS: The 2009 models were substantially improved, and these changes have been carried over to the 2010 models. Both cars are practically identical, though there may be a few hundred dollars difference in their MSRP. **Best alternatives:** Honda CR-V or Element, Hyundai Tucson, Subaru Forester, and Toyota RAV4. But remember, none of these other models can follow the Wrangler off-road. **Options:** The three-piece Freedom Top and the Sunrider soft top are nice touches, but beware of water and wind leaks (see below). Keep an eye out for the optional suspension system, which includes larger shock absorbers and heavy-duty springs. An aftermarket anti-theft system is also a plus. Ditch the Firestone tires. **Rebates:** The 2009 models are practically sold out, and they are expected to stay in short supply as fuel prices rise. Therefore, expect to buy a 2010 with a discount of no more than five percent on the higher-end models, if you are lucky. **Depreciation:** Faster than average, despite their overall popularity. A 2007 2-door X model that sold for $19,995 is worth barely $10,000 today. **Insurance cost:** Higher than average. **Parts supply/cost:** Higher than average, especially for AC, transmission, and ABS components. **Annual maintenance cost:** Repair costs are average during the warranty period, but if Chrysler goes down for the count, these expenses become your responsibility. **Warranty:** Bumper-to-bumper 3 years/60,000 km; powertrain 5 years/100,000 km; rust perforation 5 years/160,000 km. **Supplementary warranty:** Get an extended powertrain warranty. Also, brake, powertrain, and exhaust system repairs should be carried out by agencies that provide extensive warranties on their work (lifetime). **Highway/city fuel economy:** 10.8/14.1 L/100 km; *auto.*: 10.5/14.3 L/100 km.

OWNER-REPORTED PROBLEMS: Owners report frequent airbag failures, fuel-tank leaks, fuel-pump failures, malfunctioning fuel gauges, chronic engine stalling when accelerating or decelerating, front end torsion bar failures and fluid leaks, and clutch master and slave cylinder leaks and premature replacement. The 6-speed manual transmission sometimes pops out of gear; the automatic transmission slips erratically in and out of Second gear and leaks fluid; the power steering locks up; and there's excessive and premature brake wear, leading to brake failures. Other brake complaints concern the vehicle pulling to the left when braking; the rear brakes suddenly locking up while driving in the rain and approaching a stop sign; and the vehicle going into open throttle position when the brakes are applied. There have also been many instances where drivers mistook the accelerator for the brake because the pedals are so close together. Body welds and seams are susceptible to premature rusting, and there have been frequent complaints about peeling paint and water leaks:

> Soft top leaks on both sides in the front. Seats getting stained and the carpet is starting to smell. Water stains on the doors, steering column, and down the dash.

•

WIND NOISE/WATER LEAK AT SOFT TOP HEADER

BULLETIN NO.: 23-010-09 DATE: APRIL 17, 2009

SOFT TOP—WATER LEAK OR WIND LIKE SOUND AT HEADER

OVERVIEW: This bulletin involves replacing the header seal plate with a new design.

2007–09 Wrangler

WATER LEAK AT UPPER A-PILLAR DOOR SEALS

BULLETIN NO.: 23-005-09 DATE: MARCH 24, 2009

SOFT TOP—WATER LEAK AT UPPER A-PILLAR DOOR SEAL TO DOOR RAIL INTERFACE

OVERVIEW: This bulletin involves the addition of foam to eliminate a possible water leak at the upper A-Pillar.

2007–09 Wrangler

> Freedom top has leaked and stained my seats. Dealership just fixed it a month ago. Also, the Jeep was leaking oil, dealership just fixed the intake manifold gasket 3 weeks ago. It is scheduled to go back to dealership for this steering issue and it is rusting on both doors. Poor, poor quality.

The worst leaks occur at the bottom of the windshield frame. An easy way to check for this is to examine the underside of the frame to see if there's excessive rust. This has consistently been a problem area for Jeeps; hence all of the ads for aftermarket windshield frames. Watch for corroded windshield bracket bolts. The good news is that you can replace the windshield frame and all of the seals relatively cheaply. One failure that *can't* be repaired cheaply is a cracked windshield, another common Wrangler owner complaint.

Ford

Can It Jump a Lake of Fire?

> I guess these are inauspicious days to launch a pickup. The light-vehicle market has gone China Syndrome; the chief executives of the Detroit Three are groveling in their pinstripes on Capitol Hill; and there is, in the air, a diffuse but real sense of repudiation toward full-size pickups. The F-150, perennially the bestselling vehicle in America, has fallen on hard times. Sales are down 26% this year, and Ford will be lucky to move 500,000 F-150s this year, down from about 700,000 in 2006... Aesthetic and athletic, with tremendous build quality and dozens of fall-in-love features, the new F-150 refutes the easy dismissal of American automaking as somehow feckless and inefficient. These days, selling lots of pickups may be harder than swinging in a giant centrifuge or jumping lakes of fire. But I do believe the F-150 will survive just fine.

DAN NEIL
LOS ANGELES TIMES
NOVEMBER 28, 2008

Ford Job 1: Survive

For the past decade, Ford has had three ongoing problems that could still end up bankrupting the company: bad products, bad quality, and bad management. In spite of the sales success of its Escape SUV, Focus, Fusion, and F-Series pickups, Ford has been steadily going downhill (though not as fast as bankrupt Chrysler and GM), according to virtually every yardstick used to measure automotive success.

But there is a glimmer of hope. The company has come the farthest of the Detroit Three, and has done so with very little government stimulus funding. Its recent models, in particular, have been more competitive from both a performance and a reliability standpoint. In fact, most of its vehicles have scored average or higher in *Consumer Reports*' reliability surveys. For example, Ford improved considerably its F-Series pickups last year, the Ford Flex crossover looks ready to challenge the imports, and the freshened Fusion and Mercury Milan sedans combine good fuel economy with performance and quality. As far as hybrids go, the Fusion looks good, but the Escape hybrid has proven itself since 2004 to be as good as or better than the Toyota Prius hybrid.

This is not to say that most of Ford's models are just as good performers and are as reliable as the Asian competition. They aren't. A good example is the redesigned Ford Taurus. It has more trunk space, highway performance has been cranked up several notches, and the interior is more user-friendly, with better-quality materials and more attention paid to ensuring a proper fit and finish. On the other hand, the car's interior feels closed in, visibility is limited, and there's not much rear-seat room. In effect, the car is "three steps forward and two steps back" after its revamping.

This isn't just a Taurus problem. Ford's other models are mostly midpack contenders, as well. Some older models haven't been updated in years, and most of the company's SUVs (Explorer, for example) lack refinement and style. The 2011 Explorer will become a more competitive SUV by replacing its trucklike body-on-frame platform with a carlike unibody chassis. Just this one design change will improve handling, smooth out the ride, and provide better fuel economy. With any luck, powertrain "gear hunting" and intake manifold leaks won't reappear.

The Ford Taurus.

Ford is also finally shifting its product mix to smaller vehicles that use more reliable Japanese components and are assembled more cheaply in Mexico or offshore. Models like the Ford Fusion, Mercury Milan, and Lincoln Zephyr mid-sized cars, all based on the successful Mazda6, are built in Hermosillo, Mexico. Ford intends to extend this practice by copying European designs and importing some models directly from Europe. The next-generation 2010 Focus, for example, will be modelled upon the highly rated European variant and include a plug-in electric version for 2011. A small Fiesta four-door sedan/hatchback will be imported from Europe during the 2010 model year. This way, Ford keeps production costs down and also quickly puts out agile, fuel-efficient, and highway-proven vehicles that follow the marketplace's shift to downsized cars and trucks.

Poor Quality

Ford has its own poor-quality woes, just like Chrysler and GM, as the service bulletin summary below clearly shows.

2008 FORD F-150 FOUR-WHEEL DRIVE 4.6L V8

All Technical Service Bulletins

NUMBER	DATE	TITLE
09L03	04/24/2009	Campaign—Tire Valve Stem Inspection/Maintenance
08-25-5	12/22/2008	Body—L/H Cowl Panel Popped Up
08-24-8	12/08/2008	Body—Sunroof Water Leaks During High Pressure Car Wash
08-24-2	12/08/2008	Wheels/Tires—Steering Wheel Nibble/Vibration
08-23-6	11/24/2008	A/C—Cannot Control Output Temperature
08-21-11	10/27/2008	4×4/AWD System—Shudder On Accel/Decel/Binding On Turns
08-12-9	06/23/2008	Keyless Entry—Transmitter May Not Operate
08-11-1	06/09/2008	Brakes—Vibration At 45 MPH/Park Brake Partial Release
08-8-9	04/28/2008	A/C—Grinding Noise When Changing Modes
08-5-1	03/17/2008	Audio System—Radio Won't Seek Sirius Radio Channels
08-4-2	03/03/2008	Engine—Cold Start Drive Belt Whistle/Hoot Noise
08-4-4	03/03/2008	Engine Controls—Cold Start Hesitation/Intake Backfire
08-2-9	02/04/2008	Fuel System—Erratic Fuel Gauge/MIL ON/DTC P0460/P0463
07-25-2	12/24/2007	Body—Rattle Noise From Tailgate
07-24-7	12/10/2007	A/C—Compressor Shuts Off in High Temperatures
07-22-7	11/12/2007	Interior—Instrument Panel Scratch/Mar Repair Tips
07-21-3	10/29/2007	Power Steering—Cold Weather High Pressure Line Leakage
07-10-9	05/28/2007	Drivetrain—Highway Speed Vibration

One gets the feeling that Ford, unlike Chrysler and General Motors, is on top of the above-listed problems and won't let them carry over from year to year.

In the past decade, powertrain defects, faulty suspensions and steering components, and premature brake wear and brake failures were the primary concerns of Ford owners. The company's engine and automatic transmission deficiencies affected most of its products and have existed since the early '80s, judging by *Lemon-Aid* reader reports, NHTSA complaints, and confidential Ford internal documents and technical service bulletins. The quality of body components has traditionally remained far below Japanese and South Korean standards.

On top of this, Ford has managed to profoundly tick off its suppliers, dealer body, and customers. Parts suppliers have been berated by Ford management for simply following the company's insane cost-cutting orders. The dealer body no longer trusts the company that has shut down Mercury in Canada, cut warranty payouts with its Blue Oval program, and made dealers beg for after-warranty assistance for customers screwed by the automaker's abysmal quality control.

Over the past three decades, *Lemon-Aid* has warned a succession of Ford Canada presidents that quality control and management had to improve dramatically, or sales and profits would plummet. The only Canadian president who ever listened and acted on *Lemon-Aid*'s complaints was Bobbie Gaunt. But she never got the backing of Ford USA. And Ford is now reaping what its arrogance and incompetence has sown.

FOCUS ★★★

RATING: Average. **Strong points:** Excellent handling and road-holding; a commanding view of the highway; plenty of interior space for occupants and cargo; well appointed for an entry-level vehicle; user-friendly control layout; improved quality control; and impressive fuel economy. Impressive reliability during the last five years, which is all the more surprising because the 2000–04 models were quintessential lemons. NHTSA gave the two-door 2010 Focus five stars for frontal crashworthiness, three stars for side protection, and four stars for rollover resistance. The four-door model was rated a bit differently: It got five stars for side protection, four stars for frontal crashworthiness, and three stars for rollover resistance. IIHS gave its top ("Good") rating for frontal offset and side crash protection. **Weak points:** Mediocre acceleration, excessive engine and road noise, and head-restraint/rear crash protection given only an "Average" rating. No stability control. **New for 2010:** Nothing significant. Ford will introduce a redesigned third-generation Focus in 2010 as a 2011 model, with a battery-powered all-electric version following a year later.

OVERVIEW: The 2010 Ford Focus will be a lame duck, though it's still a competent small car. It provides good mileage and a surprisingly supple ride at competitive prices. The four-door sedan is a better dollar value than the cramped two-door coupe. The hatchback and a roomy wagon have been dropped.

TECHNICAL DATA

PRICES: *Sedan S:* $14,799, *Sedan SE:* $16,199, *Coupe:* $16,499, *SES:* $18,999 **FREIGHT:** $1,350 **ORIGIN:** U.S. **SALES:** Down 35%

POWERTRAIN (FRONT-DRIVE)
Engines: 2.0L DOHC 4 (132 hp) • 2.0L DOHC 4 (140 hp); Transmissions: 5-speed man. • 4-speed auto.

DIMENSIONS/CAPACITY
Passengers: 2/3; Wheelbase: 103 in.; H: 56.3/L: 175.1/W: 68.0 in.; Headroom F/R: 5.0/2.0 in.; Legroom F/R: 39.0/26.5 in.; Cargo volume: 14 cu. ft.; Fuel tank: 53L/regular; Tow limit: 1,185 lb.; Load capacity: 825 lb.; Turning circle: 36 ft.; Ground clearance: 5.5 in.; Weight: 2,720 lb.

COST ANALYSIS: The Focus is for drivers who feel fuel economy is more important than sophisticated styling or performance. The car is still using the basic chassis/platform it began with its year 2000 model. The 2009 and 2010 aren't very different; smart shoppers will wait for the more-refined 2011 model. **Best alternatives:** Honda Civic, Hyundai Accent or Elantra, Mazda3, and Nissan Versa. **Options:** Ditch the original equipment Firestones. **Rebates:** $2,000 to $3,000 as the 2011 models start appearing. **Depreciation:** Average. **Insurance cost:** Average. **Parts supply/cost:** Average. **Annual maintenance cost:** Average. **Warranty:** Bumper-to-bumper 3 years/60,000 km; powertrain 5 years/100,000 km; rust perforation 5 years/unlimited km. **Supplementary warranty:** A good idea for the powertrain. **Highway/city fuel economy:** 5.7/8.5 L/100 km with the manual transmission; 6.0/8.5 L/100 km with the automatic.

OWNER-REPORTED PROBLEMS: Some engine stalling and surging; leaking, inoperative AC compressor; brake failure and premature wear complaints; windshield stress fractures; and a moderate number of reports relative to poor fit and finish. Head restraints also come in for criticism for being angled downward too sharply, forcing the head to bend forward. Both wheels can lock up when the brakes are applied, or the car may accelerate when the brakes are applied.

FUSION, MILAN, ZEPHYR ★★★★

The Ford Fusion.

RATING: Above Average. This trio of practically identical mid-sized sedans has a lot going for it—most of which comes from Mazda. Slightly smaller than the Ford Five Hundred, the Fusion is set on a Mazda6 platform that has been lengthened a few centimetres. Added rigidity and additional chassis tweaking have resulted in a car that will comfortably seat five passengers and handle quite well, particularly when cornering. Standard four-wheel disc brakes do a good job stopping the car, with little fading after repeated stops. **Strong points:** Very reasonably priced; good acceleration and handling; and Mazda's 4-cylinder and V6 engines are competent, thrifty, and dependable. The Hybrid can run on one or both of its power sources to balance acceleration and fuel economy and requires no plug-in charging. Flawless transmission performance; steering is tight, precise, and vibration-free; and comfortable rear seating. NHTSA gives the Fusion and the Fusion Hybrid five stars for front and side crashworthiness and four stars for rollover resistance. The car has also shown exemplary reliability during its four years on the Canadian market. **Weak points:** A noisy 4-cylinder engine; stability control, traction control, and ABS are extra-cost features. Super-fast depreciation: It will likely lose 57 percent of its value after three years, making the Fusion an ideal used car but a poor new-car investment, unless you plan to keep it eight or more years. **New for 2010:** The mid-size Fusion gets many changes, with updated styling inside and out, a new 2.5L base engine, a revised 3.0L V6, and a new 263 hp 3.5L Sport model. The 2010 Fusion Hybrid uses an Atkinson-cycle version of the 2.5L engine, and its fuel economy estimates are better than the Toyota Camry and Nissan Altima hybrids.

TECHNICAL DATA

PRICES: *SE:* $22,799, *SEL V6:* $28,799, *SEL V6 AWD:* $30,799, *Hybrid:* $31,999 **FREIGHT:** $1,350 **ORIGIN:** Mexico **SALES:** *Fusion:* Up 4%

POWERTRAIN (FRONT-DRIVE)

Engines: 2.5L 4-cyl. (175 hp) • 2.5L 4-cyl. hybrid (191 hp) • 3.0L V6 (240 hp) • 3.5L V6 (263 hp); Transmissions: 6-speed man. • 6-speed auto. • CVT

DIMENSIONS/CAPACITY (FUSION)

Passengers: 2/3; Wheelbase: 107 in.; H: 56.9/L: 190.6/W: 72.0 in.; Headroom F/R: 2.5/2.5 in.; Legroom F/R: 40.5/28.0 in.; Cargo volume: 16 cu. ft.; Fuel tank: 45L/regular; Tow limit: No towing; Load capacity: 850 lb.; Turning circle: 39 ft.; Ground clearance: 5.0 in.; Weight: 3,285 lb.

OVERVIEW: This four-year-old four-door, mid-sized sedan offers four engines: two 4-cylinders, one of which is a hybrid, and two V6s. The smaller engines can be coupled to either a 6-speed manual or a 6-speed automatic transmission; there's no choice with the V6, which comes with a 6-speed automatic. The 4-cylinder comes solely in front-drive; the 3.0L is available in front-drive or all-wheel drive, while the 3.5L is uniquely AWD. The 2010 hybrid variant is a spinoff of the Mazda6 and the Ford Escape Hybrid.

COST ANALYSIS: The 2010 models were substantially improved; don't shortchange yourself with last year's leftovers. **Best alternatives:** Honda Accord, Hyundai Elantra or Tucson, Mazda6, Nissan Altima, and the Toyota Camry. **Options:** Electronic stability control is a worthwhile option. Pass on the sunroof and original equipment Firestone/Bridgestone tires. **Rebates:** Don't expect much. The 2009 models are practically all gone, but that's fine because the 2010's many improvements warrant the higher cost. Set as your goal a 2010 discounted by

5 percent on the higher-end models. **Depreciation:** Much faster than average. A first-year, base 2006 Fusion that sold for $23,000 is now worth only $9,500. **Insurance cost:** Average; the hybrid premium will be more than average. **Parts supply/cost:** Average. Hybrid parts costs are moderately expensive; availability is no problem since parts are taken from the Mazda or Escape hybrid bins. **Annual maintenance cost:** Repair costs have been lower than average during the three-year warranty period. **Warranty:** Bumper-to-bumper 3 years/60,000 km; powertrain 5 years/100,000 km; rust perforation 5 years/160,000 km. **Supplementary warranty:** Not needed. Their first three years on the market have shown the Fusion and its brothers to be exceptionally well made. **Highway/city fuel economy:** *2.5L:* 6.9/9.4 L/100 km; *3.0L:* 7.4/11.3 L/100 km; *3.0L AWD:* 7.8/11.8 L/100 km; *3.5L:* 7.4/11.7 L/100 km; *Hybrid:* 5.4/4.6 L/100 km.

OWNER-REPORTED PROBLEMS: Nothing yet on the 2010s. *2009:* Engine threw a rod; windshield cracked for no reason; head restraints are angled too far forward:

> Front seat head restraints are mounted at an extreme angle which forces your head forward at an uncomfortable angle. The head restraints need to be more straight up and down instead of curving forward.

Trunk takes too much effort to close and sometimes pops open when vehicle is underway; excessive front end drift/pull, forcing driver to continually correct the steering:

> This car will run off the road in a matter of seconds and is a considerable safety hazard. Ford's response to the problem is to instruct their dealers through an internal memo not to "attempt a repair for this problem." This is unacceptable for a company that is touting their cars to be vastly improved over Toyota and Honda. At least their cars go straight down the road with little effort having to be given by the driver. I have driven two of these cars (one of which I own) and both do the same thing.

MUSTANG ★★★★★

RATING: Recommended. The Mustang keeps getting better and better. Unlike some of Ford's front-drives, few warranty complaints are lodged against the rear-drive Mustang. **Strong points:** Base models come equipped with a host of safety, luxury, and convenience features. Fast acceleration, and impressive handling, braking, and resale value. Better-than-average past crashworthiness, standard stability control, and good overall reliability. **Weak points:** Insufficient rear-seat room and limited cargo space. The ride is a bit stiff and the car tends to understeer. **New for 2010:** Restyled and now offered with standard anti-lock brakes, electronic stability control, Easy Fuel Fill capless filler, and SOS Post Crash Alert System on all models. Ride and handling are greatly improved and the GT's V8 is now up to 315 hp. A New V6 Coupe Value Leader is available, and the 4.6L V8 adds cold air induction on the GT for increased horsepower and torque. *Shelby:* The Shelby GT500 gets a power boost; the body has been modified from the stock Mustang to improve engine cooling and performance. Ford says its revamped transmission and final-drive gearing give better acceleration off-the-line with improved fuel economy on the highway. The GT500 will come in both coupe and convertible versions.

TECHNICAL DATA

PRICES: *Coupe:* $25,499, *Convertible:* $29,699, *Coupe GT:* $36,999, *Convertible GT:* $41,199 **FREIGHT:** $1,350
ORIGIN: U.S. **SALES:** Down 22%

POWERTRAIN (REAR-DRIVE)

Engines: 4.0L V6 (210 hp) • 4.6L V8 (315 hp); • 5.4L V8 Supercharged (540 hp); Transmissions: 5-speed man. • 6-speed man. • 5-speed auto.

DIMENSIONS/CAPACITY

Passengers: 2/2; Wheelbase: 107.1 in.; H: 55.6/L: 188.1/W: 73.9 in.; Headroom F/R: 5.0/1.0 in.; Legroom F/R: 40.5/23.5 in.; Cargo volume: 13 cu. ft.; Fuel tank: 61L/regular; Tow limit: 1,000 lb.; Load capacity: 720 lb.; Turning circle: 39 ft.; Ground clearance: 4.5 in.; Weight: 3,585 lb.

OVERVIEW: The perfect "back to the future" retro sports car, the Mustang's body panel creases reign supreme. Four decades after its debut, the original "pony car" concept is back, and it looks quite handsome. The car offers either V6 or V8 (in the GT) engines, both more powerful than recent Mustang powerplants. Body assembly since the 2005 redesign is much improved. All bets are off on the GT500 powertrain; Ford's dismal history with high-performance powertrains made by Yamaha would give Freddy Kruger nightmares.

COST ANALYSIS: There are only a few unsold 2009s around, so bide your time until discounts and rebates are "sweetened" early in 2010 and then pounce on a relatively fresh Mustang built in March 2010 or later. This is to make sure most of the redesign glitches have been debugged at the factory. **Best alternatives:** Other cars worth considering are Acura's RSX, the Mazda Miata, and Toyota's Celica. Why not the resurrected Camaro? Confidential internal reports show a high number of assembly-line deficiences in this first-year's production (see the Camaro rating). **Options:** An anti-theft system that includes an engine immobilizer and good tires recommended by *www.tirerack.com*. **Rebates:** $3,000 plus low-interest financing through Ford's own financing firm (an advantage neither Chrysler nor GM have). **Depreciation:** A bit slower than average. **Insurance cost:** Way higher than average. **Parts supply/cost:** Inexpensive and easily found among independent suppliers; some delays getting engine and body components.

Annual maintenance cost: Lower than average: Most independent mechanics will be able to fix a Mustang. **Warranty:** Bumper-to-bumper 3 years/60,000 km; powertrain 5 years/100,000 km; rust perforation 5 years/unlimited km. **Supplementary warranty:** Not necessary; put your money into handling options and theft protection. **Highway/city fuel economy:** *4.0L V6:* 7.8/12.5 L/100 km; *auto.:* 8.5/13 L/100 km; *4.6L V8:* 8.7/13.8 L/100 km; *auto.:* 9.3/13.9 L/100 km; *5.4L V8:* 10.1/15.5 L/100 km.

OWNER-REPORTED PROBLEMS: The automatic transmission, fuel system, front suspension, brakes, electrical system, steering components, and fit and finish remain the primary weak spots; body assembly quality is not up to the level of Japanese vehicles. Numerous complaints of convertible roof, door, and trunk water leaks, as well as side windows that leak when it rains. Owners also report that the engine surges when shifting from Third to Fourth gear; child safety seat tethers in the convertible may not be attached due to the interference from the power convertible top when it is lowered; the hood scoop will lift when the car is underway; and there are windshield distortions:

> The driver owns a 2009 Ford Mustang. The windshield is magnified and distorted. While driving in the rain the visibility is unclear and presents a safety risk. The dealer agreed to replace the windshield.

ESCAPE, TRIBUTE ★★★★

The Ford Escape.

RATING: Above Average; points were taken away for the Escape's mediocre braking and reliability concerns. The Tribute is Mazda's version of the Escape, but without a hybrid variant. **Strong points:** Peppy V6 performance and a roomy interior that includes a large rear bench seat; a quiet interior; standard stability control; convenient Sync voice-control system; and impressive safety scores. NHTSA gave the Escape and Escape Hybrid top marks (five stars) for front and side crashworthiness; three stars were awarded for rollover resistance. IIHS also gave its top rating ("Good") to the Escape for frontal offset, side, and rear crash protection (head-restraint effectiveness). **Weak points:** The 4-cylinder engine lacks grunt in the upper gear ranges; mediocre braking performance; the Escape takes 7.6 metres (25 feet) longer to stop than its rivals, which is an unacceptably poor showing for an ABS-equipped vehicle (bean-counters decided to change the rear brakes from a disc set-up to drum brakes); and the folding second seat isn't very user-friendly. **New for 2010:** Very little; most of the major changes happened last year. Side mirrors now include a small convex section in the corner, which shows vehicles in the blind spots.

TECHNICAL DATA

PRICES: *4x2:* $23,999, *3.0L:* $26,699, *4x4:* $27,499, *LTD 3.0:* $34,899, *Hybrid 4x2:* $32,399, *4x4:* $34,799 **FREIGHT:** $1,350 **ORIGIN:** U.S. **SALES:** Down 5%

POWERTRAIN (FRONT-DRIVE)

Engines: 2.5L 4-cyl. (171 hp) • 2.5L 4-cyl. hybrid (177 hp) • 3.0L V6 (240 hp); Transmissions: 5-speed man. • CVT • 6-speed auto.

DIMENSIONS/CAPACITY

Passengers: 2/3; Wheelbase: 103 in.; H: 70/L: 175/W: 70 in.; Headroom F/R: 3.0/4.0 in.; Legroom F/R: 40.5/28.0 in.; Cargo volume: 37.5 cu. ft.; Fuel tank: 61L/regular; Tow limit: 3,500 lb.; Load capacity: 1,000 lb.; Turning circle: 42 ft.; Ground clearance: 7.0 in.; Weight: 3,605 lb.

OVERVIEW: Redesigned in 2008, this small SUV now looks more like its larger siblings, the Explorer and the Expedition. The biggest change is under the hood, where last year Ford cranked up the horsepower in both the 4- and 6-cylinder engines and replaced the old 4-speed with a smoother-shifting 6-speed automatic transmission. Cruise control and antilock brakes, formerly optional on the lower trims, became standard last year. The hybrid still uses a 4-cylinder powerplant, but a new engine processor allows the Escape to switch from electric to gasoline mode almost imperceptibly.

COST ANALYSIS: Most of the 2009s have sold out, so you will have to spring for the extra bucks for a 2010 version. **Best alternatives:** Honda CR-V, Kia Rondo, Mazda5, Subaru Forester, and Toyota Matrix. **Options:** Nothing that is essential. **Depreciation:** Average. **Insurance cost:** Average. **Parts supply/cost:** Expensive and hard-to-get hybrid parts: A cooling pump cost $640 (U.S.). Reasonably priced parts for gasoline-powered models, but parts are frequently back-ordered:

> They told me it has a bad transfer case. When the part never came in, I was informed that there was a stop shipment on the part because of a defect they found in the manufacturing. Almost a month later they have received the part.

Annual maintenance cost: Average. **Warranty:** Bumper-to-bumper 3 years/60,000 km; powertrain 5 years/100,000 km; rust perforation 5 years/unlimited km. **Supplementary warranty:** Getting an extended powertrain warranty is a good idea. **Highway/city fuel economy:** *2.5L:* 7.2/9.2 L/100 km; *auto.:* 7.2/10.1 L/100 km; *2.5L AWD:* 7.9/10.9 L/100 km; *3.0L V6:* 7.7/11.5 L/100 km;

3.0L *AWD:* 8.3/12.1 L/100 km; *Hybrid:* 6.4/5.8 L/100 km; *Hybrid AWD:* 7.4/7.0 L/100 km.

OWNER-REPORTED PROBLEMS: Airbags deploy inadvertently; airbags fail to deploy when needed; the front passenger side wheel separates from the lower control arm; transmission loses Third gear (6-speed transmission) and goes into default Fifth gear, as transmission fluid spews out through the dipstick, creating a fire hazard; transmission fluid leakage (one cause: a faulty AC condenser hose):

> Car would not accelerate—car would roll backwards on incline—car would stall out. Took in for service, dealer advised transmission fluid is leaking due to crack in the transmission cooler. Defect is not covered by powertrain because they say this part is not part of the transmission, it is a cooling unit. Approximately $750 to fix.
>
> •
>
> Transmission fluid leak within A/C condenser resulting in transmission damage and gear slippage. The vehicle would suddenly not accelerate or would lurch forward. There is no evidence to suggest it was caused by an outside source; rather a faulty line that cracked. This repair was not covered under warranty and occurred shortly after 36K mile [60,000 km] warranty expired. Total cost for repair was $1,025, plus out of pocket tow because it turned out not to be covered under a warranty repair.
>
> •
>
> Transmission fluid leak has been recalled for many other Ford SUVs but not the Escape. Started leaking just after my 36,000 [mile] [60,000 km] warranty ran out so they gave me an estimate of $750 to repair. My car is 1 year old.

Oil filler tube is located directly above the exhaust manifold, creating another fire risk; original equipment tires have defective valve stems that cause the tire to go flat; accelerator cable lines fail, causing pedal to become inoperable; vehicle will not hold when stopped on an incline; sudden loss of braking ability; and spontaneous windshield cracks. One vehicle's parking brake failed, and the vehicle rolled backwards down a hill. *Hybrid:* Surprisingly for a pickup that has such a complicated electrical system, there are just a handful of complaints concerning the 2005–09 models. One would normally expect to see, on average, 50 or so reports per model year. With the current model, owners report some brake failures and defective tire valve stems.

EXPLORER, SPORT TRAC ★★

RATING: Below Average. **Strong points:** Prices are set too high, but they can easily be haggled down as dealers make room for the arrival of the redesigned 2011 versions. Standard stability control; average reliability with the V6 engine. NHTSA gave the Explorer five stars for frontal and side crashworthiness and three stars for rollover resistance, while IIHS scored frontal offset protection "Good" and side

The Ford Explorer.

protection and head-restraint effectiveness "Acceptable." **Weak points:** The Explorer has a history of costly powertrain failures in addition to faulty brake, electrical system, and suspension components. You also get truck-like handling, a stiff ride, and poor fuel economy. The V8 engine is less reliable than the V6. **New for 2010:** Largely unchanged for what is its final model year with the current design. Both the Explorer and Sport Trac get Trailer Sway Control as a standard feature this year.

OVERVIEW: This midsize SUV uses traditional body-on-frame, truck-type construction (this will change with the 2011 version). It offers rear-drive, all-wheel drive, or four-wheel drive that can be left engaged on dry pavement and has a low-range gear for off-roading. Trim levels include XLT, Eddie Bauer, and Limited. Available safety features include ABS, traction control, anti-skid system, side curtain airbags, and front side airbags. A third-row seat increases carrying capacity to seven passengers. Explorer's capless fuelling system allows owners to fill their fuel tanks without having to remove a gas cap, and the optional Sync voice-activated cell phone and MP3 player control system is particularly useful.

TECHNICAL DATA

PRICES: *Explorer XLT:* $35,999, *XLT V8:* $37,499, *Eddie Bauer V6:* $42,399, *Eddie Bauer V8:* $43,899, *Limited V8:* $48,299, *Sport Trac 4x2:* $32,099, *LTD V8:* $37,899, *4x4:* $35,199, *LTD V8:* $41,000 **FREIGHT:** $1,350 **ORIGIN:** U.S. **SALES:** Down 51%

POWERTRAIN (REAR-DRIVE/4×4/AWD)

Engines: 4.0L V6 (210 hp) • 4.6L V8 (292 hp); Transmissions: 5-speed auto. • 6-speed auto.

DIMENSIONS/CAPACITY

Passengers: 2/3/2; Wheelbase: 114 in.; H: 73/L: 193/W: 74 in.; Headroom F/R1/R2: 2.5/4.0/0.5 in.; Legroom F/R1/R2: 40.5/28.0/27.0 in.; Cargo volume: 48 cu. ft.; Fuel tank: 85L/regular; Tow limit: 5,210 lb.; Load capacity: 1,275 lb.; Turning circle: 38 ft.; Ground clearance: 7.0 ft.; Weight: 4,905 lb.

Explorer Sport Trac

The Ford Explorer Sport Trac.

Essentially an Explorer with a pickup bed, the Sport Trac debuted in 2001 as one of the first pickups with four full-size doors, a comfortable four-passenger cabin, and a short cargo bed. Set on the Explorer's wheelbase, stretched by about 17 inches, it is offered with either a V6 or V8 engine, with a top towing capacity of 7,160 lbs. Its pluses and minuses mirror those of its brother, and defects affecting the one usually also affect the other, likely to be dropped in 2010.

COST ANALYSIS: In addition to the Explorer's many truck-based peers, numerous car-based crossover SUVs now occupy this price range, and many of them are just as family-friendly, while offering more safety features, better fuel economy, and a more-refined cabin and powertrain. This is why it's best to steer clear of the Explorer until the redesigned 2011 model arrives at the end of 2010. The 2011 model will use a car-like unibody design to improve the ride, handling, and fuel economy. Plus, Ford's antiquated and problematic powertrain will be replaced by a more-refined system. **Best alternatives:** Honda's CR-V or Ridgeline, Hyundai Tucson or Santa Fe, and the Toyota RAV4. **Options:** Be wary of the $1,700 Ironman Package. You are essentially getting larger tires, heated seats, a roof rack, and floor mats. **Rebates:** Look for $3,000 rebates, $2,000 discounts, and zero percent financing on 2009 and 2010 Explorers. **Depreciation:** Much faster than average. **Insurance cost:** Above average. **Parts supply/cost:** Parts are easy to find and are reasonably priced. **Annual maintenance cost:** Average while under warranty; higher than average thereafter, primarily because of powertrain breakdowns. **Warranty:** Bumper-to-bumper 3 years/60,000 km; powertrain 5 years/100,000 km; rust perforation 5 years/unlimited km. **Supplementary warranty:** Getting an extended powertrain warranty would be wise. **Highway/city fuel economy:** *4.0L:* 11.0/16.2 L/100 km; *4.6L:* 10.4/15.5 L/100 km; *Sport Trac 4.0L:* 10.8/15.9 L/100 km; *Sport Trac 4.6L:* 9.8/14.4 L/100 km; *4.0L 4×4:* 11.0/16.2 L/100 km; *4.6L 4×4:* 10.4/15.5 L/100 km.

OWNER-REPORTED PROBLEMS: Engine and automatic transmission failures and fit and finish deficiencies. Owners continue to complain that the head restraints are literally a pain in the neck and can be dangerous if the airbag deploys:

> The driver owns a 2009 Ford Explorer. Upon entering the vehicle, he noticed that the head rest pushes the driver's head towards the windshield due to its perpendicular design... If the air bag were to deploy, the driver could become seriously injured. The contact called the manufacturer and was informed that the vehicle was designed in that manner and no compensation would be provided.

F-150, F-250 PICKUP ★★★★

The Ford F-150.

RATING: Above Average. The F-150 has seen the best of times and the worst of times and is now coming out of a multi-year sales slump that almost forced Ford into bankruptcy. **Strong points:** Easily negotiated prices as fuel prices rise and truck prices fall. Handling is a breeze, although the ride is a bit stiff; a roomy cab with lots of convenient storage bins; a power-opening centre rear window; and a spring-assisted tailgate. NHTSA gave the 2010 F-150 five stars for front and side crashworthiness and four stars for rollover resistance. The F-250 wasn't tested. IIHS also gave the F-150 top marks ("Good") for frontal offset, side, and rear crashworthiness. **Weak points:** The powertrain is a bit rough and loud, and braking is just acceptable. Long-term reliability has yet to be determined. This is especially important because these trucks have disappointed owners after each redesign since the mid '80s. **New for 2010:** A restyled Harley-Davidson edition returns, but the big changes are reserved for the F-150 SVT Raptor, Ford's "ultimate off-road performance truck." It gets a new front suspension with a wider track, Fox Racing Shox internal-bypass shock absorbers, and 35-inch all-terrain tires on 17-inch wheels. The Raptor is 7 inches wider than the standard F-150 and is also styled differently. The first Raptors will be powered by a 320 hp 5.4L V8, with a new 6.2L V8 arriving later in the year.

OVERVIEW: The Ford F-Series ruled the roost for 30-odd years as the bestselling pickup in North America. And then Ford's house of cards came tumbling down. Abetted by lousy diesel engines; failure-prone powertrains, suspensions, and steering assemblies; and body construction that would make the Marquis de Sade proud, Ford began to lose market share a decade ago. It has never recovered.

TECHNICAL DATA

PRICES: *F-150 XL:* $24,199, *XLT:* $26,899, *XLT Super Cab:* $30,899, *XLT Super Crew:* $31,199, *XLT:* $26,899, *F-250 XL:* $29,699, *XL Super:* $32,799, *XLT:* $33,699, *XLT Super Cab:* $37,199, *Lariat Super:* $46,599, *King Ranch Crew:* $53,919 **FREIGHT:** *F-150:* $1,300, *F-250:* $1,350 **ORIGIN:** U.S. **SALES:** Down 30%

POWERTRAIN (REAR-DRIVE/PART-TIME 4x4/AWD)

Engines: 4.6L V8 (248 hp) • 4.6L V8 (292 hp) • 5.4L V8 (320 hp) • 5.4L V8 supercharged (457 hp) • 6.8L V10 (362 hp) • 6.4L V8 turbodiesel (350 hp); Transmissions: 4-speed auto. • 5-speed auto. • 6-speed auto. • 6-speed man.

DIMENSIONS/CAPACITY

Passengers: 3/3; Wheelbase: 121 in.; H: 69/L: 201/W: 77 in.; Headroom F/R: 4.5/3.5 in.; Legroom F/R: 40.0/29.5 in.; Cargo volume: N/A; Fuel tank: 98.4L/regular, *Raptor:* 94L/regular, *Harley-Davidson:* 136L/regular; Tow limit: *F-250:* 12,500 lb.; Load capacity: 1,540 lb.; Turning circle: 48 ft.; Ground clearance: 8.5 in.; Weight: 5,620 lb.

However, its 2009–10 models give hope that some of the worst design deficiencies have been corrected and Ford is finally on the road to solvency. For 2010, Ford offers three V8 engines, three cabs, and two bed lengths.

COST ANALYSIS: Unless you are looking for a high-performance Raptor, buy a 2009 model that's similar to the 2010, but with a 10 percent discount. **Best alternatives:** Chrysler's Ram, the Honda Ridgeline, and Nissan's Titan. Some trucks that are ideal for lighter duties: Ford Ranger, Mazda B-Series, and Nissan Frontier or King Cab. **Options:** Take a pass on the heated seats and Lariat Chrome package. **Rebates:** $4,000 rebates and low-cost financing on the larger trucks. **Depreciation:** Much faster than average. **Insurance cost:** Above average. **Parts supply/cost:** Reasonably priced parts are easy to find, mainly because many independent suppliers specialize in new and used F-Series parts. **Annual maintenance cost:** Average. **Warranty:** Bumper-to-bumper 3 years/60,000 km; powertrain 5 years/100,000 km; rust perforation 5 years/unlimited km. **Supplementary warranty:** Getting an extended bumper-to-bumper warranty is a good idea. **Highway/city fuel economy:** *4.6L V8:* 10.6/14.7 L/100 km; *4.6L V8 6-speed:* 9.8/14.4 L/100 km; *4.6L V8 4×4:* 10.8/15.6 L/100 km; *5.4L V8 4×4:* 11.3/15.7 L/100 km.

OWNER-REPORTED PROBLEMS: During rainy conditions, the instrument panel lights fail to illuminate; the lights only come on when there's a specific degree of darkness. The sensor on top of the dash doesn't sense enough darkness to turn on the headlights. Sudden acceleration when merging; the gas pedal becomes stuck and the steering column locks up; the SYNC computer system interferes with the backup camera transmission; the window regulator is faulty; and head restraints are uncomfortable and dangerous:

> Headrest forces driver's chin into the chest. Dealer stated that this is the new safety design. Headrests are non-adjustable. Also, they are very wide and, in conjunction with the frame post at the rear of the doors, create a blind spot on both sides of the pickup.

•

> The truck ownder stated that the driver's and passenger side headrests were not adjustable and constantly struck him in the back of the neck. The manufacturer stated that this was a new design for safety. He was concerned that his neck could be seriously injured due to the air bags in the event of a crash.

Take note that Ford has a secret warranty extension covering fuel injector replacements on 2008 and 2009 F-250 through F-550 trucks equipped with a 6.4L diesel engine (Customer Satisfaction Program #09B08). Until March 31, 2010, Ford will replace, free of charge, injectors that have prematurely worn O-rings. After that date, only "emergency" repairs will be covered. This free repair also applies to subsequent owners.

General Motors

GM's 60-Day Satisfaction Guarantee

> It's going to be such a pain in the ass to do the return most people won't even bother. The dealers are going to make this as hard and time consuming on you as possible, if they and GM are still around in two months. If you're going into buying a car with the hesitation that you might want to return it, you shouldn't be buying it anyway.
>
> *www.digg.com/autos/GM_Launches_60_Day_Money_Back_Guarantee*

GM: Geriatrics Manor

Shoppers don't want a car that they can take back. They want a vehicle they can rely on.

North America's largest automobile manufacturer has recently emerged from bankruptcy and still doesn't know what it's doing. Having cut four of its eight brands (Pontiac, Saturn, Hummer, and Saab), thrown its dealers under its unsold buses, trucks, and cars, and spent billions of dollars on overseas factories in China, the company now says it has learned its lesson.

Has it?

General Motors is still run by the same old geezers who got it into trouble in the first place. Sure, Wagoner the old prez was kicked out at the U.S. government's urging, but is his replacement any different? Have you seen the ads where GM's latest president walks the bustling GM hallways and stiffly extols the virtues of the company's 2010 lineup? Cobalt? Aveo? Pitiful. It's obvious he's not an auto man, no matter how much he puts on a Lee Iacocca front and brags about GM's products. All that's missing is his telling us to "Buy a car, and get a cheque."

GM is in much worse financial shape than Ford, but it won't likely be sold whole, as was the Chrysler group, or go bankrupt again, as some auto pundits predict.

GM minivans were always maxi-trouble.

Instead, GM will be nibbled into nothing by Asian investors picking at its entrails. Smart money says Toyota will pick up the restructured company for a song, as it methodically bought up GM's assets in the GMAC finance unit and GM's shares in other companies, like Subaru and Isuzu.

GM is desperately trying to stir up buyer enthusiasm and put some money in the till by focusing on its four remaining divisions (Buick, Cadillac, Chevrolet, and GMC) and increasing sales in Europe and China—two markets where its products are still popular and production costs are minimal. To further cut costs, the automaker dropped its infamously failure-prone front-drive minivans to make room for a 2010 crossover model based on the Saturn Outlook's SUV platform.

Rather than rejuvenate Buick (an impossible task), GM needs to close it down and market through Chevrolet whatever Buicks sell the best. Closing Pontiac and

ENGINE OIL LEAK AT REAR COVER ASSEMBLY AREA

BULLETIN NO.: 05-06-01-034H **DATE: SEPTEMBER 14, 2009**

ENGINE BLOCK POROSITY RTV REPAIR PROCEDURE

2004–07 Buick Rainier
2008–09 Buick LaCrosse Super, Allure Super (Canada Only)
2005–10 Cadillac CTS-V
2007–10 Cadillac Escalade, Escalade ESV, Escalade EXT
2003–09 Chevrolet TrailBlazer
2003–10 Chevrolet Corvette
2004–06 Chevrolet SSR
2005–10 Chevrolet Silverado, Silverado SS
2006–07 Chevrolet Monte Carlo SS
2006–09 Chevrolet TrailBlazer SS
2006–09 Chevrolet Impala SS
2007–10 Chevrolet Avalanche, Suburban, Tahoe
2009–10 Chevrolet Colorado Pickup
2010 Chevrolet Camaro
2003–09 GMC Envoy
2003–10 GMC Sierra
2004–05 GMC Envoy XUV
2007–10 GMC Yukon XL, Yukon Denali, Yukon XL Denali
2009–10 GMC Canyon
2004–06 Pontiac GTO
2005–08 Pontiac Grand Prix GXP
2008–09 Pontiac G8 GT
2009 Pontiac G8 GXP
2005–09 Saab 9-7X 5.3i
2008–09 Saab 9-7X Aero
2003–10 HUMMER H2
2006–10 HUMMER H3
with 5.3L, 5.7L, 6.0L, 6.2L, 7.0L VORTEC™ GEN III or GEN IV V8 Engine (All Aluminum Block Gen III and Gen IV V8 Engines)

GM tells us it has learned from its mistakes. If so, why are GM engines still leaking oil through the 2010 model year?

throwing money away on its Buick and Cadillac divisions is incredibly stupid, akin to the automaker buying Saab or paying a $2 billion penalty for reneging on its promise to buy Fiat.

An $18,000 2009 Saturn Opel...er, Astra—now that same car new for about $7,000 less!

And GM must stop lurching from discounts to rebates in an effort to "sell the deal" rather than selling its cars and trucks. Overpricing products in the fall and then cutting prices by 20 percent several months later doesn't build customer loyalty; it fosters customer anger and suspicion and tells shoppers that GM prices are a con. At first, only GM employees got rebates, then it was close relatives, then third-cousin Billy Bob, then it was your first date (not your first cousin, at least in Canada)...wink wink, nudge nudge.

How do you build customer confidence in your pricing when everybody but you gets a special deal? Would you buy another GM after paying the high-end price—especially after learning that savvy buyers, cousins, and girlfriends got additional discounts that you didn't?

GM's Volt Electric Car

While paying lip service to hybrid engines, GM is gaining time and PR points by promoting the 2011 Volt electric car. Reminds me of a Hydro-Québec press conference 18 years ago when, with great fanfare, the Québec utility boasted it would corner the North American market for electrically powered vehicles. It never happened, and never will. GM's $40,000 (U.S.) Volt will endure the same fate. *Mais oui!*

Be skeptical of the fuel-saving figures that are bandied about. Nissan says that its 2011 Leaf EV achieves the equivalent of 0.6 L/100 km (367 mpg). Chevrolet says its Volt EV, scheduled for a 2010 introduction, gets 1.0 L/100 km (230 mpg). For those of us wishing to go green and break our petroleum habit, these are tantalizing numbers. But the fuel economy figures are at best premature and at worst misleading.

The U.S. government's Environmental Protection Agency devises test procedures for determining miles per gallon, but the formula for electric vehicles is still in draft form, so EV mileage numbers come from an equivalency calculation of gasoline and electrical energy content, an imperfect measure at best. In fact, it's not clear that mpg is the appropriate benchmark anymore. Will the Chevy Volt, which uses gasoline for its "extended-range EV" backup, actually go 230 miles for each gallon in its tank? And what's the meaning of 367 mpg when the Nissan Leaf uses none of the stuff at all?

Let's imagine it's late 2010 and I'm the proud owner of a Chevy Volt. A topped-up battery gives me its claimed 64 kilometres (40 miles) of pure EV range. After this, its gasoline engine takes over and drives a generator that powers electric propulsion. GM hasn't disclosed the fuel efficiency of this "series hybrid" operation in reaching its next plug-in. Furthermore, how many thousands of dollars will the battery packs cost to replace after eight years or so? And what is the environmental footprint of adding another vehicle to the car population, rather than recycling a used model? GM and Nissan are mum when asked these questions.

Better Warranties, Mediocre Quality Control

I like GM's just-announced 60-day money-back guarantee (if you drive no more than 4,000 km and keep up your payments). A PR move? Of course it is. But it doesn't work for long in boosting sales. GM has done this in the past with Saturn and other vehicles that weren't very well made. Apparently, owners complain, but few go through the hassle of taking their car back. They just tell their friends never to buy another of the same model. GM says it expects a vehicle-return rate near 2 percent of its sales; the company won't disclose the return rate with its earlier programs.

GM's quality control needs serious improvement, and its recent bankruptcy has made that almost impossible. GM doesn't have the time or the resources to make the supplier and production changes needed to improve the quality sufficiently to

2008 CHEVY SILVERADO 1500 FOUR-WHEEL DRIVE 4.3L V6

All Technical Service Bulletins

- Drivetrain—Whine or Click Type Noises from Front Axle
- Mirrors—Driver's Door Mirror Glass Shakes/Flutters
- Engine Controls—MIL ON/Multiple DTCs
- Body—Front or Rear Side Door Window Multiple Problems
- Body—High Pitched Squeak Noise at Left/Right A-Pillar
- Fuel System—Driveability Issues/MIL/Multiple DTCs
- Instruments—Fuel Gauge Inaccurate/DTC P0463
- A/T—Shift Flare/Harsh 2–3 Shifting
- Body—Soft Tonneau Cover Appears Loose/Won't Latch
- Navigation Radio—Various Malfunctions
- Interior—Front Seat Cushion Cover Becomes Detached
- Body Controls—Unable to Reprogram Body Control Module
- Keyless Entry—Intermittently Inoperative
- Body—Front Door Window Regulator Squeaks
- Body—Front/Rear Door Wind Noise/Water Leaks
- Suspension—Front End Clunking/Popping/Squeaking Noise
- Interior—Steering Wheel Cover Warped/Paint Peeling
- Electrical—Various Electrical Malfunction/Systems Inoperative
- Interior, A/C—Front Heated Seat Inoperative
- Ignition System—MIL ON/Runs Rough/Misfire DTCs Set
- Body—Marks/Stains on Windshield When Wet
- Body—Accessory Toolbox Key Cylinder Won't Unlock
- Steering—Fluid Leaks from the Steering Gear/Rack
- Body—Various Sunroof Water Leaks
- Body—Rattle/Flutter Noise When Closing Door(s)
- Restraints—Seat Belt Warning Lamp On/Buckling Issues
- Restraints—SRS Lamp ON/Multiple DTCs Stored In Memory
- Exhaust System—Sulfur Odor Explanation
- Tire Monitor System—Tire Pressure Light Stays On

Restraints—Passenger Presence Sensing System Info
Tires—Slight/Mild Edge Feathering Information
Wheels/Tires—Vibration While Driving
Electrical—Intermittent MIL/DTC P2138/Reduced Power
Restraints—Air Bag Lamp On/Multiple DTCs Set
Electrical—Reducing Intermittent Electrical Concerns
Body—Roof Panel Flutters When Closing
Interior—Elimination of Unwanted Odors
A/T—4T65E Fluid Leaking From A/T Vent
A/C—Defaults to Full Hot or Full Cold
Body—Exterior Emblem Discoloration/Blistering/Peeling
Body/Frame—Underbody Pop/Clunk When Turning
A/T Controls—Multiple DTCs/Electrical Malfunctions
Lighting—Dome/Reading Lamps Inoperative
Interior—Wear Spots on Vinyl/Rubber Floor Covering
Navigation Radio—Weak or No GPS Signal Information
A/T—Water or Coolant Contamination Information
Electrical—Various Rear Door Electrical Malfunctions
Navigation Radio—Various Noises Explained
Lighting—Brake Lamps Turn Off After Stop/Pedal Applied
Battery—Drain Diagnostic Tips and Recommendations
Charging System—Low Voltage Display/Battery Discharged
Cooling System, A/C—Aluminum Heater Cores/Radiators
Engine—Drive Belt Chirping Noise
Campaign—Tire Bead Inspection/Tire Replacement
Electrical—No Start/No Crank/Electrical Operations
Mirrors—Heated Mirror Defrosting Time
Instruments—Compass/Temperature Display Information
Drivetrain—Driveline Clunk Information
Body—Front/Rear Fender Liners Warped/Wavy
A/T—Slight Vehicle Movement in Park at Start Up
Instruments—Bulb Outage Detection Restoration
Audio System—Whine from Speakers When Using OnStar
Audio System—Static/Ignition Noise on AM Band
Emission—Emissions Programming Warranty Coverage
A/T—Fluid Leak from Bell Housing Area
A/T—Gear Engagement Time Information
Lighting—Exterior Lamp Condensation Guidelines
A/T—4T80E, Slips in Gear/L/H Axle Seal Leaks
Wheels/Tires—Tire Slowly Loses Air/Low Tire Message
Body—Hard Tonneau Cover Edges are Rough
Body—Ticking Noise from the Windshield Area
Interior/Steering—Steering Wheel Cover Warped/Loose
Body—Sunroof Water Leak onto Headliner
Interior—Front Door Panel Rattles Loose
A/C—Blower Motor is Inoperative
Interior—Passenger Air Bag Not Flush with Dash
Body—Squeak/Itch Noise in Upper Door Area
Wipers/Washers—Washer Fluid Leak on the Driver's Side
Electrical—L/H/R/H Power Mirror(s) Inoperative
Remote Starting System—System Inoperative Diagnostics
Instruments—Nav. Radio Clock/Clock Tab Malfunctions
Interior—Slit/Cut in Front Carpet/Rubber Covering
Steering—Power Steering Pump Replacement Tips
Exhaust System—Moan/Vibration Noises
Fuel System—E85 Fuel Usage Precaution
Exhaust System—Catalytic Converter Precautions
Wheels—Chrome Wheel Brake Dust Accumulation/ Pitting
Body—Vehicle Glass Distortion Information
Brakes—Rotor Lateral Runout Correction Information
Wheels/Tires—Low Tire Pressure
OnStar—Incorrect GPS Position Reported During Call
OnStar—Negative Impact of Cloth/Vinyl Roofs
Interior—Poor Carpet/Rubber Mat Fit/Loose/Bulging
A/C—Does Not Cool/Can't Change Mode/DTCs Set
OnStar—Loss of GPS Signal/Hands Free Issues
Tire Monitor System—Various Concerns
Accessories—Tonneau Cover Handle Separates from Latch
Body—Metal Body Panel Corrosion Protection
Suspension—Squeak from Rear of Vehicle
Restraints—Seat Belt Latch Stop Button Availability
A/C—Compressor/Belt Noise, Reprogram PCM
Campaign—Navigation System DVD Upgrade
Body—Water Enters Accessories Side Storage Tool Box
Electrical—Multiple Electrical Concerns
A/C—Control Module A/C Indicator Blinking
Starting System—Starter Cranks After Key Released
Fuel System—E85 Fuel Usage Precautions
Suspension—Rear Leaf Spring Slapping or Clunking Noise
Restraints—Front Seat Belt Belt Twisted
Body—Buzz/Rattle from R/H Front Fender on Accel.
A/C—Odors in Hot/Humid Conditions
A/T—2–3 Upshift or 3-2 Downshift Clunk Noise

get buyers into its showrooms. GM's supplier base is decimated, employees are sullen, bankers are skeptical, dealers are afraid, and buyers are suspicious. Its engines and automatic transmissions still aren't as reliable or as durable as those of the Asian competition. Furthermore, GM brake and electronic components often fail prematurely and cost owners big bucks to diagnose and repair. The quality and assembly of body components remains far below Japanese and European standards. Take a look at the preceding confidential service bulletin chart. Many of these problems are carried over for three to five years. Not the sign of a company that sincerely believes in quality products.

GM's China Connection

China is the world's second-largest automotive market, selling more small cars and trucks than Japan or Germany. So it's no wonder that GM, Ford, and Chrysler are staking out the country as both a production centre and a sales market for new products. For example, General Motors is seriously considering building a cheap compact car in China that could be sold worldwide for less than $10,000 (U.S.) each, as France's Renault has done with their popular $7,800 (U.S.) Logan model in Europe. That car is built by Romanian automaker Dacia, known in Canada for the failure-prone ARO SUV sold principally in Quebec during the mid '70s. If GM exports its Chinese-made cars to North America, forget about quality and expect American worker anger to explode. GM will have shot itself in the heart with a rice bullet.

The Chery QQ.

It is unlikely that exports from Chinese manufacturers will pose much of a threat to GM or other North American automakers in the short run. Most of the Chinese automakers are small and will have to work overtime just supplying their domestic market with cars and parts. Also, North American consumers aren't likely to buy cars made in China. They are rightfully distrustful of a country that exports poisoned pet food, sells lead-laced toys, and tries to rip off American automakers by selling their new car as a Chevy (changed to Chery after a flurry of lawyers' letters from GM).

COBALT, G5 ★★

The Chevrolet Cobalt.

RATING: Below Average; you can get better performance and reliability from the Asian competition. Soon, the G5, formerly called the Pursuit, will disappear along with the rest of the Pontiac division. **Strong points:** Very reasonably priced; good acceleration with both engines, though the supercharged engine has the best throttle response and handling prowess. Still, the fuel-injected 2.2L 4-cylinder engine provides adequate power, if not pushed too hard. Comfortable riding; the optional suspension package offers better handling at highway speeds and the best ride control on bad roads. Plenty of front-passenger and cargo room; well appointed for an entry-level vehicle; and split rear seatbacks add to storage capacity. Disc/drum braking is just acceptable. NHTSA gives the Cobalt and G5 five stars for side crash protection and four stars for frontal crashworthiness and rollover resistance. IIHS says the cars scored "Good" for frontal offset crash protection and head restraint effectiveness and "Acceptable" for side protection. **Weak points:** Noisy, fuel-thirsty 2.2L engine; steering and handling are only average; excessive lean when cornering under power, and standard tires corner poorly; and the steering is decidedly over-assisted, resulting in constant corrections and insufficient road feel. Cramped rear seating; cheap interior; mediocre fit and finish; small

TECHNICAL DATA

PRICES: *LS Coupe:* $15,325, *LT Coupe:* $18,295, *SS:* $25,445, *SS Sedan:* $25,446 **FREIGHT:** $1,400 **ORIGIN:** U.S. **SALES:** *Cobalt:* Down 55%, *G5:* Down 50%

POWERTRAIN (FRONT-DRIVE)

Engines: 2.2L 4-cyl. (155 hp) • 2.0L 4-cyl. Turbo (260 hp); Transmissions: 5-speed man. • 4-speed auto.

DIMENSIONS/CAPACITY

Passengers: 2/3; Wheelbase: 103 in.; H: 57/L: 180/W: 68 in.; Headroom F/R: 4.0/2.5 in.; Legroom F/R: 41/26 in.; Cargo volume: 14 cu. ft.; Fuel tank: 49L/regular; Tow limit: 1,000 lb.; Load capacity: 890 lb.; Turning circle: 37 ft.; Ground clearance: 4.5 in; Weight: 2,920 lb.

trunk opening; and problematic rear entry and exit on the coupe. Real-world fuel economy is much less than what's advertised. Rear spoiler on the SS blocks visibility. Quality control still need improvement, and without the optional side airbags on the 2009s, IIHS says side crashworthiness is "Poor." **New for 2010:** Curtain airbags. *Team Canada Edition:* Standard satellite radio and premium sound system. *SS:* Standard USB connector and XM satellite radio. *SS Coupe:* Standard sunroof, performance display, and limited slip differential; the sedan version is gone after just one year of production.

OVERVIEW: Both the Cobalt and G5 use GM's Opel Astra platform and offer a base 155 hp 2.2L 4-cylinder engine that is a competent performer, although a bit noisy. A more powerful, supercharged 2.0L 4-cylinder engine is standard on the SS version.

COST ANALYSIS: Sales are very slow; expect a 10 percent discount on the 2009s and 2010s. Actually, with this year's side curtain airbags and other refinements, the 2010 is worth a few extra loonies. **Best alternatives:** With competitors like the Honda Civic, Toyota's Yaris and Corolla, and the Mazda3, the Cobalt and G5 are also-rans, running way in the distance. Even Hyundai, Kia, and GM's Daewoo-sourced Aveo look good in comparison. **Options:** Get the enhanced suspension, power windows and locks, and remote keyless entry. Forget about the rear spoiler; it looks silly and doesn't add to the car's performance. The LS, LS Sport, and performance packages aren't worth the extra cost. Owners say sunroofs are prone to air and water leaks. Pass on the original-equipment tires and contact *www.tirerack.com* for advice on the cheapest and best tires for your needs. **Rebates:** Expect to see $1,000–$3,000 rebates as these small Opels live out their last days. **Depreciation:** Average. **Insurance cost:** Average. **Parts supply/cost:** Parts are easy to find, and reasonably priced by independent suppliers. **Annual maintenance cost:** Average. **Warranty:** 60-day money-back guarantee as long as you don't drive more than 4,000 km. Bumper-to-bumper 3 years/60,000 km; powertrain 5 years/160,000 km; rust perforation 6 years/160,000 km. **Supplementary warranty:** Yes, but only for the powertrain if you'll be keeping the car for more than five years. **Highway/city fuel economy:** *2.2L:* 5.8/8.4 L/100 km; *2.0L:* 6.7/9.4 L/100 km; with the base engine and a 4-speed automatic. Although these figures look good, owners report that real-world consumption is much higher.

OWNER-REPORTED PROBLEMS: Sudden acceleration when shifted into Reverse or when the cruise control is activated; chronic stalling; airbags fail to deploy; frequent brake failures; automatic transmission failures and grinding when shifting. More recent owner-reported problems include front vacuum leaks causing the vehicle to lose power; hard starts; chronic stalling; frequent steering failures and noisy steering; extreme pulsation when braking; and water leaks from rainstorms seeping through the sunroof and soaking the headliner. Voluntary Customer Satisfaction Program to correct AC malfunctions and 2.2L engine stalling; oil leaks from the automatic transmission vent; various shifting/ignition cylinder issues; inoperative dash panel backlighting in daylight; and inability to adjust the driver-side rear-view mirror sufficiently to provide a clear view:

> The mirror has a limited adjustment range and could not be adjusted for a clear rear view before the adjustment lever reach[ed] the end of its range. The dealership reported that many customers complain of the same defect, but as yet the factory has provided no solution. I believe this factory defect has potential to cause serious accidents or mishaps.

The use of OnStar to transmit a signal that the vehicle has been in a collision has come under considerable fire from owners of cars equipped with the system installed by all automakers. They say it simply doesn't work:

> Air bags did not deploy in a 2009 Chevrolet Cobalt crash that caused $7,200 in damage and OnStar did not call or report the crash. When I asked why, I was told "Because the 'brains' of OnStar [were] 'knocked out' in the crash, that shut down the air bag system and other safety measures." Fortunately, this crash did not cause any bodily harm to the person involved, but the whole front end of the car was pushed in, radiator was pushed back, with lots of other damage. The person in the car was fine, but if the engine would have been pushed further in, it could have been in the lap or, even worse, the chest of the person driving. I do not have OnStar for it to be "disabled" in a crash because of where it is placed in the vehicle. This seriously needs to be examined and fixed before someone does really get hurt, if this had not happened already.

MALIBU, MALIBU HYBRID ★★★

The Chevrolet Malibu.

RATING: Average. The Malibu's performance strengths are compromised by the car's so-so reliability. **Strong points:** Good V6 powertrain set-up. Well-appointed; provides a comfortable though firm ride; better-than-average handling thanks to an independent suspension that doesn't sacrifice solid handling for passenger

TECHNICAL DATA

PRICES: *LS:* $23,395, *2LT:* $26,995, *LTZ:* $31,795, *Hybrid:* $28,295 **FREIGHT:** $1,400 **ORIGIN:** U.S. **SALES:** Down 14%
POWERTRAIN (FRONT-DRIVE)
Engines: 2.4L 4-cyl. Hybrid (164 hp) • 2.4L 4-cyl. (169 hp) • 3.6L V6 (252 hp); Transmissions: 4-speed auto. • 6-speed auto.
DIMENSIONS/CAPACITY (MALIBU)
Passengers: 2/3; Wheelbase: 112 in.; H: 57/L: 192/W: 70 in.; Headroom F/R: 4.0/2.0 in., 5.0/4.5 in.; Legroom F/R: 41.5/30.0 in.; Cargo volume: 15.1 cu. ft., *Hybrid:* 13.5 cu. ft.; Fuel tank: 61L/ regular; Tow limit: 1,000 lb., *Hybrid:* Not recommended; Load capacity: 915 lb.; Turning circle: 42 ft.; Ground clearance: 5.0 ft.; Weight: 3,460 lb.

comfort. Plenty of passenger and luggage space, and few squeaks and rattles. NHTSA gives the Malibu a five-star crashworthiness score for front and side protection and four stars for rollover resistance. Standard stability control. **Weak points:** The base 4-cylinder engine is barely adequate for highway driving with the automatic transmission and a full load. Rear head restraints block visibility. Expect lots of brake problems. IIHS gives the Malibu a "Marginal" rating for head-restraint effectiveness. **New for 2010:** The LT models come with a 6-speed automatic transmission.

OVERVIEW: The Malibu is a popular front-drive, mid-sized sedan, distinguished by its nice array of standard features. The base Malibu is "powered" by GM's wimpy 169 hp 2.4L 4-cylinder powerplant, found on many of its compact cars. Most buyers will be tempted to pay extra for the torquier and smoother 252 hp 3.6L V6.

The Malibu's styling is quite conservative and uncluttered. A fold-flat passenger seat and a 60/40-split rear folding bench seat maximizes the interior room. Other useful standard amenities include a driver-seat power height adjuster; a telescoping steering column that also tilts; power windows, door locks, and outside mirrors; and power-adjustable brake and accelerator pedals (LS and LT).

The Hybrid is a "mild" hybrid; it can't run solely on its battery, but the electric motor boosts the gasoline engine on acceleration. It also shuts off fuel during deceleration, and has an auto-stop mode that switches the engine off during idle. The battery is recharged through regenerative braking.

COST ANALYSIS: The 2010's 6-speed automatic is worth the extra cost. **Best alternatives:** The Honda Accord has more usable interior space and quicker and more accurate steering, and the Toyota Camry is plusher, though not as driver-oriented. Both Japanese competitors are also far more reliable. Other cars worth considering are the Hyundai Elantra or Tiburon, Mazda6, and Nissan Sentra. **Options:** The V6 and premium tires. **Rebates:** $3,500 rebates should kick in sometime during the new year. **Depreciation:** Average. **Insurance cost:** Higher than average. **Parts supply/cost:** Malibu uses GM generic parts that are found everywhere and are reasonably priced. **Annual maintenance cost:** Average. **Warranty:** 60-day money-back guarantee as long as you don't drive more than 4,000 km. Bumper-to-bumper 3 years/60,000 km; powertrain 5 years/160,000 km; rust perforation 6 years/160,000 km. **Supplementary warranty:** A wise investment. **Highway/city fuel economy:** *2.4L:* 6.5/9.5

L/100 km; *2.4L 6-speed:* 5.9/9.4 L/100 km; *V6:* 7.8/12.2 L/100 km; *Hybrid:* 7.9/5.8 L/100 km.

OWNER-REPORTED PROBLEMS: At the top of the list are engine and transmission failures, electrical system glitches (door locks that open and close randomly, for example), the frequent replacement of brake and suspension components, AC malfunctions, and very poor fit and finish. Safety-related complaints include airbags that deploy inadvertently or fail to deploy; severe glare from the dash onto the windshield; the Park gear won't hold the vehicle parked on a hill; the 6-speed transmission hesitates before shifting; and the vehicle has a tendency to wander to the left side of the road into oncoming traffic:

> I own a 2009 Chevy Malibu with a 6-cylinder engine. It has a severe and significant torque steer on acceleration (most noticeable from a stop) causing car to dramatically and dangerously pull to left. Has almost caused accidents more than once. In addition it requires a lot of pressure to put the emergency (parking) brake down to where it will hold the car on a hill. Have had this checked out by 3 separate Chevrolet dealers and all tell me they are design issues, normal conditions that cannot be corrected.

The door locks cannot be disabled to extricate an accident victim:

> My new 2009 Chevrolet Malibu does not provide for disabling the auto door locking feature. Having worked in law enforcement and been involved in accident investigations, I know that rescuers have a more difficult time of removing someone from a vehicle involved in an accident if the doors are locked especially if that person is a good Samaritan with no heavy tools. Both the dealer and GM have refused to acknowledge this problem or do anything to remediate it.

Sudden brake loss; premature warpage of the brake rotors; very loose steering; steering loss; sudden steering lock-up; chronic steering shimmy; frequent stalling for unexplained reasons; cruise control doesn't hold the set speed; original-equipment tires don't have gripping power and fail prematurely; and inaccurate fuel gauges.

IMPALA, LACROSSE ★★ / ★★★

RATING: *Impala:* Below Average. *LaCrosse:* Average. The Allure has been renamed the LaCrosse, its American moniker. **Strong points:** *Impala:* Comes with an array of standard features, provides a comfortable ride, and has an easily accessed interior, highlighted by a convenient flip-down centre console in the middle of the bench seats, and rear seatbacks that fold flat, opening up cargo storage space. NHTSA gave the Impala a five-star crashworthiness rating for front and side protection and four stars for rollover resistance. *LaCrosse:* The 3.0L V6 provides smooth acceleration and works well with the 6-speed automatic transmission, though it could use more high-speed torque. Handling and ride are better than

The Chevrolet Impala.

TECHNICAL DATA

PRICES: *Impala LS:* $26,6254, *LTZ:* $30,625, *LaCrosse CX:* $32,745, *CXL:* $34,745, *AWD:* $38,245, *CXS:* $40,745 **FREIGHT:** $1,400 **ORIGIN:** *Impala:* Canada *LaCrosse:* Just moved from Canada to the U.S. **SALES:** *Impala:* Down 57%, *LaCrosse:* Down 50%

POWERTRAIN (FRONT-DRIVE/AWD)

Engines: *Impala:* 3.5L V6 (211 hp) • 3.9L V6 (224 hp) • 5.3L V8 (303 hp), *LaCrosse:* 2.4L 4-cyl. (182 hp) • 3.0L V6 (255 hp) • 3.6L V6 (280 hp); Transmissions: *Impala:* 4-speed auto., *LaCrosse:* 6-speed auto.

DIMENSIONS/CAPACITY

Passengers: 2/3; Wheelbase: *Impala:* 110.5 in., *LaCrosse:* 111.7 in.; *Impala:* H: 58.7/L: 200.4/W: 72.9 in.; *LaCrosse:* H: 58.9/L: 197.0/W: 73.1 in.; Headroom F/R: 4.0/1.5 in.; Legroom F/R: *Impala:* 40.5/26 in., *LaCrosse:* N/A; Fuel tank: 64L/ reg./prem.; Cargo volume: 16 cu. ft.; Tow limit: 1,000 lb.; Load capacity: *Impala:* 945 lb., *LaCrosse:* 915 lb.; Turning circle: *Impala:* 41.0 ft., *LaCrosse:* 38.8 ft.; Ground clearance: *Impala:* 6.0 in., *LaCrosse:* N/A; Weight: *Impala LS, LT:* 3,555 lb., *LTZ:* 3,649 lb., *LaCrosse CX:* 3,948 lb.

Adequate rear legroom and a front bench seat. A much better reliability record than the Impala. The LaCrosse got five stars for front crash protection and four stars for rollover resistance; side protection with airbags merited three stars. Stability control is a standard LTZ feature. **Weak points:** *Impala:* The automatic 4-speed transmission is sometimes slow to downshift, and the Overdrive is clunky; this is a car that cries out for a 6-speed automatic gearbox. Rear seating is uncomfortable for three; bland styling; and obstructed rear visibility. Engine and transmission deficiencies have been commonplace. Subpar body construction, which puts the Impala on par with Chrysler's poor performers. Stability control isn't standard on the entry-level models. **New for 2010:** *Impala:* The V8-powered Impala SS has been discontinued, leaving the 3.5L and 3.9L V6s as the sole engine choices. *LaCrosse:* Completely redesigned; all-wheel drive on the CXL model; and the V8 engine has been dropped.

OVERVIEW: GM's Impala is yesterday's sedan. With the V8 option gone, the car is overwhelmed by its unimpressive highway performance and overall lack of quality. The mid-level 3.9L V6 does offer cylinder deactivation, which improves fuel economy by shutting off half the engine's cylinders when they aren't needed.

The 2010 mid-size LaCrosse has been completely restyled, and its four-wheel independent suspension has been retuned for improved ride and handling qualities. CX and CXL models will initially be powered by an all-new 255 hp 3.0L V6 hooked to a 6-speed automatic transmission; in early 2010, the CX will get a 182 hp 2.4L 4-cylinder engine as its base powerplant. CX models come with front-drive, while the CXL's all-wheel drive is optional. The top-of-the-line CXS is now powered by a 280 hp 3.6L V6, 6-speed automatic, and front-drive. The CXL features dual-zone automatic climate control, fog lamps, and mirrors with integrated turn signals and puddle lamps. The available all-wheel-drive system employs a limited-slip differential to send torque to whichever wheel has more traction for better control on slippery roads. The CXS adds 18-inch alloy wheels, an active damping system, and heated leather seats.

COST ANALYSIS: 2009 Impalas are discounted about 15 percent and are practically identical to the 2010s. **Best alternatives:** The more reliable, better-performing Honda Accord, Mazda6, Hyundai Elantra, and Toyota Camry or Avalon. Those wanting a bit more performance should consider the BMW 3 Series. More room and better performance can be had by purchasing a Hyundai Tucson or a Honda CR-V. **Options:** Pass on the Impala's rear spoiler, which obstructs rear visibility and is of doubtful utility. **Rebates:** *Impala:* The Impala is in a marketing segment that's steadily losing ground to Japanese entries. The longer you wait, the cheaper these cars will become. Look for a savings of at least $3,000. *LaCrosse:* The redesign will create some buying buzz, but GM will use sizeable $4,000+ rebates in the winter to move these large cars. **Depreciation:** *Impala:* Incredibly fast; a 2007 Impala LS that sold new for $25,230 is now worth only $12,500. *LaCrosse:* Again, depreciation is a big minus. A 2007 LaCrosse (Allure) CX that sold for $26,395 is now worth $13,000. **Insurance cost:** Higher than average. **Parts supply/cost:** Moderately priced parts that aren't hard to find. **Annual maintenance cost:** Higher than average. Independent garages can perform most non-emissions servicing; however, cylinder deactivation makes you a prisoner of GM dealer servicing. **Warranty:** 60-day money-back guarantee as long as you don't drive more than 4,000 km. Bumper-to-bumper 4 years/80,000 km; powertrain 5 years/160,000 km; rust perforation 6 years/160,000 km. **Supplementary warranty:** Essential, especially after the third year of ownership. **Highway/city fuel economy:** *Impala sedan 3.5L:* 6.7/10.8 L/100 km; *3.9L:* 7.4/12.0 L/100 km; *LaCrosse 3.0L:* 8.7/13.1 L/100 km.

OWNER-REPORTED PROBLEMS: Electrical system problems are common. Front and rear brakes rust easily and wear out early, and the discs warp far too often. Shock absorbers and MacPherson struts wear out or leak prematurely. The power rack-and-pinion steering system degenerates quickly after three years and is characterized by chronic leaking. Poor body fit, particularly around the doors, leads to excessive wind noise and water leaking into the interior. *Impala:* Airbag failures; chronic stalling; engine sputters, hesitates; driver-side wheel falls off; vehicle jerks when passing over rough pavement; car rolls back at a stop; excessive front-end vibration; brake rotors on one vehicle had to be replaced at 7,500 km; popping sound on stopping, starting, and turning; left and right control-arm, lower control-arm, ball joint, and steering failures; and a poorly designed Reverse lighting feature:

GM's use of reverse lights as "perimeter lighting" is extremely poorly thought out. Reverse lights indicate that a vehicle is in reverse motion. They should not be used for any other purpose. Using them as perimeter lighting is extremely confusing to other motorists. Picture this. A vehicle pulls into a parking space. One person exits the passengers side and the reverse lights come on. Approaching drivers are going to expect that the vehicle is about to back out of the parking space, not that the driver has turned off the engine and is waiting for someone to return.

LaCrosse: Distracting mirror reflection; vehicle wanders all over the road; brake pad, caliper, and rotor failures.

LUCERNE ★★★★

RATING: Above Average. **Strong points:** A nice array of useful standard equipment at an affordable base price, but costs go up quickly as the options grow. Good V8 powertrain performance. The electronic 4-speed transmission works imperceptibly, but it exacts a high fuel penalty. Cruise control is much smoother without all those annoying downshifts we've learned to hate in GM cars. Handling is acceptably predictable, though a bit slow with variable-assist power steering. A comfortable ride and a plush interior. Quiet running; plenty of passenger and cargo room. NHTSA gave the Lucerne its top five-star rating for front crash protection and rollover resistance; side crashworthiness scored four stars. IIHS says the car's frontal offset crash protection is "Good," and side protection is "Acceptable." **Weak points:** Giving the "Super" model a powerful Cadillac Northstar-derived V8 and then hooking it to a rudimentary 4-speed automatic is worse than taking a shower in a raincoat. Acceleration isn't breathtaking with the base V6 either; at higher revs, torque falls off quickly. The V8 tends to fishtail when at full throttle. Power steering is a bit vague at highway speeds. Fuel-thirsty; poor-quality mechanical and body components; obstructed front and rear visibility;

ponderous handling caused partly by a mediocre suspension and over-assisted steering; car fishtails at full throttle; and panic braking causes considerable nose-diving, which compromises handling. IIHS gives a "Marginal" rating for head-restraint effectiveness. **New for 2010:** Nothing significant. The fog lights and rocker panels from last year's Super are now standard, and all models get a backlit instrument cluster. The Lucerne will most likely be discontinued next year, leaving the LaCrosse as the flagship car.

TECHNICAL DATA

PRICES: *CX:* $31,995, *CXL:* $34,995, *Super:* $47,995 **FREIGHT:** $1,400 **ORIGIN:** U.S. **SALES:** Down 40%
POWERTRAIN (FRONT-DRIVE)
Engines: 3.9L V6 (227 hp) • 4.6L V8 (292 hp); Transmission: 4-speed auto.
DIMENSIONS/CAPACITY
Passengers: 2/3; Wheelbase: 116 in.; H: 58/L: 203/W: 74 in.; Headroom F/R: 3.0/2.5 in.; Legroom F/R: 42.5/31.5 in.; Cargo volume: 17 cu. ft.; Fuel tank: 70L/regular; Load capacity: 925 lb.; Tow limit: 1,000 lb.; Turning circle: 47 ft.; Ground clearance: 5.0 in.; Weight: 4,095 lb.

OVERVIEW: Buick's Lucerne is a competent front-drive family car that replaced the LeSabre and Park Avenue in 2006. It's not a very fuel-efficient four-door sedan, but generous discounting will give you plenty of change in your pockets to buy the extra gas. Clean body lines and a large platform make for an aerodynamic, pleasing appearance and a roomy interior—with more rear seatroom than the Allure. The standard 3.9L V6 engine has seven fewer horses than the old LeSabre and is rough-running and noisy when pushed. CXS models are powered by a high-performance V8, which offers much better low- and mid-range throttle response.

COST ANALYSIS: Get a 20-percent discounted, almost-identical 2009 model. **Best alternatives:** Ford Taurus, Hyundai Genesis Coupe, and Lexus ES series. **Options:** Go for the more powerful V8. **Rebates:** $5,000–$6,000+. **Depreciation:** Faster than average. **Insurance cost:** Higher than average. **Parts supply/cost:** Parts aren't hard to find, but they can be pricey. **Annual maintenance cost:** Average. **Warranty:** 60-day money-back guarantee as long as you don't drive more than 4,000 km. Bumper-to-bumper 4 years/80,000 km; powertrain 5 years/160,000 km; rust perforation 6 years/160,000 km. **Supplementary warranty:** It'll come in handy. **Highway/city fuel economy:** *3.9L V6:* 7.3/12.2 L/100 km; *4.6L V8:* 8.7/13.8 L/100 km.

OWNER-REPORTED PROBLEMS: Below average quality. Owners single out the brakes, suspension, and fit and finish as the most troublesome areas. No airbag deployment; cruise control causes the vehicle to surge; steering linkage bolts detach, causing steering failure; speedometer and fuel gauge can't be read in daylight; the driver-side mirror doesn't give a clear view to the rear; mirror fogs up; front pillars create a blind spot; and the fuel gauge gives inaccurate readings. Safety-related complaints logged by NHTSA include sudden, unintended acceleration while parking; low-beam headlights switch to high-beams and won't return to low; alcohol fumes permeate the cabin, source unknown; and door stoppers don't hold the door open on a moderate incline.

CAMARO ★

bad buy

TECHNICAL DATA

PRICES: *LS Coupe:* $26,995, *2LT:* $31,595, *1SS Coupe:* $36,995, *2SS:* $40,995 **FREIGHT:** $1,400 **ORIGIN:** Canada **SALES:** Brisk

POWERTRAIN (FRONT-DRIVE)

Engines: 3.6L V6 (304 hp) • 6.2L V8 (400–426 hp); Transmissions: 6-speed man. • 6-speed auto.

DIMENSIONS/CAPACITY

Passengers: 2/2; Wheelbase: 112.3 in.; H: 54.2/L: 190.4/W: 75.5 in.; Headroom: N/A; Legroom: N/A; Cargo volume: 11.3 cu. ft.; Fuel tank: 71.9L/regular; Tow limit: No towing; Load capacity: N/A; Turning circle: 37.7 ft.; Ground clearance: N/A; Weight: 3,750–3,913 lb.

RATING: Not Recommended during its first year on the market. **Strong points:** Nicely styled, with a mixture of retro and modern touches. Impressive V6 and V8 acceleration with reasonable fuel economy and nice steering/handling. NHTSA awarded the Camaro five stars for side crashworthiness and rollover resistance; four stars were given for frontal crash protection. IIHS has not yet tested the car. **Weak points:** No headroom; if you are 6'2" or taller your head will be constantly brushing up against the headliner; uncomfortable seats; rear seating is a "knees-to-chin" affair; not much cargo room; some of the gauges are mounted at shin-height on the console, where they can barely be seen; much of the interior trim looks and feels cheap; and owners report that first-year fit and finish glitches are everywhere. Obstructed driver visibility. **New for 2010:** Everything.

OVERVIEW: The 2010 Chevrolet Camaro resurrects General Motors' iconic "pony car" high-performance two-door coupe; a two-door convertible version is due early next spring. LS, 1LT, 2LT, 1SS, and 2SS models are offered with one of two engines: a V6 or a V8. The 3.6L V6 produces 304 hp. It's available on LS and LT versions. SS versions with a manual transmission are equipped with a 426 hp 6.2L V8. Automatic-equipped SS models get the same V8, but with "only" 400 hp and GM's Active Fuel Management cylinder deactivation. Available safety features include ABS, traction control, anti-skid system, front side airbags, and side curtain airbags.

COST ANALYSIS: Over 25,000 Camaros have been sold so far, which means dealers can ask for and get the full suggested retail price. Smart buyers will wait on the better-made and more reasonably priced 2011 models. **Best alternatives:** The Ford Mustang and Hyundai Genesis Coupe. The base Camaro is a better choice than the base V6 Mustang because GM's rear-drive powertrains are smoother. However, when you compare V8s, the Mustang GT is the clear winner where price is concerned. Normally, the Dodge Challenger would also be a "challenger," but buying any limited-production car from tottering Chrysler is a risky deal. **Options:** Integrated child safety seats. The GPS navigation aids can be useful, but don't waste your money on the power sunroof, leather upholstery, or heated seats. **Rebates:** Rebates and discounts of $3,000–$5,000. **Depreciation:** Too early to tell. **Insurance cost:** Much higher than average. **Parts supply/cost:** Not easily found and costly. At present, dealers have a monopoly on parts and service. **Annual maintenance cost:** Higher than average; there's no competition. **Warranty:** 60-day money-back guarantee as long as you don't drive more than 4,000 km. Bumper-to-bumper 4 years/80,000 km; powertrain 5 years/160,000 km; rust perforation 6 years/unlimited km. **Supplementary warranty:** A very good idea, considering that the Camaro is a first-year car. **Highway/city fuel economy:** *3.6L V6:* 6.8/12.3 L/100 km; *auto.:* 6.9/11.4 L/100 km; *6.2L V8:* 8.2/13.2 L/100 km; *auto.:* 8.2/13.2 L/100 km.

OWNER-REPORTED PROBLEMS: The cable running from the trunk-mounted battery may fray on the starter motor and ground out, causing a complete loss of power. Also, GM suspended shipments last summer of Camaro SSs (V8-engine) with manual transmissions while engineers looked into reports of failed output shafts.

Although the Camaro hasn't been on the road long enough to get reliable failure rates on its various components, one group of owners and Camaro enthusiasts at *www.camaro5.com/forums/index.php* prepared a table of defects seen with the most recently delivered 2010 models, which included the issues listed below. The group also points out those areas that require special scrutiny.

> Loose bolts that hold fluid back causing leaks (example: on oil pan, tranny fluid). • Trunk locking mechanism (issues with opening w/o adding down pressure to top of trunk first and/or emergency release appears to be loose keeping the trunk from locking properly). • Trunk may not open with remote switch. • Loose plastic paneling around the 4-gauge cluster, launch control, cigarette power plug as well as loose left and right A-pillar trim, sill trim, and dash panel trim where doors and dash meet. • Uneven dash (driver's side is lower then passenger's side. • Loose spoiler (re-torque spoiler bolts). • Wiper transmission cable overheats creating a short circuit. • One headlight may be brighter than the other. • Mismatched paint or paint that is easily chipped. • Missing or peeling paint between trunk lid and spoiler (right rear section). • Loose rocker panel that peels off. • Faulty ambient door lighting. • Radiator leaks. • Hood release/latch won't unhook to open the hood. • Gap at base of OnStar antenna. • Incorrect speedometer readings; also keeps shutting off. • Transmission failure. • Clunking noise when changing gears. • Key sticks in the ignition. • Non-RS taillights installed on RS-equipped cars. • Faulty taillights. • Rocker panel mis-aligned with body and clipped incorrectly. • Look for

mis-aligned body and door panels as well as the hood not centered. • Loose bumper. • Ambient lighting on driver's door should be as bright as the lighting on the passenger door. • Doors gaps and poor alignment. • Door panel may be scratched from the seat belt. • Sometimes, only one door will unlock. • Side fenders may be mis-aligned (wheel cover well needs to be taken off and the fender bolt loosened). • Dirt/bubbles in rally stripes. • Shift knobs quickly wear out. • AC blows cold air intermittently. • Possible blockage in AC drainage and/or AC draining into the car instead of beneath it. • Check that USB drive and auxillary port work. • Squeaky brakes. • Rims and tires may have been damaged in transport. • Check the locking mechanism of both doors. • Scraping sound when backing up. • Loose SS emblem on trunk. • Loose interior windshield trim. • GFX may be installed incorrectly and the front GFX lip may be loose. • Check that the front brake rotors are not worn. • Check that the hood latch handle retracts properly. • Look for scratches on the seats. • Check for oil cooler leaks. • Fuel gauge may give incorrect readings. • Driver's side roof light (the one with the toggle switch) may only work when it's toggled over to the passenger side. • Drive-shaft connection to the differential may crack when dropping the clutch. • Tachometer needle sticks. • Wiper motor wiring comes through bottom of the cowling-well in front of the driver. • Engine makes continuous clicking noise, beginning roughly 5 seconds after the engine starts. • Door sill plates may be wrinkled on the outside edges. • Trunk gasket at bottom of rear window may come off. • Loose weather stripping at back of the rear windows. • Driver's seat makes clicking noises when set all the way back.

CORVETTE ★★★

RATING: Average; a brawny, bulky sport coupe that's slowly evolving into a more refined machine. But quality control continues to be subpar, and safety-related transmission and body deficiencies are common. The Corvette does deliver high-performance thrills along with suspension kickback, numb steering, and seats that need extra bolstering. Overall, get the quieter and less temperamental base Corvette; it delivers the same cachet for a lot less money. **Strong points:** Powerful and smooth powertrain that responds quickly to the throttle; the 6-speed gearbox performs well in all gear ranges and makes shifting smooth, with short throws and easy entry into all gears. Easy handling; enhanced side-slip angle control helps to prevent skidding and provides better traction control. No oversteer, wheel spinning, breakaway rear ends, or nasty surprises, thanks partly to standard electronic stability control. Better-than-average braking; the ABS-vented disc brakes are easy to modulate, and they're fade-free. The car has a relatively roomy interior, user-friendly instruments and controls, and lots of convenience features. There's a key-controlled lockout feature that discourages joy riding by cutting engine power in half. All Corvettes are also equipped with an impressively effective PASS KEY theft-deterrent system that uses a resistor pellet in the ignition to disable the starter and fuel system when the key code doesn't match the ignition lock. **Weak points:** Vague steering; limited rear visibility; inadequate storage space; poor-quality powertrain; mediocre fit and finish; cabin amenities and materials that are not up to the competition's standards; and no crashworthiness or rollover data available from NHTSA or IIHS. The Corvette's sophisticated electronic and powertrain components have low tolerance for real-world conditions. The car is so low that its front air dam scrapes over the smallest rise in the road. Expect lots of visits to the dealer's repair bays. **New for 2010:** Standard side airbags, and revised interiors. Convertibles get a trunk spoiler, and cars equipped with manual transmissions get a Performance Traction Management (PTM) system that modulates the engine's torque output for fast starts. This feature also manages engine power when the driver floors the accelerator when coming out of a corner.

TECHNICAL DATA

PRICES: *Base Coupe:* $66,145, *Convertible:* $75,985, *Z06:* $94,715, *ZR1:* $127,545 **FREIGHT:** $1,400 **ORIGIN:** U.S. **SALES:** Down 50%

POWERTRAIN (REAR-DRIVE)

Engines: 6.2L V8 (430 hp) • 7.0L V8 (505 hp) • 6.2L V8 Supercharged (638 hp); Transmissions: 6-speed man. • 6-speed auto.

DIMENSIONS/CAPACITY

Passengers: 2; Wheelbase: 106 in.; H: 49/L: 175/W: 73 in.; Headroom: 4 in.; Legroom: 41 in.; Cargo volume: 11 cu. ft.; Fuel tank: 68.1L/premium; Tow limit: Not recommended; Load capacity: 390 lb.; Turning circle: 42 ft.; Ground clearance: 4.5 in.; Weight: 3,280 lb.

OVERVIEW: Standard models come with a 430 hp 6.0L V8 mated to a 6-speed manual or optional automatic transmission, Keyless Access with push-button start, large tires and wheels (18-inch front, 19-inch rear), HID xenon lighting, power hatch pull-down, heated seats, and AM/FM/CD/MP3 player with seven speakers and in-dash six-CD changer. The base design is more flowing and muscular than previous stylings.

Z06

Although not quite as fast as the Dodge Viper, this is the fastest model found in the Corvette lineup (0–100 km/h in 3.6–4.2 seconds). It's also the lightest Z06 yet, thanks to the magic of Detroit re-engineering. Instead of just adding iron and components to carry extra weight, GM has reinforced the rear axle and 6-speed clutch, installed coolers everywhere, adopted a dry-sump oil system to keep the engine well oiled when cornering, and added wider wheels and larger, heat-dissipating brakes. These improvements added about 50 kg of weight, which was trimmed by using cast-magnesium in the chassis structure and installing lighter carbon-fibre floorboards and front fenders. Net result: a monster 'Vette that is rated for 300+ km/h and weighs less than the base model.

To be honest, the Z06 chassis isn't very communicative to the driver, so the car doesn't inspire as much driving confidence as does the European competition, although it does feature standard stability control for when you get too frisky.

COST ANALYSIS: Go for a 2009 base model minus the Performance Traction Management (PTM) system and forego jackrabbit starts and high-speed cornering. Keep in mind that premium fuel and astronomical insurance rates will further drive up your operating costs. A word about the ZR1: It's like investing in Nortel—don't! A 2009 model that sold new for $127,545 is now worth $105,000. A $22,000 loss. **Best alternatives:** Other sporty models worth considering are the Ford GT or Shelby GT500 Mustang, and Porsche 911 or Boxster. The Nissan 370Z looks good on paper, but its quality problems carried over year after year make it a risky buy, much like Nissan's attractively styled Quest. **Options:** Remember, performance options rarely increase performance to the degree promised by the seller; the more performance options you buy, the less comfort you'll have, the more things can go wrong, and the more simple repairs can increase in complexity. Run-flat tires are not a good investment, either. They are hard to find and expensive. Forget about the head-up instrument display that projects speed and other data onto the windshield; it's annoyingly distracting, and you'll end up turning it off. **Rebates:** The Corvette is so popular that GM normally doesn't have to offer rebates to boost sales, but there will be some discounting starting late in 2009 as fuel costs rise and sales return to the basement. **Depreciation:** Much faster than you would imagine and nowhere near the resale prices promised by salespeople. For example, an entry-level 2003 Corvette that sold for almost $70,000 new is now worth about $20,000. **Insurance cost:** Astronomical. **Parts supply/cost:** Fair availability, but parts are pricey. **Annual maintenance cost:** Higher than average. **Warranty:** 60-day money-back guarantee as long as you don't drive more than 4,000 km. Bumper-to-bumper 3 years/60,000 km; powertrain 5 years/160,000 km; rust perforation 6 years/160,000 km. **Supplementary warranty:** A smart idea to protect you from drivetrain failures. **Highway/city fuel economy:** *6.2L man.:* 7.7/12.9 L/100 km; *auto.:* 8.1/14.3 L/100 km; *7.0L man.:* 8.2/14.2 L/100 km; *auto.:* 8.2/14.2 L/100 km.

OWNER-REPORTED PROBLEMS: Harsh, delayed transmission shifts; squeaks and rattles caused by the car's structural deficiencies. The car was built as a convertible and, therefore, has too much body flex. Servicing the different sophisticated fuel injection systems isn't easy, even (especially) for GM mechanics. NHTSA-logged safety-related complaints: The headliner sags and block the rear-view mirror view; right rear axle suddenly snaps in half; chronic stalling and excessive steering vibration; and fuel tank will only take half a tankful of gasoline:

> 2009 Covette will only take a half-tank of gas before auto-shutoff is activated. To fill tank I have to turn nozzle upside down. This method causes fuel overflow and spillage on the ground.

CTS ★★★

RATING: Average. As Cadillac reinvents itself in a futile attempt to lure younger buyers, its cars are becoming more complex and less distinctive. **Strong points:** Roomier cabin than other cars in this class (the Sport Wagon's generous cargo space is especially noteworthy); a tasteful, well-appointed interior loaded with high-tech gadgetry; competent and secure handling; and available all-wheel drive. NHTSA has given five stars for side crashworthiness and four stars for front crash protection and rollover resistance. IIHS awarded its top rating of "Good" for frontal offset crashworthiness, side impact protection, and head-restraint effectiveness. **Weak points:** Not as agile as its rivals; sport suspensions may be hard on the kidneys; poor rear visibility; and an awkward driving position caused by uneven pedal depth and limited knee room, due to the intrusion of the centre stack. Owners also complain of fit and finish deficiencies and frequent electronic malfunctions. Rear-seat access requires some acrobatics due to the low rear roof line, and the rear seatback could use additional bolstering. Also, the trunk's narrow opening adds to the difficulty of loading bulky items. **New for 2010:** A two-door CTS will appear with powertrain choices similar to the CTS Sedan. *CTS Sedan:* A 270 hp 3.0L V6 replaces the 3.6L as the standard engine; the 304 hp 3.6L will be optional. Also new: a cabin air filtration system and an upgraded steering

TECHNICAL DATA

PRICES: *Base:* $40,485, *AWD:* $44,810, *Auto Navi.:* $46,200 **FREIGHT:** $1,400
ORIGIN: U.S. **SALES:** Down 35%
POWERTRAIN (REAR-DRIVE/AWD)
Engines: 3.0L V6 (270 hp) • 3.6L V6 (304 hp) • 6.2L V8 (556 hp); Transmissions: 6-speed man. • 6-speed auto.
DIMENSIONS/CAPACITY (BASE CTS)
Passengers: 2/3; Wheelbase: 113 in.; H: 58/L: 192/W: 73 in.; Headroom F/R: 3.0/1.5 in.; Legroom F/R: 44.0/28.5 in.; Cargo volume: 14 cu. ft.; Fuel tank: 70L/premium; Tow limit: 1,000 lb.; Load capacity: 890 lb.; Turning circle: 38 ft.; Ground clearance: 5.0 in.; Weight: 3,940 lb.

wheel and shifter. *CTS Sport Wagon:* Slightly shorter than the CTS sedan, the CTS Sport Wagon will provide 7.6 metres (25 feet) of cargo space accessible via a power-assisted liftgate. The Sport Wagon will also carry a base 3.0L and optional 3.6L V6 and employ either a rear-drive or all-wheel-drive system, plus a suspension that can be adjusted from cushy to sporty (firm). *CTS-V Sedan:* This 556 hp "muscle" Cadillac returns for 2010 with no significant changes.

OVERVIEW: Cadillac's rear-drive, entry-level CTS sport sedan is available with two V6 engines. Rear-drive and a 6-speed manual are standard with both, while a 6-speed automatic and all-wheel drive are optional. Standard safety features include anti-lock disc brakes, traction control, stability control, front-seat side airbags, full-length side curtain airbags, and GM's OnStar emergency communications system.

COST ANALYSIS: Go for the more-refined 2010 version. Once all the rebates and other sales incentives kick in sometime in late winter, the slightly higher cost will be insignificant. **Best alternative:** Acura TL SH-AWD, BMW 3 Series, Hyundai Genesis, Infiniti G37, and the Lincoln MKS, MKZ, or Town Car. **Options:** Neither the adaptive cruise control nor the advanced DVD navigation system is worth the extra money. **Rebates:** \$4,500–\$6,000 in sales incentives. **Depreciation:** Unbelievably fast. A 2003 CTS that sold new for \$40,000 is now worth a little over \$7,000. **Insurance cost:** Higher than average. **Parts supply/cost:** Parts are often back-ordered and electronic components are quite pricey. **Annual maintenance cost:** Higher than average. **Warranty:** 60-day money-back guarantee as long as you don't drive more than 4,000 km. Bumper-to-bumper 4 years/80,000 km; powertrain 5 years/160,000 km; rust perforation 6 years/160,000 km. **Supplementary warranty:** A good thing to have. **Highway/city fuel economy:** N/A.

OWNER-REPORTED PROBLEMS: Engine and transmission failures, electrical system malfunctions, and fit and finish glitches. The CTS doesn't have a spare tire, jack, or lug wrench; the sunroof can implode; and there's excessive vibration and power-train drone/boom when the car is underway:

> When driving a 2009 Cadillac CTS the car generates a drone, boom and vibration. This happens when accelerating to or driving at highway speeds. I bought the car new and there has been a problem...with this car since I took delivery from the Cadillac dealer. GM has issued a service bulletin (#08-07-30-044B) to install rubber insulators and reprogram the transmission control module. This "fix" did not help. It only moved the onset of the vibration to a higher rpm/speed. When the vibration occurs the car does not feel safe. I am not sure if a mechanical component is going to fail. The drone is constant, distracting and annoying while driving. There is also a boom noise at 5 mph [8 km/h] when coming to a stop. This is not a smooth, quiet, safe car. The Cadillac service manager says he does not hear anything. I do not agree. Cadillac also says the noises are inherent in the vehicle and have no fix.
>
> •
>
> Heavy vibration and low pitch hum at approx. 45 mph [72 km/h].

2009 Cadillac CTS 3.6 direct inject engine. Starting at 700 miles [1,126 km] vehicle started shuddering between 40–75 mph [64–121 km/h]. Per GM they are aware of the design flaw but there is currently no fix for this engineering issue.

SILVERADO 1500, 2500, SIERRA ★★★

The GMC Sierra.

RATING: Average. **Strong points:** *1500:* Good choice of engines and transmissions; standard electronic stability control; comfortable seating; lots of storage capability; good fuel economy. Since its 2008 redesign, the Silverado handles much better, offers a steadier, more controllable ride (no more "Shakerado"), and has a more refined, comfortable cabin. NHTSA gave the Silverado 1500 and Hybrid five stars for frontal crash protection and four stars for rollover resistance; the truck wasn't tested for side crash protection. IIHS has given the Silverado 1500 a "Good" rating for frontal offset protection and an "Acceptable" score for head-restraint effectiveness. *2500:* These heavy-duty work trucks are built primarily to be load-carrying vehicles capable of working off-road. Therefore, don't fault them for their ponderous handling and harsh ride. The standard engine is a powerful 360 hp 6.0L V8 backed up by a 365 hp 6.6L turbodiesel. **Weak points:** *1500:* Powertrain smoothness and reliability doesn't measure up to what the Dodge Ram, Honda Ridgeline, and Nissan Titan can provide. The steering is over-assisted; there's excess body lean when cornering; climate controls aren't very user-friendly; and the servicing network is rather limited. IIHS says the 1500's side crashworthiness merits a "Poor" rating. *2500:* Stiff riding and barely acceptable handling. **New for 2010:** All V8s are flex-fuel capable, and the 4.8L and 5.3L

TECHNICAL DATA

PRICES: *1500 Regular Cab 4×2:* $23,990, *1500 Crew Cab Hybrid:* $46,725 **FREIGHT:** $1,400 **ORIGIN:** U.S. and Mexico **SALES:** *Silverado:* Down 40%, *Sierra:* Down 35%

POWERTRAIN (FRONT-DRIVE)

Engines: 4.3L V6 (195 hp) • 4.8L V8 (302 hp) • 5.3L V8 (315 hp), *Hybrid:* 6.0L V8 (332 hp) • 6.2L V8 (403 hp); Transmissions: 4-speed auto. • 6-speed auto., *Hybrid:* CVT

DIMENSIONS/CAPACITY

Passengers: *1500:* 2/1, *2500:* 3/3; Wheelbase: *1500:* 144 in., *2500:* 153 in.; *1500:* H: 74/L: 230/W: 80 in., *2500:* H: 77/L: 240/W: 80 in.; Headroom F/R: *1500:* 6.5/6.0 in., *2500:* 6.0/5.0 in.; Legroom F/R: 41.5/29 in., *2500:* 40.5/27 in.; Cargo volume: N/A; Fuel tank: 129L/ regular; Tow limit: *Hybrid:* 6,100 lb., *1500:* 7,500 lb., *2500:* 13,600 lb.; Load capacity: *1500:* 1,570 lb., *2500:* 2,260 lb.; Turning circle: *1500:* 50 ft., *2500:* 55 ft.; Ground clearance: 9.5 in.; Weight: *1500:* 5,435 lb., *2500:* 6,920 lb.

engines get variable valve timing. Trucks with the 5.3L engine also get a 6-speed automatic transmission and a revised rear axle ratio. All 1500 models have standard electronic stability control, seat-mounted side airbags, and side curtain airbags. All stereos also get a USB port.

OVERVIEW: The 2010 Chevrolet Silverado 1500 won't get a new turbodiesel V8 engine because GM is broke. Basically, this large pickup is a twin of the GMC Sierra and is offered in regular-, extended-, and crew-cab body styles. Regular cabs seat up to three passengers; extendeds and crews can carry six. There are three bed lengths: 5.8, 6.6, and 8.0 feet. Silverados offer two interiors: "pure pickup" and "luxury inspired." Available engines: 195 hp 4.3L V6; 302 hp 4.8L V8; 315 hp 5.3L V8; and 403 hp 6.2L V8. All V8s can run on ethanol-blended fuel. The 5.3 V8 saves fuel through Active Fuel Management cylinder deactivation. V6 and 4.8L V8 Silverados are coupled to a 4-speed automatic transmission. A 6-speed automatic is used with the 5.3L and 6.2L V8s. Rear-drive is standard and two four-wheel-drive systems are optional: a part-time setup that shouldn't be left engaged on dry pavement, and GM's Autotrac, which can go anywhere. Both have a low-range gear for off-roading.

The Silverado 1500 Hybrid has a 6.0L V8 that pairs with an electric motor producing 332 hp. It can run on one or both of its power sources, depending on driving demands, and doesn't need to be plugged-in. The hybrid has a continuously variable automatic transmission (CVT) and a maximum towing capacity of 6,100 lb.

COST ANALYSIS: Buy the almost identical 2009 versions and keep in mind that GM Canada is offering up to $9,500 in discounts and rebates on the 2500 series. Just be careful that the suggested retail price hasn't been inflated. Take 10 percent off that amount and work your way back from there. **Best alternatives:** The Dodge Ram pickup, Ford F-Series, and Honda Ridgeline. **Options:** Consider the $600 Exterior Plus package, which includes a remote starter, fog lights, a garage door opener, and a locking tailgate with the EZ Lift feature. Also, consider getting adjustable gas and brake pedals if you need to put extra space between you and the steering-wheel-mounted airbag. **Rebates:** $9,500 in sales incentives on the 2009 model 2500. **Depreciation:** Faster than average. **Insurance cost:** Much higher than average. **Parts supply/cost:** Parts aren't hard to find and are competitively priced by independent suppliers. **Annual maintenance cost:** Higher than average. **Warranty:** 60-day money-back guarantee as long as you don't drive more than 4,000 km. Bumper-to-bumper 4 years/80,000 km; powertrain 5 years/160,000 km; rust perforation 6 years/160,000 km. **Supplementary warranty:** Recommended. **Highway/city fuel economy:** *4.3L 2WD:* 10.0/14.1 L/100 km; *4.3L 4WD:* 11.3/14.9 L/100 km; *4.8L 2WD:* 10.6/14.7 L/100 km; *4.8L 4WD:* 11.1/15.4 L/100 km; *5.3L 2WD:* 10.1/14.5 L/100 km; *5.3L 4WD:* 10.3/14.7 L/100 km; *6.2L AWD:* 10.8/17.7 L/100 km; *Hybrid 2WD:* 9.2/9.8 L/100 km; *Hybrid 4WD:* 9.8/10.5 L/100 km.

OWNER-REPORTED PROBLEMS: Powertrain, fuel system, suspension, and fit and finish deficiencies. Safety-related complaints include sun visors that don't block the sun's rays sufficiently, and engine surging when the brakes are applied.

The Dodge Ram.

Both the Ram and F-Series outclass GM's truck lineup.

The Ford F-Series.

ASIAN VEHICLES

Hyping the Hybrids

The savings in fuel and taxes don't do enough for me to alleviate the pain of the sticker price and the cost of a new battery down the road.... Why not buy a Civic HX that gets 44 mpg [5.3 L/100 km] highway for $13,700 and use the extra money to plant a few hundred trees?

REILLY BRENNAN
MOTOR TREND
APRIL 2004

Our present economic depression has not only forced two of America's largest automakers and more than 2,000 dealers into bankruptcy but also savaged car markets worldwide, including Japan's. It's no secret that Isuzu, Suzuki, and Mitsubishi are struggling. But Toyota? Indeed, Japan's automotive powerhouse posted its first full-year operating loss in seven decades last year. In the first quarter of 2009, Toyota lost $7.87 billion (U.S.), or almost $3 billion more than General Motors.

This year, the main difference between Asian vehicles and Detroit's best is that the Asians are coming back with more-reliable, smaller, fuel-efficient models, sold through low-cost financing and leasing deals. Many American models aren't coming back at all. And adding injury to injury, Hyundai, Kia, and Mazda are prowling the streets trolling for dealers terminated by Chrysler and General Motors. This means more competition for the Detroit Three, more import dealers selling multiple makes, and more servicing outlets for Asian and European vehicles. In the final analysis, it means the death of Detroit and the rise of the imports.

Nissan's Murano combines a powerful V6 with respectable fuel economy.

No market segment is safe from the Asian invasion (except, possibly, full-sized vans). In response to high fuel prices, Honda, Nissan, and Toyota are bringing "micro" cars to North America this year; Hyundai, Mazda, and Mitsubishi will be working overtime to supply rebadged small cars to Chrysler and Ford; and almost everyone is expanding their product lines to include more hybrids and "crossover" tall wagons. Also watch for better-performing and more-economical large pickups, as well as high-performance models from Honda, Nissan, and Lexus that target GM's new Camaro and Corvette.

South Korean vehicles—once the laughing stock of car columnists and consumer advocates—are catching up to the Japanese competition in quality and sales. Hyundai is putting better-quality parts in its Kia subsidiary's cars, SUVs, and minivans.

The emerging BRIC (Brazil, Russia, India, and China) economies are major players also, in both the production and sale of new vehicles to Asian, European, and North American manufacturers. For example:

- Brazil is a big producer of ethanol and ethanol-fuelled vehicles, which it sells to its own burgeoning market and throughout the world. The country is also a major builder of conventional cars and car parts.
- Russia's car industry is booming from both a production and sales standpoint. Unfortunately, Russian cars are almost as badly built as what China spews out.
- Although struggling, India's Tata Motors is ramping up production at both the high and low ends of the auto market. Its March 2008 purchase of Jaguar and Land Rover from Ford (Ford took a $3 billion bath) reinforces the truism that the best English afternoon tea isn't served in England; it's found in Hong Kong and India. Tata's low-end $2,500 Nano car is remarkably cheap and practical, though basic to the extreme. It's scheduled to arrive in North America in late 2010 as a 2011 model and sell for $7,000.
- Look at China's Sichuan Tengzhong Heavy Industrial Machinery Co.'s on-and-off purchase of General Motors' Hummer division. The sale marks the first time that a Chinese buyer has acquired a brand from one of the struggling U.S. automakers. Usually, China simply pirates a design and then sells the vehicle as its own. ("What? We can't sell it as a Chevy? Okay, we'll call it a 'Chery.'") Nevertheless, GM simply winces and continues to operate successful car plants in Shanghai as it posts impressive sales gains throughout China and Southeast Asia. GM expects its vehicle sales in China, its second-largest market, to grow by more than 20 percent this year, as the fast-growing market remains unaffected by the company's U.S. bankruptcy.

With the exception of Chinese automakers that make some of the least crashworthy and poorest quality vehicles one can find, Asian manufacturers have a lock on reliable, fuel-sipping vehicles. Whether they're cars, minivans, sport-utilities, or pickups, and whether they're built in Japan, Canada, Mexico, or the United States, Asian cars give you much more performance and fuel economy for your money than if you were to buy the equivalent vehicle made by Chrysler, Ford, or General Motors—or by most European automakers, for that matter. Most of all, you can also count on Asian vehicles to be easy to repair and slow to depreciate in an auto market that is rapidly changing.

You don't always have to pay top dollar, either. You can get exceptionally good deals by purchasing Japanese vehicles that are rebadged as American models or built as co-ventures in Japanese, American, or Canadian factories—cars like the Toyota Matrix/Pontiac Vibe, for example. GM has announced that the Vibe will be gone at the end of the 2009 model year. The identical Toyota Matrix will carry on, however. Inasmuch as the $16,550 (U.S.) Matrix is made in Cambridge, Ontario, it has also benefited from that manufacturing plant's high quality scores.

Japanese vehicles usually sell at a 10–20 percent premium over their Detroit equivalents, although higher resale values wipe out the difference. In the past, Asian automakers have tried to keep costs down through "content cutting" and by keeping prices high. But this approach produced disastrous results in the not-too-distant past. Less content led to lower quality, and, for example, manufacturers like Honda, Toyota, and Lexus were forced to extend their powertrain warranties retroactively up to eight years to cover catastrophic engine and automatic transmission failures seen with their 1997–2004 models.

Many Toyota Camrys had transmission and engine hesitation problems.

One gets the impression that some Japanese automakers, like Toyota and Nissan, have become complacent after winning so many quality awards from CAA and other groups and are now coasting on their reputations. This attitude would explain why we've seen such an upswing in safety- and performance-related defects over the past decade: Nissan brought 200 engineers from Japan to fix the 2004 Quest's defects; many 1997–2004 Honda models had transmission failures; and 1997–2006 Toyota models were plagued by engine sludge and stinky exhausts, plus the Avalon has been failure-prone. It certainly has nothing to do with American versus Japanese manufacturing plants—these companies' poor-quality components have come from factories located around the world.

There are several important differences, however. Asian models and car manufacturers have a high degree of the public's confidence in the reliability of their vehicles and the financial stability of their companies. Chrysler, General Motors, and Ford do not. Also, Asian automakers have a more realistic mix of models that can withstand the vagaries of the marketplace as fuel prices rise and fall. And they know how to squeeze the most profit out of small cars and how to sell to emerging markets.

Acura

Acura, a division of Honda, sells six cars under its nameplate: the Canada-exclusive CSX entry-level compact and its Type-S high-performance luxury sedan, the RL, the TL, the TSX, and the MDX and RDX crossover wagons.

Let's not kid ourselves—most Acura products are basically fully loaded Hondas with a few additional features. Despite the fact that dealers try to enforce a no-haggle policy, these cars are generally good buys because maintenance costs are low, depreciation is much slower than average, and reliability is outstanding. What few defects they have are usually related to squeaks and rattles, minor trim glitches, and accessories such as the navigation, climate control, and sound systems.

CSX, TYPE-S ★★★★ / ★★★

RATING: *CSX:* Above Average; *Type-S:* Average. If the CSX was as different to the Civic as the TL is to the Accord, I'd be more enthusiastic. Strictly for drivers desperate to pay extra cash for an Acura cachet. **Strong points:** The CSX is a very well-balanced car that is both practical and fun to drive. It has more than enough power; handling is better than average; interior room is adequate, with lots of thoughtful storage areas; controls are a breeze to decipher and access; visibility is fairly good; outstanding workmanship and top-quality materials are evident everywhere (all automakers' Ontario plants are renowned for high quality control); its resale value is extraordinarily high; and low-cost leases are available. All CSX models use the same energy-absorbing frame structure that's found on the Civic, so crashworthiness should equal the Civic's five-star rating for frontal collisions, four stars for side impacts, and four stars for rollover resistance. **Weak points:** Prices are firm, and freight charges are excessive. The 5-year/unlimited km corrosion perforation warranty is rather chintzy when compared with what is offered by less-prestigious automakers. **New for 2010:** Very little.

KEY FACTS

PRICES: $26,990–$33,400 **FREIGHT:** $1,370 **ORIGIN:** Ontario **SALES:** N/A

POWERTRAIN (FRONT-DRIVE)

Engine: 2.0L 4-cyl. (155 hp) • 2.0L 4-cyl. (197 hp); Transmissions: 5-speed man. • 5-speed auto. • 6-speed man.

DIMENSIONS/CAPACITY

Passengers: 2/3; Wheelbase: 106.2 in.; H: 56.4/L: 178.8/W: 68.9 in.; Headroom F/R: N/A; Legroom F/R: 41.8/36.3 in.; Cargo volume: 12 cu. ft.; Fuel tank: 50L/ reg./prem.; Tow limit: 1,000 lb.; Load capacity: 850 lb.; Turning circle: 39 ft.; Weight: 2,848 lb.

OVERVIEW: CSX came on the scene as the 2006 model replacement for the discontinued entry-level EL, a successful Honda spin-off that was made in Canada for Canadians. (The EL debuted in 1997 with the Acura 1.6 EL, and later came the 1.7 EL.) The CSX is essentially a restyled, more-powerful luxury version of the Honda Civic sedan.

The four-door CSX is sold in two trim levels: a base model and a Tech Package version. Base models offer many useful features, like electronic stability control, anti-lock brakes, side and side curtain airbags, heated mirrors with integrated turn signals, steering-wheel audio controls, a CD/MP3 player, automatic climate control, cruise control, auto up/down windows, and a 60/40 split-folding rear seat. The Tech Package model sells for $29,990 and comes with more-gimmicky features.

COST ANALYSIS: Get a discounted 2009 model with additional rebates. **Best alternatives:** Consider the Honda Civic Si and the BMW 3 Series. **Options:** Ditch the Bridgestone tires for Michelin, Yokohama, or Pirelli. **Rebates:** $3,000 rebates; limited discounting. **Depreciation:** Very slow. **Insurance cost:** Higher than average. **Parts supply/cost:** Average. **Annual maintenance cost:** Less than average. **Warranty:** Bumper-to-bumper 5 years/100,000 km; rust perforation 5 years/unlimited km. **Supplementary warranty:** A waste of money. **City/highway fuel economy:** *CSX:* 8.7/6.4 L/100 km. *Type-S:* 10.2/6.8 L/100 km.

OWNER-REPORTED PROBLEMS: Most complaints are about premature front brake caliper and rotor wear, causing the car to shudder or pull sharply to one side when braking. Other niggling glitches concern the climate control and electrical systems.

Type-S

This is a $33,400 sportster for people who want that race-car feeling imparted by the peppy engine and close-ratio 6-speed manual transmission. Additional performance features include a speed-sensitive electric power-steering system, drive-by-wire throttle control, four-wheel disc ABS, vehicle stability assist with traction control, a sport suspension with stiffer springs, upgraded stabilizer bars front and rear, and 17-inch tires.

On the minus side: Most of the high-performance and luxury features are available in the Civic Si for thousands less, and the Accord V6 is quite a bit more powerful and luxurious but much less high-strung (it uses regular fuel). The car's engine tends to hold its speed when downshifting; it is a little unstable when encountering strong side winds; the leather interior feels cheap; and fuel consumption is on the high side.

TL ★★★★★

best buy

RATING: Recommended. **Strong points:** Comes in front-drive and all-wheel-drive versions. Very good fuel economy; impressive acceleration; handles fairly well; rides comfortably; well constructed, with quality mechanical and body components; and impressive crashworthiness scores compiled by NHTSA and IIHS. **Weak points:** An ugly front grille; suspension may be too firm for some; and not as agile as the BMW 3 Series. **New for 2010:** A manual shifter in December. The 2009 revamped model was made larger, with more rear seatroom, and features a choice of two V6 engines, all-new electric power steering, and a new interior and styling. A new $44,490 SH-AWD (Super Handling All-Wheel Drive) model was introduced; the Tech version sells for $3,500 more.

KEY FACTS

PRICES: $39,990–$47,990 **FREIGHT:** $1,825 **ORIGIN:** Ohio **SALES:** Down 25%

POWERTRAIN (FRONT-DRIVE/AWD)

Engine: 3.5L V6 (280 hp) • 3.7L V6 (305 hp); Transmissions: 5-speed auto. • 6-speed man.

DIMENSIONS/CAPACITY

Passengers: 2/3; Wheelbase: 109.3 in.; H: 57.2/L: 195.5/W: 74 in.; Headroom F/R: 3.5/3.5 in.; Legroom F/R: 42/27.5 in.; Cargo volume: 13.1 cu. ft.; Fuel tank: 50L/prem.; Tow limit: 1,000 lb.; Load capacity: 850 lb.; Turning circle: 38.4 ft.; Weight: 3,699–3,948 lb.

OVERVIEW: The TL combines luxury and performance in a nicely styled front-drive, five-passenger sedan that uses the same chassis as the Accord and CL coupe. Two engines are offered and mated to either a 5-speed Sequential SportShift automatic transmission or a 6-speed manual. A limited-slip differential provides impressive acceleration in a smooth and quiet manner. Handling is exceptional, with the firm suspension and the responsive and precise steering making it easy to toss the TL around turns without losing control. Bumps can be a bit jarring, but this is a small price to pay for the car's high-speed stability.

Interior accommodations are better than average all around; the cockpit layout is very user-friendly, in part because of the easy-to-read gauges and accessible controls. Visibility fore and aft is unobstructed.

Standard safety features include ABS, stability and traction control, front seat belt pretensioners, childproof door locks, three-point seat belts, head-protecting airbags, and a transmission/brake interlock. Crash tests give four stars for driver and passenger crash protection in frontal collisions, four and five stars for side-impact protection, and four stars for rollover resistance. The offset crash rating is also five stars. Head restraints are given a "Good" rating by IIHS.

COST ANALYSIS: Get the 2009 model to take advantage of the car's many upgrades while profiting from additional rebates as dealers make room for the almost identical 2010 models. **Best alternatives:** Consider the Audi A6, the Cadillac CTS, and the Infiniti G37 sedan. **Options:** Don't waste your money on the satellite navigation system; it's confusing to calibrate and hard to see. Ditch the Bridgestone tires for better-performing Michelin, Yokohama, or Pirelli. **Rebates:** $3,500 rebates; some discounting. **Depreciation:** Much slower than average. **Insurance cost:** Higher than average. **Parts supply/cost:** Easily found and moderately priced, especially most mechanical and electronic components, but with the exception of some body parts. **Annual maintenance cost:** Less than average. **Warranty:** Bumper-to-bumper 5 years/100,000 km; rust perforation 5 years/unlimited km. **Supplementary warranty:** Not needed. **City/highway fuel economy:** *3.5L:* 11.6/7.5 L/100 km. *3.7L:* 12.3/8.1 L/100 km.

OWNER-REPORTED PROBLEMS: Very few complaints, except for minor body fit and finish deficiencies and electrical short circuits.

TSX ★★★

RATING: Average. This car is essentially a European Accord. Buyers comparing the TSX with the Accord or TL will quickly discover that the TSX has less head and shoulder room up front and a more cramped rear-seat area. A deal breaker? Perhaps. **Strong points:** Great steering and handling; well laid-out instruments and controls; improved navigation system controls; well built; good fuel economy; and good crashworthiness scores compiled by NHTSA and IIHS. A 5-year/100,000 km bumper-to-bumper warranty. **Weak points:** The 4-cylinder is underpowered, and the V6 is overpriced. Premium fuel negates the small engine's fuel-sipping savings; the interior is a bit snug, especially in the rear; the low roofline hampers rear access; overly sensitive seat sensors may disable the airbag, even when an average-sized adult is seated; and the rear seats have insufficient thigh support. **New for 2010:** Totally redesigned last year. This year's models come with a powerful 3.5L V6, new suspension tuning, and stiffer front springs and revised dampers. A switch was made to 18-inch alloy wheels (versus 17 inches on the 4-cylinder) with wider all-season Michelins. Acura also enhanced the brake system with new rear pads, a larger master cylinder, and a new brake booster. The front end is also slightly restyled.

KEY FACTS

PRICES: $32,900–$40,300 **FREIGHT:** $1,725 **ORIGIN:** Japan **SALES:** Down 23%

POWERTRAIN (FRONT-DRIVE)
Engines: 2.4L 4-cyl. (201 hp) • 3.5L V6 (280 hp); Transmissions: 5-speed auto. • 6-speed man.

DIMENSIONS/CAPACITY
Passengers: 2/3; Wheelbase: 107 in.; H: 57/L: 186/W: 73 in.; Headroom F/R: 3.0/2.5 in.; Legroom F/R: 41/27.0 in.; Cargo volume: 13 cu. ft.; Fuel tank: 70L/prem.; Tow limit: 1,000 lb.; Load capacity: 850 lb.; Turning circle: 36.7 ft.; Weight: 3,440 lb.

OVERVIEW: Essentially a more luxurious, sportier, and smaller version of the Accord, the TSX is an entry-level sports car equipped with a 280 hp 3.5L V6 engine that competes in a luxury-sedan niche where V6 power is commonplace. It gets excellent gas mileage but runs on premium fuel only. The car is sportier than the TL, yet it isn't as harsh as the discontinued high-performance RSX. This year's models correct the vague steering and excessive cabin noise found with previous models. Nevertheless, brake fade is still present after successive stops, manual shifts aren't as quick as with other cars in this class, and the V6 option doesn't give you sportier handling than the 4-banger does.

Crash tests give five stars for driver and passenger crash protection in frontal collisions and side impacts, and five stars for rollover resistance. The offset crash rating is also five stars, and head restraints are given a "Good" rating by IIHS.

COST ANALYSIS: Get a cheaper 2009 model to take advantage of the car's many upgrades. Acura is throwing in a cornucopia of standard safety, performance, and convenience features—like standard stability and traction control and head-protecting side airbags—to make this luxury sedan attractive to shoppers who don't feel size and V6 power are everything. Yet, when you consider the TSX's price is about $8,000 more than a 4-cylinder Honda Accord, you have to wonder whether the vehicle has a lot of cachet—or if its manufacturer has a lot of nerve. **Best alternatives:** Other cars worth considering, although they aren't as well made as the TSX, are the Audi A4, BMW 335i, Infiniti G37, Lexus IS 350, and Lincoln MKZ. The TSX is better styled than the Infiniti G37 or the Lexus IS. The BMW 3 Series and Mercedes C-Class look good but aren't as reliable as the TSX and will likely cost a bundle to maintain. The TSX's size and good looks outclass the TL by far, and the V6 puts it about where the former TL was in size and power. **Options:** Don't waste your money on the satellite navigation system; it's confusing to calibrate and hard to see. Ditch the Bridgestone tires for better-performing Michelin, Yokohama, or Pirelli. **Rebates:** $3,500 rebates; some discounting. **Depreciation:** Much slower than average. **Insurance cost:** Higher than average. **Parts supply/cost:** Easily found and moderately priced, especially most mechanical and electronic components, but with the exception of some body parts. **Annual maintenance cost:** Less than average. **Warranty:** Bumper-to-bumper 5 years/100,000 km; rust perforation 5 years/unlimited km. **Supplementary warranty:** Not needed. **City/highway fuel economy:** *4-cylinder manual:* 10.5/7.0 L/100 km. *4-cylinder automatic:* 9.6/6.5 L/100 km.

OWNER-REPORTED PROBLEMS: Unstable driver's seat that squeaks and creaks with every body movement; poor body fits; and malfunctioning accessories.

RL ★★★

RATING: Average. A Honda Legend to the rest of the world. **Strong points:** Acceptable acceleration that's smooth and quiet in all gear ranges; average steering and handling; loaded with goodies; above average reliability; top-quality body and mechanical components; impressive five-star ratings for front and side occupant protection and rollover resistance; IIHS rates rear, offset, and side occupant protection "Good"; and there's a comprehensive 5-year/100,000 km bumper-to-bumper warranty. **Weak points:** Bland styling; way overpriced and overweight; suspension may be overly firm for some; slow steering response; mediocre handling; interior feels cramped (the less-expensive TL is almost as roomy); dash console looks and feels disorganized; audio and navigation systems aren't easy to use; high fuel consumption; and problematic navigation system controls. **New for 2010:** A slightly restyled front end. (Please fix that ugly front grille!) For 2011, Acura will make the car a rear-drive and add a 420 hp V8 option. The new engine will use cylinder deactivation for better fuel economy.

OVERVIEW: Acura's flagship luxury sedan got the MDX's V6 last year, hooked to a standard 5-speed automatic gearbox and all-wheel drive (stick shift isn't available). The RL is loaded with innovative high-tech safety and convenience features, like

KEY FACTS

PRICE: $63,900 **FREIGHT:** $1,895 **ORIGIN:** Japan **SALES:** Down 55%

POWERTRAIN (AWD)

Engine: 3.7L V6 (300 hp); Transmission: 5-speed auto.

DIMENSIONS/CAPACITY

Passengers: 2/3; Wheelbase: 110.2 in.; H: 57.2/L: 195.7/W: 72.7 in.; Headroom F/R: 5.0/2.5 in.; Legroom F/R: 42.4/36.3 in.; Cargo volume: 13.2 cu. ft.; Fuel tank: 73.3L/premium; Tow limit: 1,000 lb.; Load capacity: 850 lb.; Turning circle: 36.1 ft.; Weight: 4,110 lb.

heated front seats, front and rear climate controls, a rear-seat trunk pass-through, xenon headlights (get used to oncoming drivers flashing their headlights at you), "smart" side airbags, front seat belt pretensioners, ABS, traction control, and an anti-skid system. No other engine but the 3.7L is available, and the only option offered is Acura's ubiquitous GPS.

Power is delivered in a smooth and quiet manner. The car handles nicely, with a ride that's less firm than the TL's—although steering response doesn't feel as crisp. Interior accommodations for four occupants are excellent up front and in the rear because the RL uses a larger platform than the TL does. All seats are well cushioned and give plenty of thigh support. Good all-around visibility.

COST ANALYSIS: Get the practically identical 2009 model. Be wary of the untested rear-drive platform and V8 on the 2011 model, slated to go on sale in late 2010. **Best alternatives:** BMW 535xi, Cadillac STS V6 AWD, Chrysler 300C AWD, and Infiniti M35x. You may want to take a look at the TL sedan, as well. **Options:** Forget the satellite navigation system. **Rebates:** There are at least $10,000 worth of rebates and discounts you can use to bring the MSRP down to a more-rational level. **Depreciation:** Much slower than average. **Insurance cost:** Higher than average. **Parts supply/cost:** Most mechanical and electronic components are easily found and moderately priced. Body parts may be hard to come by, and they can be expensive. **Annual maintenance cost:** Less than average. **Warranty:** Bumper-to-bumper 5 years/100,000 km; rust perforation 5 years/unlimited km. **Supplementary warranty:** Not needed; the base warranty is fairly applied. **City/highway fuel economy:** 13.1/9.0 L/100 km.

OWNER-REPORTED PROBLEMS: Chronic stalling, noisy brake pads, and premature brake wear. Malfunctioning power accessories and entertainment systems. Vehicle suddenly stalled while exiting a freeway. Dashboard display is unreadable in daylight. In a crash, seat belt did not restrain driver.

MDX ★★★

RATING: Average. **Strong points:** Power is supplied smoothly, with a minimum of engine noise in all gear ranges; average steering and handling is helped by the Super Handling All-Wheel Drive (SH-AWD) and Active Damper System (the latter is available in the Elite edition); loaded with goodies; above average reliability; top-quality body and mechanical components; a five-star crashworthiness rating for front occupant protection, and a four-star rating for rollover resistance; IIHS rates rear, offset, and side occupant protection "Good"; and there's a comprehensive 5-year/100,000 km bumper-to-bumper warranty. **Weak points:** Overpriced and overweight; acceleration and handling are acceptable but not confidence inspiring; the default suspension setting degrades emergency handling; the rear third seat is a tight fit; the dash console isn't user-friendly; audio and navigation systems are needlessly complicated; and high fuel consumption. **New for 2010:** Slightly restyled front and rear ends.

KEY FACTS

PRICES: $52,500–$62,200 **FREIGHT:** $1,855 **ORIGIN:** Ontario **SALES:** Down 45%

POWERTRAIN (AWD)

Engine: 3.7L V6 (300 hp); Transmission: 5-speed auto.

DIMENSIONS/CAPACITY

Passengers: 2/3/2; Wheelbase: 108.3 in.; H: 68.2/L: 190.7/W: 78.5 in.; Headroom F/R: 4.0/4.0 in.; Legroom F/R: 41/30 in.; Cargo volume: 42 cu. ft.; Fuel tank: 72.7L/premium; Tow limit: 5,000 lb.; Load capacity: 1,160 lb.; GVWR: 5,732 lb.; Turning circle: 40 ft.; Ground clearance: 5.0 in.; Weight: 4,548 lb.

OVERVIEW: Introduced as a 2001 model, the MDX got its first complete redesign for the 2007 model year, making this mid-sized sport-utility more competitive with the better-performing BMW X5, Porsche Cayenne, and Mercedes M-Class. Acura's revamping has smoothed out the powertrain's functions, made the vehicle a bit more agile, and softened the suspension. On the other hand, the car loses its grip during avoidance manoeuvres and has a cramped interior when carrying a full passenger load, and the busy dashboard has tiny buttons everywhere.

COST ANALYSIS: Get the practically identical 2009 version. There are plenty of unsold models available with low-coast leases and financing deals. **Best alternatives:** The Lexus RX series, the BMW X5, and the Buick Enclave, GMC Acadia, and Saturn Outlook trio. Would you like comparable Asian performance and reliability for about $11,000 less? Try a Honda Pilot (the MDX's cheaper cousin) for its additional passenger- and cargo-hauling capability, or a Nissan Xterra or Toyota Highlander. The Volvo XC90 and Mercedes ML320, ML350, or ML550 have adequate cargo room with all the rows down, but they have neither comparable cargo room behind the second row nor a comparable level of quality control and dealer servicing. Furthermore, Ford's announcement that it may sell Volvo could make its future in North America even shakier. **Options:** Forget the satellite navigation system. **Rebates:** Look for $3,000+ rebates on the 2009 models, and a similar amount in the late fall, applicable to the early 2010 models. **Depreciation:** Much slower than average. **Insurance cost:** Higher than average. **Parts supply/cost:** Most mechanical and electronic components are easily found and moderately priced. Body parts may be hard to come by, and they can be expensive. **Annual maintenance cost:** Average. **Warranty:** Bumper-to-bumper 5 years/100,000 km; rust perforation 5 years/unlimited km. **Supplementary warranty:** Not needed; the base warranty is fairly applied. **City/highway fuel economy:** 13.8/10.0 L/100 km.

OWNER-REPORTED PROBLEMS: Noisy brake pads and premature brake wear; malfunctioning power accessories and entertainment systems; vehicle suddenly stalled while exiting a highway; dashboard display is unreadable in daylight; and in a crash, seat belt did not restrain driver. One complaint that the 2009 model's rear seat belts may be hazardous to children:

> The seat belt that hangs from the ceiling to the middle seat became wrapped around the child's neck. The child was unable to breath[e] properly. The child was seated in the rear driver's side seat.

RDX ★★★★

RATING: Above Average. **Strong points:** Plenty of power, and handling is effortless, agile, and secure. Handles like a tall sports car: tight and responsive. Seating and driving positions work for occupants of all sizes. The nicely appointed interior is well laid-out, with plenty of small storage areas; the seats have good thigh and back support (a criticism against the CR-V); above average reliability; top-quality mechanical components; a five-star crashworthiness rating for front and side occupant protection, and a four-star rating for rollover resistance; IIHS rates rear, offset, and side occupant protection "Good"; and there's a comprehensive 5-year/100,000 km bumper-to-bumper warranty. **Weak points:** A fuel-thirsty small engine; stiff-riding, with some jostling when passing over uneven terrain; more pavement noise than one would expect in a luxury car; the interior pillars look very unrefined, with some misaligned plastics; the trim on the exterior bottom of the driver's door is not in line with the passenger door trim; computerized audio, climate, and navigation systems are nearly impossible to learn and use; no full-size spare tire; no engine temperature gauge; and the cargo space, like in most compact SUVs, isn't quite big enough for bicycles. **New for 2010:** Nothing significant. If the 2010 model comes with direct fuel injection (DFI), the leftover 2009 models' prices will fall dramatically and CR-V sales will be cannibalized by the RDX.

KEY FACTS

PRICES: $41,400–$45,100 **FREIGHT:** $1,855 **ORIGIN:** Ontario **SALES:** Down 49%

POWERTRAIN (AWD)
Engine: 2.3L 4 Turbo (240 hp); Transmission: 5-speed auto.

DIMENSIONS/CAPACITY
Passengers: 2/3/2; Wheelbase: 104.3 in.; H: 65.2/L: 180.7/W: 73.6 in.; Headroom F/R: 4.0/3.5 in.; Legroom F/R: 40.5/27.5 in.; Cargo volume: 29.5 cu. ft.; Fuel tank: 72.7L/premium; Tow limit: 1,000 lb.; Load capacity: 870 lb.; GVWR: 5,732 lb.; Turning circle: 41 ft.; Ground clearance: 5.5 in.; Weight: 3,924 lb.

OVERVIEW: Essentially a three-year-old Honda CR-V clone, the RDX carries Honda's first turbocharged 4-cylinder engine, which makes it a hoot to drive. The RDX takes over from the MDX as Acura's entry-level crossover SUV. Although its dimensions are similar to that of the Honda CR-V, the RDX uses a unique platform developed to handle the vehicle's advanced all-wheel-drive system and peppy, turbocharged engine.

COST ANALYSIS: Get the practically identical 2009 model. To carry the CR-V and RSX comparison further, there are plenty more RDXs than CR-Vs piling up on dealer lots, and they're available with significant discounts and low-cost leases and financing. The $8,000 premium for the RDX can be whittled down to about half as much through smart haggling. The extra dough gets you a more-powerful drivetrain, a more-refined interior, more tech gadgets, and front-end styling without an underbite. If these things are not interesting to you, then save yourself the $4K–$8K with a CR-V. **Best alternatives:** BMW X3, Honda CR-V, Infiniti EX, and Mazda CX-7. **Rebates:** Look for $6,000+ rebates on the 2009 models, and a similar amount in the late fall, applicable to the early 2010 models. Remember, 2009 RDX sales have been a disaster, while CR-V sales have increased by about 20 percent. **Options:** The Bluetooth satellite navigation system should be compared with the less-expensive Garmin devices. The $4,000+ technology package—the 10-speaker Elliot Scheiner audio system with satellite radio and the full computerized navigation package with backup camera—is a money-waster. **Rebates:** With a top price of $45,100, there are at least $10,000 worth of rebates and discounts that you can use to bring the suggested list price down to a more-rational level. **Depreciation:** Much slower than average. **Insurance cost:** Higher than average. **Parts supply/cost:** Most mechanical and electronic components are easily found and moderately priced. Body parts may be hard to come by, and they can be expensive. **Annual maintenance cost:** Average. **Warranty:** Bumper-to-bumper 5 years/100,000 km; rust perforation 5 years/unlimited km. **Supplementary warranty:** Not needed. **City/highway fuel economy:** 12.5/9.3 L/100 km.

OWNER-REPORTED PROBLEMS: Poor audio reception, and malfunctioning gauges. Most of the problems reported by Acura owners concern accessories like the gauges, instruments, AC, and entertainment system and electrical short circuits.

Honda

Like Toyota's sales during the past year, Honda's sales have been quite poor for almost all of its model lineup, with the exception of the CR-V SUV. The two biggest sales laggards are the Civic, Canada's former perennial bestseller, and the Odyssey minivan. It is too early to tell how well the just-reborn Honda Insight hybrid will do, though first indications through last June show below-average sales, while sales of the company's new Ridgeline truck are stagnating.

Honda is moving downscale and upscale at the same time as fuel prices rise and fall continually. The company is importing into North America "micro" cars, like the Fit, which sold for years as the Jazz in other countries. Honda originally intended to name the car "Fitta," but shortened the name in some markets and renamed it completely in others upon discovering that "fitta" is a popular slang word for "vulva" in several Nordic languages. The 2010 Insight hybrid has been resurrected (after a three-year hiatus) in a second attempt to market popular, though money-losing, "green" cars. Honda engineers have also tweaked the performance of all models to enhance fuel economy, safety, comfort, and convenience. In this way, Honda hopes to cover all its bases even though the game is continually changing and the fans are now more fickle.

FIT ★★★★

RATING: Above Average. This four-door, five-passenger mini hatchback is surprisingly roomy and reasonably fuel-efficient (but don't believe all you are told), thanks to its small, 1.5L 4-cylinder engine mated to a 5-speed manual transmission. Slotted below the Civic, this little economy car is the best choice among the 2010 econocars. **Strong points:** Plenty of smooth, quiet power with either the manual or automatic transmission; handles and brakes like a sports car; good interior ergonomics; standard power accessories, ABS, and side curtain airbags; versatile interior; above-average crashworthiness ratings; quality craftsmanship; and a high resale value. **Weak points:** No solid safety defect data is available yet; one report that the airbag failed to deploy; rear view is a bit narrow; transmission seal leaks; weak AC; small gas tank; fuel sloshing noise heard under the front seats; no floormats; touchy, squeaky brakes; vehicle sways and wanders when encountering moderate side winds; jerky acceleration when driving in traffic; excess gear shifting over hilly terrain; some interior engine and road noise; bland exterior and interior styling; paint peeling and delamination; no centre armrest; dealers won't budge on prices; owners say fuel economy is overstated by about 30 percent; and reports that manual transmission–equipped Fits are rare and seldom sell for their suggested retail price. **New for 2010:** Nothing important; the car was revamped for 2009. A redesigned 2011 Fit may be right around the corner in the fall of 2010.

KEY FACTS

PRICES: $14,980, *Sport:* $19,280
FREIGHT: $1,370 **ORIGIN:** Japan **SALES:** Down 25%
POWERTRAIN (FRONT-DRIVE)
Engine: 1.5L 4-cyl. (109 hp);
Transmissions: 5-speed man. • 5-speed auto.
DIMENSIONS/CAPACITY
Passengers: 2/3; Wheelbase: 97 in.; H: 60/L: 157/W: 66 in.; Headroom F/R: 5.5/3.5 in.; Legroom F/R: 40/26 in; Cargo volume: 21 cu. ft.; Fuel tank: 41L/regular; Tow limit: No towing; Load capacity: 850 lb.; Turning circle: 34.3 ft.; Weight: 2,535 lb.

OVERVIEW: Selling for $14,980 for a base DX, the Fit sips fuel without compromising performance. Yes, its 1.5L engine produces only 109 hp, but that power is used so efficiently that you will seldom realize you're driving a minicompact. At a little over nine seconds to 100 km/h using a manual gearbox, it beats most competitors, and it's no slouch with an automatic, either. Handling is easy and predictable, but the ride is somewhat choppy due to the car's small size. Innovative seats allow you to lift the rear seat's base up against the backrest to make room for bulky items, or the seat can be folded flat, which doubles the cargo space and creates a flat floor. You can even configure the seats to make a small bed.

NHTSA gives the Fit its top rating of five stars for occupant protection in a frontal collision; five stars for the driver and three stars for passenger protection in a side impact; and four stars for rollover prevention. Reliability should be above average, judging by European owner reviews of the Jazz.

COST ANALYSIS: Save money buying a practically identical 2009 version. **Best alternatives:** Other good econocars this year are the Hyundai Accent, Suzuki

Aerio, Nissan Versa, and Toyota Yaris. The Chevy Aveo, Dodge Caliber, and Mercedes Smart Car bring up the rear of the pack. **Options:** Nothing worth the extra money. **Rebates:** Look for $1,000+ rebates on the 2009 models this year, and a similar amount in the late fall, applicable to the early 2010 models. Remember, 2009 sales have fallen below expectation, making dealers willing to discount. **Depreciation:** Slower than average. **Insurance cost:** Average. **Parts supply/cost:** No trouble finding parts at a fair price. **Annual maintenance cost:** Less than average. **Warranty:** Bumper-to-bumper 5 years/100,000 km; rust perforation 5 years/unlimited km. **Supplementary warranty:** Basic warranty is sufficient. **City/highway fuel economy:** *Manual:* 7.2/5.7 L/100 km. *Automatic:* 7.1/5.5 L/100 km.

OWNER-REPORTED PROBLEMS: Periodic brake failures; paint chipping and premature cosmetic rusting; insufficient legroom causes drivers to apply the brakes and accelerator at the same time; road debris easily destroys the AC condenser—an expensive repair not covered under warranty—but discounts are given under a "goodwill" warranty; dash lights are on all the time, giving the driver the impression they are illuminated when they aren't; dashboard's elevated design obstructs forward visibility; tail light jarring can cause the sockets to fall out of their housing; in a smash-up, seat belts broke and airbags failed to deploy; and the tire jack may bend sideways when lifting the car.

CIVIC ★★★★★

best buy

RATING: Recommended. The Honda Civic is one of the best performing, most dependable small cars money can buy. It's a comfortable, refined vehicle that comes with most of the features that people want, without paying for extras. Honda was the first Japanese car company to start production in Ontario, where it manufactures the Civic, Canada's top-selling car for the past 11 years. **Strong points:** Good acceleration; smooth-shifting automatic transmission; great handling and good cornering control; responsive, direct steering; a comfortable, firm ride; the reworked two-tier instrument panel is nicely done and fits well into a friendly cabin environment that houses easily accessed instruments and controls; a tilt/telescoping steering wheel is standard; interior space is more than adequate for most adults, though not to the extent that Honda represents it to be; better-than-average reliability; and a high resale value. **Weak points:** Limited price haggling. The coupe's steeply raked front windshield cuts forward visibility; long front roof pillars impede corner views; the expansive dash shelf and sloping nose make it tough to judge distance

KEY FACTS

PRICES: $16,190–$26,680 (Si) **FREIGHT:** $1,010 **ORIGIN:** Ohio and Ontario **SALES:** Down 40%

POWERTRAIN (FRONT-DRIVE)

Engines: 1.8L 4-cyl. (113 hp) • 1.8L 4-cyl. (140 hp) • 2.0L 4-cyl. (197 hp); Transmissions: 5-speed man. • 6-speed man. • 5-speed auto.

DIMENSIONS/CAPACITY

Passengers: 2/3; Wheelbase: 106.3 in.; H: 56.5/L: 176.7/W: 69 in.; Headroom F/R: 3.0/2.0 in.; Legroom F/R: 40.5/28 in.; Cargo volume: 12 cu. ft.; Fuel tank: 50L/regular; Tow limit: 1,500 lb.; Load capacity: 850 lb.; Turning circle: 39 ft.; Weight: 2,628 lb.

when parking, and rear visibility isn't impressive, either; the suspension may be too firm for some; coupe's interior noise is less isolated than in the sedan; the latest redesign has decreased overall passenger room slightly, although outward dimensions are larger; coupe's rear access takes some effort, and seating is a bit cramped; trunk hinges intrude into the cargo area; and some fit and finish problems, highlighted by interior rattles. **New for 2010:** Carried over with only a few minor improvements.

OVERVIEW: The Civic is one of the most refined and competent subcompacts on the market today. Few larger and more-expensive cars can match its quality, performance, and roominess. Earlier improvements include offering more powerful base engines on the Civic, Si, and Hybrid; additional standard safety features like front and side airbags and head-protecting side curtain airbags; improved brakes; electronic stability control on the sporty Si and Hybrid; sleeker styling (Saturn-like up front); more interior room; and a more rigid body to reduce rattles and vibrations.

The coupe version uses the same powertrain as the sedan, though it is set on a smaller wheelbase. It has 8 cm (3 in.) less height, and has a front windshield with a steeper rake (tall drivers will need to stop well in back of overhanging traffic lights).

COST ANALYSIS: Some limited price dickering with leases and financing charges. Although new Civics have lost their sales lead, they are still very popular and continue to be sold for a few thousand dollars more than the Detroit Three's similar offerings. Fortunately, Civics also retain higher resale values than most cars, taking the sting out of the excess loonies you may have originally paid. **Best alternatives:** Other cars worth considering that are cheaper are mostly not as refined, like the Hyundai Accent, Mazda3, and Toyota Yaris. **Options:** Try to get a free extra set of ignition keys written into the contract; Honda's anti-start, theft-protection keys may cost as much as $150 per set. Steer clear of the standard-issue radio and Firestone or Bridgestone tires. **Rebates:** Minimal, and mostly related to leasing and low-cost financing. **Depreciation:** What's that? **Insurance cost:** Average. **Parts supply/cost:** Reasonably priced and easily found at dealers and independent suppliers. **Annual maintenance cost:** Much less than average. **Warranty:** Bumper-to-bumper 3 years/60,000 km; powertrain 5 years/100,000 km; rust perforation 6 years/unlimited km. **Supplementary warranty:** Not needed. **City/highway fuel economy:** *1.8L (140 hp) manual:* 7.8/5.7 L/100 km. *1.8L (140 hp) automatic:* 8.2/5.7 L/100 km. *2.0L manual:* 10.2/6.8 L/100 km.

OWNER-REPORTED PROBLEMS: Despite the Civic's legendary reliability and its Recommended rating in this guide, some Honda engineers and designers have been asleep at the switch during the past few years. As a consequence, too many owners report serious safety-related failures and chronic performance glitches. For example, why does the pillar between the windshield and side window cause such an annoying blind spot, and does rear visibility have to be obstructed by the head restraints?

Other factory-related annoyances: Hard starts, won't crank, or suddenly stalls; engine oil leaks; car won't move in Drive; automatic transmission fluid leaks and noisy engagement; stalling in Reverse or Drive; manual transmission grinds when shifting into Third gear; heater blower motor overheats or blows a fuse; malfunctioning alternator; wheel bearing, brake pedal booster, clutch pedal, or master cylinder noise; A-pillar or dash rattles; sunroof rattling; windows bind or come out of run channels; faulty door lock cylinders; doors and trunk lid hard to close; inoperable fuel-door handle; and body and bumper paint peeling and cracking. Also oil leaks from the lower engine block crack; motor mounts failure; faulty main rear crankshaft seal; sluggish performance when it rains or when passing through a large puddle; transmission periodically wouldn't shift into Third or Fourth gear (torque converter replaced); premature wheel bearing replacement; excessive steering shimmy; and front strut leakage causes noise and difficult handling. Electrical system and fit and finish deficiencies include a poorly mounted driver's seat; inoperable door locks and power windows; a driver-side window that won't roll back up; sun visors that fall apart; an erratic fuel gauge, speedometer, and tachometer; an interior light that hums as it dims; lousy radio speakers; water leaks through the door bottoms, from the tail light into the trunk, and onto the driver-side footwell carpet; windows often come off their tracks; AC condenser is easily destroyed by road debris and doesn't cool properly, and condensate drips from under the glove compartment (heating core needs to be replaced to fix the problem); dashboard buzzing; front and rear windshield creaking. Loose, rattling seat belt adjusters, door panels, and door latches:

> Creaking and rattling from interior of car in several areas—most notable [in] the rear. General feeling of parts falling apart or coming loose while driving. The loudest and most troublesome noise sounds like it is coming from where the rear interior shelf and rear window meet. The noise is loudest when the car is cold and happens mostly while driving over rough patches of highway, crossing road reflectors, or when the stereo is on. There is also a "creaking" noise coming from all areas of the front dash and console around the front windshield during all driving conditions.

And then there are the defects than threaten life and limb: Fire ignited in the seat belt wiring under the passenger seat; seat belts tighten up progressively when connected; child injured when he became entangled in an unfastened rear centre shoulder belt, which retracted, cutting off his air; seat belt doesn't always retract into the harness; seat belts failed to lock up in a sudden panic stop; many complaints that the airbags failed to deploy in a frontal collision; Airbag warning light stays lit even though an adult passenger occupies the seat; inadvertent side airbag deployment; broken engine serpentine belt tensioner bolt; fractured front tie rod, causing complete steering loss; sudden acceleration or surging when AC or heater is engaged, or when the steering wheel is turned sharply; brake and accelerator pedal are mounted too close together. Sudden acceleration:

> Sudden acceleration surge, to the point of having to completely hold the brake with both feet. At one point, after putting car into Neutral, the engine revved to 7000 rpm before owner could turn car off. The initial surging resulted in the owner's wife hitting her passenger mirror against another vehicle when the engine surged while in reverse.

Cruise control doesn't stay at its set speed; chronic stalling accompanied by steering-wheel lock-up. Engine momentarily maintains high rpm when decelerating:

> When lifting foot off the accelerator car continues without decelerating for more than 1 second.... I must anticipate my deceleration or use the brake pedal suddenly when I would not have to in another car. I believe this presents a significant risk. Further when deceleration does occur it is extremely abrupt. If I am turning and I lift off the throttle the sudden deceleration and its unpredictable onset can cause lift-throttle oversteer or a tightening of the line on which the car travels. In short, the car can unpredictably go not where it was pointed.

Fuel leakage into the engine compartment while vehicle was underway; car has to warm up a few minutes before brakes will work properly; vehicle rolls back when stopped on an incline with automatic transmission engaged; transmission surges forward when put into Reverse (blamed on transmission solenoid); automatic transmission will suddenly downshift in traffic; when accelerator pedal is tapped at less than 5 km/h, vehicle suddenly passes from Drive to Neutral to Reverse; transmission won't easily go into First gear; steering wheel wouldn't lock when parked; steering wheel shakes when turned sharply to the left or right, and sometimes the tire rubs on the fender; taller drivers' vision blocked by nonadjustable, windshield-mounted rear-view mirror; loose driver's seat. Head restraint pushes head too far forward:

> I am five feet four inches tall and I like my seat to be more upright. Unfortunately, when you put the seats in this position, the head rest forces your head down, chin to chest. This would not be a problem if I were a man with large shoulder muscles or if I liked my seat to be in a reclining position. My reaction to the restraints is that they feel very unsafe. When I checked the federal web site, I found that the government tested only for the size of an average man. Will the rest of us die or sustain incredible injury?

Windshield cracked suddenly; difficult to see through bottom of windshield; with AC engaged at night, a film covers rear windshield (said to be caused by either an engine head gasket failure or "outgassing" from the interior's plastic trim). AC blamed for emitting toxic fumes:

> The HVAC (air conditioning/heating system/defroster) immediately started spewing toxic mold/mildew spores on a new vehicle test-driven at the dealer's. It occurs while driving, after running the air conditioning for a few minutes, turning the air conditioning off (while leaving the fan running) and waiting a few minutes. It then stinks for a few minutes and then disappears.

Trunk springs failed; exterior and interior lights dim to an unsafe level; rear running lights fail due to a faulty fuse box; heated side mirrors gradually lose their reflective ability; tire rims easily collect snow, ice, and dirt; and Dunlop and Firestone tires have tread separation.

CIVIC HYBRID ★★

RATING: Below Average. Why go through all the expense and bother if you won't end up driving the excessive mileage needed to amortize the high retail cost and maintenance fees? **Strong points:** A fuel-sipper; smooth-shifting, comfortable ride; AC can run off of the electric motor; excellent crashworthiness scores; standard electronic stability control on most models; and good front and rear visibility. **Weak points:** Fuel economy is hyped by at least 20–30 percent, encouraging drivers to sneak up on lights to save fuel; less-effective drum brakes in the rear; excessive noseplow in tight turns due to the fuel-saver tires; repairs and servicing are dealer-dependent; rescuers are wary of cutting through the high-voltage electrical system to save occupants after an accident; only average depreciation; and you have to drive several hundred thousand kilometres to amortize the Hybrid's start-up costs. **New for 2010:** Nothing major. The Civic Hybrid will likely be dumped if the Fit and Insight cannibalize any more of its sales, particularly since Honda and Toyota are planning to go hybrid with their 2011 Fit and Yaris models.

KEY FACTS

PRICE: $26,350 **FREIGHT:** $1,010

ORIGIN: Japan **SALES:** N/A

POWERTRAIN (FRONT-DRIVE)

Engines: 1.3L 3-cyl. (110 hp); Transmission: CVT

DIMENSIONS/CAPACITY

Passengers: 2/3; Wheelbase: 106.3 in.; H: 56.3/L: 176.7/W: 69 in.; Headroom F/R: 3.0/2.0 in.; Legroom F/R: 42.2/34.6 in.; Cargo volume: 10.4 cu. ft.; Fuel tank: 47L/regular; Tow limit: No towing; Load capacity: 850 lb.; Turning circle: 34.8 ft.; Weight: 2,875 lb.

OVERVIEW: Launched in March 2002, the Hybrid looks and feels just like a Civic, both inside and out. You should get the same high levels of reliability and durability. On top of that, its powertrain uses gasoline-electric technology that lets you travel up to 1,047 km (650 mi.) on a single tank of gas, and the battery recharges itself as you drive.

On the downside: Owners report that similar fuel economy can be achieved with cheaper, conventional Honda or Toyota small cars that aren't burdened with complex technology. This opinion has been seconded by a report in the September 2004 issue of *Car and Driver* magazine that concluded that one would have to drive a hybrid 266,000 km (165,285 mi.) to amortize its higher costs. Furthermore, the car's unique dual powerplants can make for risky driving, as this Hybrid owner warns:

> [With a] 2003 Honda Civic Hybrid on a snowy road, coming over a small rise while going around a moderate curve under 40 mph [64 km/h], the battery charging function, activated by driver taking foot off the gas before cresting the hill, produced

> progressively stronger engine braking effect on the front wheels, equivalent to an unwanted downshift and causing fishtailing and poor response to corrective steering, so that the car slid across the road and into a snow bank and concrete abutment, causing $6,000 (U.S.) in damage. If there had been oncoming traffic, there could have been serious injuries or fatalities.

COST ANALYSIS: Get a second-series 2009 Hybrid to benefit from its powertrain improvements with fewer redesign glitches. **Best alternatives:** The Honda Civic or Fit, Hyundai Accent, Nissan Versa, and Toyota Prius or Yaris are all good fuel-frugal choices. The VW Jetta TDI just doesn't cut it, unless fifth-year engine and electrical problems and head-scratching servicing are your cup of tea. **Options:** Nothing worth buying, except tires to replace the original-equipment Firestone or Bridgestone rubber bands. **Rebates:** $1,500. **Depreciation:** Average, but resale value after five years is less certain; it'll be a rough market for a used Civic Hybrid with an old-generation hybrid powertrain and a $5,000 battery pack that may soon need replacing. **Insurance cost:** Higher than average, because it's easier to "total" the car than to replace its expensive, high-tech parts. **Parts supply/cost:** Parts are often on several weeks' back order, and costs are moderately high **Annual maintenance cost:** Average. **Warranty:** Bumper-to-bumper 3 years/60,000 km; powertrain 5years/100,000 km; rust perforation 6 years/unlimited km. The Hybrid's battery pack has a 10-year/160,000 km warranty; a replacement battery costs about $3,000 (U.S.)! **Supplementary warranty:** A toss-up. **City/highway fuel economy:** 4.7/4.6 L/100 km, but owners complain they get 20–30 percent less fuel economy in real-world driving conditions.

OWNER-REPORTED PROBLEMS: Much less fuel economy than promised:

> The advertised mpg of my Honda hybrid for city driving is 48 mpg [4.9 L/100 km]. I have never gotten better than 38 mpg [6.2 L/100 km]. Honda says there's nothing they can do about it and just advertising that it will get 48 mpg doesn't mean it will get that actual mileage. I believe it should at least be close, not 20 percent less than advertised.

Vehicle loses power when merging with traffic, due to a low battery charge; rough shifting; rotten-egg smell intrudes into the cabin; premature brake and rear strut wear; Airbag light remains lit; AC condenser failed after it was hit by road debris. Walter W., a B.C.-based engineer and *Lemon-Aid* correspondent, is concerned about the Hybrid's vulnerability to road debris and premature corrosion:

> During a recent major model redesign, the steering arms were moved from under the wheel axle to over the axle (according to Honda service). In order to allow the free movement of the steering arm, a section of the forward wheelwells' lining was removed. This removal allows the entry of water, gravel, and salt into the engine bay when the car wheels are off centre during a turn.

Vehicle extremely unstable due to poor rear suspension alignment; many complaints of excessive rear tire wear (faulty camber) have led to Honda discounting replacement tires by 50 percent; rear bumper cover may fall off, not be aligned or flush, or come loose and chip paint; window binds or comes out of run channel; door lock cylinder sticks; clutch pedal has a notchy feel; erratic average fuel mileage display; fix for a deformed windshield moulding; a spare-tire kit is available free of charge for owners dissatisfied with receiving a can of sealant instead of a spare tire; airbags failed to deploy; trunk caught fire while vehicle was parked; sudden, unintended acceleration when foot was taken off of the accelerator pedal; vehicle lost all forward power while cruising on the highway; vehicle rolled backward before accelerating on a level surface. Chronic stalling and no-starts:

> The car on 8 occasions has not restarted when in the auto stop mode when I take my foot off the brake. My dealer and American Honda refuse to address the problem since it is intermittent. I am stuck in traffic until I restart the car by going to Park. I feel I am a sitting duck and sooner or later will be rear-ended.

Excessive brake vibration; front wheels locked up when brakes were tapped lightly. Transmission "lurch and lag" when accelerating or decelerating in a turn (often mistakenly blamed on low battery charge):

> Honda updated the CVT (transmission) software. A service bulletin (SB 08-014) was issued for this concern on March 1, 2008. The service bulletin stated that the transmission could experience problems similar to the one I had. I believe this model car should be recalled. Honda's service bulletin was not effective in addressing this issue.

Axle suddenly broke while vehicle was underway; shaking, steering wobble, and pull to the right when going downhill or driving in the rain; and trucks cannot hear the Hybrid's weak horn.

INSIGHT ★

RATING: Not Recommended. **Strong points:** The Insight hybrid will save you a bit on fuel, and it costs less than the more-refined Toyota Prius. It also has a versatile hatchback design. **Weak points:** Little discounting, due to the Insight's flavour-of-the-month status. For the little bit of savings over a Prius, you'll have to contend with lethargic acceleration; poor handling; a jumpy, jerky ride; a hard-to-access interior; cheap-looking plastics and carpeting; and cramped, poorly supported, knees-to-your-chin rear seats that are real head-bangers every time the car passes over uneven terrain. Get used to a raspy exhaust and moaning CVT gearbox when accelerating. Reliability can be expected to be only average or worse during the car's first year on the market. **New for 2010:** A five-door hatchback.

OVERVIEW: The Insight's pricing is set below the Accord's, and the car comes with multiple airbags, automatic climate control, power windows, locks, and heated mirrors, CD audio with auxiliary jack, and anti-lock brakes. The EX gives you

Bluetooth connectivity, a USB interface, paddle shifters, stability control, and a navigation system of doubtful utility.

KEY FACTS

PRICES: $23,900–27,500 **FREIGHT:** $1,370 **ORIGIN:** Japan **SALES:** Just arrived

POWERTRAIN (FRONT-DRIVE)

Engine: 1.3L 4-cyl. (98 hp); Transmission: CVT

DIMENSIONS/CAPACITY

Passengers: 2/3; Wheelbase: 100 in.; H: 56/L: 172/W: 67 in.; Headroom F/R: 5.0/1.5 in.; Legroom F/R: 40.5/26.5 in.; Cargo volume: 12 cu. ft.; Fuel tank: 50L/regular; Tow limit: N/R.; Load capacity: 850 lb.; Turning circle: 36 ft.; Weight: 2,725 lb.

COST ANALYSIS: This car has very little to offer except for some fuel savings and the cachet of buying a "green" car. **Best alternatives:** The Ford Escape Hybrid, Hyundai Accent, Mazda3, Nissan Sentra, Suzuki Aerio, and Toyota Prius or Yaris. **Options:** Steer clear of the standard-issue radio and Firestone or Bridgestone tires. **Rebates:** $1,500 early in the year. **Depreciation:** Average. **Insurance cost:** Higher than average. **Parts supply/cost:** Electronic parts are expensive and hard to find. **Annual maintenance cost:** Average, so far, but long-term costs are likely to be high. **Warranty:** Bumper-to-bumper 3 years/60,000 km; powertrain 5 years/100,000 km; rust perforation 6 years/unlimited km. **Supplementary warranty:** Not needed. **City/highway fuel economy:** 4.8/4.5 L/100 km.

OWNER-REPORTED PROBLEMS: Nothing, yet.

CR-V ★★★★★

RATING: Recommended. **Strong points:** The 2010 CR-V has a more-powerful, smoother-running 4-banger that gives more power than some competitors' similar small engines. Still, owners could use a bit more grunt for merging. Fuel economy and handling are much better than before—especially with standard electronic stability control (though Honda's ESC system does have some drawbacks)—but gas mileage is less than what Honda touts. The ride is firm but comfortable, with communicative steering, progressive brake pedal feel, and a 5-speed automatic transmission that performs flawlessly. The lift-up tailgate is much more convenient than the swing-out version used in previous years. More legroom than ever before, thanks to the roomy rear seats that recline and slide independently and fold down to create a flat cargo floor. **Weak points:** Strong sales make for few discounts. No V6, and ABS is a standard feature only as part of the high-trim CR-V EX package. High-speed cornering is not recommended, due to excessive body lean and the cost of replacement tires. Its stopping distance is not the

KEY FACTS

PRICES: $27,790–$37,090 **FREIGHT:** $1,560 **ORIGIN:** Ohio **SALES:** Up 10%

POWERTRAIN (FRONT-DRIVE/AWD)

Engine: 2.4L 4-cyl. (166 hp); Transmission: 5-speed auto.

DIMENSIONS/CAPACITY

Passengers: 2/3; Wheelbase: 103.1 in.; H: 66.1/L: 177.8/W: 71.6 in.; Headroom F/R: 4.0/4.0 in.; Legroom F/R: 40.1/29.0 in.; Cargo volume: 25.5 cu. ft.; Fuel tank: 50L/regular; Tow limit: 1,500 lb.; Load capacity: 850 lb.; Turning circle: 39 ft.; Ground clearance: 7.2 in.; Weight: 3,404 lb.

best in its class; the latest restyling has reduced cargo space and visibility; the temperature controls have to be reset each time (an analog dash would be more user-friendly); and Honda still needs to tweak the powertrain controls to correct a serious problem with hesitation right before acceleration that crops up from time to time in owner reports. The mirrors are skewed in a way that makes it difficult to park; the steering is still a bit stiff; the ride is bumpy at times; and annoying highway noises are omnipresent when at cruising speeds. **New for 2010:** A new 2.2L (138 hp) diesel 4-cylinder is scheduled to appear in late 2010 as a 2011 model.

OVERVIEW: One of Honda's few bestsellers during these hard economic times, the CR-V has distanced itself from the Toyota Sienna and enhanced the driving experience by making a driver-communicative SUV that is as reliable as it is cheap to service. This is a driver's car, with a peppy, fuel-saving 4-cylinder engine that has sufficient power for most occasions (okay, going uphill fully loaded isn't the 4-banger's forte) and sips gas. You always feel in control, contrary to the experience in many of the larger SUVs where the vehicle cocoons the driver into a quasi-somnolent state.

The 2009 redesign improvements made the CR-V equally manoeuvrable in tight quarters as on winding roads, and it doesn't get blown about as much in stiff cross-winds when cruising. The Real Time four-wheel drive system works well on slippery roads, where the feature automatically engages the wheels for maximum traction. Another interesting high-tech improvement is the Grade Logic Control, which automatically downshifts or upshifts when driving up or down a hill. Also, Honda has reduced engine idle vibration and noise.

COST ANALYSIS: Recently redesigned last year, so buying this year's model will get you virtually the same equipment and give you the same overall performance as a more-expensive 2010 version. **Best alternatives:** The $27,790 CR-V remains one of the most reliable and easiest to drive small SUVs around. Its biggest competitor is the $26,500 Toyota RAV4. If you don't mind going downscale a bit, consider a Hyundai Tucson. **Options:** Get a free extra set of ignition keys written into the contract; Honda's anti-start, theft-protection keys may cost as much as $150 per set. Steer clear of the standard-issue radio and Continental, Firestone, or Bridgestone tires. **Rebates:** Not likely. **Depreciation:** Much slower than average. **Insurance cost:** Average. **Parts supply/cost:** Reasonably priced and easily found at dealers and independent suppliers. **Annual maintenance cost:** Much less than average. **Warranty:** Bumper-to-bumper 3 years/60,000 km; powertrain 5 years/100,000 km; rust perforation 6 years/unlimited km. **Supplementary warranty:** Not needed. **City/highway fuel economy:** *Front-drive:* 10.3/7.3 L/100 km. *AWD:* 10.7/7.8 L/100 km.

OWNER-REPORTED PROBLEMS: One frequent remark we hear from owners is that Honda's service and warranty advisors are in desperate need of attending Dale Carnegie seminars. Generally, owners find there are too many safety-related failures that involve electrical system shorts, premature brake wear, and vibrations and rattles. Examples include airbags that fail to deploy, an AC condenser that's destroyed by road debris (a chronic failure on most of Honda's lineup), bent wheel studs that can easily snap, brake rotors that wear out prematurely; windshield washer nozzles that freeze up in cold weather, engine oil pan leaks, and a serious right-rear blind spot:

> I have serious visibility problems when backing up and changing lanes in heavy traffic.... I backed into a sign pole in a parking lot in mid April, damaging the rear right corner of the vehicle. Two days ago, while I was very slowly and carefully backing out of a parking space, I came very close to a woman pushing a baby in a cart.

There's also a malfunctioning traction control:

> Traction control doesn't work well during winter. It doesn't work well too when the vehicle is parked on a parking that slopes up with about 6 inches of snow. I was in a hurry to go to work but I got towed the first time when my 2008 CRV was only 5 months old because it could not go forward when it was in the parking that slopes up even if I already plowed the snow. It could only reverse but didn't want to go forward.

And poor stability and rapid tread wear with Continental original-equipment tires:

> Continental OEM tire on Honda CRV causes vehicle to slide out of control on snow covered roads and constantly lose traction in rear. We have had numerous near accidents because of the poorly designed low rated tires. My wife is afraid of driving the CRV now. (2) Honda dealers inspected vehicle for possible vehicle stability assist problem and both dealers confirmed that VSA was functioning properly. Dealer #2 stated that he had similar issues with other CRV owners because of the tires. Looking at tire reviews on line the Continental Contact 4x4 is rated as a very poor tire that wears out very quickly and with similar issues as I have stated. Even the authorized Continental dealer in my area says the tires are poor quality and has rarely seen them make 20,000 miles [32,187 km].

RIDGELINE

RATING: Recommended. The mid-sized Ridgeline was first launched in Canada as a 2006 model and sold between $35,000 and $42,000; the 2010 model is expected to cost $34,490 to $42,990. So, in spite of its added equipment over five model years, the pickup costs about the same as its original introductory price, plus it has the best estimated gas mileage in its class. **Strong points:** Some price haggling, mostly on financing and leasing deals. Good, quiet acceleration; a smooth-shifting automatic transmission; secure handling, and good cornering control; communicative, direct steering; a comfortable, supple ride; a friendly cabin environment where everything is easily accessible and storage spaces abound; a tailgate that opens either vertically or horizontally; an all-weather, lockable trunk beneath the cargo bed; and there isn't an intrusive wheel arch in the five-foot-long bed. Reliability and overall dependability are legendary, and crashworthiness is exemplary. **Weak points:** High sales price; bed is too small for some needs; not well-suited for off-roading; and unusual styling for a pickup. **New for 2010:** This year, we will see a restyled front end and more components shared with the Pilot. Honda is apparently putting many additional features (a diesel engine and an upgraded suspension, for example) on hold until the truck market sorts itself out.

KEY FACTS

PRICES: $34,490–$42,990 **FREIGHT:** $1,56 **ORIGIN:** Ontario **SALES:** Down 60%
POWERTRAIN (FRONT-DRIVE)
Engines: 3.5L V6 (250 hp); Transmission: 5-speed auto.
DIMENSIONS/CAPACITY
Passengers: 2/3; Wheelbase: 122 in.; H: 70.3/L: 207/W: 69 in.; Headroom F/R: 6.5/4.5 in.; Legroom F/R: 42/28 in.; Cargo volume: N/A.; Fuel tank: 83.3L/regular; Tow limit: 5,000 lb.; Load capacity: 1,554 lb.; Turning circle: 42.6 ft.; Ground clearance: 7.5 in.; Weight: 4,504 lb.; GVWR: 6,050 lb.

OVERVIEW: The Ridgeline mixes performance with convenience. It's an ideal truck for most jobs, as long as you keep it on the highway. Off-road, this unibody pickup offers only medium performance relative to its nearest body-on-frame competitors, the Toyota Tacoma and the Nissan Frontier. Its long wheelbase and independent rear suspension give the Ridgeline an impressive in-bed trunk and excellent road manners but make it difficult for the truck to traverse anything that's rougher than a stone road or has a breakover angle greater than 21 degrees. NHTSA crashworthiness ratings are outstanding: front and side occupant protection is rated five stars, and rollover protection is given four stars. IIHS gives also gives the 1996–2009 models its top, "Good" score for frontal and side occupation protection and qualifies head-restraint protection as "Good" for all models, except the 2006–08 RTL, which gets a "Marginal" score.

COST ANALYSIS: Small and mid-sized pickups retain a higher resale value than most cars, taking the sting out of the excess you may have paid. **Best alternatives:** Other pickups worth considering are the Nissan Frontier and the Toyota Tacoma. **Options:** Steer clear of the Firestone and Bridgestone original-equipment tires. **Rebates:** Look for $2,000–$4,000 rebates in the winter of 2010. **Depreciation:** Much slower than average; a 2006 model is still worth more than half its original price. **Insurance cost:** Higher than average. **Parts supply/cost:** Mostly reasonably priced and easily found at dealers and independent suppliers. Body parts are a bit costly and harder to find. **Annual maintenance cost:** Laughably low. **Warranty:** Bumper-to-bumper 3 years/60,000 km; powertrain 5 years/100,000 km; rust perforation 6 years/unlimited km. **Supplementary warranty:** A waste of money. Less than 50 safety-related incidents have been reported to NHTSA federal investigators within the last four model years, while 200 complaints would be the average for most vehicles. **City/highway fuel economy:** 14.1/9.8 L/100 km.

OWNER-REPORTED PROBLEMS: Vehicle went out of control without either the vehicle stability assist (VSA) or ABS activated; engine surges when coming to a stop; premature failure of the automatic transmission; brake and accelerator pedals are mounted too close together; many AC heater failures due to defective wiring or fan motor switch (one fire reported); centre sliding portion of the rear window exploded for no reason. Snow collects under the wipers while driving and freezes them to the cowl:

> The wipers shut off under the increased momentary load. The only way to get them to reset is to stop, turn the vehicle off and restart it. This is very difficult to do when you are completely blinded with slush looking forward.

Loose tailgate cables cause the tailgate to malfunction; side wall tread suddenly flew off of the original-equipment Michelin LTX tires; and the heated seats heat up even when the switch is turned off.

ACCORD 

RATING: Above Average. The Accord is the benchmark for dependability and performance in the family-sedan niche. **Strong points:** This is a driver's car, while its primary competitor, the Toyota Camry, is basically the Japanese version of your dad's Oldsmobile. Accord provides excellent acceleration with all engines; a 6-speed manual transmission is available on more models; it's roomy and well equipped with user-friendly instruments and controls; telescoping steering column; easy handling, thanks to large tires and a sturdy chassis; standard stability control; a comfortable ride; good craftsmanship, except for some fit and finish; above-average reliability; few factory-related glitches on the 2009s; and a high resale value. NHTSA crashworthiness scores for front, side, and rollover protection were five, four, and five stars, respectively. The Accord was also given a "Good" rating by IIHS for head-restraint effectiveness, frontal offset, and side-impact protection. **Weak points:** Mediocre fuel economy with the V6, and some road noise intrusion into the cabin area. An astoundingly high number of performance and reliability defects on the 2008 models, with apparently biodegradable brakes topping the list. Annoying windshield dash reflection; distorted windshields; and creaks and rattles. Many owner reports of airbags that explode for no reason or fail to deploy, brake failures, and sudden acceleration. **New for 2010:** An all-new crossover, the Accord Crosstour, goes on sale in the fall of 2009 as a 2010 model. It targets the Toyota Venza in the "cool hatchback" category. Actually, the Venza looks much better and shares little with the car it's based on. However, the Honda should be a better drive. The Crosstour will be styled and equipped similarly to the Acura 2010 ZDX four-door sport coupe, also out in the late fall.

KEY FACTS

PRICES: $25,090–$36,990 **FREIGHT:** $1,310 **ORIGIN:** Japan **SALES:** Down 30%
POWERTRAIN (FRONT-DRIVE)
Engines: 2.4L 4-cyl. (177 hp) • 2.4L 4-cyl. (190 hp) • 3.5L V6 (271 hp); Transmissions: 5-speed man. • 5-speed auto. • 6-speed man.
DIMENSIONS/CAPACITY (SEDAN)
Passengers: 2/3; Wheelbase: 110.2 in.; H: 58.1/L: 194.1/W: 72.7 in.; Headroom F/R: 6.5/3.5 in.; Legroom F/R: 41.5/30 in.; Cargo volume: 14 cu. ft.; Fuel tank: 65L/regular; Tow limit: 1,500 lb.; Load capacity: 850 lb.; Turning circle: 37.7 ft.; Weight: 3,230 lb.

OVERVIEW: Almost a perfect family car, the redesigned 2008 Accord jumped leagues ahead of the Altima, Mazda6, and Camry competition by combining quality craftsmanship with superior road performance. Now, two model years later, Honda has made slight improvements to the revamped models and has priced them more realistically.

If you want good fuel economy and performance with a conventional powertrain, choose one of the two 4-cylinder engines. The V6 is a bit of a gas hog and is needed only for highway travel with a full load. Ride comfort and responsive handling are assured by a suspension and steering set-up that enhances driver control. And what about space? Accord sedans are roomier than ever before, with interior dimensions and capacity that provide more interior space than you'll likely need.

Fast and nimble without a V6, this is the mid-sized sedan of choice for drivers who want maximum fuel economy and comfort along with lots of space for grocery hauling and occasional highway cruising. With the optional V6, the Accord is one of the most versatile mid-sized cars you can find. It offers something for everyone, and its top-drawer quality and high resale value mean there's no way you can lose money buying one.

COST ANALYSIS: Get a cheaper, 4-cylinder-equipped 2009 leftover, financed through one of Honda's low-interest programs. **Best alternatives:** BMW 3 Series, Chevrolet Malibu, Hyundai Elantra, Mazda6, and Toyota Camry. **Options:** The V6 gives a smoother ride and has lots of reserve power for passing and merging. The DVD navigation with voice control found on the EX and V6 coupe is a bit gimmicky, but it's easier to use and understand than most of the competition's systems. **Rebates:** Not likely, except for some attractive leasing and financing deals. **Depreciation:** Slower than average for all models. **Insurance cost:** Higher than average. **Parts supply/cost:** Good availability, and moderately priced. **Annual maintenance cost:** Less than average. **Warranty:** Bumper-to-bumper 3 years/60,000 km; powertrain 5 years/100,000 km; rust perforation 5 years/unlimited km. **Supplementary warranty:** Not needed. The less you deal with "headquarters," the better off you'll be. **City/highway fuel economy:** *Base 2.4L 4-cylinder manual:* 9.4/6.4 L/100 km. *Base 2.4L 4-cylinder automatic:* 9.9/6.5 L/100 km. *3.5L V6 6-speed manual:* 12.6/7.8 L/100 km.

OWNER-REPORTED PROBLEMS: Until the 2008 revamping, each Accord model year would usually have a few dozen reliability problems reported by owners to various government agencies and to *Lemon-Aid*; however, this is no longer the case. Honda's 2008 Accord has accounted for an incredible 400 consumer complaints logged by NHTSA alone, mostly relating to powertrain, brake, and body defects. Yet the 2009 models show barely a couple dozen complaints, leading one to conclude that either Honda fixed many of the factory-related glitches or the problems are still ticking away, waiting to fail when the two-year mark is reached.

Here are some of the most frequent problems reported: Hard starts; steering wheel locked up when making a left-hand turn; chronic premature wearout of the front and rear brake pads (especially the rear pads). Loud and constant brake squealing on the 2008 and 2009 models (not a brake rotor/pad failure):

> Dealer has checked to be sure there has not been a re-design of pads—and there has not been. A check on *Consumer Reports* web site under the forum for Honda shows this is a widespread problem. Although most got at least 12 to 15 thousand miles [19,000–24,000 km]. I live in hills which may explain part of the difference. Having to replace rear brake pads every 9,000 or 10,000 miles [14,500–16,000 km] is a safety problem.
>
> •
>
> There is an abnormal number of complaints online regarding 2008 Honda Accord's premature brake wear. (*www.carcomplaints.com/Honda/Accord/2008/brakes/premature_brake_wear.shtml*)

Hole in AC condenser likely caused by road debris; metal creaking sound around the rear shelf deck likely due to broken spot welds in the rear shelf of the car; when the AC is activated, the headlights and interior lighting dim or flicker; and remote door locking and unlocking failures. Service bulletins for the 2009 model confirm problems with the instrument time display and a rattling rear shelf.

ODYSSEY

best buy

RATING: Recommended. Odyssey outclasses the Toyota Sienna in reliability and driving pleasure. In a Sienna, the driver is "driven"; in an Odyssey, the driver does the driving by being more actively involved in the overall performance of the vehicle. There have, however, been frequent reports of safety- and performance-related failures on previous-year Odysseys. Of particular concern are airbag malfunctions and brake defects leading to sudden brake loss, and the frequent replacement of the brake calipers and rotors. **Strong points:** Plenty of power for high-speed merging; a spacious, versatile, and quiet interior; and numerous safety and convenience features. Additional mid-range torque means less shifting when the engine is under load. Carlike ride and handling; plenty of interior space; comfortable seats; second-row middle seats can be folded down as an armrest or removed completely, much like the middle-row captain's chairs, which can slide fore or aft, in unison or separately; second-row power windows; floor-stowable, 60/40 split third-row seats; easy back seat entry and exit; a convenient second driver-side door and a power tailgate; an extensive list of standard equipment; most controls and displays are easy to

KEY FACTS

PRICES: $31,490–$48,890 **FREIGHT:** $1,540 **ORIGIN:** Alabama **SALES:** Down 25%

POWERTRAIN (FRONT-DRIVE)

Engine: 3.5L V6 (244 hp); Transmission: 5-speed auto.

DIMENSIONS/CAPACITY

Passengers: 2/3/3; Wheelbase: 118.1 in.; H: 68.8/L: 202.1/W: 77.1 in.; Headroom F/R1/R2: 4.5/5.5/2.0 in.; Legroom F/R1/R2: 41.5/31/28 in.; Cargo volume: 38.4 cu. ft.; Fuel tank: 80L/regular; Tow limit: 3,500 lb.; Load capacity: 1,320 lb.; Turning circle: 36.7 ft.; Ground clearance: 5 in.; Weight: 4,387 lb.

reach and read; above-average quality control; and better fit and finish than with the Sienna. The Odyssey also has standard vehicle stability assist and traction control to prevent rollovers and enhance handling, side curtain airbags with rollover sensors for all rows, and adjustable brake and accelerator pedals. NHTSA gives the 2010 Odyssey five stars for front and side crashworthiness and four stars for rollover protection. IIHS says head restraints offer "Good" protection to occupants, and also give a "Good" frontal and side protection rating. **Weak points:** Fuel consumption isn't as low as Honda promises, despite its innovative cylinder deactivation system. Unlike with the Sienna, all-wheel drive isn't available; middle-row seats don't fold flat like in other minivans, so they need to be stowed somewhere else; second-row head restraints block visibility; front-passenger legroom is marginal, owing to the restricted seat travel; you can't slide your legs comfortably under the dash; some passengers bump their shins on the glove box; third-row seat is suitable only for children; the narrow back bench seat provides little legroom unless the middle seats are pushed far forward, inconveniencing passengers in those seats; radio control access is blocked by the shift lever, and it's difficult to calibrate the radio without taking your eyes off the road; some tire rumble, rattles, and body drumming at highway speeds; and rear-seat head restraints impede side and rear visibility. The storage well won't take any tire larger than a "space saver"—meaning you'll carry your flat in the back. **New for 2010:** Carried over unchanged; the 2011 model will be redesigned.

OVERVIEW: No longer simply an Accord masquerading as a minivan, the Odyssey is longer, wider, taller, and more powerful, thanks to its 2005 redesign. It has a lean look, but the interior is wide and long enough to accommodate a 4'× 8' sheet of plywood laid flat. Sliding doors are offered as standard equipment, and if you buy the EX version, they will both be power-assisted.

Odyssey is powered by a competent 3.5L V6, which includes variable cylinder deactivation to increase fuel economy. Gas consumption may be cut up to 10 percent by the engine's ability to automatically switch between 6-cylinder and 3-cylinder activation, depending on engine load. Although this feature produced disastrous results when first used by GM several decades ago, Honda's system has performed fairly reliably during the past three years.

COST ANALYSIS: Because sales have been almost halved this year, Honda dealers are discounting their products by as much as 15 percent through lower transaction prices and attractive lease/loan programs. There is room for some price negotiation, with savings in the $2,000–$3,500 range, but make sure you have a specific delivery date spelled out in the contract, along with a protected price, in case there's a price increase while you're waiting for delivery. **Best alternatives:** If you want better handling and reliability, the closest competitor to the Odyssey is Toyota's Sienna minivan. Chrysler's Caravan and the Mazda5 are acceptable choices for different reasons: the Mazda has less room but burns less fuel, without a high-tech engine add-on, and Chrysler's minivans aren't as reliable as the Odyssey but offer better prices, lots of room for people and things, and plenty of convenience and safety features. The Hyundai and Kia minivan twins (Entourage and Sedona) are also acceptable choices, though the Entourage has been dropped from the lineup. GM's quality-challenged Montana, Relay, Terraza, and Uplander are no longer in the running, because they were dropped as part of the automaker's bankruptcy restructuring. However, GM is in the running if you're looking for lots of towing "grunt" and plenty of usable living space; in that case, rear-drive GM full-sized vans are good buys. **Options:** Remember, if you want the gimmicky video entertainment and DVD navigation system, you also have to spring for the expensive (and not-for-everyone) leather seats. Ditch the original-equipment Firestone tires. You don't need the extra risk. **Rebates:** Any patient haggler should get a few thousand dollars cut from the base price. Low-cost financing and leasing programs will also help bring down the transaction price. **Depreciation:** Slower than average. **Insurance cost:** Higher than average. **Annual maintenance cost:** Average. **Parts supply/cost:** Moderately priced parts; availability is better than average because the Odyssey uses many generic Accord parts. CVT transmission and cylinder deactivation parts may be costly, and they may be available only from Honda dealers. **Warranty:** Bumper-to-bumper 3 years/60,000 km; powertrain 5 years/100,000 km; rust perforation 5 years/unlimited km. **Supplementary warranty:** Not needed. **City/highway fuel economy:** 12.3/7.8 L/100 km.

OWNER-REPORTED PROBLEMS: Airbags didn't deploy after a severe rear-ender; airbag cover warps; early engine and automatic transmission replacement (engine front case seal leakage); windshield shattered for no reason; excessive wind noise from the passenger and driver pillar area; poor paint job; steering pulls continually to the right; third-row folding seat collapsed and broke a child's fingers; many complaints of road debris destroying the AC condenser; premature front brake wear and excessive brake grinding noise are common problems that afflict all Hondas, but the 2007–08 brake system is particularly vulnerable; sudden brake loss after the VSA light comes on (some dealers suggest unplugging the VSA); brake loss when backing out of a parking lot; and a history of mushy braking:

> We noticed the brakes appeared to be soft and spongy. When I finally took it in for service, I was told it needed a new master cylinder (at 2,800 miles [4,500 km]), which they replaced. After I picked it up, I drove it a few miles and the brakes still felt soft and spongy, so I drove back to the dealership. The service manager then drove the car and told me, "That's the way the Odyssey brakes are."

ELEMENT ★★★★

RATING: Above Average. **Strong points:** Easy handling; standard electronic stability control and side curtain airbags; wide doorways make loading and unloading cargo a breeze; a spacious interior and washable floor; good fit and finish; all seats fold back to make a small bed; and versatile rear seats can fold to the side or be removed completely. NHTSA-tested crashworthiness is rated five stars for front and side occupant protection and three stars for rollover protection. IIHS says frontal offset and side-impact protection and head restraint effectiveness are "Good." **Weak points:** The automatic transmission hobbles the 4-cylinder engine; a stiff, jerky ride; large roof pillars obstruct outward visibility; driving position is uncomfortable for some; the rear-hinged rear side doors don't open independently of the front doors; and excessive road noise. With both the Element and Pilot, Honda maintains a death grip on dated boxy styling that screams out, "I am old!" **New for 2010:** Carried over mostly unchanged. A new Dog Friendly option package includes equipment that makes for easier and safer canine transportation. It includes a cargo-area pet bed, a cargo-area ramp for pet entry and exit, and all-weather floormats. 2011 models will be redesigned.

KEY FACTS

PRICES: $26,990–$32,090 **FREIGHT:** $1,540 **ORIGIN:** Ohio **SALES:** Down 55%
POWERTRAIN (FRONT-DRIVE/AWD)
Engine: 2.4L 4-cyl. (166 hp); Transmission: 5-speed auto.
DIMENSIONS/CAPACITY
Passengers: 2/2; Wheelbase: 101.3 in.; H: 70.3/L: 169.9/W: 77.1 in.; Headroom F/R: 7.5/2.0 in.; Legroom F/R: 41/31 in.; Cargo volume: 74.5 cu. ft.; Fuel tank: 80L/regular; Tow limit: 1,500 lb.; Load capacity: 675 lb.; Turning circle: 36 ft.; Ground clearance: 7.0 in.; Weight: 3,527 lb.

OVERVIEW: Based on the Honda Civic platform, the Element is a small, boxy SUV that is more of a cargo-hauler than a passenger-carrier. This doesn't take away the fact that the vehicle comes well-appointed and is powerful enough with its 4-banger and automatic transmission to accomplish most driving chores.

COST ANALYSIS: Element sales are now less than half what they were in 2008. Hungry dealers will haggle. Unless your heart is set on pampering your pooch, your best buy is a carried-over 2009 version, discounted by about 15 percent. That leaves enough dough for all sorts of canine comforts. **Best alternatives:** Try to get your mind around a less-quirky-looking and more-versatile wagon or hatchback, like the Chevrolet HHR, Honda Fit, Hyundai Elantra, Kia Rondo or Soul, Mazda5, Nissan Versa, Pontiac Vibe, Saturn Astra, Suzuki SX4, and Toyota Matrix. **Options:** Be wary of poorly performing Bridgestone and Firestone original-equipment tires. **Rebates:** Good leasing and low-finance deals; discounts of about 15 percent. **Depreciation:** Slower than average. **Insurance cost:** Average. **Annual maintenance cost:** Average. **Parts supply/cost:** Parts are easy to find and relatively inexpensive. **Warranty:** Bumper-to-bumper 3 years/60,000 km; powertrain 5 years/100,000 km; rust perforation 5 years/unlimited km. **Supplementary warranty:** Not necessary. **City/highway fuel economy:** *Front-drive:* 10.5/8.1 L/100 km. *AWD:* 11.0/8.3 L/100 km.

OWNER-REPORTED PROBLEMS: Reliability has proven to be much better than average. Nevertheless, you can expect problems with the premature wearout of key brake components (preceded by mushy braking), mysterious windshield cracks, and malfunctioning tire-pressure sensors.

PILOT ★★★★

RATING: Above Average. The second-generation Pilot has grown into a large-sized people-carrier that offers a comfortable ride, first-class handling, and plenty of passenger space. **Strong points:** Adequate power for highway cruising; superb handling; a versatile interior; seating for up to eight; the third-row seat folds flat into sections to free up storage space; and there's a small storage area in the floor. Chock full of safety and convenience features and excellent crashworthiness scores (five-star protection in frontal, offset frontal, and side collisions, four-star ranking for rollover protection, and "Good" head-restraint protection). Overall reliability has been excellent. The Pilot also has standard vehicle stability assist and traction control to prevent rollovers and enhance handling, side curtain airbags with rollover sensors for all rows, and adjustable brake and accelerator pedals. Fuel consumption can be improved by using the V6 engine's cylinder-shut-off system. The GPS and voice operation feature are easy to operate with a little practice. **Weak points:** Mediocre acceleration accompanied by some torque steer; so-so braking; and a boxy exterior. Unimpressive fuel economy—the much-heralded cylinder deactivation system doesn't save as much fuel as Honda fantasizes, and it makes the vehicle seriously underpowered. Interior plastic materials and overall fit and finish aren't up to Honda's reputation for quality, and road noise is omnipresent. The centre console can be a little confusing to operate until you've studied it a little while. Make sure your navigation disc is up to date; some owners report the discs may be two years old. The storage box between the front seats needs to accommodate smaller items without them rolling around (a coin tray would help). Honda also needs to make the radio and AC operation more user-friendly, with fewer buttons. **New for 2010:** Carried over unchanged; another redesign is scheduled for 2011.

KEY FACTS

PRICES: $36,820–$49,920 **FREIGHT:** $1,540 **ORIGIN:** Ontario **SALES:** Down 25%

POWERTRAIN (FRONT-DRIVE/AWD)

Engine: 3.5L V6 (250 hp); Transmission: 5-speed auto.

DIMENSIONS/CAPACITY

Passengers: 2/3/3; Wheelbase: 109.2 in.; H: 71.0/L: 190.9/W: 78.5 in.; Headroom (Honda specs.) F/R1/R2: 40/39.8/38.2 in.; Legroom (Honda specs.) F/R1/R2: 41.4/38.5/32.1 in.; Cargo volume: 18 cu. ft.; Fuel tank: 79.5L/regular; Tow limit: 3,500-4,500 lb.; Load capacity: 1,320 lb.; Turning circle: 36.7 ft.; Ground clearance: 8.0 in.; Weight: 4,319 lb.

OVERVIEW: It's the mouse that roared. The Pilot is trucklike on the outside, but it's a much tamer vehicle when you look closely. It combines carlike comfort and handling in a crossover package where ride comfort, utility, and passenger accommodations are foremost.

COST ANALYSIS: After a major redesign last year, the Pilot sees no major changes for 2010; therefore, pricing should remain about the same. There are many unsold Pilots on dealers' lots that are eligible for all kinds of automaker and dealer incentives. Be prepared to walk away if salespeople won't haggle, especially since Honda's larger vehicle sales are hurting. Each uptick in fuel prices is another downtick in market share. **Best alternatives:** GM's heavily discounted Tahoe and Yukon are perhaps not as reliable as Honda's lineup, but GM dealers are hungry to sell their large SUVs at bargain prices. **Options:** Nothing essential. **Rebates:** Look for $3,000–$5,000 discounts and attractive low financing rates and special leasing prices. **Depreciation:** Slower than average. **Insurance cost:** Higher than average. **Annual maintenance cost:** Below average. **Parts supply/cost:** Average availability. Most parts are moderately priced, except for cylinder deactivation components, which may be costly because only Honda dealers sell them. **Warranty:** Bumper-to-bumper 3 years/60,000 km; powertrain 5 years/100,000 km; rust perforation 5 years/unlimited km. **Supplementary warranty:** A waste of money. **City/highway fuel economy:** 12.7/8.7 L/100 km.

OWNER-REPORTED PROBLEMS: Airbags failed to deploy; unstable driver's seat; broken timing belt; driver's head restraint rises on its own; and headlights dip too low to be effective.

Hyundai

Hyundai and Kia are climbing the North American sales charts, and now account for more than 7 percent of the vehicles sold in the United States. These two manufacturers, owned by the same South Korean conglomerate, sell many of the same vehicles under different names. So far this has been a very successful strategy, and both companies have seen sales surge while their competitors face double-digit losses.

These two automakers are racking up impressive sales across Canada for three reasons: Their vehicles are competitively priced, their quality is almost equal to the best that comes from Japan or Detroit, and owners can count on getting a comprehensive base warranty. Increased sales and positive quality surveys indicate the company is on a much surer footing than it was in the late '70s, when Hyundai Canada was run by a ragtag gang of Toronto-based auto newbies. They made money by dumping cheap but poor-quality Pony and Stellar compacts into the market to compete against equally poor-quality American small cars. At that time, Detroit iron was too expensive and not very fuel-efficient and fuel prices were going through the roof. However, when fuel became relatively cheap again, you couldn't give a Hyundai away.

Korean Quality?

Don't laugh. Hyundai is now building cars and minivans that are as reliable and defect-free as the best that Japan offers—and selling them for much less. This quality turnaround has been accomplished through the use of better-made components and corporate espionage. In fact, Hyundai hired away one of Toyota's top quality-control engineers in 2003—and got a satchel-full of Toyota's secret documents in the bargain. Following a cease-and-desist letter from Toyota,

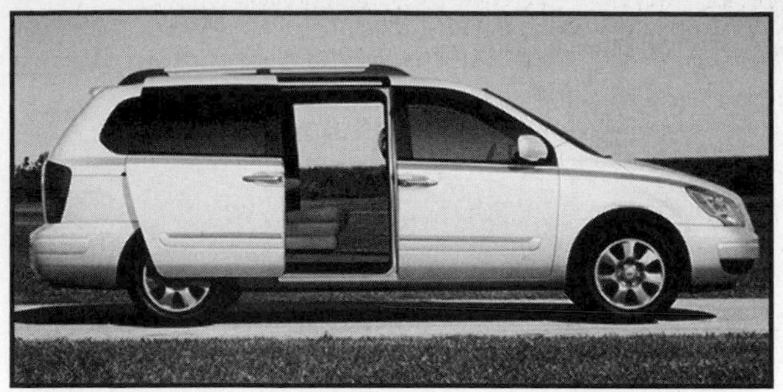

Bye-bye, Entourage.

Hyundai fired the engineer in August 2006 and returned the pilfered documents. Hyundai says it never looked at the stolen Toyota documents (wink, wink; nudge, nudge), but insiders say the privileged information figured prominently in Hyundai PowerPoint presentations.

Hyundai and Kia are also copying the successful international marketing strategy that's been employed by Japanese automakers over the past four decades: Secure a solid beachhead in one car segment, and then branch out from there. Models that don't sell get dumped, like the Entourage minivan, Elantra, Tiburon, and Azera. Hyundai is also sharing components with its Kia subsidiary to keep production costs down while raising quality. Owner surveys of these blended cars indicate that there has been an appreciable rise in quality since the reworked 2006 models arrived.

If you still have doubts as to Hyundai's car quality, check out the most recent J.D. Power survey reports, or click on to NHTSA's online consumer complaints database (*www-odi.nhtsa.dot.gov/cars/problems/complain*).

The South Koreans are investing heavily in North America as they troll for dealers recently dumped by bankrupt Chrysler and General Motors. They are bringing out an extensive lineup of fuel-efficient new cars, minivans, and SUVs, and targeting increasingly upscale customers without forgetting their entry-level base. For example, Hyundai has just enhanced its luxury lineup with the 2009 Genesis luxury sedan and a Camaro/Mustang stalker, the 2010 Genesis Coupe. Waiting in the wings is the 2011 Equus, a $70,000, V8-powered, rear-drive luxury sedan that is aimed at the BMW 5 Series and the Mercedes-Benz E-Class. The Equus was developed on the rear-drive Genesis sedan platform, but the wheelbase was stretched 10.9 cm (4.3 in.). It's 29 cm (11.4 in.) longer than the 2010 Mercedes E-Class.

At the other end of the fuel economy spectrum, both Hyundai and Kia intend to launch several new fuel-frugal small cars in the near future and offer drivers fuel-saving technology that includes a hybrid Sonata, smaller engines, direct-injection gasoline engines, plug-in hybrids, and fuel cell technology. Hyundai calls the fuel economy initiative "Blue Drive": a fancy name for cheaper models with less content, less weight, and more miles per gallon. For example, Blue Edition models will have a lower gear ratio and tires with less rolling resistance. Power windows and door locks, as well as other formerly standard amenities, will become optional, thereby trading convenience for cash savings.

ACCENT ★★★★★

RATING: Recommended, if you're using your Accent primarily as a fuel-sipping urban dweller consigned to occasional forays on the highway. Think of it as a more-refined and peppier Metro/Sprint from South Korea, built for light duty around town. **Strong points:** Reasonably priced, and very well-appointed; good fuel economy; adequate engine and automatic transmission performance in most situations; easy handling; a comfortable and quiet ride; a fair amount of interior room; comfortable driving position with good visibility and height-adjustable, form-fitting bucket seats that provide plenty of support; an incredibly good reliability record, with few complaints relative to safety or quality control; and it's cheap on gas. A 5-year/100,000 km bumper-to-bumper warranty. Some impressive but conflicting crashworthiness scores (see the "Weak points"): NHTSA gives the Accent five stars for front-impact protection and four stars for side collision and rollover protection. **Weak points:** Automatic transmission hobbles horsepower; engine could use a bit more torque and noise-vibration dampening; ride is on the firm side; numb steering feel; and acrobatic rear-seat entry/exit with the hatchback. Frontal offset crash protection rated only "Acceptable" by IIHS, and head restraints and side crash protection were rated "Poor." **New for 2010:** Carried over practically unchanged, except for the introduction of a cheaper Blue Edition ("less for less"). A redesign is expected for the 2011 or 2012 model year.

KEY FACTS

PRICES: $13,595–$18,645 **FREIGHT:** $1,345 **ORIGIN:** South Korea **SALES:** Up 15%

POWERTRAIN (FRONT-DRIVE)

Engine: 1.6L 4-cyl. (110 hp); Transmissions: 5-speed man. • 4-speed auto.

DIMENSIONS/CAPACITY

Passengers: 2/3; Wheelbase: 98.4 in.; H: 57.9/L: 159.3/W: 66.7 in.; Headroom F/R: 4.5/2.0 in.; Legroom F/R: 40.5 /25.5 in.; Cargo volume: 12 cu. ft.; Fuel tank: 45L/regular; Tow limit: N/A; Load capacity: 850 lb.; Turning circle: 36 ft.; Weight: 2,590 lb.

OVERVIEW: Accent lends its basic design to the Rio from Hyundai's Kia division, making this front-drive, entry-level sedan one of the cheapest feature-laden small cars sold in North America. Carrying a homegrown 1.6L 4-cylinder engine coupled to a 5-speed manual or 4-speed automatic transmission, the Accent offers bare-bones motoring without sacrificing basic amenities, including AC, a height-adjustable driver's seat with lumbar support, and split-folding rear seats.

COST ANALYSIS: The Accent is hot—and almost impossible to find. No surprise, when one sees the transaction price dipping below $10,000. Buy a practically identical 2009, and haggle down the price without giving up content. Remember, cheaper 2010s mean less equipment. **Best alternatives:** Honda Civic or Fit, Mazda3, Nissan Versa or Sentra, Suzuki SX4, and Toyota Yaris. **Options:** Not needed. **Rebates:** $1,000–$2,000 through low-cost financing, leasing deals, and discounting. **Depreciation:** Slower than average, now that fuel prices are rising. **Insurance cost:** Average. **Parts supply/cost:** Parts aren't hard to find, and they're reasonably priced. **Annual maintenance cost:** Average. **Warranty:**

Bumper-to-bumper 5 years/100,000 km; rust perforation 5 years/unlimited km. **Supplementary warranty:** No longer needed, such is the improvement in quality control. **City/highway fuel economy:** *Manual:* 7.4/6.0 L/100 km. *Automatic:* 7.9/5.6 L/100.

OWNER-REPORTED PROBLEMS: Airbags failed to deploy; car suddenly lost power and misfired when cruising on the highway; engine surging when stopped at a traffic light; delayed automatic transmission engagement; power-steering pump whine; turn signal malfunctions; and Kumho tire premature wear and blistering. One owner reports that the car's undercarriage cables attract groundhogs who love to snack on them, thereby disabling the tranny and key dash gauges:

> I put down moth balls and fox scent to ward the hogs off, but they love Accent wires; losing the transmission and speedometer can make driving a little dangerous.

ELANTRA

RATING: Above Average. **Strong points:** Carried-over engine delivers adequate, not spectacular, power; smooth-shifting automatic transmission; good handling and a quiet, comfortable ride; electronic stability control comes with the SE trim; well-appointed and spacious interior; comfortable seats; seatback slides far enough back to easily accommodate six-foot-plus drivers; classy, quiet interior; and above-average crashworthiness scores. For example, NHTSA gives the car five stars for frontal crash protection and four stars for side and rollover protection. A good base warranty is standard. **Weak points:** Not a lot of grunt at low engine rpm; steering feels light; noisy brakes; soft suspension is "floaty," and it dips when passing over rough spots; side airbags are standard only with the higher-end models; excessive engine noise when accelerating; brakes are a bit grabby and take some skill to modulate; cheap-looking plastic door panels; at night, the radio lights glare into the driver's eyes; a narrow trunk opening, and the trunk lid hinges cut available space; small trunk pass-through; some wind noise; and fairly rapid depreciation. **New for 2010:** A cheaper Blue Edition with less content. Hyundai plans to redesign the car for the 2012 model year. In homage to the discontinued sporty Tiburon, a new front-drive coupe will be launched as a 2012 model.

KEY FACTS

PRICES: $15,845–$23,795 **FREIGHT:** $1,345 **ORIGIN:** South Korea **SALES:** Down 30%

POWERTRAIN (FRONT-DRIVE)

Engine: 2.0L 4-cyl. (138 hp); Transmissions: 5-speed man. • 4-speed auto.

DIMENSIONS/CAPACITY

Passengers: 2/3; Wheelbase: 104.3 in.; H: 58.3/L: 177.4/W: 69.9 in.; Headroom F/R: 2.5/2.0 in.; Legroom F/R: 43.5/35 in.; Cargo volume: 14.2 cu. ft.; Fuel tank: 53L/regular; Tow limit: 2,000 lb.; Load capacity: 850 lb.; Turning circle: 37 ft.; Weight: 2,723 lb.

OVERVIEW: Elantra's latest redesign is hard to miss, with its bubbly exterior styling, fat rear end, unique nose, tall shape, large headlights, and high-mounted tail lights. The roomy interior pushes the car into the mid-size category. A wagon version, called the Touring, arrived in early 2009. A 138 hp 2.0L 4-cylinder powerplant hooked to a 4-speed automatic transmission supplies much-needed power that competes well with most other cars in this price range. The ride and handling are also quite good, owing mainly to the Elantra's long wheelbase and sophisticated suspension.

COST ANALYSIS: Get the discounted 2009 model, since the base 2010 version won't be as well equipped. **Best alternatives:** The Chevrolet Cobalt, Honda Civic, Kia Spectra5, Mazda3, Mitsubishi Lancer, and Toyota Corolla. **Options:** Electronic stability control is a must-have. Also, opt for the automatic transmission: It's quieter and shifts more smoothly than the manual, and fuel economy isn't much affected. **Rebates:** $1,500 rebates and low-cost financing. **Depreciation:** Average. **Insurance cost:** Average. **Parts supply/cost:** Parts are easy to find and reasonably priced, with heavy discounting by independents. **Annual maintenance cost:** Average. **Warranty:** Bumper-to-bumper 5 years/100,000 km; rust perforation 5 years/unlimited km. **Supplementary warranty:** Not needed. **City/highway fuel economy:** *Manual:* 8.4/6.0 L/100 km. *Automatic:* 8.2/6.0 L/100 km. *Touring manual:* 8.9/6.4 L/100 km. *Touring automatic:* 8.7/6.5 L/100 km.

OWNER-REPORTED PROBLEMS: Airbags failed to deploy:

> My wife and I were involved in an accident. Another car ran the red light and hit us. My wife and I were injured and our car was totaled. None of the airbags went off on our brand new Hyundai Elantra. We were later told by Hyundai that passenger airbags don't always go off because of weight variations in some adults. My wife is 5' 4" and her weight is normal for her height.

Defective solenoids blamed for early transmission failures; car may roll away even with emergency brake applied; sudden steering lock-up; brakes freeze up when vehicle is driven through snow; cruise control suddenly resets itself to a higher speed; throttle sensor sticks when cruising; chronic stalling, believed to be a fuel-pump-related problem; Airbag light and tire-pressure monitoring system alert come on for no reason; and in-dash front panel squeaks.

SONATA ★★★★

RATING: Above Average. The 2009 model's engine and interior refinements gave the Sonata all of the safety and performance features it needs to play in the big leagues against Japan's and Detroit's family sedans. **Strong points:** A credible alternative to most Detroit-bred family cars, and it's priced at thousands of dollars less. Well equipped and stylish; sizzling V6 power, and it burns only about 1.0 L/100 km more than the 4-banger does; good handling; comfortable ride; user-friendly controls and gauges; spacious trunk, and a conveniently low lift-in height; fairly quiet cabin that seats three comfortably in the back; and much-improved quality control. NHTSA awarded Sonata five stars for front- and side-impact occupant protection

KEY FACTS

PRICES: $21,995–$31,495 **FREIGHT:** $1,415 **ORIGIN:** Alabama **SALES:** Down 7%
POWERTRAIN (FRONT-DRIVE)
Engines: 2.4L 4-cyl. (162 hp) • 3.3L V6 (235 hp); Transmissions: 5-speed man. • 5-speed auto.
DIMENSIONS/CAPACITY
Passengers: 2/3; Wheelbase: 107 in.; H: 58/L: 189: 72 in.; Headroom F/R: 3.0/3.0 in.; Legroom F/R: 41/29.5 in.; Cargo volume: 16.3 cu. ft.; Fuel tank: 67L/regular; Tow limit: 2,000 lb.; Load capacity: 860 lb.; Turning circle: 39 ft.; Weight: 3,253 lb.

and four stars for rollover resistance. IIHS gave the Sonata a "Good" rating for front offset protection and head-restraint effectiveness and an "Acceptable" rating for side-impact protection. Backed by a comprehensive base warranty. **Weak points:** Prices have been boosted by a couple thousand dollars during the past few years; fuel economy could be better; the suspension is somewhat bouncy and noisy; lots of body lean under hard cornering; and the steering lacks feedback. **New for 2010:** Carried over unchanged. A hybrid-powertrain-equipped 2011 model will arrive at the end of 2010. The 2011 redesigned Sonata goes on sale in early 2010 with the automaker's first direct-injection 4-cylinder gasoline engine and, possibly, a double-clutch transmission.

OVERVIEW: This is the mid-sized sedan that Hyundai should have built years ago. Sure, incremental engine and suspension improvements over the years made the Sonata a pleasant car to own, but it lacked the refinement of a Honda or Toyota. That's no longer true.

Styled similarly to the Honda Accord, the redesigned Sonata meets or exceeds the engine performance standards of its competitors, although its fuel economy isn't as good. The Sonata rides on a double-wishbone front suspension and a multi-link rear suspension that is more softly sprung than usual, making the car a bit "bouncier" than its competitors.

Hyundai has again put the emphasis on safety, giving buyers a lot more safety features for their money than they get with competing models. For example, Sonatas include four-wheel ABS; stability and traction control; front, side, and curtain airbags; front and rear seat belt pretensioners; an integrated rear child safety seat; and a "smart" passenger-side airbag that won't deploy if the passenger weighs less than 30 kg (66 lb.). Well, at least that's the theory—in practice, owners report the airbag is often disabled no matter what the passenger's weight.

COST ANALYSIS: Buy a discounted 2009 model made after March 2009. **Best alternatives:** The Honda Accord, Mazda5 or Mazda6, and Toyota Camry. **Options:** Choose the V6 engine for better performance and handling; you will lose only a bit of fuel economy. If you get the 4-banger, keep in mind that good fuel economy means putting up with a bit more engine noise. Be wary of the sunroof; it eats up a lot of headroom and has a history of leaking. **Rebates:** Expect $3,000 rebates and zero percent financing or attractive leasing deals on all models. **Depreciation:** Average. **Insurance cost:** Average. **Parts supply/cost:** Easy to find, and relatively inexpensive. **Annual maintenance cost:** Average. **Warranty:** Bumper-to-bumper 5 years/100,000 km; rust perforation 5 years/ unlimited km. **Supplementary warranty:** Not needed. **City/highway fuel**

economy: *4-cylinder manual:* 9.7/6.2 L/100 km. *4-cylinder automatic:* 9.5/6.2 L/100 km. *V6:* 10.8/6.9 L/100 km.

OWNER-REPORTED PROBLEMS: Sudden, unintended acceleration when passing other cars; cruise control resets itself to a higher speed; premature wearout of the rear brakes; and noisy shocks/struts.

AZERA ★★★★

RATING: Above Average. **Strong points:** Refined, roomy, well equipped, and reasonably priced; solid V6 performance, accompanied by smooth transmission shifts and a manual shiftgate that works especially well when passing over hilly terrain; the solid body structure keeps creaks and rattles out of the cabin; a comfortable ride that doesn't compromise handling; good braking; standard electronic stability control; plenty of front seatroom and comfort; good all-around visibility; impressive fit and finish; and three-year reliability scores have been good. NHTSA awarded four stars for rollover resistance and front-impact occupant protection and five stars for side protection, while IIHS gave the Azera a "Good" rating for front offset protection and an "Acceptable" rating for side-impact and head-restraint protection. Excellent base warranty. **Weak points:** Excessive body lean and front-end plowing when cornering; large turning circle; and fuel economy is unimpressive. **New for 2010:** Nothing important; the Azera is living on borrowed time.

KEY FACTS

PRICES: $36,995 **FREIGHT:** $1,565
ORIGIN: South Korea **SALES:** Down 80%
POWERTRAIN (FRONT-DRIVE)
Engine: 3.3L V6 (234 hp) • 3.8L V6 (263 hp); Transmission: 5-speed auto.
DIMENSIONS/CAPACITY
Passengers: 2/3; Wheelbase: 109 in.; H: 59/L: 193/W: 73 in.; Headroom F/R: 4.0/3.5 in.; Legroom F/R: 40/29 in.; Cargo volume: 17 cu. ft.; Fuel tank: 75L/regular; Tow limit: 2,000 lb.; Load capacity; 860 lb.; Turning circle: 41 ft.; Weight: 3,629 lb.

OVERVIEW: This front-drive, four-door, five-passenger luxury sedan has been on the market for four years as the Hyundai XG350's replacement. Sales have been disappointing.

COST ANALYSIS: A well-equipped, refined car that has a roomy interior and a reasonable base price that undercuts similarly equipped Toyota Camrys or Avalons and Buick Allures or Lucernes. Look for a second-series 2009 (made after March 2009) that's discounted by at least 25 percent. Dealers will want to rid themselves of these cars before they are formally discontinued and their value plummets. **Best alternatives:** A fully equipped Honda Accord or a discounted Toyota Avalon or Camry V6. **Options:** Nothing needed, because this car comes with practically everything. Don't waste your money on the heated seats, rear-window blind, rain-sensitive windshield washers, or overpriced sunroof. **Rebates:** Look for $3,000 rebates, deep discounting, and low-percentage financing when the competition heats up in 2010. **Depreciation:** Predicted to be average.

Insurance cost: Higher than average. **Parts supply/cost:** Mechanical parts should be mostly generic and reasonably priced, but body parts may be expensive and in short supply until independent suppliers start stocking them. **Annual maintenance cost:** Should be average. **Warranty:** Bumper-to-bumper 5 years/100,000 km; rust perforation 5 years/unlimited km. **Supplementary warranty:** Not needed. **City/highway fuel economy:** 12.2/7.8 L/100 km.

OWNER-REPORTED PROBLEMS: Airbag warning light comes on for no reason; engine loses power when hot; and driver's seatback suddenly moved forward while the vehicle was underway.

GENESIS ★

RATING: Not Recommended. A new model, plus a year-old recession, plus hundreds of new dealers add up to possible major quality and servicing problems. Also, the Genesis is an unexceptional car, without a price advantage and with similar features found on well-proven, better-performing competitors. **Strong points:** Acceptable acceleration, but the V6 and V8 engines produce less torque at higher rpm than the Chrysler 300 or Pontiac G8 does. First-class interior fit and finish; a quiet, vibration-free, and spacious cabin; and clear and easy-to-read gauges. Impressive crashworthiness rankings: NHTSA gave the sedan its top, five-star rating for front, side, and head-restraint occupant protection; IIHS frontal offset crashworthiness was rated "Acceptable" to "Good," while side-impact and head-restraint protection were "Good." The coupe version posted similar results, except that frontal protection was not tested. **Weak points:** Unimpressive fuel economy; ho-hum styling; and excessive body roll in hard cornering. A "floaty" suspension makes for a wandering ride and imprecise steering (Infiniti M and BMW models have stiffer suspensions that produce a more-secure feeling). Hyundai mechanics say the suspension is tuned for a full load, so anything less makes the vehicle wander. Original-equipment Dunlop tires may be too sensitive to the crown in the road. Navigation and audio system controls are cumbersome. Hyundai recommends premium fuel for extra horsepower from the V8, but it's not worth the higher fuel cost for just eight more horses. Long-term reliability has yet to be determined; however, most of Hyundai's newly introduced vehicles have had fewer factory glitches than the competition. **New for 2010:** Launched as a 2009 model, the sedan returns with standard integrated Bluetooth that works with the car's audio system; a retuned suspension; improved bushings, spring rates, and

KEY FACTS

PRICES: *Coupe:* $24,495–$34,995, *Sedan:* $37,995–$48,995 **FREIGHT:** $1,565 **ORIGIN:** South Korea **SALES:** Good—newly arrived

POWERTRAIN (REAR-DRIVE)
Engines: 2.0L 4-cyl. Turbo (212 hp) • 3.8L V6 (290 hp) • 3.8L V6 (306 hp) • 4.6L V8 (375 hp); Transmissions: 6-speed man. • 5-speed manumatic • 6-speed manumatic

DIMENSIONS/CAPACITY (SEDAN)
Passengers: 2/3; Wheelbase: 115.6 in.; H: 58.3/L: 195.6/W: 73.4 in.; Headroom: N/A; Legroom: N/A; Cargo volume: 15.9 cu. ft.; Fuel tank: 65L–73L/regular/premium; Tow limit: 5,000 lb.; Load capacity; N/A; Turning circle: 36 ft.; Weight: 3,748 lb.

shocks; adaptive cruise control; an electronic parking brake with automatic vehicle hold; and touch-screen navigation that's optional on the 3.8L and standard on the base 4.6L. A slight restyling and an 8-speed automatic transmission are planned for the 2011 model year.

OVERVIEW: Hyundai's largest luxury car targets BMW and Mercedes-Benz big spenders with its own luxury rear-drive. Genesis sedans are equipped with a 290 hp 3.8L V6 or a 375 hp 4.6L V8. A new base model with a 3.3L V6 may join the sedan lineup in late 2009. All sedan engines are hooked to a 6-speed automatic transmission that has a manual shiftgate.

The smaller 2010 Genesis Coupe was launched a year after the sedan and targets the Chevrolet Camaro and Ford Mustang. It features two performance-focused engines: a 212 hp 2.0L turbocharged 4-cylinder and a range-topping, all-aluminum 306 hp 3.8L V6. The base 2.0L coupe has a starting price of just $24,495, or only 10 percent more than what the same version costs in the States. If you want more power, the 3.8L V6 will cost you $32,995. In the States, the difference is only a few thousand dollars instead of $8,500. The basic version comes standard with a 6-speed manual; shoppers looking for a 5-speed Shiftronic automatic with manual mode will pay a few thousand dollars more. The R-Spec is aimed at the high-performance crowd ("tuners") who mix and match aftermarket improvements to enhance the Genesis' style and performance. It costs less than the 2.0T Track model and comes with all the same features as the Track, except for leather seats, xenon lights, and navigation assistance. The V6 model comes standard with a leather interior.

These luxury cars are loaded with high-tech safety gear that includes ABS, traction control, an anti-skid system, side curtain airbags, front side airbags, and rear side airbags. There's also a heated and cooled driver's seat, wireless cell phone link, a navigation system with hard drive for storing digital music files, a rear-view camera, and front- and rear-obstacle detection. A knob in the centre console governs audio, navigation, and other functions.

COST ANALYSIS: The rear-drive 2010 Genesis sedan is no bargain as it goes through its second year on the market. Granted, it may have much-needed suspension improvements, but the car is still a risky, unproven investment. **Best alternatives:** *Sedan:* The BMW 3 Series, Cadillac CTS, Chrysler 300C, Ford Taurus, Lincoln MKS, Mercedes-Benz E-Class, Pontiac G8 (recently departed), and Toyota Avalon. *Coupe:* The Chevrolet Camaro, Ford Mustang, and—for sheer sportster thrills without the bills—Mazda MX-5. **Options:** Stay away from the overly complicated navigation system. **Rebates:** Look for $3,000–$5,000 rebates, deep discounting, and sweet financing deals when the competition heats up in 2010 as the lacklustre Genesis models "rust in peace" on dealers' lots. **Depreciation:** Already much faster than average for an Asian luxury car. For example, a 2009 base Genesis sedan that originally sold for $37,995 is now—just a year later—worth $26,000–$28,000; a Toyota Avalon equivalent is worth about $5,000 more. **Insurance cost:** Higher than average. **Parts supply/cost:** Parts are likely to be expensive and in short supply until independent suppliers start stocking them. **Annual maintenance cost:** Should be average. **Warranty:** Bumper-to-bumper 5 years/100,000 km; rust perforation 5 years/unlimited km. **Supplementary warranty:** Not needed. **City/highway fuel economy:** *3.8L (290 hp):* 11.4/7.2 L/100 km. *4.6L:* 12.6/8.1 L/100 km.

OWNER-REPORTED PROBLEMS: Some lower control-arm and bushing failures, and a jarring oscillation or road wander when passing over small bumps or driving over a wavy roadway.

TUCSON

RATING: Recommended. **Strong points:** Reasonably priced and well equipped; V6 engine provides smooth, sustained acceleration; sure-footed (thanks to the standard stability control) and smooth-riding; roomy and easily accessed cabin; and above-average reliability. NHTSA gave it a five-star crashworthiness rating for front- and side-impact occupant protection and a four-star rating for rollover protection. IIHS rated side-impact protection as "Acceptable," and head restraints were designated "Good." **Weak points:** The 4-cylinder engine struggles with a full load, and the expected fuel economy doesn't materialize. Vehicle isn't as agile as others in its class. **New for 2010:** The redesigned 2010 Tucson crossover will be unveiled at the Los Angeles Auto Show this December. It is reported that it will be larger and powered only by a stronger 4-cylinder engine. A hybrid 2011 model will arrive at the end of 2010.

KEY FACTS (2009)

PRICES: $21,195–$30,995 **FREIGHT:** $1,610 **ORIGIN:** South Korea **SALES:** Down 35%

POWERTRAIN (FRONT-DRIVE/AWD)

Engines: 2.0L 4-cyl. (140 hp) • 2.7L V6. (173 hp); Transmissions: 5-speed man. • 4-speed manumatic

DIMENSIONS/CAPACITY

Passengers: 2/3; Wheelbase: 103.5 in.; H: 68.1/L: 170.3/W: 70.7 in.; Headroom F/R: 5.0/4.0 in.; Legroom F/R: 41/29 in.; Cargo volume: 65.5 cu. ft.; Fuel tank: 58L/regular; Tow limit: 1,000 lb.; Load capacity: 860 lb.; Turning circle: 35.4 ft.; Ground clearance: 7.0 in.; Weight: 3,240 lb.

OVERVIEW: The Tucson is Hyundai's compact crossover that was first introduced for the 2005 model year. It is smaller than the Santa Fe and built on the same Elantra-based platform as the Kia Sportage. The standard powerplant in all Tucsons is a 2.0L DOHC 4-cylinder engine. Through the 2009 model year, the Tucson has been offered with an optional 2.7L V6, pushing horsepower up to 173 at 6000 rpm. With the GLS, owners can choose between a 5-speed manual transmission and a 4-speed Shiftronic automatic. The optional all-wheel-drive system can send 99 percent of the power to the front wheels, or split the traction between the front and rear wheels.

COST ANALYSIS: Buy a 2009 to have the option of getting the better-performing V6. **Best alternatives:** The Honda CR-V, Kia Sorento, and Toyota RAV4. **Options:** Choose the V6 engine for better performance and handling; you will lose only a bit of fuel economy. If you get the 4-banger, keep in mind that good fuel economy means putting up with a bit more engine noise and slow merging with fast-moving traffic. **Rebates:** Expect $2,000 discounts, zero percent financing, and attractive leasing deals on all models. **Depreciation:** Average. **Insurance cost:** Average. **Parts supply/cost:** Easy to find, and relatively inexpensive. **Annual maintenance cost:** Less than average. **Warranty:** Bumper-to-bumper 5 years/100,000 km; rust perforation 5 years/unlimited km. **Supplementary warranty:** Not needed. **City/highway fuel economy:** *Manual:* 10.5/7.6 L/100 km. *Manumatic:* 10.2/8.0 L/100 km. *2.7L:* 11.3/8.4 L/100 km. *AWD:* 11.6/8.8 L/100 km.

OWNER-REPORTED PROBLEMS: Firewall insulation caught fire; rear of the vehicle slides as if it were on ice; rear-tire lock-up; excessive vibrations at 100 km/h; windshield wipers malfunction; and windshield wiper fluid leaks out of the filler neck.

best buy

SANTA FE ★★★★★

RATING: Recommended. This SUV does almost everything right. **Strong points:** Acceptable acceleration with the base 2.7L V6, but the 3.3L gives you more power without much fuel wasted. Smooth-shifting automatic transmission; good steering response; fairly agile; comfortable, controlled ride; standard stability/traction control and full-body side curtain airbags; lots of interior room; and much-improved quality control. A spacious interior allows for an optional pair of flat-folding third-row seats. Owner complaints are rare. NHTSA and IIHS gave the Santa Fe their top ratings for offset and front- and side-impact protection. Rollover resistance got four stars, and head-restraint effectiveness was rated "Good." **Weak points:** Needs more zip, a better ride, and handling balance; fuel economy is disappointing; tall drivers may need more headroom. **New for 2010:** Carried over unchanged. The 2011 models will be redesigned, and a 4-cylinder engine and 6-speed automatic transmission will be added. They may also carry turbodiesel engines.

KEY FACTS

PRICES: $21,995–$31,495 **FREIGHT:** $1,610 **ORIGIN:** Alabama **SALES:** Down 10%

POWERTRAIN (FRONT-DRIVE/AWD)
Engines: 2.7L V6 (185 hp) • 3.3L V6 (242 hp); Transmissions: 5-speed man. • 4-speed auto. • 5-speed manumatic

DIMENSIONS/CAPACITY
Passengers: 2/3/2; Wheelbase: 107 in.; H: 58/L: 189: 72 in.; Headroom F/R1/R2: 3.0/4.5/0.0 in.; Legroom F/R1/R2: 41/27.5/26 in.; Cargo volume: 37.5 cu. ft.; Fuel tank: 75L/regular; Tow limit: 3,500 lb.; Load capacity: 1,120 lb.; Turning circle: 39 ft.; Ground clearance: 7.0 in.; Weight: 3,253 lb.

OVERVIEW: Redesigned in 2007, the Santa Fe is a competitively priced family SUV that offers impressive room, good build quality, and many standard safety and performance features. This mid-size crossover comes with front-drive or with all-wheel drive that allows locking in a 50/50 front/rear power split.

COST ANALYSIS: Don't waste your money on a 2010. Instead, buy an almost identical, discounted 2009 for about $4,000 less. **Best alternatives:** Jeep Liberty (if Chrysler stays in business), Kia Sorento, Nissan Xterra, Saturn Outlook, and

Toyota RAV4 or Highlander. **Rebates:** Expect $3,000 rebates, zero percent financing, and cheap leases on all models. **Depreciation:** Average. **Insurance cost:** Average. **Parts supply/cost:** Easy to find, and relatively inexpensive. **Annual maintenance cost:** Average. **Warranty:** Bumper-to-bumper 5 years/100,000 km; rust perforation 5 years/unlimited km. **Supplementary warranty:** Not needed. **City/highway fuel economy:** Manual: 9.7/6.2 L/100 km. Automatic: 9.5/6.2 L/100 km. 3.3L: 10.8/6.9 L/100 km.

OWNER-REPORTED PROBLEMS: Sudden acceleration accompanied by loss of braking; passenger-side airbag is disabled when an average-sized passenger is seated; sudden brake failure, with pedal going to the floor; horn needs to be pounded in the right spot to activate; rear window exploded for no reason; excessive engine and steering vibration when underway; door lock failures; low-beam headlights don't give far enough illumination; steel belts may unravel on Bridgestone Dueler tires; and tire-pressure monitor system light comes on for no reason.

VERACRUZ ★★★★

RATING: Above Average. **Strong points:** The powerful V6 and 6-speed automatic transmission perform flawlessly to deliver smooth acceleration and a comfortable ride. NHTSA and IIHS gave the Veracruz their top ratings for offset and front- and side-impact protection. Rollover resistance got four stars, and head-restraint effectiveness was rated "Acceptable." Backed by a comprehensive base warranty. **Weak points:** Some suspension noise, and not as agile as some of its rivals. **New for 2010:** Carried over unchanged; the Veracruz is likely to be dropped after its 2010 model year.

KEY FACTS (2009)

PRICES: $36,995–$47,295 **FREIGHT:** $1,760 **ORIGIN:** South Korea **SALES:** Same as last year

POWERTRAIN (FRONT-DRIVE/AWD)

Engine: 3.8L V6 (260 hp); Transmission: 6-speed auto.

DIMENSIONS/CAPACITY

Passengers: 2/3/2; Wheelbase: 110.4 in.; H: 68.9/L: 190.6/W: 76.6 in.; Headroom F/R1/R2: 3.0/4.0/1.0 in.; Legroom F/R1/R2: 39/29.5/25.5 in.; Cargo volume: 41.5 cu. ft.; Fuel tank: 78L/regular; Tow limit: 3,500 lb.; Load capacity: 1,160 lb.; Turning circle: 36.7 ft.; Ground clearance: 8.1 in.; Weight: 3,253 lb.

OVERVIEW: The seven-passenger Veracruz uses a stretched Santa Fe platform and offers all of the safety, performance, and convenience features you'll find on SUVs that cost $10,000 more.

COST ANALYSIS: Buy a discounted 2009, inasmuch as the 2010s are practically identical. **Best alternatives:** Competes mostly with other higher-end mid-sized crossovers, like the Honda Pilot, Nissan Murano, and Lexus RX series. **Options:** Stay away from original-equipment Bridgestone or Dunlop tires; Michelins are much better performers and are more durable. **Rebates:** Expect $5,000 rebates, low-interest financing, and sweet leasing deals. **Depreciation:** Faster than average. A 2007 Limited that sold originally for $46,000 is now worth barely $26,000. **Insurance cost:** Above average. **Parts supply/cost:** Not easy to find; moderately expensive powertrain components. **Annual maintenance cost:**

Higher than average. **Warranty:** Bumper-to-bumper 5 years/100,000 km; rust perforation 5 years/unlimited km. **Supplementary warranty:** Not needed. **City/highway fuel economy:** 13.4/8.7 L/100 km.

OWNER-REPORTED PROBLEMS: Sudden, unintended acceleration while vehicle was in Reverse. Premature wearout of brake calipers, and out-of-round rotors:

> Hyundai has brake and rotor issues and won't do anything about it.... The vehicle off the lot had rotor problems. Had them shaved, then replaced and they were worn out within a year.... They can offer this 100,000 mile warranty [in the United States] because the consumer pays for brakes everytime they step foot in dealership.... If you search Internet you will find brake issue with all vehicles from Hyundai.... They will not do anything about this problem.... Cheap material on vehicle!

Opened rear hatch may suddenly fall down; sudden stalling and no-starts likely caused by a poor-quality fuel pump; high- and low-beam headlights can't be adjusted separately, causing the high beams to shoot up way too high, and low beams are too low; and the key fob opens the rear liftgate when the Open Door key is punched.

Infiniti

Unlike Toyota's Lexus division, which started out with softly sprung vehicles akin to your dad's fully loaded Oldsmobile, Nissan's number one alter ego has historically stressed performance over comfort and opulence, and it has offered buyers lots of high-performance features at what were initially very reasonable prices. But the company got greedy during the mid '90s. Its Infiniti lineup became more mainstream and lost its price and performance edge, particularly after the company stripped out or downgraded the Q45's features, resurrected its embarrassingly incompetent G20, and dropped the J30 and J30t.

But Infiniti is fighting to get that performance edge back. There are now greater differences between Nissan and Infiniti vehicles, even though most models share the same platform. Infinitis usually add more-powerful engines, more gears, steering and suspensions tweaked for sportier driving, and more-luxurious interior appointments. These improvements have produced a new roster of sporty luxury vehicles: the Infiniti G, EX, FX, M, and QX.

A stylish convertible has been added to the G37 lineup.

Like Lexus and BMW models, all Infinitis come fully equipped and offer owners the prestige of driving a reliable and nicely styled luxury car with lots of standard performance and safety features. Nevertheless, the company has a ways to go. After two decades of challenging BMW, Infiniti still sells annually barely half the 17,000 cars sold by BMW (most of which are the 3 Series, with more choice of models and engines).

Although Infinitis are sold and serviced by a small dealer network across Canada, this limited support base doesn't compromise either the availability or quality of servicing, since any Nissan dealer can carry out most non-warranty maintenance work. Furthermore, these cars are generally quite dependable, so there is less need for service. The only drawback is that powertrain and body parts may be in short supply. Incidentally, do-it-yourselfers will benefit from accessing technical service bulletins and owner's manuals at Infiniti's website (*www.infiniti-techinfo.com*). This costs $19.99 (U.S.) a day for a single-day access. Your subscription also allows you access to info on all of Nissan's models (insert "nissan" wherever you see "infiniti" in the URL).

G37

RATING: Above Average. The G37 coupe and sedan are basically the 2008 G35, but with a larger engine and additional performance and convenience features. **Strong points:** A powerful, smooth, and responsive powertrain; predictable handling; and a firm but comfortable, ride. The car is fairly agile, quiet, and comfortable. The convertible has five horses less than the coupe (325 hp) but lots more than you'll find with the equivalent BMW or Mercedes. Crashworthiness is impressive: NHTSA gives the G37 a five-star ranking for frontal, side, and rollover occupant protection, and IIHS gives it a "Good" rating for frontal offset and side crashworthiness. **Weak points:** Like the EX, the G series comes with a small rear seat and cargo area; towing is not advised; and IIHS rated head-restraint effectiveness as "Marginal." The convertible model has even less room and has yet to be crash tested. **New for 2010:** Sedan gets interior refinements and a slightly restyled front end; new G37x colours, navigation system, and option packages; and a convertible joins the lineup.

KEY FACTS

PRICES: *Sedan:* $37,090, *Coupe:* $45,200, *Sport:* $47,700 **FREIGHT:** $1,825 **ORIGIN:** Japan **SALES:** Down 34%
POWERTRAIN (REAR-DRIVE/AWD)
Engine: 3.7L V6 (330 hp); Transmissions: 6-speed man. • 7-speed auto.
DIMENSIONS/CAPACITY
Passengers: 2/3; Wheelbase: 112.2 in.; H: 54.7–55.3/L: 183.1/W: 71.8 in.; Headroom F/R: 2.5/1.5 in.; Legroom F/R: 41/27.5 in.; Cargo volume: N/A; Fuel tank: 76L/premium; Tow limit: N/A; Load capacity: 900 lb.; Turning circle: 38 ft.; Ground clearance: 4.5 in.; Weight: 3,642–3,847 lb.

OVERVIEW: The G37 is a premium midsize car with SUV pretensions. It is sold as a two-door coupe or 4-door sedan, along with a two-door convertible with a power-retractable hardtop. The G37 targets shoppers who normally buy the Acura RDX or the BMW X3. Not for off-road, but definitely a comfortable, well-equipped, and versatile vehicle for most driving needs. It is priced in the same range as the Infiniti G series and is essentially a G35 wagon. The just-launched convertible model will sell for about $57,400, or about $12,000 more than the G37 Coupe but right within striking range of BMW's 328i/335i Cabriolet ($48,900/$55,600) and the new 2010 Lexus IS 250 or IS 350 C convertibles ($52,100/$60,400). The Mercedes-Benz CLK350 AMG Edition Cabriolet ($78,400) has priced itself out of that market.

COST ANALYSIS: Get the 2009 G37 because it's practically identical to the costlier 2010 version. **Best alternatives:** The Infiniti EX35 and the BMW 3 Series. **Options:** The limited-slip differential in the Sport Package. **Rebates:** $4,500+ discounts, low-cost financing, and attractive leases; discounts will be sweetened in early 2010. **Depreciation:** Average. **Insurance cost:** Higher than average. **Parts supply/cost:** Expensive parts that can be easily found in the Maxima parts bin. **Annual maintenance cost:** Lower than average. **Warranty:** Bumper-to-bumper 4 years/100,000 km; powertrain 6 years/110,000 km; rust perforation 7 years/unlimited km. **Supplementary warranty:** Not needed. **City/highway fuel economy:** 11.7/7.6 L/100 km. *Sport:* 12.2/7.8 L/100 km.

OWNER-REPORTED PROBLEMS: Engine surges when braking (confirmed by TSB #ITB07-048); engine tapping, clicking sound at start-up requires the use of a costlier "factory" oil; the anti-traction feature activated on its own and caused the wheels to lock on a rainy day; defective Bridgestone Pole Position tires; Tire Pressure light did not come on when tire went flat; premature brake replacement; the area between the gas pedal and centre console get quite hot; audio system malfunctions; and poor fit and finish.

EX35 ★★★★

RATING: Above Average. The EX and G series are entry-level Infinitis with the most to offer from a price and quality perspective—as long as you have short legs, or never ride in the rear seat. **Strong points:** Drives like a car with power to spare, and the smooth, responsive automatic/manual transmission works flawlessly with the well-calibrated V6; overall the car is much more agile, quiet, and comfortable than the G series. A classy, though small, interior. NHTSA gives the EX35 a five-star ranking for side-impact occupant protection and four stars for frontal and rollover safety. IIHS gives it an all-around "Good" rating. **Weak points:** Not as sporty as Infiniti's sport sedans, or some of BMW's crossovers; really a four-seater; limited cargo space; back seat occupants must keep a knee-to-chin posture when the front seats are pushed all the way back; taller drivers will want more headroom (especially with the sunroof-equipped Journey model); right-rear visibility is compromised by right-rear head restraint and side pillar; no towing; and fuel economy is unimpressive. **New for 2010:** Infiniti promises more legroom (the 2009 Acura RDX has 22.9 cm (9 in.) more rear legroom, and Lincoln's MKX has 25.4 (10 in.) more).

OVERVIEW: Offering the room of a small station wagon, the EX35 is a small, upscale SUV wannabe that targets shoppers who would normally buy the Acura RDX or

KEY FACTS

PRICES: $40,900 **FREIGHT:** $1,825
ORIGIN: Japan **SALES:** Down 40%
POWERTRAIN (AWD)
Engine: 3.5L V6 (297 hp); Transmission: 5-speed manumatic
DIMENSIONS/CAPACITY
Passengers: 2/3; Wheelbase: 110.2 in.; H: 62.6/L: 182.3/W: 71 in.; Headroom F/R: 3.0/3.0 in.; Legroom F/R: 42/26 in.; Cargo volume: 18.6 cu. ft.; Fuel tank: 76L/premium; Tow limit: N/A; Load capacity: 860 lb.; Turning circle: 39 ft.; Ground clearance: 5.5 in.; Weight: 3,915 lb.

the BMW X3. Smaller than the Infiniti FX, it is priced in the same range as the Infiniti G series and is essentially a G35 wagon. Not for off-road, but definitely a comfortable, well-equipped, and versatile vehicle for most driving needs.

COST ANALYSIS: Sales are 50 percent less than what the Infiniti suits predicted, so discounts are easy to get. Don't buy the 2010, unless Infiniti delivers on its promise to add more rear legroom. **Best alternatives:** Acura RDX, BMW 3 Series or X3, Cadillac SRX, and Lincoln MKX. **Options:** The Navigation Package is overpriced and mostly fluff. **Rebates:** $4,000+ discounts, low-cost financing, and cheaper leases; discounts will become even more generous in early 2010 as the temperature drops and the competition heats up. **Depreciation:** Average. **Insurance cost:** Higher than average. **Parts supply/cost:** Expensive parts that can be easily found in the Maxima parts bin. **Annual maintenance cost:** Lower than average. **Warranty:** Bumper-to-bumper 4 years/100,000 km; powertrain 6 years/110,000 km; rust perforation 7 years/unlimited km. **Supplementary warranty:** Not needed. **City/highway fuel economy:** 12.9/8.5 L/100 km.

OWNER-REPORTED PROBLEMS: There have been fewer problems reported with this model than for any of the other vehicles in the Infiniti lineup. The one continuing beef owners have is the poor-quality body hardware. For example, the hitch will break if you tow anything at all. Says one owner:

> It will probably do damage even if you only use it for a bike rack. It is a very nicely built part which fits exactly as advertised, however, it mounts to the bumper supports which are made of a very flimsy sheet metal. As a result, continued up and down motion such as a bouncy bike rack or the routine undulations of a trailer captured by the ball mount will fatigue and break the metal that holds the bumper mounting supports to the car.

FX37, FX50

RATING: Above Average. **Strong points:** Both engines have power to spare, delivered by a smooth and quiet drivetrain. Handling is precise and secure. Decent towing capacity and torque. NHTSA gives the vehicles five stars for frontal collision crashworthiness and three stars for rollover protection. **Weak points:** A tight cabin; limited rear visibility; and some reliability concerns. **New for 2010:** Nothing important.

OVERVIEW: These are well-appointed, agile luxury crossover SUVs that drive and ride like sports sedans. The primary difference between the two vehicles is their engines, plus a few additional features.

COST ANALYSIS: It will be hard to haggle, due to the popularity of the FX series. **Best alternatives:** BMW X6 xDrive. **Options:** Nothing is needed. **Rebates:** Look for discounts of about 10 percent as well as some very attractive leasing deals in the first quarter of 2010. **Depreciation:** Average. **Insurance cost:** Higher than average. **Parts supply/cost:** Expensive powertrain and body parts that aren't easily available. **Annual maintenance cost:** Higher than average. **Warranty:** Bumper-to-bumper 4 years/100,000 km; powertrain 6 years/110,000 km; rust perforation 7 years/unlimited km. **Supplementary warranty:** Not needed. **City/highway fuel economy:** *FX35:* 13.3/9.3 L/100 km. *FX50:* 14.6/10.1 L/100 km.

KEY FACTS

PRICES: *FX37* $51,800, *FX50:* $59,900 **FREIGHT:** $1,825 **ORIGIN:** Japan **SALES:** Down 10%

POWERTRAIN (REAR-DRIVE/AWD)
Engine: 3.5L V6 (303 hp) 5.0L V8 (390 hp); Transmission: 7-speed auto.

DIMENSIONS/CAPACITY
Passengers: 2/3/; Wheelbase: 113.6 in.; H: 66.1/L: 191.3/W: 75.9 in.; Headroom F/R: N/A; Legroom F/R: N/A; Cargo volume: 62 cu. ft.; Fuel tank: 90L/premium; Tow limit: 3,500 lb.; Load capacity: N/A; Turning circle: 36.7 ft.; Ground clearance: 7.4 in.; Weight: 4,299 lb., 4,575 lb.

OWNER-REPORTED PROBLEMS: The only two problem areas are the early replacement of brake calipers and rotors, and sound system malfunctions. Surprisingly, body hardware and fit and finish get top marks, unlike with the top-of-the-line QX56.

M35, M45 ★★★★

RATING: Above Average. These vehicles are the high-performance successors to the discontinued Q45. The major difference between the M35 and M45 is engine size, plus additional performance and convenience gadgets. **Strong points:** Well appointed; superior acceleration and handling; easy entry and exit; head restraints lower into the seatback; and low depreciation. **Weak points:** Some road noise, and the vehicles require premium fuel while delivering disappointing fuel economy. **New for 2010:** They return relatively unchanged.

OVERVIEW: The M35 and M45 are rear-drive/AWD luxury sedans that ride on a four-wheel independent suspension and carry a 303 hp V6 or a 325 hp V8. The M cars share the QX's drivetrain but are set on a shorter wheelbase. Because of their lighter curb weight and their potent engines, these cars can do 0–100 km/h in less than six seconds. Forget about fuel economy, though.

KEY FACTS

PRICES: *M35:* $54,900–$55,200, *M45:* $68,950 **FREIGHT:** $1,850 **ORIGIN:** Japan **SALES:** N/A

POWERTRAIN (REAR-DRIVE/AWD)
Engines: 3.5L V6 (303 hp) • 4.5L V8 (325 hp); Transmissions: 7-speed auto. • 5-speed auto.

DIMENSIONS/CAPACITY
Passengers: 2/3; Wheelbase: 114.2 in.; H: 60/L: 194.1/W: 71.6 in.; Headroom F/R: 4.0/3.0 in.; Legroom F/R: 41/30 in.; Cargo volume: 14.9 cu. ft.; Fuel tank: 90L/premium; Tow limit: N/A; Load capacity: 860 lb.; Turning circle: 36.7 ft.; Weight: 3,889 lb., 4,012 lb.

COST ANALYSIS: The M35 is Infinti's entry-level M model ($54,900), while the M45 piles on the safety, performance, and convenience options to give shoppers more high-performance thrills and luxury for about $14,000 more. It comes packed with all the techno-goodies car companies stuff into their vehicles to impress shoppers who have more money than good sense. Get the cheaper, practically identical, 2009 version. **Best alternatives:** Other cars you may wish to consider are the Acura RL V6, Audi A6, Cadillac DTS, and BMW 5 Series. **Options:** The limited-slip differential in the Sport Package. **Rebates:** $4,500+ discounts, low-cost financing, and attractive leases; discounts will be sweetened in early 2010. **Depreciation:** Average. **Insurance cost:** Higher than average. **Parts supply/cost:** Expensive parts that can be easily found in the Maxima parts bin. **Annual maintenance cost:** Lower than average. **Warranty:** Bumper-to-bumper 4 years/100,000 km; powertrain 6 years/110,000 km; rust perforation 7 years/unlimited km. **Supplementary warranty:** Not needed. **City/highway fuel economy:** *M35 rear-drive:* 12.6/8.1 L/100 km. *M35 AWD:* 13.3/9.1 L/100 km. *M45 rear-drive:* 13.5/9.4 L/100 km. *M45 AWD:* 15.5/10.2 L/100 km.

OWNER-REPORTED PROBLEMS: *M35:* Since the 2007 model year, owners say there is a "rocks rattling in a can" sound coming from underneath the car. Other concerns: Steering pulls hard to one side and wanders (tramlining) at all speeds, making the vehicle almost impossible to control (some relief is gained by replacing the Goodyear Eagle RS-A tires with Michelin Primacy MXV4 tires or by changing the steering rack); and a variety of sound system malfunctions.

QX56 ★★★

KEY FACTS

PRICES: $71,900 **FREIGHT:** $1,825
ORIGIN: Japan **SALES:** Down 47%
POWERTRAIN (AWD)
Engine: 5.6L V8 (320 hp); Transmission: 5-speed auto.
DIMENSIONS/CAPACITY
Passengers: 2/3/3; Wheelbase: 123.2 in.; H: 62.6/L: 206.9/W: 67.5 in.; Headroom F/R: N/A; Legroom F/R: N/A; Cargo volume: 97.1 cu. ft.; Fuel tank: 105L/premium; Tow limit: 8,900 lb.; Load capacity: N/A; Turning circle: 40.8 ft.; Ground clearance: 8.3 in.; Weight: 5,913 lb.

RATING: Average. The QX is merely a gussied-up Nissan Armada with a plusher interior and a standard navigation system—all for a $19,000 premium. (No kidding!) **Strong points:** V8 power makes the QX a "go anywhere, do anything" vehicle with a smooth-shifting automatic transmission and lots of towing capacity and torque; plenty of interior room; and predictable, responsive handling, thanks to the independent rear suspension. NHTSA gives the QX56 a five-star ranking for front-impact occupant protection and three stars for rollover safety. **Weak points:** Way overpriced; fuel economy is nonexistent; a stiff, jarring ride accompanied by lots of engine noise; and an unusually small third-row seat. Reliability has been worse than average. **New for 2010:** Nothing important.

OVERVIEW: This is Infiniti's SUV luxury flagship that is loaded with every conceivable safety, performance, and convenience feature one could ever imagine. Yet, someone forgot to design a decent-sized third-row rear seat that's large enough for most people. Nevertheless, the QX56 has been on the market in Canada since 2004, and it has a loyal following, judging by its increased sales in a dismal economy.

COST ANALYSIS: It will be hard to haggle, due to the popularity of the QX series. **Best alternatives:** An almost identical Nissan Armada will save you almost 20 grand. **Options:** Nothing is needed. **Rebates:** Look for discounts of about 10 percent as well as some very attractive leasing deals in the first quarter of 2010. **Depreciation:** Average. **Insurance cost:** Higher than average. **Parts supply/cost:** Expensive parts that aren't easily found with independent suppliers. **Annual maintenance cost:** Higher than average. **Warranty:** Bumper-to-bumper 4 years/100,000 km; powertrain 6 years/110,000 km; rust perforation 7 years/unlimited km. **Supplementary warranty:** Not needed. **City/highway fuel economy:** 18.2/11.8 L/100 km.

OWNER-REPORTED PROBLEMS: Body hardware and fit and finish deficiencies; frequent brake repairs; excessive steering shake and shimmy when passing over small bumps in the road; power accessories that malfunction; and a failure-prone sound system.

Kia

Functionality, Fuel Economy, and Fresh Styling

While Kia-owner Hyundai goes upscale with high-tech and good fuel economy offerings, Kia is putting its money into an expanded lineup of fuel-efficient vehicles that carry more standard features and are freshly styled. Positive reports from buyers of Kia's recently redesigned cars, minivans, and SUVs have led industry analysts to conclude that Hyundai's product improvement efforts are paying off with some Kia models; principally, the Optima, Rondo, and Sportage. On the other hand, models like the Sedona, Sorento, and Spectra continue to anchor the quality ratings.

Sins of the Past

Kia has long suffered from a reputation for making primitive, low-quality vehicles that are risky buys. However, over the past few years, Kia has posted impressive sales gains, thanks to low prices, a comprehensive base warranty, and better-made vehicles.

Kia still needs to offer better-quality vehicles, and it also must work to improve engine and suspension performance. Kia's quality control, particularly when it comes to automatic transmissions and electronic sensors (also Hyundai and Daewoo bugaboos), has been abysmal. Before, the company simply offered a longer base warranty as a substitute for quality components (much like Chrysler), and routinely paid warranty claims instead of improving the product. But Kia says that is no longer the case. I don't believe it—at least not for the vehicles mentioned above.

For 2010, Hyundai will continue to strengthen both automakers' dealer network by improving quality and service while it trolls for first-class dealers in prime locations who got dumped during Chrysler's and GM's Chapter 11 bankruptcies. On the manufacturing side, Kia will share more platforms and key components with Hyundai in order to put out cheap and fuel-efficient small cars. Some of those new small cars will be the Soul, a youth-oriented, boxy five-door hatchback, and the Forte sedan and Forte Koupe replacements for the Spectra. Compared with the Spectra, these econocars will sit on a new platform, have more horsepower, give better fuel economy, and offer more standard features, like ABS, electronic stability control, and Bluetooth wireless capability.

RIO, RIO5

RATING: Average. The Rio sedan and Rio5 hatchback combine good fuel economy and interior room with useful standard features. **Strong points:** The 1.6L engine is usually adequate for most chores, and handling is acceptable, with plenty of steering feedback and good brakes; the ride is also comfortable, though sometimes busy; and passenger and cargo room are better than average. NHTSA gave the Rio four stars for frontal, side, and rollover crash protection. IIHS rates the Rio's frontal offset protection as "Acceptable." **Weak points:** Slow acceleration with the automatic transmission; insufficient highway passing power; excessive engine noise at higher speeds; harsh ride when passing over small bumps; trunk lid hinges intrude into the trunk area; actual fuel consumption is much higher than what is promised; poor rear-corner visibility with the Rio5; and below-average IIHS crashworthiness scores for side collisions and head-restraint effectiveness. **New for 2010:** Carried over relatively unchanged, except for a revised interior. The car will likely be dropped next year.

KEY FACTS

PRICES: $15,695–$20,995 **FREIGHT:** $1,650 **ORIGIN:** South Korea **SALES:** Down 45%

POWERTRAIN (FRONT-DRIVE)

Engine: 1.6L 4-cyl. (110 hp); Transmissions: 5-speed man. • 4-speed auto.

DIMENSIONS/CAPACITY

Passengers: 2/3; Wheelbase: 98.4 in.; H: 57.9/L: 166.9/W: 66.7 in.; Headroom F/R: 4.5/2.0 in.; Legroom F/R: 40/25 in.; Cargo volume: *Rio:* 11.9 cu. ft., *Rio5:* 15.8 cu. ft.; Fuel tank: 45L/regular; Tow limit: N/A; Load capacity: 850 lb.; Turning circle: 33.1 ft.; Weight: 2,312 lb.

OVERVIEW: The base Rio sedan won't spoil you. It comes with only a manual transmission, wind-up windows, and manual door locks. On the other hand, safety features that are extra-cost items on more-expensive cars—like front seat belt pretensioners, disc brakes on all four wheels, and six airbags (dual frontal, front-seat side-impact, and full-coverage side curtain)—are standard features.

COST ANALYSIS: The discounted 2009s are cheaper buys than the almost identical 2010 version. **Best alternatives:** The Honda Fit, Kia Soul (but wait a year), Hyundai Accent, Nissan Versa, and Toyota Yaris are more-refined small cars that offer better performance while also conserving fuel. **Options:** Nothing important. **Rebates:** Look for $1,500 rebates or discounts and low financing rates in early 2010. **Depreciation:** Slower than average. **Insurance cost:** Average. **Parts supply/cost:** Average costs; parts aren't hard to find. **Annual maintenance cost:** Less than average. **Warranty:** Bumper-to-bumper 5 years/100,000 km; powertrain 5 years/100,000 km; rust perforation 5 years/unlimited km. **Supplementary warranty:** A wise buy, considering Kia's previous powertrain troubles. **City/highway fuel economy:** *Manual:* 7.3/5.9 L/100 km. *Automatic:* 7.7/5.6 L/100 km.

OWNER-REPORTED PROBLEMS: Sharing the Accent platform and using more Hyundai components has undoubtedly improved Kia's quality, judging by J.D. Power survey results and the lower number of owner complaints. Nevertheless, owners have reported the following problems: automatic transmission malfunctions; poor fit and finish; premature brake repairs; electrical shorts; airbags failed to deploy in a frontal collision; passenger-side airbag was disabled, even though an average-sized occupant was seated; sudden acceleration in Reverse, with loss of brakes; brakes locked up when applied; and the rear window shattered when the driver's door was closed.

SOUL ★

RATING: Not Recommended during its first year on the market, particularly in view of Kia's high number of factory powertrain glitches in first-year cars. **Strong points:** Inexpensive and well equipped with safety devices like ABS, stability control, six airbags, and active head restraints—features that are rare on entry-level small cars. User-friendly controls; plenty of interior room; comfortable seats; a competent engine (the 2.0L is a better choice for reserve power); a compliant suspension, without undue body roll or front-end plow; fairly agile when cornering, with good steering feedback; a smoothly shifting transmission; and fewer rattles and body glitches than normally seen on Kias. NHTSA gives the Soul five stars for frontal and side occupant crash protection. Rollover protection was given four stars. **Weak points:** Base engine could use more grunt at low engine rpm; automatic transmission needs a Fifth gear; limited cargo room when compared to its rivals; some wind and road noise; a busy highway

KEY FACTS

PRICES: $15,495–$20,995 **FREIGHT:** $1,650 **ORIGIN:** South Korea **SALES:** N/A

POWERTRAIN (FRONT-DRIVE)

Engines: 1.6L 4-cyl. (122 hp) • 2.0L 4-cyl. (142 hp); Transmissions: 5-speed man. • 4-speed auto.

DIMENSIONS/CAPACITY

Passengers: 2/3; Wheelbase: 100.4 in.; H: 63.4/L: 161.6/W: 70.3 in.; Headroom F/R: N/A; Legroom F/R: N/A; Cargo volume: 19.3 cu. ft.; Fuel tank: 48L/regular; Tow limit: N/A; Load capacity: N/A; Turning circle: 34.4 ft.; Weight: 2,560 lb.

ride; fuel economy is seriously overstated; and the car has not yet been crash tested. **New for 2010:** Everything.

OVERVIEW: This little four-door hatchback/wagon combines safety with performance, while keeping your fuel bills low. The best combination is the 2.0L engine hooked to a 5-speed manual transmission. If you get the 4-speed automatic shifter, understand that the engine will seem sluggish without a Fifth gear. Invest in the ABS and stability control by moving upscale to the Soul 2u. Forget the space-robbing sunroof. Confirming this to be a car aimed at the younger Scion and Cube crowd, check out the USB/iPod inputs; they allow you to carry your music on a "stick."

COST ANALYSIS: Best Alternatives: Other contenders are the Honda Civic, Hyundai Elantra, Nissan Cube or Versa, Scion xB, and Toyota Yaris or Corolla. **City/highway fuel economy:** 8.5/6.6 L/100 km.

bad buy

FORTE, FORTE KOUP ★

RATING: Not Recommended during the Forte's first year on the market. Kia slew the poor-quality dragon; now, its newest compact sedan gets the engine and suspension refinements Kia's lineup lacked in the past. **Strong points:** Good acceleration; four-wheel disc brakes; exemplary fit and finish; nicely bolstered front seats; plenty of interior room up front, with comfortable seats; competent engines at high revs, with plenty of reserve power and a smoothly shifting automatic transmission; sure-footed and precise handling, and a comfortable ride; standard Bluetooth and steering wheel controls with voice activation; heated sideview windows; fewer rattles and body glitches; a large dealer network with both Kia and Hyundai providing servicing; and a comprehensive base warranty. **Weak points:** Steering wheel tilts but doesn't telescope (EX trim excepted); rear seating is cramped for three; long-term reliability is unproven; the vehicle has not yet been crash tested; and prices are likely to stay firm as higher fuel costs add to the overall popularity of these new econocars. **New for 2010:** Everything.

KEY FACTS

PRICES: $15,695–$20,995 **FREIGHT:** $1,650 **ORIGIN:** South Korea **SALES:** N/A

POWERTRAIN (FRONT-DRIVE)

Engines: 2.0L 4-cyl. (156 hp) • 2.4L 4-cyl. (173 hp) Transmissions: 5-speed man. • 6-speed man. • 4-speed auto. • 5-speed auto.

DIMENSIONS/CAPACITY

Passengers: 2/3; Wheelbase: 104.3 in.; H: 55.1/L: 176.4/W: 69.5 in.; Headroom F/R: N/A; Legroom F/R: N/A; Cargo volume: 12.6 cu. ft.; Fuel tank: 51.9L/regular; Tow limit: N/A; Load capacity: N/A; Turning circle: 33.8 ft.; Ground clearance: 5.5 in.; Weight: 2,701 lb.

OVERVIEW: This compact sedan and coupe have what it takes to satisfy the needs of the daily commuter as well as excite the most ardent high-performance fan. Two different 4-cylinder engines deliver more than enough power, without wasting fuel. In fact, the SX features an upgraded 2.4L inline 4-banger that delivers 173 hp—more than the most powerful versions of the Toyota Corolla, or even the Mazda3. Handling is a breeze, thanks to the Forte's front-drive unibody frame and four-wheel independent suspension, which provide a smooth and sporty ride, with a minimum of noise, vibration, and harshness.

COST ANALYSIS: **Best Alternatives:** The Ford Focus, Honda Civic, Hyundai Elantra, Mazda3, and Toyota Corolla **City/highway fuel economy:** *2.0L manual:* 8.3/5.8 L/100 km. *2.0L automatic:* 8.1/5.8 L/100 km. *2.4L manual*: 9.2/6.2 L/100 km. *2.4L automatic:* 9.0/6.3 L/100 km.

RONDO ★★★★

RATING: Above Average. **Strong points:** Competent engines; offers small-car dimensions with minivan utility; can carry seven passengers to the Mazda5's six; easy entry and exit; a comfortable and quiet ride; good fit and finish; and standard stability control and side curtain airbags. NHTSA gave the Rondo five stars for frontal and side crash protection. Rollover protection earned four stars. **Weak points:** Not as agile as its Mazda5 rival; and mediocre fuel economy with the V6. **New for 2010:** Nothing important; scheduled to be restyled in 2011.

KEY FACTS

PRICES: $19,995–$26,595 **FREIGHT:** $1,650 **ORIGIN:** South Korea **SALES:** Down 48%

POWERTRAIN (FRONT-DRIVE)

Engines: 2.4L 4-cyl. (175 hp) • 2.7L V6 (192 hp); Transmissions: 4-speed auto. • 5-speed auto.

DIMENSIONS/CAPACITY

Passengers: 2/3/2; Wheelbase: 106.3 in.; H: 65/L: 178.9/W: 71.7 in.; Headroom F/R1/R2: 6.0/5.0/0.0 in.; Legroom F/R1/R2: 40/28/23 in.; Cargo volume: 33 cu. ft.; Fuel tank: 60L/regular; Tow limit: 1,500; 2,000 lb.; Load capacity: 825 lb.; Turning circle: 39 ft.; Ground clearance: 6.1 in.; Weight: 3,333 lb.

OVERVIEW: Kia's Rondo is one of the best compact hatchbacks on the market; it's a pity that it's so often overlooked. Seating seven, it offers an impressive amount of room for its size, although third-row seating is for children only.

COST ANALYSIS: The Rondo and Mazda5 cost practically the same; however, Mazda dealers aren't quick to offer discounts, while Kia dealers try harder to close the deal. **Best alternative:** The Mazda5. **Options:** The V6 engine is essential if you intend to carry full loads. **Rebates:** Look for $3,000 rebates and low financing rates in early 2010. **Depreciation:** A bit faster than average. **Insurance cost:** Average. **Parts supply/cost:** Average. **Annual maintenance cost:** Average. **Warranty:** Bumper-to-bumper 5 years/100,000 km; powertrain 5 years/100,000 km; rust perforation 5 years/unlimited km. **Supplementary warranty:** A toss-up; extra powertrain coverage is all that is needed. **City/highway fuel economy:** *2.4L:* 10.6/7.5 L/100 km. *2.7L:* 11.5/7.7 L/100 km.

OWNER-REPORTED PROBLEMS: Owners complain mostly about climate control malfunctions and frequent brake component replacements (calipers and rotors); passenger Airbag warning light stays on for no reason; severe vibration and shaking when cruising at 90 km/h; low-beam headlights don't illuminate up to a safe distance forward; transmission stalling and grinding; fuel consumption is much higher than what's promised by Kia; and vibration and loud cabin roar if one of the windows is opened while the vehicle is underway.

MAGENTIS ★★★

RATING: Average. Consider buying a competitor with more refinement and a proven history for reliability and good quality control. **Strong points:** Nicely appointed; good overall visibility; plenty of front headroom; firm, supportive front bucket seats with plenty of fore and aft travel; better-than-average fuel economy with regular fuel; nice ride quality and handling; spacious trunk; four-star front and side crashworthiness rating, and five stars awarded for rollover resistance; and servicing can be carried out by both Hyundai and Kia dealers. A 5-year/100,000 km all-inclusive warranty. **Weak points:** An underpowered 4-cylinder engine; only average V6 performance; mediocre braking; average rear headroom; considerable body lean when turning; excessive wind and tire noise; trunk has a small opening; stability and traction control are optional on base models and standard only on the higher-end versions; and fit and finish isn't up to Honda's or Toyota's standards. **New for 2010:** Nothing major; Kia is coasting on last year's redesign.

KEY FACTS

PRICES: $21,995–$28,195 **FREIGHT:** $1,650 **ORIGIN:** South Korea **SALES:** N/A

POWERTRAIN (FRONT-DRIVE)
Engines: 2.4L 4-cyl. (175 hp) • 2.7L V6 (190 hp); Transmissions: 5-speed man. • 5-speed auto.

DIMENSIONS/CAPACITY
Passengers: 2/3; Wheelbase: 107 in.; H: 58.2/L: 188.9/W: 71 in.; Headroom F/R: N/A; Legroom F/R: 39.7/38 in.; Cargo volume: 14.8 cu. ft.; Fuel tank: 62L/regular; Tow limit: 2.4L: No towing, 2.7L: 1,000–2,000 lb.; Load capacity: N/A; Turning circle: 35.4 ft.; Weight: 3,157 lb.

OVERVIEW: Kia's mid-sized sedan is essentially a rebadged Hyundai Sonata, sold also as the Optima in the States. All models include front side airbags and side curtain airbags, seat belt pretensioners, ABS, four-wheel disc brakes, and anti-whiplash head restraints that have received IIHS's top safety rating.

COST ANALYSIS: Save money with a 2009. Since the 2010s are carryovers from last year, hold out for major discounting and generous rebates to cut the retail price by at least 15 percent. **Best alternatives:** Consider the Chevrolet Malibu, Honda Accord, Hyundai Elantra, and Toyota Camry. **Options:** Save your money. **Rebates:** Look for $2,500 rebates or discounts and low financing rates early in 2010. **Depreciation:** Slower than average. **Insurance cost:** Average. **Parts supply/cost:** Average. **Annual maintenance cost:** Average. **Warranty:** Bumper-to-bumper 5 years/100,000 km; powertrain 5 years/100,000 km; rust perforation 5 years/unlimited km. **Supplementary warranty:** A wise buy for the engine and transmission. **City/highway fuel economy:** *2.4L manual:* 9.4/6.2 L/100 km. *2.4L automatic:* 9.4/6.2 L/100 km. *2.7L:* 10.5/7.0 L/100 km.

OWNER-REPORTED PROBLEMS: Passenger-side airbag is disabled when passenger of any size is seated; seat belt harness's shoulder belts were nonfunctional in a collision; when downshifting, the engine surges at about 40 km/h; parked car will roll down an incline, despite being put in First gear; vehicle pulls to the right when underway; windows leak air; low-beam headlights don't illuminate far enough; and headlights dim when applying the brakes or when slowing down.

AMANTI ★★

RATING: Below Average. **Strong points:** The V6 is fairly powerful, and the car gives a comfortable ride. Good overall visibility; plenty of headroom and legroom; a spacious trunk; and servicing is available from both Hyundai and Kia dealers. Rollover protection for the 2006 model was given four stars by NHTSA, and IIHS rates frontal offset and side crash protection as "Good." **Weak points:** Ponderous handling, vague steering, and lots of body roll; fuel economy is nowhere near what Kia represents; below-average reliability; no frontal or side NHTSA crashworthiness tests have been performed; head-restraint protection is rated "Marginal" by IIHS; mediocre braking; and stability control is optional. **New for 2010:** Carried over relatively unchanged; a remake is scheduled for 2011.

KEY FACTS

PRICES: $29,995–$37,195 **FREIGHT:** $1,650 **ORIGIN:** South Korea **SALES:** Up 40%

POWERTRAIN (FRONT-DRIVE)

Engine: 3.8L V6 (264 hp); Transmission: 5-speed manumatic

DIMENSIONS/CAPACITY

Passengers: 2/3; Wheelbase: 110.2 in.; H: 58.5/L: 196.8/W: 72.8 in.; Headroom F/R: 3.0/4.0 in.; Legroom F/R: 41/28.5 in.; Cargo volume: 15.9 cu. ft.; Fuel tank: 70L/regular; Tow limit: 3,500 lb.; Load capacity: 860 lb.; Turning circle: 42 ft.; Ground clearance: 5.0 in.; Weight: 3,770 lb.

OVERVIEW: This large front-drive sedan stresses ride comfort over satisfactory handling. Its overall styling is reminiscent of the Mercedes-Benz E-Class.

COST ANALYSIS: There's no reason to buy a 2010, but if you do, cut the price by 15–20 percent. If buying a 2009, take an extra 10 percent off. **Best alternatives:** The Honda Accord, Hyundai Elantra, Nissan Maxima, and Toyota Camry or Avalon. **Options:** Save your money. **Rebates:** Look for $3,000 rebates or discounts and low financing rates early in 2010. **Depreciation:** Faster than average. **Insurance cost:** Higher than average. **Parts supply/cost:** Average. **Annual maintenance cost:** Average. **Warranty:** Bumper-to-bumper 5 years/100,000 km; powertrain 5 years/100,000 km; rust perforation 5 years/unlimited km. **Supplementary warranty:** A wise buy for the engine and transmission. **City/highway fuel economy:** 12.6/8.2 L/100 km.

OWNER-REPORTED PROBLEMS: Sudden acceleration when the brakes are applied:

> Since I can never know when it might happen, all driving of the car makes me very anxious—afraid it will happen, for example, when I approach a crosswalk full of children. I feel I have no choice but to get rid of the car. I will, of course, feel morally obligated to reveal the problem when I trade the car in and will thus no doubt take

a significant financial loss. This will be better than hurting someone either inside or outside of the car.

SEDONA ★

RATING: Not Recommended. In theory, this should be the minivan everyone should buy. But, sadly, a good idea has been hobbled by poor execution. The Sedona and Entourage are expected to meet similar fates due to slow sales: Hyundai's Entourage will be dropped by year's end, and the Sedona isn't expected to last beyond the 2011 model year. **Strong points:** An entry-level Sedona will cost about $6,000 less than the equivalent Honda or Toyota minivan. Sedona is well-appointed, and stability control is a standard feature. The engine supplies more than enough power in all gear ranges; the automatic transmission shifts smoothly and quietly; the ride is comfortable; and handling is very responsive. A low ground clearance adds to stability and helps passengers access the interior. Important interior features include a low step-in; a convenient "walk-through" space between front seats; second-row seats that flip and fold for access to the third row; a split rear bench that folds into the floor (a Honda idea); well laid-out, user-friendly instruments and controls; lots of storage areas; active head restraints; and side curtain airbags for head protection in all three rows. There's also good visibility, minimal engine and road noise, excellent crashworthiness scores, good braking, traction control and stability control, and a comprehensive base warranty. **Weak points:** Reliability, reliability, and reliability. Both the Sedona and Entourage are riddled with factory-related defects affecting primarily the powertrain, brakes, electronic system, suspension, and fit and finish. Fuel consumption is also much higher than what Kia and Transport Canada represents. **New for 2010:** Nothing significant. Both Sedona and Entourage are "dead vans, walking."

KEY FACTS

PRICES: $26,745–$38,895 **FREIGHT:** $1,650 **ORIGIN:** South Korea **SALES:** Up 28%

POWERTRAIN (FRONT-DRIVE)

Engine: 3.8L V6 (250 hp); Transmission: 5-speed auto.

DIMENSIONS/CAPACITY

Passengers: 2/2/3; Wheelbase: 119 in.; H: 69./L: 202/W: 78 in.; Headroom F/R1/R2: 5.0/2.0/3.0 in.; Legroom F/R1/R2: 40/31/28 in.; Cargo volume: 65 cu. ft.; Fuel tank: 80L/regular; Tow limit: 3,500 lb.; Load capacity: 1,155 lb.; Turning circle: 43 ft.; Ground clearance: 5.0 in.; Weight: 4,802 lb.

OVERVIEW: Sedona leapfrogged over most of the competition when it was restyled and reengineered a few years ago. The latest model refines those changes and offers buyers a minivan that's similar in size to the Honda Odyssey and Toyota Sienna; full of standard safety, performance, and convenience goodies; and backed by a comprehensive warranty.

COST ANALYSIS: Without a doubt, this is a cheaper minivan than the Japanese competition, but the money you save may be spent on expensive repairs later on. **Best alternatives:** Consider the Honda Odyssey, Mazda5, and Toyota Sienna. Chrysler's minivans are good second choices that will be cheaper and feature-loaded as well. Their only drawback will be the need for you to buy an extended warranty to protect yourself from tranny failures. **Options:** The $5,000 EX Luxury option is a waste of money on nonessentials. Stay away from the power-sliding doors. **Rebates:** Look for $3,500 rebates, low financing rates, and attractive leases. **Depreciation:** Faster than average. **Insurance cost:** Average. **Parts supply/cost:** Average costs, but availability has been spotty. **Annual maintenance cost:** Higher than average. **Warranty:** Bumper-to-bumper 5 years/100,000 km; powertrain 5 years/100,000 km; rust perforation 5 years/unlimited km. **Supplementary warranty:** A wise buy, considering Kia's previous transmission troubles and the installation of a new set-up on the 2006s. **City/highway fuel economy:** 13.2/8.8 L/100 km.

OWNER-REPORTED PROBLEMS: Erratic opening and closing of the power-sliding door (a common failure with all minivans' power-assisted doors); the Sedona eats brakes and tires; front axle failure due to bearing and seal defect; vehicle rolled back while in Park. Suddenly accelerated to 145–161 km/h when passing another car:

> I could not get the van to slow down even though I was pushing the brake to the floor. At one point I was doing between 90 and 100 mph [145–161 km/h]. I finally managed to get the van stopped and my brakes were smoking extremely bad. I took it to the dealer and they said it was a bad brake switch. The dealer acted like it was no big deal. I explained that we could have been injured or even killed.

Chronic stalling while underway or turning into an intersection; engine constantly misfires. Electrical malfunctions:

> With only 700 miles [1,127 km] on Sedona minivan I have had an air bag sensor go bad, a drivers side sliding door sensor go bad, a passenger side front door sensor go bad, the IP computer (fuse box inside vehicle near drivers side) burned up completely.

SPORTAGE ★★★★

RATING: Above Average. The Sportage is reasonably priced and has a better reliability record than the Sorento does. **Strong points:** A lively V6, and a comfortable, quiet ride; dependable handling, thanks to the responsive steering and firm suspension; and standard stability control and curtain airbags. NHTSA gives the Sportage five stars for frontal and side occupant crash protection; rollover protection was given three stars. "Acceptable" IIHS scores. **Weak points:** Mediocre fuel economy with the V6, and overall fuel consumption with the 4-cylinder is much higher than represented. The 4-cylinder is also a bit underpowered and buzzy. Lack of interior storage room. **New for 2010:** Nothing worth spending the extra money for. The 2010 or 2011 Sportage redesign will feature only 4-cylinder engines, as with the Hyundai Tucson makeover.

OVERVIEW: The Sportage has been around forever. Now—in its downsized configuration, resting on the Hyundai Tucson's frame, and with its use of Kia's ubiquitous 2.7L V6—Sportage offers power, carlike handling, and better dependability. Standard equipment for the base LX version, which has a 4-cylinder engine hooked to a manual 5-speed transmission, includes power windows and door locks, cruise control, tilt steering, power side mirrors, and four-wheel disc brakes with ABS.

KEY FACTS

PRICES: $21,695–$30,935 **FREIGHT:** $1,650 **ORIGIN:** South Korea **SALES:** Up 28%

POWERTRAIN (FRONT-DRIVE/AWD)
Engines: 2.0L 4-cyl. (140 hp) • 2.7L V6 (173 hp); Transmissions: 5-speed man. • 4-speed auto.

DIMENSIONS/CAPACITY
Passengers: 2/3; Wheelbase: 103.5 in.; H: 66.7/L: 171.3/W: 70.9 in.; Headroom F/R: 4.0/5.0 in.; Legroom F/R: 40/29 in.; Cargo volume: 31 cu. ft.; Fuel tank: 58L–65L/regular; Tow limit: 1,000–2,000 lb.; Load capacity: 860 lb.; Turning circle: 38 ft.; Ground clearance: 6.0 in.; Weight: 3,230–3,527 lb.

COST ANALYSIS: Although the V6 is a gas-burner, it's the engine of choice for its extra power. And, as for the high fuel cost, word is out that the Sportage is in its last days—which is driving down both new and used prices, compensating purchasers for the extra money they'll spend on fuel. **Best alternatives:** The Ford Escape, Honda CR-V, Hyundai Tucson, Kia Rondo, Mazda Tribute, and Toyota RAV4. **Options:** The LX V6; the EX version is padded with nonessentials. Forget the rear spoiler. **Depreciation:** Average. **Insurance cost:** Average. **Parts supply/cost:** Average cost; some delays for parts. **Annual maintenance cost:** Average. **Warranty:** Bumper-to-bumper 5 years/100,000 km; powertrain 5 years/100,000 km; rust perforation 5 years/unlimited km. **Supplementary warranty:** Worth considering. **City/highway fuel economy:** *2.0L manual:* 10.3/7.8 L/100 km. *2.0L automatic:* 10.2/8.0 L/100 km. *2.0L AWD:* 10.8/8.3 L/100 km. *2.7L:* 11.5/8.5 L/100 km. *2.7L AWD:* 11.7/8.8 L/100 km.

OWNER-REPORTED PROBLEMS: Not as many complaints as with the Sorento and Sedona. Instrument panel failures; tire-pressure sensor comes on for no reason; and the gas tank is vulnerable to road debris.

SORENTO

RATING: Below Average. What, $39,000 for this? Poor reliability and future orphanhood make Sorento's 2010 carryover model a poor buy. **Strong points:** Okay, it is well appointed and you get more SUV for fewer bucks, but what you do get may be all show and no go—and not very reliable, as well. (Not really "strong points," eh?) The base engine will do what is required. You also have standard stability control and a fairly roomy interior with good fit and finish. At first glance, this is an off-roader's delight, with low-range gearing and good ground clearance, but there's always that pesky reliability thing. NHTSA gives five stars for front and side crash protection and four stars for rollover protection. IIHS says frontal offset crashworthiness and head-restraint protection are "Good." **Weak points:** Your off-roading fun will end as soon as the tranny or brakes give out. (Did we mention reliability?) Fuel consumption is much higher than represented, and IIHS says side-impact crashworthiness is "Poor." **New for 2010:** Nothing significant this year; Sorento will adopt a unibody platform and add its third-row seat for the 2011 model year, if it makes it that far.

OVERVIEW: Sorento represents good value in theory, with its strong towing capacity and excellent safety ratings. However, it falls short on reliability, fuel economy, and ride quality.

COST ANALYSIS: The 2009s are selling for a song, now that word is out that the Sorento won't likely stay around for another model year. **Best alternatives:** The Honda CR-V, Hyundai Tucson, and Toyota RAV4. **Options:** The Sport Package isn't worth its cost. **Rebates:** Look for $3,500 rebates and low financing and leasing rates in early 2010. **Depreciation:** Faster than average for an Asian make. **Insurance cost:** Average. **Annual maintenance cost:** Higher than average. **Warranty:** Bumper-to-bumper 5 years/100,000 km; powertrain 5 years/100,000 km; rust perforation 5 years/unlimited km. **Supplementary warranty:** A wise buy, considering Kia's previous transmission troubles. **City/highway fuel economy:** *3.3L:* 14.0/9.2 L/100 km. *3.8L:* 14.0/9.8 L/100 km.

KEY FACTS

PRICES: $29,995–$39,295 **FREIGHT:** $1,650 **ORIGIN:** South Korea **SALES:** Up 13%

POWERTRAIN (REAR-DRIVE/4WD)
Engines: 3.3L V6 (242 hp) • 3.8L V6 (262 hp); Transmissions: 5-speed man. • 5-speed auto.

DIMENSIONS/CAPACITY
Passengers: 2/3; Wheelbase: 119 in.; H: 69./L: 202/W: 78 in.; Headroom F/R: 4.5/5.0 in.; Legroom F/R: 40/28 in.; Cargo volume: 32 cu. ft.; Fuel tank: 80L/regular; Tow limit: 5,000 lb.; Load capacity: 880 lb.; Turning circle: 38 ft.; Ground clearance: 7.0 in.; Weight: 4,274 lb.

OWNER-REPORTED PROBLEMS: Many owner complaints logged by NHTSA and *Consumer Reports*. Same old story of the passenger-side airbags being disabled when an adult passenger is seated. Other concerns: engine fire; engine harmonic balancer failure; airbags failed to deploy; automatic transmission failures; transmission torque converter locks up; vehicle jerks, stutters, and stalls; driveline vibration; faulty wiring harness, early brake wearout; headlight illumination is too short; speedometer reads slower than the actual speed; and tire valve stem air leakage.

BORREGO ★★

RATING: Below Average. The Borrego lacks the refined ride comfort and handling found in other luxury three-row SUVs, due to its trucklike body-on-frame construction. **Strong points:** The V6 performs quite well in all driving situations and can handle heavy loads with ease. The V8 cranks up the towing capability to 7,500 lb., with plenty of power in reserve for serious stump pulling. There's also a smooth-shifting automatic transmission, a quiet interior, user-friendly controls, ample third-row seating, a standard trailer hitch and electric harness, and standard stability control. NHTSA gives the Borrego five stars for frontal and side occupant crash protection. Rollover protection was given four stars. Few owner complaints over reliability, so far. **Weak points:** A hard, jolting ride; poor emergency

KEY FACTS

PRICES: $36,995–$43,495 **FREIGHT:** $1,650 **ORIGIN:** South Korea **SALES:** N/A
POWERTRAIN (REAR-DRIVE/4WD)
Engines: 3.8L V6 (276 hp) • 4.6L V8 (337 hp); Transmissions: 5-speed manumatic • 6-speed auto.
DIMENSIONS/CAPACITY
Passengers: 2/3/2; Wheelbase: 114 in.; H: 71/L: 192/W: 75 in.; Headroom F/R1/R2: 3.5/5.0/3.0 in.; Legroom F/R1/R2: 40.5/29/26 in.; Cargo volume: 41.5 cu. ft.; Fuel tank: 78L/regular; Tow limit: 5,000–7,500 lb.; Load capacity: 1,155 lb.; Turning circle: 38 ft.; Ground clearance: 7.5 in.; Weight: 4,735 lb.

handling; head restraints are too close to the back of the head; lacks a power tailgate; and fuel consumption is much higher than represented. **New for 2010:** Nothing major; Borrego is selling poorly and may not make it through the 2010 model year.

OVERVIEW: Borrego is a truck. It's a nicely appointed truck, but a truck just the same. This means you can carry a family of seven in comfort, tow practically anything, go off-roading (within reason), and manoeuvre in small areas due to the Borrego's tight (for its size) turning circle. For these and other truck-like attributes, the Borrego outshines the Ford Explorer. On the other hand, you won't find any styling breakthroughs (Kia thinks boxy is beautiful), the vehicle struggles in some off-road areas, and fuel economy is nonexistent.

COST ANALYSIS: Lots of deal making is going on with this gas-guzzler as the price of fuel moves upward. **Best alternatives:** Nissan Pathfinder and Toyota 4Runner for trucklike attributes. Vehicles with more carlike qualities are the Chevy Traverse, Ford Flex, Honda Pilot, and Mazda CX-9. **Options:** Skid plate protection, if going off-road. Forego the heated leather seats, chrome wheels, and space-stealing sunroof. **Rebates:** Look for $5,000 rebates, low financing rates, and leasing deals in early 2010. **Depreciation:** Much faster than average: A $43,000, top-of-the-line 2009 Borrego EX V8 sells used for less than $30,000. **Insurance cost:** Much higher than average. **Parts supply/cost:** Moderately expensive, and hard to find; expect long delays for parts. **Annual maintenance cost:** Expected to be much higher than average. **Warranty:** Bumper-to-bumper 5 years/100,000 km; powertrain 5 years/100,000 km; rust perforation 5 years/unlimited km. **Supplementary warranty:** A wise buy, considering Kia's previous transmission troubles and its 2009 revamping. **City/highway fuel economy:** *3.8L manumatic:* 13.0/9.4 L/100 km. *3.8L automatic:* 14.4/9.7 L/100 km. *4.6L:* 14.4/9.7 L/100 km.

OWNER-REPORTED PROBLEMS: Nothing significant, yet.

Lexus

The first Lexus, the LS 400, appeared in 1989 and didn't share any major components with previous Toyotas. Equipped with a V8 engine and noted for its outstanding engine performance, quietness, well-appointed interior, and impressive build quality, the car was an immediate success. Now the Lexus name has supplanted Cadillac as a term for luxury and quality, and it has been chosen as the most popular luxury car company in Germany.

Lexus continues to be a luxury automaker on its own merits, even though some models have mostly been dressed-up Camrys (only the ES 350 fits that description now). Unlike Acura and Infiniti, Lexus has become the epitome of luxury and comfort, with a small dab of performance thrown in. Lexus executives know that no matter how often car enthusiast magazines say that drivers want "road feel," "responsive handling," and "high-performance" thrills, the truth of the matter is that most drivers simply want to travel from point A to point B in safety and comfort, without interruption, in cars that are more than fully equipped Civics or warmed-over Maximas. Lexus figures that hardcore high-performance aficionados can move up to its sportier, rear-drive IS 350 and the rest will stick with the Camry-based "Japanese Oldsmobile" ES series.

Although these imports do set advanced benchmarks for quality control, they don't demonstrate engineering perfection, as a recent spate of engine failures—including sludge buildup and automatic transmissions that hesitate and then surge when shifting—proves. And yes, cheaper luxury cars from Acura, Hyundai, Kia, Nissan, and Toyota give you almost as much comfort and reliability, but without as much cachet and resale value.

Technical service bulletins show that these cars have been affected by electrical malfunctions, faulty emissions-control components, computer module miscalibrations, and minor body fit and trim glitches. Most owners haven't heard of these problems, because Lexus dealers have been particularly adept at fixing many of them before they become chronic.

ES 350 ★★★

RATING: Average. A near-luxury sedan that's really an all-dressed Camry clone. **Strong points:** Good acceleration; pleasantly quiet ride; and excellent quality control and warranty performance. Five-star NHTSA crashworthiness rating for frontal and side impacts, and four-star rollover protection. IIHS gave "Good" ratings for front- and side-impact protection. **Weak points:** Dangerous automatic transmission that hesitates and surges when shifting; primarily a four-seater, as three adults can't sit comfortably in the rear; headroom is inadequate for tall occupants; steering feel is muted; manual shifting system isn't very user-friendly, and overall handling isn't as nimble as with its BMW or Mercedes rivals; trunk space is limited (low liftover, though); rear-corner visibility is hampered by the high rear end; and head restraints were rated "Marginal" by IIHS. **New for 2010:** This year's ES offers more room, more horsepower, and

KEY FACTS

PRICES: $39,950 **FREIGHT:** $1,895
ORIGIN: Japan **SALES:** Down 20%
POWERTRAIN (FRONT-DRIVE)
Engine: 3.5L V6 (272 hp); Transmission: 6-speed auto.
DIMENSIONS/CAPACITY
Passengers: 2/3; Wheelbase: 109.3 in.; H: 57.1/L: 191.1/W: 71.7 in.; Headroom F/R: 2.5/1.5 in.; Legroom F/R: 42/2859 in.; Cargo volume: 14.7 cu. ft.; Fuel tank: 70L/premium; Tow limit: N/A; Load capacity: 900 lb.; Turning circle: 38.7 ft.; Ground clearance: 4.0 in.; Weight: 3,580 lb.

more safety features than the model it replaces did. Also standard this year are stability control and a power-adjustable steering wheel.

OVERVIEW: This entry-level Lexus front-drive carries a 272 hp V6 mated to an electronically controlled 6-speed automatic transmission that handles the 3.5L engine's horses effortlessly, without sacrificing fuel economy. All ES 350s feature dual front and side airbags, anti-lock brakes, double-piston front brake calipers, an optional Adaptive Variable Suspension, power-adjustable pedals with memory setting, 60/40 split-folding rear seats, a DVD navigation system, a 10-way power-adjustable driver's seat with memory, rain-sensing wipers, and one of the rarest features of all: a conventional spare tire.

COST ANALYSIS: The improved 2010 is your best choice; however, the usurious freight/PDI fee should be at least halved. **Best alternatives:** The all-dressed Camry, the Acura TL, the BMW 3 Series, and the Toyota Avalon. **Options:** Run like the wind if the dealer asks for another $7,000 for the "Emperor's New Clothes" Ultra Luxury Package. **Rebates:** Mostly low-cost financing. **Depreciation:** Much lower than average. **Insurance cost:** Much higher than average. **Parts supply/cost:** Good availability, and parts are moderately priced. **Annual maintenance cost:** Below average. **Warranty:** Bumper-to-bumper 4 years/80,000 km; powertrain 6 years/120,000 km; rust perforation 6 years/unlimited km. **Supplementary warranty:** May be needed to cover automatic transmission malfunctions. **City/highway fuel economy:** 10.9/7.2 L/100 km.

OWNER-REPORTED PROBLEMS: Automatic transmission shifts erratically, suddenly accelerates, or slips and hesitates before going into gear; some minor transmission malfunctions, radio system glitches, and fit and finish imperfections; tire side wall blew out after a low-speed impact with the curb when parking; tire monitor system malfunctions; engine ticking (replace camshaft housing or camshaft); Bluetooth cell phone voice distortion; rubbing noise from rear of vehicle; and an inoperative moonroof.

IS 250, IS 350, IS F ★★★★

RATING: Above Average. **Strong points:** More standard safety, performance, and convenience features than with the IS 300; the car is wider, longer, and more solid-looking; a competent standard IS 350 3.5L engine; easy handling, and effective braking; an upgraded interior; optional navigation screen is user-friendly and easily read; pleasant riding; low beltline provides a great view; and first-class workmanship. NHTSA crashworthiness figures: five stars for side-impact and rollover protection, and four stars for front-impact protection. IIHS gives a "Good" rating to frontal offset protection and an "Acceptable" score to head-restraint protection. *IS F:* Lots of tire-smoking power; high-performance handling; and a relatively quiet, high-quality interior. **Weak points:** The IS 250 feels rather sluggish when pushed. Handling on both the 250 and 350 models doesn't feel as sharp or responsive as with the BMW competition, owing in a large part to an intrusive Vehicle Dynamics Integrated Management system that automatically eases up on the throttle during hard cornering. Emergency braking also isn't a confidence-builder. Cramped rear seating. The car requires premium fuel and has outrageously high freight charges. *IS F:* A bone-jarring, teeth-chattering ride; a too-firm suspension; no manual transmission option; and a tiny cabin. **New for 2010:** The IS F gets upgraded handling and weight reduction. The hardtop convertible version of the IS makes its long-awaited debut. Both IS engines will be available, and the new convertibles will be known as the IS 250C and IS 350C.

KEY FACTS

PRICES: *IS 250:* $32,350, *IS 350:* $43,850, *IS F:* $65,300 **FREIGHT:** $1,895
ORIGIN: Japan **SALES:** Down 33%
POWERTRAIN (REAR-DRIVE/AWD)
Engines: 2.5L V6 (204 hp) • 3.5L V6 (306 hp) • 5.0L V8 (416 hp); Transmissions: 6-speed man. • 6-speed auto.
DIMENSIONS/CAPACITY
Passengers: 2/3; Wheelbase: 107.5 in.; H: 55.7/L: 182.5/W: 70.9; Headroom F/R: 2.0/2.0 in.; Legroom F/R: 41.5/25.5 in.; Cargo volume: 10.8 cu. ft.; Fuel tank: 65L; Tow limit: 1,500 lb.; Load capacity: 825 lb.; Turning circle: 33.5 ft.; Ground clearance: 4.7–5.3 in.; Weight: 3,814 lb.

OVERVIEW: Targeting BMW's 3 Series, Lexus's entry-level IS 250 and IS 350 rear-drive sports-compact sedans come with either a 204 hp 2.5L V6 or a 306 hp 3.5L V6. The F version ups the ante considerably with its 416 hp 5.0L V8 powerplant, which is going into its third year on the market. Owner comments have been positive, and the car's residual value has been quite strong.

COST ANALYSIS: **Best alternatives:** Try the Audi A5, Acura TL, BMW 3 Series, and Infiniti G35. Audi's A4 would be a contender, were it not for its poor quality-control history. **Options:** Don't waste money on the sunroof, heated seats, or leather upholstery. **Rebates:** Expect $2,000–$3,000 discounts early in 2010, along with attractive financing and leasing deals. **Depreciation:** Much lower than average. **Insurance cost:** Higher than average. **Parts supply/cost:** Average availability, though parts may be quite expensive because of the lack of independent part suppliers. **Annual maintenance cost:** Below average. **Warranty:** Bumper-to-bumper 4 years/80,000 km; powertrain 6 years/120,000 km; rust perforation 6 years/unlimited km. **Supplementary warranty:** Not necessary. **City/highway fuel economy:** *IS 250 manual:* 11.4/7.5 L/100 km. *IS 250 automatic:* 11.8/6.5 L/100 km. *IS 250 AWD:* 10.5/7.6 L/100 km. *IS 350:* 10.9/7.8 L/100 km. *IS F:* 13.0/8.5 L/100 km.

OWNER-REPORTED PROBLEMS: Mostly problems with premature brake wear, poor audio, and fit and finish imperfections. Other concerns: sunroof shattered while vehicle was underway; loss of transmission fluid; and AC mildew odour (Lexus replaced vehicle).

GS 350, GS 450H, GS 460 ★★★★

RATING: Above Average. An exercise in passive driving—an abundance of electronic gadgetry cannot transform these luxury sedans into sports cars. **Strong points:**

KEY FACTS

PRICES: $51,200, *AWD:* $53,200 **FREIGHT:** $1,895 **ORIGIN:** Japan **SALES:** Down 55%

POWERTRAIN (REAR-DRIVE/AWD)
Engines: 3.5L V6 (303 hp) • 3.5L V6 Hybrid (340 hp) • 4.6L V8 (342 hp); Transmissions: 6-speed auto. • 8-speed auto. CVT

DIMENSIONS/CAPACITY
Passengers: 2/3; Wheelbase: 112.2 in.; H: 56.1/L: 190/W: 71.7; Headroom F/R: 2.0/2.0 in.; Legroom F/R: 41.5/28 in.; Cargo volume: 14.8 cu. ft.; Fuel tank: 70L/premium; Tow limit: N/A; Load capacity: 815 lb.; Turning circle: 37.1 ft.; Ground clearance: 5.0 in.; Weight: 3,685 lb.

Good high-performance powertrain set-up; pleasantly quiet ride; acceptable handling and braking; average fuel economy, though premium fuel must be used; and exceptional quality control. **Weak points:** Primarily a four-seater with limited headroom for six-footers; the Audi A6 offers more rear legroom; middle-rear passengers, as usual in rear-drive sedans, get to ride the powertrain hump and thump the low roof with their heads; high window line impedes rear visibility; and some instruments are hidden by the steering wheel. No NHTSA crashworthiness data available. **New for 2010:** Everyone agrees little is new since the latest generation GS debuted in 2005. Key changes for the GS line are new colour schemes—two for the exterior and one for the interior—slightly restyled front ends, and active front headrests. Lexus finally joins the 21st century and ditches the standard cassette player in favour of iPod, satellite radio, and Bluetooth connectivity. An updated navigation system includes voice recognition. As for the hybrid GS 450h, 2010 brings several cosmetic changes.

OVERVIEW: The GS 350 luxury sedan comes with a 303 hp 3.5L V6 engine hooked to a 6-speed automatic transmission with sequential manual shift. The GS 460 and the GS 450h gas-electric hybrid are powered by a 342 hp V8 and a 340 hp V6, respectively. The GS 450h can run on one or both of its power sources, uses a continuously variable automatic transmission (CVT), and doesn't need plug-in charging. Standard safety features include traction/anti-skid control, ABS, front knee airbags, front side airbags, side curtain airbags, a rear-view camera, and a Pre-Collision System designed to automatically cinch seat belts and apply the brakes if an unavoidable crash is detected. Other standard features include driver-adjustable shock absorbers (460 and 450h models), leather upholstery, and dual-zone climate controls, plus oodles of other safety, performance, and convenience features.

COST ANALYSIS: The GS models continue to be comfortable, polished luxury sedans, but sporty performers they are not. The Infiniti M, for example, allows for more driver input and is more satisfying to drive, owing mainly to smooth power delivery, crisper shifts, precise steering, more-predictable brakes, and a less-intrusive stability system. **Best alternatives:** The Acura TL and the BMW 5 Series. **Options:** Lexus has now packaged GS options so that it is almost impossible to get the essential without getting the frivolous or dangerous. Try to stay away from the in-dash navigator; it complicates the calibration of the sound system and climate controls. Other money-wasting options: a power sunshade, moonroof, the Mark Levinson stereo, XM radio, ventilated seats, spoiler, Intuitive

Park Assist parking sensors, and rain-sensing wipers with Adaptive Front Lighting swivelling headlights. Be wary of the Dynamic Radar Cruise Control that reduces your speed when cars cut you off; if it malfunctions, as other systems have, you are toast. **Rebates:** By early winter, expect $3,000 rebates, zero percent financing, "giveaway" leasing terms, and discounting on the MSRP by about 10 percent. **Depreciation:** Slower than average. **Insurance cost:** Much higher than average. **Parts supply/cost:** Parts aren't easily found outside of the dealer network, and they're fairly pricey. **Annual maintenance cost:** Much less than average. **Warranty:** Bumper-to-bumper 4 years/80,000 km; powertrain 6 years/120,000 km; rust perforation 6 years/unlimited km. **Supplementary warranty:** Not necessary. **City/highway fuel economy:** *GS 350:* 10.9/7.4 L/100 km. *GS 350 AWD:* 11.6/8.0 L/100 km. *GS 450h:* 8.7/7.8 L/100 km. *GS 460:* 12.4/8.1 L/100 km.

OWNER-REPORTED PROBLEMS: Car suddenly accelerated as it was being parked.

RX 350, RX 450H ★★★★ / ★★★

RATING: *RX 350:* Above Average. Lexus invented the luxury crossover segment with the RX series in 1998, and it has since been a perennial bestseller. *RX 450h:* Average. Some fuel savings, but at a heavy price. Its price will plummet as you get closer to the battery pack's replacement time. **Strong points:** Now in its third generation, the 2010 doesn't disappoint with its attractive styling, great safety ratings, lots of luxury in a spacious cabin, and a smooth, carlike ride. RX received a "Top Safety Pick" award from IIHS. To earn that status, vehicles must be ranked as "Good"—the institute's top crash rating—in front, side, and rear impacts and be equipped with electronic stability control. Improved braking response and feel; more back-seat legroom; and the backrest's recline lever is more easily accessible. Also, the RX has excellent gas mileage for a luxury crossover. **Weak points:** High, firm prices; car doesn't feel as agile as its competition (this year's 350 model has 400 more pounds); no third-seat option; expensive options packages; less steering feedback when compared to the RX 450h, although the latter version takes more effort to turn; modest cargo capacity; and excessive road noise. The hybrid's acceleration is slower, thanks to its 300 extra pounds this year, and its Remote Touch multifunction joystick and screen forces you to take your eyes off the road. **New for 2010:** The redesigned 2010 is about one inch bigger everywhere, and the exterior has been slightly restyled, with a less-pointy nose. The interior has been revamped

KEY FACTS

PRICES: *RX 350:* $46,900, *RX 450h:* $53,650 **FREIGHT:** $1,895 **ORIGIN:** Ontario **SALES:** Down 5%

POWERTRAIN (FRONT-DRIVE/AWD)
Engines: 3.5L V6 (275 hp) • 3.5L V6 Hybrid (295 hp); Transmissions: 6-speed auto. • CVT

DIMENSIONS/CAPACITY
Passengers: 2/3; Wheelbase: 107.9 in.; H: 66.3/L: 187.8/W: 74.2 in.; Headroom F/R: 3.5/4.0 in.; Legroom F/R: 40.5/29.0 in.; Cargo volume: 40 cu. ft.; Fuel tank: 70L/regular/premium; Tow limit: 3,500 lb.; Load capacity: 925 lb.; Turning circle: 37.1 ft.; Ground clearance: 7.3 in.; Weight: 4,178 lb.

with better-quality materials and more user-friendly gauges, instruments, and controls. The model's powertrain has been reworked, as well, and the V6 now boasts 275 hp, up from 270 hp. A 6-speed automatic replaces last year's 5-speed.

OVERVIEW: Exterior styling is slightly different in the latest RX. Suspension is independent all around, and the progressive electronic power-steering system is speed sensing for enhanced control. The front-drive and all-wheel-drive RX models come identically equipped. Rear cargo room has been increased slightly, and anti-lock brakes, stability control, traction control, and 10 airbags are standard.

COST ANALYSIS: Get the 2010 for the improvements, but take a good 7 percent off the list price. **Best alternatives:** The BMW 5 Series, Cadillac SRX, Hyundai Veracruz, and Lincoln MKX. **Options:** Stay away from the moonroof option. Not only is it nonessential and often failure-prone, but it also comes in packages that include other frivolous features. Be wary of the Adaptive Cruise Control; it may behave erratically. **Rebates:** Expect $2,000 rebates, zero percent financing, good leasing terms, and discounting on the MSRP by about 10 percent. Discounting and rebates will become more attractive in the summer of 2010. **Depreciation:** Slower than average. **Insurance cost:** Much higher than average. **Parts supply/cost:** Parts are hard to find from independent sources; prices are on the high side. **Annual maintenance cost:** Less than average. **Warranty:** Bumper-to-bumper 4 years/80,000 km; powertrain 6 years/120,000 km; rust perforation 6 years/unlimited km. **Supplementary warranty:** Not needed. **City/highway fuel economy:** *RX 350:* 11.6/8.2 L/100 km. *RX 450h:* 6.6/7.2 L/100 km.

OWNER-REPORTED PROBLEMS: Audio system problems and poor fit and finish are the major owner grievances. Other concerns: excessive dust/powder blows from the AC vents; driver's door rattles; engine ticking (replace camshaft housing and camshaft); fluid leaks from the transfer case; tire monitor system malfunctions; liftgate-area water leaks; inoperative moonroof; and the vehicle pulls to the right.

Mazda

Back to the Future

Mazda has come full circle. Following its debut four decades ago as a small automaker selling inexpensive econocars and a rotary-engine-powered 1968 R100 coupe, followed by the RX-7 roadster (1978–2002), Mazda went upmarket and almost went bankrupt in 1994. Then Ford stepped in to turn the company around, and Mazda soon turned profitable through better management and an exciting new array of small cars and trucks. (The company's sole minivan, the MPV, never got any traction and was taken off the market in 2006.)

The peppy and fuel-efficient Mazda3 goes into its seventh model year after replacing the long-running Protegé, bringing the company back to its compact-car roots and adding some performance thrills. The Mazda3's larger brother, the Mazda6, returns with a hatchback and a wagon to accompany its sedan version. The model hasn't sold very well, so expect lots of discounting. Mazda B-Series trucks, the Tribute (Ford's Escape SUV twin), and the C-7 and C-9 have all weathered the recession relatively well.

MAZDA3 ★★★★★

RATING: Recommended. These cars have brought the fun back into driving at a reasonable cost. **Strong points:** Good powertrain set-up, with plenty of reserve power for passing and merging; easy, predictable handling; good steering feedback; small turning radius; rear multi-link suspension gives the car great stability at higher speeds; spacious, easy-to-load trunk; user-friendly instruments and controls; and better-than-average workmanship. NHTSA's front- and side-impact crashworthiness rating is five stars, and rollover resistance scored four stars. IIHS gives the Mazda3 its top, "Good" score for frontal offset protection. **Weak points:** Mazda3 has a history of automatic transmission malfunctions (but no more than with Honda or Toyota vehicles), prematurely worn-out brake rotors and pads, and fit and finish deficiencies. Some road noise intrudes into the cabin; a very small trunk; a high deck cuts rear visibility; limited rear footroom; and be wary of Mazda dealers overcharging for scheduled maintenance. IIHS rated side crashworthiness as "Poor" and head-restraint effectiveness as "Marginal." **New for 2010:** A minor exterior restyling; the MazdaSpeed3 hatchback continues with a turbocharged 263 hp 4-cylinder engine similar to the turbo engine used in the MazdaSpeed6; also look for some handling refinements. This year's redesigned front end has gone from "unique" to Stephen King–like "bizarre."

KEY FACTS

PRICES: \$15,995, *Sport 2.5:* \$23,595 **FREIGHT:** \$1,395 **ORIGIN:** Japan **SALES:** Down 25%

POWERTRAIN (FRONT-DRIVE)
Engines: 2.0L 4-cyl. (148 hp) • 2.5L 4-cyl. (167 hp) • 2.3L 4-cyl. Turbo (263 hp); Transmissions: 5-speed man. • 6-speed man. • 5-speed auto.

DIMENSIONS/CAPACITY (SEDAN)
Passengers: 2/3; Wheelbase: 103.9 in.; H: 57.9/L: 180.7/W: 69.1 in.; Headroom F/R: 5.5/2.0 in.; Legroom F/R: 41.5/27 in.; Cargo volume: 11.8 cu. ft.; Fuel tank: 55L/regular; Tow limit: N/A; Load capacity: 850 lb.; Turning circle: 17.1 ft.; Ground clearance: 5.0 in.; Weight: 2,868 lb.

Hey, Mazda3 Sport, wipe that grin off your face!

OVERVIEW: Going into its seventh year, the Mazda3 is an econobox with flair that pleases commuters and "tuners" alike. With considerable engineering help from Ford and Volvo, these cars use a platform that will also serve future iterations of the Ford Focus and Volvo S40. The car offers spirited acceleration and smooth, sporty shifting. Handling is enhanced with a highly rigid body structure, front and rear stabilizer bars, a multi-link rear suspension, and four-wheel disc brakes. Interior room is quite ample with the car's relatively long wheelbase, extra width, and straight sides, which maximize headroom, legroom, and shoulder room.

COST ANALYSIS: A cheaper and virtually identical 2009 version is recommended, but it may be hard to find. Hatchback models give you the most versatility. **Best alternatives:** The Honda Civic. **Options:** Don't accept the original Goodyear Eagle RS-A tires; go to The Tire Rack online to find some better tires for less money. The 5-speed automatic transmission with AC is a good start, although the 6-speed manual is lots more fun to drive. **Rebates:** Not likely. **Depreciation:** Much slower than average. **Insurance cost:** Average. **Parts supply/cost:** Parts are easy to find. **Annual maintenance cost:** Less than average, so far. **Warranty:** Bumper-to-bumper 3 years/80,000 km; powertrain 5 years/100,000 km; rust perforation 5 years/unlimited km. **Supplementary warranty:** Not needed. **City/highway fuel economy:** *2.0L manual:* 8.1/5.9 L/100 km. *2.0L automatic:* 8.7/6.0 L/100 km. *2.5L manual:* 10.1/6.9 L/100 km. *2.5L automatic:* 9.2/6.8 L/100 km.

OWNER-REPORTED PROBLEMS: Airbags failed to deploy; weak rims may fracture after hitting a small pothole; sudden stalling while cruising on the highway; delayed acceleration; manual transmission may go into Reverse when shifted into Fourth gear; car rolls away when parked on an incline; car tends to pull to one side; premature power-steering pump failures first seen as a stiffening of the steering. Goodyear Eagle RS-A 205/50 R17 tires provide little traction on ice or snow and may wear out prematurely. Goodyear refuses claims, saying there is no proof of "poor workmanship" on their part—the tires simply wear out quickly. Shameful!

> This car/tire combination provided extremely low traction on packed snow and ice. The dealership and Mazda have been unwilling to provide adequate tires so the car is no longer being driven when there is snow or ice on the roads.

Other concerns are mostly transmission and brake deficiencies. The transmission can be hard to shift, especially from Third to Fourth gear or when gearing down; premature wearout of brake pads and rotors, accompanied by an annoying grinding sound and pulling to one side when the brakes are applied; brake rotors are easily grooved; whine in the steering system; body vibration and steering-wheel shimmy; and a snap, then a clunk noise may be heard when opening the windows.

MAZDA5 ★★★★

RATING: Above Average. The Mazda5 is basically a compact miniwagon that's based broadly on the Mazda3 and carries six passengers in three rows of seats. Used mostly for urban errands and light commuting, the "5" employs a peppy, though fuel-frugal, 2.3L 153 hp 4-cylinder engine hooked to a standard 5-speed manual transmission or a 5-speed automatic. So far, the engine has had few problems during the past four years the Mazda5 has run in Canada. **Strong points:** All the advantages of a small minivan, without the handling or fuel penalties; reasonably priced; decent fuel economy; adequate 2.3L engine; a comfortable ride; and relatively quiet interior (except for omnipresent road noise—a common trait with small wagons). NHTSA's front- and side-impact crashworthiness rating is five stars, and rollover resistance scored four stars. **Weak points:** The small 4-cylinder engine doesn't have much torque ("grunt," or pulling power) for heavy loads or hill climbing, and towing isn't recommended. There isn't much room for passengers in the third-row seat. There's also a history of automatic transmission malfunctions (but no more than with Honda or Toyota vehicles), prematurely worn-out brake rotors and pads, and fit and finish deficiencies. **New for 2010:** Just a few minor equipment changes.

KEY FACTS

PRICES: $22,495–$27,495 **FREIGHT:** $1,325 **ORIGIN:** Japan **SALES:** Down 3%
POWERTRAIN (FRONT-DRIVE)
Engine: 2.3L 4-cyl. (153 hp); Transmissions: 5-speed man. • 5-speed auto.
DIMENSIONS/CAPACITY
Passengers: 2/2/2; Wheelbase: 108.3 in.; H: 64.2/L: 181.5/W: 69.1 in.; Headroom F/R1/R2: 4.5/4.5/2.0 in.; Legroom F/R1/R2: 41/29.5/22 in.; Cargo volume: 39 cu. ft.; Fuel tank: 60L/regular; Tow limit: No towing; Load capacity: 1,020 lb.; Turning circle: 37 ft.; Ground clearance: 5.0 in.; Weight: 2,815 lb.

OVERVIEW: This is a relatively tall and narrow car, with a thick, obtrusive front A-pillar. Nevertheless, it handles well, despite some body roll and steering that's a bit vague. Drivers will find this vehicle a breeze to park and easy to manoeuvre, and it's fairly spacious inside. Two wide-opening sliding doors make for easy entry and exit.

COST ANALYSIS: Get a 2009 with a sizeable discount of at least 15 percent. **Best alternatives:** The Honda Civic, Hyundai Tucson, and Toyota Matrix. **Options:** Any good tires, instead of Bridgestone or Firestone. **Rebates:** Not likely. **Depreciation:** Much slower than average. **Insurance cost:** Average. **Parts supply/cost:** Easy to find. **Annual maintenance cost:** Less than average, so far. **Warranty:** Bumper-to-bumper 3 years/80,000 km; powertrain 5 years/100,000 km; rust perforation 5 years/unlimited km. **Supplementary warranty:** Not needed. **City/highway fuel economy:** *Manual:* 9.2/6.7 L/100 km. *Automatic:* 9.4/6.9 L/100 km.

OWNER-REPORTED PROBLEMS: A few automatic transmission failures; transmission gear hunting and fluid leaks; power-steering malfunctions; electrical system shorts; early suspension replacement; and rapid brake and tire wear.

MAZDA6

RATING: Average. A car enthusiast's family sedan, although not as refined as Toyota's Camry or as sporty as Honda's Accord. The car stands out for its sharp styling and sporty driving dynamics. **Strong points:** Adequate powertrain set-up; very agile, with good overall handling; responsive, precise steering; all-independent suspension; impressive braking; comfortable seating; and better-than-average workmanship. High prices are easily bargained down. NHTSA gives its top, five-star score to the Mazda6 for front, side, and rollover protection. Also, IIHS gives

KEY FACTS

PRICES: $22,695–$33,400 **FREIGHT:** $1,325 **ORIGIN:** Japan **SALES:** Down: 28%
POWERTRAIN (FRONT-DRIVE)
Engines: 2.5L 4-cyl. (170 hp) • 3.7L V6 (272 hp) • 2.3L Turbo-4 (274 hp); Transmissions: 6-speed man. • 5-speed auto. • 6-speed auto.
DIMENSIONS/CAPACITY
Passengers: 2/3; Wheelbase: 109.8 in.; H: 57.8/L: 194.4/W: 72.4 in.; Headroom F/R: 4/2 in.; Legroom F/R: 40.5/29 in.; Cargo volume: 16.6 cu. ft.; Fuel tank: 64L/regular; Tow limit: No towing; Load capacity: 850 lb.; Turning circle: 41 ft.; Ground clearance: 5.1 in.; Weight 3,549 lb.

its top, "Good" score for frontal offset protection. Excellent fit and finish. **Weak points:** Manual and automatic transmission shifting isn't all that smooth; hard riding over uneven pavement; torque steer (pulling) to the right when accelerating; excessive road noise intrudes into the cabin; and IIHS rates side-impact protection as "Poor" and head-restraint effectiveness as "Marginal." Mazda has a history of automatic transmission and fit and finish deficiencies and scheduled maintenance overcharges. Mediocre fuel economy numbers. One major Mazda6 drawback may be its price—although prices are very fluid, there's not enough difference to lure Honda, Hyundai, Kia, Nissan, or Toyota buyers away. **New for 2010:** Nothing important.

OVERVIEW: Blame it all on Nissan. They kicked off the family feud over mid-sized sedans by revamping their Altima to offer a sweet combination of high performance, a capacious interior, and clean, aerodynamic styling. Then Toyota reworked its Camry, and Honda responded with its seventh-generation Accord. And then it was Mazda's turn, so voila! We have the Mazda6.

COST ANALYSIS: The 2009s underwent a major redesign, and leftovers should be cheaper than the carried-over 2010 version. **Best alternatives:** The Ford Fusion, Honda Accord, Hyundai Tucson, Nissan Altima, and Toyota Camry or Matrix. **Options:** Options are pricey; be wary of the Bridgestone and Firestone tires. **Rebates:** $3,000 enticements and low-cost leases and financing are most likely. **Depreciation:** Average. **Insurance cost:** Average. **Parts supply/cost:** Easy to find. **Annual maintenance cost:** Average. **Warranty:** Bumper-to-bumper 3 years/80,000 km; powertrain 5 years/100,000 km; rust perforation 5 years/unlimited km. **Supplementary warranty:** Not needed. **City/highway fuel economy:** *2.5L:* 10.4/6.9 L/100 km. *3.7L:* 12.1/8.0 L/100 km.

OWNER-REPORTED PROBLEMS: Some minor problems with the transmission and electrical and fuel systems. Other owners have reported that the automatic transmission "weep hole" leaks fluid, the engine makes a ticking sound at low rpms, and the remote door lock feature often malfunctions.

MX-5 ★★★★★

best buy

RATING: Recommended. An exceptional, reasonably priced roadster. **Strong points:** Well-matched and beefier powertrain provides better-than-expected acceleration and top-end power at the 7000 rpm range; classic sports car handling; perfectly weighted steering with plenty of road feedback; a firm but comfortable suspension; impressive braking; mirrors are bigger and more effective than those found in most luxury sports cars; a user-friendly, manually operated top; engine is fairly quiet, and less road noise intrudes into the cabin; instruments and controls are easy to read and access; a slightly roomier interior; good fuel economy; no safety-related complaints, and few performance-related ones; and a high resale value. The 2005 earned five stars for rollover protection, four stars for frontal crashworthiness, and three stars for side-impact protection, but NHTSA hasn't crash tested the MX-5 since then. IIHS gave it an "Average" rating for head-restraint effectiveness. **Weak points:** All the things that make roadsters so much "fun": limited passenger and cargo room (still not much room for six-footers); difficult entry and exit; restricted rear visibility with the top up; and a can of tire sealant instead of a spare tire. Optional stability control. **New for 2010:** Almost everything has been redesigned or tweaked, including the exterior styling, interior trim and fittings, engine, suspension, and exhaust. Look for more top-end power, slicker manual shifts, and an easier way to go from automatic to manual mode. The engine now has a raspier sound; there's an iPod socket in the cabin; and tall drivers find the door pockets less intrusive.

KEY FACTS

PRICES: \$28,995–\$39,995 **FREIGHT:** \$1,395 **ORIGIN:** Japan **SALES:** Down 33%

POWERTRAIN (REAR-DRIVE)

Engine: 2.0L 4-cyl. (170 hp);
Transmissions: 5-speed man. • 6-speed man. • 6-speed auto.

DIMENSIONS/CAPACITY

Passengers: 2; Wheelbase: 89.2 in.; H: 49/L: 157.1/W: 67.7 in.; Headroom: 1.5 in.; Legroom: 40 in.; Cargo volume: 5.3 cu. ft.; Fuel tank: 48L/regular; Tow limit: N/A; Load capacity: 340 lb.; Turning circle: 33 ft.; Ground clearance: 4.0 in.; Weight: 2,440 lb.

OVERVIEW: The MX-5 is a stubby, lightweight, rear-drive, two-seater convertible sports car that combines new technology with old British roadster styling reminiscent of the Triumph, the Austin-Healy, and the Lotus Elan. It comes in a variety of trim levels: The three convertibles are the Sport, Touring, and Grand Touring. The fourth model is the Touring (Power-Retractable) Hard Top. The lineup begins with the soft-top-only Sport; a removable hardtop is available as an option. All models come with a heated glass rear window.

It's amazing how well the MX-5 is put together, considering that it isn't particularly innovative and most parts are borrowed from Mazda's other models. For example, the engine is borrowed from the Mazda3 and Mazda6, and the suspension is taken from the RX-8. A 5-speed manual gearbox is standard fare, and the 6-speed automatic is optional, as is the 6-speed manual. The MX-5 is shorter than most other sports cars; nevertheless, this is a fun car to drive, costing much less than other vehicles in its class.

COST ANALYSIS: Get the improved 2010. It will cost more, but you will recoup the extra expense come trade-in time. **Best alternatives:** The BMW Z cars, Chevrolet Camaro, Mercedes-Benz SLK, Pontiac Solstice (before they're dropped), and Porsche Boxster. **Options:** The 6-speed manual transmission is a toss-up, since the 5-speed is so smooth. **Rebates:** Look for \$3,000 discounts by year's end. **Depreciation:** Slower than average. **Insurance cost:** Higher than average.

Parts supply/cost: Parts are easy to find, but they often cost more than average. **Annual maintenance cost:** Much less than average, particularly when compared to other roadsters. **Warranty:** Bumper-to-bumper 3 years/80,000 km; powertrain 5 years/100,000 km; rust perforation 5 years/unlimited km. **Supplementary warranty:** Not needed. **City/highway fuel economy:** *5-speed manual:* 9.2/7.1 L/100 km. *6-speed manual:* 9.7/7.1 L/100 km. *6-speed automatic:* 10.1/7.2 L/100 km.

OWNER-REPORTED PROBLEMS: Some minor driveline, fuel system, and fit and finish complaints.

RX-8 ★

RATING: Not Recommended. Mazda's most unreliable vehicle since the MPV minivan was dumped in 2006. **Strong points:** A quiet, smooth rotary powerplant that hits its stride in the mid-rpm range; engine's front mid-ship layout assures competent handling and responsive steering; reinforced chassis reduces body-flexing squeaks, rattles, and leaks; upscale, well-appointed interior; and good rear-seat access to comfortable, well-bolstered seats. NHTSA gives its top, five-star score for rollover protection and a four-star rating for front and side protection. **Weak points:** Major reliability problems for years; acceleration isn't all that impressive; the multi-link suspension and 18-inch tires make for a slightly harsh ride, but it's a bit smoother than with the Nissan Z cars; interior is somewhat cramped, and large doorsills add to the feeling of isolation; head restraints and side pillars obstruct outward visibility; little rear legroom; and a small trunk opening. Poor fuel economy and premium gas increase costs. Stability control depends upon the model chosen. **New for 2010:** Nothing significant; a redesign is scheduled for the 2011 model year.

KEY FACTS

PRICES: $37,295–$42,395 **FREIGHT:** $1,325 **ORIGIN:** Japan **SALES:** Down 45%
POWERTRAIN (REAR-DRIVE)
Engines: 1.3L Rotary (212 hp) • 1.3L Rotary (232 hp); Transmissions: 6-speed man. • 6-speed auto.
DIMENSIONS/CAPACITY
Passengers: 2/2; Wheelbase: 106.4 in.; H: 52.8/L: 175.6/W: 69.7 in.; Headroom F/R: 1.5/1.5 in.; Legroom F/R: 40/26 in.; Cargo volume: 7.6 cu. ft.; Fuel tank: 60L/premium; Tow limit: N/A; Load capacity: 680 lb.; Turning circle: 34.8 ft.; Ground clearance: 4.7 in.; Weight: 3,111 lb.

OVERVIEW: The rotary is back! Mazda has brought back its latest iteration of the Wankel-inspired rotary engine in its rear-drive, four-door RX-8 sports coupe. And this time, the price is right—about $11,500 less than what the $48,795 RX-7 sold for back in 1995.

COST ANALYSIS: Weak demand and the car's poor reputation has pushed prices down. **Best alternatives:** The BMW M Coupe and Honda R2000. **Options:** Nothing extra is needed. **Rebates:** Look for $3,000 discounts by year's end. **Depreciation:** Slower than average. **Insurance cost:** Higher than average.

Parts supply/cost: Parts are easy to find, but they often cost more than average. **Annual maintenance cost:** Average. **Warranty:** Bumper-to-bumper 3 years/80,000 km; powertrain 5 years/100,000 km; rust perforation 5 years/unlimited km. **Supplementary warranty:** Don't drive without one. **City/highway fuel economy:** *6-speed manual:* 12.8/9.2 L/100 km. *6-speed Sport manumatic:* 12.9/8.6 L/100 km.

OWNER-REPORTED PROBLEMS: Chronic powertrain failures; fuel and electrical system malfunctions; very poor fit and finish; and frequent brake repairs.

B-SERIES TRUCKS ★★★★★

RATING: Recommended. Good, reliable small trucks, if you don't mind a stiff ride, a small cabin, and thinly padded seats. **New for 2010:** Mazda has dropped this popular pickup that's the Ford Ranger's twin.

OVERVIEW: The B-Series trucks have been around for decades and are simple in design and quite reliable. Although the rear seats are more suitable for cargo than for people, these pickups are quite capable of doing all the chores a light truck is expected to carry out.

COST ANALYSIS: Higher fuel costs are driving prices down to where 15 percent discounts are commonplace. **Best alternatives:** The Ford Ranger, Nissan Frontier, and Toyota Tacoma. **Options:** Bucket seats will make up for the lack of bolstering with original-equipment seats. **Rebates:** Look for $3,000 discounts by year's end. **Depreciation:** Slower than average. **Insurance cost:** Higher than average. **Parts supply/cost:** Parts are easy to find, but they often cost more than average. **Annual maintenance cost:** Average. **Warranty:** Bumper-to-bumper 3 years/80,000 km; powertrain 5 years/100,000 km; rust perforation 5 years/unlimited km. **Supplementary warranty:** Don't drive without one. **City/highway fuel economy:** *B2300 manual:* 9.9/7.5 L/100 km. *B2300 automatic:* 10.6/8.3 L/100 km. *B4000 manual:* 14.0/9.7 L/100 km. *B4000 automatic:* 13.4/9.7 L/100 km.

KEY FACTS

PRICES: *B2300:* $15,395, *B4000:* $18,995–$22,995 **FREIGHT:** $1,535
ORIGIN: Japan **SALES:** Down 50%
POWERTRAIN (REAR-DRIVE/AWD)
Engines: 2.3L 4-cyl. (143 hp) • 4.0L V6 (207 hp); Transmissions: 5-speed man. • 5-speed auto.
DIMENSIONS/CAPACITY
Passengers: *B2300:* 2/1, *B4000:* 2/3; Wheelbase: 111.6.4 in.; H: 64.9/L: 187/W: 69.4 in.; Headroom F/R: N/A; Legroom F/R: N/A; Cargo volume: 7.6 cu. ft.; Fuel tank: 62.4L/regular; Tow limit: 5,600 lb.; Load capacity: 680 lb.; Turning circle: 38 ft.; Ground clearance: 6.7 in.; Weight: 3,064 lb.

OWNER-REPORTED PROBLEMS: Sudden, unintended acceleration, a sticking throttle, and frequent brake repairs.

Mitsubishi

Make-or-Break Time

Mitsubishi has had a rocky road in Canada, particularly since 2003, mainly because of its practically nonexistent dealer network, maladministration, and the rise of many Japanese and South Korean makes that are more refined and better accepted by shoppers. The automaker's two redesigned models—the 2007 Endeavor and 2008 Lancer—were expected to showcase the company's engineering and styling prowess, but they floundered in the economic recession that hit in mid 2008.

Mitsubishi sells the following models in Canada: the compact Lancer ($16,598–$22,298) and its variants, the Sportback ($23,498), Ralliart ($32,998), Lancer Sportback Ralliart ($33,498), and Evolution ($41,498); the mid-sized Galant ($23,998–$27,998; Ralliart: $32,998); the Eclipse GS ($25,998–$34,798), GT ($32,998), and Spyder (GS: $32,298; GT-P: $37,798); and the Endeavor ($35,998; 4×4: $39,298) and Outlander ($24,998; 4×4: $26,998–$32,198) sport-utilities.

All things considered, Mitsubishis are acceptable, cheap buys—mechanically. However, when you buy the product, you also buy the management, and that part is rotten to the core. The purchase of any Mitsubishi product is particularly risky for Canadians because of the company's weak dealer network. Moreover, insiders say that after a quarter century the automaker is seriously considering leaving the North American market, after the recession caused joblessness and weak consumer confidence, which decimated Mitsubishi sales. In fact, North American car sales for July 2009 fell 56 percent to just over 3,000 units, and SUV sales dropped 20 percent to 1,500 vehicles.

Will Mitsubishi pull out of North America? Yes, it's just a matter of time before the company follows truckmaker Isuzu.

RATING: All Mitsubishis are Average buys, with easily negotiated base prices. Its cars are fairly reliable; however, servicing is a problem on models with complicated fuel-delivery systems or other high-tech features. Problems they all share: poor Yokohama tire traction; sudden loss of brakes, and premature replacement of the brake pads and rotors; early clutch failures; and airbags that don't deploy when they should. Mostly four- and five-star crash protection.

COST ANALYSIS: Although the Endeavor mid-sized SUV is the best of the lot, its maintenance is highly dealer-dependent. When Mitsubishi leaves town, repairs and parts will be hard to find. **Best alternatives:** The Honda Civic; Hyundai Accent, Elantra, or Tucson 4×4; Mazda3; Nissan Sentra; and Toyota Yaris or Matrix. **Options:** Electronic stability control is recommended, but stay away from any of the models equipped with a turbocharged engine. Turbo repairs will devour your wallet. **Rebates:** Look for $3,000 discounts on the small cars and

$5,000 on the SUVs. The Eclipse Spyder sportster, on the other hand, will continue to sell at its full retail price. **Depreciation:** Average. **Insurance cost:** Above average for the SUVs and Spyder. **Parts supply/cost:** Parts are easy to find. **Annual maintenance cost:** Average, so far. **Warranty:** Bumper-to-bumper 3 years/80,000 km; powertrain 5 years/100,000 km; rust perforation 5 years/unlimited km. **Supplementary warranty:** A good idea, if the warranty is sold by an insured independent company.

Nissan

Nissan—or should I say Renault's Nissan division?—has risen from the dead so many times, it should star in a George A. Romero zombie flick. And it looks as if the automaker will do it again, by surviving this recession with a few feathers plucked but carrying a lineup of models that covers almost every marketing niche.

While many manufacturers continue to dial back on their product development activities, Nissan plows ahead into the 2010 model year with the introduction of the all-new 370Z Roadster and the additional refinement of popular Nissan vehicles such as the Altima, Sentra, Versa, Armada, and Rogue. These changes, of course, are in addition to the late-2009 model year introduction of the uniquely styled Nissan Cube and the June debut of the new NISMO 370Z.

Nissan, like Mazda, makes many dependable cars, trucks, and minivans that fly under the media radar and go unheralded by the motoring press. But word has gotten around, and shoppers are now visiting Nissan showrooms to buy highly styled and reasonably priced models that combine good fuel economy with cutting-edge technology and breathtaking performance.

VERSA ★★★★

RATING: Above Average. **Strong points:** Good-quality interior appointments; tilt steering column; and standard side-impact and side curtain airbags. A 6-speed manual transmission is available, whereas most small cars offer only a 4- or 5-speed gearbox. NHTSA awarded the Versa four stars for front, side, and rollover crash protection. IIHS gave the car its top, "Good" score for head-restraint, offset, and side crash protection. As CanadianDriver columnist Paul Williams put it, the Versa is the "jumbo shrimp" of micro cars. The car's larger wheelbase makes for a smooth ride and creates a lot more interior room than what is offered by other small cars in its class. A tall roofline makes for easy access. Visibility is first rate, and there's minimal road noise. The fuel tank dwarfs the mini-car field, where most tanks are 45 L; standard 15-inch wheels are used, versus the competition's 14-inchers; and the Versa carries a 122 hp engine, while the other micro cars get by with 103–110 hp powerplants. The 1.8L 4-cylinder engine provides plenty of power, and handling is responsive and predictable, thanks to the tight, power-assisted steering and

KEY FACTS

PRICES: *Sedan:* $12,498, *Hatchback:* $13,998 **FREIGHT:** $1,325 **ORIGIN:** Japan **SALES:** Down 18%

POWERTRAIN (FRONT-DRIVE)
Engines: 1.6L 4-cyl. (107 hp) • 1.8L 4-cyl. (122 hp); Transmissions: 5-speed man. • 6-speed man. • CVT • 4-speed auto.

DIMENSIONS/CAPACITY
Passengers: 2/3; Wheelbase: 102.4 in.; H: 60.4/L: 169.1/W: 66.7 in.; Headroom F/R: 5.0/3.5; Legroom F/R: 40/30 in.; Cargo volume: 17.8 cu. ft.; Fuel tank: 50L/regular; Tow limit: N/A; Load capacity: 860 lb.; Turning circle: 37 ft.; Ground clearance: 5.0 in.; Weight: 2,780 lb.

independent front suspension. **Weak points:** Engine lacks "grunt" at higher rpms, and produces an annoying drone when pushed; the manual 6-speed is a bit clunky, and the suspension is tuned more to the soft side; very little price haggling, due to the popularity of these little cars; less-effective rear drum brakes; no stability control on all models; and owners say real-world fuel economy is about 20 percent less than what is represented. **New for 2010:** Slightly restyled; new wheels; and standard fog lights. ABS and traction control added to the Versa 1.8SL

OVERVIEW: The Versa is Nissan's first "micro" car since the Micra was dropped in 1991 and the Sentra became the company's entry-level model. Targeting mainly the GM Aveo, Honda Fit, Hyundai Accent, and Toyota Yaris, Versa is the largest of these small cars.

COST ANALYSIS: Get the 2009 hatchback coupled to a 6-speed manual transmission for the best overall performance and highest residual value. **Best alternatives:** Honda Fit and Toyota Yaris. Nevertheless, the Versa's strong engine and larger body make it stand out. **Options:** The 6-speed transmission is a much better performer than the CVT. **Rebates:** Not likely. Expect a little discounting by early summer. **Depreciation:** Below average. **Insurance cost:** Average. **Parts supply/cost:** Parts aren't hard to find and are relatively inexpensive. **Annual maintenance cost:** Predicted to be much less than average. **Warranty:** Bumper-to-bumper 3 years/60,000 km; powertrain 5 years/100,000 km; rust perforation 5 years/unlimited km. **Supplementary warranty:** Not needed. **City/highway fuel economy:** *6-speed manual:* 7.9/6.3 L/100 km. *4-speed automatic:* 8.5/6.2 L/100 km. *CVT:* 7.9/6.1 L/100 km. Owners say their real gas consumption is much higher than these estimates.

OWNER-REPORTED PROBLEMS: Driver-side windshield wiper throws water onto the passenger side of the windshield after the wiper has passed, ensuring that the passenger-side windshield is never cleaned. Brake failures; reduced braking effectiveness; and many complaints of hard starting.

SENTRA ★★★★

RATING: Above Average. **Strong points:** 2.5L engine provides lots of power; occupants are treated to a quiet, comfortable, "floaty" ride; easy handling, if not pushed hard; plenty of cabin space, and the rear seat cushion can be folded forward, permitting the split rear seatback to fold flat with the floor; a commodious trunk; the locking glove box could house a laptop; and good quality control, with few safety- or performance-related defects. **Weak points:** The 2.0L engine is underpowered; manual transmission shifter's location may be too high and forward for some drivers; some body lean when cornering under power, and the rear end tends to fishtail; lots of road wander; long braking distances probably due to the use of rear drum brakes instead of the more-effective disc brakes; and the front side pillar obstructs the view forward. **New for 2010:** Slightly restyled; new headlights, tail lights, and fog lights; new utility box; stability/traction control extended to other models; and the 6-speed manual transmission has been dropped.

KEY FACTS

PRICES: $14,798–$22,198 **FREIGHT:** $1,231 **ORIGIN:** Japan **SALES:** Down 40%
POWERTRAIN (FRONT-DRIVE)
Engines: 2.0L 4-cyl. (140 hp) • 2.5L 4-cyl. (177 hp) • 2.5L 4-cyl. (200 hp); Transmissions: 6-speed man. • CVT
DIMENSIONS/CAPACITY
Passengers: 2/3; Wheelbase: 100 in.; H: 55.5/L: 178/W: 67 in.; Headroom F/R: 6.0/2.0 in.; Legroom F/R: 41/26.5 in.; Cargo volume: 11.6 cu. ft.; Fuel tank: 50L/reg./prem.; Tow limit: 1,000 lb.; Load capacity: 850 lb.; Turning circle: 35.4 ft.; Ground clearance: 5.5 in.; Weight: 2,695 lb.

OVERVIEW: Unlike many bare-bones economy cars, entry-level Sentras offer dependable motoring with lots of safety, performance, and comfort. Besides making for a roomier interior, the large body produces a quieter, smoother ride. These entry-level small sedans come in three trim levels: a fuel-frugal base 140 hp 2.0L 4-cylinder engine and two 2.5L 4-bangers, producing 177 and 200 horses, respectively.

COST ANALYSIS: Get the practically identical and cheaper 2009. **Best alternatives:** Sentra's engine and body dimension improvements over the past few years have made it a good competitor to the Honda Civic, Hyundai Elantra, and Mazda3. **Options:** Choose the 177 hp 2.5L 4-cylinder for the best power and fuel economy combination. **Rebates:** Expect $1,500 rebates in early 2010. **Depreciation:** Average. **Insurance cost:** Average for the base models. **Parts supply/cost:** Inexpensive parts can be found practically anywhere. Suspension parts and parts needed for recall campaigns are often back ordered. **Annual maintenance cost:** Less than average. **Warranty:** Bumper-to-bumper 3 years/60,000 km; powertrain 5 years/100,000 km; rust perforation 5 years/unlimited km. **Supplementary warranty:** Not needed. **City/highway fuel economy:** *2.0L manual:* 8.4/6.4 L/100 km. *2.0L CVT:* 8.0/5.9 L/100 km. *2.5L manual:* 9.7/6.9 L/100 km. Note that many owners report getting about 30 percent less fuel economy than advertised.

OWNER-REPORTED PROBLEMS: Owners complain that they never receive notices of recall campaigns. Airbags failed to deploy; gas pedal is mounted too close to the brake pedal; sudden, unintended acceleration; early replacement of Bridgestone Turanza EL400 tires. Premature wearout of rear tires due to factory misalignment of the rear suspension:

> Rear suspension was inspected and I was informed that it was out of alignment, and they could not bring it to within specs. The fix was a total rear suspension replacement.... I now have a front strut bearing gone and have been waiting 2 months for parts...with my front end alignment out because of this, and no word on part arrival.

Engine piston slap; blown engine head gasket; power-steering failure; unstable front seats; seat belts snap back so quickly that they can cause injury; bottom of the windshield may be distorted; and tire-pressure indicator malfunctions.

ALTIMA ★★★★

RATING: Above Average. **Strong points:** A powerful 4-cylinder engine that delivers good fuel economy, and an even better V6 that provides scintillating acceleration while sipping fuel; flawless automatic transmission shifting; good braking; well laid-out instruments and controls; and better-than-average interior room. The 2.5 S handles well and is relatively softly sprung, whereas the 3.5 SE corners better but delivers a stiffer, more-jittery ride. Quality problems have abated during the last two model years. NHTSA gave the two-door Altima five stars for side and rollover crash protection; four stars were awarded for front crashworthiness. The four-door version got five stars for front crash protection and four stars for rollover protection. IIHS scored frontal offset and side crash protection as "Good," and head restraints as "Acceptable." **Weak points:** Pricier 3.5 SE models come equipped with a firmer suspension and wider tires that degrade ride comfort. Electronic stability control isn't available with the base model. Limited rear headroom; snug rear seating for three adults; and the 3-year/60,000 km warranty is too short. *Hybrid:* Less fuel savings than advertised; a small trunk; and cycling between gasoline and electric power is a bit rough. **New for 2010:** An all-new SR model and a restyled front end.

KEY FACTS

PRICES: $22,698–$32,298 **FREIGHT:** $1,400 **ORIGIN:** Japan **SALES:** Down 30%
POWERTRAIN (FRONT-DRIVE)
Engines: 2.5L 4-cyl. (175 hp) • 2.5L 4-cyl. (198 hp) • 3.5L V6 (270 hp); Transmissions: 6-speed man. • CVT
DIMENSIONS/CAPACITY (2.5S)
Passengers: 2/3; Wheelbase: 109 in.; H: 58/L: 190/W: 71. in.; Headroom F/R: 4.5/2.0 in.; Legroom F/R: 41.5/29 in.; Cargo volume: 8–15.3 cu. ft.; Fuel tank: 76L/regular; Tow limit: 1,000 lb.; Load capacity: 900 lb.; Turning circle: 39 ft.; Ground clearance: 4.0 in.; Weight: t3,115 lb.

OVERVIEW: Nissan's front-drive, mid-sized sedan stakes out the territory occupied by the Honda Accord, Mazda6, and Toyota Camry. The car's base 4-cylinder engine is almost as powerful as the competition's V6 powerplants, and the optional 270 hp 3.5L V6 has few equals among cars in this price and size class. And, when you consider that the Altima is much lighter than most of its competitors, it's obvious why this car produces sizzling (and sometimes uncontrollable) acceleration with little fuel penalty. Four-wheel independent suspension strikes the right balance between a comfortable ride and sporty handling. The 3.5 S, 3.5 SE, and new-for-2010 SR models add even more performance and luxury enhancements.

COST ANALYSIS: No need to buy a 2010 model; a discounted 2009 equipped with the V6 engine is just as good—and cheaper, as well. **Best alternatives:** The Honda Accord, Hyundai Elantra or Sonata, Mazda6, and Toyota Camry. **Options:** Watch out for option loading after you agree to a reasonable base price. Canny Nissan sales agents pretend that some options *must* be purchased, or that some can't be bought without having others included. **Rebates:** $3,000 rebates or discounts and zero percent financing on fully loaded models. Attractive leasing deals are also common. **Depreciation:** Slower than average, especially the much-coveted V6-equipped models. For example, a 2006 SE-R high-performance model is still worth almost half its $36,000 original cost. **Insurance cost:** Higher than average. **Parts supply/cost:** Slightly higher than average, but most parts are easily found. **Annual maintenance cost:** Average. **Warranty:** Bumper-to-bumper 3 years/60,000 km; powertrain 5 years/100,000 km; rust perforation 5 years/unlimited km. **Supplementary warranty:** Not needed. **City/highway fuel economy:** *2.5 S:* 8.9/6.1 L/100 km. *2.5 S CVT:* 8.9/6.3 L/100 km. *3.5 S, 3.5 SE CVT:* 10.7/7.7 L/100 km. *3.5 SE manual:* 11.4/7.3 L/100 km.

OWNER-REPORTED PROBLEMS: Passenger-side airbags are disabled even though an average-sized adult is seated; a fusible link failure may cause the vehicle to shut down completely; transmission popped out of gear; and faulty tire stems and tire-pressure sensors cause tires to leak air.

MAXIMA ★★★★

RATING: Above Average. **Strong points:** Competent powertrain performance, decent handling, and a comfortable ride. Last year's redesign didn't degrade quality, as evidenced by the small number of safety- and performance-related complaints reported to public and governmental agencies. **Weak points:** Handling is a bit ponderous when compared with the competition; 18-inch tires produce high-speed tire whine; tall occupants may find rear seating a bit cramped; the latest redesign produced a shorter, though wider, car; small trunk opening limits what luggage you can carry; requires premium fuel; and many incidents of the SkyView roof suddenly shattering. **New for 2010:** Refinements to the exterior, interior, and option packages.

OVERVIEW: After its recent redesign, the front-drive, mid-sized Maxima soldiers on as Nissan's luxury flagship, a competent and roomy sedan that's a mini-step above the bestselling Altima. Its 290 hp 3.5L V6 is coupled to a continuously variable automatic transmission, and it comes with an impressive array of standard equipment and a host of performance and safety features, such as large front brakes with full

KEY FACTS

PRICES: $37,000–$43,150 **FREIGHT:** $1,425 **ORIGIN:** Japan **SALES:** Up 5%

POWERTRAIN (FRONT-DRIVE)

Engine: 3.5L V6 (290 hp); Transmission: CVT

DIMENSIONS/CAPACITY

Passengers: 2/3; Wheelbase: 109 in.; H: 58/L: 191/W: 73 in.; Headroom F/R: 3.0/2.5 in.; Legroom F/R: 43.9/ 36.5 in.; Cargo volume: 14.2 cu. ft.; Fuel tank: 76L/premium; Tow limit: 1,000 lb.; Load capacity: 900 lb.; Turning circle: 37.4 ft.; Ground clearance: 5.6 in.; Weight: 3,555 lb.

brake assist, a power driver's seat, xenon headlights, and 18-inch wheels. Granted, you get plenty of horsepower, comfort, and gadgets, but unfortunately the car isn't backed up with the technical refinements and quality components provided by its Honda and Toyota rivals.

COST ANALYSIS: The revamped 2009 is your best buy from a quality and cost perspective. **Best alternatives:** The Acura TSX, BMW 3 Series, and automatic transmission–equipped versions of the Honda Accord V6, Lexus IS, 5-speed Mazda6 GT V6, and Toyota Camry V6. **Options:** Traction control wouldn't be a bad idea if you are lead-footed; otherwise, keep things simple. **Rebates:** $3,500 discounts and low-interest financing and leasing in early 2010. **Depreciation:** Average. **Insurance cost:** Higher than average. **Parts supply/cost:** Moderate parts prices, and some powertrain parts may be back ordered. **Annual maintenance cost:** Average. **Warranty:** Bumper-to-bumper 3 years/60,000 km; powertrain 5 years/ 100,000 km; rust perforation 5 years/ unlimited km. **Supplementary warranty:** Not needed. **City/highway fuel economy:** 10.8/7.7 L/100 km.

OWNER-REPORTED PROBLEMS: Unstable driver's seat rocks back and forth; passenger-side airbag is disabled when the seat is occupied; electrical problems knock out the interior lights, door locks, and other controls; and the adjustable steering wheel may stick in its highest position.

QUEST

RATING: Below Average; a poor-quality embarrassment. **Strong points:** Soft prices are easily bargained down; smooth V6 engine; impressive highway performance (as long as you aren't carrying a full load); the 5-speed automatic transmission is smooth and quiet; braking performance is quite good (when the brakes are working properly); and NHTSA crashworthiness scores are almost perfect: five stars for front and side protection, and four stars for rollover resistance. Highway stability is above reproach, aided by excellent forward visibility and easy, no-surprise, carlike handling. Occupants get a comfortable ride with lots of seating choices, wide side sliding doors, second- and third-row seats that fold flat when not in use, small handgrips that are easily accessed by children, and an airy cabin that provides plenty of passenger and cargo room. **Weak points:** The electrical system, braking components, and fit and finish are all subpar and not dependable. Plus, these fuel-thirsty minivans are heavyweights that the 3.5L 235 hp engine has to go all out to carry. The powertrain set-up trails the Honda Odyssey in acceleration and passing. Other minuses: a soft suspension that bottoms out on rough roads; a quirky dash and cheap-looking interior styling; an instrument panel that produces windshield glare; a thick pillar that obstructs over-left-shoulder visibility; a control layout that can be a bit confusing; a heavy third-row seat; and excessive engine, wind, and road noise. Buyers also deserve a longer base warranty to fix the many factory glitches that inevitably appear. IIHS rated head-restraint effectiveness as "Poor." **New for 2010:** The Quest is moving from stateside production to Japanese production, so until we get a brand new model, the Nissan Quest will continue to be sold as a 2009 through early 2010. It may be replaced by a new, highly styled crossover-type vehicle.

KEY FACTS

PRICES: $29,998–$44,998 **FREIGHT:** $1,450 **ORIGIN:** Japan **SALES:** Down 52%
POWERTRAIN (FRONT-DRIVE)
Engine: 3.5L V6 (235 hp); Transmission: 5-speed auto.
DIMENSIONS/CAPACITY
Passengers: 2/2/3; Wheelbase: 124 in.; H: 70/L: 204/W: 78 in.; Headroom F/R1/R2: 5.5/8.5/2.0 in.; Legroom F/R1/R2: 40/33/27 in.; Cargo volume: 60 cu. ft.; Fuel tank: 76L/regular; Tow limit: 3,500 lb.; Load capacity: 1,205 lb.; Turning circle: 45 ft.; Ground clearance: 4.5 in.; Weight: 4,550 lb.

OVERVIEW: The 2009 Quest is one of the most stylish, smoothest-running, and (sigh) priciest minivans on the road. Set on the Altima/Murano platform, it offers all the standard high-tech safety, performance, and convenience features one could want. Its long wheelbase allows for the widest-opening sliding doors among front-drive minivans, rear-seating access is a breeze, and a capacious interior allows for flexible cargo and passenger configurations that can easily accommodate 4' × 8' objects with the liftgate closed. Standard fold-flat third-row seats and fold-to-the-floor centre-row seats allow owners to increase storage space without worrying about where to store the extra seats; head restraints must be removed before the seats can be folded away.

Although it feels a bit heavy in the city, the Quest is very carlike when driven on the highway. Ride and handling are enhanced by a four-wheel independent suspension, along with front and rear stabilizer bars and upgraded anti-lock brakes.

COST ANALYSIS: A 2009 with a 30 percent or higher discount would be your best bet. If a redesigned 2010 model does come out, run for the hills. Nissan's last redesign of the Quest for 2005 took engineers three years to correct. Delay your purchase until mid-2010 so as to take advantage of the expected huge discounts and rebates given out as Nissan struggles to liquidate the huge buildup of Quest inventory. **Best alternatives:** The Honda Odyssey, Chrysler minivans, Mazda5, and Toyota Sienna. **Options:** Nothing really worthwhile; run-flat tires may cause more problems than they are worth. **Rebates:** Expect huge discounts as dealers try to unload this beast before it is euthanized or replaced: about $5,000 in early 2010. **Depreciation:** Much faster than average. Imagine: A 2006 entry-level Quest that originally sold for $32,000 is now worth barely a third of that amount. **Insurance cost:** Higher than average. **Parts supply/cost:** Parts are often on back order and can be expensive. **Annual maintenance cost:** Average. **Warranty:** Bumper-to-bumper 3 years/60,000 km; powertrain 5 years/100,000 km; rust perforation 5 years/unlimited km. **Supplementary warranty:** An extended warranty isn't needed. **Maintenance/repair costs:** Higher than average. **City/highway fuel economy:** 12.9/8.4 L/100 km.

OWNER-REPORTED PROBLEMS: Chronic problems with the electrical and climate control systems, brakes, and body fit and finish.

ROGUE ★★★★

RATING: Above Average. More car than truck. **Strong points:** Standard features abound, with stability control, curtain airbags, active head restraints, and anti-lock brakes. The fuel-thrifty 2.5L 4-banger gets a bit noisy when pushed, but the fuel savings are worth it. The quiet-running CVT transmission smoothes out the power delivery. Handling is a pleasure. Well-crafted interior, comfortable front seating, and impressive braking. Interestingly, fit and finish elicits few complaints, whereas this has been a chronic problem with Nissan's other models. NHTSA gives the 2010 Rogue five stars for side crashworthiness and four stars for rollover resistance. IIHS gave its top, "Good" rating for frontal offset, side, and head-restraint protection. **Weak points:** Some of the standard features are fairly basic, and those that are in the premium packages should be standard; engine sounds like a diesel when accelerating, and it could use a bit more "grunt"; lacks cargo space and rear-seat versatility; and poor rearward visibility. **New for 2010:** Chrome door handles, and a Value Package option.

KEY FACTS

PRICES: $23,798–$28,398 **FREIGHT:** $1,500 **ORIGIN:** Ontario **SALES:** Up 2%

POWERTRAIN (FRONT-DRIVE/AWD)

Engine: 2.5L 4-cyl. (170 hp); Transmission: CVT

DIMENSIONS/CAPACITY

Passengers: 2/3; Wheelbase: 106 in.; H: 65/L: 183/W: 71 in.; Headroom F/R: 3.5/4.0 in.; Legroom F/R: 42/30 in.; Cargo volume: 24.5 cu. ft.; Fuel tank: 60L/regular; Tow limit: 1,500 lb.; Load capacity: 900 lb.; Turning circle: 37.4 ft.; Ground clearance: 8.3 in.; Weight: 3,535 lb.

OVERVIEW: This compact SUV is based on the Sentra sedan and gives carlike handling and better fuel economy than the competition that's still wedded to truck platforms. Nevertheless, the Rogue's car DNA becomes all the more evident as the engine protests going through the upper reaches of the CVT when accelerating.

COST ANALYSIS: The 2009 model was redesigned, so paying more for an almost identical 2010 version doesn't make sense. Delay your purchase until early 2010 so as to take advantage of the inevitable discounts and rebates. **Best alternatives:** The Buick Enclave, GMC Acadia, Ford Escape, and Saturn Outlook. **Options:** Consider getting the top-drawer Bose audio system, but stay away from the failure-prone, expensive, and back-ordered run-flat tires. **Rebates:** $2,000 by late 2009, in addition to low-cost financing and leasing. **Depreciation:** Average. **Insurance cost:** Higher than average. **Parts supply/cost:** Parts are easily found in the Sentra bin, and are reasonably priced. **Annual maintenance cost:** Average. **Warranty:** Bumper-to-bumper 3 years/60,000 km; powertrain 5 years/100,000 km; rust perforation 5 years/unlimited km. **Supplementary warranty:** Not needed. **City/highway fuel economy:** *Front-drive:* 9.1/7.2 L/100 km. *AWD:* 9.4/7.7 L/100 km.

OWNER-REPORTED PROBLEMS: Early transmission failures; steering wheel, gear shifter, and brakes suddenly locked up; and tire-pressure monitoring systems are so sensitive that they often give false alerts, so drivers end up ignoring them.

MURANO ★★★★

RATING: Above Average. **Strong points:** Nicely equipped with a refined, responsive powertrain that includes a smooth V6 coupled to a quiet CVT transmission; sports car–like performance; a plush, easily accessed, comfortable, and roomy interior; standard stability control; a comfortable ride, good fuel economy; no-surprise, responsive carlike handling; and better-than-average reliability. NHTSA gives the Murano five stars for side crash protection and four stars for frontal and rollover crashworthiness. At IIHS, the Murano gets "Good," a perfect score, for frontal offset, side, and head-restraint protection. **Weak points:** Cargo space behind the second row is less than the competition's; limited rear visibility; and requires premium fuel. **New for 2010:** LE model added; standard security system and roof rails on the SL, and a moonroof on the LE.

KEY FACTS

PRICES: $37,648–$47,498 **FREIGHT:** $1,500 **ORIGIN:** Japan **SALES:** Down 30%

POWERTRAIN (FRONT-DRIVE/AWD)

Engine: 3.5L V6 (265 hp); Transmission: CVT

DIMENSIONS/CAPACITY

Passengers: 2/3; Wheelbase: 111 in.; H: 67/L: 189/W: 74 in.; Headroom F/R: 3.0/3.0 in.; Legroom F/R: 40.5/28 in.; Cargo volume: 31 cu. ft.; Fuel tank: 82L/premium; Tow limit: 3,500 lb.; Load capacity: 900 lb.; Turning circle: 40 ft.; Ground clearance: 6.5 in.; Weight: 4,190 lb.

OVERVIEW: The mid-size Murano continues to be the car-based "ying" to the Pathfinder's truck-based "yang." Both vehicles embody strong, in-your-face styling and are loaded with many standard safety, performance, and convenience features.

COST ANALYSIS: The 2009 model was redesigned, so paying more for an almost identical 2010 version doesn't make sense. Delay your purchase until early 2010 so as to take advantage of the inevitable discounts and rebates—in addition to allowing time for the redesign factory glitches to be corrected. **Best alternatives:** The Buick Enclave, GMC Acadia, and Saturn Outlook. **Options:** Don't buy the failure-prone, expensive, and back-ordered run-flat tires. **Rebates:** $3,000 by late 2009. **Depreciation:** Average. **Insurance cost:** Higher than average. **Parts supply/cost:** Parts are sometimes hard to find and can be costly. **Annual maintenance cost:** Higher than average. **Warranty:** Bumper-to-bumper 3 years/60,000 km; powertrain 5 years/100,000 km; rust perforation 5 years/unlimited km. **Supplementary warranty:** Not needed. **City/highway fuel economy:** *Front-drive:* 11.8/8.7 L/100 km.

OWNER-REPORTED PROBLEMS: Generally, owners have pointed out frequent brake replacements (calipers and rotors) and poor body fit and finish, including paint defects and water/air leaks. Other concerns: Airbag warning light comes on continually, even after multiple resets by the dealer; vehicle rolls down incline when stopped in traffic; Check Engine light comes on after each fill-up (cap must be resealed); headlights may suddenly shut off; the Start/Stop ignition button can be accidently pressed, and this can suddenly shut down the vehicle when it's underway; remote-controlled door locks operate erratically; inoperative sunroof; and excessive vibration (fixed by reducing tire pressure from 41 psi to 36 psi).

Nissan/Suzuki

FRONTIER/EQUATOR

RATING: Recommended. **Strong points:** Well equipped; carries a powerful V6, with more horsepower than any other V6 engine in its class; the 4-cylinder engine is acceptable for light chores; handling is quick and nimble; an accommodating interior; plenty of storage in the centre console; and outstanding reliability. NHTSA gives the Frontier and Equator four stars for frontal crash protection and three stars for rollover crashworthiness. **Weak points:** Ride is a bit stiff; stability control is optional; rear seatroom is tight in the Crew Cab; and you'll need to eat your Wheaties before attempting to lift the tailgate. **New for 2010:** Standard side curtain airbags on all models; Vehicle Dynamic Control on V6-equipped models.

KEY FACTS

PRICES: $22,598–$39,198 **FREIGHT:** $1,440 **ORIGIN:** Japan **SALES:** *Frontier:* Down 50%, *Equator:* N/A

POWERTRAIN (FRONT-DRIVE/AWD)

Engines: 2.5L 4-cyl. (152 hp) • 4.0L V6 (261 hp); Transmissions: 5-speed man. • 6-speed man. • 5-speed auto.

DIMENSIONS/CAPACITY

Passengers: 2/3; Wheelbase: 125.9 in.; H: 68.7/L: 205.5/W: 72.8 in.; Headroom F/R: 3.0/3.5 in.; Legroom F/R: 40/27 in.; Cargo volume: 60 cu. ft.; Fuel tank: 80L/regular; Tow limit: 3,500–6,500 lb.; Load capacity: 967–1,455 lb.; Turning circle: 43.3 ft.; Ground clearance: 8.7 in.; Weight: 3,716 lb.

OVERVIEW: This year's Frontier continues to be joined by its Suzuki twin, the Equator. They are gutsy pickups that are compact in name only. The PRO-4X model offers serious off-road features seldom found among compact trucks, like a locking rear differential, Bilstein dampers, and skid plates.

COST ANALYSIS: For the same model year, and almost identical pickup, Suzuki dealers are more amenable to haggling than the Nissan crowd. A cheaper 2009 Frontier/Equator will give most everything that's offered with the 2010 version. Delay your purchase until early 2010 so as to take advantage of the inevitable discounts and rebates. **Best alternatives:** The Mazda B-Series and Toyota Tacoma. **Options:** Run away from the failure-prone, expensive, and back-ordered run-flat tires. **Rebates:** $3,000 by late 2009. **Depreciation:** Average. **Insurance cost:** Higher than average. **Parts supply/cost:** Parts are everywhere, and they don't cost much. The Frontier shares many parts with the Pathfinder, Xterra, and Titan. **Annual maintenance cost:** Average. **Warranty:** Bumper-to-bumper 3 years/60,000 km; powertrain 5 years/100,000 km; rust perforation 5 years/unlimited km. **Supplementary warranty:** Not needed. **Maintenance/repair costs:** Less than average. **City/highway fuel economy:** *2.5L manual:* 10.7/8.7 L/100 km. *2.5L automatic*: 12.6/9.2 L/100 km. *4.0L manual*: 13.5/10.0 L/100 km. *4.0L automatic:* 14.4/10.0 L/100 km.

OWNER-REPORTED PROBLEMS: Faulty fuel-level sending unit sensor:

I went online to *Nissanhelp.com* after performing a search, I came across many others who have experienced the same problem. Apparently it has something to do with the fuel sending unit. A similar problem was found on the 2000–2004 Xterra models and a recall was performed when the vehicle would stop after not getting any fuel.

Subaru

Whenever I see a Subaru passing, my thoughts turn to the musical *The Music Man*. In the early '90s, no one believed in an ugly little import called the Subaru. And then along came Malcolm Bricklin, part genius and part flim-flam entrepreneur. He brought Subaru to North America, but by 1995, Subaru realized it was losing the battle with Honda and Toyota for buyers of its front-drive compact cars, so it bet the farm on building versatile and reasonably priced all-wheel-drive Outback and Forester models—and on Paul Hogan (a.k.a. Crocodile Dundee), an Australian actor *cum* Subaru pitchman. Sales soared, with most cars selling close to their MSRP and keeping much of their value come trade-in time.

Even in these hard economic times, when nine out of 10 automaker's models are in the cellar, buyers are clamouring for Subaru's all-wheel-drive Forester, Impreza, and Legacy. And the company doesn't intend to risk its success with any dramatic changes: Subaru's overall product lineup this year stands pat, with most of the redesigns and styling changes scheduled for 2011 and later.

Although all Subarus provide full-time AWD capability, studies show that most owners don't need the off-road prowess; only 5 percent will ever use their Subaru for off-roading. The other 95 percent just like knowing they have the option of going wherever they please, whenever they please—and they don't seem to care that an AWD burns about 2 percent more fuel. And, as one retired Quebec mechanic told me: "All-wheel drive simply means that you will get stuck deeper, further from home. It's no replacement for common sense."

FORESTER, IMPREZA, WRX, STI ★★★★ / ★★★ / ★

RATING: *Forester:* Above Average. *Impreza:* Average. *WRX and STI:* Not Recommended. The Forester and WRX have been downgraded mainly because the competition has raised the performance and reliability bar, while Subaru simply coasts along as it adds more expensive standard features. **Strong points:** Impressive acceleration with the base 2.5L engine; however, the WRX, STI, and STI Limited sedans have even more powerful 305 hp engines. But with that power comes complexity, requiring good access to parts and service that is frequently lacking. Competent handling, without any torque steer; Forester passengers are spoiled by agile and secure handling, thanks to a tight turning circle; a roomy cabin; lots of storage space with the wagons; a nice control layout; and average

KEY FACTS

PRICES: *Forester:* $25,795–$34,895, *Impreza:* $20,995, *WRX:* $30,995, *STI:* $39,995 **FREIGHT:** $1,495 **ORIGIN:** Japan
SALES: *Forester:* Up 28%, *Impreza:* Up 2%
POWERTRAIN (AWD)
Engines: 2.5L 4-cyl. (170 hp) • 2.5L 4-cyl. Turbo (224 hp) • 2.5L 4-cyl. Turbo (305 hp); Transmissions: 5-speed man. • 6-speed man. • 4-speed auto.
DIMENSIONS/CAPACITY (FORESTER)
Passengers: 2/3; Wheelbase: 103 in.; H: 66/L: 180/W: 70 in.; Headroom F/R: 6.5/6.5 in.; Legroom F/R: 41/29.5 in.; Cargo volume: 35.5 cu. ft.; Fuel tank: 64L/reg./prem.; Tow limit: 2,400 lb.; Load capacity: 900 lb.; Turning circle: 34 ft.; Weight: 3,235 lb.

quality control. Impressive NHTSA crash test results. *Forester and Impreza:* Five stars for front and side crash protection, and four stars for rollover resistance. The Forester also excelled in IIHS crash tests, getting the Institute's top, "Good," mark for frontal offset, side, and head-restraint protection and for roof strength. The Impreza WRX would likely post similar results. **Weak points:** Keep in mind, there is nothing remarkable about Subaru's lineup except for the inclusion of AWD in all models. If you don't need the AWD capability, you're wasting your money. Last year's extra height and ground clearance and increased suspension travel create more body roll when cornering; AWD cuts fuel economy; the outdated 4-speed automatic transmission shifts roughly and wastes fuel; and the Outback Sport doesn't ride as comfortably or handle as well as other Imprezas. There's also problematic entry and exit, and the seats require additional lumbar bolstering. WRX and STI require premium fuel. **New for 2010:** A slightly restyled Impreza.

OVERVIEW: The Forester is a cross between a wagon and a sport-utility. Based on the shorter Impreza, it uses the Legacy Outback's 2.5L engine, or an optional turbocharged version of the same powerplant, coupled to a 5-speed manual transmission or an optional 4-speed automatic. Its road manners are more subdued, and its engine provides plenty of power and torque for off-roading.

Redesigned last year, the Forester now comes with a roomier rear seat; an upgraded interior; standard curtain airbags; more-responsive, precise steering with greater road feel; and a much more comfortable ride. Its two "boxer" 4-cylinder engines are both competitive in terms of power and fuel economy, despite being coupled to an outmoded 4-speed automatic transmission.

The Impreza is essentially a shorter Legacy with additional convenience features. It comes as a four-door sedan, a wagon, and an Outback Sport wagon, all powered by a 170 hp 2.5L flat-four engine or a 224 hp turbocharged 2.5L. The rally-inspired WRX models have a more-powerful turbocharged engine—a 305 hp 2.5L variant—lots of standard performance features, a sport suspension, an aluminum hood with functional scoop, and higher-quality instruments, controls, trim, and seats.

COST ANALYSIS: Be wary of Subaru's high-performance WRX and STI models. They require special parts and specialized mechanical know-how that may be hard to find in these trouble times. Instead, buy an upgraded 2009 Forester or Impreza, preferably one made in mid 2009, and haggle for a 10 percent discount. Remember, WRX versions are expensive, problematic Imprezas, but when they run right, they'll equal the sporty performance of most of the entry-level Audis and BMWs—cars that cost thousands of dollars more. **Best alternatives:** If you don't really need a 4×4, here are some front-drives worth considering: the Honda Civic, Hyundai Elantra, Mazda6, and Toyota Corolla or Matrix (and any leftover GM Vibes). **Rebates:** $1,000 rebates, and low-interest financing. **Options:** Larger tires to smooth out the ride. **Depreciation:** Slower than average, and faster than average. Foresters hold their value best: A 2006 Forester that originally sold for $28,000 is still worth a respectable $13,000. But WRX models lose their value quickly: A 2006 entry-level WRX that sold for $35,500 is now worth $14,000. **Insurance cost:** Higher than average. **Parts supply/cost:** Parts aren't easy to find, and they can be costly; expect delayed recall repairs. **Annual maintenance cost:** Higher than average. Mediocre, expensive servicing is hard to overcome because independent garages can't service Subaru AWD powertrains and turbochargers. **Warranty:** Bumper-to-bumper 3 years/60,000 km; powertrain 5 years/100,000 km; rust perforation 5 years/unlimited km. **Supplementary warranty:** Quality control and customer service could be better. Protect yourself with an extended powertrain warranty. **City/highway fuel economy:** *Base 2.5L manual:* 10.7/7.5 L/100 km. *Base 2.5L automatic:* 10.4/7.8 L/100 km. *2.5L turbo manual:* 12.0/8.3 L/100 km. *2.5L turbo automatic:* 11.4/8.5 L/100 km.

OWNER-REPORTED PROBLEMS: Many complaints of sudden, unintended acceleration:

> While driving approximately 15 mph [24 km/h] on normal road conditions, there was sudden, aggressive, and forceful acceleration. The driver immediately depressed the brake pedal, but there was no response. The driver placed the gear shifter into Park, but the vehicle failed to slow down. The vehicle crashed into a brick wall. The failure occurred without warning. The police and ambulance were called to the scene and a police report was filed. The driver sustained severe back injuries. The vehicle was completely destroyed.

When accelerating, there's also a serious shift lag, then the vehicle surges ahead; defective engine had to be replaced; head restraints push head forward at an uncomfortable angle, causing neck strain and backache; and the moonroof system cavity allows debris and small animals to enter between the headliner and interior walls—the perfect place for fungi and mould to incubate.

LEGACY, OUTBACK ★★★

RATING: Average. This car is all about full-time all-wheel drive. It handles difficult terrain without the fuel penalty or clumsiness of many truck-based SUVs. Without the AWD, the Outback would be just a raised wagon variant that's well equipped but outclassed by most of the import competition. **Strong points:** A refined and reliable AWD system; a well-balanced 6-cylinder engine; precise, responsive handling, and a comfortable ride; interior materials and fit and finish have been substantially upgraded; standard electronic stability control; the GT version handles best and has power to spare; and lots of cargo room. NHTSA gives the

KEY FACTS

PRICES: $23,995–$38,395 **FREIGHT:** $1,495 **ORIGIN:** Japan **SALES:** Down 5%
POWERTRAIN (AWD)
Engines: 2.5L 4-cyl. (170 hp) • 2.5L 4-cyl. Turbo (265 hp) • 3.6L V6 (256 hp); Transmissions: 5-speed man. • 6-speed man. • 4-speed auto. • 5-speed auto. • CVT
DIMENSIONS/CAPACITY
Passengers: 2/3; Wheelbase: 105 in.; H: 56/L: 186/W: 68 in.; Headroom F/R: 3.0/1.0 in.; Legroom F/R: 41/28 in.; Cargo volume: 14.7 cu. ft.; Fuel tank: 70L/reg./prem.; Tow limit: 2,700; Load capacity: 850 lb.; Turning circle: 36.8 ft.; Ground clearance: 8.7; Weight: 3,540 lb.

Legacy five stars for front and side protection; rollover resistance scored four stars. IIHS gives it its top, "Good" rating for frontal offset, side, and rollover crash protection. **Weak points:** The base 2.5L engine is a sluggish performer, undoubtedly because of the car's heft. On the other hand, the more-powerful GT version is a fuel hog. Fuel economy, though improved for 2010, still trails rivals like the Toyota Camry, Chevrolet Malibu, and Ford Fusion. Another mixed blessing: The stability control feature (VDC) adds exponential complexity to a vehicle that is already complicated to repair. Other minuses: Crosswinds require constant steering correction; excessive engine and road noise; limited rear access; front seats need more padding; interior garnishes look and feel cheap; stereo dials are minuscule; entertainment system doesn't let you change playlists, albums, or artists unless the car is stopped; the Mazda6 and Ford Fusion offer more cargo space; the V6 engine requires premium fuel; and these cars are very dealer-dependent for parts and servicing. God help you if the dealer goes under, or you need parts when dealers are cutting back on inventory. **New for 2010:** A bigger back seat with more legroom and thigh support; new doors with window frames; the active head restraints have been changed for new, whiplash-mitigating head restraints; and improved fuel economy.

OVERVIEW: A competent, full-time 4×4 performer for drivers who want to move up in size, comfort, and features. Available as a four-door sedan or five-door wagon, the Legacy is cleanly and conventionally styled, with a hint of the Acura Legend in the rear end.

Legacy spec.B sedan

For 2010, the current spec.B—a real sleeper—has a firmer ride calibration. The spec.B mid-sized sedan comes equipped with a high-performance variant of the turbocharged 2.5L engine. It is mated to the same 6-speed manual transmission that is found in the WRX STI and comes with a Bilstein sport suspension. The spec.B also has a feature called SI-Drive (short for Subaru Intelligent Drive), which is a rotary dial that allows the driver to select one of three engine performance settings. Subaru's continuing to sell the spec.B in Canada is good news for enthusiasts who need a little more space and comfort with their AWD performance car than what is offered with the WRX.

COST ANALYSIS: Get an upgraded 2010 model; it is projected to cost about $1,000 less than last year's version. **Best alternatives:** The Honda CR-V, Hyundai Tucson or Santa Fe, and Toyota RAV4. **Options:** Base models hooked to an automatic transmission are severely performance-challenged. Stay away from the Firestone and Bridgestone original-equipment tires. **Rebates:** $2,000, and low-interest financing. **Depreciation:** Slower than average. **Insurance cost:** Average. **Parts supply/cost:** Parts aren't easily found, and they can be costly. **Annual maintenance cost:** Average. **Warranty:** Bumper-to-bumper 3 years/60,000 km; powertrain 5 years/100,000 km; rust perforation 5 years/unlimited km. **Supplementary warranty:** A good idea. **City/highway fuel economy:** *Base 2.5L:* 10.6/7.5 L/100 km. *3.0L:* 12.1/8.3 L/100 km.

OWNER-REPORTED PROBLEMS: Owners complain about poorly designed head restraints, showing this to be a problem with 2009 models that affects more than just the Forester (the 2010 head restraints have been redesigned):

> 2009, head rests are so uncomfortable I am actually developing lower back pain for the first time in my life. You have sacrificed [the prevention of] permanent disabling back problems for a safety issue. The head is pushed too far forward, straining my neck.

Owners have to pay $50 twice per year to have the federally mandated tire-pressure monitoring system reset:

> There is no customer reset for this federal mandated device on my 2009 Subaru Legacy. I have to pay $50.00 each time to have it reset at the dealer when I change tires in the spring and fall. Thanks a lot for this fix that was not thought out by my elected representatives.

Suzuki

Suzuki, like Mitsubishi, is on its last legs in North America. Sales have been dismal since 2003. The company has little product available, except for a three-year-old SX4 crossover (the Aerio's replacement) and a new Equator light-duty pickup, which is really a rebadged Nissan Frontier (see the Frontier/Equator rating on page 300). Suzuki ditched its Swift, Vitara, and XL-7 models, and dealers are running for the hills.

All of this sounds hard to believe. After all, Suzuki has been making very good entry-level small cars and acceptable sport-utility vehicles for well over a decade—just the kinds of cars that should be hot sellers in a recession. But they aren't.

Suzuki proves that simply building good, cheap cars and SUVs isn't enough to succeed as an auto manufacturer in North America. You also have to have a large advertising budget and almost perfect timing in your launches and promotion. Suzuki never put much money into advertising, and it has had a revolving door of incompetent executives who have run the company into the ground. Most shoppers don't give the company a second thought, since many of its products were sold under GM's name. And many of those who do recognize the Suzuki badge blame the company for selling unreliable Daewoo entry-level compacts under its own name.

The Name Game

GM has long had a manufacturing and retail partnership with Suzuki. In 2002, GM bought a controlling interest in the assets of bankrupt Korean automaker Daewoo and convinced Suzuki Canada to sell two of the Daewoo cars as the Suzuki Swift+ (Aveo) and Verona (Epica). Prior to that deal, Suzuki had made considerable progress in raising its quality scores to a level that rivalled other Japanese models.

Unfortunately, Suzuki's rebadged Daewoo cars gave Suzuki a black eye in 2005, when J.D. Power announced that Suzuki had finished last in its Initial Quality Study of 36 nameplates. One of the cars that contributed most to the poor quality rating was the Suzuki Forenza, sold in Canada as the Optra. Suzuki never recovered from the bad publicity and poor administration. And as we go into another period of high fuel costs, where a rising tide should raise all compact-car-sales boats, Suzuki and Mitsubishi will probably be washed out to sea.

SX4 ★★★★

RATING: Above Average. This roomy little car is a winner because of its better-than-average overall performance, low price, and versatile body styles that rival many wagons and hatchbacks. What's worrisome is the company's huge losses and rumours that it will soon quit the North American market, where it has lost millions of dollars over the past seven years. **Strong points:** All models are bargain-priced, and they deliver a lot of content. On the road, the SX4 performs fairly well. Its lightweight and relatively powerful engine gets it quickly up to cruising speed; handling is fairly nimble; the automatic transmission shifts smoothly; the ride quality is good; and brakes are adequate, though a bit soft. The tall roofline ensures plenty of headroom for all passengers, makes for easy passenger access, and enhances overall visibility. There's a surprising amount of occupant and cargo room, and legroom is on par with or better than most of its competition. Lots of glass all around, making the cabin appear much larger than it is. ABS and front/side curtain airbags are standard. NHTSA gives the car five stars for side-impact occupant protection and four stars for frontal and rollover crashworthiness. IIHS rates frontal offset and side-impact crashworthiness as "Good." **Weak points:** Excessive engine and road noise, and the ride is jarring when passing over small bumps; fuel economy is sharply reduced with the AWD, but not so much with the automatic transmission; and stability control is optional. IIHS rates head-restraint protection as "Marginal." **New for 2010:** An SX4

SportBack model. Suzuki has also partnered with Garmin GPS to provide a standard navigation system for the SX4 Sport and Sport Touring models, making the SX4 the first vehicle for less than $16,000 (U.S.) to offer this feature standard in the States.

KEY FACTS

PRICES: $17,395–$23,195 **FREIGHT:** $1,395 **ORIGIN:** Japan **SALES:** Down 35%
POWERTRAIN (FRONT-DRIVE/AWD)
Engine: 2.0L 4-cyl. (143 hp); Transmissions: 5-speed man. • 4-speed auto.
DIMENSIONS/CAPACITY (BASE MODEL)
Passengers: 2/3; Wheelbase: 98.4 in.; H: 60.8/L: 177.6/W: 68.1 in., H: 60.8/ L: 162.8/W: 68.1 in.; Headroom F/R: 4.0/3.0 in.; Legroom F/R: 40/26 in.; Cargo volume: 15.5 cu. ft.; Fuel tank: 50L/regular; Tow limit: No towing; Load capacity: 815 lb.; Turning circle: 37 ft.; Ground clearance: 5.5 in.; Weight: 2,668 lb.

OVERVIEW: "The cure for the common Corolla," says *Car and Driver* magazine. Available in both front-drive and all-wheel-drive trims, the SX4 crossover is a fun-to-drive, inexpensive, small SUV-like hatchback with interior features and performance qualities that make it a great alternative to the top-ranked small cars. Practical dimensions, combined with a lengthy list of features and sporty dynamics, make the SX4 a good choice for anyone who's put off by the higher-priced competition. Reliability hasn't been a major issue, but a limited servicing network, less than average fuel economy, and a cheap-looking plastic-wrapped cabin has turned many buyers away.

COST ANALYSIS: Get the 2009 model, if it's offered with a 20 percent discount/rebate. **Best alternatives:** The Honda Fit or Civic, Mazda3, Nissan Versa or Rogue, and Toyota Yaris or Matrix are affordable alternatives that have more-established reputations. **Options:** Stay away from the Firestone and Bridgestone original-equipment tires. The Garmin GPS option looks like a real bargain. **Rebates:** $3,000 and low-interest financing. **Depreciation:** Higher than average. **Insurance cost:** Average. **Parts supply/cost:** Parts aren't easily found, and can be costly. **Annual maintenance cost:** Average. **Warranty:** Bumper-to-bumper 3 years/60,000 km; powertrain 5 years/100,000 km; rust perforation 5 years/unlimited km. **Supplementary warranty:** A good idea. **City/highway fuel economy:** Although these "official" fuel consumption figures shouldn't be trusted completely, it's interesting to see that the automatic transmission doesn't impose a fuel penalty with either the hatchback or the sedan. *Front-drive manual:* 9.2/6.5 L/100 km. *Front-drive automatic:* 9.0/6.5 L/100 km. *AWD:* 9.9/7.1 L/100 km.

OWNER-REPORTED PROBLEMS: Passenger Airbag warning light comes on randomly; tire-pressure monitoring system malfunctions and gives alert for no reason; fuel smell in the cabin; hard starting; condensation builds up in the AC and drips onto the floor when the car is shut down; rainwater cascades down from the roof and stains the upholstery whenever the door is opened; and paint is easily chipped, and the unprotected metal is quick to rust.

Toyota

Toyota Bounces Back

The biggest argument we have that American automakers aren't entirely responsible for their own demise is to look at the billions of dollars that Toyota has lost during the present recession, despite its popular car lineup and conservative, frugal ways.

Nevertheless, sales are back on an upswing for most automakers, and Toyota is coming back into the marketplace better positioned than ever. Its hybrid models are starting to pay off, and they now make an estimated profit of about $3,100 (U.S.) for each unit sold—an amount similar to what Toyota makes on small gasoline-powered vehicles. Toyota also has easy access to leasing and financing, which can be the ace up its sleeve in closing deals while money is tight.

Toyota Quality Myth

Toyota's image as a builder of quality vehicles has been legendary. Then in the late '90s, that reputation took a battering when angry owners refused to pay $6,000–$9,000 to repair sludged-up engines, used on most of Toyota's lineup. The company relented and quietly settled most claims (see *www.oilgelsettlement.com*).

More recently, Toyota has stonewalled owners over dangerously defective drivetrains that possibly affect all of its 1999–2009 lineup. A look at NHTSA's safety complaint database shows a ton of complaints alleging the vehicles have a "lag and lurch" problem when accelerating, decelerating, or turning.

> Difficulty shifting my 2004 Camry from Park to Reverse, then upon shifting into Drive the car accelerated uncontrollably, would not stop, collided with a mobile home, airbags did not deploy, resulting in the death of one passenger and injury of driver.

•

> My 2002 Lexus ES 300's transmission gets confused when shifting into and out of the lower gears, then spends too long trying to figure out what gear to be in. This causes dangerous delays in acceleration, the effect is the same as a momentary engine stall. We have had this happen on several occasions, freeway ramp entrances are certainly the most dangerous place that this has occurred. Dealer acknowledges that there have been complaints about the shifting delays but they say no fix is available. This is our third ES 300, the previous models used a cable between the gas pedal and the throttle, this new one uses what is called "fly by wire," a position sensor on the accelerator that a computer is supposed to use to figure out what to tell the engine and transmission. It isn't working very well. If not rectified, this problem will certainly lead to a crash someday—then we'll get to see how good the safety equipment is.

Yes, it does appear that Toyota has been skating on its reputation for the past few years, while Honda, Kia, Mazda, and Hyundai have continued to improve their overall quality.

A perusal of *Lemon-Aid* readers' letters and emails, as well as NHTSA reports, shows that recent-model Toyotas have been plagued by engineering mistakes that put occupants' lives in jeopardy. These include Corollas that wander all over the road, Prius hybrids that lose their brakes, and Tundra trucks with rear ends that bounce uncontrollably over even the smoothest roadways. Other safety failures include engine and transmission malfunctions; fuel spewing out of cracked gas tanks; sudden, unintended acceleration; gauge lights that can't be seen in daylight; and electrical system glitches that can transform a power door into a guillotine. This year's *Lemon-Aid* has lowered the ratings on a number of Toyota's most popular models to reflect these dangers and to warn buyers of the potential for harm.

When running properly, Toyotas do hold up very well over the years, are especially forgiving of owner neglect, and cost very little to service at independent garages. But the kicker for most buyers is how little most Toyotas depreciate; it's not unusual to see a five-year-old Camry or Avalon selling for over half its original selling price—a value reached by most Detroit Three vehicles after only their third year of ownership. But this is not the case with Toyota hybrids, which depreciate quite rapidly as word gets out that their fuel economy is not all that impressive when one considers that a $3,000 (U.S.) battery pack replacement can buy a lot of gas.

Hybrid

PRIUS ★★

RATING: Below Average. The 2009 Prius has some serious sudden acceleration, braking, and steering issues. I doubt all these issues were addressed in this recession-dominated model year. I am also concerned that dealers don't have the money to invest in Prius inventory, or to hire mechanics specialized in hybrid repairs. Bottom line: Don't buy a Prius until at least mid 2010. **Strong points:** Good fuel economy; much-improved acceleration and handling in most situations; smooth transition to battery-recharge mode; and less cabin noise. NHTSA gave Prius a five-star rating for side crash protection, and four stars for front-impact protection and rollover resistance. IIHS gave its top, "Good" rating for frontal offset, side, and head-restraint protection. **Weak points:** It's pricey—Honda's Insight sells for about $3,500 less. Poorer performance in cold weather; battery pack will eventually cost about $3,000 (U.S.) to replace; fuel

KEY FACTS

PRICES: $27,500–$36,565 **FREIGHT:** $1,420 **ORIGIN:** Japan **SALES:** Down 29%
POWERTRAIN (FRONT-DRIVE)
Engine: 1.8L 4-cyl. (134 hp); Transmission: CVT
DIMENSIONS/CAPACITY
Passengers: 2/3; Wheelbase: 106.3 in.; H: 58.3/L: 175.6/W: 68.7 in.; Headroom F/R: 4.0/2.0 in.; Legroom F/R: 40.5/30 in.; Cargo volume: 15.7 cu. ft.; Fuel tank: 45L/regular; Tow limit: No towing; Load capacity: 810 lb.; Turning circle: 34.2 ft.; Ground clearance: 5.5 in.; Weight: 3,042 lb.

economy may be 20 percent less than advertised; 50 percent depreciation after three years; higher-than-average insurance premiums; dealer-dependent servicing means higher servicing costs; rear seating is cramped for three adults; sales and servicing may not be available outside of large urban areas; and the CVT cannot be easily repaired by independent agencies. Owners say the Prius is slow-steering, has lots of body roll when cornering, and is stall-prone. Braking isn't very precise or responsive, and the car is very unstable when hit by crosswinds. Highway rescuers are wary of the car's 500-volt electrical system, and are taking special courses to prevent electrocution and avoid toxic battery components. Reliability data is a mixed bag. **New for 2010:** The 1.5L 4-cylinder engine is replaced by a more fuel-efficient 1.8L 4-banger. Toyota offers what it says is an improved nickel-metal hydride (NiMH) battery. There are three new driving modes the driver may "dial in": Depending on your driving situation, you can now select from EV, Eco, and Power modes. Improved ride and handling; the top of the roof has been pushed back about 10 cm (4 in.); rear lights use LED bulbs; headlights have a blue-tinted lens; a small increase in length and width; cabin's centre stack is now a storage bin; dials and controls seem more upscale; and displays are easier to see.

OVERVIEW: This third-generation Prius contains a 1.8L DOHC 16-valve 4-cylinder engine. It may sound hard to believe, but the bigger engine doesn't have to work as hard. So at highway speeds, the lower rpms save about 1.3 km/L (3 mpg). The gasoline engine delivers a total of 98 hp, and when combined with the hybrid system, you get 134 hp—24 more horses than with last year's model. The Prius is now approaching the Camry in size, and its powerplant is more sophisticated, powerful, and efficient than what you get with similar vehicles in the marketplace. Interestingly, because the car relies primarily on electrical energy, fuel economy is better in the city than on the highway—the opposite of what one finds with gasoline-powered vehicles.

An electric motor is the main power source, and it uses an innovative and fairly reliable CVT for smooth and efficient shifting (these transmissions have been troublesome when used on Detroit cars, like the Saturn Vue). The motor is used mainly for acceleration, with the gasoline engine kicking in when needed to provide power. Braking automatically shuts off the engine, as the electric motor acts as a generator to replenish the environmentally "unfriendly" NiMH battery pack. Interestingly, this year's Solar Panels option uses solar energy to keep the vehicle cool when it's parked.

COST ANALYSIS: Buy the 2010 late in the year for all of the powertain, safety, and convenience improvements, after allowing the factory time to fix the glitches caused by this year's revamping. Delivery delays have shortened; nevertheless, ask the dealer to give you a "protected" price to prevent price gouging from the time the contract is signed to when the car is delivered. **Best alternatives:** The Honda Civic, Fit, or Insight; Hyundai Accent; Nissan Versa; and Toyota Yaris. In a Prius versus Insight match-up, the Prius gets better fuel economy but is more expensive. The Insight, despite its fewer horses, is more fun to drive, though it's not as fast as the Prius. **Options:** Stability control, and the 17-inch wheels will add to your driving pleasure with a quicker steering response and better road feedback. **Rebates:** The Prius' popularity rises and falls in tandem with fuel prices, so $1,000 maximum rebates will quickly come and go. **Depreciation:** Unbelievably fast. A 2003 Prius that sold for $30,000 is now worth about $8,000, or just over a quarter of its original price; a similar Honda Accord EX sold originally for $1,000 less and is now worth $3,000 more ($11,000). **Insurance cost:** Higher than average. **Parts supply/cost:** Parts aren't easily found, and they can be costly. **Annual maintenance cost:** Average, so far. **Warranty:** Bumper-to-bumper 3 years/60,000 km; powertrain 5 years/100,000 km; hybrid-related components (battery, battery-control module, inverter with converter) 8 years/unlimited km; major emissions components 8 years/130,000 km; rust perforation 5 years/unlimited km. **Supplementary warranty:** Not needed. **City/highway fuel economy:** 4.0/4.2 L/100 km.

OWNER-REPORTED PROBLEMS: Airbags failed to deploy. Extremely vulnerable to side winds:

> Prius had extremely poor stability at highway speeds with 25 mph [40 km/h] gusty crosswind. Directional stability was extremely poor—wind gust would shift direction of the car 10–15 degrees. Little road feedback in steering wheel, required great attention from driver to control car at 60 mph [95 km/h]. Less capable driver...probably would end up in a wreck.

Poor braking at low speeds, and often the car accelerates when the brakes are applied:

> These incidents caused me to search the web for similar experiences of others, and I have found many, some with severe consequences.... I sometimes hear a slight grinding disk sound when I brake, and I have on a few occasions noticed that the brakes are skipping and the ABS engaging, as if I were on a slippery or graveled surface.... In retrospect, after having experienced the acceleration at the stop sign, I realize that these other odd braking issues might be symptoms of the bigger braking issue.

•

> While driving 5 mph [8 km/h] into a parking space, the brakes did not work when the pedal was depressed. On two separate occasions, the vehicle struck a garage door and the contact rear-ended another vehicle due to the brake failure.

Inaccurate fuel readings:

> Unable to properly fill the fuel tank. The fuel bladder collapses.

Traction control engages when it shouldn't; and headlights go on and off intermittently.

YARIS ★★★★

RATING: Above Average. The Yaris feels about right as the classic commuter car, where functionality trumps style and driving pleasure. Not a sporty performer by any stretch. **Strong points:** Roomy, economical, and versatile, with a wee bit of styling flash. Plenty of usable power, accelerates a bit faster than the Honda Fit or Hyundai Accent; excellent fuel economy; and lots of interior space up front, along with an incredible array of storage areas, including a huge trunk and standard 60/40 split-folding rear seats. Well-designed instruments and controls; comfortable high front seating; easy rear access; and excellent visibility fore and aft. Yaris passes over uneven terrain with less jarring movements than do other minicompacts. Quite nimble when cornering. Surprisingly quiet for an economy car. NHTSA gives the Yaris four stars for frontal, side, and rollover crash protection; liftback versions get five stars for front and side protection. IIHS rates frontal offset and side crashworthiness protection as "Good." **Weak points:** Higher priced than most of the competition, and not overly generous with standard features (get used to roll-down windows and manual locks). Says the *Chicago Sun-Times*, "The Yaris five-door is basically a hood, hatch and four doors attached to a metal skeleton supported by four wheels." Interior ergonomics are not the best; cramped rear seating; and tall profile and light weight make the car vulnerable to side-wind buffeting. The base tires provide poor wet traction; excessive torque steer (sudden pulling to one side when accelerating); some wind noise from the base of the windshield; and the steering wheel is mounted too far away for some drivers. IIHS rates head-restraint protection as "Marginal." **New for 2010:** A five-door hatchback.

KEY FACTS

PRICES: $14,300–$18,815 **FREIGHT:** $1,140 **ORIGIN:** Japan **SALES:** Down 40%
POWERTRAIN (FRONT-DRIVE)
Engine: 1.5L 4-cyl. (106 hp); Transmissions: 5-speed man. • 4-speed auto.
DIMENSIONS/CAPACITY
Passengers: 2/3; Wheelbase: 100.4 in.; H: 56.7/L: 169.3/W: 66.5 in.; Headroom F/R: 3.5/1.5 in.; Legroom F/R: 40.5/27 in.; Cargo volume: 12.9 cu. ft.; Fuel tank: 42L/regular; Tow limit: 700 lb.; Load capacity: 845 lb.; Turning circle: 34.1 ft.; Ground clearance: 5.1 in.; Weight: 2,315 lb.

OVERVIEW: This entry-level, five-passenger econocar gives decent fuel economy without sacrificing performance. It's essentially a spin-off of Toyota's popular Echo hatchback, a Canada-only hatch that was built specifically for the Canadian market and whose demise is deeply lamented.

Positioned just below the Corolla, the Yaris costs about $1,200 less yet offers about the same amount of passenger space, thanks to a tall roof, low floor height, and upright seating position. The Yaris has a more-modern look than the Echo it replaced, and its interior improvements—like large windows, additional legroom, and high-quality trim and seats—give it the allure of a much more expensive car.

COST ANALYSIS: Get the cheaper 2009 model. **Best alternatives:** The Honda Fit is worth the extra money—it's got more room and is a lot more fun to drive. The Honda Civic, Hyundai Accent, Nissan Versa, Suzuki Aerio, and Mazda3 are worthwhile candidates also. **Options:** Consider snow tires and better-quality 14-inch tires for improved traction in inclement weather. Beware of option loading, where you have to buy a host of overpriced, nonessential, impractical features in order to get one or two amenities you require. **Rebates:** 2009 models get $1,500–$2,000 rebates. **Depreciation:** Much slower than average. **Insurance cost:** Below average. **Parts supply/cost:** Easily found and reasonably priced. **Annual maintenance cost:** Costs over the long term are predicted to be low. **Warranty:** Bumper-to-bumper 3 years/60,000 km; powertrain 5 years/100,000 km; rust perforation 5 years/unlimited km. **Supplementary warranty:** Not needed. **City/highway fuel economy:** *Manual:* 6.9/5.5 L/100 km. *Automatic:* 7.0/5.7 L/100 km.

OWNER COMPLAINTS: Passenger-side airbag is disabled when an average-sized passenger is seated, requiring that the warning light be constantly reset; airbags did not deploy in a high-speed frontal collision; ignition sticks in the starter position; and the daytime running lights are too bright.

COROLLA ★★

RATING: Below Average. The Corolla has dropped two notches in *Lemon-Aid*'s rating due to its hazardous steering assembly. **Strong points:** Pleasant ride; good braking; better quality control than with the Detroit Three; improved interior ergonomics (lots more space); improved crashworthiness scores; and a high resale value. **Weak points:** It's hard to keep the vehicle in a straight line without your eyes glued to the road and both hands keeping a tight grip on the steering wheel. Sound like fun? Average acceleration requires constant shifting to keep in the pack; automatic transmission–equipped versions are even slower still; clumsy emergency handling; lots of high-speed wind and road noise; limited front legroom; head restraints block rear visibility; many report that these cars literally stink because of a rotten-egg exhaust smell entering the interior; and some reports of airbags deploying inadvertently or failing to deploy. Side and side curtain airbags are optional on the CE but standard on the LE and Sport. Stability control is also optional. IIHS rates head-restraint protection as "Poor." **New for 2010:** Nothing significant.

KEY FACTS

PRICES: $15,160–$22,250 **FREIGHT:** $1,140 **ORIGIN:** U.S. and Canada **SALES:** Down 60%

POWERTRAIN (FRONT-DRIVE)
Engines: 1.8L 4-cyl. (132 hp) • 2.4L 4-cyl. (158 hp); Transmissions: 5-speed man. • 4-speed auto. • 5-speed auto.

DIMENSIONS/CAPACITY
Passengers: 2/3; Wheelbase: 102.4 in.; H: 57.7/L: 178.7/W: 69.3 in.; Headroom F/R: 4.0/2.0 in.; Legroom F/R: 41/28 in.; Cargo volume: 12.3 cu. ft.; Fuel tank: 50L/regular; Tow limit: 1,500 lb.; Load capacity: 825 lb.; Turning circle: 37.1 ft.; Ground clearance: 5.8 in., XRS: 5.3 in.; Weight: 2,722 lb.

OVERVIEW: A step up from the Yaris, the Corolla has long been Toyota's conservative standard-bearer in the compact sedan class. Over the years, however, the car has grown in size and price, to the point where it can now be considered a small family sedan. All Corollas ride on a front-drive platform with independent suspension on all wheels. There are three variants: the value-leader CE and the more upscale LE and S models. Power is supplied by a torquey 132 hp 1.8L twin-cam four, teamed with a standard 5-speed manual gearbox or optional 4- or 5-speed automatics.

COST ANALYSIS: Selling prices are soft due to poor sales through the summer. Make sure the car is road tested on the highway for excessive road wander and instability. **Best alternatives:** Other small cars that represent good investments are the Honda Civic, Hyundai Elantra, and Mazda3 or Mazda6. **Options:** The built-in rear child seat is a sound buy. For better steering response and additional high-speed stability, order the optional 185/65R14 tires that come with the LE. **Rebates:** $1,000 rebates, low-interest financing, and modest discounting early in 2010. **Depreciation:** Much slower than average. **Insurance cost:** Average. **Parts supply/cost:** Parts are easily found and reasonably priced. **Annual maintenance cost:** Lower than average. **Warranty:** Bumper-to-bumper 3 years/60,000 km; powertrain 5 years/100,000 km; rust perforation 5 years/unlimited km. **Supplementary warranty:** Not needed. **City/highway fuel economy:** *1.8L manual:* 7.5/5.6 L/100 km. *1.8L automatic:* 7.4/5.6 L/100 km. *2.4L manual:* 9.5/6.7 L/100 km. *2.4L automatic:* 9.4/6.5 L/100 km.

OWNER-REPORTED PROBLEMS: A major steering defect makes the Corolla unsafe to drive. Steering tends to allow the vehicle to wander all over the road; car cannot track a straight line on a flat road (alignments and a new steering rack doesn't help):

> It is very difficult to keep the vehicle within the lane. If it deviates (which is normal) and a correction is made, the car over-reacts and the vehicle veers to the other side of the lane. Another correction puts the vehicle back to the other side. So the vehicle moves side to side.

Driver cannot open the rear window with the other windows closed without producing a dramatic vibration and shaking inside the vehicle; car can be parked on a small hill with the parking brake applied and still roll away; harsh downshift when stopping; the vehicle stalls in the rain; side plastic airbag housing pops off; bolts holding the door come lose; inner and outer tie rods bent; instrument-panel rattling; windshield back glass ticking; front-seat squeaking, and the front power seat grinds and groans.

Option

CAMRY, CAMRY HYBRID ★★★ / ★★

RATING: *Camry:* Average. *Camry Hybrid:* Below Average. **Strong points:** Last year's redesign corrected most of the Camry's safety and performance gaps; a retuned SE trim level delivers sporty handling; the base 4-cylinder is a competent, responsive performer; surprisingly, the 3.5L V6 powertrain set-up delivers almost as good a fuel economy as the base 4-banger; there's a nice array of new standard safety and convenience features that include a telescoping steering column, side airbags, and stability control; pleasant ride; quiet interior; well laid-out instrumentation and controls; nicely padded dash and door panels; lots of interior passenger and storage space; and a high resale value. NHTSA gives the Camry five stars for frontal and side crashworthiness and four stars for rollover resistance; IIHS rates the Camry's frontal offset and side protection as "Good." **Weak points:** Owners report long service waits for their Hybrids. Safety-related failures are particularly worrisome because they have been mentioned year after year, and can be particularly lethal to older drivers with slower reflexes, who may not correct in time for sudden engine surging or delayed transmission engagement when accelerating, merging, passing, or turning. IIHS rates head-restraint effectiveness as only "Marginal." Hybrid fuel economy is overstated by almost 30 percent, says *Consumer Reports* and almost everyone else. **New for 2010:** A slight restyling until the 2012 redesign.

KEY FACTS

PRICES: *Camry:* $24,000, *Hybrid:* $31,790 **FREIGHT:** $1,240 **ORIGIN:** Kentucky **SALES:** Down 35%

POWERTRAIN (FRONT-DRIVE)

Engines: 2.4L 4-cyl. Hybrid (187 hp) • 2.5L 4-cyl. (169 or 179 hp) • 3.5L V6 (268 hp); Transmissions: 6-speed man. • 6-speed auto. • CVT

DIMENSIONS/CAPACITY

Passengers: 2/3; Wheelbase: 109.3 in.; H: *Camry:* 57.9, *Hybrid:* 57.5/L: 189.2/ W: 71.7 in.; Headroom F/R: 5.0/2.0 in.; Legroom F/R: 42/29 in.; Cargo volume: *Camry:* 15 cu. ft., *Hybrid:* 10.6 cu. ft.; Fuel tank: *Camry:* 70L, *Hybrid:* 65L/ reg./prem.; Tow limit: *Camry:* 1,000 lb., *Hybrid:* Not advised; Load capacity: 900 lb.; Turning circle: 36.1 ft.; Ground clearance: *Camry:* 5.3 in., *Hybrid:* 5.9 in.; Weight: *Camry:* 3,307 lb., *Hybrid:* 3,638 lb.

OVERVIEW: The Camry is available only as a four-door sedan based on the Avalon platform. Power is supplied by a peppy 169 hp 2.5L 4-cylinder engine (179 hp with the SE), a 187 hp 2.4L gas-electric hybrid 4-cylinder, and a 268 hp 3.5L V6. The base engine can be coupled to a 6-speed manual or a 6-speed automatic, and the V6 uses a 6-speed automatic. Hybrids come with a continuously variable transmission (CVT). There are many standard features available. For example, side airbags, side curtain airbags, a driver's knee airbag, and anti-lock four-wheel disc brakes are standard on all Camrys, plus stability and traction control can be found on the higher-end models and the Hybrid (traction/anti-skid control). Rear seats have shoulder belts for the middle passenger; low-beam lights are quite bright; and the headlights switch on and off automatically as conditions change.

COST ANALYSIS: Buy a cheaper, almost identical 2009 model. **Best alternatives:** The Honda Accord, Hyundai Elantra, Mazda6, and Nissan Sentra. **Options:** Stay away from the optional moonroof; it robs you of much-needed headroom and exposes you to a deafening wind roar, rattling, and leaks. **Rebates:** $2,000 rebates, plus low-interest financing and very attractive leasing deals in the early winter of 2010. **Depreciation:** Slower than average. **Insurance cost:** Higher than average. **Parts supply/cost:** Parts are easily found and moderately priced. **Annual maintenance cost:** Average. **Warranty:** Bumper-to-bumper 3 years/60,000 km; powertrain 5 years/100,000 km; rust perforation 5 years/ unlimited km. **Supplementary warranty:** Not needed. **City/highway fuel economy:** *Hybrid:* Supposedly averages 5.7 L/100 km for city and highway driving combined, but many owners say their vehicle's real-world fuel consumption is closer to 7.6 L/100 km. *2.5L manual:* 9.6/6.4 L/100 km. *2.5L automatic:* 9.5/6.2 L/100 km. *3.5L V6:* 10.7/7.0 L/100 km.

OWNER-REPORTED PROBLEMS: Sudden, unintended acceleration without any brakes when passing; vehicle hesitates before accelerating after coming to a stop; vehicle constantly pulls you to the left, into oncoming traffic, no matter how many alignments you get; car caught on fire after being plugged into a block heater; Hybrid's lower beam lights are inadequate for lighting the highway; driver-seat backrest lumbar support may be painful to some drivers; passenger window fell out; front windshield distortion looks like little bubbles are embedded in the glass; rear window-defrosting wires don't clear the upper top of the windshield; water leaks onto the headliner/footwell area; engine ticking noise; front-seat squeaking; power-seat grinding, groaning; moonroof makes a knocking noise; radio noise; excessive dust from vents; console door won't open; transmission control module (TCM) updates for shift improvement; torque converter shudder on light acceleration; and paint is stained under the Rapguard protective wrap.

AVALON ★★★★

RATING: Above Average. The Avalon is a "geezer teaser" that can turn deadly through delayed shifts and engine surging. **Strong points:** Excellent powertrain performance, and acceptable handling and ride; a roomy, limousine-like interior with reclining backrests and plenty of storage space; large doors make for easy front- and rear-seat access; comfortable seats; a quiet interior; exceptional reliability when compared with some of Toyota's other models; and a high resale value. NHTSA gives the car five stars for front and side crash protection and four stars for rollover resistance. IIHS rates rollover resistance and frontal offset and side crashworthiness as "Good." **Weak points:** Rear-corner blind spots; mushy brake pedal; a "floaty" suspension and ultra-light steering degrades handling; and a bit fuel-thirsty. **New for 2010:** Nothing new; the 2012 model will have all the changes.

KEY FACTS

PRICES: $37,755 **FREIGHT:** $1,490
ORIGIN: Japan **SALES:** Down 40%
POWERTRAIN (FRONT-DRIVE)
Engine: 3.5L V6 (268 hp); Transmission: 6-speed auto.
DIMENSIONS/CAPACITY
Passengers: 2/3; Wheelbase: 111 in.; H: 59/L: 197.6/W: 73 in.; Cargo volume: 14.4 cu. ft.; Fuel tank: 70L/regular; Headroom F/R: 3.0/2.5 in.; Legroom F/R: 41/31 in.; Tow limit: Not recommended; Load capacity: 875 lb.; Turning circle: 36.9 ft.; Ground clearance: 5.3 in.; Weight: 3,567 lb.

OVERVIEW: This five-passenger, near-luxury four-door offers more value and reliability than do other cars in its class that cost thousands of dollars more. A front-engine, front-drive, mid-sized sedan based on a stretched Camry platform, the Avalon is similar in size to the Ford Taurus and bigger than the rear-drive Cressida it replaced. Yet, despite its generous interior space, the car has a relatively small profile.

COST ANALYSIS: Buy an identical 2009 model. It should be discounted by about 20 percent due to slow sales and rumours the car may soon be dropped. **Best alternatives:** The Honda Accord V6, Mazda6, and Toyota Camry V6. **Options:** The engine-immobilizing anti-theft system and dealer-installed towing package are worthwhile items. Stay away from the navigation control system; it's a pain to program. Sonar cruise control doesn't let other drivers know you may suddenly slow down. **Rebates:** $3,000+ on the 2009s, plus low-interest financing. **Depreciation:** Average. **Insurance cost:** Higher than average. **Parts supply/cost:** Parts are relatively inexpensive and easily found. If the Avalon *is* discontinued, parts still won't be a problem, because so many were sold and the model hasn't changed much over the years. **Annual maintenance cost:** Less than average. **Warranty:** Bumper-to-bumper 3 years/60,000 km; powertrain 5 years/100,000 km; rust perforation 5 years/unlimited km. **Supplementary warranty:** Not needed. **City/highway fuel economy:** 10.7/7.0 L/100 km.

OWNER-REPORTED PROBLEMS: Practically all of the owner complaints relate to poor fit and finish. Water leaks into the headliner/footwell area; engine ticking noise; transmission control module (TCM) updates needed to improve shifting; windshield back glass ticking noise; and a front power-seat grinding, groaning noise.

SIENNA

RATING: Above Average. One of the Big Three of minivans (the other two are the Honda Odyssey and Chrysler's minivans). There has been a resurgence of safety-related defects since the 2004 model was redesigned; however, the comfort, performance, and convenience features make Sienna an above-average buy in its class—almost as good as the Odyssey. **Strong points:** Smooth 3.5L V6 powertrain (most of the time); optional full-time AWD; standard stability control; three-row side curtain airbags; a comfortable, stable ride; plenty of standard safety, performance, and convenience features; a fourth door; a tight turning circle; a good amount of passenger and cargo room; and good reliability. NHTSA gives the Sienna four stars for frontal collision protection and rollover crashworthiness, and five stars for side protection. IIHS gives its top, "Good" rating for frontal offset and side crashworthiness. **Weak points:** Recommended options are bundled with costly gadgets; nondescript styling; an unusually large number of body rattles and safety-related complaints; mediocre braking; third-row head restraints are mounted too low; fast-wearing and expensive-to-replace run-flat tires; and rear head-restraint effectiveness is rated "Poor" by IIHS. **New for 2010:** Nothing significant.

KEY FACTS

PRICES: $29,500–$39,990 **FREIGHT:** $1,490 **ORIGIN:** Japan **SALES:** Down 40%

POWERTRAIN (FRONT-DRIVE/AWD)

Engine: 3.5L V6 (266 hp); Transmission: 5-speed auto.

DIMENSIONS/CAPACITY (LE)

Passengers: 2/3/3; Wheelbase: 119.3 in.; H: 68.9/L: 201/W: 77.4 in.; Headroom F/R1/R2: 3.5/4.0/2.5 in.; Legroom F/R1/R2: 40.5/31.5/2.5 in.; Cargo volume: 43.6 cu. ft.; Fuel tank: 79L/regular; Tow limit: 3,500 lb.; Load capacity: 1,120 lb.; Turning circle: 36.7 ft.; Ground clearance: 6.9 in.; Weight: 4,270–4,545 lb.

OVERVIEW: Toyota built the Sienna for comfort and convenience. If you want more performance and driver interaction, get a Honda Odyssey. Sienna's V6 turns in respectable acceleration times, and the handling is also very carlike, but not as agile as with the Odyssey. However, the spacious interior accommodates up to eight passengers. All models come with standard four-wheel disc brakes, and all-wheel drive is available.

Sienna offers dual power-sliding doors with optional remote controls, and its interior is well detailed. The third-row seats split and fold away; head restraints don't have to be removed when the seats are stored; and second-row bucket seats are easily converted to bench seats. Other nice interior features are a telescoping steering wheel and power-assisted second-row windows.

COST ANALYSIS: Toyota is keeping most prices near last year's levels, making the 2010 your best buy. Prices are firm, at first, but with Sienna sales in the cellar, dickering can be effective. **Best alternatives:** The Chrysler Caravan, *et al.*; Honda Odyssey; and Mazda5 (a mini-minivan). Chrysler's extensive reworking of its minivans' interiors and its competitive prices, innovative styling, and improved quality have made its minivans good second choices for the past several years. Why not Nissan's Quest? It has been seriously glitch-afflicted with factory-related redesign deficiencies. **Options:** Power windows and door locks, rear heater, and AC unit. Be wary of the power-sliding door. As with all minivans offering this feature, these doors can injure children and pose unnecessary risks to other occupants. Go for Michelin or Pirelli original-equipment tires. Don't buy Bridgestone or Dunlop run-flats. **Rebates:** *2009 models:* $2,000. Dealers want to make room for the arrival of the revamped 2010s in the late fall. *2010 models:* $1,000. **Depreciation:** Much slower than average. **Insurance cost:** Higher than average. **Parts supply/cost:** Excellent supply of reasonably priced parts taken from the Camry's parts bin. But run-flat tire replacements are expensive and hard to find. **Annual maintenance cost:** Less than average. **Warranty:** Bumper-to-bumper 3 years/60,000 km; powertrain 5 years/100,000 km; rust perforation
5 years/unlimited km. **Supplementary warranty:** An extended warranty isn't necessary. **City/highway fuel economy:** *Front-drive:* 11.7/8.1 L/100 km. *AWD:* 13.3/9.5 L/100 km.

OWNER-REPORTED PROBLEMS: In a nutshell, recent Toyotas continue to have fuel delivery failures and serious body panel defects, side-door hazards, and poor fit and finish. A driver accelerated to pass another car, and his Sienna suddenly accelerated out of control, while the brakes were useless:

> The cruise control stuck while accelerating and would not disengage by pressing the brake pedal or by pulling the cruise control lever (located on the steering column) towards the driver.

Passenger-side sliding door is still failure-prone after a decade of complaints:

> After using some online blogs I discovered that there is a lot of Sienna owners with the very same problem, beside the fact I am driving two 5 year old kids in this van every day and this clearly creates a very dangerous safety concern.

Multiple warning lights come on, and the vehicle cannot be shifted; engine ticking; more ticking from the windshield/back glass; and transfer-case fluid leaks.

RAV4 ★★★★

RATING: Above Average. **Strong points:** Base models offer a nice array of standard safety, performance, and convenience features, including electronic stability control; 4-cylinder acceleration from a stop is acceptable with a full load; excellent V6 powertrain performance; precise handling and a comfortable ride are big improvements over earlier, more firmly sprung models; RAV4 seats five, but an optional third-row bench on Base and Limited models increases capacity to seven; comfortable seats; a quiet interior; cabin gauges and controls are easy to access and read; exceptional reliability; good fuel economy with the 4-cylinder engine (the V6 is almost as fuel-frugal); and a high resale value. NHTSA gives the RAV4 five stars for front and side crashworthiness and four stars for rollover protection. IIHS says head-restraint protection and frontal offset and side crashworthiness are "Good." **Weak points:** Transmission is hesitant to shift to a lower gear when under load, and sometimes produces jerky low-speed shifts; some noseplow and body lean when cornering under power; long-legged drivers may wish for more legroom; rear seating is a bit cramped; and lots of road and wind noise (mostly wind rush from the base of the front windshield). **New for 2010:** Returns largely unchanged.

KEY FACTS

PRICES: $26,500–$33,890 **FREIGHT:** $1,895 **ORIGIN:** Japan **SALES:** Down 25%

POWERTRAIN (FRONT-DRIVE/AWD)
Engines: 2.5L 4-cyl. (179 hp) • 3.5L V6 (269 hp); Transmissions: 4-speed auto. • 5-speed auto.

DIMENSIONS/CAPACITY
Passengers: 2/3/2; Wheelbase: 104.7 in.; H: 68.7/L: 181.9/W: 71.5 in.; Cargo volume: 35.9 cu. ft.; Fuel tank: 70L/regular; Headroom F/R: 6.55/4.0 in.; Legroom F/R: 41.5/29 in.; Tow limit: 1,500–3,500 lb.; Load capacity: 825 lb.; Turning circle: 37.4 ft.; Ground clearance: 7.5 in.; Weight: 3,360–3,500 lb.

OVERVIEW: This five-passenger, near-luxury four-door SUV offers more value and reliability than do other cars in its class that cost thousands of dollars more. Essentially a mid-sized sedan based on a stretched Camry platform, the RAV4 is slightly larger than the rear-drive Cressida it replaced. Yet, despite its generous interior space, the car has a relatively small profile.

COST ANALYSIS: Look for an identical 2009 model, discounted by about 15 percent. The styling and equipment upgrades given the 2009 RAV4 will do until 2012, when it will be fully redesigned and a gas-electric hybrid model will be added. The 2010 and 2011 RAV4s won't change much, but they could cost more. **Best alternatives:** The Honda CR-V, Hyundai Tucson, or Nissan X-Trail. **Options:** The engine-immobilizing anti-theft system and dealer-installed towing package are worthwhile items. **Rebates:** $2,000+ on the 2009s ($1,000 on the 2010s), plus low-interest financing and leasing. **Depreciation:** Slower than average. **Insurance cost:** Higher than average. **Parts supply/cost:** Parts are relatively inexpensive and easily found. **Annual maintenance cost:** Less than average. **Warranty:** Bumper-to-bumper 3 years/60,000 km; powertrain 5 years/100,000 km; rust perforation 5 years/unlimited km. **Supplementary warranty:** A waste of money. **City/highway fuel economy:** *2.5L front-drive:* 9.4/6.9 L/100 km. *2.5L AWD:* 9.7/7.2 L/100 km. *3.5L front-drive:* 10.7/7.4 L/100 km. *3.5L AWD:* 11.1/7.7 L/100 km.

OWNER-REPORTED PROBLEMS: Practically all of the owner complaints relate to poor fit and finish and audio system malfunctions. Owners also deride the flimsy glove box lid, loose sun visor, constantly flickering traction control light, sticking ignition key, uncomfortable head restraints, squeaks and rattles from the dashboard and rear-seat area, and wide rear roof pillars that obstruct visibility. Other, more serious concerns include sudden, unintended acceleration:

> I was going through a drive through carwash, auto in Neutral. Reached the end, put foot on brake, put auto into Drive. The vehicle accelerated on its own, going straight out of the end of the carwash. Had the brakes on but they didn't stop the vehicle. Turned the car to miss a telephone pole and went out into 4-lane hwy., crashing into another vehicle, stopping my vehicle, finally. Vehicle would not stop at all.

Fire erupted in the engine compartment; original-equipment Yokohama tires may blow out their side walls; spare-tire cover becomes loose (elastic deteriorates) and blows off; defroster system is weak; and mice enter the vehicle through the clean-air filter—dealer suggested buying a mouse trap.

VENZA ★★★

RATING: Average. This combination of a small SUV and wagon has to prove itself for another year. **Strong points:** Powerful and efficient engines; a roomy interior; a pleasant driving demeanour; a comfy ride; innovative interior storage areas; an automatic headlight dimmer; easy entry and exit; foldable rear seats, a large cargo area and rear hatch opening; a low rear loading height; and standard stability and traction control. NHTSA gave the Venza a five-star rating for front and side crashworthiness, while rollover protection garnered four stars. IIHS rated the vehicle as "Good" for frontal offset and side protection, and head-restraint effectiveness was seen as "Acceptable." **Weak points:** Can't tow or haul as much as other crossovers; not an exciting drive; no third-row seat; high-intensity discharge headlights are annoying to other drivers, are often stolen, and are expensive to replace. **New for 2010:** No major changes until the 2012 hybrid arrives.

OVERVIEW: Toyota's Venza is a five-passenger wagon sold in two trim levels that match the two available engines. Going into its second year, the car offers the styling and comfort of a passenger car with the flexibility of a small SUV. A perfect alternative for Toyota customers who need more vehicle than what the Camry offers but not as much as the Highlander.

COST ANALYSIS: Most of the 2009s have been sold. Expect to pay full list price for a 2010. **Best alternatives:** The Ford Edge, Nissan Murano, and Toyota Highlander. **Options:** Stay away from the panoramic roof option and backup camera; both are expensive gadgets of doubtful utility. **Rebates:** $1,000+ on the 2009s, plus low-interest financing. **Depreciation:** Too early to know. **Insurance cost:** Average. **Parts supply/cost:** Parts are average-priced and easily found. **Annual maintenance cost:** Should be less than average. **Warranty:** Bumper-to-bumper 3 years/60,000 km; powertrain 5 years/100,000 km; rust perforation 5 years/unlimited km. **Supplementary warranty:** Not needed. **City/highway fuel economy:** *2.7L front-drive:* 10.0/6.8 L/100 km. *2.7L AWD:* 10.2/7.1 L/100 km. *3.5L front-drive:* 11.0/7.6 L/100 km. *3.5L AWD:* 11.5/7.9 L/100 km.

KEY FACTS

PRICES: *Front-drive:* $28,720, *AWD:* $29,720 **FREIGHT:** $1,490 **ORIGIN:** Kentucky **SALES:** N/A

POWERTRAIN (FRONT-DRIVE/AWD)
Engines: 2.7L 4-cyl. (182 hp) • 3.5L V6 (268 hp); Transmission: 6-speed auto.

DIMENSIONS/CAPACITY
Passengers: 2/3; Wheelbase: 109.3 in.; H: 63.4/L: 189/W: 75 in.; Cargo volume: 34 cu. ft.; Fuel tank: 67L/regular; Headroom F/R: N/A; Legroom F/R: N/A; Tow limit: 2,500–3,500 lb.; Load capacity: 875 lb.; Turning circle: 39.1 ft.; Ground clearance: 8.1 in.; Weight: 3,760 lb.

OWNER-REPORTED PROBLEMS: Improperly installed rubber mat caused accelerator pedal to stick; transmission would not go into Reverse; and the Hill-Start Assist feature doesn't prevent the car from rolling back when stopped on a hill in traffic:

> I feel Toyota should immediately send out a safety notice requiring all employees be briefed about the Hill-Start Assist feature, how it doesn't activate automatically, and how to activate the feature when stopped on an uphill slope.

HIGHLANDER ★★★★

RATING: Above Average. **Strong points:** Powerful engines and a smooth, refined powertrain; the Hybrid can propel itself on electric power alone; a quiet interior enhances the comfortable ride; responsive handling; roomy second-row seating is fairly versatile. NHTSA gives the vehicle five stars for frontal and side crashworthiness, and four stars for rollover resistance. IIHS rates the vehicle as "Good" for frontal offset, side, and head-restraint protection. **Weak points:** Steering is somewhat vague, and the vehicle isn't very agile. The third-row seat is a bit tight and doesn't fold in a 50/50 split. **New for 2010:** Nothing of importance.

OVERVIEW: A trucky alternative to a minivan, this competent, refined, family-friendly SUV puts function ahead of style and provides cargo and passenger versatility along with a high level of component and workmanship quality. V6-equipped models best represent the Highlander's attributes, as the Hybrid models' higher prices will take years to offset in fuel savings.

KEY FACTS

PRICES: $46,900, *Hybrid:* $53,650 **FREIGHT:** $1,895 **ORIGIN:** Japan **SALES:** Up 10%

POWERTRAIN (FRONT-DRIVE/AWD)

Engines: 2.7L 4-cyl. (187 hp) • 3.3L V6 (270 hp) • 3.5L V6 (270 hp); Transmissions: 5-speed auto. • 6-speed auto. • CVT

DIMENSIONS/CAPACITY

Passengers: 2/3/2, Hybrid: 2/3; Wheelbase: 109.8 in.; H: 69.3/ L: 188.4/W: 75.2 in.; Cargo volume: 10.3 cu. ft.; Fuel tank: 72.5L/regular; Headroom F/R1/R2: 3.5/5.0/0.0 in.; Legroom F/R1/R2: 41.5/32/23.5 in.; Tow limit: 3,500–5,000 lb.; Load capacity: 1,200 lb.; Turning circle: 38.7 ft.; Ground clearance: 7.8 in.; Weight: 4,050–4,641 lb.

COST ANALYSIS: Look for an identical 2009 model, discounted by about 15 percent. **Best alternatives:** From the SUV side: the Buick Enclave, GMC Acadia, and Saturn Outlook. The Honda Odyssey is a suitable minivan choice. **Options:** Yes to the engine-immobilizing anti-theft system; no to the failure-prone and high-maintenance-cost tire-pressure monitoring system. **Rebates:** $2,000+ on the 2009s, plus low-interest financing and leasing. **Depreciation:** Slower than average. **Insurance cost:** Higher than average. **Parts supply/cost:** Parts are relatively inexpensive and easily found. **Annual maintenance cost:** Average. **Warranty:** Bumper-to-bumper 3 years/60,000 km; powertrain 5 years/100,000 km; rust perforation 5 years/unlimited km. **Supplementary warranty:** Not needed. **City/highway fuel economy:** *Base:* 10.4/7.3 L/100 km. *Hybrid:* 7.4/8.0 L/100 km.

OWNER-REPORTED PROBLEMS: Practically nonexistent. However, NHTSA's safety-defect log sheet notes that the remote keyless park feature allows the vehicle to be shut off even when it isn't in Park, and the tire-pressure monitoring system has to be reset by the dealer when the tires are changed ($135 twice a year).

TACOMA ★★★

RATING: Average. This cheap and reliable light-duty truck would have been rated Recommended if it weren't for owner reports of Toyota's infamous decade-old lag and lurch transmission problem spilling over to the 2009s. **Strong points:** Well-chosen powertrain and steering set-up; ideal for off-road work with the optional suspension; good acceleration; standard electronic stability control; very responsive handling; a well-garnished, roomy interior; plenty of storage space; and impressive reliability. Given five stars by NHTSA for frontal crashworthiness, and four stars for rollover resistance. IIHS rates front and side protection as "Good." **Weak points:** The ride is a bit jolting, and the driving position seems low when compared with the competition. IIHS says rear head-restraint effectiveness is only "Marginal." Delayed transmission engagement is still present. **New for 2010:** Nothing significant; a redesign is scheduled for the 2012 model year.

OVERVIEW: Toyota's entry-level pickup isn't as utilitarian as its predecessors or some of the competition, but it returns with more power and a retuned suspension that enhances handling and ride comfort. If you opt for the optional off-road suspension, you will quickly notice the firmer ride and increased road feedback.

COST ANALYSIS: Look for an identical 2009 model, discounted by about 10 percent. **Best alternatives:** The Mazda B-Series and Nissan Frontier. **Options:** The stiffer suspension for off-roading, and a better-quality substitute for the JBL model. The engine-immobilizing anti-theft system and dealer-installed towing package are also worthwhile items. **Rebates:** $1,500+ on the 2009s, plus low-interest financing. **Depreciation:** Slower than average. **Insurance cost:** Average. **Parts supply/cost:** Inexpensive and easily found. **Annual maintenance cost:** Average. **Warranty:** Bumper-to-bumper 3 years/60,000 km; powertrain 5 years/100,000 km; rust perforation 5 years/unlimited km. **Supplementary warranty:** Not needed. **City/highway fuel economy:** *2.7L manual:* 10.5/7.8 L/100 km. *2.7L automatic:* 11.0/7.9 L/100 km. *4.0L 6-speed manual:* 13.5/10.1 L/100 km.

KEY FACTS

PRICES: $20,215–$33,305 **FREIGHT:** $1,490 **ORIGIN:** Japan **SALES:** Up 10%
POWERTRAIN (REAR-DRIVE/AWD)
Engines: 2.7L 4-cyl. (159 hp) • 4.0L V6 (236 hp); Transmissions: 5-speed man. • 6-speed man. • 4-speed auto. • 5-speed auto.
DIMENSIONS/CAPACITY
Passengers: 2/2; Wheelbase: 127.8 in.; H: 65.7/L: 208.1/W: 72.2 in.; Cargo volume: N/A; Fuel tank: 80L/regular; Headroom F/R: 4.0/3.0 in.; Legroom F/R: 42.5/28 in.; Tow limit: 3,500–6,500 lb.; Load capacity: 1,100 lb.; Turning circle: 44.6 ft.; Ground clearance: 8.1 in.; Weight: 3,560 lb.

OWNER-REPORTED PROBLEMS: Premature automatic transmission failure. Automatic transmission lag and lurch, especially when coming out of a turn:

> The transmission in my 2009 Tacoma 4WD V6 does not shift down smoothly as the truck slows down into a turn and begins to accelerate out of a turn or in a straight away. The issue is pronounced in speeds of 35 mph [56 km/h] and less. There seem[s] to be a delay in response when accelerating...until the transmission responds and the truck lurches forward. I checked with the Toyota dealer, and the dealer does not think there is a problem. I checked Toyota forums and found out numerous complaints about the same issue that I have.

Vehicle began to accelerate on its own as driver waited for pedestrians to clear the crosswalk; throttle stuck when passing another vehicle; JBL radio operates erratically. The truck doesn't carry the payload advertised:

> The truck bottoms out at about half the payload capacity of 1,295 pounds [587 kg]. A 652 lb. [296 kg] ATV caused the truck to bottom out. There is a TSB out for 2005–2008 models and Toyota claims it has remedied the problem but the same exact parts are still in use on the 2009 models.

bad buy

TUNDRA ★

RATING: Not Recommended. An excellent concept, but poorly executed. The Tundra's lag and lurch transmission/throttle problem and dangerous rear-end bounce make the truck a poor choice. **Strong points:** Strong powertrain performance; a roomy interior with plenty of storage space; large doors make for easy front- and rear-seat access; comfortable seats; and a quiet interior. **Weak**

KEY FACTS

PRICES: $24,995–$35,790 **FREIGHT:** $1,490 **ORIGIN:** Texas **SALES:** Down 55%
POWERTRAIN (REAR-DRIVE/AWD)
Engines: 4.6L V8 (310 hp) • 5.7L V8 (381 hp); Transmissions: 6-speed auto.
DIMENSIONS/CAPACITY
Passengers: 2/2; Wheelbase: 145.6 in.; H: 75.7/L: 228.71/W: 79.9 in.; Cargo volume: N/A; Fuel tank: 100L/regular; Headroom F/R: 5.5/3.5 in.; Legroom F/R: 42.5/28.5 in.; Tow limit: 8,900–10,800 lb.; Load capacity: 1,755–1,900 lb.; Turning circle: 44 ft.; Ground clearance: 10.4 in.; Weight: 4,830 lb.

points: Engines are fuel-thirsty, and handling is degraded by excessive rear-end bounce; powertrain lag and lurch is hazardous to all; TRD package gives a stiff ride; and interior design looks early Paleolithic. **New for 2010:** A subtle facelift, and the 4.7L V8 engine is replaced by a thriftier, more-powerful 4.6L V8 that has 30 more horsepower and about 0.9 km/L (2 mpg) better mileage.

OVERVIEW: A heavy, full-sized truck that has more glitches than goodies, this year's freshened Tundra has an all-new V8 that's smaller but stronger, lighter, and more fuel-efficient than the 4.7L engine it replaces. Paired with a new 6-speed automatic transmission, it's expected to decrease gas consumption by about 5 percent. Thanks, Toyota. Now get off your butt and fix the Tundra's powertrain and suspension problems.

COST ANALYSIS: Go for the 2010 model to get the more-refined 4.6L V8, after waiting six months for Toyota to iron out its suspension bounce/vibration and transmission lag problems. Haggle for a 10 percent discount. **Best alternatives:** GM's Sierra or Silverado. **Options:** The engine-immobilizing anti-theft system is worthwhile. Stay away from the Bridgestone and Firestone tires. Make sure the spare tire is the same make and size as your regular tire; some dealers have given out smaller Michelin spares. **Rebates:** $4,000+ on the leftover 2009s, plus low-interest financing. **Depreciation:** Average. **Insurance cost:** Higher than average. **Parts supply/cost:** Parts are moderately expensive and sometimes hard to find. **Annual maintenance cost:** Average. **Warranty:** Bumper-to-bumper 3 years/60,000 km; powertrain 5 years/100,000 km; rust perforation 5 years/unlimited km. **Supplementary warranty:** Yes, on the powertrain. **City/highway fuel economy:** *4.6L rear-drive:* 15.2/11.7 L/100 km. *4.6L 4×4:* 15.9/12.2 L/100 km. *5.7L rear-drive:* 15.2/10.9 L/100 km. *5.7L 4×4:* 16.6/11.7 L/100 km.

OWNER-REPORTED PROBLEMS: Sudden, unintended acceleration; stuck accelerator; rear wheel came off the vehicle because the lug nuts weren't tightened sufficiently at the factory. Engine failure caused by a poorly designed Toyota oil filter:

> The perforated steel center tube will come off in the old oil filter and will fail by collapsing in fairly short order and cause total engine failure. $22,000 to $30,000 for a new engine.

Engine lag and lurch when accelerating; engine knocking caused by a piston striking the cylinder wall of the 5.7L V8 engine; repeated failure of the transmission and transfer case; vehicle will stall in any gear. Owners complain the truck is a "Shake-undra":

> Anyone familiar with "shaken baby" syndrome will recognize this defect. On certain sections of pavement and at certain speeds, this vehicle sets up a harmonic vibration and shakes so violently that infants are at risk.

Excessive bed bounce when going over smooth roadways; water leaks into the headliner/footwell area; engine ticking noise; TCM updates needed to improve shifting; heat/AC/ventilation system is a "rodent lair"—the inside air is laced with rodent feces; inoperative instrument lighting for the power-mirror control (must turn on dome light to see); windshield back glass ticking noise; front power-seat grinding, groaning noise; lots of owner complaints relate to poor fit and finish; blue paint is easily scratched and looks bad; and sudden Bridgestone Dueler tire side wall blowout.

Scion - 2012

EUROPEAN VEHICLES

Don't get Smart!

Those Fickle Germans

Readers of the latest ADAC brand-satisfaction rankings may be surprised to find that the German automobile club puts Smart, DaimlerChrysler's cult city car brand, in last place. It's not that customers are dissatisfied with the car itself, according to survey results. No, they are bothered by the way they get treated at the dealership.

That's no wonder. Smart customers bear the brunt of the brand's constantly changing sales strategy. They are nomads in a service desert, always looking for the next dealership. When the brand was launched, there were Smart Centers to visit. But the people working in them quite often had a relationship with automobiles that can only be described as aloof.

The centers mostly are history, and Mercedes has taken over the brand's sales and service. But Smart customers now must stand around among SL-, E- and S-class owners and feel as out of place as rock fans at the annual festival of Wagner operas in Bayreuth, Germany.

www.gilbran.com/news
DECEMBER 4, 2006

VW Auto-Eroticism

First it was prostitutes. Then it was luxury foreign trips. Yesterday, however, the sex scandal at the German car manufacturer Volkswagen deepened when a former manager admitted he had supplied members of the firm's works council not just with female company, but also with Viagra.

THE GUARDIAN
SEPTEMBER 30, 2005

Europe Goes Bust

In the first six months of 2008, demand for new cars across Europe dipped merely 2 percent, with commercial vehicle sales down by just 0.4 percent. By the end of that year, markets for all types of vehicles crashed: In the final quarter, car sales fell 19.3 percent, with some countries reporting a decline of more than 50 percent in December alone. Demand for new commercial vehicles across Europe decreased by 24 percent, and continued the sharp downturn in the first quarter of 2009. The drop in passenger-car registrations recovered somewhat, to a still-formidable 15 percent, supported by the introduction of "cash for clunkers" incentives in a number of European Community countries.

The year-old, worldwide economic recession may end up saving the auto industry after all. After losing billions of dollars in sales, getting some government handouts from France, Germany, Italy, and Spain, and wallowing in red ink, the European auto industry is poised to bring common sense back into a business that had taken leave of its senses over the past four decades by losing sight of its core business. With bankruptcy court authority, European automakers can legally renege on most of their labour and franchise contracts, pare their dealer bodies down to Toyota's size, make alliances with no fear of anti-trust lawsuits, drop duplicate models, focus on more fuel-efficient vehicles, and cut car prices to more-affordable levels.

Ta-ta, Jaguar; Ta-ta, Land Rover

European automakers have been especially hard hit by poor sales and have taken many different routes to sustainability by going to two extremes, where they focus on entry-level econocars and on luxury high-performance vehicles. Key to this strategy is making joint production deals with competitors, no matter the quality of the product they produce. Fiat, for example, will replace many of Chrysler's trucks with its own Fiats, and Ford will bring to North America most of its European small product lineup, reliving the dismal history of its Cortina, Fiesta, and XR4Ti past. *Lemon-Aid* predicts both companies will lose millions by using European products as their lifelines to financial stability.

And then there's the *Slumdog Millionaire* twins Jaguar (priced at $60,000) and Land Rover (priced at $45,000). They are now part of India's Tata auto conglomerate, which builds $2,500 econoboxes with optional windshield wipers. Tata also considers cows to be sacred—unless they're used for leather seats.

GM has sold Saab to Koenigsegg Group AB, a tiny Swedish maker of $1 million "supercars," and Volvo is still pimping its wares around the world—with few takers. Surprisingly, Volvo has been treated with benign neglect by the Swedish government, which has never forgiven the automaker for selling out to Ford a decade ago for $6.45 million (U.S.). The company has been told politely to go work another street corner. As for Opel, General Motors' sole European refugee, the on-and-off deal with Canada's Magna International and its Russian Sberbank partner should be resolved soon. Opel says it has only enough dough to last through Christmas.

Now we come to Audi, Porsche, and Volkswagen, a past powerhouse of German engineering and creative design. Still, the recession has taken its toll, cutting July's year-to-year total North American sales for Audi by 15 percent, for Porsche by almost 40 percent, and for VW by about 20 percent. In this triad, Volkswagen has the best chance of quickly bouncing back as fuel prices soar. It has the most fuel-saving and high-performing vehicles, its North American marketing presence is relatively intact, with minimal dealer attrition, and the company is well positioned to ride the upcoming diesel craze to fatter future profits as hybrids and electric-car sales falter.

Finally, we'll say a few words about BMW and Mercedes-Benz, the two remaining iconic European companies and perennial sales leaders that have taken it on the chin this year. First, some surprising statistics: BMW sales through July 2009 were down about 30 percent—an incredible decline for such a prestigious automobile company. Yet, Mercedes hasn't done much better. Its sales are down over the same period by more than 30 percent, and even its cute, fuel-frugal minicompact Smart Car's sales have dropped almost 25 percent.

Luxury Lemons

European vehicles are generally a driver's delight and a frugal consumer's nightmare. They're noted for having a high level of performance combined with a full array of standard comfort and convenience features. They're fun to drive, well-appointed, and attractively styled. But they're also unreliable, overpriced, and a pain in the butt to service.

This last point is important to remember because in hard economic times such as these, cash-strapped dealers do not invest in a large inventory or mechanic training to adequately service what they sell. For them, the present is chaotic and the future is unknown and threatening. If you insist on buying a European make, be sure you know where it can be serviced by independent mechanics if the dealership's service falters or servicing costs are too high. Also, buy a model that's been sold for years in relatively large quantities and that has parts that are available from independent suppliers.

Why aren't European cars selling? First, they can't withstand performance and durability comparisons with cheaper Asian competitors. Who wants a Mercedes when offered a Lexus? Why get a VW Jetta when you can have more fun with a Mazda3 Sport (with a stupid grin on its front grille)? Second, when times get tough, European automakers get out of town; Asians, on the other hand, tough it out. Remember ARO, Dacia, Fiat, Peugeot, Renault, Skoda, and Yugo? And, finally, European vehicles aren't that dependable and tend to be poorly serviced, with maintenance bills that rival the cost of a week at Cannes. Shoppers understandably balk at these outrageously high prices, and European automakers respond by adding nonessential, problem-prone gadgets that drive up costs even more. In effect, they are selling the sizzle because the steak is *pourri*.

Writes British independent automotive journalist Robert Farago on his website The Truth About Cars (*www.thetruthaboutcars.com*):

> Once upon a time, a company called Mercedes-Benz built luxury cars. Not Elk aversive city runabouts. [An allusion to the Smart Car.] Not German taxis. Not teeny tiny hairdressers' playthings. And definitely not off-roaders.... In the process, the Mercedes brand lost its reputation for quality and exclusivity. In fact, the brand has become so devalued that Mercedes themselves abandoned it, reviving the Nazi-friendly Maybach marque for its top-of-the-range limo. Now that Mercedes has morphed with Chrysler, the company is busy proving that the average of something good and something bad is something mediocre.

You won't read this kind of straight reporting from the cowering North American motoring press as they fawn over any new techno-gadget-laden vehicle hailing from England, Germany, or Sweden. It's easy for them; they get their cars and press junkets for free.

Buyers aren't falling for the car ads' appeal to snobbery. They are still wary of European automakers' reputations for poor quality, high parts and servicing costs, and weak dealer networks. And they have independent data to support their misgivings. One MIT study concluded over two decades ago that European automakers built poor-quality vehicles and then, much like the Detroit Three, attempted to fix their mistakes at the end of the assembly line. As one reviewer of *The Machine That Changed the World*, by James P. Womack, Daniel T. Jones, and Daniel Roos (HarperCollins, November 1991), wrote:

> This study of the world automotive industry by a group of MIT academics reaches the radical conclusion that the much-vaunted Mercedes technicians are actually a throwback to the pre-industrial age, while Toyota is far ahead in costs and quality by building the automobiles correctly the first time.
>
> J.L.

Lemon-Aid readers who own pricey European imports invariably tell me of nightmarish electrical glitches that run the gamut from annoying to life-threatening. Other problems noted by owners include premature brake wear and excessive brake noise, AC malfunctions, faulty computer modules leading to erratic shifting, poor driveability, hard starts, and frequent stalling. Interestingly, although Ladas were low-quality Soviet imports, their deficiencies pale in comparison to what I've seen coming out of the European luxury corral. Maybe that's the logic behind GM's co-venture with Lada to market a Cavalier/Lada 4×4 to European consumers: payback for all of those European lemons shipped to North America over the past five decades.

Service with a Shrug

Have you visited a European automaker's dealership lately? Although poor servicing is usually more acute with vehicles that are new on the market, it has long been the Achilles' heel of European importers. Owners give them low ratings for mishandling complaints, inadequately training their service representatives, and hiring an insufficient number of mechanics—not to mention for the abrasive, arrogant attitude typified by some automakers and dealers who bully customers because they have a virtual monopoly on sales and servicing in their regions. Look at their dealer networks, and you'll see that most European automakers are crowded in Ontario and on the West Coast, leaving their customers in eastern Canada or the Prairies to fend for themselves. This makes their chances of finding someone to do competent repairs about as likely as those of getting Bloc Québécois leader Gilles Duceppe to vote Liberal.

In light of all their shortcomings, why are European vehicles popular? Basically, because they are stylish and fun to drive due to their precise, responsive steering, drivetrain, and brakes. Buyers also like their many techno-gadgets; plush, driver-friendly interiors; and high residual values. For example, a year-old 2009 Mini Cooper that originally cost $23,000 now has a resale value of about $20,000; after five years, it will be worth about $12,000.

Audi

Saddled in the early '80s with a reputation for making poor-quality cars that would suddenly accelerate out of control, Audi fought back for two decades and staged a spectacular comeback with well-built, moderately priced front-drive and AWD Quattro sedans and wagons. Through an expanded lineup of sedans, coupes, and a Cabriolet during the last decade, Audi has gained a reputation for making sure-footed all-wheel-drive luxury cars that are loaded with lots of high-tech bells and whistles and look drop-dead gorgeous.

The Audi TT Coupe.

As with most European makes, Audis excel in comfort and performance. But quality control, servicing, and warranty support remain problematic and are not expected to get much better as the company struggles to keep its head up in a sea of red ink. Nevertheless, Audi sales are on the upswing. So, with a strong backing of its warranty and better quality control, Audi may finally sell vehicles that last as well as they perform.

The fact that Audi warrants the powertrain only up to 4 years/80,000 km is far from reassuring, since engines and transmissions have traditionally been Audi's weakest components and many other automakers cover their vehicles up to 5 years/100,000 km. Fortunately, owner complaints relative to poor quality have been quite rare during the past several years that the A3 has been sold. Whether this is a long-awaited trend or just a blip on the quality screen will be determined during the car's crucial fourth and fifth years.

The following models have been discontinued for the 2010 model year lineup: the A3 3.2, A4 3.2, TT 3.2, TT 2.0T front-drive, A5 3.2 manual (the automatic continues), S8, and A8 W12. New models for 2010 are the S4, A5 2.0T, A5 and S5 Cabriolets (launching later this year), and R8 5.2 V10.

A5 and S5 Coupe: A new 2.0T Quattro with Tiptronic and manual variants; the 3.2 manual variant is discontinued (3.2 Tiptronic continues); introduction of a new Quattro with Sport Rear Differential (varies torque between the rear wheels to eliminate under-steer); an upgraded navigation system (as on the Q5); and standard LED tail lights.

A8: The S8 and A8 W12 are discontinued.

Q5: Not Recommended, even though you're dealing with a well-known engine and few complicated systems. All of the below-listed caveats for the Q7 apply even more to this newer five-passenger compact crossover. On the market less than a year, Audi's $43,400 crossover wagon carries a 270 hp 3.2L V6 hooked to a 6-speed transmission. There is no diesel option. Sales of the Q5 have been one-third better than those for the Q7. NHTSA has given the Q5 five stars for front and side crash protection and four stars for rollover resistance. IIHS has posted similar accolades: frontal offset, side, and head-restraint protection all earned "Good" scores.

Q7: Not Recommended. These are complicated five- or seven-passenger machines that are new to the market and made from bits and pieces of VW's other models. About three a day are sold in all of North America, and this represents a sales decline of close to 45 percent. Selling from $54,200 to $77,200, the Q7 is a VW Touareg/Porsche Cayenne combo with an Audi badge. On the market only three years, its off-road prowess is not as great as Touareg's or Cayenne's. Furthermore, early owner feedback indicates that this large crossover AWD wagon has a host of factory-related defects affecting its fuel and electrical systems, powertrain components, and fit and finish—exactly the problems owners find with Porsche and VW models. The standard engine is an overwhelmed 280 hp 3.6L V6, but the optional 350 hp 4.2L V8 is a gas-guzzler. Better to opt for the newly arrived 225 hp 3.0L turbodiesel option to save fuel and to get more torque (grunt) in the lower speeds in order to move this 2,480 kg (5,467 lb.) behemoth. Poor servicing and recurring factory glitches are to be expected, and the new diesel engine will require specialized mechanics to figure out the latest emissions modifications. NHTSA gives the Q7 five stars for front and side crash protection and four stars for rollover resistance. IIHS gives its top, "Good" score for frontal offset, side, and head-restraint protection.

R8: Carries a 525 hp 5.2L V10 in manual and R tronic variants.

S8: New for 2009 was a standard trunk lid with integrated spoiler; 19-inch wheels; and ventilated/massage seats.

A3 ★★★

RATING: Average. **Strong points:** The freight fee is half of what most automakers charge, plus depreciation will likely be much slower than average. The car's a superb highway performer, thanks to its powerful and smooth-running engines and transmissions. Handling is crisp, steering is accurate, and cornering is accomplished with minimal body roll. Lots of safety, performance, and convenience features, and superior fit and finish. Audi rates the A3 as capable of carrying five passengers; however, the three back-seat passengers had better be friends. IIHS rates the A3 as "Good" for head-restraint protection and in protecting occupants in frontal offset and side crashes. **Weak points:** Fairly expensive for an entry-level Audi; nevertheless, most vehicles will sell for their full price because of their cachet. Premium gas is required, and insurance premiums are higher than average. Judging by past Audi launches, the A3 may have numerous factory-related problems affecting primarily the electrical system, powertrain, brakes, and accessories as its warranty ends. No NHTSA crashworthiness data. **New for 2010:** The A3 will offer the 2.0L "clean" diesel engine found in the 140 hp Jetta TDI, hooked to a 6-speed S tronic twin-clutch automatic transmission. The 3.2L variant and the Audi magnetic ride have been dropped, and the navigation system has been upgraded. A new A3 is on the way for the 2011 model year. Along with a hatchback and a convertible (currently sold in markets outside North America), Audi is reportedly considering a Jetta-sized sedan version.

KEY FACTS

PRICES: *6-speed manual:* $32,300, *Premium Quattro 6-speed automatic:* $39,950 **FREIGHT:** $800 **ORIGIN:** Germany **SALES:** Down 40%

POWERTRAIN (FRONT-DRIVE/AWD)
Engine: 2.0L 4-cyl. (140 hp) • 2.0L 4-cyl. (200 hp); Transmissions: 6-speed man. • 6-speed auto.

DIMENSIONS/CAPACITY
Passengers: 2/3; Wheelbase: 102 in.; H: 57/L: 169/W: 77 in.; Headroom F/R: 4.5/2.0 in.; Legroom F/R: 42.5/25.5 in.; Cargo volume: 19.5 cu. ft.; Fuel tank: 55L/premium; Tow limit: Not recommended; Load capacity: 990 lb.; Turning circle: 35 ft.; Ground clearance: 4.0 in.; Weight: 3,305 lb.

OVERVIEW: Based on the redesigned Volkswagen Golf, the A3 is Audi's latest entry-level compact four-door hatchback. It's a well-appointed, generously powered vehicle that arrived in the summer of 2005 and sells for $32,300 for the base 2.0T and $39,950 for the top-of-the-line model. The A3 comes in Standard and Premium trim levels, with a choice of two engines: 2.0 T versions have a 200 hp 2.0L turbocharged 4-cylinder engine, available with a 6-speed manual or 6-speed automatic transmission, and the 2.0 TDI has a 140 hp 4-cylinder turbodiesel with the automatic only. The V6-powered 3.2 S line has been discontinued. All A3s are available in front-drive, and Audi's Quattro all-wheel drive is available on automatic transmission 2.0 Ts. Standard safety features include ABS, traction control, an anti-skid system, front side airbags, rear side airbags, and side curtain airbags.

COST ANALYSIS: This four-door hatchback is smaller and less costly than Audi's A4 compacts, and is just as much fun to drive. Inasmuch as these cars are mostly carryovers from the 2009s, look for a discounted second-series 2009, unless you really lust after diesel economy. If so, wait until the better-made models arrive in the summer of 2010. **Best alternatives:** Acura TSX, BMW 3 Series, Ford Taurus, Volvo V50, and a fully loaded VW Jetta TDI. **Rebates:** Not likely, though prices will likely soften in late summer. **Depreciation:** Average. Audi values no longer nosedive when the base warranty expires. **Insurance cost:** Higher than average. **Parts supply/cost:** Pure hell! Owners report months-long waits for the fuel system and other powertrain components to arrive to fix an all-too-common lurch and lag condition. The present recession is making the problem of limited part supplies and high parts costs untenable—sufficient reason alone not to buy this Audi this year. Independent suppliers scratch their heads when you ask about Audi parts. **Annual maintenance cost:** Predicted to be much higher than average. **Warranty:** Bumper-to-bumper 4 years/80,000 km; rust perforation 10 years/unlimited km. **Supplementary warranty:** Don't leave the dealership without getting at least powertrain coverage for five years. **Highway/city fuel economy:** 2.0 *front-drive manual:* 6.7/10.4 L/100 km; 2.0 *front-drive automatic:* 6.9/9.4 L/100 km; 3.2 *Quattro:* 8.0/11.3 L/100 km; 2.0 *turbo:* 7.5/9.6 L/100 km.

OWNER-REPORTED PROBLEMS: Blinking headlights and interior lights when the brakes are applied; vehicle suddenly shuts down in the middle of the highway; and transmission engages and then disengages when accelerating away from a stoplight:

> We thought it may have been just bad gas. It seems the problem is getting worse and more frequent as of late. Reading forums and articles online, it seems to be the symptoms of the transmission which is a DSG/S-tronic transmission.

A4, S4, RS 4 ★★

RATING: Below Average. The recession has made Audi quality and servicing problems worse. You cannot lose almost one-half of your sales in a one-year period and still pay the best mechanics, keep a costly parts inventory, and repair factory

The Audi RS4

glitches through "goodwill" programs. On the positive side, so many of these vehicles have been sold for so long that sustained digging will usually find you the part and the mechanic who can service the vehicle competently. But part back orders? I see no solution before a couple of years of restructuring. **Strong points:** Loaded with safety, performance, and convenience features. The base 2.0L engine provides gobs of low-end torque and accelerates as well with the automatic transmission as it does with the manual. The turbocharger works well, with no turbo delay or torque steer. The manual gearbox, Tiptronic automatic transmission, and CVT all work flawlessly. Comfortable ride; exceptional handling, though not as sporty as Acura's TSX; impressive braking performance (when the brakes are working properly); and lots of cargo room in the wagon. NHTSA gave its top, five-star crashworthiness score for front, side, and rollover protection; IIHS posted similar impressive scores, giving a "Good" rating to frontal offset, side, and head-restraint protection. **Weak points:** Not as fast as its rivals; the ride is stiff at low speeds, and a bit firm at other times; some body roll and brake dive under extreme conditions; braking is a bit twitchy at times; some tire drumming and engine noise; and limited rear seatroom, where the front seatbacks continually press against rear occupants' knees. **New for 2010:** *A4:* The 3.2 variant is dropped; Bluetooth and HomeLink are combined; and an upgraded navigation system appears. *S4:* The arrival of a new S4

KEY FACTS

PRICES: *A4:* $38,300–$43,600, *S4:* $52,500–$54,100 **FREIGHT:** $800 **ORIGIN:** Germany **SALES:** Down 20%

POWERTRAIN (FRONT-DRIVE/AWD)
Engines: 2.0L 4-cyl. (211 hp) • 3.0L SC V6 (333 hp) • 3.2L V6 (265 hp); Transmissions: 6-speed man. • 6-speed auto. • 7-speed auto. • CVT

DIMENSIONS/CAPACITY (A4 SEDAN)
Passengers: 2/3; Wheelbase: 110.6 in.; H: 56.2/L: 185/W: 71.9 in.; Headroom F/R: 3.5/2.5 in.; Legroom F/R: 41.5/24.5 in.; Cargo volume: 13 cu. ft.; Fuel tank: 62L/premium; Tow limit: Not recommended; Load capacity: 1,060 lb.; Turning circle: 37.4 ft.; Ground clearance: 4.2 in.; Weight: 3,750 lb.

sedan with a 3.0 T supercharged V6 in manual and S tronic variants. Introduction of a new 7-speed S tronic and a new Quattro version with Sport Rear Differential (varies torque between the rear wheels to eliminate understeer).

OVERVIEW: This is Audi's bread-and-butter model, probably because it comes in so many variations, including sedans, Avant wagons, and convertibles, plus the lineup includes high-performance models that are sold under the S4 and RS 4 labels. The A4 bills itself as Audi's family sport sedan and targets the BMW 3 Series and Volvo S40/S60 customer by featuring a roomy interior, a 6-speed manual or continuously variable automatic transmission (CVT) with manual-shift capability, all-wheel drive, independent suspension, low-speed traction enhancement, automatic climate control, and more airbags than you can imagine.

The 2010 Audi A4 lineup also includes a restyled, upgraded supercharged S4 sedan model, along with four-door sedans and Avant wagons. The Cabriolet convertible is redesigned and is sold as part of Audi's A5 lineup. Sedans and wagons continue to offer Audi's Quattro all-wheel drive, and some versions of the sedan are available as front-drives. Sedans and Avants come as the 2.0 T and feature a turbocharged 211 hp 2.0L 4-cylinder engine. A continuously variable automatic transmission is standard on front-drive 2.0 Ts. The 2.0 T Quattro models may be hooked to a 6-speed manual or 6-speed automatic transmission. The S4 is powered by a powerful 333 hp 3.0L supercharged V6 mated to either a 6-speed manual or a 7-speed automatic. This new powerplant has impressive torque, which comes on at just 2500 rpm and remains constant through 4850 rpm, making the car especially responsive in everyday driving. The S4 has 18-inch wheels and unique exterior and interior features. Available safety features include ABS, traction control, an anti-skid system, front side airbags, rear side airbags, and side curtain airbags. Other features include a navigation system; Audi Drive Select, which allows the driver to customize steering and suspension settings; a blind-spot alert; keyless entry and engine start; a wireless cell phone link; and a rear-view camera.

COST ANALYSIS: The A4 and A5 are dressed-up VW Passats, so don't get mesmerized by the Audi badge. There's nothing like mixing a deaf and isolated bureaucracy with heaping spoonfuls of arrogance, and then stirring with 50 percent fewer car sales this year. Result? Go for the redesigned 2009, or get this model used, and get your servicing from an independent agency with a reputation for performing competent repairs. **Best alternatives:** If you like the S4 Quattro tire-burner, also consider the BMW M3 convertible or 5 Series and the Porsche 911 Carrera. A4 alternatives are the Acura TL or TSX, Audi TT Coupe, BMW 3 Series, Cadillac CTS, Infiniti G35, Lexus ES 350 or IS series, Subaru Legacy GT, and Toyota Avalon. **Options:** An automatic transmission and all-wheel drive. Think twice about getting the power moonroof if you're a tall driver. **Rebates:** \$3,000–\$6,000 rebates, and a variety of dealer incentive plans and low-interest financing programs. **Depreciation:** Very slow. Audi values no longer nosedive when the base warranty expires and repair costs become the owner's responsibility. **Insurance cost:** Higher than average. **Parts supply/cost:** Often back ordered and expensive. Forget about saving money by getting parts from independent suppliers; they carry few Audi parts. **Annual maintenance cost:** Higher than average, but not exorbitant. **Warranty:** Bumper-to-bumper 4 years/80,000 km; rust perforation 10 years/unlimited km. **Supplementary warranty:** Don't leave the dealership without it. **Highway/city fuel economy:** *2.0 front-drive manual:* 6.5/9.0 L/100 km; *2.0 front-drive automatic:* 7.4/10.1 L/100 km; *2.0 Quattro manual:* 7.4/10.1 L/100 km; *2.0 Quattro automatic:* 7.2/10.8 L/100 km; *3.2 Cabriolet:* 7.7/12.1 L/100 km. Remember, AWD models trade fuel economy for better traction.

OWNER-REPORTED PROBLEMS: Overall quality control has improved over the past several years, but it's still horrendous. The following problems have all taken these cars out of service for extended periods in the past: airbag fails to deploy; excessive steering shake due to a faulty lower control arm; engine, fuel-system, and powertrain component failures; defective brakes; electrical shorts; and abysmal fit and finish. The electrical system is the car's weakest link, and it has plagued Audi's entire lineup for the past decade. Normally, this wouldn't be catastrophic; however, as the cars become more electronically complex and as competent mechanics are fired, you're looking at poor-quality servicing, long waits for service, and unacceptably high maintenance and repair costs.

A6, S6, R8 ★★★

The Audi A6.

RATING: Average. **Strong points:** A potent base engine; superb handling; comfortable seating; plenty of passenger and cargo room (it beats out both BMW and Mercedes in this area); easy front and rear access; and very good build quality.

The Avant wagon performs like a sporty sport-utility, with side airbags, high-intensity discharge (HID) xenon headlights, and excellent outward visibility. IIHS considers offset crash protection to be "Acceptable" and head-restraint protection to be "Good." **Weak points:** The V8 is a bit "growly" when pushed; no real-world performance or reliability data on the V10 yet; firm suspension can make for a jittery ride; radio and navigation controls aren't easily accessed and are counterintuitive; some tire thumping and highway wind noise; the wagon's two-place rear seat is rather small; no NHTSA crashworthiness ratings; limited availability of the most popular models; a chintzy powertrain warranty; and servicing can be problematic. **New for 2010:** *A6:* A new 3.2L engine with Audi's valvelift system and 10 more horses. *S6:* Standard heated rear seats.

KEY FACTS

PRICES: *A6:* $52,900–$72,900, *S6:* $99,500, *R8:* $141,000–$173,000 **FREIGHT:** $800 **ORIGIN:** Germany **SALES:** *A6:* Down 45%, *S6:* Down 52%, *R8:* Unchanged

POWERTRAIN (FRONT-DRIVE/AWD)

Engines: 3.2L V6 (265 hp) • 4.2L V8 (420 hp) • 5.2L V10 (525 hp); Transmissions: 6-speed auto. • 6-speed manual and R tronic • CVT

DIMENSIONS/CAPACITY

Passengers: 2/3; Wheelbase: 111.9 in.; H: 57.5/L: 193.5/W: 79.2 in.; Headroom F/R: 3.0/3.0 in.; Legroom F/R: 42/27.5 in.; Cargo volume: 16 cu. ft.; Fuel tank: 80.1L/premium; Tow limit: 2,000 lb.; Load capacity: 1,100 lb.; Turning circle: 40 ft.; Ground clearance: *A6:* 5.0 in.; *S6:* N/A; *R8:* N/A; Weight: 3,836 lb.

OVERVIEW: Audi's A6 3.2 is essentially a larger, fully equipped A4, and the S models are high-performance, feature-laden variants. A6 is a comfortable, spacious front-drive luxury sedan or wagon that offers standard dual front side airbags and head-protecting side curtain airbags; torso side airbags are optional. Also standard are ABS, an anti-skid system, and xenon headlights (thieves love 'em). There's also a multi-tasking joystick control for all the entertainment, navigation, and climate-control functions. It's similar in function to BMW's iDrive system, which has been roundly criticized as being both confusing and dangerously distracting. The A6 sedan comes with a base 255 hp 3.2L V6 or an optional 350 hp 4.2L V8. Both engines are mated to a 6-speed automatic transmission with manual-shift capability; Audi's Quattro all-wheel drive is also available.

The 2010 Audi R8 is an all-wheel drive, two-seat coupe with a mid-mounted engine; it gets more power this year. The entry-level 4.2 has a 420 hp 4.2L V8 engine, but the 5.2L has a 525 hp V10. Both models are available with a manual transmission or Audi's R tronic automated manual.

COST ANALYSIS: **Best alternatives:** Other vehicles worth taking a look at are the Acura TL, BMW 5 Series, and Volvo V70. **Options:** Think twice about getting the power moonroof if you're a tall driver. **Rebates:** $5,000 rebates and low-interest financing. **Depreciation:** Slower than average. **Insurance cost:** Higher than average. **Parts supply/cost:** Very dealer-dependent and expensive. Independent suppliers carry few Audi parts. **Annual maintenance cost:** Low during the warranty period, and then it climbs steadily. **Warranty:** Bumper-to-bumper 4 years/80,000 km; powertrain 4 years/80,000 km; rust perforation 10 years/ unlimited km. **Supplementary warranty:** A prerequisite to Audi ownership, and it guarantees a good resale price. **Highway/city fuel economy:** *3.2:* 7.4/11.4

L/100 km; 4.2 *Quattro:* 8.8/13.1 L/100 km; *S6* 5.2: 10.4/15.2 L/100 km; *R8* 5.2: 11.6/19.1 L/100 km; *auto.*: 11.2/16.5 L/100 km.

OWNER-REPORTED PROBLEMS: Moisture accumulation in headlights; OnStar loses vehicle location; airbags fail to deploy; front seat fails to stay anchored in a rear-ender; severe hesitation on acceleration; vehicle loses power or stalls when making right turns; premature transmission failure; transmission slips from automatic to manual mode without warning; chronic hesitation at low speeds; faulty gas-tank sensors transmit the wrong measurement of remaining fuel; and distorted front windshield.

TT COUPE ★★★★★

best buy

RATING: Recommended. **Strong points:** Impressive acceleration with the base 200 hp powerplant; all-wheel drive available; good handling and road holding; very well appointed and tastefully designed interior; comfortable, supportive seats; plenty of passenger and cargo space (especially with the rear seatbacks folded); standard ABS; "smart" dual front airbags; standard stability control; and a predicted high resale value. **Weak points:** Base engine lacks low-end torque; excess weight limits handling; poor rear and side visibility; ride may be too firm for some; confusing interior controls; a useless back seat; difficult rear-seat access; lots of engine and road noise; and limited availability. No crashworthiness data available. **New for 2010:** Discontinued 3.2L variants and 2.0 T front-drives; improved standard navigation system; 18-inch wheels; and Bluetooth and HomeLink.

2010 TT

Redesigned in 2009, the TT Coupes carry two engines both reserved for the AWD Quattro versions: a 200 hp 2.0L turbocharged 4-banger, a 265 hp variant of the same engine, and a 250 hp 3.2L V6. On the safety front, all of the 2010 models will have self-supporting run-flat tires; a tire pressure warning system; full-sized dual-stage front airbags, triggered in two stages; and side (head/thorax) and knee airbags. There's also a connection for playing and charging your iPod located in the glove box, which you can control via the radio or the multi-function steering wheel. A Bluetooth mobile telephone feature allows for hands-free operation with voice-controlled capabilities.

TECHNICAL DATA

PRICES: $49,350, *Cabriolet:* $52,350, *TTS Cabriolet:* $61,900 **FREIGHT:** $800
ORIGIN: Germany **SALES:** Down 65%
POWERTRAIN (FRONT-DRIVE/AWD)
Engines: 2.0L 4-cyl. (200 hp) • 2.0L 4-cyl. Turbo (265 hp) • 3.2L V6 (250 hp); Transmissions: 6-speed man. • 6-speed manumatic
DIMENSIONS/CAPACITY
Passengers: 2/2; Wheelbase: 97 in.; H: 53/L: 165/W: 73 in.; Headroom F/R: 3.5/N/A in.; Legroom F/R: 41/N/A in.; Cargo volume: 13.1 cu. ft.; Fuel tank: 62L/premium; Tow limit: No towing; Load capacity: 770 lb.; Turning circle: 36 ft.; Ground clearance: N/A; Weight: 2,965 lb.

OVERVIEW: Although these cars usually hold their value well, bargains abound. Selling for an estimated $49,350 (plus $800 for freight/PDI), the TT Coupe Quattro debuted in the spring of 1999 as a $49,000 sporty front-drive hatchback with 2+2 seating, set on the same platform used by the A4 and the VW Golf, Jetta, and New Beetle. By 2006, the base price had been boosted to an unheard-of $55,980. That first-generation TT is now worth between $8,000 and $11,000; a 2003 entry-level TT that originally sold for $49,000 now sells used for $13,000 to $14,000; a Quattro version of the same model year that originally cost $54,000 is now worth about $14,000, as well; and the $51,650 Cabriolet is worth a paltry $16,000 today. A two-seat convertible version TT Quattro sells for $61,650. The base 200 hp 2.0L 4-cylinder turbocharged engine and optional 250 hp 3.2L V6 are both coupled to a manual 6-speed gearbox; however, the V6 can also be used with the 6-speed manumatic set-up. The 2.0L comes with front-drive only; the V6 model is Quattro only. Shorter and more firmly sprung than the A4, the TT's engines are turbocharged, though only the optional engine comes with standard AWD. A spoiler and anti-skid system are also standard.

More beautifully styled and with better handling than most sporty cars, the TT comes with lots of high-tech standard features that include four-wheel disc brakes, airbags everywhere, stability and traction control, a power top (Quattro), a heated-glass rear window, and a power-retractable glass windbreak between the roll bars (convertible). An alarm system employs a pulse radar system to catch prying hands invading the cockpit area.

COST ANALYSIS: Go for an identical 2009, priced thousands of dollars cheaper. **Best alternatives:** The BMW Z Series, Chevrolet Corvette, Chrysler Crossfire, Honda S2000, Infiniti G35 Coupe, Mazda Miata, Mercedes-Benz CLK or SLK, and Porsche Cayman. **Options:** Think twice about getting the power moonroof if you're a tall driver. **Rebates:** $5,000 rebates and low-interest financing. **Depreciation:** Slower than average. **Insurance cost:** Higher than average. **Parts supply/cost:** Very dealer-dependent and expensive. Independent suppliers carry few Audi parts. **Annual maintenance cost:** Low during the warranty period, and then it climbs steadily. **Warranty:** Bumper-to-bumper 4 years/80,000 km; powertrain 4 years/80,000 km; rust perforation 10 years/unlimited km. **Supplementary warranty:** A prerequisite to Audi ownership, and it guarantees a good resale price. **Highway/city fuel economy:** *2.0:* 6.3/9.0 L/100 km; *3.2 Quattro:* 8.1/12.6 L/100 km.

OWNER-REPORTED PROBLEMS: Airbags fail to deploy; and front seat fails to stay anchored in a rear-ender. Premature transmission failure; transmission slips from automatic to manual mode without warning; chronic hesitation at low speeds; vehicle suddenly surges forward once stopped at a light; severe hesitation on acceleration; vehicle loses power or stalls when making right turns; transmission shifts erratically:

> When I try to accelerate quickly or move my automatic transmission from Drive to Sport there are times when my car feels like it shifts into Neutral instead of down shifting into the next lower gear. There are also times at low speed when the car will have a harsh shift from First to Second and occasionally the automatic transmission will almost stall when trying to start from a stop on a hill.

Faulty gas-tank sensors transmit the wrong measurement of remaining fuel; and screws that secure the oil pan can puncture the pan if hit by road debris. Premature brake wear and electrical system/electronic malfunctions are commonplace. Xenon headlights make it difficult to see the sides of the road; and moisture accumulates in headlights. Front windshield is distorted; central computer causes door locks to jam; windshield wipers often stop working; and side mirrors do not extend out far enough to get a good view of the road.

BMW

BMW is stunned. Long the European sales leader through thick and thin economic times, the latest economic recession has sent the automaker reeling. Sales of cars and trucks (X3, X5, and X6) are down almost 30 percent, and the automaker has had to use rebates, generous leasing programs, and discounts to move its vehicles.

Only BMW's 1 Series has sold relatively well, and that includes a 10% decline through July.

BMW 1 Series: On the market over a year, the 1 Series is BMW's compact, entry-level sedan and convertible, selling for $33,900 and $39,900, respectively. About the same size as the 3 Series of 20 years ago, most of the car's mechanicals have been proven in other countries, where it has been available since late 2004. It is a light, quick car with its base

3.0L 230 hp 6-cylinder engine; however, it cranks out 300 hp when equipped with the turbocharger option. Steering and handling are exceptional. Parts availability should be no problem inasmuch as the 1 Series uses the 3 Series running gear. The car remains unrated by *Lemon-Aid* until more actual driving data is available early next year.

X1: A new entry-level crossover SUV, the X1 is scheduled to go on sale in late 2009 as a 2010 model. The X1 will offer rear-drive or all-wheel drive. Powertrains have not been announced, but it's a safe bet the 3L inline-six found in the 1 and 3 Series will be used.

5 Series: A new hatchback version of the 5 Series, called the Gran Turismo (GT for short), will be introduced towards the end of 2009.

BMW continues to build well-appointed cars that are well built and excel at handling and driving comfort. No matter if fuel prices rise or fall, BMW has a product that will be appropriate for the times. Entry-level shoppers have the 1 and 3 Series; families with more spendable income may opt for the 5 and 6 Series; and for those who have the cash to buy loads of cachet, there's always the flagship 7 Series. Sport-utility fans also have three vehicles to choose from: the compact X3 and larger X5 and X6.

BMWs have excellent road manners, depreciate slowly, and have an "I got mine!" cachet that buyers find hard to resist. Unfortunately, they also have an incredibly complicated centre-console-mounted iDrive feature that some have renamed the "iDie" controller. An article in *Popular Science* titled "uDrive Me Crazy" describes it this way:

> With a push, turn, or shove, this automotive supermouse controls 700 functions, which are displayed in menus on the screen above. Most features that 7 Series drivers had previously selected and modulated via switches, knobs, sliders, pushbuttons, and stalks are now operated by the knob.... It's somewhere between silly and wonderful. It's more a step sideways than a step forward—a few good ideas, a few good features, and a whole bunch of bad implementation.

Lately, BMW has made the iDrive more user-friendly, but the system still takes some getting used to.

Other BMW minuses: limited interior room (except in the high-end models), some quality-control deficiencies (notably the electrical system, brake pads, and fit and finish), and its vehicles can be difficult and expensive to service. A good website that lists BMW problems and fixes is *www.roadfly.com*.

Other than cachet, there are many acceptable reasons for buying a BMW, including fair overall reliability; impressive, high-performance road handling; and a low rate of depreciation. Keep in mind, though, that there are plenty of other cars that cost less, offer more interior room, and are more reliable and better-performing.

So, if you're buying a BMW, remember that this is not the year to try out new fuel, electrical, or powertrain systems. Stick with the cars that have had the fewest changes, and if that means buying a leftover 2009, then so be it; you will likely save on the retail price as well. The entry-level versions of these little status symbols are more show than go, and just a few options can blow your budget. Adding to that, the larger, better-performing high-end models are much more expensive and don't give you the same standard features as many Japanese and South Korean imports do. Also, be prepared to endure long servicing waits, body and trim glitches, and brake, electrical, powertrain, and accessory problems.

MINI COOPER ★★★★

RATING: Above Average. **Strong points:** Better handling than earlier models; more rear legroom and storage capability; distinctively styled; slow depreciation; good offset, front, and side crash protection; head-restraint effectiveness given an "Above Average" rating by IIHS; and NHTSA says this little tyke merits a four-star rating for its resistance to rollovers. Owner reliability complaints have been few, and there's a 4-year/80,000 km all-inclusive base warranty. **Weak points:** A high retail price and freight/PDI fee; mediocre fuel economy, considering the powertrain components; a kidney-pounding ride; and limited front and rear visibility. Stability and traction control are standard only with the upscale models. **New for 2010:** BMW is planning to expand its Mini brand into a multi-model line. The mainstay two-door hatchback hardtop, redesigned for '08, is being joined by the extended-body Clubman, a unique-looking, more-rugged version of the standard mini station wagon.

OVERVIEW: Insiders predict the car will adopt AWD, although its off-road prowess will remain limited due to its low ground clearance, among other things. Next is an updated Mini convertible based on the redesigned hatchback, and again offering Cooper and supercharged Cooper S versions some time in late 2009. In early 2010, we will see the introduction of a Mini E electric car, the first all-electric production car offered to the American buying public by a major manufacturer, beating the rest to the market. Initially this will be an American-only car. The fast-charging E is going to be built in a batch of only 500 cars, 250 for greater Los Angeles and 250 for greater New York, and leased for $850 a month, or $500 more than a conventional lease. A 240-volt, 50-amp charging unit will take 2 hours to recharge the battery. Household current from a 110-volt outlet will take 24 hours. A fully-charged Mini will have a 257-km (160-mi.) driving range.

TECHNICAL DATA

PRICES: *Cooper:* $22,800–$38,390, *Clubman:* $26,400–$39,990 **FREIGHT:** $1,350 **ORIGIN:** Germany **SALES:** Down 20%

POWERTRAIN (FRONT-DRIVE)

Engines: 1.6L 4-cyl. (118 hp) • 1.6L 4-cyl. Turbo (172 hp) • 1.6L 4-cyl. Turbo (208 hp); Transmissions: 6-speed man. • 6-speed auto.

DIMENSIONS/CAPACITY

Passengers: 2/2; Wheelbase: 97 in.; H: 55.4/L: 146.0/W: 66.0 in.; Headroom F/R: 3.5/2.0 in.; Legroom F/R: 41.5/22.0 in.; Cargo volume: 6.0 cu. ft.; Fuel tank: 50L/premium; Tow limit: No towing; Load capacity: 815 lb.; Turning circle: 35.1 ft.; Ground clearance: 4.8 in.; Weight: 2,535 lb.

COST ANALYSIS: Okay, so the Mini's no longer cheap, nor is it as fast as the competition—but stylish it remains, with its uniquely hunkered-down, cute look. It has more interior space than the Austin did (weren't we all smaller back then?), there are 50/50 split-folding seats for additional storage space, and the fully independent suspension carries a body that we're told is much more rigid than what's offered by the competition. Plus, it's almost as cheap to drive as walking. **Best alternatives:** The Mazda Miata and Porsche Boxster. The Ford Mustang convertible is the perfect muscle car to contrast with the Mini's less-is-more ethos. The Mustang possesses style in droves and offers an exciting driving experience—with more fuel consumption and more weight. Or you could consider a classic roadster, such as the Mazda Miata. Though it comes as a two-seater only, it's perhaps the closest to the Mini Cooper's lightweight joy, its controls and responses a seeming extension of the driver's wishes. **Highway/city fuel economy:** *1.6L engine with a manual transmission:* 5.3/7.1 L/100 km; *1.6L auto.:* 5.7/7.9 L/100 km; *S manual:* 5.7/7.8 L/100 km; *S automatic:* 6.2/8.7 L/100 km.

OWNER-REPORTED PROBLEMS: Engine idle dip and poor acceleration; AC whistling, sunroof squeaking, and rear hatch/door window rattling; a seat heater that gets too hot or too cold; windshield stress cracks; speedometer needle vibration; and inoperative interior lights. See *www.mini.ca* and *www.mini2.com/forum* for a good overview of ownership pros and cons.

3 SERIES ★★★/★

RATING: Average. *M3:* Not Recommended; the transmission hesitation upon acceleration or deceleration can get you killed. Many competitors deliver more interior room and standard features for less money. Smart BMW buyers will stick with the simple, large-volume, entry-level models until the recession blows over. **Strong points:** Very well-appointed: recently upgraded cockpit amenities include a standard tilt/telescope steering wheel, optional power-memory seats, power lumbar adjustments, an in-dash CD player, steering wheel audio and cruise controls, standard traction and stability control, and rear side-impact airbags. Good acceleration (highlighted by the $69,900 M3's incredibly fast performance); the 6-cylinder engines and the transmissions are the essence of harmonious cooperation, even when coupled to an automatic transmission—there's not actually that much difference between the manual and the automatic from a performance perspective. Light and precise gear shifting with easy clutch and shift action; competent and predictable handling on dry surfaces; no-surprise suspension and steering make for crisp high-speed and emergency handling; lots of road feedback, which enhances rear-end stability; smooth, efficient braking that produces short stopping distances; and top-notch quality control. NHTSA give its top crashworthiness five-star score for front

TECHNICAL DATA

PRICES: $34,900–$65,600 **FREIGHT:** $1,350 **ORIGIN:** Germany **SALES:** Down 30%

POWERTRAIN (REAR-DRIVE/AWD)

Engines: 3.0L 6-cyl. (230 hp) • 3.0L 6-cyl Turbo (300 hp) • 3.0L 6-cyl. Diesel (265 hp) • 4.0L V8 (414 hp); Transmissions: 6-speed man. • 6-speed auto. • 7-speed auto.

DIMENSIONS/CAPACITY

Passengers: 2/2; Wheelbase: 109 in.; H: 56/L: 178/W: 72 in.; Headroom F/R: 3.5/2.5 in.; Legroom F/R: 40.5/27.5 in.; Cargo volume: 11 cu. ft.; Fuel tank: 63L/premium; Tow limit: No towing; Load capacity: 1,060 lb.; Turning circle: 19.4 ft.; Ground clearance: N/A; Weight: 3,485 lb.

and side protection; rollover resistance received four stars. **Weak points:** A somewhat harsh ride (the M3 is harsher than most); insufficient front headroom and seat lumbar support for tall occupants; limited rear-seat room and cargo area; tricky entry and exit, even on sedans; confusing navigation system controls; excessive tire noise, especially with the M3; and premium fuel required. **New for 2010:** The 2010 BMW 3 Series sedans and wagons will be carried over relatively unchanged after their 2009 freshening and the introduction of a diesel engine. The coupes and convertibles may be slightly restyled. The 3 Series model lineup, with its entry-level 328, mid-line 335, and high-performance M3, remain practically unchanged; 328i's should continue to be available with rear-wheel drive or with BMW's xDrive AWD hooked to a 230 hp 3.0L 6-cylinder engine. All of the other models will remain powered by a turbocharged 300 hp version of the 3.0L 6-cylinder. The rear-drive 335d will return with its 265 hp 3.0L 6-cylinder turbodiesel powerplant. M3 models return with last year's 414 hp 4.0L V8.

All BMW 3 Series gasoline engines should remain available with a 6-speed manual transmission. Most likely remaining available on the 328i and 335i, and standard on the 335d, is a 6-speed automatic. The M3 will return with its 7-speed automatic.

OVERVIEW: With BMW's recent mechanical upgrades, styling changes, and increased exterior and interior dimensions, the 3 Series has come to resemble its more expensive big brothers, with super-smooth powertrain performance and enhanced handling. The 3 Series Sedan and Coupé come as 328i, all-wheel-drive 328xi, and 335i models, plus there's a Canadian-only 323i ($35,000); the Touring wagon is designated as a 328xi model. They all have a base 3.0L inline 6-cylinder engine, except the 323i, which has a 2.5L. The 328i and 328xi versions have a 230 hp engine that replaces the 215 hp version sold with the 325i. The 255 hp 330i models have been replaced by the 300 hp turbocharged 335i.

COST ANALYSIS: Buy a cheaper 2009 for that year's upgrades; the 2010s have little that is new apart from diesel power, which is worth staying away from during its first few years on the market. **Best alternatives:** Other cars worth considering are the Audi A4 and the Lexus IS series. **Options:** If you buy a convertible, invest $1,500 in the rollover protection system that pops up from behind the rear seat. The optional Sport suspension does enhance handling and steering, but it also produces an overly harsh, jiggly ride on rough pavement. Wider tires compromise traction in snow. Stay away from the Turanza run-flats and Bridgestone tires:

> Bridgestone tire exhibits unsafe characteristics in wet weather, with noticeable drift and hydroplaning in any amount of standing water, even as little as 1/16 inch [1.5 mm]. In heavy rains, even with no standing water present, the tire seems incapable of dispersing water as quickly as it falls, again leading to vehicle instability. From a ride quality point of view the tire is also unsatisfactory in that it flat spots every morning, especially in cool weather but even in warmer weather as well, leading to vibrations in the initial miles of any drive. It is also especially harsh over roadway expansion joints, and is so loud on concrete pavements that it poses a safety hazard

> due to driver fatigue induced by the continuous noise. I also understand that there may be an issue regarding the rating as an "all season tire" with many owners reporting that this tire is virtually useless in any kind of snow conditions.

Rebates: Not likely. Dealers will push generous leases and low-interest financing. **Depreciation:** Slower than average. **Insurance cost:** Higher than average. **Parts supply/cost:** Parts are less expensive than those for other cars in this class. Unfortunately, they aren't easily found outside of the dealer network, where they're often back-ordered. That said, parts and repairs are far easier to find than with Audi, Jaguar, Mini, Porsche, and Saab. **Annual maintenance cost:** Average until the warranty runs out, and then your mechanic starts sharing your paycheque. **Warranty:** Bumper-to-bumper 4 years/80,000 km; rust perforation 6 years/unlimited km. **Supplementary warranty:** Not needed. **Highway/city fuel economy:** *128i Cabriolet:* 7.0/11.3 L/100 km; *auto.:* 7.3./11.4 L/100 km; *323i 2.5L:* 6.9/11.1 L/100 km; *auto.:* 6.7/11.2 L/100 km; *M3 Cabriolet:* 10.1/15.7 L/100 km; *Coupe:* 9.7/15.3 L/100 km.

OWNER-REPORTED PROBLEMS: Fire originated in the fog light socket (see *www.bmw-fire.com*); engines, brakes, electrical system (telematics), and some body trim and accessories are the most failure-prone components; engine overheating is a serious problem, and it's most common on past models; premature tire wear, and noisy run-flat tires—owners forced to pay for tire failures. *325i:* Excessive hesitation on acceleration:

> When the driver demands a sudden increase in acceleration, the car hesitates anywhere from 1.5 to 3 seconds. This is a dangerous condition when someone is making a left turn in traffic, or getting onto a highway, or passing on a 2 lane country road, etc. Other cars traveling at 60 mph [96.5 km/h] are moving at 88 ft./sec. [27 m/s]. The amount of leeway this car needs is much too excessive.

Bridgestone tire-tread separation and side wall buckling:

> Bridgestone Potenza RE050A runflat tires. The tires buckled on the side wall after less than 8,000 miles [12,870 km]. Out of curiosity I checked the Bimmerfest www.*bimmerfest.com/forums/showthread.php?t=146728* forum and discovered this is a widespread problem among BMW owners.

328: Airbag failed to deploy; premature tire failure (bubbles in the tread); sudden acceleration; when accelerating, engine cuts out and then surges forward (suspected failure of the throttle assembly); severe engine vibrations after a cold start as Check Engine light comes on; and rear-quarter blind spot with the convertibles. *330i:* Side airbag deployed when vehicle hit a pothole; vehicle overheats in low gears; and vehicle slips out of Second gear when accelerating. *335i:* Sunroof suddenly exploded. Engine stalling and loss of power fixed by replacing the fuel pump; now exhaust is booming, fuel economy has dropped, and there's considerable "turbo lag" when accelerating. Many other cases of the high-pressure fuel pump failing, with some owners having to replace the pump four times. *M3:* Tail light socket overheats, blowing the bulb and shorting other lights: costs $600 to rewire. Vehicle loses power due to faulty fuel pumps; transmission hesitates when accelerating in Second gear (see *www.roadfly.com*):

> There are times, however, when the car is decelerating but not coming to a full stop (when taking a turn at an intersection, for example), that the transmission will begin its automated downshifts but then become incredibly unresponsive. In these cases, if I press on the accelerator before coming to a full stop, I'll notice a significant lag before the engine actually revs up.

bad buy

X3, X5, X6 ★

The BMW X5.

RATING: Not Recommended. This triad of SUVs is totally unremarkable. Sales trailed appreciably through July 2009, even though the decade-old X5 has been less affected than the newer X3 and X6. A larger X3 is known to be in the works and will likely show up sometime during 2010. Expect the X3 to grow by nearly a foot. The X5 and X6 get a new M version with a 555 hp twin-turbo V8, stiffer suspension, and racy body trim.

The X1 is BMW's new entry-level crossover SUV, which goes on sale in Europe this fall and will be introduced later to North America in 2011. The European version will offer three diesel engines and one gasoline-powered unit. It is expected that the U.S.- and Canada-destined X1 will get a 258 hp 3.0L inline-six, all-wheel drive, and a sticker price of $33,000–$38,000.

X3: A small crossover SUV for the upscale crowd, which wants a compact 5-seater SUV that behaves like a sports sedan. **Strong points:** Responsive handling; precise, predictable steering; abundant cargo space; and a quiet, nicely appointed

TECHNICAL DATA

X3

PRICES: $45,300 **FREIGHT:** $1,350 **ORIGIN:** Austria, South Carolina **SALES:** Down 70%

POWERTRAIN (REAR-DRIVE/AWD)
Engine: 3.0L 6-cyl. (260 hp); Transmissions: 6-speed man. • 6-speed auto.

DIMENSIONS/CAPACITY
Passengers: 2/3; Wheelbase: 110 in.; H: 66/L: 180/W: 73 in.; Headroom F/R: 4.0/3.0 in.; Legroom F/R: 41.5/27.5 in.; Cargo volume: 33 cu. ft.; Fuel tank: 67L/premium; Tow limit: 3.500 lb.; Load capacity: 1,005 lb.; Turning circle: 38.4 ft.; Ground clearance: 8.0 in.; Weight: 4,065 lb.

X5

PRICES: $58,200–$71,500 **FREIGHT:** $1,350 **ORIGIN:** South Carolina **SALES:** Down 21%

POWERTRAIN (REAR-DRIVE/AWD)
Engines: 3.0L 6-cyl. (230 hp) • 3.0L 6-cyl. (260 hp) • 3.0L Diesel 6-cyl. (265 hp) • 4.8L V8 (350 hp); Transmission: 6-speed auto.

DIMENSIONS/CAPACITY
Passengers: 2/3/2; Wheelbase: 116 in.; H: 70/L: 191/W: 76 in.; Headroom F/R: 3.5/2.5 in.; Legroom F/R: 40/27.5 in.; Cargo volume: 36 cu. ft.; Fuel tank: 93L/premium; Tow limit: 6,000 lb.; Load capacity: 1,350 lb.; Turning circle: 42 ft.; Ground clearance: 8.3 in.; Weight: 5,025 lb.

X6

PRICES: $63,900–$78,100 **FREIGHT:** $1,350 **ORIGIN:** South Carolina **SALES:** Down 47%

POWERTRAIN (REAR-DRIVE/AWD)
Engines: 2.5L 6-cyl. (200 hp) • 3.0L 6-cyl. (230 hp) • 3.0L 6-cyl. (300 hp); Transmissions: 6-speed man. • 6-speed auto.

DIMENSIONS/CAPACITY
Passengers: 2/3/2; Wheelbase: 116 in.; H: 67/L: 192/W: 78 in.; Headroom F/R: 3.5/2.5 in.; Legroom F/R: 40/27.5 in.; Cargo volume: N/A; Fuel tank: 85L/premium; Tow limit: No towing; Load capacity: 1,190 lb.; Turning circle: 42 ft.; Ground clearance: 8.5 in.; Weight: 4,895 lb.

interior. **Weak points:** This little SUV wannabe responds to a need no one has expressed. Way overpriced; options are a minefield of inflated charges; mind-spinning depreciation; a stiff ride; a narrow interior; serious fit and finish problems; audio system malfunctions; power equipment failures; and electrical system glitches. *X5:* BMW's first crossover SUV, this mid-size seven-seater has been on the market since 1999. **Strong points:** All three X5 engines deliver plenty of power, and there's a turbocharged diesel option; smooth, responsive power delivery, secure handling, and good steering feedback; comfortable first- and second-row seating; and a well-appointed interior. **Weak points:** During the past decade, the X5 has built a reputation for poor quality control and major deficiencies in body integrity, fit and finish, powertrain, and electrical components. Following its recent redesign, the X5 needs to be taken back to the shop. The ride is just as stiff and choppy as before (a characteristic it shares with the X3); the complicated shifter and iDrive controls can be hard to master without a lot of patience and frustration; and the third-row seats are for kids only. *X6:* An X5 spin-off, the X6 gives you many of the X5 advantages and disadvantages, but in a larger box. **Strong points:** On the market only two years, the X6 is billed as BMW's "sports activity" coupe because it is loaded with high-performance features. It carries a standard turbocharged 3.0L 6-cylinder engine and a powerful optional 4.4L V8, seats only four, and is a bit taller than most coupes. The AWD system can vary the torque from side to side to minimize under-steer. A hybrid X5 is in the offing for next year. **Weak points:** New on the market, so servicing and parts availability may be problematic.

OVERVIEW: Here is where BMW took on the Asian automakers and came out second best. Despite BMW's recent mechanical upgrades, styling changes, and increased exterior and interior dimensions, the X3, X5, and X6 SUVs are not very impressive from either a performance or a comfort/convenience perspective. Despite tax credits and superior gas mileage figures, BMW is reportedly having a tough time selling its new diesels on the 2009 X5 xDrive35d and the 335d sports sedan.

COST ANALYSIS: Buy an almost identical, cheaper 2009, or wait for the X1's arrival next year. **Best alternatives:** *X3:* Acura RDX, Audi Q5, Honda CR-V, Mercedes GLK, and Volvo XC60. *X5, X6:* GM Acadia, Enclave, Escalade, and Outlook; Lexus RX Series, Mercedes ML-Class, Toyota Land Cruiser, and Volvo V70 Cross Country. **Rebates:** \$4,000–\$7,000 discounts along with low-rate financing and generous leasing terms. **Depreciation:** Average. **Insurance cost:** Higher than average. **Parts supply/cost:** Moderately expensive; they aren't easily found outside of the dealer network, where they're often back-ordered. **Annual maintenance cost:** Average until the warranty runs out, and then your mechanic gets to know you real well. **Warranty:** Bumper-to-bumper 4 years/80,000 km; rust perforation 6 years/unlimited km. **Supplementary warranty:** A wise decision. **Highway/city fuel economy:** *X3:* 8.2/12.5 L/100 km; *auto.:* 8.4/12.2 L/100 km; *X5:* 9.3/13.6 L/100 km; *diesel:* 7.5/10.7 L/100 km; *V8:* 10.2/15.6 L/100 km; *X6:* 10.0/14.4 L/100 km; *V8:* 11.0/17.1 L/100 km.

OWNER-REPORTED PROBLEMS: Parts are scarce outside of major metropolitan areas, and independent mechanics are rare. All of the foregoing servicing deficiencies are being accentuated by poor sales, a shaky dealer network, and unreliable suppliers. *X3:* Fewer owner complaints than for the X5. Owners target the fit and finish, power equipment, audio system, fuel system, and transmission as most in need of special attention. *X5:* Owners report problems with the powertrain, electrical system, climate controls, brakes, audio system, body integrity, and fit and finish. During the X5's 10-year tenure in North America, it has earned an unenviable reputation for poor quality and unreliable performance. Insiders say that the quality problems surged during the first few years because the X5 was a totally new kind of BMW, rushed to production with many components that were not compatible with the new vehicle's structure and hadn't been proven under real driving conditions. Why are the problems still there today? Because BMW decided to turn its attention to the core passenger car market and let the X series simply stumble along. Now, the economic recession has again diverted the company's attention away from correcting the X's deficiencies. From the NHTSA complaint log:

> A Florida dealer had to replace every rotor-pad and sensor on my 2009 X5, and less than 2 weeks later the rear brakes and sensors needed replacement, again. Do not buy an X5 from this company, because even after their own [service] manager states to replace the vehicle they say there is nothing wrong and don't give a damn about your safety.

•

2008 BMW X5 has a faulty fuel injector pump and battery. The vehicle suddenly stopped in the middle of the highway. It stopped again in the middle of the highway after the fuel pump was supposedly replaced. The car owner was told again the fuel pump was faulty. The sunroof was inoperative and the camera used that gives guidance when backing out of spaces was inoperative, as well.

•

My 2008 BMW X5 is reporting high battery drain and it's only 13 months old with 5,000 miles [8,050 km]. The dealer states the issues is because the vehicle is not driven at least 25 miles [40 km] a day. If this is a requirement to owning the vehicles it was never mentioned when I purchased the vehicle. My own research on the Internet indicates this is a well known problem.

•

The problem with my 2008 X3 is that the transmission is not reactive, and causes major hesitation, delayed shifting, and awkward responses from the throttle which is a serious issue when merging or passing, etc. The car does not get up to speed, and at times literally "chokes," which can cause an accident as someone behind you can just begin to accelerate and plow right into you.

Jaguar

Not Recommended. Jaguar isn't a car, it's an image—an image of what was so great with British cars that were quite like us in the '60s: adventurous, rebellious, and independent.

But that time is long-passed, and Jaguar's image now is that of a doddering old uncle who's had multiple hip replacements, suffers from Alzheimer's, and has been thrown out of his American rest home and is now in intensive care somewhere in India.

Jaguar is proof positive that the British can't build quality cars; the Americans don't want to build performance cars; and India's Tata Motors, Jaguar's latest keeper, doesn't give a damn either way. Although the cars' styling, ride, handling, and comfort still entice motoring masochists full of nostalgia for the British cars of the 1960s, what they get instead is a hodgepodge of Ford Taurus and Lincoln parts thrown together with a Jaguar badge. No wonder Taurus-sourced powertrain, electronic, and body problems persist—problems such as sudden, unintended acceleration; automatic transmission and brake failures; shimmying; and excessive noise when driving with the rear windows open. What's all the more surprising is that even with these serious defects, insiders say these pseudo-Jags are better built than the original versions. Moreover, the Jaguar's poor-quality image lives on despite fewer complaints recorded over the past few years. This is probably why these luxury cars have such a high rate of depreciation (a 2009 XJ8 entry-level Jaguar that originally sold for $80,500 is now worth $50,000) and why prudent buyers prefer to lease rather than purchase their Jags.

When Ford bought Jaguar, it had three goals: Improve quality, make the cars more affordable, and make the division profitable. Consequently, Ford has introduced two cheaper models, the S-Type and X-Type, joined by the more upscale XJ8 and XK8. As far as making Jaguar profitable—it never happened. Jaguar continues to lose money, recently posting a more than $500-million operating loss that it blames on the economy, its workers, and unsophisticated shoppers. (Oh no, it's not the cars!)

High-end Jaguars have excess weight that makes it necessary to install lots of complicated and difficult-to-troubleshoot devices, as well as larger engines encased in aluminum bodies, in order to make them decent highway performers. Entry-level Jags have a different problem: convincing buyers that the X-Types are more than gussied-up Ford-Tata-Nanos. Jaguar models are discussed in more detail in Appendix I.

Mercedes-Benz

The Mighty Have Fallen

In the first seven months of 2009, Mercedes announced a 17.5 percent drop-off in sales to 638,100 cars, almost half the percentage of the industry's sales decline (36.6 percent). And this wasn't simply a reaction to the recession, the drying up of discretionary funds, or higher fuel prices. In fact, sales of Mercedes' Smart minicar were down an unexpected 15.9 percent on the year, at 10,400 cars in July.

M-B's parent firm Daimler posted a loss of $1.6 billion (U.S.) in the second quarter of 2009 before taxes, and trumpeted that this result was better than expected. A billion-dollar loss is good news? Daimler says it is also continuing to be hit by the expense of giving up its former 19.9 percent stake in Chrysler, which saw it write off Chrysler's outstanding loans and agree to pay $200 million a year into Chrysler's pension fund. It said that this continuing exposure to Chrysler losses has already cost the German automaker $400 billion during the last quarter.

Nevertheless, Mercedes expects to see a return to profit in 2010, helped mainly by predicted sales of the new E-Class, which went on sale earlier this year. Stung by mounting criticism and souring sales as a result of the earlier, post-2002 E-Class's reliability and quality woes, Mercedes has introduced hundreds of changes designed to improve the model's looks and performance.

Poor Quality Still Haunts Mercedes

Still, the poor quality reputation lingers on. In a 2007 *Consumer Reports* survey of 36 leading automobile brands, Mercedes-Benz ranked dead last in predicted reliability. In *CR*'s April 2009 Auto Guide edition, Mercedes' 2003 through 2008 models have more "Poor Reliability" black spots than Walt Disney's *101 Dalmatians*. Even so, *Consumer Reports*' April edition recommends the E-Class, M-Class, and S-Class models. *Lemon-Aid* gives the E-Class an Average rating and considers the M-Class Not Recommended.

Way before *Consumer Reports* got involved, except for some hapless buyers, everyone knew that Mercedes' 1998 M-Class sport-utilities were abysmally bad. You couldn't have made a worse vehicle, judging by the unending stream of desperate-sounding service bulletins sent by the head office to dealers following the vehicles' official launch. Two bulletins stand out in my mind. One was an authorization for dry-cleaning payouts to dealers whose customers' clothing had been stained by the dye from the burgundy-coloured leather seats. The other was a lengthy explanation as to why drivers were "tasered" by static electricity when entering or leaving their vehicles.

Car columnists have always known that Mercedes has made some bad cars and SUVs, but it took business reporters (not auto beat writers) from the gutsy *Wall Street Journal* to spill the beans. In a February 2, 2002, article titled "An Engineering Icon Slips," the *WSJ* cited several confidential industry-initiated surveys that showed that Mercedes' quality and customer satisfaction had fallen dramatically since 1999—to a level below that of GM's Opel, a brand that had one of the worst reputations for poor quality in Europe.

An earlier J.D. Power and Associates study of vehicle durability in the States put Mercedes 12th in its ranking, behind Lincoln, Cadillac, and (gasp!) Jaguar. Its chief failings were in the transmission and features/controls categories. Following this study, J.D. Power and Associates announced to a National Automobile Dealers Association convention that Mercedes' rating for overall quality had been lowered to "Fair" from "Good."

The quality issue first surfaced in various quality surveys and then again after the launch of the technically advanced E-Class in 2003. It was then reflected in slipping positions in customer satisfaction polls. In a recent *Consumer Reports* U.S. subscriber survey, the 2004 Mercedes-Benz E-Class was the most problem-ridden car. Among 2001 models, the C-Class was the worst car and the M-Class the worst SUV.

Industry insiders give me different reasons why Mercedes-Benz quality has fallen. They say quality control has been diluted by the more than doubling of M-B's product lineup since 1997. Helpful, too, were the company's aggressive PR campaigns and the Teutonic mindset that tended to blame the driver rather than the product—both spectacularly successful in keeping the quality myth alive in the media until the *Wall Street Journal* broke the story. Neither mindset nor PR worked to mitigate owners' displeasure over M-B's engine sludge stonewalling, though. It cost Mercedes $32 million (U.S.) to settle after the company denied that there was a factory-related problem.

For a small taste of how well Mercedes manages the press circling its vehicles, look on the Internet for stories relating to the A-Class "Baby Benz" (a Smart Car predecessor sold mainly in Europe) flipping over during its press launching, allegations involving M-B's Holocaust involvement, its tight-lipped reaction to the above-cited quality surveys, and reports that Mercedes' residual values have fallen dramatically. For example, a 2003 C-Class C230 that originally sold for $34,500 is now worth only $7,000, and a 2003 E-Class E320 mid-range sedan once priced at $70,000 can now be bought for $15,000.

Mercedes 2010 Changes

Mercedes knows that if it is to claw its way back up the sales charts, the company has to improve servicing, ship new products to dealer showrooms, and simplify its model lineup. Consequently, Mercedes is re-engineering and trimming its 2010 models, offering fuel-frugal compacts like the B-Class and Smart Car, and introducing hybrid variants throughout its model lineup. Mercedes will also launch the B-Class F-CELL in the summer of 2010, the production vehicle with a local, zero-emission fuel-cell drive.

The S-Class hybrid will be Mercedes' single largest mechanical update for 2010, bringing what is billed as the first widely marketed lithium-ion battery in a hybrid. The new hybrid will come with the rest of the S-Class in early 2010. The standard S-Class sedans will also get new standard wheels and new driver assistance systems, including Attention Assist, Nightview Assist PLUS, and Lane Keeping Assist.

Other key changes include a renaming of the firm's diesel offerings from GL320, ML320, and R320 to GL350, ML350, and R350. Be warned: The numbers don't indicate an engine upgrade; the same V6 turbodiesel lies under their hoods. GL-Class cars also get a facelift, POST-SAFE post-accident safety system, and a few new options. The M-Class SUV lineup adds a ML450 hybrid to its family. It arrives at year's end with a full hybrid powertrain, capable of producing 335 hp with a specially adapted V6 engine.

Also new for 2010 will be the ML350 BlueTEC, which will be replacing the ML320 BlueTEC. Unchanged for 2010 will be rear-drive and AWD models of the gas-powered ML350, AWD ML550, and performance-oriented ML63 AMG.

SMART ★★

RATING: Below Average; this vehicle is smaller than small. **Strong points:** Once the car gets up to highway speeds (which may seem like forever), it manages to keep up with traffic; fuel-frugal; highly practical for city driving and parking; good short-term reliability reports; slow depreciation; distinctive styling; the engine bay isn't as crammed as with many small cars; responsive steering and transmission performance; and the ride is almost comfortable, thanks to well-bolstered seats, a longer wheelbase, and a wider track than provided with earlier models. NHTSA gives the 2010 Smart four stars for frontal collision occupant protection, five stars for side protection, and three stars for rollover resistance. It also received "Good" ratings (the top rating) for front and side crash protection in IIHS tests. Standard stability control, side airbags, and ABS. Sold in most of Canada's 45-some Mercedes-Benz dealerships with a 4-year/80,000 km all-inclusive warranty. **Weak points:** You pay a maxi price for a minicar that's less refined than cheaper Honda, Hyundai, Kia, Nissan, Suzuki, or Toyota microcars; dealer-dependent servicing (trips must be planned carefully for servicing accessibility); slow

TECHNICAL DATA

PRICES: *Fortwo Coupe:* $14,990–$18,250, *Fortwo Cabriolet:* $21,250
FREIGHT: $1,795 **ORIGIN:** Germany
SALES: Down 15.9%
POWERTRAIN (REAR-DRIVE)
Engines: 3-cylinder 1.0L (71 hp); Transmission: 5-speed manumatic
DIMENSIONS/CAPACITY
Passengers: 2; Wheelbase: 73.5 in.; H: 60.7/L: 106.1/W: 61.4 in.; Headroom F/R: N/A; Legroom F/R: N/A; Cargo volume: 12.0 cu. ft.; Fuel tank: 37.8 L/premium; Tow limit: No towing; Load capacity: N/A; Turning circle: 28 ft.; Ground clearance: N/A; Weight: 1,808 lb.

acceleration from a stop; the automated manual shifter is annoyingly slow and rough. NHTSA says that during its side impact test, the driver door unlatched and opened. A door opening during a side impact crash increases the likelihood of occupant ejection resulting in serious injury or death. Also, in an April 2009 64 km/h (40 mph) frontal offset crash test between a Smart Fortwo and a Mercedes C-Class, IIHS rated the Fortwo "Poor," noting that "Multiple injuries, including to the head, would be likely for a real-world driver of a Smart in a similar collision." You must use premium fuel. **New for 2010:** An all-electric Smart is expected in late 2010; it will cost $35,000 (U.S.), or $5,000 less than the GM Volt gas/electric car.

OVERVIEW: This minicompact two-seater made its European debut in October 1998. Since then, it has run Mercedes into the hole to the tune of $3 billion. It arrived in Canada in the fall of 2004 and was greeted by record sales and an almost cult following—until the last couple of years, when shoppers flocked to the more refined econoboxes sold by Asian automakers. Over 10,000 Smarts have been sold in Canada, three times more than expected, and a third of those sales were in Quebec. Not bad for a tiny, two-seat, French-built runabout that's based on a car that rolled over at its European press launching.

Smarts are powered by a 3-cylinder engine that produces 71 hp—nowhere near the 106 horses offered by Toyota's smallest car, the $13,000+ Yaris. Furthermore, the Smart is only 2.5 metres long and weighs in at only 730 kg, compared to the 1,040-kg Yaris. These factors combine to give the Smart a 4.8/5.9 L/100 km fuel consumption rating for the Coupe and Cabriolet, much better than the Yaris's estimated highway/city fuel economy of 5.5 L/100 km and 6.9 L/100 km, respectively, and much more than the outrageously inaccurate fuel savings claims bandied about by Honda and Toyota when they hype their hybrids that cost far more than a Smart.

Is the Smart safe?

It's safer than many cars, thanks to stability control, ABS, and side airbags. NHTSA and Australian crash researchers give it high crashworthiness marks, generally. The Smart is undoubtedly as safe a car as others in its class—but there's the dilemma: its size will always make it vulnerable to the basic laws of physics. In fact, IIHS recently crash-tested several small cars, including the Chevy Aveo and Honda Fit, and five of the eight models—including some with side curtain airbags—fared poorly.

What is risky? The car's long-term viability.

As Mercedes continues "Americanizing" the Smart—making it heavier, larger, and less fuel-efficient—the car becomes less distinctive and more costly to own. Also, cheaper, more refined, and just as fuel-efficient competitors will soon look better in comparison. Finally, as fuel prices rise and fall with the lunar cycle (or so it seems), fewer buyers will accept the Smart's disadvantages in exchange for lower fuel costs.

As things now stand in the States, Smart is an automotive orphan placed in the Penske Child Care Centre until Mercedes can make up its mind as to the car's future. If it decides that Smart is more of a drain than a gain, you can expect owners to be left high and dry, judging by Mercedes' record with its small, entry-level "Baby Benz" 190 models, introduced over a decade ago and then quickly abandoned. Now this wouldn't be much of a problem if Smarts were conventional small cars backed by an extensive dealer network and a large parts inventory. But that's not the case. Furthermore, unlike with old MGs and Triumphs, there isn't a body of independent repairers and parts suppliers who can step into the breach.

B-CLASS ★★

RATING: Below Average. First launched as a 2006 model, this car is sold mainly in Canada and Europe. It's Mercedes' second-smallest car, following the Smart. It is feature-laden, with four-wheel disc brakes, side airbags, and stability control. Fuel economy figures aren't that impressive (*manual:* 6.7/9.2 L/100 km; *CVT:* 7.2/9.2 L/100 km; *turbo and CVT:* 7.4/9.5 L/100 km; *turbo and 6-speed manual:* 6.9/10.3 L/100 km), and the car isn't as fuel-efficient as some of the Japanese competition. The retail price could also be trimmed by at least $5,000. It's seriously overpriced and not as cheap to drive as represented. Furthermore, it has an unusually large turning circle, which cuts its urban usefulness. Shoppers would be wise to consider the equivalent Mazdas, or Japanese microcars like the Honda Fit, Nissan Versa, and Toyota Yaris. Granted, the car represents a solid commitment by M-B to offer smaller, more economical compacts through its own dealer network. But the company's last step in this direction, the 190 Series "Baby Benz" (1990–93), was a quality- and performance-challenged flop. And the question remains: Is the B-Class worth a $29,900 price tag? **New for 2010:** A slight restyling, giving the car more of a C-Class hatchback look. Fuel-cell power is coming, but we don't yet know how much the cars will cost, or how well they will be serviced. Again, *Lemon-Aid* cautions readers: Tough times are not good times for servicing vehicles with new high-tech systems.

TECHNICAL DATA

PRICES: $29,900–$34,400 **FREIGHT:** $1,795 **ORIGIN:** Germany **SALES:** N/A
POWERTRAIN (FRONT-DRIVE)
Engines: 2.0L 4-cyl. (134 hp) • 2.0L Turbo 4-cyl. (193 hp); Transmissions: 5-speed man. • 6-speed man. • CVT
DIMENSIONS/CAPACITY
Passengers: 2/3; Wheelbase: 109.3 in.; H: 63.1/L: 168.1/W: 69.6 in.; Headroom F/R: N/A; Legroom F/R: 43.0/25.5 in.; Cargo volume: 13.4 cu. ft.; Fuel tank: 54L/premium; Tow limit: No towing; Load capacity: N/A; Turning circle: 39.2 ft.; Ground clearance: N/A; Weight: 2,854 lb.

Technically, the fuel cell–powered B-Class is a joy to contemplate. Compared to the F-CELL found in M-B's A-Class, a more efficient system is used in the F-CELL B-Class. The electric motor develops maximum output of 100 kW/136 hp and a maximum torque of 320 newton metres. This means that the B-Class F-CELL offers extremely high road-holding standards that surpass those of a standard 2L gas engine. At the same time, the fuel-cell drive in this compact vehicle with a family-friendly design uses the equivalent of just 2.9L of fuel (diesel equivalent) per 100 km—and all that with zero emissions.

C-CLASS ★★★

TECHNICAL DATA

PRICES: *230:* $35,800, *63 AMG:* $63,500 **FREIGHT:** $1,795 **ORIGIN:** Germany **SALES:** Down 30%

POWERTRAIN (REAR-DRIVE/AWD)

Engines: 3.0L V6 (228 hp) • 3.5L V6 (268 hp) • 6.2L V8 (451 hp); Transmissions: 6-speed man. • 7-speed auto.

DIMENSIONS/CAPACITY

Passengers: 2/3; Wheelbase: 109 in.; H: 56.1/L: 182.0/W: 70.0 in.; Headroom F/R: 2.5/1.5 in.; Legroom F/R: 42/26 in.; Cargo volume: 12 cu. ft.; Fuel tank: 62L/ premium; Tow limit: Not recommended; Load capacity: 835 lb.; Turning circle: 35.3 ft.; Ground clearance: 4.2 in.; Weight: 3,565 lb.

-Benz

RATING: Average. These little entry-level cars lack the simplicity and popular pricing found with the Japanese competition; save up for an E-Class. **Strong points:** Plenty of high-tech safety features; strong powertrain matchup with decent fuel economy, all enhanced with AWD; a comfortable ride; easy handling; excellent braking; innovative anti-theft system; NHTSA's top five-star award for side crashworthiness; and four stars given out for front and rollover protection. IIHS crash tests gave top marks ("Good") for frontal offset, side, and head-restraint protection. **Weak points:** The light steering requires constant correction; a choppy ride with the sport suspension; complicated controls; limited rear-seat and cargo room; tight entry and exit; and some tire thumping and engine and wind noise. Also, the cars are noted for their weak resale value. Very dealer-dependent for parts and servicing. **New for 2010:** Three new diesel engine choices. There's a 2.2L 4-banger diesel available with a single turbo that puts out 170 hp and a beefy 295 lb.-ft. of torque; and another 4 cylinder, this one featuring dual turbos, 204 hp, and 369 lb.-ft. of torque. There will also be some new features and option packages available for 2010.

OVERVIEW: Four models continue in this lineup. The C300 Luxury and C300 Sport have a 228 hp 3.0L V6; the C350 Sport offers a 268 hp 3.5L V6; and the C63 AMG carries a 451 hp 6.2L V8. C300 Sport is available with manual or automatic transmission. All other C-Class cars use a 7-speed automatic. The C300 is also available with Mercedes' 4MATIC all-wheel drive. All C300 models can run on ethanol-blended E85 fuel. Sport models have a sport suspension and unique interior and exterior styling. Available safety features include ABS, traction control, antiskid system, front and rear side airbags, and curtain side airbags. Newly standard are front hip-protecting side airbags. Newly available on the 2010 Mercedes-Benz C-Class are keyless entry/engine start and rearview camera. Also available on rear-drive Sport models is a Dynamic Handling Package, which includes active suspension, specific 18-inch wheels, and steering-wheel shift paddles on cars with an automatic transmission.

COST ANALYSIS: Take a pass on this year's models until prices come down by mid-2010. **Best alternatives:** Take a look at the Audi TT and BMW 3 Series. **Options:** The Bose sound system is a good investment. **Rebates:** $4,000–$5,000 rebates, generous leasing deals, and low-interest financing. **Depreciation:** Faster than average: A $37,000 2006 C-Class Coupe is now barely worth $17,000. **Insurance cost:** Higher than average. **Parts supply/cost:** Limited availability, and parts are expensive. **Annual maintenance cost:** Average. **Warranty:** Bumper-to-bumper 4 years/80,000 km; powertrain 5 years/120,000 km; rust perforation 5 years/120,000 km. **Supplementary warranty:** Not needed. **Highway/city fuel economy:** *3.0L:* 7.7/11.7 L/100 km; *auto.:* 7.8/11.7 L/100 km; *4Matic:* 8.0/12.0 L/100 km; *3.5L:* 8.0/12.2 L/100 km; *3.0L:* 7.7/11.7 L/100 km; *4Matic:* 8.2/12.5 L/100 km; *AMG:* 10.4/17.2 L/100 km.

OWNER-REPORTED PROBLEMS: Transmission, fuel, electrical and climate control systems, brakes, body hardware and paint, power system, audio devices, and fit and finish deficiencies. Side-view mirror cracks:

> I'd had the car in my possession for a little less than two weeks when I woke one chilly morning to discover a crack in the driver's side mirror. I immediately phoned the dealership and was told to bring the car in for evaluation. Service assessed the damage and advised me that they'd recently (the day before) become aware that the heating elements were cracking the mirrors in the C-Class models. They then apologized for the inconvenience, gave me a loaner car (free of charge) while my car was being repaired (free of charge), and advised me that, although Mercedes-Benz does not allow preemptive repairs, they would repair the passenger side mirror (free of charge) should it crack in the future. They told me that the passenger side would be fixed even if the warranty had otherwise expired. The part repaired was the auto defrosting/dimming driver's side mirror.

Sudden steering lockup; power steering failure; electronic stability control and seatbelt fail to activate during a collision; vehicle rolls away on a hill:

> While parked on a hill and attempting to place the gear shifter into reverse, the vehicle would roll forward instead of backwards. The vehicle would roll forward approximately one foot as if it were in neutral. During this time, the steering would lock and the brakes would lose power. It would take tremendous force to depress the brake pedal and stop the vehicle.

E-CLASS ★★★

TECHNICAL DATA (E350)

PRICES: *320:* $52,900, *350 AWD:* $74,500, *550 AWD:* $85,300, *AMG:* $121,100 **FREIGHT:** $1,795 **ORIGIN:** Germany **SALES:** Down 28%

POWERTRAIN (REAR-DRIVE/AWD)

Engines: 3.5L V6 (268 hp) • 5.5L V8 (382 hp) • 6.3L V8 (507 hp); Transmission: 7-speed auto.

DIMENSIONS/CAPACITY

Passengers: 2/3; Wheelbase: 113.1 in.; H: 57.7/L: 191.7/W: 71.9 in.; Headroom F/R: 3.5/3.0 in.; Legroom F/R: 42.5/28.0 in.; Cargo volume: 16 cu. ft.; Fuel tank: 80L/premium; Tow limit: N/A; Load capacity: 1,010 lb.; Turning circle: 36.2 ft.; Ground clearance: 4.1 in.; Weight: 3,825 lb.

RATING: Average. *This* is the Mercedes to buy—not some smaller "Baby Benz" with a lower price and quality to match. It delivers reasonable fuel economy and dazzling highway performance. **Strong points:** Solid acceleration in the higher gear ranges; well-appointed with many new safety, performance, and convenience features added this year; good engine and transmission combo; 4Matic all-wheel drive operates flawlessly; easy handling; good braking; comfortable ride; roomy interior; lots of cargo room (4Matic Wagon); innovative anti-theft system; excellent quality control; NHTSA awarded the 2009 model four stars for driver and passenger frontal crash protection; rollover resistance and side protection rated five stars; IIHS designated the same model year "Good" for offset crashworthiness and head-restraint effectiveness; side-impact protection was rated "Acceptable." **Weak points:** The car feels much slower than it actually is due to lack of low-end torque, and handling is not quite as crisp as with the BMW 5 Series; suspension is still a bit soft; complicated electronic control centre and navigation system controls are a pain to use; the steering column–mounted automatic transmission control is easily confused for the wipers; a surprisingly small trunk; and tall drivers may be bothered by the knee bolsters. **New for 2010:** This year's models are restyled, with a more masculine shape and a conservative interior look. AMG's Sports package will be standard equipment on all E-Class models. The 2010s ride on an all-new platform borrowed from the C-Class that is longer, lower, and wider. Fuel economy is slightly better, despite using the same engines, thanks to some engine tweaking and a more aerodynamic body that matches the slippery 2010 Toyota Prius. There are also many new safety and comfort technologies handed down from the S-Class. As for diesel changes, a new E350 BlueTEC, powered by a 210 hp 3.0L V6, will arrive in 2010. Finally, there's the new Adaptive High-Beam Control headlight system, which allows the driver to keep the high beams on at all times. When meeting an oncoming vehicle, or a vehicle in front, the beams are automatically lowered. One caveat: This feature doesn't work too well on curvy roads. My dad's '64 Buick had that same "new" feature. Next, they will "invent" the side vent window.

OVERVIEW: Mercedes' E-Class cars have always been *Lemon-Aid* favourites because they've improved incrementally over the years and have not suffered as much from content-cutting and poor quality control (except for the electronics) as M-B's other offerings. This year, we rate the E-Class as Average, and shoppers are cautioned to be wary of the 2007 and later re-engineered diesel-equipped models. Besides adding to the retail cost, the new diesels haven't had the quality or servicing support of gasoline-powered engines. Plus, cautious dealers who are hunkering down during the present economic recession aren't likely to hire specialized mechanics or invest in expensive diesel inventory or diagnostic machines until profits start flowing.

The E-Class is your father's Oldsmobile—if he was German. Redesigned only a few times during the past decade, these family sedans and wagons do everything well, and they manage to hold five people in relative comfort. They're first-class in combining performance, road manners, and comfort. True, they're not the best riding, handling, or accelerating cars available, but they're able to perform each of these tasks almost as well as the best cars in each specific area, without sacrificing some other important elements in the driving equation.

COST ANALYSIS: Diesel buyers should be wary—diesels have been radically changed since 2007 and are much less reliable and much harder to have serviced competently. Performance enthusiasts will want to check out the E500's supercharged V8. All others should look for a heavily discounted 2009 sedan or wagon. **Best alternatives:** The Hyundai Genesis, which has a low-$40,000 price tag, a fantastic interior, rear-drive power delivery, and a nearly 400 hp V8. Other choices: the Acura RL, Audi A6, BMW 5 Series, Infiniti M35x, Lexus GS 350 AWD, and Volvo S80. **Options:** Nothing is needed. **Rebates:** $4,000+ rebates/discounts, generous leasing deals (keep the residual value high), and low-interest rate financing. **Depreciation:** Faster than average: A $74,300 2006 E350 rear-drive is now worth about a third of its original price. **Insurance cost:** Higher than average. **Parts supply/cost:** Hard to find outside of the dealer network, and they can be expensive at times (body and electronic parts, especially). **Annual maintenance cost:** More than average. **Warranty:** Bumper-to-bumper 4 years/80,000 km; powertrain 5 years/120,000 km; rust perforation 5 years/120,000 km. **Supplementary warranty:** Not needed. **Highway/city fuel economy:** *3.5L V6:* 8.0/12.2 L/100 km; *4Matic:* 8.2/12.5 L/100 km.

OWNER-REPORTED PROBLEMS: Automatic transmission malfunctions; inoperative climate control; premature replacement of brake rotor and pads; body hardware and fit and finish deficiencies; power equipment and audio system breakdowns; inadvertent airbag deployment; and the "Check Engine" light comes on for no reason.

bad buy

M-CLASS ★

RATING: Not Recommended. This is the Mercedes to *not* buy. **Strong points:** A luxurious interior; the ride is comfortable and quiet, while handling is responsive and fairly predictable. Good off-road performance, despite the lack of a low-range gear. NHTSA gives the M-Class five stars for front and side crash protection and four stars for rollover resistance, while the IIHS ranked the M-Class "Good" for frontal offset, side, and head restraint protection. **Weak points:** Way overpriced; incredibly poor quality control; the V6 is a competent but fuel-thirsty powerplant; and the 7-speed shifter is poorly calibrated, leading to rough, jerky shifting. Confusing controls (love those Germans: "It's our customers, not our cars"); and

the electronic column shifter can be mistakenly knocked into Neutral. **New for 2010:** The ML450 Hybrid debuts in December with a full hybrid powertrain that is capable of producing 335 hp and will consume almost 50 percent less fuel than the ML550 does and 30 percent less fuel than a V6-powered M-Class. Mercedes achieves this fuel savings with a specially designed 3.5L Atkinson-cycle V6 connected with a continuously variable transmission (CVT), twin electric motors, four clutches, and the company's 4Matic all-wheel drive. Also new in the late fall will be the ML350 BlueTEC, which will replace the ML320 version.

TECHNICAL DATA

PRICES: *63 AMG:* $57,400–$97,500
FREIGHT: $1,795 **ORIGIN:** Germany
SALES: Down 40%
POWERTRAIN (REAR-DRIVE/AWD)
Engines: 3.0L V6 TD (215 hp) • 3.5L V6 (268 hp) • 5.0L V8 (382 hp) • 5.5L V8 (503 hp); Transmission: 7-speed auto.
DIMENSIONS/CAPACITY
Passengers: 2/3; Wheelbase: 115 in.; H: 70/L: 189/W: 75 in.; Headroom F/R: 6/5 in.; Legroom F/R: 42/28 in.; Cargo volume: 40.5 cu. ft.; Fuel tank: 95L/premium; Tow limit: 5,000 lb.; Load capacity: 1,165 lb.; Turning circle: 38 ft.; Ground clearance: 8.5 in.; Weight: 3,745 lb.

OVERVIEW: If you pay the high sticker price for an M-Class, you have more money than common sense. This is a huge SUV that costs an arm and a leg to own and has one of the worst quality/reliability records of any SUV put on the market in the past several decades, including those made by that infamous quintet of Kia, Lada, Land Rover, Porsche, and Volkswagen. No, I take that back. The M-Class and VW Touareg are tied for "worst in class" honours. Consider this: The 2010 Mercedes-Benz M-Class ranked 8 out of 15 luxury midsize SUVs in the *U.S. News and World Report*'s analysis of 64 published reviews and test drives of the M-Class and a check of reliability and safety data. Think about it: $57,400–$97,500 spent for an SUV that doesn't even place in the middle of the pack?

Okay, the M-Class *does* come with more bells and whistles than your high school band. It has a spacious interior and plenty of modern techno-gadgets to fiddle with while the car's in the service bay or when waiting for a tow truck, and it still doesn't match the base power of competitors. Oh, did I mention poor quality?

There are a few nice things to say about the 2010 models. Like that the few reviewers who have driven the upcoming hybrid are impressed with its smooth ride and excellent fuel economy. They say it's one of the best-performing and most fuel efficient luxury SUVs on the market. In short, the hybrid SUV drives pretty much like its non-hybrid sibling.

The 2010 Mercedes-Benz M-Class is available in several trims: the V6-powered ML350, diesel-powered ML350 BlueTEC (formerly the ML320), ML450 hybrid, V8-powered ML550, and ultra-performance ML63 AMG.

COST ANALYSIS: Diesel buyers should consider the 2010 upgraded models that may have fewer glitches than the post-2007 models, which were rushed into production. Opposite advice relative to the new hybrid models: Stay away from them until they have been on the market at least a year. **Best alternatives:** The GM Acadian, Enclave, or Outlook; Infiniti FX; and Lexus RX 350 or Hybrid. **Options:** Stay away. **Rebates:** Look for generous leases, low-interest financing, and $5,000+ in discounts/rebates. **Depreciation:** Faster than a speeding bullet: A $56,000 2006 350 AWD is now worth...$25,000. **Insurance cost:** Higher than average. **Parts supply/cost:** Hard to find outside of the dealer network, and they are usually quite expensive. **Annual maintenance cost:** Higher than average. **Warranty:** Bumper-to-bumper 4 years/80,000 km; powertrain 5 years/120,000 km; rust perforation 5 years/120,000 km. **Supplementary warranty:** A must-have. **Highway/city fuel economy:** *ML320 BlueTEC diesel:* 8.2/11.8 L/100 km; *ML350:* 10.2/14.2 L/100 km; *ML550:* 11.2/16.0 L/100 km.

OWNER-REPORTED PROBLEMS: Although these cars are built for safety, ironically many failure-prone components actually put drivers in harm's way. One driver put the vehicle into Park with the engine running; when he started unloading books from the right passenger side, the vehicle advanced one metre and fractured his foot. Loose steering; sudden acceleration:

> I was pulling into my gym's parking lot. As I attempted to brake, the car continued to accelerate. I kept pumping on the brake only to have the car make a grinding sound as it continued to accelerate (as if it were resisting my attempts to stop it). Eventually, and thankfully before it hit the building, the car stalled to a stop. The car actually ascended three wooden porch steps and hit a wooden porch column before stopping.

Volkswagen

VW Beat the Recession...Almost

You can hear the chortling chorus all the way from Wolfsburg, Germany.

While almost every automaker is losing millions of dollars from the two-year-old recession, Volkswagen/Audi/Bentley has kept its losses to a minimum and is poised to become the world's third-largest automaker. Last year, Ford Motor Company for the first time ceded second place in U.S. auto sales to Toyota. Volkswagen now says that it beat Ford in global sales for the first six months of the year by selling 3.31 million vehicles, about 220,000 more than Ford. In fact, VW increased sales by 7.2 percent for the period, while Ford sales declined 3.4 percent. That puts VW behind Toyota Motor Corp. and General Motors in the race to the top.

How did VW increase market share during a recession? It was a combination of diesel popularity, less exposure to the slumping American market than other automakers, the right mix of vehicles that respond well to up-and-down fuel prices, and a solid international footing. Volkswagen is huge internationally, with well-established operations in Latin America; an expanding presence in China, Russia, and India; and a dominant role in Western Europe, where it also markets its Seat and Skoda brands.

VW's small, fuel-efficient cars and diesel improvements have touched a nerve with Canadian shoppers in much the same way as the company's first Beetle captured the imagination and support of consumers in the mid-'60s. Building on that support, this August, Volkswagen began delivery of its clean-diesel car, rated at 7 L/100 km (34 mpg)—a figure that beats most cars, except hybrids and the Smart Fortwo. And instead of slowing production and idling some plants, as other automakers are doing, VW will soon build a $1 billion plant in Chattanooga, Tennessee, to create a new Jetta for the U.S. market.

This Jetta will be retooled to suit North American tastes. For example, it will have a softer suspension, and the gas and brake pedals will be farther apart in response to American complaints that it is easy to accidentally press both simultaneously. And VW will drop the bulky dials used to recline seats in European cars.

Volkswagen sells the City Golf, City Jetta (2009), Rabbit, GTI, New Beetle, New Beetle Convertible, Jetta, Jetta TDI Clean Diesel, GLI, Jetta Wagon, Jetta Wagon TDI Clean Diesel, Eos, Passat, Passat CC, Passat Wagon, Tiguan, Routan, Touareg, and Touareg TDI Clean Diesel through nearly 130 independent Canadian dealers.

Sales of VW's huge Touareg SUV have been dismal, and the Routan, a minivan made in partnership with Chrysler, has done so poorly that it is scheduled to be dropped at the end of the 2009 model year. Other big losers: the Eos, GTI, New Beetle, Passat, and Rabbit. On the other hand, Volkswagen has done particularly well with its two-year-old Tiguan small sport-utility; sales have soared 145 percent through August 2009. Jetta sales have been lukewarm, without any great losses or gains.

As with most European cars, Volkswagens are practical drivers' cars that offer excellent handling and great fuel economy without sacrificing interior comfort. But overall reliability isn't very good (particularly after the fifth year of ownership), and servicing is often better and much cheaper at independent garages, which have grown increasingly popular as owners flee more expensive VW dealerships. Unfortunately, parts are fairly expensive, and both dealers and independent garages have trouble finding them due to chaotic parts distribution following dealer and supplier closures this year.

Diesel Savings Illusory?

Keep in mind that unless you travel more than 30,000 km a year, diesel cost savings may be illusory. Granted, there are usually fewer things to go wrong with diesel engines, and their fuel economy is high, but gasoline-powered Asian compacts are much more reliable, their parts are cheaper and more easily found, and their vehicles are almost as fuel frugal. And here's the danger with diesels for the 2010 model year: They have been completely reworked to be as emissions-free as possible. Mechanics aren't yet familiar with them. Backup parts are still "in the pipeline," supposedly, and dealers aren't rushing to buy replacement parts until they can sell their old stock. Therefore, wise shoppers will steer clear of VW's diesel-equipped vehicles at least until the 2011 model year, when servicing know-how and parts distribution are improved.

Don't Buy a VW This Year

After telling you why you shouldn't buy a diesel-equipped VW this year, I will now tell you why you shouldn't buy a Volkswagen at all. Every year I peruse thousands of U.S. government automobile owner reports of safety-related incidents. In looking at the 2009 models—yes, vehicles not even a year old—I am astounded to see the large number of VWs that have automatic transmissions that lag and lurch or suddenly drop into Neutral until the car is stopped and restarted. This deadly defect apparently affects VW's entire lineup and has done so for a number of years.

Let me be clear: *Lemon-Aid* will not recommend any 2010 model year VW until there are assurances that the transmission failures have been fixed at the factory level. Keep in mind that Volkswagen finished 34th out of 37 brands in one J.D. Power Initial Quality Study, after which VW vowed to take firm control over its dealer network to improve service. Poor servicing has long been a source of irritation among owners who have complained about bad after-sales service on top of quality problems, which include powertrain and electrical system malfunctions and early brake replacements.

VW Eos

Names change at VW, but the models aren't all that different. For example, the new Golf is really the old Rabbit, and the new Eos is a revamped Cabrio (Europeanese for "convertible"). The Jetta-based Eos four-seater convertible is equipped with a retractable roof and powered by a 200 hp 2.0L turbocharged 4-cylinder engine or a 250 hp 3.2L V6. Of the two powerplants, the 4-cylinder is the better performer, if fuel economy is important. Two important features: a standard 6-speed manual and optional 6-speed automatic transmission, and standard head-protecting side curtain airbags. It's a good-handling car, if you can put up with all of the road- and wind-noise intrusion into the cabin when the top is closed, and practically unsupportable when the top is open. Incidentally, the latest research shows that convertibles driven with the top down contribute to premature hearing loss. There are two models to choose from: the $36,575 Trendline, or the $43,375 Comfortline. The freight charge is $1,335. Sales were off by 50 percent through August 2009, so there is some bargaining room. Eos has not yet been tested by NHTSA, but IIHS gave the car a "Good" rating for frontal offset and side crashworthiness; head restraint effectiveness was judged to be "Marginal." For 2010, the Volkswagen Eos increases its list of standard or available features. All models receive park distance control, Bluetooth, a revamped instrument cluster, a wind blocker, and a leather-wrapped steering wheel with audio controls. Competitors are the Audi A4 Cabriolet, BMW 3 Series Cabriolet, Mercedes-Benz CLK-Class Cabriolet, and Mitsubishi Eclipse Spyder.

Eos uses most of the same components that VW has put into its other models, so servicing and parts availability may be less of a problem than with other models (except for roof components and body panels). Nevertheless, short-term reliability reports are negative. Owners of two- and three-year-old models reports serious problems with the body integrity and hardware, power equipment, and audio system. Not to mention a deadly "lag and lurch" problem:

> I was making a right turn when the car switched into Neutral causing the car behind me to hit the brakes so as not to hit me. My car then switched into Drive and lurched forward causing me to hit the brakes so as not to hit the car in front of me. This is the third time since I leased the car that it has shifted into Neutral and then into Drive.

•

> A valve that measures the temperature of the clutch malfunctioned. As a "safety" precaution the transmission will not change gears if the clutch temperature is too high.

This valve malfunctioned while I was on the freeway. The car operated as though I put it in Neutral and revved the engine. Once out of oncoming traffic, it took me three tries to restart my car. I proceeded to exit the freeway and get to a safer destination. While doing so, this malfunction occurred two more times. Upon taking my car to the dealer to be repaired I was initially told that the engine switch malfunctioned. [It was] only upon demanding to speak with the head mechanic and being asked to fully describe the situation that the true problem was discovered. It was made clear to me that this is a common problem with this model.

Bad

NEW BEETLE ★

bad buy

RATING: Not Recommended. Like the Mini Cooper, the New Beetle is an expensive trip down memory lane. Personally, I don't think it's worth it. No matter how they stir the pot (Beetle Turbo, Turbo S, and the Beetle Convertible), the soup is cold and old. **Strong points:** Competent 5-cylinder engine; easy handling; sure-footed and comfortable, though firm, ride; impressive braking; standard traction and stability control; most instruments and controls are user-friendly; comfortable and supportive front seats with plenty of headroom and legroom; cargo area can be expanded by folding down the seats; upgraded head-protecting airbags and front head restraints. NHTSA rates the vehicle five stars for side occupant crash protection and four stars for frontal and rollover protection. IIHS gives the New Beetle a "Good" rating for frontal offset crash protection and head restraint effectiveness. **Weak points:** The noisy, 2.5L engine doesn't excite; serious safety defects reported by owners; 2006 diesel engine fuel economy is overstated; easily buffeted by crosswinds; large head restraints and large front roof pillars obstruct front visibility; limited rear legroom and headroom; excessive engine noise; and skimpy interior storage and trunk space. IIHS says side crash protection is "Poor." Worse than average reliability. **New for 2010:** Restyled and re-engineered. Watch out for price creep: The New Beetle is now sold only with the Comfortline

TECHNICAL DATA

PRICES: *Coupe:* $24,175, *Convertible:* $29,175 **FREIGHT:** $1,335 **ORIGIN:** Mexico **SALES:** *Coupe:* Down 40.8%; *Convertible:* Down 63.5%
POWERTRAIN (FRONT-DRIVE)
Engine: 2.5L 5-cyl. (150 hp); Transmissions: 5-speed man. • 6-speed auto.
DIMENSIONS/CAPACITY
Passengers: 2/2; Wheelbase: 99 in.; H: 58/L: 161/W: 68 in.; Headroom F/R: 8.0/1.0 in.; Legroom F/R: 42.0/23.5 in.; Cargo volume: 5 cu. ft.; Fuel tank: 55L/ regular; Tow limit: N/A; Load capacity: 770 lb.; Turning circle: 35.8 ft.; Ground clearance: 4.6 in.; Weight: 3,280 lb.

trim package, which was previously the mid-range model. What do you get for the higher price? Reduced Roadside Assistance, a standard leather-wrapped steering wheel and shifter knob, and Sirius satellite radio. Whoopee!

OVERVIEW: Why was there so much press coverage for the return of an ugly German import that never had a functioning heater, was declared "small on safety" by Ralph Nader and his Center for Auto Safety, and carried a puny 48 hp engine? The simple answer is that in its original incarnation, it was cheap and it represented the first car most of us could afford as we went through school, got our first job, and dreamed of getting a better car. Time has taken the edge off the memories of the hardships the Beetle made us endure—like having to scrape the inside windshield with our nails as our breath froze—and left us with the cozy feeling that the car wasn't that bad, after all. But it was that bad.

Now VW has resurrected the Beetle and produced a more refined and safer front-engine, front-drive compact car—set on the chassis and running gear of the Golf hatchback. The 150 hp base engine is a big improvement over previous engines. There's still not much room for rear passengers, engine noise is disconcerting, front visibility is hindered by the car's quirky design, and storage capacity is at a premium.

COST ANALYSIS: Shop for a cheaper 2009 model, and seek a 10 percent discount. **Best alternatives:** Other cars worth considering are the Hyundai Elantra, Mazda6, Mini Cooper (if you have the cash for extra cachet), and Toyota Corolla. **Options:** Nothing important. The $1,650 Luxury package is all fluff. Save a cow—eschew the $2,910 Luxury Leather package. **Rebates:** Dealers have some unsold inventor, yet rebates and discounts are quite modest ($1,000–$2,000). **Depreciation:** Much slower than average, especially during the first two years. **Insurance cost:** Higher than average. **Parts supply/cost:** Parts aren't hard to find, since they're taken from the Golf/Jetta parts bin, but they aren't cheap. **Annual maintenance cost:** Average during the first three years. After this, expect repair costs to climb dramatically. **Warranty:** Bumper-to-bumper 4 years/80,000 km; powertrain 5 years/100,000 km; rust perforation 12 years/ unlimited km. **Supplementary warranty:** A good idea. **Highway/city fuel economy:** 7.1/10.4 L/100 km.

OWNER-REPORTED PROBLEMS: Sudden acceleration; delayed acceleration; chronic stalling; steering wheel locks up when accelerating; and in one incident, the vehicle surged forward while stopped at a red light. When vehicle is cruising on the highway, it suddenly loses most of its power for about 30 seconds, and then returns to normal. Key sticks in the ignition and causes starter to burn out:

> I began experiencing problems with the key not being able to turn in the starter. I found I had to use a great deal of force and over the course of the next four months broke two keys off in the ignition. In March 2009, I was down to my last key when the starter became stripped, with the key spinning and not triggering the starter at all. At this point, the car was towed to the VW dealer, which ordered a replacement starter. I waited 17 days for the repair to be completed because, I was told, there were hundreds of backorders nationally for this starter part. When I received the car back with the new part, I immediately began experiencing the same problem. I also noted the same problem in two loaner cars (2009 models of the VW Beetle).

In one incident, the side airbag deployed for no reason, injuring the occupant; in another, the side-impact airbags did not deploy, resulting in death. In many incidents, the driver-side airbag didn't deploy. Airbag light won't go off; Check Engine light comes on for no reason; temperature gauge warning light malfunctions and reservoir tank sensor fails, causing vehicle to overheat; steering wheel shakes excessively and pulls vehicle to the right; back glass suddenly explodes; rear windshield glass hard to see through; driver seatback fails following a rear-end collision; the headrest is 15 cm (6 in.) too high to fit driver's head and obstructs rear visibility; busted fuel tank leaks fuel; plastic fuel tank is easily punctured because of its vulnerable, low-mounted position; open sunroof sucks exhaust fumes into the cabin; driver-side window doesn't operate correctly; the left front strut slips down through the spindle, causing the spindle to hit the wheelwell; brake and turn signal lights cannot be seen by other drivers in bright sunlight because of the sloped design; and windshield wipers quit working in a storm. Won't shift from Reverse to Drive, slams into Forward gear, or downshifts abruptly when coming to a stop. Frequent mass airflow sensor failures; intermittent automatic transmission leaks; front and rear windshield distortion; broken air vents; horn failure; axle oil-pan and oil-pump failures; high-maintenance brakes because of prematurely worn pads and rotors; malfunctioning dashboard gauges; glitch-prone convertible top; poor fit and finish accompanied by omnipresent squeaks, rattles, and buzzing; inoperative power windows. Driver door and trunk won't shut; radio is faulty; and window regulators are often broken.

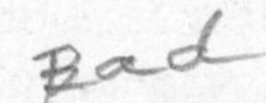

GOLF, CITY, RABBIT, JETTA ★

bad buy

RATING: Not Recommended, until we can see improved quality and powertrain performance. **Strong points:** Good all-around front-drive performers when coupled to a manual shifter; the turbocharged 200 hp 2.0L 4-cylinder engine delivers high-performance thrills without much of a fuel penalty. The 2.5L 5-cylinder engine is well suited for city driving and most leisurely highway cruising, thanks mainly to the car's light weight and handling prowess. First-class

The Volkswagen Golf.

handling; excellent braking; a comfortable ride; plenty of front legroom, and easily accessed cargo room; standard tilt/telescope steering wheel; a low load floor; and good fuel economy. Good crashworthiness scores from both NHTSA and IIHS: five stars for side crash protection and four stars for frontal collision and rollover protection from NHTSA and a "Good" rating for head restraint effectiveness and frontal offset and side crash protection from IIHS. IIHS didn't test the Golf for side crashworthiness. **Weak points:** The base City 115 hp 4-cylinder engine is the runt of the litter and doesn't perform well with an automatic transmission. Diesel engine–equipped models with cruise control can't handle small hills very well, and usually drop 10–15 km/h. Excessive engine and road noise; difficult entry and exit; limited rear legroom due to the extra-long front seat tracks; restricted rear visibility; and folding rear seats don't lie flat. ESP stability control is optional in Canada on the Golf hatch, standard on the wagon, and standard on all VWs in the USA. Make sure your insurance company knows, because ESP could lower your insurance premiums. A high number of safety-related complaints have been logged by NHTSA. Many incidents reported of airbags deploying for no reason and injuring or killing occupants. Maintenance costs increase dramatically after the fifth year of

TECHNICAL DATA

PRICES: *Golf, City:* $15,300, *Jetta Trendline Wagon:* $21,950 **FREIGHT:** $1,335 **ORIGIN:** Germany **SALES:** *Rabbit:* Down 61.6%, *Jetta:* Down 3%

POWERTRAIN (FRONT-DRIVE)

Engines: 2.0L 4-cyl. (115 hp) • 2.0L TDI 4-cyl. (140 hp) • 2.5L 5-cyl. (170 hp); 2.0L Turbo 4-cyl. (200 hp); Transmissions: 5-speed man. • 6-speed man. • 6-speed auto.

DIMENSIONS/CAPACITY (JETTA)

Passengers: 2/3; Wheelbase: 102 in.; H: 58/L: 166/W: 69 in.; Headroom F/R: N/A; Legroom F/R: 41.3/33.3 in.; Cargo volume: 15 cu. ft.; Fuel tank: 55L/regular; Tow limit: 2,000 lb.; Turning circle: 35.7 ft.; Ground clearance: Weight: 3,137 lb.

ownership. **New for 2010:** The City Jetta has been dropped, leaving only the City Golf, which returns unchanged for its last year. Jetta's TDI version gets a new instrument cluster and steering wheel. The 2010 Jetta sedan will continue to use a fifth-generation body with some minor cosmetic sixth-generation updates; the 2010 Jetta/Golf station wagon gets cosmetic updates but does not use a full sixth-generation body; the 2010 Golf uses the full sixth-generation body, exterior, and interior. These differences are due to the rolling transition from fifth to sixth generation, and because the Jetta station wagon is very popular in Europe (but is called the Golf variant there). VW is updating the look of the wagon only (without updating the underlying body) so that all Golf models look the same. The model name "Jetta sportwagen" will be replaced with "Golf Wagon" in Canada, so the station wagon will be called a Golf everywhere except the US, where it will be called the Jetta sportwagen. Volkswagen will reintroduce the Golf TDI, which uses the same 140 hp 2L turbodiesel engine found in the 2009 Jetta TDI.

OVERVIEW: Practical and fun to drive: That pretty well sums up the main reasons that these VWs continue to be so popular. Yet they offer much more, including lots of front interior room, plenty of power, responsive handling, and great fuel economy. Too bad overall reliability is so iffy.

Again, we raise the caveat that this first-year new diesel design will likely have servicing and parts availability problems and, for this reason alone, buyers should delay their purchase until the 2011 model year. That said, diesel is the best alternative to high fuel prices at the moment. As *Autoweek* magazine so aptly put it, "For comfort, quiet and highway handling, our drivers found the TDI had significant advantages over every other car in the test. It would have been our choice, in other words, for an easy daytrip on the interstates, regardless of fuel economy. And we topped the hybrids by driving with just a little attention to fuel economy, not making it an obsession."

COST ANALYSIS: Even though fuel prices are off their highs, there are few 2009 diesel-equipped VWs left on dealers' lots, and the early 2010 models are going for their full retail price. There is no guarantee that prices will come down in the winter, as they usually do, if fuel costs keep rising. **Best alternatives:** Other cars worth considering are the Honda Civic or Accord, Mazda6, Nissan Sentra, and Toyota Corolla or Matrix. **Options:** Stay away from the electric sunroof; it costs a bundle to repair and offers not much more than the well-designed manual sunroof. On top of that, you lose too much headroom. **Rebates:** $2,000 rebates on non-diesels, low-interest financing and attractive leases (use the *Red Book* to set a low residual price). **Depreciation:** About average, especially the Jetta. **Insurance cost:** Higher than average. **Parts supply/cost:** Not hard to find, but parts can be more expensive than with most other cars in this class. Diesel parts may be harder to find and much more expensive. **Annual maintenance cost:** Less than average while under warranty. After that, repair costs start to climb dramatically. **Warranty:** Bumper-to-bumper 4 years/80,000 km; powertrain 5 years/100,000 km; rust perforation 12 years/unlimited km. **Supplementary warranty:** A good idea. **Highway/city fuel economy:** *City Golf 2.0L:* 7.0/9.8

L/100 km; *auto.:* 6.9/9.9 L/100 km; *Jetta 2.5L:* 7.0/10.7 L/100 km; *auto.:* 7.2/10.5 L/100 km; *Jetta TDI:* 4.9/6.8 L/100 km; *Jetta wagon:* 7.0/10.7 L/100 km; *diesel wagon:* 4.8/6.8 L/100 km.

OWNER-REPORTED PROBLEMS: 2009 Jetta owners have reported 58 safety-related failures to NHTSA, mostly relating to the vehicle suddenly shifting into Neutral while underway on the highway:

> 2009 VW TDI Sportswagen DSG will randomly shift into Neutral. This has occurred at various times varying from being stopped to cruising at highway speeds. The vehicle has been in the shop twice for the problem. During the first visit, the dealer was unable to replicate the problem. The second time, we took a video of the event and showed it to the lead mechanic. The shop has determined a temperature sensor in the transmission is overheating and causing the car to slip into Neutral. The part is reportedly on back order and we do not have any estimate as to when the repairs will be completed.

If you survive the unintended shifting into Neutral, there's always sudden steering lockup:

> When driving into a sweeping curve at 45–65 mph [72–104 km/h], the steering mechanism or rack and pinion system locks and fails on my '09 Jetta Wolfsburg Edition sometimes leading to a short skid and temporary loss of steering control. I previously owned the exact same year and make vehicle that exhibited the same defect. Due to this and other defects, the manufacturer replaced the vehicle. I'm now starting to experience the same issue with the new replacement vehicle.

Severe engine hesitation with diesel engines; premature rear brake replacement; burnt clutch (dual mass flywheel failure?); overheated front brakes; airbag warning light comes on for no reason; cooling fan module failure. Heated seats are fire-prone, or as one owner so succinctly wrote to government investigators:

> My heated seats caught fire and burnt my ass...

PASSAT ★

RATING: Not Recommend until Volkswagen improves quality and recalls vehicles that slip out of gear, lurch, and lag. **Strong points:** Well-appointed and holds its value fairly well. Impressive acceleration with the turbocharged engine. Great performance with the manual gearbox; smooth and quiet shifting with the automatic gearbox. The 4Motion full-time all-wheel drive shifts effortlessly into gear; refined road manners; sophisticated, user-friendly all-wheel drive; no turbo lag; better-than-average emergency handling; impressive with the AWD system and quick and predictable steering; handling outclasses most of the competition's, and the suspension is both firm and comfortable. Quiet-running; plenty of

passenger and cargo room; impressive interior fit and finish; and exceptional driving comfort. Good crashworthiness scores from both NHTSA and IIHS. NHTSA gave it five stars for side crash protection and four stars for frontal collision and rollover protection. IIHS gave the vehicle a "Good" rating for head restraint effectiveness and frontal offset and side crash protection. **Weak points:** Both engines hesitate when accelerating; excessive brake fade after successive stops; rear-corner blind spots and rear head restraints impede rear visibility; many safety and performance complaints (faulty airbags and transmissions, distorted windshields, and chronic stalling); plus, these models are expensive to purchase and give poor fuel economy. **New for 2010:** Automatic Passats now get the problem-prone 6-speed Direct Shift Gearbox transmission. All Passats get Bluetooth phone connectivity and a leather-wrapped steering wheel with audio controls as standard features. Wagons get fog lights. Rear and side sunshades have been eliminated, and the 2.0T model loses its heated side mirrors.

TECHNICAL DATA

PRICES: \$31,975–\$44,975 **FREIGHT:** \$1,335 **ORIGIN:** Germany **SALES:** Down 64.6%

POWERTRAIN (FRONT-DRIVE/AWD)
Engines: 2.0L 4-cyl. (200 hp) • 3.6L V6 (280 hp); Transmissions: 6-speed man. • 6-speed auto.

DIMENSIONS/CAPACITY
Passengers: 2/3; Wheelbase: 107 in.; H: 58/L: 188/W: 72 in.; Headroom F/R: 4.0/3.0 in.; Legroom F/R: 43/29 in.; Cargo volume: 14 cu. ft.; Fuel tank: 70L/premium; Tow limit: 2,000 lb.; Load capacity: 975 lb.; Turning circle: 38 ft.; Ground clearance: 5.2 inches; Weight: 3,465 lb.

OVERVIEW: The Passat is an attractive mid-sized car that rides on the same platform as the Audi A4. It has a more stylish design than the Golf or Jetta, but it still provides a comfortable, roomy interior and gives good all-around performance for highway and city driving. The car's large wheelbase and squat appearance give it a massive, solid feeling, while its aerodynamic styling makes it look sleek and clean. Base 2.0T Passats come with a turbocharged 200 hp 4-cylinder engine and front-wheel drive, while the 3.6L models use a 280 hp V6 harnessed to a front-wheel drive or 4Motion all-wheel-drive powertrain. In addition to the standard 6-speed manual transmission found on 4-cylinder models, an optional 6-speed automatic is available, though it's standard on 3.6Ls. Passats come fully loaded with anti-lock four-wheel disc brakes, traction and anti-skid control, front side and side curtain airbags, tinted glass, front and rear stabilizer bars, and full instrumentation.

COST ANALYSIS: Get an identical 2009 model with a sizeable discount (at least 15 percent). **Best alternatives:** The BMW 3 Series, Honda Accord, Saturn Aura, and Toyota Camry. **Options:** A good anti-theft system. The AWD is an excellent investment if you need the extra sure-footedness and traction. Not so the adaptive cruise control; it frequently malfunctions. **Rebates:** $3,000–$5,000. **Depreciation:** Average. **Insurance cost:** Higher than average. These cars are favourites with thieves—whether for stealing radios, wheels, VW badges, or entire cars. **Parts supply/cost:** Parts are getting harder to find as dealers and suppliers close their doors. **Annual maintenance cost:** Higher than average. **Warranty:** Bumper-to-bumper 4 years/80,000 km; powertrain 5 years/100,000 km; rust perforation 12 years/unlimited km. **Supplementary warranty:** A must-have. Maintenance costs are higher than average once the warranty expires. **Highway/city fuel economy:** 6.6/10.0 L/100 km; *auto.:* 7.1/10.8 L/100 km; *wagon:* 6.6/10.0 L/100 km; *4Motion:* 8.3/12.7 L/100 km.

OWNER-REPORTED PROBLEMS: The transmission lines are positioned in such a way that the cooling fan motor cut the lines, causing catastrophic transmission failure. Chronic stalling; delayed steering response:

> While driving between 55–70 mph [88–113 km/h], a delay occurs when one turns the steering wheel. The steering does not respond normally and the vehicle drifts while driving forward. There is a recall on the Internet, but this vehicle was not included.

TIGUAN ★

bad buy

RATING: Not Recommended; long-term reliability has not been proven. **Strong points:** Well equipped with an upscale interior ambiance; roomy; easy handling; and provides a comfortable ride. The small turbocharged engine is an impressive performer, without exacting much of a fuel penalty. Excellent crash scores from both NHTSA and IIHS: five stars for frontal and side crash protection and four stars for rollover protection from NHTSA, and a "Good" rating for frontal offset and side crash protection and head restraint effectiveness from IIHS. **Weak points:** Pricey compared to the competition; limited cargo space; side airbags for rear passengers are optional; and the 998 kg (2,200 lb.) towing limit is about 590 kg (1,300 lb.) less than V6-powered rivals. **New for 2010:** Mirror tips down when shifting into Reverse (with automatic transmission), new instrument cluster and climate controls; Comfortline and Highline have standard black roof rails, heated washer nozzles, premium six-CD stereo, Sirius satellite radio, and heated seats. Unlimited mileage Roadside Assistance is cut back to 4 years/80,000 km.

TECHNICAL DATA

PRICES: *Trendline:* $27,875, *Highline:* $37,775 **FREIGHT:** $1,550 **ORIGIN:** Germany **SALES:** Down 64.6%

POWERTRAIN (FRONT-DRIVE/AWD)

Engine: 2.0L 4-cyl. Turbo (200 hp); Transmissions: 6-speed man. • 6-speed auto.

DIMENSIONS/CAPACITY

Passengers: 2/3; Wheelbase: 102.5 in.; H: 66.0/L: 174.3/W: 71.2 in.; Headroom F/R: 5.0/1.5 in.; Legroom F/R: 42/28 in.; Cargo volume: 23.8 cu. ft.; Fuel tank: 70L/premium; Tow limit: 2,200 lb.; Load capacity: 1,110 lb.; Turning circle: 39.4 ft.; Ground clearance: 6.9 in.; Weight: 3,397 lb.

OVERVIEW: Based on the Rabbit platform, the Tiguan has been a sales success mainly because it is well-positioned between moderately priced small SUVs like the Honda CR-V and more upscale offerings like the Acura RDX.

COST ANALYSIS: Most of the 2009s have been sold, so you will have to pay full price for a 2010 version. **Best alternatives:** A Honda CR-V or a Hyundai Tucson. **Options:** Be careful of option packages—they are pricey and full of non-essential features. Consider getting a good anti-theft system from an independent agency (usually better choice and cheaper prices). Think twice about the AWD option. It will drive up you fuel consumption and only ensure that you get stuck deeper, farther from home. **Rebates:** Not likely; VW knows it has a winner. **Depreciation:** Slower than average. **Insurance cost:** Average. **Parts supply/cost:** Parts are no problem inasmuch as many are available from the Rabbit inventory. **Annual maintenance cost:** Predicted to be average. **Warranty:** Bumper-to-bumper 4 years/80,000 km; powertrain 5 years/100,000 km; rust perforation 12 years/unlimited km. **Supplementary warranty:** Always a good idea with cars that are relatively new to the market. **Highway/city fuel economy:** 7.6/11.2 L/100 km; *auto.:* 8.1/11.4 L/100 km; *AWD:* 8.3/11.6 L/100 km.

OWNER-REPORTED PROBLEMS: The fuel line "quick-connect" fittings in the engine compartment (passenger-side firewall area) disconnected while one vehicle was underway. It stopped dead with the engine covered with fuel. Driveshaft bolts stripped because they were improperly torqued at the factory; AWD axle came loose while driving; sudden unintended acceleration when braking:

> I was traveling west bound on a typical south Florida day, very hot and humid clear day. Just then a pick-up truck [pulled] out very fast in front of me. I slammed on my brakes with plenty of time to stop, but just before I came to a complete stop, the engine roared and I hit the truck very hard. At first I though my foot slipped off the brake to the gas, but no way, I broke my foot because I hit the brake so hard.

Volvo

Waiting for *Rigor Mortis*

Half in jest, I've always said it's easy to see why Volvos are so popular with NDPers. Volvo has always distinguished itself from the rest of the automotive pack through its much-vaunted standard safety features, crashworthiness, and engineering that emphasized function over style. But unfortunately, these noteworthy features were eclipsed by bland styling, ponderous highway performance, inconsistent quality control that compromised long-term reliability and drove up ownership costs, and chancy servicing by a small dealer network. I hesitate to say why Conservatives love large GM SUVs and my Liberal friends dig European cars.

Asian automakers have successfully encroached on Volvo territory by bringing out new products in smaller packages: cars that are as safe and comfortable as Volvos to drive, with greater reliability and servicing support thrown in. Granted, several years ago Volvo met the Asian competition by dramatically restyling its cars and cranking up their performance capabilities by several notches. It dumped its boxy station wagons and rediscovered rounded edges, all-wheel drive, and high-performance powertrains and handling. The automaker's curvy AWD XC models are the latest examples of a mindset change that is in full swing.

But all this is too little, too late.

There are four problems that remain: price-gouging, poor servicing, poor quality control, and Ford's maladministration of its Volvo acquisition. Furthermore, the cars' additional performance features have priced most Volvos out of the reach of the average car buyer. And as more complicated features are added, these vehicles become a nightmare to service for mechanics whose job is complicated by the mixing and matching of parts and platforms from other automakers and recession-ravaged dealers who can't invest in inventory.

But the worst news has been saved for last. Ford wants to dump Volvo, but nobody wants the company. Apart from several Chinese firms, there are few serious bidders for the beleaguered European automaker that's awash in red ink. In the meantime, Volvo dealers are closing their doors, mechanics have turned off the lights, and Volvo owners have fewer places to service their cars or honour their warranties.

Bottom line: Don't buy any Volvo until we see where the company's headed.

C30 ★

RATING: Not Recommended. Volvo seems headed for bankruptcy, and you don't want to go there with them. **Strong points:** The car is loaded with standard safety features like child safety seats, electronic traction and stability control, head- and side-protecting passenger airbags, four-wheel antilock brakes and remote keyless entry. **Weak points:** Handling is much less sporty than advertised. **New for 2010:** A slightly restyled front end with a honeycomb grille and new body panels, headlights, and bumper. New standard equipment includes Bluetooth phone connectivity, cruise control, a trip computer, adjustable head restraints, a leather-and-aluminum gearshift knob, and a leather-wrapped handbrake. R-Design models also get fog lights.

TECHNICAL DATA

PRICES: $27,695–$33,695 **FREIGHT:** $1,615 **ORIGIN:** Belgium **SALES:** N/A
POWERTRAIN (FRONT-DRIVE/AWD)
Engines: 2.5L Turbo 5-cyl. (227 hp); Transmissions: 5-speed man. • 6-speed man. • 5-speed auto.
DIMENSIONS/CAPACITY
Passengers: 2/2; Wheelbase: 103.9 in.; H: 57/L: 167/W: 70 in.; Headroom F/R: 3.0/2.5 in.; Legroom F/R: 41.5/28.0 in., 41/26 in.; Cargo volume: 15 cu. ft.; Fuel tank: 52L/premium; Tow limit: 2,000 lb.; Load capacity: 1,040 lb.; Turning circle: 36 ft.; Ground clearance: 5.3 in.; Weight: 3,175 lb.

OVERVIEW: The C30 is a two-door hatchback that was spun off of the S40 and V50. Ford's contribution is the platform, which is based on a combination of the S40 and the very popular Mazda3.

COST ANALYSIS: Go for the almost identical 2009 version, if you can get a good price. If not, sit tight and wait for prices on this year's models to come down early in 2010, if the company is still solvent. **Best alternatives:** Other cars worth considering are the Acura TL or TSX, the BMW 3 Series, the Mazda3, the Mini Cooper, and Toyota's Matrix. **Options:** Xenon headlights, a sunroof, and heated seats may be more trouble than they're worth. Headlights cost $350 each, and an opened sunroof is noisy. **Rebates:** Look for major price cuts in the new year as Ford scrambles to unload piled-up inventory. **Depreciation:** Much faster than average, as the sharks circle in the water. For example: a 2007 C30 that sold originally for $27,495 is now worth about $16,000. **Insurance cost:** Higher than average. **Parts supply/cost:** Parts are getting hard to find and are much more expensive than average. **Annual maintenance cost:** Higher than average because of a small dealer network that is low on morale and new products. **Warranty:** Bumper-to-bumper 4 years/80,000 km; powertrain 5 years/80,000 km; rust perforation 12 years/unlimited km. **Supplementary warranty:** A must-have in view of Volvo's precarious financial position. **Highway/city fuel economy:** *2.4L manual:* 7.1/10.5 L/100 km; *2.5L T5 Turbo manual and automatic:* 7.0/10.7 L/100 km.

OWNER-REPORTED PROBLEMS: Brake and gas pedal are mounted too close together, and the side airbag sensors may inadvertently set off the airbags.

V70, XC60, XC70, XC90 ★

RATING: Not Recommended. Volvos are so dealer-dependent that poor servicing and back-ordered parts can make your life a nightmare. And that's what you can expect as Volvo is dumped by Ford and taken over by the Chinese. Why am I not thrilled by Chinese ownership? It would be an administrative nightmare in which low prices would trump quality. Plus, according to one article ("Total Recall," *The National Interest*, March 2008, Dali L. Yang), there is the Chinese attitude to safety to consider, which seems to be: "Okay, perhaps our pet food will kill your dog. So we will sell it to you for half price." Also, go to *www.crashtest.com* and look at the crash test results for Chinese luxury vehicles. Is there a score lower than one star? **Strong points:** Practical to the extreme. These cars have plenty of high-range power with their base engines, especially when coupled to a manual gearbox. The 281 hp 3.0L turbocharged 6-cylinder is a lively performer that is relatively quiet and smooth. There's no turbo lag, and the engine posted better-than-average acceleration times with plenty of torque. Both the manual and automatic gearboxes are smooth and quiet. Better-than-average emergency handling, with minimal body roll, good control, and a predictable, rapid steering response that handles

This horrifying 64 km/h (40 mph) offset frontal crash test video of the 2007 China-made Brilliance luxury sedan shows damage that can be described as catastrophic at best. The A-pillar collapses and folds up like a cheap suitcase, forcing the driver's door to pop largely out of its frame, while the lower portion of the car buckles like it's made of recycled pop cans. Imagine the travesty of putting a Volvo badge on *that*.

TECHNICAL DATA

PRICES: *V70:* $43,995, *XC60:* $39,995–$44,495, *XC70:* $44,095–$51,595, *XC90:* $48,595–$70,595 **FREIGHT:** $1,615 **ORIGIN:** Belgium **SALES:** *XC90:* Down 65% **POWERTRAIN (FRONT-DRIVE/AWD)** Engines: 2.4L 5-cyl. (168 hp) • 2.5L 5-cyl. Turbo (208 hp) • 2.5L 5-cyl. Turbo (300 hp) • 3.2L 6-cyl. (235 hp) • 3.0L 6-cyl. Turbo (281 hp) • 4.4L V8 (311 hp); Transmissions: 5-speed man. • 6-speed man. • 5-speed auto. • 6-speed auto. • 6-speed manumatic **DIMENSIONS/CAPACITY (V70/XC70)** Passengers: 2/3/2; Wheelbase: 111 in.; H: 63/L: 191/W: 73 in.; Headroom F/R: 3.0/4.0 in.; Legroom F/R: 42.0/28.5 in.; Cargo volume: 36.5 cu. ft.; Fuel tank: 70L/premium; Tow limit: 3,300 lb.; Load capacity: 900 lb.; Turning circle: *V70:* 36.7 ft., *XC70:* 37.7 ft.; Ground clearance: *V70:* 5.6 in.; *XC70:* 8.3 in.; Weight: *V70:* 3,895 lb.; *XC70:* 4,160 lb. **DIMENSIONS/CAPACITY (XC60)** Passengers: 2/3; Wheelbase: 109.2 in.; H: 67.4/L: 182.2/W: 84.3 in.; Headroom F/R: 3.5/3.5 in.; Legroom F/R: 43.0/28.5 in.; Cargo volume: 30.8 cu. ft.; Fuel tank: 70L/premium; Tow limit: 3,300 lb.; Load capacity: 1,285 lb.; Turning circle: 38.4 ft.; Ground clearance: 9.0 in.; Weight: 4,250 lb. **DIMENSIONS/CAPACITY (XC90)** Passengers: 2/3/2; Wheelbase: 112.4 in.; H: 70.2/L: 189.2/W: 75 in.; Headroom F/R: 3.5/3.5 in.; Legroom F/R: 43.0/28.5 in.; Cargo volume: 41.5 cu. ft.; Fuel tank: 68L/premium; Tow limit: 5,000 lb.; Load capacity: 1,210 lb.; Turning circle: 42 ft.; Ground clearance: 8.5 in.; Weight: 4,645 lb.

sudden steering corrections very well. When the XC60 is pushed when cornering, it tends to understeer, but the standard electronic stability control kicks in and keeps it on track. This important safety feature works similarly on the other Volvos, as well. Lots of cargo room; well-designed instruments and controls are easy to read and access; many standard safety features; and excellent crashworthiness scores. Standard side-impact airbags and standard traction control are a nice touch. Other safety features include rear head restraints; reinforced anti-roll bars; front and rear crumple zones; a practical roof-mounted interior cargo net, and rear three-point seat belts. As with Volvo's other models, IIHS has awarded the V70 its highest rating for frontal offset crashworthiness and rear head-restraint protection. Fewer reliability problems reported than with Volvo's other models; still, chronic stalling complaints are worrisome. **Weak points:** Steering response is a bit slow and vague; the ride deteriorates progressively as the road gets rougher and passenger weight is added—a particularly jarring ride with vehicles equipped with 16- and 17-inch wheels. Excessive engine, wind, and road noise; the XC60's wide dashboard centre stack cuts into the driver's knee room; its displays lack contrast; leg and toe room is surprisingly limited; the tilt-telescoping steering wheel could telescope a bit more; confusing navigation system controls. A two-step starting system: you insert the ignition key and then push a button (for $550 (U.S.) you can get a one-step key). Turbo models are fuel-thirsty; limited rear visibility; and a worrisome number of safety- and performance-related factory defects reported to the U.S. government. The XC70 is less comfortable than the V70, its steering is numb and imprecise, and fuel economy suffers. Owners report that the XC70 "floats" over uneven terrain and exhibits body roll in cornering, owing to its tall body. Roadside Assistance has been cut back to 80,000 km. **New for 2010:** *C70:* The hardtop convertible gets new front- and rear-end styling. *S40:* The 2.4i can be had with a 5-speed manual transmission, while the T50 AWD R-Design comes with a 6-speed (front-drive T5s are still automatic-only) and automatic climate control. *V50:* Now available with a manual transmission. *V70:* A new R-Design model includes 18-inch wheels, a sport-tuned chassis, tailgate spoiler, and unique trim inside and out. All V70s get a new grille and silver roof rails. *XC60:* Everything's new. *XC70:* The 3.2 gets a new grille, more chrome trim, and an updated navigation system. The T6 AWD gets more standard features, like leather upholstery, power passenger seat, integrated child booster seats, and wood interior trim. *XC90:* Volvo's largest SUV gets more standard equipment, including leather seats with power adjustment for both driver and passenger, a third-row seat, three-row climate control, a moonroof, rear park assist, and an integrated centre booster seat. The V8 gets a wood-trimmed cabin, heated front seats, headlight washers, a cabin filter, and rain-sensing wipers. The car also comes with a new City Safety feature that automatically applies the brakes if the car senses you are closing in on another vehicle too fast. The feature works only at 30 km/h (19 mph) or less. The V8 R-Design model has been discontinued.

OVERVIEW: *V70:* The quintessential Volvo wagon and Volvo's bestselling line, the V70 has two models available: a base front-drive and an AWD. Front-drives and AWD use a 208 hp 2.5L 5-cylinder engine hooked to a 5-speed automatic. Three powertrains are offered: a 168 hp 2.4L 5-cylinder, the aforementioned 208 hp variant, and the V70 R's 300 hp 2.5L 5-cylinder equipped with a high-pressure turbocharger. As expected with Volvo, these cars are loaded with safety and convenience features that include four-wheel disc brakes, head/chest front and side airbags, and high-tech seatbacks designed to minimize whiplash.

XC60, XC70, XC90

XC60: Going through its first year on the market, the XC60 occupies a rung just below the Volvo XC90 and offers only one powertrain combination, a turbocharged T6 hooked to all-wheel drive, at a base price of $45,495. Later in 2010, Volvo will introduce the 3.2L engine with front drive, which will be priced at $39,995, and $44,495 in all-wheel drive. The T6 will then be upgraded with the addition of several new features, which will boost its starting price to $49,995. Did we mention Volvo may be pricing itself out of the market? *XC70:* Essentially a renamed V70 station wagon, the XC70 is an SUV wannabe that offers five-passenger seating, a high ground clearance, sleek styling, and AWD versatility—all for $44,095–$51,595 (T6). Its mechanical components are practically identical to those of Volvo's other sedans. The XC70's engine is a 235 hp 3.2L 6-cylinder hooked to a 6-speed automatic gearbox. A 300 hp variant is available. *XC90:* XC90 models start at $48,595 and offer five- or seven-passenger seating, along with either a 235 hp 3.2L 6-cylinder engine or a 311 hp 4.4L V8 hooked to a 6-speed automatic.

COST ANALYSIS: Discounted 2009s are the best choice, since they are practically identical to the 2010 versions. **Best alternatives:** Other cars worth considering are the Acura TL and the BMW 5 Series Touring wagon. XC60 buyers may wish to consider the BMW X3, the Mercedes-Benz GLK, and the Acura RDX. **Options:** Integrated child safety seats and a full-sized spare tire are good choices. The leather seats are quite slippery and the tilt-telescopic steering wheel may not telescope sufficiently. Also, take a pass on the complex Navigation System option. A rear-view camera is only available as part of a $2,700 (U.S.) multimedia package. **Rebates:** Look for $5,000+ rebates and many low-financing and discounting programs to kick in before year's end. **Depreciation:** Much faster than average, and values are likely to plummet as soon as the new owners are named. Already, a 2006 XC90 AWD that sold originally for $50,000 is now only worth about $22,000. **Insurance cost:** Higher than average. **Parts supply/cost:** Parts for the most recent XC60 model are hard to find, few independents stock them, and they are moderately expensive. Parts for the other models are easier to find because of the many V70s that were sold. XC70s may have back-ordered drivetrain components, though. **Annual maintenance cost:** Average; higher than average for the XCs. **Warranty:** Bumper-to-bumper 4 years/80,000 km; rust perforation 8 years/unlimited km. **Supplementary warranty:** Recommended. The most frequent complaint concerns the brakes, an item excluded from most supplementary warranties. **Highway/city fuel economy:** *2.4L:* 7.8/11.0 L/100 km; *XC60:* 9.1/13.5 L/100 km; *XC70 3.2L AWD:* 8.8/13.7 L/100 km; *XC70 3.2L T6:* 9.0/13.7 L/100 km; *XC90 3.2L:* 9.8/14.6 L/100 km; *AWD:* 10.0/15.0 L/100 km; *V8:* 10.6/16.2 L/100 km.

OWNER-REPORTED PROBLEMS: C30, S60, S80, XC60, and XC70 owners have registered fewer owner complaints than those who own the C70, S40, V40/50, and XC90. Most of the problem areas are the fuel and electrical systems, suspension, brakes, and subpar fit and finish. Other problem areas are limited to frequent brake maintenance (rotors and pads); chronic stalling; electrical shorts and body faults like inoperative moonroofs, door locks, and gauges; notably excessive windshield/dash glare; and side windows that won't easily close. Poor fuel economy is a frequent refrain. Rear shock-absorber noise; the ball joint nut securing the front control arm may lose its initial tension. *V70:* One vehicle's engine repeatedly stopped in traffic because of what one Volvo insider called a "weak" fuel pump that is said to affect many V70 and S80 models; the same engine problem is blamed on debris in the fuel line. Vehicle runs out of gas, despite gauge showing sufficient fuel left in the tank; electronic throttle hampered by a delay in fuel getting into the engine; one car rolled forward down an incline, despite being put into Reverse; brake and gas pedals are mounted too close together; seat belt tightens progressively; seat belt crosses at the neck; fuel spews out of fuel-filler pipe; vehicle continually pulls to the right when underway; many complaints that forward visibility is seriously compromised by the dash reflecting onto the windshield (the creamy-beige colour is the worst offender); front doors will slam shut on a moderate slope; and coffee can spill from the cupholder onto the airbag computer module, causing a huge expense. *XC90:* Won't start for long periods; brakes frequently lock up; and original-equipment Michelin tires have poor traction and are unsafe on wet roads. One vehicle's hatch fell on a driver's head, fracturing his neck. *XC70:* Vehicle accelerates without warning; vehicle suddenly shuts down on the highway; loss of brakes; power steering hose failure; vehicle rolls back when stopped on an incline;

convertible top obscures visibility of the right rear side; driver's seatback locks up if it's folded toward the steering wheel; non-adjustable shoulder belt crosses at the neck; painful front-seat design causes seat to press into driver's back; and xenon low beam headlights don't give enough light when going down a hill. Faulty fuel pump and module left one motorist stranded on the highway, even though fuel gauge indicated plenty of fuel was left; incorrect fuel tank readings, and dealers refusing to carry out the subsequent recall campaign for non-customers:

> The consumer was trying to get a recall issue resolved regarding the fan control module. However, he was told [preference] was given to clients that purchased vehicles from them and the part would have to be ordered. The consumer went to another dealer and was told the part would be replaced within three days, even though the consumer purchased his vehicle elsewhere.

XC90: Shift/brake interlock failed:

> My 4-year-old son was in an accident with our brand new Volvo XC90. I got out of [the] car to take a picture (leaving the engine on for air conditioning) and he shifted the car out of park, crashing thank goodness into a fence that slowly stopped him. Knowing he cannot reach the brake, I immediately tested the gear shift and found that it easily shifts out of park without your foot on the brake. We have returned the car to the dealer who has admitted "The car's shifter is broken." We asked to check another new XC90; it functioned properly. This could have been a fatal accident if it happened in any other location.

Appendix I

MINI-REVIEWS AND PREVIEWS

The vehicles rated in this section aren't bestsellers, and they may not have been on the market a long time. Nevertheless, they are important niche models in the annual new car, truck, and SUV lineup.

General Motors

The sun set on Saturn last October when auto investor Roger Penske backed out of his deal with GM at the last moment, after learning no one would make the Saturn models for him. That leaves him with only the Smart Car franchise in the States. More bad news: Hummer's sale to the Chinese has been settled for $150 million (though GM told the bankruptcy court Hummer would fetch $500 million), and that money will be paid only if the Chinese government approves the purchase sometime in 2010.

GM's U.S. turnaround plan assumes it can maintain slightly more than 19 percent of the U.S. market, which is a modest goal considering that GM, flush with $50 billion of emergency U.S. government support, had 19.5 percent of the U.S. auto market in the third quarter of 2009. The automaker's share of U.S. sales has declined steadily since peaking at 51 percent in 1962. GM held almost 29 percent in 2002, but those days are long gone.

GM's few sales gains in September are due mostly to the new Chevrolet Equinox crossover, the Cadillac CTS sports wagon, and the Buick LaCrosse sedan. Equinox increased sales by 93 percent, and the new Traverse did almost as well. The Suburban saw a modest 23 percent increase, and the Tahoe declined by a mere 1 percent.

The Chevrolet Equinox increased sales in a dismal market.

Here's what GM's September results show isn't selling: Buick was down 33 percent, Chevy fell 40 percent, GMC dropped 53 percent, and Cadillac declined 8.8 percent. GM's cast-off divisions did even worse: Pontiac –52.5 percent, Saab –73 percent, Hummer –81.5 percent, and Saturn –83.8 percent.

GMC's truck and SUV sales are catastrophic, having dropped by more than half in September. Acadia fell 52.7 percent, Sierra dropped 61 percent, and the new

Terrain posted feeble sales. Yukon and Yukon XL fell 11.4 percent and 7.8 percent respectively.

On the Chevy side, Aveo posted –52.4 percent, Cobalt –55.3 percent, Impala –52 percent, and the Malibu –46.9 percent. The Silverado and Chevy's full-size pickups both fell by just over 61 percent, and the HHR was down 38.2 percent.

Chrysler

As for Chrysler, there's little to preview. The company has no new products, and what it does have isn't reliable enough to recommend. In fact, Thrifty Car Rental has announced it is reducing the proportion of fleet cars it buys from Chrysler for 2010 from 76 percent to 30 percent. Ford will make up 34 percent of its fleet and GM another 20 percent. It's doubtful that Chrysler will last through 2010.

Ford

Ford is chugging along with a good product mix, nice overseas positioning, stronger European sales, and money enough to last through the next year or so. That should be time enough for the company to retool American factories for small cars and bring in other small cars through its European connections. On the downside, Ford's overall sales are still below sea level and the company continues to hemorrhage cash, although not as quickly as the remaining Detroit automakers. Furthermore, Ford put its money-losing Volvo division on the block in December 2008, as it shed overseas luxury lines to focus on its core brands. Geely, China's biggest private automaker, has made an offer of $2 billion for Volvo—less than one-third what Ford paid for the company in 1999.

Chrysler, Ford, and GM minivans have a long history of premature automatic transmission failures.

Imports

While rival automakers struggled amid a 27 percent drop in total U.S. sales in the first nine months of the year, Canadian sales were off almost half as much. Hyundai and Kia were the best-selling Asian brands, with 26 and 20 percent sales increases, respectively. On the European front, Audi, BMW, and Volkswagen are recovering better than most. And even Jaguar and Land Rover boosted their sales in Canada by 78 percent over the same period (1,972 units), proving that hope does spring eternal.

Finally, a word about Toyota, an automaker that has taken hit after hit during the past year over its poor sales; patent infringement with key components in its Prius hybrid; allegations of hiding damning evidence in rollover trials; reports of poor quality control leading to dangerously rust-cankered Tacoma and Tundra trucks; deaths and injuries caused by sudden, unintended acceleration; and faulty steering rods.

Toyota's sales are down 18 percent in Canada. Its sales incentives have increased by 90 percent since 2007 and 22 percent (a U.S. average of $1,620) this year to move unsold 2009s. In a word, Toyota is in trouble.

2009–11 Models

These are volatile times, with the price of cars going down, while fuel and insurance costs go through the roof. You don't need the economic burden of buying an unproven car that has been radically changed this year, or one that's on the market for the first time. Nor should you invest in a vehicle that doesn't have a positive reliability history, merely because it looks nice. And you certainly don't want to overpay for a car or minivan simply to be the first in your town with something "different." The uniqueness will pass; the repairs will remain constant.

Consider these tips:

1. If you really want to save money, try to buy a vehicle that's presently being used by one of your family members. Although you may risk a family squabble somewhere down the road, you'll likely get a good buy for next to nothing, you'll have a good idea of how it was driven and maintained, and you can use the same repair facilities that have been repairing your family's vehicles for years. Don't worry if a vehicle is almost 10 years old—that's becoming the norm for Canadian ownership, particularly the farther west you go.
2. Get a fuel-efficient car. Be wary of diesel-equipped or hybrid cars that may require more-expensive dealer servicing that could wipe out any fuel consumption savings. Don't trust hybrid fuel economy hype: Sometimes it can be off by 40 percent. Also, don't buy a "lemon" simply because it's touted as being fuel-efficient: A failure-prone Chrysler Caliber may cost you more to

repair than to fuel, and a 4-cylinder minivan, though cheap to run, can make highway merging a white-knuckle affair.

3. Use *www.insurancehotline.com* to find out which cars are the cheapest to insure. Remember, having an additional licensed driver in the family places your policy in a higher risk category, with accompanying higher premiums. Not giving that extra driver permission to use the car has little bearing on your rates—you'll still pay more.
4. Used is always a better buy than new—there's little depreciation or upfront costs, and the cars have been pre-dented, pre-stained, and pre-rusted.
5. If you do buy used, buy privately. Look for high-mileage vehicles sold by a major rental agency that offers simply worded money-back guarantees and reasonably priced extended warranties. Franchised new-car dealers can also give you a good deal if they include all of the car's repair history. Keep the vehicle for at least 10 years and then resell it privately (back to the family, perhaps?).
6. Delay buying a new car until early 2010, when automaker and dealer clearance rebates bring down new prices, and lots of inexpensive trade-ins reduce used prices, as well. Also, refuse all preparation charges, wear and tear insurance, and "administration" fees. It's uncanny how automakers and dealers create problems and then sell you the solution. For example, extended warranties are bought because the car industry rejects so many valid claims. Now, wear and tear insurance, selling for about $700, is used to "protect" those who lease their car and are afraid of the dealer's chargeback for accelerated wear and tear.
7. Buy an entry-level Asian model or Asian/American co-venture from dealer stock for better price leverage.
8. Stay away from most American front-drives—more frequent failures and costlier repairs are a given. Besides, American automakers are now returning to rear-drives.
9. Be wary of all European models. Even the venerable *Consumer Reports* now agrees with *Lemon-Aid*: European makes are way overpriced, parts and servicing can be a problem, and quality control is another language.
10. Don't buy "nostalgia" cars: They aren't as good as the memories they invoke. New Beetles, PT Cruisers, and GM's HHR van are all heavily depreciated. Only BMW's limited-production Mini Cooper has kept a high resale value.

Audi

Q5

RATING: Not Recommended during the Q5's first year on the market. **Price:** $43,500–$48,500 (soft). The Q7's smaller brother debuted this year as a stylish five-passenger luxury crossover compact that's full of high-tech gadgetry, all ready to go awry. Most notable is the car's adaptive suspension that allows for firm, sporty handling, if so desired. Q5 power comes by way of a 3.2L 270 hp V6 and the latest rear-biased version of AWD. **Strengths:** Stylish, luxury appointments;

excellent handling; and full of nifty safety, performance, and convenience goodies. **Weaknesses:** New to the Canadian market; servicing is highly dependent upon a weak dealer network; parts are problematic; and servicing quality will depend on how well mechanics get to know a vehicle new to the market and sold in small volume. Unlike the Q7, there is no diesel option. **Crashworthiness:** NHTSA awarded five stars for front and side crashworthiness and four stars for rollover protection.

Ford

Econoline/E-Series

RATING: Average. These gas-guzzling full-size vans quickly lose their value, making them a better deal used. Going into 2010, the E-Series and the Transit are the only vans in the Ford lineup in North America. **Price:** *Commercial:* $30,099; *passenger van:* $34,499 (very soft). **Strengths:** Parts are plentiful and repairs aren't dealer-dependent. **Weaknesses:** Vulnerable to side winds; rapid brake wear; poor-quality original equipment tires; electrical system shorts; oil leaks into coolant; and excessive turbocharger carbon deposits, causing surging, power loss, or black/white smoke (6.0L engines). Harsh automatic transmission shifts, improper gear selection, erratic converter clutch operation, or improper shift feel. **Crashworthiness:** NHTSA gives the van three stars for rollover protection.

Edge/MKX

RATING: Above Average. A five-passenger wagon/SUV crossover based on the same platform as the Fusion sedan, the Edge comes in either all-wheel drive without low-range gearing, or front-drive. The only engine available is a 265 hp V6 hooked to a 6-speed automatic transmission. Standard features include ABS, traction/anti-skid control, and front side and side curtain airbags. **Price:** $30,499–$40,699 (negotiable). **Strengths:** The vehicle accelerates nicely, though there is some hesitant downshifting. Although softly sprung, handling is better than average for a crossover. Good passenger and cargo room combined with a comfortable ride. **Weaknesses:** Mediocre fuel economy, lots of engine noise, and spongy-

feeling brakes. Parts are a bit scarce and repairs are highly dealer-dependent. Optional equipment you don't need to buy: Ford's Vista Roof (a glass roof with a sliding glass sunroof over the front seats), a navigation system, a DVD entertainment system, leather upholstery, and larger wheels. Lincoln's MKX is a more luxury-laden spin-off. **Crashworthiness:** NHTSA gives the Edge and MKX five stars for front and side protection and four stars for rollover protection.

Flex

RATING: Above Average. This front-drive boxy four-door wagon shares many components with Ford's Edge and Taurus X crossover SUVs. The Flex seats either six or seven on three rows of seats. Power comes from a 3.5L 262 hp V6 mated to a 6-speed automatic transmission, and all-wheel drive is available. Safety features include ABS, traction control, an anti-skid system, front side airbags, and curtain side airbags. Some of Flex's other features include a rear-view camera, power liftgate, voice-activated navigation system with real-time traffic and weather updates, four-panel glass roof, and a refrigerated centre console. Other available features include Ford's Sync, which is a voice-activated system that controls some cell phone and MP3 player functions. **Price:** \$32,699–\$46,599 (soft). Other vehicles worth considering: Chevrolet Traverse, GMC Acadia, Honda Pilot, Hyundai Santa Fe, Mazda CX-9, Saturn Outlook, and Toyota Highlander. **Strengths:** Acceptable acceleration and handling; a roomy interior; third-row seating is a pleasure; entry/exit is made easy with the wide doors and low step-up; the cabin is generally quiet; and the soft, compliant suspension gives a comfortable ride for seven and car-like handling. Good overall visibility. **Weaknesses:** Pricey; loses value quickly; a gas-burner; Flex is new to the market, so servicing is very

dealer-dependent; steering is a bit too light; excessive nose dive upon hard braking; a moderate amount of engine noise when accelerating; an inoperative power liftgate; and reports of driveshaft seal leaks:

INTERMEDIATE SHAFT SEAL LEAKS

BULLETIN NO.: TSB 09-8-10 **DATE: MAY 4, 2009**

RIGHT HAND INTERMEDIATE SHAFT SEAL LEAKS

2008–09 Taurus X, Taurus; 2009–08 Edge; 2009 Flex; 2009 MKS; 2007–09 MKX; 2008–09 Sable

ISSUE: Some 2007–08 Edge, MKX, 2008 Taurus, Taurus-X, and Sable vehicles may experience a fluid leak at the power take-off unit (PTU) right hand (RH) intermediate shaft seal. The online Workshop Manual (WSM), Section 308-07B has been updated with new tools and service procedures to assist with resolving leaks in this area. In addition, two (2) new seal kits were developed and depending on the location of the leak must be used to prevent repeat repairs.

A harsh, uneven idle; power locks cycle on their own; airbags fail to deploy in a head-on collision; sudden brake failure and chronic stalling:

> 2009 Ford Flex engine dies while driving without any warning. The problem is intermittent but certainly present in numerous 2009 Ford Flex vehicles. Follow this link: *www.fordflex.net/forums/viewtopic.php?f=3&t=711.* This incident has happened to me twice. The dealer was supposed to have fixed the problem after the first occurrence.

Crashworthiness: NHTSA gave the Flex five stars for front and side protection and four stars for rollover resistance.

Taurus

RATING: Average. Be wary of buying this revised Taurus before it is road-tested for at least a year. **Price:** $34,998–$40,499 (a bit firm). The front-drive 2010 version returns this year considerably improved, with a restyled exterior and interior, new features, and the return of Ford's high-performance Taurus SHO (MIA since 1999). All-wheel drive is offered on the SEL and Limited models, which use the same 3.5L 263 hp V6 engine hooked to a 6-speed automatic transmission. The SHO (super high-output) returns with an EcoBoost turbocharged 3.5L 365 hp V6 engine, 6-speed automatic transmission, and AWD. SHO models have performance-oriented steering, suspension tuning, and brakes. Later in the model year, SHO models will get upgraded brakes and 20-inch summer performance tires. **Strengths:** Excellent overall reliability. Good acceleration and steering/handling with the SHO version; the base Taurus does reasonably well. A quiet interior and a comfortable ride. **Weaknesses:** Automatic transmission performance degraded by frequent gear-hunting (non-SHO); limited rear seat headroom; and the SHO ride can be uncomfortably firm. Electrical and suspension glitches reported, and roof pillars obstruct rearward vision. **Crashworthiness:** NHTSA gives the Taurus four stars for rollover resistance.

Transit

RATING: Not Recommended. Wait until the Transit has been road-rested for at least a year to better judge overall reliability and servicing support. **Price:** $26,799–$27,299 (soft). The 2010 Transit Connect is new to North America, but other countries have been using this Focus-inspired compact van since 2002. It is aimed at the small business commercial market and fits between the compact Chevrolet HHR and the recently dropped humongous and problematic Dodge Sprinter (now sold exclusively by Mercedes-Benz). Powered by a puny 2.0L 136 hp 4-cylinder engine and a rather primitive fuel-thirsty 4-speed automatic transmission, the Transit is longer, wider, and heavier than a Focus. Ford says the Connect has more than 135 cu. ft. of total cargo capacity and a payload of up to 1,600 pounds. Just don't be in a hurry to get anywhere. **Strengths:** An easily accessed, capacious rolling box with traction control; an anti-skid system, a vehicle tracking device, and an Internet connection. Handling is fairly good. Fuel economy is only acceptable. **Weaknesses:** Lethargic acceleration caused by a sluggish, uncertain transmission (a deal-breaker, for sure); very vulnerable to side winds; cheap interior materials; tall head restraints and closed rear quarter panels limit visibility; drivetrain pedals are too close to each other for such a wide interior and the pads are unusually small; you get a buggy navigation feature; and there's a symphony of engine and road noise that transform the interior into a Jamaican steel drum. Owners can expect problems with premature brake wear and powertrain glitches due to the Transit's heft. **Crashworthiness:** Good; NHTSA five-star protection from side impact injury.

General Motors

The *Buick Enclave* ($41,595–$51,995), *Chevrolet Traverse* (*LTZ AWD:* $35,620–$53,560), *GMC Acadia* ($37,800–$51,335), and *Saturn Outlook* ($35,010–$42,120) are practically identical seven- and eight-passenger crossover SUVs; the Saturn is the cheapest of the group and the Traverse is the most recent addition. The Chevy differs from its corporate cousins in pricing, features, and details. All four vehicles have five-star front and side NHTSA crashworthiness scores; rollover resistance earned four stars. Sales have been hard hit by high fuel costs and tighter credit, making 40 percent discounts not unusual with these models. Although they are fuel-thirsty SUVs, maintenance cost and mechanical/body failures aren't excessive. Still, some problem areas to note include: Side airbags sometimes fail to deploy; head restraints force your chin into your chest; transmission oil leaks and

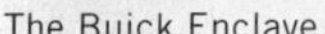

The Buick Enclave.

The GMC Acadia.

The Chevrolet Traverse.

The Saturn Outlook.

malfunctions; fuel pump flow module failures, making the engine run rough or stall; inaccurate fuel gauges; a noisy suspension; and headlight failures.

DTS

RATING: Above Average. It's essentially your father's old, comfortable, roomy, bouncy, and ponderous Oldsmobile. **Price:** $55,490–$63,835 (very soft). **Strengths:** Good reliability, parts are plentiful, and repairs aren't dealer-dependent. **Weaknesses:** Owners note problems mainly with premature brake wear and subpar fit and finish. **Crashworthiness:** Good; four- and five-star protection across the board.

Escalade/Tahoe/Yukon

RATING: Above Average, but hurry: Dealers are dumping these SUVs as GM winds down their production. Buy in late winter and you will get them for almost half price. **Price:** *Escalade:* $78,535; *Tahoe:* $47,650; *Yukon:* $48,245 (very soft). **Strengths:** Many powertrain configurations; parts aren't hard to find and are reasonably priced; and repairs can be done by independent garages. **Weaknesses:** Depreciation is so rapid that a 2009 Tahoe that sold for $43,855 is now worth only

The Cadillac Escalade.

The GMC Yukon.

$30,000. Specific problem areas include loss of brakes; faulty powertrain, suspension, and climate controls; and various body glitches. **Crashworthiness:** NHTSA gave these SUVs five stars for frontal passenger protection and three stars for rollover resistance.

STS

RATING: Average. A rear-drive/AWD Seville replacement, the STS is attractively styled and has plenty of power and performance—all available for a premium price. **Price:** Carrying a price tag of $60,920 for the 3.6L 255 hp V6 coupled with a 5-speed automatic transmission, $70,230 for the 4.6L 320 hp V8 (AWD) with a 6-speed automatic, and $89,975 for the 4.4L 469 hp V8-equipped STS-V, these cars are for the well-heeled who haven't yet given up on American cars for their thrills. **Strengths:** Undoubtedly, Cadillac's switch to rear-drive enhances the STS's balance, handling, overall performance, and reliability. The interior is first class, and rear seatroom is larger than with most of the competition. Standard features include StabiliTrak stability control, a Bose sound system with CD player, leather seats, Keyless Access with a push-button ignition start, Adaptive Remote Start, and Panic Brake Assist. STS has lots of potential as Cadillac fights a volatile market where price, fuel economy, reliability, and cachet rule.

So far, the car appears to be doing well. The STS has had few safety-related complaints posted with NHTSA. They concern the failure of the side airbags to deploy, the car's poor traction in the snow, sudden rear differential lock-up (also a CTS complaint), chronic stalling, and incomplete speedometer readings. **Crashworthiness:** NHTSA gave the STS four stars for frontal and side protection, and five stars for rollover resistance.

SRX

RATING: Not Recommended. During the first year of its redesign, the SRX will likely be more glitch-prone than ever. **Price:** $46,910–$63,350 for the V8 AWD. Prices are negotiable, but they are firming up due to solid sales. The five-passenger SRX returns for 2010 with new styling and power choices in a car that's about 5 inches shorter in both wheelbase and overall length than the previous, 2004–09 generation. Base models are front-drive, while Luxury versions include all-wheel drive; both are powered by a 3.0L 265 hp V6 hooked to a 6-speed automatic transmission, with a maximum towing capacity of 3,500 lb. Available safety features include ABS, traction control, anti-skid system, side curtain airbags, and front side airbags. Optional safety features include steering-linked headlights and adjustable pedals. **Strengths:** Good handling and a quiet interior. **Weaknesses:** Overpriced; quickly loses resale value; insufficient rear passenger room; poor fit and finish; costly, dealer-dependent servicing; and suspension may be too firm for some. Slow acceleration; the AWD model is slower to accelerate than the rear-drive, and the transmission often hesitates before downshifting. Alternative vehicles are the Lexus RX or Acura RDX. **Crashworthiness:** Not tested.

XLR

RATING: Not Recommended. Cadillac's XLR has been discontinued, but there are still a few 2009s on dealers' lots selling with huge discounts. **Price:** $103,000 reduced to about $65,000. The two-seat convertible is based on Chevrolet's Corvette, but has its own unique styling, a power-folding hardtop, and different powertrains. XLR is offered in two trims: Platinum and XLR-V. Platinum is powered by a 4.6L 320 hp V8. High-performance versions carry a supercharged 4.4L 443 hp V8. A 6-speed automatic transmission is standard, along with safety features that include ABS, traction control, an anti-skid system, run-flat tires, and an automatic adjusting suspension. Other vehicles worth considering: the Chevrolet Corvette, Porsche Boxster, and Nissan GT-R. **Strengths:** Lots of high-performance thrills. **Weaknesses:** Lots of high-performance bills. Accelerated depreciation and problematic servicing. **Crashworthiness:** Not tested.

The XLR was a Corvette wannabe that never caught on.

Aveo

RATING: Below Average. **Price:** $13,970–$16,570 (soft). **Strengths:** Parts are plentiful and repairs aren't dealer-dependent. **Weaknesses:** Depreciation is so rapid that a 2009 model sold for $14,000 is now worth only $8,500. Worse is the car's poor reliability. Almost every component has come up short. So, without adequate quality control and providing only mediocre highway performance, this Daewoo/Chevrolet is no bargain, despite its low price. Specific component failures include the powertrain and the fuel and electrical systems, and it has atrocious fit and finish. **Crashworthiness:** Better-than-average occupant protection.

Caprice

RATING: Not Recommended during its first year on the market, but this car has lots of potential if they can bring the price down. The Chevrolet Caprice will return in 2011 as a rear-drive police car, engineered and assembled by Holden in Australia. Based on the recently dropped, but much-acclaimed, Pontiac G8 platform, the car will offer a 6.0L 355 hp V8 engine at first and then launch a V6-equipped version later in the year, coupled with a 6-speed automatic transmission. The Police Cruiser Package is expected to drive the car's price through the $35,000 (CDN) ceiling. The new Caprice will compete with the Ford Crown Victoria until Ford takes that car off the market in the latter part of 2011. The 1996 Caprice was the last rear-drive sedan offered by Chevrolet with a police pursuit package; currently, Chevrolet offers a police package only on the Impala and the Tahoe.

The 2011 Caprice Police Patrol Vehicle will eventually be sold to high-performance enthusiasts.

The Chevrolet Caprice Police Patrol Vehicle is based on GM's global rear-drive family of vehicles, which also underpins the Chevy Camaro. It uses the longest wheelbase of the architecture—118.5 inches (301 cm)—along with a four-wheel independent suspension that delivers responsive high-performance driving characteristics that are crucial in some police scenarios.

Chevrolet Caprice PPV's long wheelbase also contributes to exceptional spaciousness. Compared to the primary competition, its advantages include

- A larger interior volume—3,172L (112 cu. ft.)—than the Ford Crown Victoria, including nearly 101 mm (4 inches) more rear legroom;
- A front seat that accommodates a police utility belt;
- Farther rearward positioning of the barrier between the front seat and rear seat, allowing for full front-seat travel and greater recline for officer doughnut-dining comfort and miscreant discomfort; and
- At 535L (18 cu. ft.) of free space (beyond the battery located in the trunk), enough trunk volume to accommodate a full-sized spare tire under a flat load surface in the trunk storage area, or a human body.

Additional police car–specific powertrain and vehicle system features include

- High-output alternator;
- Engine oil, transmission, and power steering coolers;
- Standard 18-inch steel wheels with bolt-on centre cap;
- Large four-wheel disc brakes with heavy-duty brake pads;
- Heavy-duty suspension components;
- Police-calibrated stability control system; and
- Driver information centre in the instrument cluster with selectable speed tracking feature.

A host of complementary features are also offered, including special equipment packages such as spotlights; lockouts for the power windows and locks; and an "undercover" street-appearance package (hmm...hard to go undercover with a resurrected 1996-*cum*-2011 Chevrolet Caprice).

Cruze

RATING: Not Recommended during its first year on the market. The Cruze's predicted price of $16,500–$19,000 makes the Ford Focus and Honda Civic more credible alternatives. The Ohio-built front-drive Cruze will debut in early 2010 as a 2011 model. It is expected to have a slightly larger wheelbase and a bit wider stance than the Chevrolet Cobalt it will eventually replace. GM says light-weight materials will be used to increase the compact's fuel economy and

The Chevrolet Cruze will replace the Cobalt.

performance, and structural rigidity will be reinforced to improve ride and handling. Powered by a 1.8L 138 hp 4-cylinder engine used by the Saturn Astra, a more frugal 1.4L 140 hp turbocharged four will also be available. Either engine can be hooked to a 6-speed manual or a 6-speed automatic transmission.

Equinox/Terrain

RATING: Above Average. Wait until mid-2010 for the usual redesign glitches to be corrected. Stay away from earlier models; they perform poorly and tend to fall apart after three years. The redesigned 2010 Equinox has been restyled and given more powerful engines, in addition to some other new features. With any luck, reliability has been improved as well. With seating for five, this four-door crossover SUV offers a choice of two engines: a base 2.4L 182 hp 4-cylinder and an optional 3.0L 264 hp V6. Both variants are teamed with a smooth-performing 6-speed automatic transmission, and front-drive and all-wheel drive are available with all models. Most of the important safety devices are standard (traction control, an anti-skid system, front side airbags, and side curtain airbags). Other handy features include remote engine start, a navigation system, wireless cell phone link, DVD entertainment, a hard drive for storing digital audio files, a rear-view camera, and a power liftgate. GMC's MultiFlex rear seat can be moved 20 cm (8 in.) fore and aft to better accommodate people and cargo. **Price:** $25,995–$34,995 (firm).

The Chevrolet Equinox.

The GMC Terrain.

The GMC MultiFlex.

GMC's Terrain shares its basic design and powertrain with the Chevrolet Equinox. Besides a plethora of airbags, the Terrain also comes with ABS, traction control, and an anti-skid system. The Terrain will use an all-new Active Noise Cancellation system on its 4-cylinder models late next year. A rear-view camera is standard on all Terrain models. **Price:** $27,465–$34,400 (firm). **Strengths:** Thrilling acceleration with the V6 and manual transmission; the 4-cylinder engine and automatic gearbox are acceptable and fairly quiet; acceptable handling and braking combined with a comfortable ride. Plenty of passenger and cargo room; a quiet interior; well-laid out controls; very comfortable seating; and a smooth-performing, fuel-sipping manual drivetrain. **Weaknesses:** V6 fuel economy is below average but a fair trade-off for the extra power; the 4-cylinder engine comes up short when passing or merging with other vehicles; some delayed downshifting with the V6, and handling is better with the Honda competition; tall head restraints cuts rear visibility; the dash buttons can be confusing because of their similar configuration; cheap-looking, easily scratched, and hard-to-keep-clean door panels and dash materials:

> The lower body molding detached from the front wheel opening, and then to the rear wheel opening. Driver's leg was cut as a consequence because the corners of the doors became extremely sharp.

•

> I failed to check where the fuel fill door was located. It is on the righthand side of the vehicle which is the wrong side. It creates a safety hazard when getting fuel (getting out into station traffic, walking between cars, and being a longer distance from the driver's door when most people leave their keys in the car when fueling). The front doors are located so that I bump my head (I have cut my head) unless the seat is back as far as possible. GM has no retrofit to move fuel fill door or unit to put seats back to give more head room.

Overall reliability has been below average, with premature brake caliper and rotor replacements the top issue. The suspension, electrical, and fuel systems have also been failure-prone, and fit and finish continue to get low marks. Some reports that the Check Engine light often comes on due to bad sensors. The Honda CR-V, Hyundai Tucson, Subaru Forester, or Toyota RAV4 are worthy alternatives. **Crashworthiness:** NHTSA gives the Equinox and its Terrain twin five stars for frontal and side protection. Although rollover resistance hasn't yet been tested, standard electronic stability control is a good sign that rollovers will be an infrequent occurrence.

Express/Savana

RATING: Recommended. These full-sized, rear-drive vans have been around forever. **Price:** $26,799–$27,299 (soft). **Strengths:** An easily accessed, capacious van. With fuel prices going higher, they are turning into "distressed merchandise" and are discounted by 30+ percent. Both vans are perfect recession buys because any independent garage can repair them, and most of their reliability issues aren't expensive to correct. **Weaknesses:** Fuel-thirsty, mediocre handling, and water leaks. **Crashworthiness:** NHTSA gives the Express 1500 cargo van five stars for frontal protection; the 1500 passenger van gets five stars for frontal protection and three stars for rollover resistance. The 2500 and 3500 12-passenger vans and the 3500 15-passenger van earned three stars for rollover resistance. But as *Lemon-Aid* has reported before, 15-passenger vans can be killers. For more, see the explanation later in this appendix.

The Chevrolet Express.

The GMC Savana.

HHR

RATING: Below Average. The HHR (Heritage High Roof) is a mini version of GM's 1949 Suburban, but it's equipped with many of the latest safety, performance, and convenience features. **Price:** $20,315–$28,900 (soft). This five-passenger crossover compact wagon uses GM's Cobalt/Pursuit platform and 4-cylinder engines to target Chrysler's PT Cruiser with a price that's $600 less than the base Cruiser's (prices are heavily discounted on both models). GM's going after commercial fleet sales with its similarly priced two-seat panel-truck version that comes with windowless side panels and rear cargo doors in place of the HHR's conventional rear doors. The 2010 entry-level LS and 1LT models use a 2.2L 155 hp 4-cylinder engine; a 2.4L 172 hp 4-cylinder is optional with the 1LT and standard with the 2LT. The high-performance, turbocharged SS has a 2.0L 250–260 hp 4-cylinder engine. It's no longer offered with the panel model. A 5-speed manual transmission is standard and a 4-speed automatic is optional. **Strengths:** Small-statured drivers moving from a minivan or SUV will appreciate the HHR's high seating position. There's also adequate rear legroom and storage space. Additionally, the vehicle's interior is easily accessed through wide-opening doors and easy-entry seats. On the road, the HHR handles quite well. Steering is accurate and responsive. **Weaknesses:** The HHR is clearly underpowered without the turbocharged engine option; the better-performing 2.4L powerplant makes passing and merging almost acceptable. GM recommends premium fuel for the 2.4L and turbocharged engines. Expect a bouncy ride; tire thump, engine buzz and turbo whine; mushy brakes; thinly padded seats; and front seatbacks that are too upright for some. Panels have no rear seating. Drivers over 6 feet tall will likely find their heads grazing the headliner, especially if a sunroof is installed. The under-floor storage bins are too shallow. Thick pillars block the view fore and aft, especially on the side-windowless panels. Forward view is impeded by the low roof design. Owners report electrical, suspension, and brake system failures in addition to a slap-dash fit and finish. These deficiencies are due partly to the HHR's use of failure-

As owners cry out for more power, GM drops the HHR's turbocharged option.

prone Cobalt-derived components. Alternative vehicles worth considering are the Chrysler PT Cruiser and the Honda Element. **Crashworthiness:** NHTSA gives the HHR five stars for frontal- and side-impact occupant protection; rollover protection hasn't been tested.

Honda

S2000

RATING: Above Average; 2009 is its last year. This convertible stepped into the void created by the Prelude's departure and is second-ranked with the Mazda Miata as one of the best-performing roadsters available in its class. **Price:** $50,600 (soft). **Strengths:** Powered by a powerful, smooth, and responsive 2.2L VTEC engine, the S2000 will reach 0–100 km/h in about the time it takes to close the convertible roof—under six seconds—without straining the high-revving engine (the tachometer has an unbelievable 9000 rpm red line). The upgraded 6-speed shifter has short throws, helped by a direct link with the gearbox, rather than shift-by-wire units used in other cars. The S2000 excels at acceleration, braking, cornering, and shifting, owing in large part to the car's powerful engine, anti-lock brakes, electronic stability control, double-wishbone body, rigid suspension, and electronically controlled rack-and-pinion steering, which enhances steering response without compromising stability. Owners report that the power top is a breeze to operate. **Weaknesses:** This car is overpriced by about $20,000. The ride can be jolting and noisy, as with many convertibles; tall drivers won't fit comfortably in the cockpit; and there are quite a few squeaks and rattles. **Crashworthiness:** NHTSA has given the S2000 four stars for driver and passenger frontal crash protection, five stars for side protection, and five stars for rollover resistance.

Hyundai

Entourage

RATING: Above Average. Surprisingly, this Kia Sedona twin has sold so poorly that Hyundai has taken the Entourage off the market for 2010. There's lots of discounting in anticipation of the new fall arrival of other models, making the Entourage one of the best bargains you'll find. **Price:** $30,995–$39,495 (very soft). **Strengths:** Reasonably priced and well appointed; a versatile, roomy interior; user-friendly controls; and the windows on the sliding doors retract.

Weaknesses: Steering is vague; lots of body lean when cornering under power; tall drivers may want more headroom; there's less cargo room than with the competition; and the third-row seating could be more accommodating for adults. Poor fuel economy. An abundance of safety-related complaints relative to faulty sliding doors logged by NHTSA (check *www-odi.nhtsa.dot.gov/complaints*). **Crashworthiness:** Excellent crash test results: NHTSA gave the Entourage five stars for front, side, and offset crash protection, and rollover resistance got four stars.

Hummer

RATING: Not Recommended. Hummers are humongous SUV gas hogs that are poorly made and hard to handle. Dealers are scarce and parts will be harder to find as manufacturing shifts to the Chinese purchaser. **Price:** *H2 4×4:* $63,950; *H3 4×4:* $34,445–$45,445; *H3T 4×4:* $33,695–$39,695. GM bought the Hummer brand in December 1999 from AM General, which has also continued to make versions for the armed forces. Hummer's 64 percent sales decline through September from year-earlier levels was the steepest of any volume brand in the United States and effectively led to Hummer going on the auction block. In its June bankruptcy filing, GM estimated that Hummer was worth $500 million. Yet it jumped at the Chinese offer of $150 million. Hmm…does this mean we should offer hungry GM dealers less than a third of the retail prices for GM's 2010 new cars, trucks, SUVs, and vans?

Going, going, almost gone.

Future models are expected to have the useless flex fuel E85 capability, a wider variety of diesel powerplants (for overseas sales), and 6-speed transmissions. Hummers will continue to be manufactured and sold in the States through June 2011, with a possible one-year extension, under contract with GM. **Strengths:** Hummers can go practically anywhere and are great ego-boosters for insecure men. **Weaknesses:** Frequent powertrain, electrical system, and suspension breakdowns; problematic servicing and parts supply; fit and finish that only Iraqi veterans would appreciate; and wallet-busting depreciation. For example, the 2009 H2 4×4 loses $25,000 in value during its first year on the market. **Crashworthiness:** The 2010 H3 was given an NHTSA five-star rating for front and side crash protection; rollover protection garnered three stars.

Jaguar and Land Rover

RATING: Not Recommended. Jaguar and Land Rover are now owned and built by Tata Motors of India, who purchased the companies in March 2008. The $2.3 billion (CDN) purchase price is about half what Ford originally paid for the luxury brands. Nevertheless, Tata's "bargain" contributed to the company's first loss in eight years of $520 million up to March 2009. Jaguar Land Rover's unit share of the loss was $504 million. The company is seeking U.K. guarantees for more than $500 million (CDN) in loans from U.K.-based banks. If Tata doesn't get the loan guarantees, the JLR brands will likely be dropped in 2011. If the loan guarantees do come through, Tata will burn through the money and probably drop the cars at a later date.

Jaguar has completely revamped its entire model line in less than two years, and the company's tattered quality image was also given a small boost in J.D. Power's

The Land Rover LR2.

vehicle dependability survey, which gave the company high marks. For a brand that's dependably undependable, this was unexpected good news, inasmuch as quality snafus had plagued the first XF cars off the assembly line and sullied what should have been a triumphant comeback. *XF:* A smaller Jaguar that debuted in early 2008, the XF embodies a new blunt-nose and swept-back-roofline style that is now incorporated into the XJ. For 2010, the car is available with new, more powerful engines, and a high-performance XFR model has been added. Base versions reprise the 4.2L 300 hp V8, while Premium models use a 5.0L 385 hp V8. Supercharged versions crank up the horsepower to 510. All use a 6-speed automatic transmission with a rotary knob for gear selection. The car has power to spare and a well-appointed cabin, but front and rear room is limited. Reliability is still subpar, with the powertrain, electrical, and suspension systems causing the most grief. Crashworthiness hasn't been ascertained. **Price:** $59,800 for the base model (very soft and depreciates $20,000 when it leaves the showroom); $65,800 for the Premium; and $77,800 for the Supercharged version. *XJ sedan:* Jaguar's full-sized flagship sedan was launched in June 2009. It has none of the classic Jaguar looks, nor has it been as glitch-ridden as the XF. The 2010 model has freshened styling, more power, and new features. Trim levels include the base XJ, a mid-level Supercharged, and a top-line Supersport, all using different variations of the 5.0L V8 engine hooked to a 6-speed automatic transmission. The base XJ and XJL have 385 hp; the XJ Supercharged and XJL Supercharged have 470 hp. The XJ Supersport and XJL Supersport produce 510 hp and must be specially ordered. **Price:** $80,500 for the base model (very soft).

Land Rover sells four SUV models in Canada: *LR2:* $44,900; *LR3:* $53,900; *Range Rover:* $100,900; *Range Rover Sport:* $78,300, and $94,400 for the supercharged version. All of the above prices can be beaten down by 15 to 20 percent, which compensates for the car's 35 percent depreciation when it leaves the showroom. Although the 2010 LR2 returns unchanged, the restyled and re-engineered LR3 comes back as the LR4, with a new 5.0L 375 hp V8 engine, a more luxurious interior, and better handling.

The Land Rover LR3.

The Range Rover Sport.

LR2: This five-passenger SUV has all-wheel drive without a low-range gear for off-roading. The sole powertrain teams a 3.2L 230 hp 6-cylinder engine with a 6-speed automatic transmission. First launched as the Freelander, the car had so many failure-prone components that Land Rover "fixed" the name and changed it to the LR3, and then the LR2, starting in 2006. **Strengths:** A comfortable but firm ride and good handling. **Weaknesses:** Overpriced for what you get and unable to maintain a reasonable resale value. Little steering feedback, and brakes are hard to modulate. Unreliable, with a host of brake, electrical system, and powertrain problems. **Crashworthiness:** Not tested. *Range Rover:* The Range Rover flagship gets new styling and upgraded engines for 2010. The HSE has a new 5.0L 375 hp V8, and the top-line Supercharged model with a supercharged 5.0L 510 hp V8 is hooked to a 6-speed automatic with manual shift gate is the lone transmission. It's well-appointed and provides a comfortable ride. On the minus side, the car is way overpriced and is a gas-guzzler. Handling is mediocre, brakes are just acceptable, and quality control is atrocious. **Crashworthiness:** Not tested.

LAND ROVER QUALITY IS NOT "JOB 1"

Problems per 100 vehicles, compared with industry average

Year	Land Rover	Industry
2006	204	124
2005	149	118
2004	148	119
2003	190	133

Source: J.D. Power and Associates 2006 Initial Quality Study.

According to J.D. Power's 2006 Initial Quality Study (IQS), Land Rover anchored the bottom of the quality heap with 204 problems per 100 vehicles—more than two problems per vehicle, and a far cry from the industry average of 124 problems. Nevertheless, the poor showing is no surprise for the British automaker now owned by Tata Motors. It has been a perennial bottom-feeder in quality surveys for the past several decades. Industry watchers say the company's dead-last IQS finish was the result of electronic glitches that followed the replacement of Land Rover's BMW-sourced engines with Jaguar engines during the 2006 model year. For example, the 2006 Range Rover adopted the Jaguar engine but retained the original BMW electrical architecture—a sure-fire recipe for trouble and a constantly lit Check Engine light.

Land Rover also tied for last with Hummer and Porsche in *Consumer Reports*' 2006 car reliability survey, and it was only one of six makes that did not have a model whose reliability was "Good" or above, a "distinction" shared with Mercedes-Benz, Volkswagen, and Jaguar.

The following year, Land Rover placed second-to-last in the same *Consumer Reports* reliability survey. (Mercedes-Benz took the bottom spot.) The V8-equipped LR3/Discovery was ranked the second-least reliable mid-sized SUV. (The Mercedes-Benz M-Class SUV took last place.)

Nissan

RATING: *Cube and Leaf:* Not Recommended. The Cube ($16,998–$21,498; Tech Package is plus $1,300 for an automatic transmission and another $1,400 for delivery) and the 2011 Leaf ($25,000–$30,000) are both affordable, but neither one is Recommended, because they are so new to the market. The Cube is

The Cube: Not a pretty car, but better-performing than the Kia Soul.

essentially a box on wheels that has plenty of room, but no personality. It is ugly stylistically and induces a feeling of instant claustrophobia. No changes are expected for this 2010 five-passenger front-drive, 1.8L 122-hp 4-cylinder-powered people-mover. Crashworthiness hasn't been determined. In a comparison with the Kia Soul, the Cube is a better buy. Although the Kia may be cheaper, neither the ride nor the handling can touch the Nissan. Add in the fact that the Cube has been proven in other countries (it's in its third generation) and offers Nissan B– reliability/quality. Finally, Kia's reliability is at about a C level on a good day, and first-year Kia's are notoriously glitch-prone. As for the initial cash savings with the Soul, it will likely be wiped out in what will probably be a higher rate of depreciation, if the past is any guide.

Nissan's Leaf electric car: A battery is extra?

The Leaf is Nissan's all-electric car that can go 160 kilometres without stopping to recharge, a process that would take about eight hours. Nevertheless, although the Leaf costs a few thousand dollars more than the Prius, it's $15,000 less costly than the Chevrolet Volt. Nissan has suggested that it may lease or charge separately for the Leaf's battery pack. If the company actually goes through with this hare-brained idea, it can kiss this car goodbye.

Nissan does have a couple of sports cars that are worth considering, although they have yet to be crash tested. The *370Z* is a $38,998 coupe that gets a roadster running mate for 2011, costing a predicted $6,000 premium. Is either model worth the price? Yes, both are an excellent alternative to the Chevrolet Corvette, which costs $15,000 more. The Recommended Nissan *GT-R* ($89,900) is the first AWD sports car to be fitted with an independent rear axle and powered by a 485 hp twin-turbo V6.

Porsche

Now owned by Volkswagen, Porsche has also just come off one of its worst years ever. There are five Porsches to choose from: the entry-level Boxster, 911, Cayenne, Cayman, and the newest addition, the Panamera.

The Porsche Boxster.

The Porsche Panamera.

Why buy your Cayenne in Canada when it's $26,000 cheaper in the States?

RATINGS: *Boxster:* Above Average; *911, Cayenne, Cayman, and Panamera:* Not Recommended. **Price:** Porsche was forced to cut its Canadian prices by almost 10 percent when the Canadian dollar increased value in September 2007. Now that the dollar is stronger once again, look for further price cuts. Adroit haggling should get you 20 percent off the suggested retail price. *Boxster:* $58,100–$73,900; *911:* $94,800–$174,600; *Cayenne:* $56,700–$152,200; *Cayman:* $63,500–$89,100; *Panamera:* $115,100–$155,000. Incidentally, that $152,200 (CDN) price for the Cayenne S 4.8 V8 is reduced to $126,300 (U.S.) in the States, and a base Boxster costs only $46,600 (U.S.). (Yikes!)

Of these five cars, the 911 and Cayenne are Not Recommended due to their high frequency of repair scores and greater need for dealer servicing, and the Cayman and Panamera are too new to the market to judge. Both Porsche and VW are in the throes of reorganization, and many dealerships are uncertain as to their future. Parts supply is another area that is being restructured. With all these strikes going against the company, the only safe bet is the entry-level Boxster, rated Above Average, mainly due to its exceptional highway performance, high resale value, and the availability of independent servicing agencies familiar with the car. Still, its fit and finish leaves much to be desired. On the 911 and Cayenne, the powertrain, climate system, suspension, and fit and finish should be your main concern. **Crashworthiness:** Not tested.

Saab

RATING: All Saabs are rated Not Recommended. This includes the *9-3, 9-5,* and *9-7X AWD.* GM hopes someone will buy the company before it folds completely. In the meantime, Saab dealers are packing their bags; parts are caught in a practically

The Saab 9-3.

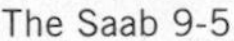

The Saab 9-5.

The Saab 9-7X.

non-existent supply chain somewhere between Sweden, the States, and Oshawa; and depreciation is cataclysmic. All three models suffer from an abundance of defective components that imperil the cars' reliability and your own financial solvency. Be especially wary of powertrain, electrical, and fuel system breakdowns; brake failures; and poor fit and finish. **Crashworthiness:** Better than average, though the 9-5 and 9-7X AWD remain untested.

Saturn

RATING: Not Recommended, except for the *Outlook* SUV, which is rated Average. The European-imported, Opel-derived *Astra* is the next best Saturn and is rated Below Average. It has fewer complaints than the other models, but parts and servicing will become increasingly problematic now that the Penske purchase of the company has fallen through. Shoppers know this and are bidding down the car's price by more than 30 percent.

The Saturn Outlook.

The Outlook shares many of the problems listed below; however, it is easily repaired and can be serviced by independent repair agencies using Chevrolet, GMC, and Buick parts.

The three most troublesome Saturns are the *Sky* (*Red Line:* $32,000–$39,660), *Vue* (*XR AWD:* $26,900–$33,920), and *Aura* (*XR V6:* $24,710–$31,965), listed from worst to just bad. All have serious fit and finish deficiencies like water leaks; squeaks, rattles, and clunks; and premature brake caliper and rotor wearout after barely a year on the road.

Other problems they all share: rolling backwards when stopped on a hill, faulty engine cam sensors, automatic transmissions that over-rev when in passing mode and are slow-shifting, steering failures, wipers that fly off their shafts, inaccurate fuel gauges caused by defective fuel-level sensor, and worst of all, airbags that deploy for no reason:

The Saturn Astra.

> While driving less than 10 mph [16 km/h] and attempting to make a right turn, the air bags deployed without impact. The seat belt locked around the contact's neck. Her neck was injured and she was transported to a physician due to the chemicals expelled from the air bags. The impact was forceful enough that the contact thought she had been shot.

The Sky has the most serious problems of the three. Over 50 owners complain of brake failure. Others write of fuel leakage from the fuel filler tube and fuel tanks, and traction and stability control malfunctions that make their vehicle shake and difficult to control. Next worst is the Vue, a vehicle redesigned in 2008 using Opel Vectra parts. Its specialty is transmission fluid leaks, poor transmission performance, a tendency to constantly downshift when in cruise-control mode, and transmission failures. Its engine tends to overheat due to a faulty heater core. The one fit and finish defect that leaps out at you is the door locks that either don't latch or won't open. Owners tell of the doors flying open when cornering, or back-seat passengers having to crawl over the front seats to exit. The Aura isn't much better. Owners report hood latch failures; Goodyear tire sidewall bulges; chronic fuel leaks, particularly when refuelling; and failure of the airbags to deploy.

Saturn production will soon cease and all dealer contracts will expire in October 2010. No, the cars won't become collectors' cars any more than the recently dropped Oldsmobiles. They will be junk, needed only for parts. Look for all the above prices to nosedive close to half their suggested retail value as we go into the new year.

Toyota

Scion xB

RATING: Average. This boxy-styled Toyota hatch coupe is carried over into 2010 with a couple of new colours, integrated USB/iPod inputs, steering-wheel controls, and an upgraded 160-watt Pioneer audio system ("boom-boom" instead of "vroom-vroom"). Two other Scions that will also arrive for 2010 are the tC compact "sport coupe" five-seat hatchback with panorama moon roof and the xD subcompact four-door hatchback.

The year 2010 will be the first year in Canada for this nicely appointed compact front-drive, five-door wagon with its handy one-piece rear liftgate. Carrying a standard-issue 2.4L 158 hp 4-cylinder engine teamed with a 5-speed manual or 4-speed automatic transmission, the xB offers a full array of safety features like ABS, traction control, an anti-skid system, side curtain airbags, and front side airbags. **Price:** $15,750, plus another $1,000 for an automatic transmission (firm). **Strengths:** Reasonably priced; a history of keeping a high resale value in the States; relatively few reports of reliability problems; and repairs can be easily done with parts taken from the Toyota generic parts bin. Additional pluses: good passenger and cargo room; easy entry/exit; good maneuverability; and a comfortable ride. **Weaknesses:** Good initial acceleration disappoints when merging or passing other cars. The automatic transmission sometimes hesitates when shifting (a familiar Toyota shortcoming), and the manual tranny is clunky to some. The car isn't as fuel-frugal as one would expect after owning the previous generation model, and the automatic transmission is an economy killer. The rear view is obstructed by claustrophia-inducing large rear pillars and low windows. There has been one complaint that the airbags failed to deploy in an accident. **Crashworthiness:** NHTSA has given the previous model a five-star rating for side crash protection and four stars for frontal crashworthiness and rollover resistance.

FJ Cruiser

RATING: Recommended; the Cruiser takes its inspiration from the Toyota FJ40 Land Cruiser, built between 1956 and 1983, and sells for $30,080–$35,590 (base price is $22,545 in the States). Its prices are negotiable and the Cruiser competes especially well off-road against the Ford Escape, Honda Element, Jeep Liberty or Wrangler, and Nissan Xterra. It is powered by a competent 4.0L 239 hp V6 that can be used for either two- or four-wheel drive. A 5-speed automatic transmission comes with both versions, and a 6-speed manual gearbox is available with the all-wheel drive. Although the FJ's turning circle is about 1.5 m (5 ft.), larger than those of similar-sized SUVs, off-roading should be a breeze if done carefully, thanks to standard electronic stability control, short overhangs, and better-than-average ground clearance. **Crashworthiness:** Interestingly, NHTSA crashworthiness scores for front and side impacts are five stars; however, rollover protection merits only three stars. This is disappointing, and it's almost never seen with vehicles that are equipped with electronic stability control.

The rear side doors are taken from the Honda Element, which means rear and side visibility is severely limited. There is also some side-wind vulnerability, and annoying wind noises are generated by the large side mirrors. Although touted as

a five-passenger conveyance, a normal-sized fifth passenger in the back seat won't be comfortable. Plus, the rear seats are hard to access, forcing front occupants to unbuckle every time a rear occupant gets in or out. Front-seat headrests may be uncomfortably positioned for short occupants. Another minus is that premium fuel must be used.

Volkswagen

Routan

RATING: Not Recommended. A Chrysler minivan cousin with a German accent, the Routan is a seven-seat spin-off of the RT platform used by the Chrysler Town & Country and Dodge Grand Caravan. 2009 was its only model year in Canada. **Price:** $27,975–$49,975 (very soft). It was manufactured in Windsor, Ontario, alongside Chrysler's minivans, and featured revised styling and firmer suspension tuning. In January 2009, VW of America asked Chrysler Canada to stop production of the Routan for the month of February after 29,000 Routans had been shipped to U.S. dealerships. By July 2009, 11,677 units had sold. Depreciation? A 2009 top-of-the-line $50,000 Execline is now worth about $35,000. If you are offered a Routan at a ridiculously low price, run—don't walk—away. The Routan has all of the Caravan's problems without the warranty backup or low prices available from Chrysler dealers. **Crashworthiness:** NHTSA

"Honey, I can't get this damn top down!" At Volkswagen, some things never change.

gives the Routan five stars for front and side crashworthiness and four stars for rollover resistance. Some of the more common safety complaints concern transmission failures, which means the transmission locks up in traffic; a poorly designed backup camera; unsafe child safety seat positioning; a power sliding door that can crush a child's hand; and unsafe power-assisted rear seats:

> My 2009 Volkswagen Routan slipped into Reverse while I was behind it today, running me over.
>
> •
>
> Back up camera on the Volkswagen Routan minivan is unusable. Video has no contrast, low color level, lacks detail, wrong colors, etc. This camera is a hazard for anyone that tries to use it for backing up. Same camera is on all Chrysler minivans. Additionally when the van is equipped with the camera, they delete the backup sensors, leaving no aids for determining if the blind spots are clear.
>
> •
>
> The third row is a bench seat, which has latch compatibility in one place. The owner's manual states that a child safety seat (booster or infant seat) can be installed using the latch system in the center seat of the third row. When a booster seat or an infant seat are, in fact, installed in this third row, the child is actually positioned in between the outboard seat and the center seat, due to the position of the latch "bars," and the child's head is in between the center and outboard headrest, and is not protected by either headrest. This also means that neither the center seatbelt or outboard seatbelt fits across my child as it should—it is not across his shoulder.
>
> •
>
> My 7 year old found buttons that powered the last row of seats. These buttons lifted the seats up and down. To my horror I all of [a] sudden heard my 3 year old screaming. He was standing in the car directly in front of the last row of seats with his foot lodged in between the seat and the floor. The power lift was still running and smashing his foot. There was no sensor that stopped the power seat. I feel this could be very dangerous. What would happen if a child's head got lodged in this mechanism? Luckily my child had Croc shoes on and was able to pull his foot out of his shoe but there was quite an indentation mark from where the seat was pushing on his foot. The doors in minivans have sensors—I believe these power lift back row seats should have some sort of sensor. I would hate to have a child get killed by this.

Touareg 2

RATING: Not Recommended; wait for the cheaper and more fuel-efficient second-series 2011 model. **Price:** $44,975–$69,975 (very soft). Volkswagen's second-generation 2010 mid-size Touareg comes with lots of style, a plush and comfortable cabin, and some of the most impressive off-road capabilities in its class. For this, you pay an outrageously high price for an SUV that doesn't offer third-row seating and has a pitifully poor reliability record and sky-high maintenance costs. The quintessential lemon, problem areas include the powertrain, fuel, and electrical systems; brakes; and fit and finish. A redesigned 2011 Touareg is expected in late 2010. Early reports say it will shed some weight for better fuel economy, cost about $5,000 to $10,000 less than the Touareg 2, offer third-row seating, and make available an optional gas/electric hybrid powertrain.

Crashworthiness: NHTSA gives the Touareg five stars for front and side crashworthiness and four stars for rollover resistance.

The 15-Passenger Van: A Death Trap on Wheels

Fifteen-passenger vans like the 1997 Ford Econoline that went out of control and killed seven basketball players and one teacher on January 13, 2008, near Bathurst, New Brunswick, are "death trap[s] on wheels," says The Safety Forum, a Washington, D.C.–based consumer consulting group. In fact, NHTSA issued four consumer safety advisories between 2000 and 2005, more than for any other vehicle type. They are considered so unsafe that the United States government has banned schools from purchasing them.

And Transport Canada sits back and smugly says, "We are studying the issue."

In 1971, the full-sized Dodge Ram Wagon passenger van, one of the oldest 15-passenger vans, came on the market. Since then, 15-passenger vans have been responsible for thousands of deaths and injuries. NHTSA says the vans are prone to fishtailing and are difficult to bring back under control, particularly at high speeds and especially when they are heavily loaded.

According to NHTSA, 1,003 people died in 15-passenger van crashes between 1990 and 2001, which included 316 rollovers. The National Transportation Safety Board (NTSB) has found that 15-passenger vans are involved in a greater number of single-vehicle accidents resulting in rollover crashes than any other passenger vehicle.

There are approximately 1.5 million 15-passenger vans registered in North America, used by schools, churches, daycare centres, retirement homes, and hotels. They were initially sold almost four decades ago as cargo vans, but automakers have left them relatively unchanged except for GM's introduction of electronic stability control on 2003 models and Ford's phase-in of the same feature on its 2006 versions.

In October 2004, IIHS released a study saying stability control systems could save up to 7,000 lives each year if they were standard equipment on all vehicles. Developed in the mid-1990s, this safety feature uses an electronic module that compares steering input with the van's actual steering arc and then, if necessary, makes quick, individual brake applications to enhance control and keep the vehicle on track. Brake pressure is automatically applied to each wheel individually when the module senses wheel slippage, understeer (plowing), or oversteer (fishtailing). If needed, engine torque may be adjusted to help the driver regain directional control.

Without stability control, the likelihood of a rollover during a sudden turn or when travelling over slippery roads increases significantly when five or more people are in the van. The van fishtails first, and because it is top-heavy and overloaded in the rear, it then rolls over. This usually results in severe injuries and many casualties.

Transport Canada has treated 15-passenger van safety with benign neglect, despite being warned by the Canadian Standards Association in the summer of 2007 that the vans are killers.

Incidentally, Ford paid $37.5 million in a 2004 Kentucky van crash case after a Scott County jury found the automaker's 15-passenger van to be responsible for three deaths.

Some Final Precautions

Here's how to check out a new or used vehicle without a lot of hassle. But if you are deceived by a seller despite your best efforts, don't despair. As discussed in Part Two, Canadian federal and provincial laws dish out harsh penalties to new- and used-car dealers who hide or embellish important facts. Ontario's *Consumer Protection Act* (*www.e-laws.gov.on.ca/html/statutes/english/elaws_statutes_02c30_e.htm*), for example, lets consumers cancel a contract within one year of entering into an agreement if a seller makes a false, misleading, deceptive, or unconscionable representation. This includes using exaggeration, innuendo, or ambiguity about a material fact, or failing to state a material fact, if such use or failure deceives or tends to deceive.

Just keep in mind the following points:

- Dealers are *presumed* to know the history, quality, and true performance of what they sell.
- Even details like a vehicle's fuel economy can lead to a contract's cancellation if the dealer gave a higher-than-accurate figure. In *Sidney v. 1011067 Ontario Inc. (c.o.b. Southside Motors)* 15, the plaintiff was awarded $11,424.51 plus prejudgment interest. The plaintiff claimed the defendant advised him that the vehicle had a fuel efficiency of 800–900 km per tank of fuel, when in fact, the maximum efficiency was only 500 km per tank.

A Check-Up Checklist

Now, let's assume you are dealing with an honest seller and that you've chosen a vehicle that's priced right and seems to meet your needs. Take some time to assess its interior, its exterior, and its highway performance with the checklist below. If you're buying from a dealer, ask to take the vehicle home overnight in order to drive it over the same roads you use in your daily activities. Of course, if you're buying privately, it's doubtful that you'll get the vehicle for an overnight test—you may have to rent a similar one from a dealer or rental agency.

Safety Check

1. Is the vehicle equipped with electronic stability control and full-torso side airbags, and has it earned a high crashworthiness ranking? Remember, a study by the Insurance Institute for Highway Safety found side airbags that include head protection cut a driver's risk of death almost in half for driver's side collisions. Another study from the same Institute concluded that electronic stability control reduces the risk of fatal single-vehicle crashes by more than half.
2. Is outward visibility good in all directions?
3. Are there large blind spots impeding vision, such as side pillars?
4. Are the mirrors large enough for good side and rear views? Do they block your view or vibrate?
5. Are all instrument displays clearly visible (not washed out in sunlight)? Is there daytime or nighttime dash glare upon the windshield? Are the controls easy to reach?
6. Are the handbrake and hood release easy to reach and use? Will they hold the vehicle on a hill?
7. Does the front seat have sufficient rearward travel to put you at a safe distance from the airbag's deployment (about 30 cm/12 in.) and still allow you to reach the brake and accelerator pedals? Are the brake and accelerator pedals adjustable and spaced far enough apart?
8. Are the head restraints adjustable or non-adjustable? (The latter is better if you often forget to set them.) Do they push your chin into your chest?
9. Are the head restraints designed to permit rear visibility? (Some are annoyingly obtrusive.)

10. Are there rear three-point shoulder belts similar to those on the front seats?
11. Is the seat belt latch plate easy to find and reach?
12. Does the seat belt fit comfortably across your chest, release easily, retract smoothly, and use pretensioners for maximum effectiveness?
13. Are there user-friendly child-seat anchor locations?
14. Are there automatic door locks controlled by the driver, or childproof rear door locks? Does the automatic side sliding door latch securely, and does it immediately stop when encountering an object as it opens or closes?
15. Do the rear windows roll only halfway down? When they are down, are your ears assailed by a booming wind noise, or does the vehicle vibrate excessively?

Exterior Check

Rust

Cosmetic rusting (rear hatch, exhaust system, front hood, door jamb) isn't unusual on new cars that have been on the dealer's lot for some time. Minor rusting is acceptable and can even help push the price way down, as long as the chassis and other major structural members aren't affected.

Knock gently on the front fenders, door bottoms, rear wheelwells, and rear doors—places where rust usually occurs first. Even if these areas have been repaired with plastic, lead, metal plates, or fibreglass, once rusting starts, it's difficult to stop. Use a small magnet to check which body panels have been repaired with non-metallic body fillers.

Use a flashlight to check for exhaust system and suspension component rust-out. Make sure the catalytic converter is present. In the past, many drivers removed this pollution-control device in the mistaken belief that it would improve fuel economy. The police can fine you for not having the converter, and you'll be forced to buy one ($400+) in order to certify your vehicle.

Tires

Be wary of tire brands that have poor durability records. Stay away from Firestone/Bridgestone tires sold with many new vehicles. Look at tire wear for clues that the vehicle is out of alignment, needs suspension repairs, or has serious chassis problems. Getting an alignment and new shocks and springs is part of routine maintenance, and it's relatively inexpensive to do with aftermarket parts. However, if your vehicle is a 4×4 or the MacPherson struts have to be replaced, you're looking at a $1,000 repair bill.

Accident damage

Most new cars have some shipping damage. In British Columbia, all accidents involving more than $2,000 in repairs must be reported to subsequent buyers.

Here are some tips on what you can do to avoid buying a damaged new or used vehicle. First, ask the following questions about the vehicle's accident history:

- Has it ever been in an accident? Was there a claim for transport damage when the vehicle was shipped from the factory? Can you show me the PDI (pre-delivery inspection) sheet? Do you have a vehicle history file?
- What was the damage and who fixed it?
- Is there any warranty outstanding? Can I have a copy of the work order?
- Has the vehicle's certificate of title been labelled "salvage"? ("Salvage" means that an expert has determined that the cost to properly repair the vehicle is more than its value. This usually happens after the vehicle has been in a serious accident.)

If the vehicle has been in an accident, you should either walk away from the sale or have the vehicle checked by a qualified auto body expert. Remember, not all salvage vehicles are bad—properly repaired ones can be a safe and sound investment if the price is low enough.

What to look for

1. If the vehicle has been repainted recently, check the quality of the job by inspecting the engine and trunk compartments and the inside door panels. Do it on a clear day so that you'll see any waves in the paint.
2. Check the paint—do all of the vehicle's panels match?
3. Inspect the paint for tiny bubbles. They may identify a poor priming job or premature rust.
4. Is there paint overspray or primer in the door jambs, wheelwells, or engine compartment? These are signs that the vehicle has had body repairs.
5. Check the gaps between body panels—are they equal? Unequal gaps may indicate improper panel alignment or a bent frame.
6. Do the doors, hood, and rear hatch open and shut properly?
7. Have the bumpers been damaged or recently repaired? Check the bumper support struts for corrosion damage.
8. Test the shock absorbers by pushing hard on a corner of the vehicle. If it bounces around like a ship at sea, the shocks need replacing.
9. Look for signs of premature rust or displacement from a collision on the muffler and exhaust pipe.
10. Make sure there's a readily accessible spare tire as well as a jack and tools for changing a flat. Also look for premature rusting in the side wheelwells, and for water in the rear hatch channel.
11. Look at how the vehicle sits. If one side or end is higher than the other, it could mean that the suspension is defective.
12. Ask the seller to turn on the headlights (low and high beams), turn signals, parking lights, and emergency blinking lights, and to blow the horn. From the rear, check that the brake lights, backup lights, turn indicators, tail lights, and licence plate light all work.

Interior Check

New vehicles often have a few hundred kilometres on the clock; used vehicles should have 20,000 km per model year. Thus, a three-year-old vehicle would ordinarily have been driven about 60,000 kilometres. The number of kilometres on the odometer isn't as important as how well the vehicle was driven and maintained. Still, high-mileage vehicles depreciate rapidly because most people consider them to be risky buys. On new cars, a few thousand kilometres showing may indicate the car was used as a demonstrator or sold and then taken back. Be suspicious. With used cars, subtract from your offer about $200 for each additional 10,000 kilometres above the average the car shows. Confirm the odometer figure by checking the vehicle's maintenance records.

The condition of the interior will often give you an idea of how the vehicle was used and maintained. For example, sagging rear seats plus a front passenger seat in pristine condition indicate that your minivan may have been used as a minibus. Delivery vans will have the paint on the driver's doorsill rubbed down to the metal, while the passenger doorsill will look like new.

What to look for

1. Watch for excessive wear of the seats, dash, accelerator, brake pedal, armrests, and roof lining.
2. Check the dash and roof lining for radio or cellular phone mounting holes (as used in police cruisers, taxis, and delivery vans). Is the radio tuned to local stations?
3. Turn the steering wheel. Listen for unusual noises and watch for excessive play (more than 2.5 cm/1 in.).
4. Test the emergency brake with the vehicle parked on a hill.
5. Inspect the seat belts. Is the webbing in good condition? Do the belts retract easily?
6. Make sure that door latches and locks are in good working order. If rear doors have no handles or locks, or if they've just been installed, your minivan may have been used to transport prisoners.
7. Can the seats be moved into all the positions intended by the manufacturer? Look under them to make sure that the runners are functioning as they should.
8. Can headrests be adjusted easily?
9. Peel back the rugs and check the metal floor for signs of rust or dampness.

Road Test

1. Start the vehicle and listen for unusual noises. Shift automatics into Park and manuals into Neutral with the handbrake engaged. Open the hood to check for fluid leaks. Do this test with the engine running and then repeat it 10 minutes after the engine has been shut down following the completion of the test drive.

2. With the motor running, check out all dashboard controls: windshield wipers, heater and defroster, and radio.
3. If the engine stalls or races at idle, a simple adjustment may fix the trouble. But loud clanks or low oil pressure could mean potentially expensive repairs.
4. Check all ventilation systems. Do the rear side windows roll down? Are there excessive air leaks around the door handles?
5. While in Neutral, push down on the accelerator abruptly. Black exhaust smoke may require only a minor engine adjustment; blue smoke may signal major engine repairs.
6. Shift an automatic into Drive with the motor still idling. The vehicle should creep forward slowly without stalling or speeding. Listen for unusual noises when the transmission is engaged. Manual transmissions should engage as soon as the clutch is released. Slipping or stalling could require a new clutch. While driving, make absolutely sure that a four-wheel drive can be engaged without unusual noises or hesitation.
7. Shift an automatic transmission into Drive. While the motor is idling, apply the emergency brake. If the motor isn't racing and the brake is in good condition, the vehicle should stop.
8. Accelerate to 50 km/h while slowly moving through all the gears. Listen for transmission noises. Step lightly on the brakes. The response should be immediate and equal for all wheels.
9. In a deserted parking lot, test the vehicle's steering and suspension by driving in figure eights at low speeds.
10. Make sure the road is clear of traffic and pedestrians. While driving at 30 km/h, take both hands off the steering wheel to see whether the vehicle veers from one side to the other. If it does, the alignment or suspension could be defective, or the vehicle could have been in an accident.
11. Test the suspension by driving over some rough terrain.
12. Stop at the foot of a small hill and then see if the vehicle can climb it without difficulty. Stop on a hill and see if the transmission holds the car in place without you giving it gas (a "hill-holder" feature).
13. On an expressway, it should take no longer than 20 seconds for most cars and minivans to accelerate from a standing start to 100 km/h.
14. Drive through a tunnel with the windows open. Try to detect any unusual motor, exhaust, or suspension sounds.
15. After the test drive, verify the performance of the automatic transmission by shifting from Drive to Neutral to Reverse. Listen for clunking sounds during transmission engagement.

Many of these tests will undoubtedly turn up some defects, which may be major or minor (new vehicles have an average of a half-dozen major and minor defects). Ask an independent mechanic for an estimate, and try to convince the seller to pay part of the repair bill if you buy the vehicle. Keep in mind that many 3- to 5-year-old vehicles with 60,000–100,000 km on their odometers run the risk of having an engine timing belt or timing chain failure that can cause several thousand dollars' worth of repairs. If the timing belt or chain hasn't been replaced, plan to do it and deduct about $300 from the purchase price for the repair.

It's important to eliminate as many duds as possible through your own cursory check, since you'll later invest two hours and about $100 for a thorough mechanical inspection. Garages approved by the Automobile Protection Association (APA) or members of the Canadian Automobile Association (CAA) usually do a good job. CAA inspections run from $100 to $150 for non-members. Remember, if you get a bum steer from an independent testing agency, you can get the inspection fee refunded and hold the garage responsible for your subsequent repairs and consequential damages, like towing, missed work, or a ruined vacation.

Appendix II

TWENTY EASY WAYS TO CUT FUEL COSTS

Before we tell you how to cut your fuel costs, let's first explain why government-disseminated fuel economy figures are a hoax.

Drivers are rightfully complaining that their real-world gas mileage is about 15 percent less than the "official" estimates given by Transport Canada and the U.S. Environmental Protection Agency (EPA). These figures are regularly included in published and online car guides, are posted on the window stickers of nearly every car and truck sold, and are showcased in automakers' advertising. Yet new vehicles that are tested for their energy consumption are never actually driven anywhere—much less to and from work—and their fuel consumption ratings are not ultimately based on how much fuel they consume. No wonder the government warns "your fuel economy may vary" while hiding the fact that its own figures are misleading and dishonest.

In fact, subsequent "real-world" tests conducted by the EPA on a dozen vehicles in its hybrid car fleet showed that far more fuel was burned than was indicated in the EPA's own posted ratings. The differences were astonishing: The Honda Civic got 6.2 L/100 km, the Honda Insight posted 5.1 L/100 km, and the Toyota Prius got

5.3 L/100 km. Yet the EPA continues to publish fuel consumption estimates that run as low as 4.6 L/100 km, 3.6 L/100 km, and 3.9 L/100 km, respectively.

Ethanol: A Boondoggle

Ethanol fuel is another "smart" government idea that has turned out to be a rathole down which Canadian and American taxpayers have poured billions of dollars. Several years ago, *Lemon-Aid* warned readers that ethanol would not save fuel and most certainly wouldn't make for a greener planet. Now we have confirmation that we were right in an article filed by Canwest News Service last October, which quotes a confidential memo sent to Natural Resources Minister Lisa Raitt by her deputy minister that says E85 fuel (85 percent ethanol and 15 percent ordinary gasoline) will do no good. In fact, Canwest concludes that E85 will bring no actual reductions in total greenhouse gas emissions, but will cost Canadian taxpayers $2.2 billion in federal subsidies, plus more from provinces, especially Ontario.

E85 has other drawbacks: You will pay more at the pump, despite huge subsidies given out to fuel companies by Ottawa; it burns 30 percent more fuel in cold weather; it's highly corrosive and requires rust-resistant tankers, storage tanks, pumps, and auto components; and in all of Canada, there are only four gas stations where you can buy E85. That means the estimated 300,000 E85 flex-fuel vehicles on the road today will likely never get near a filling station that can refuel their vehicle with the right product.

In the meantime, Canada's auto industry and its dealers are tuning FFVs to run on gasoline because they know widespread ethanol use will never happen and they don't want customers complaining that their cars' engines run poorly with gasoline.

Okay, now that we know ethanol and hybrids aren't what they pretend to be, here are 20 real ways to cut your fuel consumption and save money:

1. **Buy a small 4-cylinder vehicle that has good crashworthiness and reliability ratings**—Generally, a vehicle with a minimum of 100 horses will get you around town and will be suitable for light commuting duties. This choice will cut your fuel bills by one-third to one-half if you are downsizing from a V8 or a 6-cylinder engine—assuming that you will not load up the vehicle with fuel-burning accessories. Air conditioning and other electrical accessories will put a greater load on a vehicle's engine and, thus, reduce its fuel economy.

2. **Stay away from hybrids and diesels**—You have to do a lot of driving to make a diesel or hybrid pay off. If you do go diesel, stay away from the ones made by Ford and GM and go with the Chrysler Cummins, but get extra powertrain protection. All three U.S. automakers have chronic diesel-injector problems on their trucks and SUVs, covered by secret repair warranties.

And the situation won't get better. GM is halting its truck production for four months in 2010 to install more-complicated urea-injecting emissions components on its diesel-equipped trucks.

Hybrids are expensive, aren't as frugal as they pretend to be, keep you a captive customer, can be costly to service, and may be life-threatening. For example, only 60 volts across the chest can injure or kill, and a hybrid's NiMH battery can produce 270 volts. Furthermore, in a car accident with a hybrid, if the NiMH battery cable is damaged, heavy sparking can start a fire, toxic chemicals may be released, and the EMT rescuers must put on heavy rubber gloves before touching the car to extract passengers and get the car ready for towing. Getting this important NiMH battery information about hybrids from car dealers can be very difficult. There is also an economic angle: If your NiMH battery has an eight-year warranty, its replacement cost could almost equal the cost of the gasoline you saved. Interestingly, Nissan is thinking of selling separate battery pack leases for its Leaf electric car in order to strengthen the car's residual value as it nears the eight-year mark.

3. **Order a manual-transmission-equipped vehicle**—With rare exceptions, manual transmissions save fuel. How much depends on factors including the vehicle's size, the owner's driving style, and traffic conditions. Another benefit to manual transmissions is that they make you a more alert driver because you have to be constantly aware of traffic conditions in order to gear down to a stop or shift to accelerate. Interestingly, only 12 percent of the vehicles on North American highways use manual transmissions. In Europe, it's just the opposite—over 90 percent of drivers choose a manual gearbox.

4. **Get an automatic transmission with more gears**—If you choose an automatic, remember that a 5-speed tranny saves you more fuel than a 4-speed. Some high-end cars actually have 7-speed transmissions, and 8-speeds are being considered.

5. **Don't buy a 4×4 vehicle**—You will burn more fuel whether or not the 4×4 feature is engaged, because of its extra weight and gearing.

6. **Be wary of the cruise control**—It's a good idea to hold a steady speed on flat terrain, but if you're driving in a hilly area, the cruise control can actually make your gas mileage worse. In hilly conditions, if traffic permits, it's better to let the vehicle slow down a little on the uphill sections and then gain the speed back on the downhill side. If you use the cruise control in these conditions, it will floor the accelerator if necessary to keep your speed constant while going uphill.

7. **Use the AC sparingly**—Don't turn on the air conditioner as your first response to heat. Start your drive by slowly accelerating with the windows open to exhaust the hot air out of the rear windows, and then put on the AC, if needed. This tactic will also enable the air conditioning to work faster and

more efficiently when it is turned on. Having the AC off and the windows open will not save gas, however. Furthermore, driving any vehicle with a window or sunroof open will likely produce a painful roar in the cabin and cause excessive vibration in the steering.

8. **Keep your vehicle aerodynamic**—Resist the urge to attach accessories like roof racks, spoilers, and cargo carriers that hamper a vehicle's aerodynamics. Incidentally, pickup truck drivers won't save fuel by lowering the tailgate when driving on the highway. With the gate closed, air flows across the top of the bed and does not get caught by the tailgate. The airflow patterns are less efficient with the tailgate open or removed.

9. **Use the Internet to find cheap gas**—Websites like *www.GasBuddy.com* will show you which stations are selling cheaper fuel, sometimes up to 10 cents less than the average price. The Internet can also be helpful in calculating your real-world gas mileage and savings—*www.sciencemadesimple.net/fuel_economy.php* is an easy-to-use site to try.

10. **Use regular-grade fuel**—Unless the engine "knocks," using a higher-octane fuel than what is recommended by the manufacturer is foolish. Using premium fuel when the engine doesn't require it will not cause it to get better fuel consumption, and it may damage your emissions-control system. Some high-mileage vehicles, however, may need high-octane fuel if they "ping" (spark knocking) heavily on regular gas. Light knocking on acceleration is not a problem, but if the knocking continues at a constant speed, or if it's very loud, move up to a higher-octane fuel until it stops. Persistent, heavy knocking reduces an engine's efficiency and can damage it in extreme cases.

11. **Shop by price, not brand**—Gas is gas, and many different brands buy from the same refineries. Buy gasoline during the coolest time of day—early morning or late evening is best. During these times, gasoline is densest. Keep in mind that gas pumps measure volumes of gasoline, not densities of fuel concentration. It is also a smart idea to use credit cards that give cardholders cash rebates based on a percentage of their purchases.

12. **Coddle your throttle**—New vehicles don't usually attain their top mileage until they're broken in, which occurs at about 5,000–8,000 km of fairly gentle driving. Avoid the prolonged warming-up of the engine on cold mornings—30–45 seconds is plenty of time. Also, don't start and stop the engine needlessly. Idling your engine for one minute consumes the amount of gas equivalent to the gas used when you start the engine. Avoid revving the engine, especially just before you switch the engine off; this wastes fuel needlessly and washes oil down from the inside cylinder walls, leading to the loss of oil pressure and premature wear. Lead-footed acceleration, heavy braking, and high-speed driving all increase gas consumption. The EPA estimates that jackrabbit starts and sudden stops can reduce fuel economy by as much as a third.

13. **Drive economically**—Driving 110 km/h instead of 90 km/h will lower your car's fuel economy by 17 percent. Driving at fast rates in low gears can consume up to 45 percent more fuel than necessary. Don't worry about whether windows are open or closed—tests carried out by *Consumer Reports* and others find it doesn't make any difference. Use only your right foot for both accelerating and braking. That way you can't accidentally ride the brake and use excessive gas.

14. **Get regular tune-ups, and change the oil and air filter frequently**—Don't let the Car Care Council and other trade groups convince you that more frequent tune-ups or adjustments will increase gas mileage. Once again, test findings show that the payoff is small—simply follow the instructions in the owner's manual. Malfunctioning emissions components, however, can burn lots of fuel. Have them "scope-checked" periodically by an independent garage, who will usually charge less than the dealer. Keep the brakes properly adjusted, since dragging brakes increases resistance. Check your gas cap—one out of every five vehicles on the road has a gas cap that is either damaged, loose, or missing altogether, which allows gas in your tank to vaporize.

15. **Be tire-smart**—Inflate all tires to their maximum limits, and don't believe all the extended tire durability and fuel-saving claims made by sellers of nitrogen gas used in tire inflation. Each tire should be periodically spun, balanced, and checked for unevenness. Remove the spare tire; instead, keep a cell phone handy and join CAA. Changing a tire beside the road puts your life at risk, and it's a pain in the butt.

16. **Fight excess weight**—Remove excess weight from the trunk or the inside of the car, including extra tires, minivan back seats, and unnecessary heavy parts. Don't drive with a full fuel tank. Remember, carrying an extra 45 kg (100 lb.) in the trunk of your car may cut your car's fuel economy by 1–2 percent. An empty roof rack may cut fuel economy by 10 percent; fully loaded, it can reduce gas mileage by 18 percent. The further you run with the tank closer to empty, the further you run in a lighter car, thereby increasing the fuel mileage. Ideally, you never want to fill your tank more than a quarter- or half-tank full.

17. **Stay away from gas-saving gadgets**—They don't work, and they may cancel the manufacturer's warranty. Instead, park your car in the shade to reduce fuel evaporation, and buy a good windshield shade to keep the interior cool. Parking in your garage will help your car stay warm in winter and cool in summer, and you won't have to depend as much on your gas-guzzling air conditioning when you drive.

18. **Carpool**—Carpools reduce travel monotony and gas expenses—all riders chip in to help you buy. Conversation helps to keep the driver alert. Pooling also reduces traffic congestion.

19. **Consolidate trips**—Combine several short errands into one trip, and combine private errands with business trips as a tax write-off.

20. **Fill up in the States**—Fuel costs a heck of a lot less there than it does in Canada.

Appendix III

INTERNET INFO

Recent surveys show that close to 80 percent of car buyers get reliability and pricing information from the Internet before visiting a dealer or private seller. This trend has resulted in easier access to confidential price margins, secret warranties, and lower prices—if you know where to look.

Getting the Lowest Price

Here's what to do: First, compare a new vehicle's "discounted" MSRP prices published on different automakers' websites with invoices downloaded from sites such as *OnTheHoist.com*, the Automobile Protection Association (*www.apa.ca*), the Canadian Automobile Association (CAA, *www.caa.ca*), and a host of other agencies. Second, check the prices you find against the ones listed in this book. Third, pay particular attention to the prices charged in the States by accessing automakers' U.S. websites—just type the company name into Google and add "USA." For example, "GM USA" will take you directly to the automaker's American website, whereas "GM Canada" gives you the Canadian headquarters, models, and prices. If you find the U.S. price is substantially lower than what Canadian dealers charge, take your U.S. printout to the Canadian dealers and ask them to come closer to the American price. There is no reason why you should pay more in Canada. And this includes freight and pre-delivery inspection fees.

Confidential Reliability Info

Unearthing reliability information from independent sources on the Internet takes a bit more patience. You should first wade through the thousands of consumer complaints logged in the NHTSA database. Next, use the NHTSA and ALLDATA service bulletin databases to confirm a specific problem's existence, to find out if it's caused by a manufacturing defect, and to learn how to correct it. Augment this information with tips found on car forums and protest/information sites. *Lemon-Aid* does this for you in its guides, but you can stay current about your vehicle's problems or research a particular failure in greater depth on your own by using the above search methods.

Automobile companies have helpful—though self-serving—websites, most of which feature detailed sections on their vehicles' histories and research and development, as well as all sorts of information of interest to auto enthusiasts. Manufacturers can easily be accessed through a search engine like Google or by typing the automaker's name into your Internet browser's address bar followed by ".com" or ".ca". Or for extra fun and a more balanced presentation, type the vehicle model or manufacturer's name into a search engine, followed by "lemon."

Consumer Protection

Automobile Consumer Coalition (*www.carhelpcanada.com*)
Founded by former director of the Toronto Automobile Protection Association Mohamed Bouchama, the ACC's Car Help Canada website provides many of the same services as does the APA; however, ACC is especially effective in Ontario and Alberta and uses a network of honest garages and dealers to help members get honest and fair prices for vehicles and repairs. ACC has been especially effective in getting new legislation enacted in Ontario and obtaining refunds for its members.

Automobile Protection Association (*www.apa.ca*)
With offices in Toronto and Montreal, this consumer group fights for safer vehicles for consumers and has exposed many scams associated with new-vehicle sales, leasing, and repairs. For a small fee, it will send you the invoice price for most new vehicles.

BBC TV Top Gear (*www.topgear.com*)
Britain's automotive equivalent to Canada's CBC TV *Marketplace*, *Top Gear* blows the whistle on the best and worst European-sold vehicles, auto products, and industry practices.

CanadianDriver (*www.canadiandriver.com*)
An exceptionally well-structured and current Canadian website for new- and used-vehicle reviews, MSRPs, and consumer reports. Other car magazine websites:

- *Automotive News* (*www.autonews.com*)
- *Autonet.ca* (*www.autonet.ca*)
- *Car and Driver* (*www.caranddriver.com*)
- *Motor Trend* (*www.motortrend.com*)
- *Road & Track* (*www.roadandtrack.com*)
- *World of Wheels* (*www.wheels.ca*)

Canadian Legal Information Institute (*www.canlii.org*)
Be your own legal researcher, and save big bucks. Use these links to find court judgments from every province and territory all the way up to the Supreme Court of Canada.

CBC TV *Marketplace* (*www.cbc.ca/marketplace*)
Marketplace has been the CBC's premier national consumer show for almost forever. Staffers are dedicated to searching out scammers, airbag dangers, misleading advertising, and unsafe, poor-quality products.

Class Actions in Canada (*www.classproceedings.ca*)
After successfully kicking Ford's rear end over its front-end thick film ignition (TFI) troubles and getting a million-dollar out-of-court settlement, this powerhouse Ontario-based law firm is now taking on GM for a decade of defective

engine intake manifold gasket failures. Estimated damages are well over a billion dollars. The firm has also worked with others to force Liberty Mutual and other insurers to refund money paid by policyholders who were forced to accept accident repairs with used, reconditioned parts instead of new, original-equipment parts.

Class Actions in the U.S. (*www.lawyersandsettlements.com*)
This is a useful site if you want to use a company's class action woes in U.S. jurisdictions as leverage in settling your own Canadian claim out of court. If you decide to go the Canadian class action route, most of the legal legwork will have been done for you. The site is easy and free to search. Just type in the make of the vehicle you're investigating, and read the results.

Competition Bureau Canada (*www.competitionbureau.gc.ca*)
The Competition Bureau is responsible for the administration and enforcement of the *Competition Act*, the *Consumer Packaging and Labelling Act*, the *Textile Labelling Act*, and the *Precious Metals Marking Act.* Its role is to promote and maintain fair competition so that Canadians can benefit from lower prices, increased product choices, and quality services.

Most auto-related complaints submitted to the Bureau concern price-fixing and misleading advertising. After *Lemon-Aid*, the APA, and Mohamed Bouchama from ACC submitted formal complaints to Ottawa against Toyota's Access pricing program a few years ago, the automaker settled the case for $2.3 million. The Bureau agreed to drop its inquiry into charges that the automaker rigged new car prices.

Almost 28 years earlier, an APA complaint forced GM to pay a $20,000 fine for lying in newspaper ads touting the Vauxhall Firenza's triumphant cross-Canada "reliability run." The cars constantly broke down, and one auto journalist brought along for the ride spilled the beans to Ottawa probers. GM took the car off the market shortly thereafter.

ConsumerAffairs.Com (*www.consumeraffairs.com/automotive/manufacturers.htm*)
Expecting some namby-pamby consumer affairs site? Won't find that here. It's a "seller beware" kind of website, where you'll find the scandals before they hit the mainstream press.

***Consumer Reports* and Consumers Union** (*www.consumerreports.org/cro/cars.htm*)
It costs $5.95 (U.S.) a month to subscribe online, but *CR*'s database is chock full of comparison tests and in-depth stories on products and services.

***Protégez-Vous* (Protect Yourself)** (*www.protegez-vous.qc.ca*)
Quebec's French-language monthly consumer protection magazine and website is a hard-hitting critic of the auto industry. It contains dozens of test-drives as well as articles relating to a broad range of products and services sold in Canada.

Supreme Court of Canada (*scc.lexum.umontreal.ca/en/index.html*)
It's not enough to have a solid claim against a company or the government. Supporting your position with a Supreme Court decision also helps. Three pro-consumer judgments rendered in February 2002 are particularly useful:

- *Bannon v. Thunder Bay (City):* An injured resident missed the deadline to file a claim against Thunder Bay; however, the Supreme Court maintained that extenuating factors, such as being under the effects of medication, extended her time to file. A good case to remember next time your vehicle is damaged by a pothole or you are injured by a municipality's negligence.

- *R. v. Guignard:* This judgment says you can protest as long as you speak or write the truth and you don't disturb the peace or harass customers or workers.

- *Whiten v. Pilot Insurance Co.:* The insured's home burned down, and the insurance company refused to pay the claim. The jury was outraged and ordered the company to pay the $345,000 claim, plus $320,000 for legal costs and $1 million in punitive damages, making it the largest punitive damage award in Canadian history. The Supreme Court maintained the jury's decision, calling Pilot "the insurer from hell." This judgment scares the dickens out of insurers, who fear that they face huge punitive damage awards if they don't pay promptly.

Auto Safety

Center for Auto Safety (*www.autosafety.org*)
A Ralph Nader–founded agency that provides free online info on safety- and performance-related defects on each model vehicle.

Crashtest.com (*www.crashtest.com*)
This website has crash-test information from around the world. You can find additional crashworthiness data for cars just recently coming on to the North American market that have been sold for many years in Asia, Europe, or Australia. The Honda Fit (Jazz), Mercedes Smart, Magna's Opel lineup, and Ford's upcoming European Fiesta and Focus imports are just a few examples.

Insurance Institute for Highway Safety (*www.iihs.org*)
A dazzling site that's long on crash photos and graphs that show which vehicles are the most crashworthy in side and offset collisions and which head restraints work best.

SafetyForum (*www.safetyforum.com*)
The 'Forum contains comprehensive news archives and links to useful sites, plus names of court-recognized experts on everything from unsafe Chrysler minivan latches to dangerous van conversions.

Transport Canada (*www.tc.gc.ca/eng/roadsafety/safevehicles-defectinvestigations-index-76.htm*)
A ho-hum site that's in no way as informative as the NHTSA or IIHS sites. You can access recalls for 1970–2010 models, but owner complaints aren't listed, defect investigations aren't disclosed, and service bulletin summaries aren't provided. A list of used vehicles admissible for import is available at *www.tc.gc.ca/roadsafety/safevehicles/importation/usa/vafus/list2/menu.htm*, or by calling the Registrar of Imported Vehicles (RIV) at 1-888-848-8240.

U.S. National Highway Traffic Safety Administration (*www.nhtsa.dot.gov/cars/problems*)
This site has a comprehensive free database covering owner complaints, recall campaigns, crashworthiness and rollover ratings, defect investigations, service bulletin summaries, and safety research papers.

Mediation/Protest

GMInsideNews (*www.gminsidenews.com/forums*)
This forum is a good place to start to get a general, dispassionate feel for GM's new-car performance and technical problems.

Links to other sites include:

- GM Piston Slap (*www.pistonslap.com*): Some GM motors appear to have problems…
- GM Truck Lemon Center (*agmlemon.freeservers.com*)

Roadfly's Car Forums and Automotive Chat Rooms (*www.roadfly.org/forums*)
Another site that's no butt-kisser. Here you'll learn about BMW fan fires, upgrades, and performance comparisons. It also contains message forums for Bentley, Cadillac, Chevy, Jaguar, Lotus, Porsche, Mercedes-Benz, and others.

MyVWLemon.com (*www.myvwlemon.com*)
Lots of venting, but enough interesting and entertaining discussions to be worthwhile.

Information/Services

Alberta Government's Vehicle Cost Calculator (*www.agric.gov.ab.ca/app24/costcalculators/vehicle/getvechimpls.jsp*)
Estimate and compare the ownership and operating costs of vehicles using variations in purchase price, options, fuel type, interest rates, or length of ownership.

ALLDATA Service Bulletins (*www.alldata.com/recalls/index.html*)
Free summaries of automotive recalls and technical service bulletins are listed by year, make, model, and engine option. You can access your vehicle's full bulletins online by paying a $26.95 (U.S.) subscription fee.

The Auto Channel (*www.theautochannel.com*)
This website gives you useful, comprehensive information on choosing a new or used vehicle, filing a claim for compensation, or linking up with other owners.

Autoextremist (*www.autoextremist.com*)
Rantings and ravings from a Detroit insider.

Automobile News Groups
These Usenet news groups are compilations of email raves and gripes that cover all makes and models. They fall into four distinct areas: *rec.autos.makers.ford* (or you can substitute any automaker's name at the end); *rec.autos.tech*; *rec.autos.driving*; and *rec.autos.misc*. The easiest way to find these groups, if you don't have a news server, is to type the address into the Groups tab of the Google search engine.

CarTrackers.com (*www.cartrackers.com*)
Used cars, consumer advice, and environmental issues are all well-covered in this site, which features a terrific auto image gallery and an excellent automotive glossary.

***Kelley Blue Book* and Edmunds** (*www.kbb.com*; *www.edmunds.com*)
Prices and technical info is American-oriented, but you'll find good reviews of almost every vehicle sold in North America, plus there's an informative readers' forum.

Online Metric Conversions (*www.sciencemadesimple.net/conversions.html*)
A great place to instantly convert gallons to litres, miles to kilometres, etc.

Phil Bailey's Auto World (*www.baileycar.com*)
Phil Bailey owns his own garage and specializes in the diagnosis and repair of foreign cars, particularly British ones. He's been advising Montreal motorists for years on local radio shows and has an exceptionally well-written and informative website.

Straight-Six.com (*www.straight-six.com*)
Okay, for you high-performance aficionados, here's a website that doesn't idolize NASCAR, Earnhardt, or the Porsche Cayenne SUV (they call it the "Ca-Yawn").

Women's Garage (*www.womensgarage.com*)
Three Canadian mechanics with a combined 100 years' experience set up this site to take the mystery out of maintaining and repairing vehicles. Don't be deterred by the site's title—males will learn more than they'll care to admit.

Finally, here are a number of other websites that may be helpful:

- *forum.freeadvice.com*
- *www.lexusownersclub.com*
- *www.benzworld.org/forums*

- *www.bmwboard.com*
- *www.bmwnation.com*
- *www.carforums.com/forums*
- *www.consumeraffairs.com/automotive/ford_transmissions.htm*
- *www.datatown.com/chrysler*
- *www.epa.gov/otaq/consumer/warr95fs.txt*
- *www.flamingfords.info*
- *www.ford-trucks.com/forums*
- *www.hotbimmer.net*
- *www.ptcruiserlinks.com*
- *www.troublebenz.com/my_opinion/actions/links.htm*
- *www.vehicle-injuries.com*

Appendix IV

CROSS-BORDER SHOPPING

Every time the loonie goes up in value, thousands of Canadians buy their new or used car across the border in the United States, where vehicles are 10 to 25 percent cheaper. For example, the Canadian dollar last traded at par with the U.S. greenback in July 2008, and that year Canadian shoppers imported a record 240,000 vehicles from the United States into Canada. Imports slowed to a trickle in the first quarter of 2009 when the dollar dropped well below 90 cents (U.S.) (then only 18,800 vehicles were imported).

But with the loonie's 21 percent surge since then, Canadian buyers are again flocking to dealer showrooms in the States. And, when you consider that most Canadians live within an hour's drive of the border, it's clear that getting a cross-border bargain is easier than ever.

Furthermore, dealers on both sides of the border are hungry for sales and aren't likely to knuckle under automaker pressure to refuse warranty repairs or service on cars purchased in the States, as they attempted to do in better economic times a year ago. Also, Transport Canada has made it easier to import new and used cars from the States, and businesses on both sides of the border have sprung up to facilitate purchases for Canadians. In fact, imports were almost twice as high in September as in January.

Shopping Tips

Reported savings range from around 10 percent for subcompact and compact vehicles, compact SUVs, and small vans to over 25 percent in the luxury vehicle segment. Most manufacturers honour the warranty, and many dealers and independent garages will modify cars to Canadian standards, including speedometer and odometer labels, child tether anchorage, daytime running lights, French airbag labels, and anti-theft immobilization devices. Some will complete the import paperwork for you. Again, whether it's worthwhile importing a car from the U.S. is a personal decision. Keep in mind that there may be a few extra costs to consider. For instance, if the vehicle was not made in North America, you have to pay duty to bring it into Canada. Normally, the duty for cars is 6.2 percent of the value of the vehicle. There are also excise taxes on vehicles weighing more than 2,007 kg (4,425 pounds). A listing of Canadian border crossing spots where you can bring in a just-purchased new or used car can be found at *www.ucanimport.com/Border_Crossing_Info.aspx*.

Consumer groups like Montreal-based CarsWithoutBorders and the Automobile Protection Association (*www.apa.ca*) say buying a car in the States as part of your vacation trip and driving it back to Canada or using an auto broker is a sure money-saver and easy to do. Canadian dealers say it's unpatriotic and not fair to dealers, and that U.S. cars have softer paint and weaker batteries.

Canadian independent new- and used-car dealers aren't buying that argument; they are some of the biggest buyers of used cars in the States. Advantage Trading Ltd. in Burnaby, B.C., for example, one of the largest importers on the West Coast, says they can get U.S. cars so cheap that they can offer discounts to Canadians and still make a handsome profit. The only downside is that there is a shortage of some popular makes and models.

If you do decide to import a vehicle on your own, Transport Canada suggests you use the Registrar of Imported Vehicles' comprehensive and easy-to-follow checklist of things you must do (*www.riv.ca/ImportingAVehicle.aspx*). It covers:

- What to do before importing a vehicle
- What to do at the border
- What to do after the vehicle enters Canada
- What RIV fees will be applied
- Who to contact for vehicle import questions, including contact information for the Canada Border Services Agency (CBSA)

This list is all you need to import almost any car and get big savings. There are also independent resources listed at *www.riv.ca/HelpfulLinks.aspx* and *www.importcartocanada.info/category/faq*. The latter site goes into even greater detail by answering these questions:

- Why buy a vehicle in the U.S. and import it into Canada?
- What are the differences between Canadian and U.S. vehicle MSRP prices?
- Why are vehicle prices so much higher in Canada than in the U.S.?
- What vehicles can be imported into Canada?
- How long does it take to import a vehicle into Canada from the U.S.?
- What should I watch out for when purchasing a vehicle to import into Canada?
- What types of modifications are needed to import a vehicle into Canada?
- What kinds of documents do I need to import a vehicle into Canada?
- Do I have to pay tax when I import a vehicle into Canada from the U.S.?
- Do I have to pay duty when I import a vehicle into Canada from the U.S.?
- Is there anyone that can import the vehicle into Canada for me?
- Can I drive my U.S. vehicle into Canada without notifying U.S. Customs?
- Where can I cross the border to import a vehicle into Canada?
- What do I do at the border?
- What should I do when I arrive at home in Canada with my new vehicle?
- What happens if my vehicle fails federal inspection?
- What is a recall clearance letter?
- Can I import a vehicle into Canada that is over 15 years old?
- How do I import a vehicle into Canada from a country other than the U.S.?
- Which vehicle manufacturers honour warranties on vehicles imported into Canada?

Where To Go

AutoCanada Income Fund (*www.autocan.ca*) specializes in cross-border shopping through 22 dealerships located across Canada, offering thousands of vehicles for sale. Currently, AutoCanada sells all makes of new and used vehicles through the following dealers:

Alberta

- Capital Chrysler Jeep Dodge, Edmonton
- Crosstown Chrysler Jeep Dodge, Edmonton
- Grande Prairie Chrysler Jeep Dodge, Grande Prairie
- Grande Prairie Hyundai, Grande Prairie
- Grande Prairie Mitsubishi, Grande Prairie
- Grande Prairie Nissan, Grande Prairie
- Grande Prairie Subaru, Grande Prairie
- Ponoka Chrysler Jeep Dodge, Ponoka
- Sherwood Park Hyundai, Sherwood Park

British Columbia

- Maple Ridge Chrysler Jeep Dodge, Maple Ridge
- Maple Ridge Volkswagen, Maple Ridge
- Northland Chrysler Jeep Dodge, Prince George
- Northland Hyundai, Prince George
- Northland Nissan, Prince George
- Okanagan Chrysler Jeep Dodge, Kelowna
- Victoria Hyundai, Victoria

Manitoba

- Thompson Chrysler Jeep Dodge, Thompson

New Brunswick

- Moncton Chrysler Jeep Dodge, Moncton

Nova Scotia

- Dartmouth Chrysler Jeep Dodge, Dartmouth

Ontario

- Cambridge Hyundai, Cambridge
- Colombo Chrysler Jeep Dodge, Woodbridge
- Doner Infiniti, Newmarket
- Doner Nissan, Newmarket

We leave the last word to CarsWithoutBorders (*www.carswithoutborders.com*):

> If you are shopping for a car, tires, car parts—do yourself a favor and check out the US pricing. In most cases there is an advantage and many times a LARGE benefit. At CarsWithoutBorders we are trying to help consumers to level the playing field. Companies are scaring Canadians into buying at home at higher prices but they know several hundred thousand cars are imported from the USA every year, so it is something that is doable and worthwhile.

Appendix V

SECRET WARRANTIES AND CONFIDENTIAL SERVICE BULLETINS

Many 2009–10 models appear in confidential documents that show which cars, trucks, vans, and SUVs have major failings that are covered by secret warranties or special service bulletins. In this section, we provide examples of the latest secret warranties and service bulletin alerts that cover major failures affecting a large number of vehicles. Remember to bring a copy of the appropriate bulletin to the dealer to use as leverage in getting free extended warranty repairs for what the automaker admits is a factory-related problem.

AUTOMAKER CONTACT INFORMATION

Chrysler Canada, Inc.	1-800-465-2001 1-800-387-9983 (Quebec)
Ford Motor Company of Canada, Ltd.	1-800-565-3673
General Motors of Canada, Ltd.	1-800-263-3777 (English) 1-800-263-7854 (French) 1-800-263-3830 (TTY)
Honda Canada, Inc.	1-888-946-6329 (Honda) 1-888-922-8729 (Acura)
Hyundai Auto Canada	1-800-461-8242 (English) 1-800-461-5695 (French)
Jaguar Canada, Inc.	1-800-668-6257
Kia Canada, Inc.	1-877-542-2886
Land Rover Group Canada, Inc.	1-800-346-3493
Mazda Canada, Inc.	1-800-263-4680
Mercedes-Benz Canada, Inc.	1-800-387-0100
Nissan Canada, Inc.	1-800-387-0122
Porsche Cars Canada, Ltd.	1-800-545-8039
Subaru Canada, Inc.	1-800-894-4212
Suzuki Canada, Inc.	905-889-2677 ext 2254
Toyota Canada, Inc.	1-888-869-6828 (Toyota) 1-800-265-3987 (Lexus)
Volkswagen Canada, Inc.	1-800-822-8987 (Volkswagen) 1-800-822-2834 (Audi)
Volvo Cars Canada, Ltd.	1-800-663-8255

Secret Warranties

ACURA

TRUNK LOCK CYLINDER

BULLETIN NO.: 08-040 AUGUST 19, 2008

VALET KEY OPENS THE TRUNK

2009 TSX

BACKGROUND: Because of a manufacturing error, the valet key can open the trunk using the trunk lock behind the left rear head restraint. (The valet key should work only in the ignition switch and the driver's door lock.) A valet key that opens the trunk gives trunk access to anyone using that key, including a valet service.

CORRECTIVE ACTION: Update the trunk lock by installing a trunk key cylinder kit. This free repair ends on August 19, 2011.

GENERAL MOTORS

CONVERTIBLE TOP COVER SEPARATION

BULLETIN NO.: 08312 DATE: APRIL 21, 2009

CONVERTIBLE ROOF COVER SEPARATION—INSTALL NEW RETAINER BRACKET

2008–09 Chevrolet Corvette

THIS PROGRAM IS IN EFFECT UNTIL MAY 31, 2010.

CONDITION: The fabric roof cover may begin to separate from its retainer bracket near the top edge of the windshield. When the vehicle reaches speeds of approximately 100 mph (160 km/h) or greater, the roof cover could begin to pull away from the retainer bracket and, depending on the speed of the vehicle and duration at that speed, could tear to the rear glass.

CORRECTION: Dealers are to install a new design retainer bracket.

CLUTCH SPRING FRACTURE—REPLACE CLUTCH

BULLETIN NO.: 09160 DATE: JULY 6, 2009

2009 Chevrolet Corvette ZR1

THIS PROGRAM IS IN EFFECT UNTIL JULY 31, 2010.

CONDITION: 2009 model year Chevrolet Corvette ZR1 vehicles may have a condition in which the clutch damper spring may fracture. If this were to occur, the driver may or may not notice gear rattle and/or the transmission may be hard to shift. If the vehicle is driven with a fractured clutch damper spring, it could result in damage to the transmission.

CORRECTION: Dealers are to replace the clutch assembly.

TEMPORARY REDUCTION IN POWER BRAKE ASSIST IN EXTREME COLD WEATHER

BULLETIN NO.: 09051 **DATE: JUNE 8, 2009**

2009 Buick Enclave
2009 Chevrolet Traverse
2009 GMC Acadia
2009 Saturn Outlook
Registered in Canada, Alaska, Colorado, Idaho, Illinois, Indiana, Iowa, Maine, Michigan, Minnesota, Montana, Nebraska, New Hampshire, New York, North Dakota, Ohio, Pennsylvania, South Dakota, Vermont, Wisconsin, Wyoming
THIS PROGRAM IS IN EFFECT UNTIL JUNE 30, 2010.

CONDITION: Certain 2009 model year Buick Enclave, Chevrolet Traverse, GMC Acadia, and Saturn Outlook vehicles that are operated in temperatures of –5° to –49°F (–21° to –45°C) may have a condition in which the power brake assist may be temporarily reduced. In these extreme cold temperatures, the opening of one or both of the power break booster vacuum check valves may be delayed, resulting in reduced power brake assist. As the valve(s) warm, which could take more than 1 minute, the valve operation returns to normal and full power brake assist returns.

CORRECTION: Dealers/retailers are to repair the power brake assist.

SPECIAL COVERAGE ADJUSTMENT—ENGINE CONTROL MODULE—EMISSION RELATED REPROGRAMMING

BULLETIN NO.: 09014 **DATE: SEPTEMBER 9, 2009**

2006 Chevrolet Cobalt, HHR
2006 Pontiac Pursuit (Canada only)
2006 Saturn Ion
With 2.2L engine

CONDITION: Engine control modules on certain 2006 model year Chevrolet Cobalt, HHR; Pontiac Pursuit; and Saturn Ion vehicles, equipped with a 2.2L engine (RPO L61), may randomly fail to respond to single information requests made by an On-Board Diagnostics (OBD) emission test device, generic scan tool, or other aftermarket devices that plug into the vehicle's Data Link Connector (DLC). GM Tech 2 scan tools are not affected by this condition. It is possible that the lack of a single ECM response to an emission test tool could result in missing or inaccurate OBD emission test data (for example no or partial electronic VIN display) resulting in a customer's vehicle failing or being rejected from a state/province mandated OBD emission test (Inspection and Maintenance (I/M) Test or Smog Check).

SPECIAL COVERAGE ADJUSTMENT: This special coverage covers ECM reprogramming for the condition described above for a period of 15 years or 150,000 miles (240,000 km), whichever occurs first, from the date the vehicle was originally placed in service, regardless of ownership. ECM reprogramming will be performed at no charge to the customer.

SPECIAL POLICY ADJUSTMENT (REPLACE INJECTOR)

BULLETIN NO.: 04039 DATE: JUNE 2004

2001–02 Silverado/Sierra (6.6L Duramax Diesel)

CONDITION: Some customers of 2001–02 model year Chevrolet Silverado and GMC Sierra vehicles, equipped with a 6.6L Duramax Diesel (RPO LB7 – VIN Code 1) engine, may experience vehicle service engine soon (SES) light illumination, low engine power, hard start, and/or fuel in crankcase, requiring injector replacement, as a result of high fuel return rates due to fuel injector body cracks or ball seat erosion.

SPECIAL POLICY ADJUSTMENT: This special policy covers the condition described above for a period of 7 years or 200,000 miles (320,000 km), whichever occurs first, from the date the vehicle was originally placed in service, regardless of ownership. The repairs will be made at no charge to the customer.

PAINT CHIPPING BY WHEEL OPENINGS

BULLETIN NO.: 03-08-111-002F DATE: APRIL 30, 2007

PAINT CHIPPING BEHIND FRONT WHEELS/FRONT OF REAR WHEELS, DAMAGED LOWER DOOR/CLADDING AND ROCKER PANELS (REPAINT DAMAGED AREA, INSTALL ASSIST STEP)

2004–07 Buick Rainier, 2002–06 Chevrolet TrailBlazer EXT, 2002–07 Chevrolet TrailBlazer, 2006–07 Chevrolet TrailBlazer SS, 2002–06 GMC Envoy XL, 2002–07 GMC Envoy, 2004–05 GMC Envoy XUV, 2002–04 Oldsmobile Bravada, 2005–07 Saab 9-7X.

ATTENTION: Implementation of this Service Bulletin requires case-by-case review and approval by your District Service Manager (DVM) (U.S.) or District Service Manager (DSM) (Canada) PRIOR to the performance of any repairs.

CONDITION: Some customers may comment that the paint is chipped just behind the front wheels as well as just in front of the rear wheels. Some customers may also comment about damage to the lower door/cladding and rocker panels.

CAUSE: The rocker and lower door areas may be damaged by road debris thrown up by the tires at highway speeds.

CORRECTION: It may be necessary to perform the following repair in order to meet customer expectations and gain their product satisfaction.

In Canada, the 2007 GM Approved Refinish Materials booklet is also available on the GM infoNET under the Service and Body tab. For all of the above vehicles except TrailBlazer SS, install the assist step. For the TrailBlazer SS, install a Protector Kit. Instructions are included in the kit.

GM ENGINE OIL OR COOLANT LEAK

BULLETIN NO.: 03-06-01-010A **DATE: APRIL 2003**

ENGINE OIL OR COOLANT LEAK (INSTALL NEW INTAKE MANIFOLD GASKET)

2000–03 Buick Century; 2002–03 Buick Rendezvous; 1996 Chevrolet Lumina APV; 1997–2003 Chevrolet Venture; 1999–2001 Chevrolet Lumina; 1999–2003 Chevrolet Malibu, Monte Carlo; 2000–03 Chevrolet Impala; 1996–2003 Oldsmobile Silhouette; 1999 Oldsmobile Cutlass; 1999–2003 Oldsmobile Alero; 1996–99 Pontiac Trans Sport; 1999–2003 Pontiac Grand Am; 2000–03 Pontiac Grand Prix, Montana 2001–03 Pontiac Aztek with 3.1L or 3.4L V6 engine (VINs J, E—RPOs LGB, LA1)

CONDITION: Some owners may comment on an apparent oil or coolant leak. Additionally, the comments may range from spots on the driveway to having to add fluids.

CAUSE: Intake manifold may be leaking allowing coolant, oil or both to leak from the engine.

CORRECTION: Install a new-design intake manifold gasket. The material used in the gasket has been changed in order to improve the sealing qualities of the gasket. When replacing the gasket, the intake manifold bolts must also be replaced and torqued to a revised specification. The new bolts will come with a pre-applied threadlocker on them.

ENHANCED CALIBRATION FOR TRANSMISSION OVERHEAT IN EXTREME COLD AIR TEMPERATURES

BULLETIN NO.: 09038 **DATE: SEPTEMBER 2, 2009**

2006–08 Chevrolet Silverado HD

2006–08 GMC Sierra HD Equipped with Allison 1000 Transmission (RPO MW7) and Duramax 6.6L Diesel V8 Engine (RPO LLY/LBZ/LMM—VIN 2/D/6)

Located in Certain U.S. Cold Weather States; Alberta, British Columbia, Manitoba, Newfoundland, Northwest Territories, Ontario, Quebec, Saskatchewan, and Yukon

THIS PROGRAM IS IN EFFECT UNTIL SEPTEMBER 30, 2010.

CONDITION: Certain 2006–08 model year Chevrolet Silverado HD and GMC Sierra HD vehicles, equipped with an Allison 1000 transmission (RPO MW7) and Duramax 6.6L diesel V8 engine (RPO LLY/LBZ/LMM VIN 2/D/6), and located in certain U.S. cold weather states; Alberta, British Columbia, Manitoba, Newfoundland, Northwest Territories, Ontario, Quebec, Saskatchewan, and Yukon, may have limited or no transmission fluid (oil) flow through the transmission oil cooler after sitting for an extended period of time, such as overnight, during extreme cold temperatures, less than –40°F or °C, excluding wind chill. If the "Elevated Idle Mode", cabin heater performance option is operative and the engine is allowed to idle for an extended period of 15 to 30 minutes while cooler flow is limited, the transmission fluid may overheat, resulting in transmission damage, and subsequent failure. These low temperatures only occur in the areas listed above, and therefore, only vehicles in theses areas are involved in this program.

CORRECTION: Dealers are to reprogram the Transmission Control Module (TCM) with a new enhanced calibration.

SPECIAL COVERAGE ADJUSTMENT—EXTENDED CATALYTIC CONVERTER WARRANTY COVERAGE

BULLETIN NO.: 08300 **DATE: JUNE 11, 2009**

2006–07 Pontiac Solstice
2007 Saturn Sky
Equipped with 2.4L Engine (LE5)

CONDITION: Some customers of 2006–07 model year Pontiac Solstice vehicles, and 2007 model year Saturn Sky Vehicles, equipped with a 2.4L engine (LE5), may comment on illumination of the malfunction indicator lamp (MAL) and/or lack of engine power. This may be caused by failure of the catalytic convertor.

SPECIAL COVERAGE ADJUSTMENT: This special coverage covers the condition described above for a period of 10 years or 120,000 miles (193,000 km), whichever occurs first, from the date the vehicles was originally placed in service, regardless of ownership.

FORD

FUEL INJECTOR REPLACEMENT

BULLETIN NO.: 09B08-SUPPLEMENT #1 **DATE: AUGUST 24, 2009**

REFERENCE: Customer Satisfaction Program 09B08: Parts Update dated March 31, 2009
Certain 2008 and 2009 Model Year F-250 through F-550 Vehicles
Equipped with a 6.4L Diesel Engine

REASONS FOR THIS SUPPLEMENT:

- Add additional vehicles.
- Program Extension: The expiration date for Customer Satisfaction Program 09B08 has been extended through August 31, 2010.

NISSAN

L/H REAR SUSPENSION KNUCKLE

BULLETIN NO.: NTB09-031 **DATE: APRIL 23, 2009**

VOLUNTARY SERVICE CAMPAIGN PC005

2009 Nissan Altima and Maxima

On some 2009 Altima and Maxima vehicles, the left hand rear suspension knuckle may not be manufactured to specification, which may result in noise or vibration under certain circumstances. Although no safety issue is presented, Nissan is conducting this service campaign to identify and replace those affected units. This service will be performed at no cost for parts or labor.

TOYOTA

TOYOTA POWER REAR DOOR SHUDDER/WATER LEAKS

BULLETIN NO.: B0003-04 **DATE: MARCH 9, 2004**

BACK DOOR STAY LEAK & COLD WEATHER SHUDDER IMPROVEMENT

2004–06 Sienna

The back door stays have been redesigned to improve the operating effort of the rear hatch, provide improved resistance to seal damage, and prevent leakage. The improvement will also address the power back door shudder that can occur when operating during cold weather conditions.

Service Bulletins

ACURA

REAR SUSPENSION THUDDING/DRUMMING NOISES

BULLETIN NO.: 08-038 **DATE: FEBRUARY 6, 2009**

THUDDING OR DRUMMING FROM THE REAR SUSPENSION WHEN DRIVING OVER ROUGH ROADS

2007–09 MDX, Except Sport

PROBABLE CAUSE: The rear dampers are faulty.

CHRYSLER

LEAD OR DRIFT TO EITHER SIDE OF ROAD

BULLETIN NO.: 02-006-04 **DATE: AUGUST 20, 2004**

SPECIAL OFFSET BALL JOINT ALLOWS ADJUSTMENT TO CASTER AND CAMBER ANGLES

This bulletin involves the replacement of one or both front upper ball joints when front end alignment specifications can not be obtained using normal alignment practices.

2001–05 Wrangler

2001–04 Grand Cherokee

2001 Cherokee

SYMPTOM/CONDITION: The customer may experience a slight lead or drift to either side of the road. This condition may occur when there is no driver input to the steering system, or when the driver must maintain a constant input to the steering system in order to maintain a straight ahead direction of the vehicle.

SLIDING DOOR LOWER HINGE ASSEMBLY GRINDING NOISE

BULLETIN NO.: 23-016-09 **DATE: MAY 19, 2009**

2008–09 Town & Country/Grand Voyager

NOTE: This bulletin applies to vehicles equipped with power sliding doors (sales code JRA and JRB) built before February 2, 2009 (MDH 0202XX).

SYMPTOM/CONDITION: Some customers may experience a grinding sound when opening and closing the sliding door.

DIAGNOSIS: Open and close the sliding door multiple times. Assure there are no obstructions in the track and listen for a grinding sound originating from the lower track of the door.

If the above symptom/condition is experienced or can be verified, perform the Repair Procedure.

INOPERATIVE A/C SYSTEM

BULLETIN NO.: 24-003-09 **DATE: JULY 29, 2009**

OVERVIEW: This bulletin involves replacing the A/C discharge line and performing the refrigerant system charge procedure.

2008–09 Town & Country/Voyager/Caravan

NOTE: The bulletin applied to vehicles equipped with a 3.3L or 3.8L engine and air conditioning (Sales Code EGV or EGL with HAA or HAG or HBB).

SYMPTOM/CONDITION: Customer may complain that A/C system is inoperative or loses charge. This condition is caused by the A/C discharge line. A new discharge line addresses this issue.

GENERAL MOTORS

INACCURATE FUEL GAUGE READINGS

BULLETIN NO.: 09-08-49-005 **DATE: MARCH 27, 2009**

FUEL GAUGE READS INACCURATE OR EMPTY, LOW FUEL INDICATOR ILLUMINATED, DTCS P0461 AND/OR P0463 SET

2008–09 Buick Allure (Canada Only), Allure Super (Canada Only), LaCrosse, LaCrosse Super; 2008–09 Chevrolet Impala, and Impala SS

CONDITION: Some customers may comment that the low fuel indicator comes on and the fuel gauge reads empty when there is fuel in the tank. Other comments may be that the fuel gauge is inaccurate.

CAUSE: This condition may be due to poor terminal tension at connector X405, resulting in resistance at the affected circuits.

CORRECTION: Perform a pin drag test on all female terminals within connector X405. If a terminal is found to be loose or have poor tension, replace the affected terminal.

AUTOMATIC TRANSMISSION FLUID LEAK

BULLETIN NO.: 09-07-30-006 **DATE: MARCH 9, 2009**

TRANSMISSION FLUID LEAK DUE TO TRANSMISSION CONVERTER HOUSING SEAL (INSPECT WITH DYE AND BLACK LIGHT, REPLACE TORQUE CONVERTER FLUID SEAL)

2008–09 Buick Enclave; 2008–09 Chevrolet Equinox, Malibu; 2009 Chevrolet Traverse; 2007–09 GMC Acadia; 2007–09 Pontiac G6; 2008–09 Pontiac Torrent; 2007–09 Saturn Aura, Outlook; 2008–09 Saturn Vue

CONDITION: Some customers may comment about an oil leak. Upon further investigation, the technician may find a transmission oil leak at the transmission converter housing or transmission case to housing, at the gasket, or at the rear lower engine oil pan bolts.

BOOMING/DRONING NOISE

BULLETIN NO.: 08-07-30-044C **DATE: APRIL 29, 2009**

PHASING DRONE, BOOM, MOAN OR VIBRATION IN SEAT, FLOOR PAN OR DOOR PANEL AT 87–97 KPH (54–60 MPH) OR AT 64 KPH (40 MPH) IN 6TH GEAR OR 1000–1300 RPM WITH TORQUE CONVERTER CLUTCH ENGAGED (REPROGRAM TCM AND INSTALL WASHERS ON VEHICLES BUILT WITHOUT WASHERS)

2008–09 Cadillac CTS

A/T SHIFT FLARE/HARSH 2–3 SHIFTING

BULLETIN NO.: 09-07-30-004A **DATE: APRIL 21, 2009**

FLARE AND/OR HARSH 2–3 SHIFTS (INSTALL THREE FLUID SEAL RINGS)

2007–09 Cadillac Escalade, Escalade ESV, Escalade EXT; 2007–09 Chevrolet Silverado; 2008–09 Chevrolet Suburban; 2009 Chevrolet Avalanche, Tahoe; 2007–09 GMC Sierra, Yukon Denali, Yukon XL Denali; 2008–09 GMC Yukon XL; 2009 GMC Yukon

CAUSE: This condition may be caused by leaking 1–2–3–4 and 3–5–R clutch fluid seal rings.

DECELERATION/A/T GEAR HUNTING

BULLETIN NO.: 21-003-09 **DATE: APRIL 3, 2009**

DECEL. HUNTING/BUMP/OSCILLATION FEELING AND AUTOMATIC TRANSMISSION SHIFT IMPROVEMENTS

This bulletin involves selectively erasing and reprogramming the Powertrain Control Module.

2007–09 (JS) Sebring/Avenger/Sebring Convertible

HONK/MOAN ON HARD LEFT HAND TURNS

BULLETIN NO.: 19-001-09 **DATE: JANUARY 22, 2009**

POWER STEERING HONK, MOAN OR GRINDING SOUND ON LEFT TURNS

This bulletin involves replacing the power steering reservoir with a revised (taller) reservoir and bleeding the power steering system.

2007–09 Sebring/Avenger/Sebring Convertible; 2009 Jeep Journey

FRONT SIDE DOOR GLASS LOOSE IN CHANNEL, WIND NOISE, WATER LEAK

BULLETIN NO.: 09-08-64-020 **DATE: MAY 20, 2009**

REVISE WINDOW REGULATOR MOUNTING HOLE

2008–10 Chevrolet Cobalt (Sedan Only)

2008–10 Pontiac G5 (Sedan Only)

CONDITION: Some customers may comment that the left and/or right front side door glass may leave the rear of the front side door window weatherstrip run channel when being cycled up or down. This may also lead to wind noise and water leak issues in the upper B-pillar area.

CAUSE: This condition may be caused by the window glass rocking forward in the door as the window is cycled. This may allow the glass to disengage from the rear of the front side door window weatherstrip run channel. The rocking condition may be caused by the window regulator being improperly positioned within the door.

CREAK, POP, CLUNK NOISE, REAR STRUT, UPPER MOUNT, SUSPENSION

BULLETIN NO.: 07-03-09-001J **DATE: SEPTEMBER 15, 2009**

ENGINEERING RECOMMENDATIONS

2006–10 Chevrolet Impala

SUPERCEDE: This bulletin is being revised to end the need for information from the field and to provide engineering recommendations to correct the concern. Please discard Corporate Bulletin Number 07-03-09-001 (Section 03—Suspension).

CONDITION: Some customers may comment on a creak, pop, or clunk nose coming from the rear of the vehicle.

CAUSE: This condition may be caused by the rear strut spring rubber isolator contacting the lower spring coil.

CLUNK, KNOCK OR RATTLE NOISE FROM FRONT OF VEHICLE WHILE DRIVING OR TURNING OVER BUMPS AT LOW SPEEDS

BULLETIN NO.: 06-02-32-007F DATE: AUGUST 24, 2009

DIAGNOSE NOISE AND PERFORM OUTLINED REPAIR

2004–06 Chevrolet Malibu Maxx
2004–08 Chevrolet Malibu Classic
2008–10 Chevrolet Malibu
2005–10 Pontiac G6
2007–10 Saturn Aura

NO REVERSE/CHECK ENGINE LIGHT ILLUMINATED, DTC P0776 AND P0842

BULLETIN NO.: 09-07-30-012 DATE: JUNE 24, 2009

REPLACE 3–5 REVERSE CLUTCH PLATE WAVED

2008–09 Buick Enclave
2008–09 Chevrolet Equinox, Malibu
2009 Chevrolet Traverse
2007–09 GMC Acadia
2007–09 Pontiac G6
2008–09 Pontiac Torrent
2007–09 Saturn Aura, Outlook
2008–09 Saturn Vue

WATER LEAK IN TRUNK AREA OF VEHICLE/POSSIBLE NO AUDIO FROM RADIO

BULLETIN NO.: 09-08-57-004B DATE: SEPTEMBER 11, 2009

APPLY SEAM SEALER

2008–09 Chevrolet Malibu
2006–09 Pontiac G6
2007–09 Saturn Aura

REAR LEAF SPRING SLAP OR CLUNK NOISE

BULLETIN NO.: 03-03-09-002C DATE: JUNE 2, 2009

REPLACE SPRING INSERTS

1999–2009 Chevrolet Silverado 1500/2500 Series Pickups

2000–09 Chevrolet Suburban 2500 Series

2002–09 Chevrolet Avalanche 2500 Series

2003–09 Chevrolet Express 2500/3500 Vans with 8500 GVWR (RPO C5F), 8600 GVWR (RPO C6P) or 9600 GVWR (RPO C6Y)

1999–2009 GMC Sierra 1500/2500 Series Pickups

2000–09 GMC Yukon XL 2500 Series

2003–09 GMC Savana 2500/3500 Vans with 8500 GVWR (RPO C5F), 8600 GVWR (RPO C6P) or 9600 GVWR (RPO C6Y)

FLUID LEAK AT LEFT HAND TRANSFER CASE WEEP HOLE OR BETWEEN TRANSFER CASE AND TRANSMISSION

BULLETIN NO.: 09-04-21-004 DATE: JUNE 25, 2009

REPLACE LEFT TRANSFER CASE INPUT SHAFT SEAL OR TRANSFER CASE O-RING SEAL

2008–10 Buick Enclave

2008–09 Chevrolet Equinox Sport

2009–10 Chevrolet Traverse

2010 Chevrolet Equinox

2007–10 GMC Acadia

2010 GMC Terrain

2008–09 Pontiac Torrent GXP

2007–10 Saturn Outlook

2008–10 Saturn Vue

2007–09 Suzuki XL-7

ENGINE OIL LEAKS FROM CHARGE AIR COOLER AND TURBOCHARGER AIR INLET ADAPTER

BULLETIN NO.: 09-06-93-001 DATE: MAY 5, 2009

REPLACE CLAMP AND/OR TURBO INLET DUCT/PIPE

2004–10 Light and Medium Duty Trucks Equipped with Diesel Engines

2010 and Prior Chevrolet Kodiak, Silverado Equipped with Engine RPO—LLY, LBZ or LMM Diesel

2010 and Prior GMC Sierra, TopKick Equipped with Engine RPO—LLY, LBZ or LMM Diesel

Please Refer to GMVIS

CONDITION: Some customers may comment on an engine oil leak from the rear of the engine near the flywheel housing. Upon further investigation, a technician may find oil in the charge air cooler or turbocharger air inlet adapter.

DIESEL ENGINE OIL LEAK

BULLETIN NO.: 02-06-01-023C **DATE: JULY 20, 2004**

OIL LEAK AT OIL COOLER TO 6.6L DIESEL ENGINE BLOCK MATING SURFACE (REPLACE O-RINGS, APPLY SEALANT)

2001–04 Chevrolet Silverado 2500/3500

2001–04 GMC Sierra 2500/3500

2003–04 Chevrolet Kodiak C4500/5500

2003–04 GMC Topkick C4500/5500

CAUSE: Minor imperfections in the engine block machined surfaces at the oil cooler interface may allow oil seepage past the oil cooler O-rings.

V8 ENGINE OIL LEAKS/LOW OIL LAMP ON

BULLETIN NO.: 07-06-01-004 **DATE: MARCH 16, 2007**

LOW OIL LEVEL INDICATOR LAMP ON AND/OR ENGINE OIL LEAK (RESEAL OIL PRESSURE SENSOR)

2006–07 Buick Rainier; Cadillac Escalade, CTS-V; Chevrolet Corvette Z06, Impala SS, Monte Carlo SS; Chevrolet Avalanche, Silverado, Silverado HD, Suburban, Tahoe, TrailBlazer, TrailBlazer SS; 2006–07 GMC Envoy, Envoy Denali, Sierra, Sierra HD, Sierra Denali, Yukon, XL, Yukon Denali XL; Pontiac Grand Prix GXP; Saab 9-7X V8

CONDITION: Some customers may comment on a low oil level indicator lamp on and/or engine oil leak. Upon further investigation, the technician may find that the oil leak is at the oil pressure sensor that is threaded into the valve lifter oil manifold (VLOM) assembly and/or engine valley cover.

CORRECTION: If the engine oil leak was found to be at the engine oil pressure sensor, then remove the oil pressure sensor and reseal with a pipe sealant with Teflon or equivalent, P/N 12346004 (in Canada, P/N 10953480). Refer to Engine Oil Pressure Sensor and/or Switch Replacement in SI.

A/C TEMPERATURE WON'T CHANGE/POOR PERFORMANCE

BULLETIN NO.: 06-01-39-004A **DATE: APRIL 25, 2006**

2005–06 Montana SV6, Relay, Terraza and Uplander

ATTENTION: THIS IS NOT A RECALL. "GM of Canada" dealers are not authorized to use this bulletin. This bulletin ONLY applies to vehicles in which the customer has commented about this concern AND the EI number shows in GMVIS. All others should disregard this bulletin and proceed with diagnostics found in published service information.

CONDITION: IMPORTANT: If the customer did not bring their vehicle in for this issue, DO NOT proceed with this bulletin.

Some customers may comment that they are unable to change the HVAC mode and/or temperature. Customers may also comment that the A/C may be inoperative or have poor performance.

CORRECTION: GM Engineering is attempting to determine the root cause of this condition. GM has a need to obtain information first hand BEFORE any repairs are made.

WARRANTY INFORMATION:

Labor Operation	Description	Labor Time
D9719*	HVAC — Engineering Investigation	1.0 hr
Add	Recover and Recharge A/C System WITH Rear A/C	0.7 hr
Add	Recover and Recharge A/C System WITHOUT Rear A/C	0.5 hr

*This labor operation is for bulletin use only. It will not be published in the Labor Time Guide.

FORD

POWER STEERING FLUID LEAKS/NOISY

BULLETIN NO.: 08-19-9 **DATE: SEPTEMBER 29, 2008**

POWER STEERING LEAK/NOISY

2006–09 Focus

ISSUE: Some 2006–09 Focus vehicles built on or after 10/3/2005 may experience a customer concern of the power steering system leaking and/or system noisy. This may be due to a damaged O-ring seal at the P/S reservoir-to-pump body causing a low fluid level or fluid aeration.

ENGINE SQUEAL/CHIRP

BULLETIN NO.: 09-7-7 **DATE: APRIL 4, 2009**

ENGINE BELT SQUEAL OR CHIRP NOISE ON COLD STARTUP

2009 Mustang; 2007–08 Explorer Sport Trac, Explorer; 2007–08 Mountaineer

ISSUE: Some 2007–08 Explorer, Explorer Sport Trac, Mountaineer and 2009 Mustang vehicles equipped with a 4.0L engine may exhibit a belt squeal or belt chirp from the front end accessory drive (FEAD) belt near the power steering pulley area.

ACTION: It may be necessary to replace the generator bracket with an updated bracket or install an updated accessory drive belt.

WATER LEAK ONTO FRONT FLOOR AREA

BULLETIN NO.: 08-26-7 **DATE: JANUARY 5, 2009**

WATER LEAK—FRONT FLOOR AREA

2005–09 Mustang

ISSUE: Some 2005–09 Mustang vehicles may exhibit a difficult to diagnose water leak in the front floor area. This may be caused by loose grommets and/or sealer skips around the cowl area, loose A-pillar window weatherstrip retainer, misaligned body harness grommet through the firewall, or a misaligned body harness grommet from the passenger door.

SHUDDER ON ACCELERATION

BULLETIN NO.: 08-23-4 **DATE: NOVEMBER 24, 2008**

SHUDDER ON ACCELERATION—POSSIBLE WRONG TRANSMISSION CROSSMEMBER ASSEMBLY INSTALLED

2005–09 Mustang

ISSUE: Some 2005–09 Mustang vehicles (Excludes GI 500), equipped with either a 4.0L or 4.6L engine, may exhibit a heavy driveline shudder on acceleration from a stop or between 3–15 MPH (5–24 km/h). The wrong transmission crossmember assembly may have been installed from the factory. Similar complaints may also occur if the transmission crossmember and transmission support insulator were improperly reassembled after transmission removal.

EXCESSIVE REAR AXLE WHINE

BULLETIN NO.: 09-20-4 **DATE: SEPTEMBER 28, 2009**

AXLE WHINE

2005–10 Mustang

ISSUE: Some 2005–10 Mustangs may exhibit excessive axle whine noise.

SERVICE PROCEDURE: This condition may be corrected by installing tuned dampers on the rear axle assembly, if not already installed.

AUTOMATIC TRANSMISSION MALFUNCTIONS

BULLETIN NO.: 09-3-3 DATE: FEBRUARY 2, 2009

TRANSMISSION—ERRATIC OPERATION

2009 Crown Victoria, E-150, F-150; 2009 Town Car; 2009 Grand Marquis

ISSUE: Some 2009 F-150, E-150, Crown Victoria, Grand Marquis and Town Car vehicles equipped with 4R75E transmission and a transmission build date before 12/1/2008, may exhibit improper gear selection, converter clutch operation or improper shift feel. The cause may be an intermittent electrical open or short circuit and/or a fuse blown in the battery junction box (BJB). The most likely diagnostic trouble codes (DTCs) for this concern are related to transmission internal solenoids and they are as follows: P0750, P0753, P0755, P0758, P0740, P0743, P0748, P0962, P0963 and/or P0712. Depending on shorted circuits, an open fuse might be present at BJB location F21 in Crown Vic, Grand Marquis or Town Car; BJB location F79 in E-Series and F-Series.

ACTION: The most likely cause is a misrouted internal wiring harness being pinched between the transmission fluid pan and the main control.

FRONT BRAKES—INTERMITTENT GRUNT OR GRINDING NOISE

BULLETIN NO.: 09-18-14 DATE: SEPTEMBER 9, 2009

Ford: 2009 Flex

Lincoln: 2009 MKS

ISSUE: Some 2009 MKS vehicles built before 4/27/2009 and Ford Flex vehicles built before 5/26/2009 may exhibit intermittent grunt or grinding noise from the front brakes.

STEERING WANDER

BULLETIN NO.: TSB 09-20-7 DATE: SEPTEMBER 30, 2009

2008–10 E-150, E-250, E-350

ISSUE: Some 2008–10 E-Series 150 to 350 vehicles may exhibit steering wander or free play.

ACTION: Follow the Service Procedure steps to correct the condition.

SERVICE PROCEDURE: Several factors may contribute to steering wander or free play condition and are addressed below:

- Steering gear mesh load adjustment. Steering free play is normally attributed to low mesh load torque. But in some vehicles high mesh load torque may result in a condition called sticky on-center feel that may be misinterpreted as wander.
- Front end alignment may be adjusted to improve the wander/free play condition.
- Sticky on-center feel may also be due to ball joint tightness and/or high friction/rubbing of the intermediate shaft boot.

UN-COMMANDED TCC APPLY ON THE 1–2 SHIFT CAUSING PERCEPTION OF HESITATION AND/OR LACK OF POWER DURING SHIFT

BULLETIN NO.: TSB 02-20-14 **DATE: OCTOBER 5, 2009**

2005–10 Crown Victoria; 2005–06 Expedition; 2005–10 E-150, E-250, E-350, F-150
2005–10 Town Car; 2006–08 Mark LT
2005–10 Grand Marquis

This article supersedes TSB 6-22-7 to update the Issue Statement, vehicle model years and model line covered.

ISSUE: Some 2005–10 vehicles equipped with a 4R70/75E-W transmission may experience an un-commanded torque converter clutch (TCC) apply or TCC partial apply immediately after the 1–2 shift. This may result in the perception that the vehicle lacks power or that the transmission is up-shifting too early. Additional symptoms of uncommanded TCC apply when coming to a stop (before the 2–1 downshift is commanded), are engine stalling or lugging when engaging manual 2nd while at a stop and code P1742 may be present in continuous memory. However, the vehicle should operate normally in Park, Reverse, Neutral and manual 1st gear.

ACTION: Follow the Service Procedure for verification and repair.

2.5L ENGINE—INTERMITTENT NO CRANK/NO START WITH ONE TOUCH INTEGRATED SYSTEM (OTIS)

BULLETIN NO.: TSB 09-15-10

2010 Fusion
2010 Milan

ISSUE: Some 2010 Fusion and Milan vehicles (Excludes Hybrid) built before 7/26/2009 equipped with 2.5L engines may exhibit intermittent no crank/no start condition when cycling the key into the run position, vehicle may also exhibit one touch instant start (OTIS) time out concern with no diagnostic trouble codes (DTCs) present. This intermittent condition may be caused by radio frequency interference (RFI) intermittently corrupting the crankshaft position sensor (CKP) signal input.

RUNS ROUGH OR MISSES

BULLETIN NO.: TSB 09-12-8

2008–09 Taurus X, Taurus; 2007–09 Edge; 2009 Flex
2007–09 MKZ; 2009 MKS; 2007–09 MKX
2008–09 Sable

ISSUE: Some 2007–09 Edge, MKX, MKZ, 2008–09 Taurus, Taurus X, Sable, and 2009 Flex and MKS vehicles equipped with a 3.5L or 3.7L engine and built on or before 12/15/2008 may exhibit a malfunction indicator lamp (MIL) on with and one or more diagnostic trouble codes (DTCs) P0011, P0012, P0016, P0018, P0021, P0022. Vehicle may also exhibit rough idle or misses.

DIESEL: LOW POWER/MISFIRE/SMOKE

BULLETIN NO.: 04-23-3 **DATE: NOVEMBER 29, 2004**

2003–2005 Excursion, F-Super Duty; 2004–2005 E-Series, F-650, F-750

ISSUE: Some 6.0L vehicles may exhibit a misfire, lack of power, buck/jerk, excessive smoke, or crank/no-start. There are several potential causes for these symptoms, Including injector concerns.

ACTION: If normal diagnostics lead to an injector concern, use the following diagnostics to confirm the cause of injector failure and/or to rule out other conditions which may cause the same symptoms as a failed injector.

LOW OR NEGATIVE FUEL PRESSURE

Internal injector damage can be caused by lack of fuel system supply pressure. Restricted fuel filters and/or fuel line(s), or an inoperative fuel pump can create a low or negative fuel supply pressure. Low or negative pressures may hinder the return stroke of the injector intensifier plunger to its rest position, leading to internal injector damage. To diagnose for low or negative fuel pressure and to confirm if any injectors have been damaged:

1. Perform standard diagnostic procedures, including verification of supply fuel pressure while the symptom is evident.
2. Repair causes for low pressure on the supply side of the fuel system.
3. Diagnose for failed injector(s) only after rectifying fuel supply pressure.

COMBUSTION GAS ENTERING THE FUEL SYSTEM

1. Remove outlet fuel lines from the fuel filter housing on top of engine.
2. Install a balloon over each fuel line with a zip tie.
3. Disable the fuel pump and FICM relays.
4. Crank engine and watch for compression pulses in the balloon.
5. For each line where compression pulses are evident, remove all but one of the glow plugs from the affected cylinder head(s).
6. Crank engine and watch again for compression pulses.
7. Remove the glow plug and transfer it to the next cylinder in the head and repeat Step 6.
8. For each cylinder where compression pulses are evident remove injector(s) and inspect copper gasket and lower O-ring, replace if necessary. If gasket(s) and O-ring(s) are OK, replace injector(s). Retest to confirm repair.

ERRATIC HIGH PRESSURE OIL SUPPLY

Erratic supply of high pressure oil to injectors may cause a rough running engine. High pressure oil flow can be disrupted by faulty check valve(s) or a faulty IPR valve.

To diagnose, first perform a slow neutral run up in park/neutral. If the engine runs rough between 1200 and 1900 RPM proceed to Check Valve Diagnosis; if the engine runs rough between 3000 and 4000 RPM replace the IPR valve.

CHECK VALVE DIAGNOSIS

1. To isolate the bank with the faulty check valve, disconnect all of the injector electrical connectors on one bank.
2. Perform a Power Balance test. Engine misfires should be constant on the four disconnected cylinders and the operational cylinders should be contributing evenly.
3. Repeat steps 1 and 2 on the opposite bank.
4. If the operating contribution is erratic on one bank, replace the check valve on that bank.

WARRANTY STATUS: Eligible under provisions of New Vehicle Limited Warranty Coverage and Emissions Warranty Coverage

DIESEL ENGINE DRIVEABILITY CONCERNS

BULLETIN NO.: 03-20-12 **DATE: OCTOBER 13, 2003**

2003–04 Excursion, F Super Duty

Some vehicles may exhibit various driveability conditions listed below:

- Rough/Rolling Idle When The Engine Is Warm
- Rough/Rolling Idle And White Smoke After Hot Restart
- Lacks Power After Initial Start-Up
- Cold Idle kicker Performance At Warm Ambient Temps
- U0306 Codes After Reprogramming
- P2263 Code Set During Extended Idle
- False P0196 Codes

ACTION: Reprogram the PCM/TCM/FICM modules to the latest calibration level (B27.9) or later. This calibration should only be installed on customer vehicles that exhibit one of the conditions addressed above.

REAR AXLE WHINE OR HUM

BULLETIN NO.: 05-6-18 **DATE: APRIL 4, 2005**

1997–2005 Expedition, F-150
2002–05 Explorer
1998–2005 Navigator
2003–05 Aviator
2002–05 Mountaineer

ISSUE: Some vehicles may exhibit an axle whine or hum during acceleration, deceleration, and/or cruise.

ACTION: An axle repair kit has been developed, which incorporates most parts required for a comprehensive axle repair. The kit should be used instead of installing a complete axle assembly to repair an axle whine/hum.

ALUMINUM BODY PANELS CORROSION

BULLETIN NO.: 06-25-15 **DATE: DECEMBER 11, 2006**

ALUMINUM BODY PANELS—CORROSION—SERVICE TIP

2000–07 Crown Victoria, Taurus; 2005–06 Ford GT; 2005–07 Mustang; 2000–03 Ranger; 2000–07 Expedition; 2002–07 Explorer; 2004–07 F-150

2007 Explorer Sport Trac; 2000–06 Lincoln LS; 2000–07 Town Car, Navigator; 2000–07 Grand Marquis, Sable.

ISSUE: Some vehicles may exhibit a bubbling or blistering under the paint on aluminum body parts. This is due to iron contamination of the aluminum panel.

WATER IN THE FUEL TANK BEHIND REAR AXLE—6.0L AND 7.3L DIESEL ENGINE

BULLETIN NO.: 05-11-7

FORD:

1999–2005 F-350, F-450

ISSUE: Some 1999–2005 vehicles equipped with the 6.0L or 7.3L diesel engine and a 40-gallon (151.4L) fuel tank behind the rear axle, may exhibit water in the fuel tank. This is due to snow and ice accumulating around the mushroom vent cap, melting, and being pulled into the tank through the mushroom cap.

ACTION: Replace the mushroom cap with a vent line assembly kit.

HONDA

VEHICLE DRIFTS TO THE RIGHT

BULLETIN NO.: 03-004 DATE: JANUARY 21, 2003

2002–03 CR-V 4WD With A/T

SYMPTOM: The vehicle drifts or pulls to the right while driving at highway speeds.

CORRECTIVE ACTION: Realign the damper spring on the upper spring seat.

OUT OF WARRANTY: Any repair performed after warranty expiration may be eligible for goodwill consideration by the District Parts and Service Manager or your Zone Office. You must request consideration, and get a decision, before starting work.

LEXUS

VEHICLE PULLS TO ONE SIDE

BULLETIN NO.: L-SB-0174-08; T-SB-0391-0 DATE: DECEMBER 24, 2008

REPAIR MANUAL SUPPLEMENT: VEHICLE PULLING TO ONE SIDE

These two bulletins contain general vehicle pulling diagnosis and repair procedures along with specific information to help correct pulling complaints. This information supplements Repair Manual procedures when the symptoms are:

1. The driver holds the steering wheel without exerting steering effort while driving straight ahead, the vehicle drifts to the right or the left.
2. While driving straight ahead, the driver has to steer either to the right or the left to maintain straight driving.

NOTE: In these two bulletins, Lexus and Toyota admit that pulling to one side is a generic problem affecting almost all 2002–09 Lexus and Toyota models. Bring a copy of this service bulletin the next time your dealer feigns ignorance of the defect or you are stonewalled by Toyota inaction.

MAZDA

UNSTABLE IDLE/STALLING

BULLETIN NO: 01-007/09 **DATE: FEBRUARY 11, 2009**

UNSTABLE IDLING/ENGINE STALLS JUST AFTER STOPPING

2003–09 Mazda6 with 2.3L/2.5L (including Mazdaspeed6); 2004–09 Mazda3 (including Mazdaspeed3); 2006–09 Mazda5; 2006–09 Mazda MX-5; 2007–09 Mazda CX-7

DESCRIPTION: Some vehicles may exhibit a concern of unstable idling or, in some rare cases, stalling, just after the vehicle stops with no DTCs detected. The problem is due to the accumulation of carbon deposits inside the throttle body causing air flow to decrease.

NISSAN

FUEL GAUGE WON'T READ FULL/SLOW TO RESPOND

BULLETIN NO.: EL09-002 **DATE: FEBRUARY 5, 2009**

FUEL GAUGE DOES NOT READ FULL, OR SLOW TO RESPOND

2008–09 Rogue

IF YOU CONFIRM: Fuel level gauge does not read full when tank is full, or the fuel level gauge is inaccurate or reads erratically: For 2WD models, replace the fuel sender unit only; for AWD models, replace the fuel sender unit and sub-sender unit.

SUBARU

WATER LEAK/FRONT FLOOR AREA

BULLETIN NO.: 12-108-09 **DATE: FEBRUARY 11, 2009**

WATER LEAK, FRONT PASSENGER AREA

2008–09 Impreza; 2009 Forester

If you encounter a vehicle which has a water leak in the front driver/passenger side of the vehicle, it may be coming from the body seam located behind the front inner fender well. To correct the condition, the body seam will need to be sealed.

TOYOTA

ENGINE NOISE/VIBRATION ON ACCELERATION/SHIFTING GEARS

BULLETIN NO.: BT-SB-0068-09 DATE: FEBRUARY 19, 2009

ABNORMAL NOISE AND VIBRATION ON ACCELERATION

ISSUE: Some 2007–09 model year Yaris vehicles may exhibit an abnormal noise and vibration when accelerating from a stop, or while shifting gears.

ACTION: It may be necessary to change the transverse engine mount.

CAN'T SHIFT FROM PARK/MULTIPLE WARNINGS ON

BULLETIN NO.: T-SB-0002-09, T-SB-0047-09 DATE: JANUARY 6, 19, 2009

IG1 RELAY FREEZING

2006–09 Corolla, Highlander, Matrix, Prius, RAV4, Sienna, and Yaris

ISSUE: Some customers may experience multiple warning lights illuminated, vehicle not shifting from Park to Drive, and other accessories becoming inoperative after the vehicle has cold soaked in sub-freezing (below 14°F [–10°C]) ambient air temperatures. A new relay has been made available to improve this condition.

HARSH DOWNSHIFT WHEN STOPPING

BULLETIN NO.: T-SB-0082-09 DATE: MARCH 11, 2009

HARSH DOWNSHIFT WHEN COMING TO A STOP

2009 Corolla and Matrix

ISSUE: Some customers may experience a harsh downshift feeling when coming to a stop after the transaxle has up-shifted to 4th or 5th gear. The Engine Control Module/ECM (SAE term: Powertrain Control Module/PCM) calibration has been revised. This repair is covered under the Toyota Federal Emission Warranty. This warranty is in effect for 96 months or 80,000 miles [128,700 kilometres], whichever occurs first, from the vehicle's in-service date.

ENGINE TICKING NOISE

BULLETIN NO.: T-SB-0094-09 DATE: MARCH 19, 2009

2GR-FE ENGINE TICKING NOISE AND/OR MIL ON P0014, P0015, P0024, P0025, P0017, OR P0018

2005–09 Avalon; 2007–09 Camry; 2008–09 Highlander; 2006–09 RAV4, 2007–09 Sienna

ISSUE: Some 2005–09 model year vehicles with 2GR-FE engines may exhibit a ticking/clicking type noise from the cylinder head cover area which may be accompanied by a MIL "ON" and one or more VVT-i related Diagnostic Trouble Codes (DTCs).

WATER LEAKS ONTO HEADLINER/FOOTWELL AREA

BULLETIN NO.: T-SB-0141-08 **DATE: JULY 29, 2008**

WATER LEAK AT HEADLINER

2005–09 Avalon; 2007–09 Camry; 2004–08 Solara

ISSUE: Some customers may experience a water leak condition in the headliner that may also result in a wet foot well area. This condition may be the result of one or more moon roof drain hoses becoming loose or disconnected from a moon roof drain pan nipple.

BODY–TICKING NOISE FROM WINDSHIELD/BACK GLASS

BULLETIN NO.: T-SB-0142-08 **DATE: JULY 29, 2008**

UPPER/LOWER WINDSHIELD/REAR GLASS TICK NOISE

Almost all of the 2003–09 Toyota lineup.

ISSUE: If a creak tick or rattle noise is heard at the top or bottom of the windshield or at the top of the rear glass the source of the noise may be the two stoppers bonded to the top of the windshield/rear glass or the windshield retainers bonded to the lower edge of the windshield. This bulletin provides the recommended repair procedure to eliminate these types of noises from the windshield/rear glass area.

WATER CONDENSATION DRIPPING FROM HEADLINER

BULLETIN NO.: 0241-09 **DATE: JULY 30, 2009**

2009–10 Corolla

INTRODUCTION: Some 2009–10 Corolla vehicles may exhibit a condition where water drips from the gap between the headliner and the A-Pillar garnish.

TOYOTA NO START IN EXTREME COLD

BULLETIN NO.: EG032-06 **DATE: MAY 9, 2006**

NO START IN SUB-FREEZING AMBIENT AIR TEMPERATURES

2004–05 Sienna

Some customers may experience a “no start” condition and/or M.I.L. “ON” with DTCs P0300, P0171, and P0174 after the vehicle has cold soaked in sub-freezing ambient air temperatures. To correct this condition, a new fuel pump sub-tank assembly is now available. Follow the repair procedure to replace the fuel pump sub-tank assembly.

ICE DEFORMS LEADING EDGE OF DOOR(S)

BULLETIN NO · 5708 15 DATE: DECEMBER 10, 2008

FRONT DOOR DEFORMED BY ICE

2006–09 Rabbits

ISSUE: Water draining from the front cowl drains into the rear of the front fender area. Water seeps out behind the lower front door and freezes causing door obstruction and damage to door panel. This condition may also occur at rear lower corner of front fender

MODEL INDEX

Recommended

Above Average

Average

Below Average

Not Recommended

Corolla 313
Camry 314 Hybrid
Lexus 279
La Crosse 201
Infiniti 259
Acura 219